NAPOLEON'S VICEROY
EUGÈNE DE BEAUHARNAIS

Eugène de Beauharnais
by H. Scheffer
By permission of the Musée de l'Armée, Hôtel des Invalides

NAPOLEON'S VICEROY

EUGÈNE DE BEAUHARNAIS

BY

Carola Oman

FUNK AND WAGNALLS / NEW YORK

Preface

No life of Eugène de Beauharnais exists in the English language, hardly any information and only one full-length biography in German. Yet he was the adopted son of whom Napoleon said, "Eugène never caused me any grief," and the only son of Josephine. Today his descendants are the rulers of Sweden, Norway, Belgium and Denmark.

As the child of a broken home he was pushed from pillar to post until, according to modern theories, he might well have emerged a juvenile delinquent. But from the age of thirteen, when he lost his father by the guillotine, he was the protector and supporter of his mother, and of his sister, Hortense, Queen of Holland, eventually the mother of Napoleon III. Even before he entered the profession chosen for him by his parents—the army—he showed signs of being a remarkable character, handsome, modest, of great courage, both physical and moral. (During the last months of his life he confessed to a sympathetic secretary that he would have liked to have been sent to sea!)

As Viceroy of Italy for eight years, he displayed exemplary diligence, tact and ability. He was a devoted trainer of troops, and long after he had quitted the active scene his accomplished and inspired voice was remembered on the parade ground. He began to distinguish himself as a young aide de camp on Napoleon's gruelling Egyptian campaign; in his prime he won two outstanding victories, quite out of sight, in Hungary and Russia; he gallantly took over the command when Murat deserted from the tragedy of the retreat from Moscow, and did all that he could to restore the health and morale of what was left of the Grande Armée. He was generally admitted to be an excellent employer; he never lost his temper or his sense of humour, which astonishingly survived revolutions, *coups d'état* and four major campaigns.

Frédéric Masson, dedicated biographer of the Bonaparte family, never devoted a volume to the stepson, though the Prince Eugène was noted as present on nearly every important family occasion, and was mentioned in countless contemporary memoirs. (Everyone imaginable hastened to set down their recollections of the Napoleonic scene. Unfortunately, some of those closest to the principal figures were inexperienced as authors and employed professionals. This applies to the lively reminiscences of Constant, valet first to Eugène then to Napoleon, and to Mlle. Avrillon, first *femme de chambre* to the Empress Josephine. But where a book or article is edited by M. Jean Hanoteau, the reader may put perfect trust.) "The Beauharnais" is to be recognized in many crowd-paintings. Portraits and busts of him in uniform stare resolutely in palaces of France and Italy. Like his mother he was a great lover of gardens, particularly trees and shrubs. He planted wherever he went, and today enormous specimen conifers, ginkgos, purple beeches and Louisiana cypresses, towering in parks in France, Italy, Switzerland and Bavaria, remind the visitor that Prince Eugène was once here.

He was universally commended for his dignified bearing and refusal of any honours when his stepfather divorced his mother. He refused two crowns, perhaps three. He ended his days in retirement in his wife's country, a beloved husband and father, broken-hearted over the situation in France. His life had been hard and he died prematurely at the age of forty-three.

Few figures of the period have been worse served by historians. Largely owing to the appalling jealousy of his stepfather's family, he remained forever the eternal apprentice. He was said to have been saved from extinction in his campaigns in Italy first by being superseded in command by Massena, then by Macdonald. Facts show otherwise. He was accused of failing to come to the rescue of his stepfather in 1813 when he was strictly obeying orders. (One of his Italian aides de camp arrived in Paris asking for further instructions after the Emperor had left for Elba.) The accusations that he had deserted a ruined tyrant were re-doubled after Waterloo, but most unfairly. As his sister Hortense reminded the Emperor, he had given his word to the allies not to re-enter the field. "And you know Eugène always keeps his word." He made every possible effort during the St. Helena exile and captivity to fulfil his stepfather's orders and succour him and his staff.

A few officers and members of his household produced memoirs of Prince Eugène, Duke of Leuchtenberg, Prince of Eichstätt, soon after his death. Not one divulged.then that, like his mother, he had been incorrigibly generous, and had died in debt. (But like her also he had valuable property which could be realized.) It was not until 1860 that his nephew Napoleon III, who well remembered him, sponsored an invaluable publication in ten volumes. *Mémoires et correspondance politique et militaire du Prince*

Eugène opened with a fragment of autobiography and a brief memento of the Russian campaign, dictated by him, almost at the last, to three secretaries—Darnay, who had come to him in Italy in 1805; Hennin, his Treasurer for the Kingdom of Italy, and Planat de la Faye, who had tried to accompany the Emperor to St. Helena. The whole was edited by Baron Pierre Albert Du Casse, a military historian, a creditable product of St. Cyr. He had never seen his hero. He had produced a life of Joseph Bonaparte and was to go on to deal with two more royal brothers of the Emperor and a *Histoire anecdotique du Second Empire par un ancien fonctionnaire* in 1887. The widow of Prince Eugène was dead by the time his master-work appeared, but his children gave the editor lavish material. The prince had always been fortunate in his staff with one exception (thrust upon him and apparently indestructible): he was a good picker. His official papers and private correspondence from the date of Darnay's taking office, were in wonderful order.

The Emperor Napoleon III departed to melancholy exile and death in England and the image of Prince Eugène somewhat faded from the public eye. If anyone heard the name it suggested the Prince Eugène of Savoy-Carignan, a commander in chief who had collaborated triumphantly with Marlborough, a bachelor without any discernible private life, "a Mars without Venus", a cold and sceptical hero, a very different character.

Professeur Arthur Lévy, a brilliant lecturer, an ardent Bonapartist, produced in 1926 *Napoléon et Eugène de Beauharnais*, a slender volume, charmingly written, partisan, emotional, maddeningly deficient in exact references and containing next to nothing hitherto unobtainable. No full length biography of Eugène de Beauharnais has yet engaged a French historian of the first order. But in 1940 Adalbert, Prince of Bavaria came forward with *Eugen Beauharnais der Stiefsohn Napoleons. Ein Lebensbild.* This is the book which must be the Bible of the serious student.

The author desires to record her thanks, firstly to Adalbert, Prince of Bavaria, without whose generous co-operation this first English life of Eugène de Beauharnais would not have been possible, and to Albrecht, Duke of Bavaria, for permission to quote from the Geheimes Hausarchiv in Munich. She also wishes to thank Dr. Hans Rall, Direktor des Geheimen Hausarchivs, for assistance to inspect documents and micro-films, and Dr. Martha Dreesbach for help with illustrations from pictures at the Landeshaupstadt Museum, Munich. King Gustav VI of Sweden has given permission to quote from the diary and correspondence of Princess Auguste, wife of Prince Eugène, in the Bernadotte Archives, Stockholm. In Switzerland, Herr Jakob and Herr Willi Hugentobler, Custodians of the Napoleon Museum, Arenenberg, gave valuable information and made arrangements for the author to visit Schloss Eugensberg. At Frauenfeld, Dr. B. Meyer, Keeper of the Staats Archiv of the Canton of Thurgau, supplied information and photographs.

In France, Colonel Wemaere, Conservateur, Hôtel des Invalides. Musée de l'Armée, kindly gave details about the relics of Prince Eugène in the Museum, and the monument presiding outside. At Versailles M. Van der Kemp, Conservateur en Chef, arranged for the author to be shown the department of the Museum gallery devoted to paintings of the Consulate and Empire.

Finally, in England, the author would like to record her debt to Mrs. Joan Saunders of the Writers and Speakers Research, and to her translators, Miss Theodora Scott Fox and Mr. Peter Robert Oman Stuart.

C.O. 1966

Contents

CONTENTS

Illustrations

ILLUSTRATIONS

MAPS

CHAPTER ONE

The Heir

1779 : 1781

I

TEN DAYS before Christmas 1779 a wedding took place at the parish church of Noisy le Grand, a village on the Marne some eighteen kilometres east of Paris. The church, consecrated in 1484, was in the elaborate late gothic style, light enough even on a winter's day, but bitterly cold. The curé of the parish, the Abbé Durand, officiated. The bridegroom was "the high and puissant seigneur Alexandre François Marie, Vicomte de Beauharnais, captain in the infantry regiment of the Sarre." He was attended by two brother officers bearing younger-son titles, by his surviving parent, the Marquis de Beauharnais, once Governor-General of the French West Indies, by his elder brother, François, Comte de Beauharnais, his uncle, Claude Louis, also Comte de Beauharnais and with a son confusingly named after him, by two unexplained spinster ladies with an Italian surname, and two bureaucrats from the Marine and Metz who had witnessed the marriage contract. There was also present a solemn figure, M. Patricol, a retired professor of mathematics. He had been tutor to the Beauharnais boys and attempted to rear them in admiration of the precepts of Rousseau, Raynal, Morellet, etc.

On the bride's side there was only one male representative, the Prior of Sainte Gauburge, Louis Samuel Tascher, almoner to His Serene Highness Monseigneur le Duc de Penthièvre. He was quite a distant cousin but had been given authority to represent both her parents. Her mother was at home, on the family estate in the island of Martinique, her father "our invalid" had got no further than the Beauharnais hôtel in Paris. He had been dreadfully sea-sick and believed himself to be nearly bankrupt and dying. Neither of these facts, however was allowed to appear. When his masterful sister, Madame Renaudin, had whistled, he had obediently set sail to cross the Atlantic in the worst possible season. He had brought with him an unmarried sister "Tante Rosette" (who claimed to have tenderly nursed the bridegroom in his infancy), his only available daughter, Marie Joseph Rose, generally called Marie Rose and a mulatto maid, Euphemia, unkindly believed in Martinique to be another of his daughters. The Chevalier Joseph Gaspard Tascher de la Pagerie was an easy-going agreeable man, but long past his best, and it had not been in his power to refuse a brilliant marriage for a child, whatever the drawbacks and difficulties.

Originally, the intended bride had been his second girl, Catherine. She had been considered the most suitable in age for Alexandre, when the alliance had first been mooted. She had been three years younger than he. Catherine had died of a malignant fever. M. Tascher had hastened to offer his third girl, Marie Françoise. His eldest would not, it appeared, please the bridegroom. He had been seventeen and a half and had objected that a young lady of fifteen would be too old for him. But in the end she was the one he had to have. For when the marriage settlements began to be discussed in detail M. Tascher had to confess that his youngest, "Manette", was not yet twelve. She clung to her mother and both had howled.

Madame Renaudin began to lose patience. "Arrive with one of your daughters or with two. Whatever you do will be agreeable to us." She dreadfully hinted that if our young chevalier was kept dangling he might look elsewhere, and he was, apparently, an almost heavenly being. "All that I could tell you about him would be below his deserts—a pleasing face, a charming figure, intelligence, talent, knowledge, and (what is beyond price) all the noble qualities of soul and heart are united in him."

It could not be denied that Madame Renaudin, who had made the match for the good of her family, was a shuddery figure. She had been born Euphemia Tascher de la Pagerie, and at the age of twenty, blonde, big and cheerful, had gone to Government House, Fort Royal, as a sort of companion-attendant to the young wife of the newly arrived Governor-General. Unfortunately, he had fallen in love with her and she was not of a type to let go. He had done what seemed the most sensible thing, found her a husband on his staff. M. Alexis Renaudin had been the son and heir of one of the first families in the neighbouring island of St. Lucia, but could hardly refuse to oblige his Governor. He had been released after four years imprisonment in the fortress of Saumur, on a *lettre de cachet*, accused of having attempted to poison his father. Surprisingly, his father had held out until his last breath against the idea of his heir, however maladjusted, marrying the Governor's mistress, a woman without a dowry. But M. Renaudin, senior, had died, and the wedding arrangements had gone forward. Everything about that marriage was ill-starred. Lingering at Fort Royal to see that Renaudin did not run out, the Governor allowed an English fleet to capture Guadeloupe. He had ample reinforcements and had received repeated warnings. But it was the Governor of Guadeloupe who was disgraced, dismissed from his post and the army (with a terrible parade ceremony at Fort Royal), and despatched to France to be locked up for life. M. de Beauharnais was, it was true, recalled, but he had good friends at court. He was solaced on his retirement by being advanced to the title of marquis with an excellent pension.

Quite soon after their marriage, Madame Renaudin had accused her husband of trying to poison her—with arsenic again. He had gone to Paris and entered a plea for a legal separation, supported by her. The result had been wholly advantageous to her. She had got a fine allowance, he had never returned, and when the Governor had arrived in France she had soon taken up her old post again. His misguided and unhappy wife, who had even gone to the length of appointing Madame Renaudin godmother to her second son, Alexandre, had eventually gone to live with her mother, at Blois. When the Beauharnais boys had been seven and nine she had died. But the Marquis and Madame Renaudin could not regularize their position. There was still the wretched Renaudin alive. They continued to live together.

To a certain extent the conventions were observed. In the marriage contract Joseph Gaspard, father of the bride was mendaciously described as occupying an apartment in the home of Madame Renaudin. He was living in the Beauharnais hôtel in Paris. The only home which she did own she had bought three years earlier. It was at Noisy le Grand, opposite a farm belonging to the nuns of St. Martin, a good country house, with a couple of courtyards, stables and flower and vegetable gardens. She had bought it from a Comtesse de Lauranais, rather cheap, but spent as much redecorating and furnishing it. She was presenting it to her niece, the bride, together with the reversion of a substantial sum due to be paid to her by a Renaudin nephew. She had, in fact, advanced to her brother the first instalment of the marriage portion which he had agreed to pay. This was only fair, as in the preliminary letters about the match the marquis himself had stated genially that no portion would be asked for. But Joseph Gaspard was not allowed to handle the loan. Madame Renaudin had spent it on the trousseau. Joseph Gaspard had promised on paper to find a dowry of a hundred and twenty thousand livres. He could not produce twenty thousand. He had scarcely been able to muster credit to pay for passages for four from the West Indies to Brest. But the prize offered had been too great a temptation. Also, like the marquis, he was an easy-going man completely under the thumb of a domineering woman.

Madame Renaudin had long considered the advantages of a marriage for one of her nieces with a Beauharnais son. The elder, François, had always been promised to his first cousin, Françoise, daughter of the Comte de Beauharnais. They had now been married some years and had only one child, a daughter. The marriage was not going well. Alexandre might succeed to the marquisate and all, not only half the property at la Ferté Auvrain. In any case he would be wealthy. He had inherited from his grandmother and mother estates in San Domingo and in the Orléannais.

It would hardly have been possible to guess this from his extremely gushing letters on the subject of the alliance, but the marquis had not been fascinated by the prospect of a Tascher daughter-in-law from Martinique. However he had been gradually brought to realize that he must bow to the inevitable; and Alexandre had played into the hands of Madame Renaudin. He had imprudently sent her a letter couched in the high-flown romantic style now fashionable telling her that he had chosen Juliette as the name of "one who will be very dear to us." At seventeen he was an expectant father. The next child of Madame de Longpré, a lady eleven years his senior, with West India connections and a château near Brest, was accepted by her husband without demur and quietly absorbed into their family. It was not Juliette. It was a boy and it was christened Alexandre. Such an exploit was not at all unexampled for a young officer in a provincial garrison town, but the marquis had to agree that the sooner his son married the better. Alexandre had accepted the news unenthusiastically. "Surely, you cannot intend that I must marry

this young lady if we find that we have a mutual repugnance!"
But to be married to a girl he had never seen was the usual fate of
his contemporaries and the arrangement would bring him some
importance. After the ceremony he would assume the title of
vicomte. Hitherto he had borne simply that of chevalier.

As an infant he had been left by his parents in Martinique in
the care of old Madame Tascher de la Pagerie, grandmother of
his future bride. But as he had been sent for to join his parents at
the age of five he could have no recollection of her, and very
vague memories of the Antilles. He had been well remembered
there as a charming little boy, well-grown, fair and sharp. He had
been sent, on his arrival in Paris, with his elder brother to the
famous College of Plessis. As was customary, a private tutor—
Patricol—had accompanied them. From his tenth year until his
sixteenth Alexandre had been instructed by the mathematician.
His elder brother had soon been realized by Patricol to be un-
teachable—a complacent boy of a reactionary type, a devoted
royalist. Of Alexandre, Patricol had high hopes. The boy was
brilliant, promisingly open to modern ideas.

The trio went to Heidelberg for the youths to perfect their
German. On their return Patricol received the offer of a new and
splendid post. The Duc de la Rochefoucauld, head of one of the
noblest families of France, needed a tutor for the two Rohan
Chabot boys, sons of a sister. Alexandre de Beauharnais arrived
with his pedagogue at La Roche Guyon on the Seine, and from
that moment became an accepted hanger-on of the ducal household. Nothing could have been more fortunate. He entered a
charmed circle of wealth, intelligence and wit. The duke was an
advanced Liberal. He got Alexandre a commission in a regiment
which he commanded. Alexandre set off on a series of garrison
duties in dull towns with the happy certainty that he might always
present himself on leave either at the Rochefoucauld château, or
at one of their two palaces in Paris. (One of the Rohan Chabot
boys had come to see him married.)

The Tascher and Beauharnais families had in their backgrounds
much in common, but the records of the Taschers, now ruined,
indolent and melancholy, decidedly surpassed those of the Beauharnais in lustre. Alermic de Tascher had helped to build the
Abbey of St. Mesmin in 1142, Nicholas had received permission
from Louis le Jeune to rebuild the walls of Orleans. Regnault and
Arnaud had gone on Crusades, Ferry had been given a Seigneurie

by Philippe le Bel. They had always been soldiers—Marin had fought at the battle of St. Quentin, Jean at the siege of Turin, Jacques at the siege of Bergues. But they had not collected riches, only estates which needed money ploughed back into them. Gradually they had been obliged to sell even La Pagerie though they retained the name of that beloved estate.

The first of them to sail for the West Indies to seek his fortune had hardly prospered, except in making an advantageous marriage and producing five children. Both his sons returned to France. An uncle, Canon of Blois and almoner to the Dauphine, had got them appointed pages in the household of that lady. Her son was going to become Louis XVI, but Joseph Gaspard did not retain his employment. He went back to Martinique, aged twenty, and became a lieutenant in the marine artillery of the Militia raised to repel the English invasion. He did not succeed in this patriotic effort. Martinique became English. After a year it was returned by treaty to France and M. de Beauharnais in Paris saw to it that Joseph Gaspard got a small pension as a retired officer. He may have assisted him to win the hand of Mlle. Rose Claire des Vergers de Sannois who brought him a plantation at Trois Islets on the bay opposite Fort Royal, complete with slaves from the Guinea Coast falsely declared to number one hundred and fifty. The name Rose was thereafter largely bestowed on descendants. Joseph Gaspard's wife was believed to have noble Irish blood. Her mother had been a Mlle. Browne, of the family of Viscount Montague.

But he was not a lucky man. He never got a son and heir. His house was destroyed by an earthquake. He moved with his family into his sugar refinery which he hastily adapted and never had the means to improve.

His three daughters had as their world a verdant isle, fifteen miles by forty. Trois Islets consisted of less than fifty houses all built of wood. Only the church, which contained the Tascher de la Pagerie family vault, was of expensive stone. Marie Rose and her younger sisters lived the typical lives of young Créole ladies —no shortage of slaves to wait upon them, no insistence on any duties except the purely social. Marie Rose had a beloved and devoted mulatto attendant, "Marion," whom she never forgot. The daughters of the island were expected to have languorous grace, and wear with elegance, outlandish garish costumes, striped and dotted muslins and cottons as brilliant as the parakeets who flew above their curly turbaned heads. Paris dress-makers sometimes in hot weather had success with Créole fashions. Créole meant a person born and naturalized in the isles, either European or African, but never of mixed blood; there was in the word no connotation of colour.

The two elder girls went to convent school on Fort Royal; not the most costly one. Marie Rose's education ended when her sister died and she went home to comfort her mother. Her father's description of her to the Beauharnais hôtel sounded slightly apologetic.

"She has a very good skin, good eyes, good arms and a surprising taste for music. I gave her a teacher for the guitar while she was at the convent and she made full use of this and has a very pretty voice. It is a pity she had not the advantage of an education in France." He added that she had often asked to be taken there and burned with desire to see her good aunt.

When Madame Renaudin heard that her brother and the bride had escaped being captured at sea by the English and were actually arrived in Normandy, she set off with speed, bringing with her the bridegroom. Alexandre reported to his father that M. Tascher de la Pagerie seemed less ill than they had been led to expect. Although he had been put in terror of death for various reasons no less than ten times on their passage, he was not dying. He should be able to travel to Paris in a few days time, by easy stages. Alexandre had to tell his father that he had bought a cabriolet for their journey, drawing on their family banking house. He supplied full details. He drew to a close:

"Mademoiselle de la Pagerie will perhaps seem less pretty to you than you expect but I believe I can assure you that the honesty and sweetness of her character will surpass whatever people have been able to tell you about her." At any rate, he had not felt his dreaded repugnance. Like many young men of family before him he was preparing to make the best of his future with a girl whom he would never have chosen.

Thereafter events moved swiftly. Banns were read once only on Sunday, December 5 by special permission from the Arch-bishop of Paris. The marriage contract was sealed five days later. The wedding party which gathered in the parish church of Noisy le Grand on Monday 13 appeared at a superficial glance promisingly normal. There were imposing personages on both sides of the families—the marquis wearing his military Order of

St. Louis, Madame Renaudin, large, majestic, triumphant. The bridegroom and his brother-officers wore the becoming uniform of their corps—white cloth with silver grey cuffs and revers, light dress-swords and black tricornes with silver braid. Alexandre at eighteen was outstandingly handsome, tall, slight, fair, smiling, too easy in manner to be shy.

Only the bride, who signed herself for the last time in an unformed hand "M. J. R. Tascher de la Pagerie" seemed inadequate and aware of it. She was sixteen and a half and her father had assured her future relations that she was well developed and looked more than her age. This was indeed true. Marie Joseph Rose who was to become famous for her seductive grace had not yet fined down. She had the dreadful, almost apprehensive, burdened air of the growing girl. Even in her new Paris gown she had hardly any looks. Her figure was heavy, her face large, she moved badly. A connoisseur might have discerned that her features were not bad, and her expression was not sullen.

Nobody could possible have guessed that from this arranged marriage of provincial nobility with a West Indian connection, staged in an obscure suburban parish church, on a short winter's day, was to result descendants who would sit on almost every throne in Europe.[1]

II

Alexandre addressed his letters to his wife:

À Madame
Madame la Vicomtesse de Beauharnais
en son hôtel
Rue Thévenot
vis-à-vis la rue des Deux Portes Saint Sauveur
Paris

He wrote many letters to her in the few years of their marriage, some cheerful, teasing her about her chubby little cheeks and promising her a thousand kisses, far more very condescending, and the last ones very cruel. She kept them all and left them to her son.

The Rue Thévenot was in an old-fashioned quarter of dark sunless streets of tall noble houses with garden walls and courtyards and handsome wrought-iron railings. It had been fashionable in the days when there had been a court at the Louvre and the Tuileries, but no king had dwelt in his capital since Louis XIV. Inside the Hôtel Beauharnais there were lofty reception rooms with elegant panelling and plasterwork and an imposing entrance hall from which a beautiful grand staircase invited upstairs. In the top storeys there were numbers of small bedrooms offering no comfort at all—hot in summer, freezing in winter.[2]

This was the house in which Alexandre's great grandfather the Governor of Canada had died and in which they must expect that their children would be born. It was a family house. The legend was that such noble mansions might look like prisons outside but inside were Aladdin's caves. They were glowing with heirlooms—tapestries, paintings, porcelains, bronzes, crystal chandeliers, parquet floors, gilded furniture; fitting background for scenes of elegant revelry. The truth was that a great many of them more resembled mausoleums, inside and out, and the sounds of many clocks of different opinions telling the hours in the gaunt and creaky rooms only enhanced their melancholy. A church very close outside added deeper notes.

The Admiral's lady had been a Hardouineau from San Domingo, and so had her mother, so the new generation would have the isles over and over again in their blood. She had been a great heiress and the furniture and *décor* dated from that marriage, so was not very new. The wife of Alexandre began to learn more and more about her husband's family, dead and alive. The dead were very important. There had been a Marie Bonneau, wife of Jean Jacques de Beauharnais, Seigneur de Miramion, who had founded a female charitable order, called after her the Miramiones. The Governor of Canada had discovered some mountains called the Rockies. Another daring sea-farer had discovered a river—Mississippi. Her father in law had himself been a sailor, and this was sometimes recognizable. He seemed to care for his dead relations much more than those who were visible. Fortunately these were not very many. There was his elder brother Vice-Admiral Claude, Comte des Roches Baritaud, who had come to the wedding but would never stay in Paris while his wife was in residence. He lived in La Rochelle. She was "Tante Fanny" and celebrated, a poetess, daughter of a rich industrial. She sat on a canapé while adorers read her own poems aloud to her. Her disapproving-looking daughter was married to Alexandre's brother.

It was disappointing that the family was not larger and nobody in it except "Tante Fanny" seemed to care for entertaining. When Alexandre went off to join his regiment in July, after a long stay at Roche Guyon (without his wife) she was the only young person left in the house. She was not alone, to be sure. She had for company the marquis and Tante Renaudin, but she was really frightened of both, though they were kind. Her father was a sad object, always worrying about his liver complaint and his passage back to the isles and his debts when he got there. Tante Rosette said acid things and had no money. Poor Euphemia, the mulatto, complained of nothing, but her blue cold face was enough to make one want to weep on her bosom, and Marie Rose often did.

There was something terrible about this house, with nothing going on, and all the clocks ticking away her youth. She was seventeen. She would soon be eighteen. She knew what this house was waiting for, and everyone in it. It was her son.

III

When M. Patricol received, in June 1781, a letter from Madame Renaudin asking for advice he applied himself to the problem she posed with his usual solemnity.

It was not new to him. He had already heard at length from his best pupil. The situation was grave, for the young couple had now been married eighteen months and at last a son and heir was hoped for. (There had been a *déception* last August, a sad disappointment. Madame de Beauharnais had got as far as knitting the first of two stockings for the coming little one.)

That she never opened a book and had no idea how to write a letter did not surprise Patricol. The ladies of the isles, he knew, spent their days reclining under palms, banana trees and mangoes, in a becoming undress, fanned by slaves and listening to the music thrummed and howled by more slaves. Though one must not say so, Madame de Beauharnais had received hardly any education. It was unfortunate that she danced badly, and though supposed to be musical, could perform only on the guitar. That instrument was out of fashion. Ladies today were expected to seat themselves with aplomb at the classical harp. Her husband had sent her a master for the harp—Signor Petrini. She had good arms. The vicomte said that he had explained to madame what a letter should be and suggested that she should send him her first drafts for correction. Letters were not intended to tell the recipient such things as what your journey had been like (what a silly question! Brest was a bitch of a town!) They were an opportunity for displaying literary style and, particularly, sensibility. Her letters had improved. He could see which bits were Madame Renaudin. But his wife would never be a Madame de Sévigné. She said she had borrowed the first two volumes of the Abbé Vertot's masterpiece, *Roman Revolutions*.

At first when he had discovered the extent of her ignorance he had been inspired by the thought of moulding and directing an immature understanding. At first, too, she had seemed willing to be improved so that she could gain his affection. He had told her that he was ready to repair the fifteen wasted years of her existence. It was a great deal to have offered. She had not even thanked him. Quite soon he had come to the conclusion that she was opposing her intelligence, such as it was, to his well meant efforts. She maddened him by asking questions—where had he been? with whom? even, of what was he thinking? She was jealous. This made him cold. She wanted to be taken to large tumultuous gatherings, a thing he detested. She wanted his company. So he stayed at home with her. When they were alone, nowadays, they sat in silence. Was it to be wondered at that he had resumed his old bachelor habits? But he had married in hopes of a happy home and had not abandoned his schemes for his wife's education without sorrow.

Patricol's suggestions were tactful. As the vicomtesse would be in the country at present might it be best that she confined her reading to poetry? If M. Tascher's health permitted perhaps she could read with him some history and geography. She might like to commit to memory some *morceaux choisis* from famous French classic drama. On her return to Paris, Patricol would be happy to find for Madame la vicomtesse someone who could direct her studies next winter.

The question of her asking to be taken more into society he prudently avoided. It might be that her husband felt he would blush to see her exposing herself by her gaucherie and timidity. He had used the expression with regard to her letters. He had kindly told her she need no longer blush to address herself to whoever she chose. Patricol knew, like everybody else, that his pupil was a great favourite in the royal palaces. He was considered one of the best dancers at Versailles. He was asked to perform in the queen's own formal set dances. He had, hanging up in the Hôtel Beauharnais in Paris, many suits of extraordinary beauty—pale satins and brocades and velvets, garnished with gold and silver braid and silk floral embroidery, and paillettes and laces. His wife loved finery. When they had been first married she had been so pleased with the jewellery he had given her that she had carried it about with her, playing with it, like a child. She wanted to show it to people—two diamond candelabra earrings, two diamond bracelets, a watch and chain encrusted with diamonds, a classical medallion set in diamonds . . .[3]

Patricol thought seriously of the vicomte's complaint of his wife's jealousy. This baneful passion, if indulged, must ruin any marriage. He wished it could be represented to Madame that the wife did not occupy the same place in a man's regard as his mistress. Brusquerie and tyranny were not allowed to her. It was her duty to seek to fix his affection, to inspire sentiments of the most solid and durable kind. But he was sure that Madame Renaudin could expand better on this theme than he. He would pledge himself that the vicomte had a most tender heart and longed to be loved . . . Madame Renaudin said he had written that he was much occupied in his new garrison. However, his greatest desire would be gratified if he could obtain the means to assist at the *accouchement* of Madame de Beauharnais. Even though conditions were very hard he would get some leave.

He was obviously interested in the child-to-be. As long ago as April when her pregnancy seemed established, he had sent his wife samples of sugared almonds, pink and white and blue in little barrels, for the family to taste and pronounce upon. These were the *dragées* to be handed round at a baptism, and Verdun, where his regiment was now stationed, was the most renowned place in France for *dragées*.[4]

IV

The Vicomtesse de Beauharnais gave birth to her first child on Monday, September 3, 1781. It was a son. The child was baptized next day in the adjoining church of St. Sauveur, by the names of Eugène Rose. Rose was the name of his heiress grandmother des

Vergers de Sannois, but Eugène had never been known in the family on either side. It was the choice of his father—a neo-classical name. Four popes had borne it; one of them had been canonized. This was fortunate, for every Christian child must be given the name of some saint. And there had been a fierce little Savoy-Carignan general of Imperial armies, Prince Eugène, but he had nothing to do with the case. The hero after whom Eugène de Beauharnais was called was the French rhetorician, the Emperor Eugenius, put to death by Theodosius in the year 394.

The narrow street outside the Hôtel de Beauharnais was entirely blocked by carriages, but it was never wide enough for two to pass. At last the gloomy house seemed a happy one. The guests with a few additions were nearly all the same as those who had attended the wedding at Noisy le Grand, even to the sisters Cecconi and the bureaucrats from the Marine and Metz. Eugène's sponsors were the marquis and Madame de la Pagerie, grand-parents. Even "our invalid" was present. Now the succession was assured his sister would assist him to return to Martinique. Madame Renaudin represented the absent godmother and presented the infant at the font. It was her proudest hour.

Afterwards, in the house, by the light of many candles, the heir was carried round by his beaming and bedizened *nounou* and the little boxes of Verdun *dragées* were distributed.

Two months later, on November 1 his father departed for Italy. Even Madame Renaudin had thought that since he would never otherwise be happy Alexandre had better see Rome.[5]

CHAPTER TWO

From Pillar to Post

1781 : 1794

I

EUGÈNE DE BEAUHARNAIS had six homes before he was five, and then six more before he was thirteen. There never was a child so pushed from pillar to post.

Soon after his birth, the whole caravan from the Hôtel de Beauharnais moved to a smaller but more modern and cheerful house on the Rue Neuve St. Charles.[1] There was a church near by, St. Philippe du Roule so new that it had not yet been consecrated. The idea was that the young couple should set up house together in a home of their own when the traveller returned from Italy. Meanwhile his father and Madame Renaudin bore his wife company. Alexandre returned in July 1782 and at first, according to her report supplied to her lawyers three year later, he seemed enchanted to be with his wife again. Another child was begotten. But within two months he was on the wing again. He had applied to the Duc de la Rochefoucauld to recommend him as an aide de camp to the Marquis de Bouillé just appointed to the command in the Windward Isles. The new governor had sailed without him, but Alexandre decided to follow. He left Noisy le Grand like a thief in the night of September 6 without farewells to his family. He never lived with his wife again.

She learned gradually that his old mistress Madame de Longpré had embarked for Martinique in the same vessel with him. By a chance stranger than fiction this accomplished, enthralling woman (eleven years his senior) had become a widow eight days before he had married. Still, he continued to write friendly letters to his wife, always sending effusive messages to his little Eugène. He had thought of a fine name for the next child, or rather a choice of two. He wavered between Quintus Hor-

26

tensius (the orator, rival of Cicero) and Scipio, name of a patrician family with several distinguished members. The child born on April 17, 1783, was female. She was christened Hortense Eugénie and her godparents were Joseph Gaspard, now back in Martinique and "Tante Fanny" Beauharnais.

In Martinique, according to the Marquis de Bouillé, Alexandre de Beauharnais told him that he had been married against his will; his father had forced him to it; and now his father wanted him to separate from his wife. It might have been true. The old man was deep. But facts seemed against it. When he sent his wife an atrocious letter, accusing her of adultery and promiscuity, his family as well as hers rallied instinctively to her. He had gone round Martinique paying slaves to give him evidence of indiscretions by Marie Rose Tascher before she had left the isles to become his bride, aged sixteen. He repudiated the paternity of Hortense. Madame Tascher believed the snake in the grass was Madame de Longpré. She sent her slandered daughter a voluminous letter offering her a warm welcome back to her old home. Even "our invalid" bestirred himself to write to his graceless son in law breathing fire.

But the Vicomtesse de Beauharnais was no longer sixteen, and she had had enough of her husband. He had said that he would meet her once more only in this life, and they did finally meet in a notary's office, to settle their "amicable arrangement," but of course, as this was a story of a broken marriage in real life, the end of it could not be so tidy and painless. Almost until death did them part they bickered, each using the unfortunate children as a weapon. It seemed they could give one another no peace. They often met, and wrote, about the children, and the bills, and the furniture.

On his arrival back in France the father posted a letter from Rochefort asking for his carriage to be sent to Paris to meet him. He added he would like the mulatto Euphemia to bring his dear little Eugène. At this period nearly everyone was at work to effect a reconciliation. The child was dressed in his best and sent off. The result was fatal. The vicomte had always been fond of children, and this one was particularly attractive. On the dark morning of February 4, 1786, Alexandre de Beauharnais stole his son from the convent of Penthemont in which his wife had taken modest lodgings until her separation should be concluded. He had to give up the child speedily. It was only three. The Créole mother's piercing shrieks of anxiety and rage, although translated to paper by a secretary for presentation at the office of the Commissioner of the Châtelet, were formidable. The repercussions were in the end favourable to her. Processes which had been seemed to have come to a standstill for a year were hurried at last. Within a month of Alexandre's *gaffe* the unhappy couple met to sign their articles of separation.

The wife's complaint was of the husband's "great dissipation" and continual absences from home, of his insufferable imputations. She deposed that she had exercised patience until to endure more would be to prepare both for herself and her children, a terrible fate. On the face of it, she got off with all the honours. Her husband was ordered to make her an allowance which would have been handsome had it ever been punctually paid. He apologized for letters written in youthful loss of temper. She was free to live where she liked with her daughter, for whom provision was made. But she lost Eugène after he was five, and her jewellery.[2]

She had to stay in the convent while she considered her future. In the end she spent eighteen months there. Curious though it seemed, it was while she was immured in this extremely equivocal position that she began to experience her first social successes. The poor little Créole vicomtesse with two children beautiful as angels was found by several families of consideration to be charming. She was not exactly beautiful, but her delicate features, her swimming dark eyes and waving hair, her pallor, her slender shape and apologetic air were all very sympathetic. She was "interesting". The convent harboured many single ladies of very good family, spinsters, orphans, or like herself waiting to get rid of a husband. She was invited, and gladly accepted an invitation, to attend the ceremony of clothing a high-born novice.

The house in the Rue Neuve St. Charles was uninhabitable. Her husband had removed the furniture. It was sold. The one at Noisy le Grand which theoretically belonged to her had gone already. She would never have been able to afford to run it. She had been keeping Hortense down there with a wet-nurse whose name should surely have pleased the father—*la mère* Rousseau.

The good curé of Noisy le Grand who had married the young couple had sent Madame Renaudin a timid letter to divulge that the vicomte had made an appearance to see his daughter, and had given her some gew-gaws from the local fair which had been in progress, and had paid the nurse two months' wages. He had refused to come in, because of the company he had with him, and had gone off telling Abbé Durand that he was "diverting himself infinitely" in Paris. He continued to take inconvenient interest in his children. He insisted on Hortense being vaccinated. After another fearful family conclave the mother was advised to submit. Eugène was getting double teeth, so his ordeal was postponed. As the children ceased to be babies and became boy and girl it was clear that both had inherited their father's colouring and Hortense was the fairer. Her head was covered with silvery flaxen curls, and she had a rose-petal complexion. Eugène was sturdy and bronzed—better for a boy. They were inseparable.

Punctually on September 3, 1786, Eugène was sent off to his father. With him went Euphemia. The mother had to rely on news from the mulatto, to whom, after a week of silence, she wrote painfully. The vicomte had arranged for his son to live in a pension in the Rue de Seine with a M. Verdière who would be his tutor when he went to the Collège d'Harcourt in January. The vicomte himself was living in the little hôtel of the Rochefoucaulds which lay alongside their large hôtel, on the quayside at the end of the Rue de Seine, in the Rue des Petits Augustins. He was about to become a relation. In 1788 his first cousin on his long-forgotten mother's side, Adelaide Pyvart de Chastullé married Comte Alexandre de la Rochefoucauld.

II

Both the Beauharnais children in after-life, wrote their memoirs.[3] Neither ever mentioned that their parents had been separated. Their mother had always spoken to them with dignity about their brave father.

Looking back, Eugène de Beauharnais thought that perhaps he had gone to school too young. After three years at the Collège d'Harcourt he feared he had been backward for his age. He remembered with gratitude the immense pains that his grand-father had taken to coach him. He had very pleasant memories of the old marquis ending his days in tranquil retirement in their second home at Fontainebleau. The first had been a lodging in the Rue de Remiremont, but the second, in the Rue de France, was their own. There was to be yet a third. He went to the first house only once. It had been arranged that when his parents separated that the boy should go to his mother for his summer holidays. Fontainebleau was fine. There was a forest in which he could learn to ride. The whole family rode, mother, son and even little Hortense. When the king came to hunt, there were hounds baying and horns blowing and a tremendous turn-out of noble lords and ladies on horseback and in light carriages. His grandfather once reported that his mother had been out following the royal hunt all day, on a wet autumn day, and had come in soaked. They knew some valuable people at Fontainebleau—the very Comte de Montmiron, hereditary Governor of the palace, after whose family the street in which they lodged was called, and the Vicomte and Viscomtesse de Béthisy whose aunt had been abbess of the convent of Penthemont. But by the time the court came to Fontainebleau Eugène would always be back at college for they always came in October.[4] When his second year away from home arrived he learned that his mother and Hortense and Euphemia were going to Martinique, and there would be only his grandfather and Tante Renaudin to greet him. He was to see his mulatto nurse again but not for many years.

Hortense made the best of the situation in her memoirs.

"The brilliance of my mother's social position could not make her forget her birthplace and her family. She had left an aged mother whom she wished to see once more. It may be, too, that she felt the need of a diversion from a feeling difficult to overcome and very natural. For my father, handsome in person, remarkably gifted and accomplished, was greatly in request amongst the foremost characters, both at Court and in society. His wife, whose over-sensitive nature made her too susceptible, was wounded and even jealous, and sought a remedy in the separation of a voyage. My mother and I sailed alone. I was four years old at the time. We embarked at Le Havre where a violent squall threatened to capsize our vessel almost in port. On arriving at Martinique we were received by my mother's family with transports of joy. The quiet life that we led, sometimes in one house, sometimes in another, must have suited my mother, for we remained more than three years out of France . . .

"The Revolution caused disturbances in the colony. Monsieur de Viomesnil and Monsieur de Damas in turn became governors, but the latter was obliged to leave precipitately. We were living at Government House at the time. One night my mother received word that the cannon were to open fire on the town of Fort Royal the following day. She set out instantly to seek refuge aboard a frigate whose captain we knew. As we crossed the fields which are called savannahs, a cannon-ball fell close beside us. The next day the town was seized by the revolutionists."

Their troubles were not yet over, for they ran aground on the coast of Africa, but they made the port of Toulon early in November 1790. When Hortense saw Eugène again she claimed that she had seen more of the world than he, and Eugène, always the soul of honour, admitted that she had reason.

But he too had been seeing life, and told her an anecdote which she put in her memoirs. He had been greatly excited by the thought of attending on July 14, the first anniversary of the taking of the Bastille. The occasion was to be marked by a tremendous celebration on the military parade-ground, the Champs de Mars, between the École Militaire and the south bank. His father had explained to him the exaltation that everyone in France must feel that day at the prospect of the Freedom now before them, and the opportunity to practise the noble Roman civic virtues. He must be taken to see his father riding in the procession. Alas! the morning was one of a steady downpour. However, he set off, hand in hand with his governor at an early hour. They ran into numbers of voluntary workers still wheeling barrows of earth, to build up the ramp in the amphitheatre. Unluckily, M. l'abbé had thought fit to wear his best canonicals and this costume roused the ire of a body of fishwives. They fell upon the poor man, put him in the shafts of a little cart and insisted that he should tug them to the show. They plied whips upon his defenceless back. He set off, miserably alarmed. But his pupil, a stout little boy, ran after the vehicle and belaboured everyone in it with the only weapon he had to hand—a large wet umbrella. Surprisingly, the furies desisted and his preceptor was rescued.

The greatest treat of his Paris college days was when his father called for him and they went up together to the Hall of the Constituent Assembly which was in the old royal riding-school of the palace of the Tuileries. The king had come back to live in his capital, as he should. Eugène never forgot the thrill of arriving at the new parliament house with his father and his father's elder brother, swinging along on a sharp morning giving a hand to each. The long narrow building was badly lit, and the only heating in it came from a stove in the centre. When they arrived at the stove, the Beauharnais brothers bowed to one another and Comte

François, who was royalist, and objected to every amendment and anything new, went to the right of the President's chair and table, and Vicomte Alexandre who had embraced the principles of the Revolution with a full heart, climbed up to the group of seats on the left known as the Mountain. That was where M. de Robespierre and the principal members of the Jacobin Club sat. All the benches were covered with green cloth. There were four galleries in which a thousand people applauded as if they were in a theatre, and sometimes three or four deputies sprang to their feet and started speaking at once, often very badly, and would not leave off though M. le Président rang his bell repeatedly. Eugène attended the Assembly many times and heard his father speak wonderfully.

Patricol's best pupil, who had complained that one little Créole would not let him mould her, was now moulding France.

On June 18 he was elected President, but most annoyingly Eugène was not there to see him take the chair as he had gone for the summer holidays to Fontainebleau. So he, who had spent so many hours there, missed hearing his father make an historic announcement. On the morning of June 2 the Assembly waited breathless with expectation, for Paris had been alive with rumours since dawn. The President entered deathly pale but his *sang-froid* was perfect. "Messieurs, I have just heard from M. Bailly" (Mayor of Paris) "that the king and the royal family have left Paris during the night. Shall we proceed to business?"

"In effect," wrote Eugène "by the absence of the royal authority he became the first personage in France, and I remember when people saw me in the streets of Fontainebleau they said *"Voilà! le Dauphin."*[5]

Hortense enlarged on this. "His firm attitude, the manner in which he maintained order in Paris, aroused a momentary enthusiasm. Even in our retreat at Fontainebleau, whenever people caught sight of my brother and myself, standing at a window, someone would call out, 'Look at our Dauphin and Dauphine!' When this occurred we retired hastily, as unable to understand the cause of the demonstration as to surmise what the future held in store for us."

At the moment it held a new home. Their mother had taken a house in the Rue St. Dominique, south of the river,[6] together with a Madame de Hosten Lamotte, whose family owned great estates in San Domingo. She wanted to send Hortense as a pupil to the convent of Abbaye aux Bois and the new address was convenient for seeing both her and Eugène. The cruel rule that she got the boy only in the summer holidays was having to go by the board. The royal family had been brought back to Paris very quickly. The king had accepted a Constitution and the Constituent Assembly closed at the end of September. War against his wife's country, Austria, would be the next thing the king would be obliged to accept. Alexandre de Beauharnais decided to return to his old profession. He had never got further than being a captain of a cavalry regiment—the Royal Champagne—and then had to revert to infantry to get a majority. But now his rise in the army was as spectacular as his rapid ascent in political life. "He left Paris," wrote Hortense, "to take command of the Army of the North with the title of General." This was anticipating events a little but he was adjustant-general, brigadier-general and chief of staff at Strasbourg within twelve months. Hortense's education at the chosen church school lasted an even shorter time. The Abbaye aux Bois, like all convents for women, was closed by law on August 18, 1792. Eugène's college had been closed long before. The Beauharnais children gradually learned that they were going to be evacuated to England with some other children they knew.

Their mother had come to this dramatic decision after two periods of agonizing anxiety. On Friday, August 10, the noises in the streets and sounds from across the river alarmed her. She sent for her daughter and had hours of suspense before the child arrived safely. Rumour declared that the Tuileries palace had been stormed and burned to the ground and the whole royal family had been put to the sword. They had in fact escaped but only to be sent to prison in the tower of the Temple: their Swiss guard had fallen to a man. Less than a month later what were to be known as the September Massacres began. The nine chief prisons of Paris were over-filled with priests who had refused to take the oath to the new government, criminals who had been forging the new paper money, and a large number of royalists, "enemies of the people." The first victims were priests, outside the Abbaye prison and inside the Carmes. After five days it was reckoned that about fourteen hundred captives had been liquidated. No politician could be found to take responsibility for the slaughter. No written order for it was ever found. It was said that the people who had burst into the prisons had been amateurs, convinced that they were only just in time to stop the prisoners, who were highly organized, from bursting out. These scenes of horror had taken place, not in one district across the river near the palace, but all over Paris. Some of the prisons were quite close to the new Beauharnais home.

Neither of the children ever mentioned that they had actually been sent off for England after the September massacres.

The friend to whom their mother entrusted them was well chosen. The Princess Amalia of Hohenzollern Sigmaringen was sister to the Prince of Salm Kyrbourg who had one of the best palaces in Paris, 60 Rue de Bourbon, on the south bank almost opposite the Tuileries. Everything about this couple was magnificent, including their generosity. The children were to be taken first to a château in Artois belonging to the prince, St. Martin, near St. Pol. It was close to the coast. One night, after dark, a yacht from England would run in quietly, in answer to some beckoning light or curlew call . . . But there had now been three large emigrations of aristocrats from Revolutionary France and escapes were becoming more difficult. The affair had to be kept a dead secret. The Vicomtesse de Beauharnais writing to a château in Artois was necessarily guarded.

"Your letter gave me much pleasure, my dear Hortense. I quite appreciate the sorrow which you show at being separated from your *maman*.

"But my child, it is not for long. I hope the Princess will return in the spring, or I will come and fetch you.

"Oh! how clever you will be when you return!; how well the Princess will speak of my little ones! I have no need to bid you to love her well. I see by your letter that you are very grateful to her for all her goodness to you and your brother. Prove it to her often, my dear; this is the way to please me.

"I feel much pain in being separated from you, and am not yet consoled for it. I love my little Hortense with all my heart.

"Embrace Eugène for me.

"Farewell, my child, my Hortense; I embrace you with all my heart, and I love you just the same.

Your fond mother,
Josephine de Beauharnais."[7]

The vicomtesse had taken to signing herself by a new name. It was generally assumed afterwards that her second husband chose her new name for her, but this was not so. With her independence she had taken on a new character. She was no longer Marie Joseph Rose or Marie Rose, a sugary failure of a girl. She had quite a good circle of friends in every camp.

Eugène de Beauharnais was not to see England. General Alexandre Beauharnais was just in time to send a courier to stop his son. In forty-eight hours the parties of children would have been off. He was expecting to be made Commander in Chief of the whole Army of the Rhine; he was going to be offered the Ministry of War (and prudently refuse it). He could not possibly have it said that he had sent his children to safety in England, a country with which France was going to war at any moment, and with a German prince. Once the attempted emigration was known it had to be given up, at least for the present. The princess and her brother returned to Paris, bringing all the children. Eugène was forwarded to his father at Strasbourg.

III

He was sent to the National School at Strasbourg and found himself happier than ever in his life before. His father's head-quarters were at Weissenburg, a little more than forty miles north-east, at the foot of the Vosges. He went out often and got fine horses to ride. Strasbourg, capital of the imperial provinces of Alsace-Lorraine, was a fortress of the first rank. He lived in a world of bugle calls, marching troops, words of command and military music. The "Marseillaise" was so-called because it had come to Paris with the federal volunteers who had made the first attack on the Tuileries; but the young man who had composed it had been serving with the army of the Rhine. He had first sung it to a band of fellow recruits in Dietrich's tavern in this town. This lovely countryside had inspired it. Eugène found himself back in the atmosphere which had been so exhilarating in Paris at the outbreak of the Revolution. "Everything breathed the love of La Gloire and La Patrie."[8]

Revolutionary France had received a great shock when her troops had been ignominiously repulsed on their entry into war with Austria and Prussia. But the Battle of Valmy had proved that the material which had made her armies famous was still available, and that properly fed and led they might still be formidable. In

September 1792, when the Government had put up posters "The Country is in danger," volunteers had presented themselves at the rate of eighteen hundred a day. They were quite untrained of course and had very little idea of discipline. At Lille they had murdered their general. General "Moustache"—Custine, whom Beauharnais had succeeded—had not been murdered, but he had been recalled to Paris and it would soon be seen what was the present Government's way with unlucky generals. Alexandre spent hours writing very fine screeds to the Legislative Assembly, and presently to the Convention. About two months after his son had arrived in Strasbourg, someone in Paris scribbled a note, the result of a train of whispers. The background of the *ci-devant* Vicomte de Beauharnais was insecure. He had a brother, an *émigré*, fighting with Austria against France in the royalist regiment raised by the Duc de Condé. There had already been two glaring examples of generals with aristocratic connections deserting the colours of the Republic. The cry "We have been betrayed!" was becoming familiar.

In July 1793 General Beauharnais failed to relieve Mainz which had opened its gates to Custine's troops last year, and was being besieged by the Austrians and Prussians. Mainz fell and what was worse, he had made no attempt to regain it. He had taken sick leave. His reputation with women was well known. There was talk of an attraction at Strasbourg, the daughter of an officer in the commissariat. But naturally, there was jealousy of so successful, so fluent and so handsome a man.

"The decree which excluded the nobility from the army obliged my father to leave the Rhine," wrote Hortense. "During the *régime* of the Terror," wrote Eugène, "my father quitted the army and retired to his estates." It was not quite as simple as that. He had returned to his post and sent in his resignation before he could be dismissed, but a letter from Paris accepting it had ordered him to leave within six hours. In the end he had gone off in such a hurry he had not been able to collect his horses, his carriages and his son. He had written that he hoped the boy would go to his grandfather at Fontainebleau. In any case he could not have remained at the Strasbourg college. It was closing. It seemed Eugène de Beauharnais was never to get an education.

He only saw his father once again, and never to speak to. The *ci-devant* Vicomte General de Beauharnais fought with all the

Alexandre, Vicomte de Beauharnais
General commanding the Army of the Rhine, 1792, after
a portrait by Rouget

The First Portrait
Eugène de Beauharnais aged sixteen, as aide de camp to
General Bonaparte, 1797, by Antoine-Jean, Baron Gros
By permission of the Prince Napoléon

skill he could command to preserve himself. General Custine had been sent to the guillotine. The family of Beauharnais had been Barons de Beauville, Comtes des Roches Baritaud, Seigneurs de Villechauve Monvoy, and la Ferté. He took a house in Blois, in the district which was the cradle of his race. He became Mayor of la Ferté Auvrain, President of the Jacobin clubs of the whole canton. He never ceased to write careful letters to people in high places. La Ferté Beauharnais, twenty one kilometres from Orleans, was a small, innocent-looking place. It lay between the Loire and the Cher. It had a mouldering château on a height, one street of brick houses, crossed by the Beauvron, a small tributary of the Loire, quite a good little church with sixteenth-century choir stalls, around which some antique buildings were of wood. Lamotte Beauvron, the rendezvous for hunting, was on the edge of the plain of the Sologne, insalubrious and poor land. There were melancholy wastes of balding conifers and standing water. But the very obscurity of this landscape gave him, as autumn pased into winter, an illusion of security. Here he could dwell in peace.

"I should never have believed," he wrote to his father in October, "that on quitting such an active life as that of the army, I should find time would flow by so rapidly in the quiet of solitude. Days pass as quickly as before my retreat. To be sure my brain is not sluggish. It exhausts itself in schemes to advance the Republic, as my heart overflows with efforts for the well-being of my fellow citizens."

He had dreadful thoughts for company. His glorious revolution had taken such an unmerited twist against him. During the September massacres his school-days friend Charles de Rohan Chabot had been murdered in prison. The Duc de la Rochefoucauld, "the greatest and best revolutionary in France," had been torn in pieces by a mob at Gisors.

Early in March 1794 the long arm of authority from Paris stretched out to gather the *ci-devant* General Beauharnais into the net. A closed carriage arrived at his house and he was handed an order for his arrest by the Commissaire Sirejean. He was taken to Paris, to the Luxembourg prison, deserted palace of the Comte d'Artois, and from there transferred to Les Carmes, the carmelite convent in the Rue Vaugirard. Both were in the neighbourhood of the house in which his family were known to live—Rue St. Dominique.

IV

His mother wrote that *le citoyen* Eugène Beauharnais had arrived to her from Strasbourg two days ago. The date was September 26, 1793, and she was applying for a certificate of citizenship in the village of Croissy sur Seine. The old marquis and her aunt had obtained one as permanent residents of Fontainebleau seven months before, and he had affirmed his republican beliefs. Josephine had been taken with a villa at Croissy, on a visit soon after she had come out of the convent of Penthemont. Madame Hosten had then been living there. Experience had confirmed that it was a charming riverside resort. But this same villa which she had now taken was not gimcrack. It had belonged to a lady in waiting of the late queen, a Madame Campan, and it was well appointed with rather old-fashioned furniture. She had quite a circle of friends at Croissy—Madame Hosten who shared her Paris house and had two daughters, one just the age for Hortense, M. and Mme. de Croiseul who also had children, Mlles. des Vergennes, Mme. de Rémusat, M. Réal who had introduced M. Tallien. The new Law of Suspects had meant that everyone who could must apply for registration, and a suburb looked safer than Paris as a fixed address. But she returned to Paris for the winter months. She had a governess for the children—Mlle. de Lannoy. Hortense's report on this lady was unusually critical. "Well born, well educated and possessed of several talents, her lessons would have proved useful to me had not her attention been entirely absorbed by politics."

In January, Josephine set herself down to write a letter to Citoyen Vadier, President of the Committee of Public Safety. Her sister-in-law Francoise Beauharnais had been arrested and was in the prison of Ste. Pelagie. Almost the only lesson that Josephine seemed to have learned from her husband was how to write a letter, or at any rate not to fear to put pen to paper. She wrote with a flourish—"46, Rue St. Dominique, Faubourg St. Germain, Paris, 28 Nivôse, Year II of the French Republic, One and Indivisible." (Nivôse was January, "snow." All the old names of the months had been changed at the New Year for patriotic reasons, and the new set had been chosen by a poet and a band of mathematicians. There were now ten days in a week, and three weeks in a month, and five days for public fêtes, and every single day of the Republican year had its own name. It was enough to drive a woman wild.)

"Lapagerie Beauharnais to Vadier, Representative of the People.

"Greetings! Esteem! Confidence! Fraternity!"

"Since it is impossible for me to see you, I hope that you will consent to read this attached memorandum. Your colleague has told me of your severity, but at the same time of your pure and virtuous patriotism, and how despite your searching inquisitions into the citizenship of ex-aristos you are always interested in the unhappy victims of a mistake."

She was longwinded. She had not yet learned that busy ministers do not turn over. She also lacked clarity. What she wanted to say was that Françoise Beauharnais ought not to be in prison. True, she was the wife of the elder Beauharnais brother who was an *émigré*, but she had divorced him as an enemy of the Republic. The letter really seemed to be a defence of the younger, "good," Beauharnais, "Alexandre, your colleague and my husband. I should feel much regret, Citizen Representative, if you were to confound in your mind Alexandre and Beauharnais the elder . . . You are right in suspecting the patriotism of the ex-nobles, but it is in the realms of possibility that among them are to be found ardent friends of Liberty and Equality. Alexandre has never strayed from these principles . . . My household is a Republican household; before the Revolution my children were not different from the *sans-culottes*, and I hope they will prove worthy of the Republic . . ."[9]

Ten weeks after Josephine had sent off her letter, to which she received no reply, Vadier signed the order for the arrest of the good Beauharnais. Josephine heard that he was in the Carmes prison but could not find out on what charge. (It was for having lost Mainz.) This made it difficult but not impossible for her to write again, in his defence.

On the Black Monday morning of April 21 the children in the Rue St. Dominique woke to find that their mother had gone. She had been taken to prison during the night. She had come weeping to kiss them farewell but had told Mlle. de Lannoy, "Do not wake them. I could not bear to see them cry. I should not have the strength to part from them." She, too, was now in the Carmes. Eugène was splendid. "My brother, despite his youth, felt all the force of a noble nature, and was fired with so intense a longing to see our parents that he was convinced he would succeed." After many hours he came back, dreadfully crestfallen. It had not been possible for him to reach Deputy Tallien. Everyone had seemed terrified when they heard he was a boy whose father and mother were in prison. Still, he was sure Tallien was their man.

They set off for the prison. It became their daily journey. It was one of the worst in Paris and still stained with the blood of the many priests slaughtered there in the September massacres. It was the fullest, and the weather began to grow warm. The children were forbidden entrance, but little notes from both parents reached them. "De la Prison des Carmes, le 9 Floréal, An II. My dear little Hortense, It grieves me to be separated from you and my dear Eugène. I think without ceasing of my dear little children whom I love and embrace with all my heart. Josephine." The General's enclosed note typically urged them to behave well and work hard until the parents returned—soon, he hoped. They got one more from their mother and then letters were prohibited. "We tried to replace them by words written below the list of articles in the packages we brought. 'Your children are in good health'; but the gate-keeper was cruel enough to efface them. As a last resource we took turns in copying the list so that the sight of our two handwritings might assure our parents that we were both alive . . ."

They got the better of the ogre, though. Their *maman* had a pet pug, Fortuné, who had only to be told her name to rush off to find her. They fastened a message to Fortuné's collar, and he dashed off down the black corridors. When he came back he had a fresh twist of paper round his collar.[10] Their mother said they must write to the Convention and to the Sûreté. To be sure they would. They had kind helpers. Mlle. de Lannoy had a brother in law, M. Sabatier, and there was M. Calmelet. They had a writing master, who was an ardent Jacobin, and a Professor of History who was a fervent royalist. Best of all they had the heroic Princess Hohenzollern. Her brother the Prince of Salm was also in the Carmes, and she herself was suspect and had a Republican guard in her house. But she had the Beauharnais children for the day every Sunday, and they played with the young Prince of Salm, her nephew, and an English girl whose deluded parents had sent her to Paris to have finishing lessons.

Neither of the children ever mentioned the word Guillotine. It was too horrible. Eugène always wrote of people "perishing on the scaffold." Hortense had a bad experience one Sunday returning home after a day at the Salm palace. The usual elderly maid was not available to escort her, and Eugène had not come, as he was behind with some lessons, so she set off with a very young chambermaid. As they turned a corner they caught sight of a crowd of ferocious looking bare-armed men advancing towards them to the sound of a band. They were singing the "Marseillaise," which was noble, and the "*Ça ira*" which was not.

> "*Ah! ça ira, ça ira, ça ira*
> *Les aristocrates à la lanterne!*"

Suddenly, the streets were bare. Everyone had got out of the way. There was a noise of doors and windows slamming. Hortense and her companion huddled together trembling, under the recess of a carriage entrance. They almost died of fear when the men stopped in front of the house opposite. They had found a statue of the Virgin on it. They banged on the gates and called to the *aristos* inside for ladders, and they got ladders, and the statue was hacked and mutilated and fell into the street. Then they went on their way. "I never found out what this mob was." Hortense had been convinced that she was seeing the beginning of another Day which would be remembered for some atrocities. But this was just an ordinary Sunday evening demonstration in Paris during the Terror.

In spite of the Terror, they were young enough to enjoy playing games with the princess's other young guests on the terrace of the Salm palace. It had such a lovely view across the river. But at a certain hour every day (since sounds carry well across water), they began to hear strange noises, like an angry sea, or wild animals, swelling in volume. And they could see in the distance crowds beginning to assemble on the Place Louis XV, where there was a structure which they knew to be a scaffold with a Machine, gaunt and black against the westering skies. They used to look away, and hurry indoors, heavy hearted. They cried, for they knew people were being killed now—innocent people.[11] Both the king and queen had perished on that scaffold.

Sunday, June 8 was the Feast of the Supreme Being. The Convention, or Robespierre (who was known to dislike Atheism), had decided on setting aside a day for the solemn admission that some Supreme Being did exist. All the friends of the Beauharnais children were delighted with this development. It was rumoured that Robespierre was going to be offered a kingly crown, like Julius Ceasar, but that unlike that unlucky character he was going to accept it. Their mother's *femme de chambre*, Agathe Rible, said as she dressed Hortense, "We must make you very fine, for it might be that we shall hear today that your father and mother are released and you will be allowed to kiss them." Hortense had a white lawn gown, a broad blue sash, and her hair fell in curls on her shoulders. When they arrived at the Tuileries gardens they had a very long wait, but were able to have a good look at the ingenious pageant designed by the famous artist David. The great basin of the palace garden had been drained dry and there was a hideous, enormous statue representing Atheism who, together with Egotism, Ambition, Discord, etc., was going to be burnt to death. The weather was perfect. At last the children saw the members of the Convention coming. They filed down an improvised staircase into the garden. One walked alone, ahead and was also conspicuous in that he had powdered hair and wore knee-breeches. That was Robespierre, and they were told to listen carefully to what he had to say. They could not hear a word. At the end he was handed a lighted fuse. The beautiful idea was that he would ignite Atheism and company, who would vanish in smoke, and when that had cleared a white figure symbolising Wisdom would arise in their place out of the ashes. Unfortunately Atheism gave off a shower of sparks and one of them landed on Hortense. Her gown went up in flames and her neck was burned. She was with difficulty extricated from the mob and taken home. To crown the children's disappointment not a word had been said about freeing prisoners.

Another great patriotic fête was ordered for July 19, the "Fraternal Banquet". Every house was to have a table spread in the street, and masters and servants, men, women, and children, were to sup together happily, under penalty of arrest. 46 Rue Dominique had the list of inhabitants pasted on the door. It looked very poor. Everyone in that house was in prison except one manservant, one maid, the porter and wife, the governess and the two *ci-devant aristo* Beauharnais children. They got into trouble at first for not having placed their table in the centre of the street, but the night was balmy, and the lights set on the festal boards and in the windows of the empty houses (ordered because residential streets were too dark), made the scene curious and unusual. They persuaded Mademoiselle to take them down into the shopping quarter where there would be more life. Here some of the streets had a roof of green boughs which made a very good effect, but the feasters still lacked gaiety. Shabby men were loafing about drinking, singing, and shouting. In the poorer streets there seemed more fun, but Mademoiselle got herself kissed by a cobbler. She kept on repeating as she hurried her charges home. "A thing like that could never have happened under the old régime!" Eugène suggested that the shoemaker's action had been prompted solely by a desire to correct her haughtiness of bearing. But he looked wickedly at his sister, for anyone could see that their governess had been kissed for the first time in her life. The poor woman was extremely plain. "I am glad to be only a little girl, or that horrid man might have tried to kiss me too," said Hortense. "I should never have allowed such a thing," said Eugène, drawing himself up.

A few days later an unknown woman called at the house for the children. Mademoiselle refused to let them go and the woman produced a note in their mother's hand giving them permission. Mademoiselle let them go, still fearing a trap. The woman led them to the bottom of a garden in what Hortense believed to be the Rue de Seine, but it must have been the Rue Cassette. She took them into a gardener's cottage. Opposite there was a big dark building. A window opened, and their father and mother appeared, standing together. It was like a scene in a play. Filled with surprise and delight Hortense uttered a cry and held out her arms towards her parents. A sentinel on duty moved up with a shout and the strange woman hurried them away.[12]

Mademoiselle told them a few days after this that their father was no more. He had died the death of a hero. Of course he became a perfect hero to them. They remembered him for ever as they had last seen him, fair and calm, handsome and smiling. Much later they were allowed to see his last letter. It was very long, but there was a message for them at the end.

"I die not only with the serenity that allows us to think fondly of our dear ones but also with the courage that animates a man who recognizes no master, whose conscience is clear, whose spirit is upright, whose most ardent wish is the prosperity of the Republic.

"Farewell, dear friend. Console thyself in our children. Console them by enlightening their minds, and above all by teaching them that by their courage and patriotism they may efface the memory of my execution and recall my services and my claims to our nation's gratitude. Farewell! thou knowest those I love: be their comforter and by thy care prolong my life in their hearts. Farwell! I press thee and my dear children for the last time to my breast.   Alexandre Beauharnais"

It was sold as a pamphlet on the streets of Paris. He had prepared a noble defence but he was condemned eventually on a charge of having taken part in a conspiracy of *aristos* in the prison.

When Hortense came to write her memoirs she said that the grief she had felt for the loss of her beloved father would never diminish, but time had lessened the shock she had felt that his end should be so horrible. Eugène wrote, "He was a patriot, in the full meaning of the word. He had embraced with fervour the principles of the Revolution without foreseeing the abuses which would follow. He perished together with a body of the *élite* of France, victim of an attachment to ideals which seemed to promise a happiness and stainless glory hitherto unknown to his country. His last words were of hope for the restoration of order and justice. History will recognize his claims to gratitude, and those of other illustrious victims of his time."

The Prince of Salm had been guillotined on the same day as Alexandre Beauharnais. Terror as well as misfortune increased around the fatherless children. For the Princess Hohenzollern, with whom they now spent every day, sharing their grief, had secretly decided that she was going to leave France. She would almost certainly be killed, whether she went or stayed. There were frightening rumours that the children of persons who had perished on the scaffold were to be arrested. There were already two boys of thirteen in the Carmes prison. Eugène was now nearly thirteen. But he refused to be alarmed.

He had taken on the responsibility for his mother and sister which he was never in this life to resign. Quarter of a century later the words, "Send for Prince Eugène," wailed by one of them would, they knew, in the shortest possible time, bring a travelling carriage with Imperial liveries, which had come at top speed over the Alps, clattering into the courtyard of the Château of Malmaison. "My brother," wrote Hortense, "considered himself as the natural protector not only of myself but also of my mother. Despite his youth he already showed that decision of character and calmness in the face of danger which he has displayed since."

The children talked together almost in whispers in the dreadful empty house in the Rue St. Dominique.

"I shall never abandon you. Set your mind at rest. I won't allow you to be taken away."

"But you will not be able to prevent it."

"Oh! yes, I shall. I shall enlist. Then no one will dare touch my sister and my mother. I have been thinking. While I am with the army, and until our mother is released you must go to La Ferté Beauharnais."

"All alone? Without you? No! No! I could never do that."

"Well then, come along with me. You won't be afraid of the shooting?"

"No! that I can promise you."[13]

The next thing they heard was that all children of noble birth must learn a trade. "My brother, in spite of our governess's despair, chose that of a carpenter." He got himself apprenticed to one in the Rue de l'Echelle and went regularly in the mornings. His employer was a furious Jacobin. He proudly exhibited the king's own front-door knocker which he had looted in the sack of the Tuileries. But he was quite good to Eugène, and he was sheltering two sisters, ex-nuns, as gentle as he was terrible. These good sisters gave Eugène, under the rose, little images of the blessed Virgin and holy saints which he brought home in glee as his first wages. Hortense's profession was entered as "dressmaker". Mlle. de Lannoy was her instructress.[14]

Madame de Fontenay came to see the children. She had curly black hair and roving black eyes, and was wonderful to behold. She was Spanish and divorced; they could not know that, but anyone could see here was a woman about whom men would go mad. She caressed the children and looked mysterious and told them not to lose hope. She had herself just come out of prison. She promised to interest herself in their mother's case.

They knew that Robespierre had gone to the scaffold and people said the Terror was over. On August 6 their mother was suddenly returned to them. She had been a hundred and eight days in prison. Both Eugène and Hortense always believed that Tallien had got her out. He was about to marry Madame de Fontenay.

CHAPTER THREE

The Stepfather
1795 : 1797

I

IN AUGUST 1795 Eugène de Beauharnais arrived at his fifteenth home—371, Rue de l'Université. The street ran parallel to the Rue St. Dominique but was further north, nearer the river. It was not surprising that his mother had wished to move as soon as possible from the house from which she had been hauled off to prison in the middle of the night and in which her children had lived the lives of orphans. In any case her own apartments had been sealed up and months must pass before she got permission to reclaim her furniture. But she had emerged from Les Carmes practically destitute. She took rooms in the house of another Créole, Madame Dooé. When General Hoche offered to relieve her of her son she did not hesitate to accept.

General Hoche had risen from the ranks and was "more of a Hercules than an Apollo." He had been married shortly before his arrest, and had an infant. He had been in Les Carmes with the Beauharnais for a short time, but had then been moved to the dreaded Conciergerie, last step before that to the scaffold. Here he had been put in a separate cell and either simply or elaborately forgotten. He had been quickly released on the fall of Robespierre and given a command, against the rebels of the west—the Chouans and Vendéens. The district was the coastal lands north and south of the mouth of the Loire. The Vendéens were royalist, religious, and accustomed to a low standard of living. Their country was ideal for guerilla warfare. They were entirely fanatical and their women believed that the soldiers of the Republic ate infants. The word Chouan literally translated meant screech-owl. They were smugglers and dealers in contraband salt, and it was rumoured that their nickname imitated the uncanny cries they

46

made in the night when approaching a rendezvous. They were being ruined by the Revolution and lived in huts and caves, performing robberies and murders financed by royalists and foreign enemies of the Republic. They stopped coaches, and stripped the passengers. They fired from behind hedges. It was a world of windy skies and wild seas, shots in the night and uneasiness.

Hoche recommended an amnesty and a declaration of religious freedom. Given leave to proceed, he made peace with the Vendéans in February 1795 and with the Chouans in April. But in July a body of *émigrés* was landed under cover of an English fleet on the peninsula of Quiberon. Hoche surrounded them and attacked. Of the six thousand landed on their native shore only one thousand eight hundred escaped, to be taken off by the ships which had brought them. Nearly seven hundred were executed by court-martial. It was a horrible campaign, Frenchman fighting against Frenchman. Nobody could look back on it with pride. When, after nearly a year, the widowed ex-vicomtesse reclaimed her son, Hoche made no attempt to keep him although he had been fond of the boy.

"Hoche," explained Hortense, "believed that one cannot begin too soon to form a man's character, and despite my brother's age (he was barely thirteen) he spared him no fatigue, employed him constantly as a simple orderly and exposed him to every danger. Such was the beginning of Eugène's military career, and doubtless it was in this rough school that he learned to understand the soldier, and later to make himself beloved. But that which for him was instruction filled my mother with dismay. Moreover his regular studies were not finished. So she recalled him from the army."

Eugène believed that he had been recommended to Hoche by his father, shortly before his execution. Hoche had served under General Beauharnais on the Rhine. "My master was severe, but although my schooling was hard it was none the less good." Until he had been taken by Hoche he had still been going every morning to the carpenter's shop, quite a long walk, over the river. (Years later, when he was a prince, an old lady who had lived there loved to recount how she had often seen the young Beauharnais with a plank on his shoulder.)[1]

If the widowed ex-vicomtesse could be thinking of sending both her children to boarding school, things must be going better for her. Hoche was glad. And she had used a reason for removing her son which he must instantly accept. Nobody knew better than General Hoche how lack of education could hold a boy back. But he was sad, for as recently as May he had written to an architect friend in Paris that now he had been frustrated for the third time from getting to the capital to see what had become of a widow whom he loved, and whose son he had come to regard as his own.[2] Her failure to answer his letters was driving him to despair. He understood her silence now and accepted his congé with fortitude. All women of Paris were coquettes and most men fools. A year later he wrote to the old marquis to say that when he passed through Paris he would like to call at Fontainebleau to embrace his dear Eugène. The boy never saw him again. For General Hoche was despatched on an unsuccessful attempt to land revolutionary French troops in Ireland, and then sent to the Rhine. He died very suddenly in September 1797, mourned not only by the troops but by all France. He was officially announced to have been long a sufferer from lung trouble, but there were persistent murky stories that he had been poisoned. The wife of another general who had risen from the ranks—Junot—put it in her memoirs that he had been assassinated. She knew, said she.[3]

II

Things were indeed going better for the widow. Hortense believed that in spite of hard times they had never suffered real privations because every month "Monsieur Henry," a banker in Dunkirk, sent them money from their grandmother's estate in Martinique. So even while their mother had been in prison, their governess had been able to provide them with comforts to which they were accustomed. This was only partly true and the comforts must have come partly out of the pocket of poor mademoiselle, to whom their mother was chronically in debt. There was a M. Emmery, a benevolent figure, with sugar-trade connections with the West Indies and he did collect what he could, but it arrived irregularly and never in sufficient amounts to meet the widow's rising expenditure. Martinique had been occupied by the British. Only her mother remained at Trois Isles now; all else were dead, father, sister, Tante Rosette. The Beauharnais children were heirs to their father's San Domingo estates, in which island the slaves had revolted. From these sources, Emmery produced a meagre sustenance.

He also made loans. The year was one of famine and prices of essential commodities were rising. The cost of a pair of shoes for the little Beauharnais girl was unbelievable. Bread was so dear that it was an understood thing at many houses that guests brought their own. Only poor *Citoyenne Veuve* Beauharnais was never expected to do this and was so grateful. She had sold almost the last of her jewellery.

Within a few days of Eugène's arrival the boy signed, together with his mother and sister, a pathetic letter asking the Convention to remember the widow and infants of one who had perished owing to the machinations of the *aristos* in spite of having dedicated his life to the Revolution. His mother had become an inveterate begging letter writer. It had been pointed out to her that by the edict of 8 Pluvoise she was entitled to some relief, and she had recovered her own effects. Now she was asking that her husband's books, silver and furniture, left behind in the house at Blois, might be returned to her, or that she might receive a lump sum. She was going on to ask for sugar and coffee (which she could sell very profitably) instead of rents from her family plantations which had been wrecked by the slaves.

Both the children needed the dentist, and so did she—again, alas! Her front teeth were stopped. It did not show at a few paces; she could still pass for a young and pretty woman; but she practised tight-lipped smiles in front of her looking glass. She made several expeditions to Fontainebleau. Things there were now very bad. An ungrateful country had reduced the pension of the old marquis, too, by two-thirds. He was equally involved in the ruin of San Domingo. At a family conclave it had been decided to sell the house in the Rue de France, move into a hired one in the Rue St. Merry, and use the result in sending Eugène and Hortense to boarding schools. Madame Campan, who had opened a select seminary, had agreed to take Hortense at half price and was going to provide her with a second-hand uniform. Eugène was going to the Collège Irlandais, where the President was Patrick McDermot, who had taught Henri Campan. The Campan school, named *"Institution Nationale de St. Germain"* was in the Rue de l'Unité in the old Hôtel de Rohan. The Collège Irlandais was in the old Ursuline convent and was next door. It was arranged that Eugène should spend two hours with his sister every Sunday. St. Germain missed royalty even more than Fontainebleau, but it had been decaying much longer. Its enormous château was in ruins and had never been inhabited by a monarch since Louis XIV had lent it to the exiled Stuart king, James II. But it had one feature of surpassing beauty, a terrace walk, backed by towering trees, designed by the famous Le Nôtre, and a mile and a half long. From it the view of the Seine valley and distant Paris was magnificent.

The letters to those in high places, suggested by the Talliens, and Barras, President of the Convention, had worked wonders. Claude Beauharnais's name had been erased from the list of proscribed *émigrés*. His wife had died and he was left with a beautiful fair little girl of three, who was at present at Fontainebleau—Cousine Stéphanie. Persistent nagging had resulted in Françoise Beauharnais being released from prison at last. Her child, Émilie, was also at Fontainebleau, a year older than Eugène.

A letter to the Committee of Public Safety, alleging that General Beauharnais had left behind at Strasbourg stables and equipages, had miraculously produced a carriage and a pair of black Hungarian horses, seven years old. The widow took her children in their carriage, which might be regarded as a legacy from their heroic father, to see their new home. Kind friends had put her in the way of taking a lease of their best home yet.

Number 6 Rue Chantereine[4] stood in its own garden at the end of a fine avenue, and had a coach-house and stables in which the Veuve Beauharnais was going to keep, as well as the black horses, a red cow. The house had been built by the well-known architect Ledoux for the Marquis de Condorcet in 1791. It was a miniature pavilion, a little gem. To arrive at it was like coming into port after a rough passage—a quiet haven. It was perfectly secluded, down its own lane, surrounded by the high walls of other houses and gardens, but nevertheless desirably central. Its last owner had been Julie Carreau, wife of the rising actor Talma, who had now left her. It had been given to her by an admirer, before her marriage. She had been in a position to equip it very handsomely. Unkind visitors described it as a Temple of Love. Before she had captured the young Talma she had been the mistress of the Vicomte de Ségur and the Comte de Narbonne, and according to Paris rumour had borne three children to three different fathers. The house in the Rue Chantereine had certainly been the birthplace of the short-lived Talma twins, Castor and Pollux, in 1791. The decoration in the birthchamber was declared to be "in the Roman and Etruscan style." It was a neat little square house of two storeys with a mansard roof. It had good cellars and light kitchens, for the ground floor was raised above street level. There were five delightful reception rooms. One of them was oval and had semicircular French windows and a verandah from which people could walk down steps to sit in the garden. (Even in her worst days the widow's bills had always included those for flowers.) A circular staircase only wide enough for one at a time led up into the principal bedroom. There was an adjacent bathroom and dressing room, of which even the doors were lined with mirrors. There was a very dark little sitting room and lesser bedrooms. All these had to have rather low ceilings. The downstairs rooms must be palatial. The mantelpieces were marble, the doors mahogany; everything was of the best, though on so small a scale. It could easily be run with a man servant who could cook beautifully (the Citizen Galliot), a coachman-gardener (butler from the Rue St. Dominique, metamorphosed into the Citizen Gonthier) and a new and superior *femme de chambre* (Louise Compoint) who expected to sit down with the family. Of course, Mademoiselle de Lannoy (at a salary of 600 livres a year, very reasonable) was staying on. She was indispensable.

Madame Talma had asked a substantial sum for the furniture but she had removed a good deal to her new home in the Rue Matignon, and Talma, now settled in the Rue de la Loi, had taken some more. Veuve Beauharnais sent Mademoiselle de Lannoy out to buy enough straw-coloured china silk tufted with red and blue to make bedroom curtains and a coverlet and covers for six bedroom chairs. She had brought her own old Guadeloupe secrétaire, and yellow octagonal table to match, and a walnut writing table with a marble top, and a harp, and a white marble bust of Socrates . . . But nothing in her new surroundings was going to remind her family of past homes. In the dining-room she had four new mahogany chairs with bronze inlay and black horse-hair seats, and in the *salon* a fine piano. Her own expenditure on dress this season had been very small—material for one muslin dress and one of grey Italian silk taffeta; and three pairs of grey silk stockings, and a little shawl for warm days, and a large shawl for later.

She began her move on October 2 and on October 5 France

jettisoned the Convention and conceived a Directory, with Barras as one of the five directors. This change of government could not be effected without a whiff of grapeshot. Thirty thousand National Guards, malcontents, including it was said some royalists, had massed to coerce the Convention, established in the Tuileries. Barras was in charge of the defence of Paris. He had appointed the young artillery officer from the topographical department of the Committee of Public Safety, hereafter nicknamed General Vendémiaire, who had paralysed the revolt at its headquarters, the church of St. Roch. The casualties had not been heavy but Paris had heard again the tocsin ringing and drums beating the alarm and the crackle of musketry. On October 14 the *Moniteur* printed an edict and presently officials arrived at the Rue de l'Université demanding the surrender of all unauthorized weapons. Eugène was fourteen now and had lived hard for the past year. He said that they should take away his father's sword over his dead body. They took it, but told him that he might get it back if he applied to the General Officer in command of the regular troops in the capital. Headquarters were in the Rue des Capucines, 26. He was General Buonaparte, an Italian name. He was said to be Corsican. Eugène's mother had just been in company with him once, at the Talliens'.

III

General "Vendémiaire" Buonaparte was a thin young man, very pale, with lank black hair, shoulder-long. He might have been handsome if he had not looked so hungry. His features were regular, classical, and he had piercing light-blue eyes. His aide de camp who looked even younger, and was indeed not of age, gave the same impression of zeal. While the sabre of the late General Alexandre Beauharnais was being looked for, the general told the boy to sit and asked him some questions about his family. Where did he live? Who had taught him to have such a regard for a hero of the Republic? His widowed mother! But his father also had always impressed him with the noble Roman ideals. He wanted to be a soldier too. He had already served under Hoche. When Captain Lemarrus returned with commendable speed he was told to give the sheathed weapon to the boy. Was this his father's sword? The question need not have been asked. Tears were pouring down the boy's face as he received it. He raised it to his lips. The general told him to take it and be off. "Your certificate of permission will arrive tomorrow." When the general smiled he changed entirely. Eugène admired him wholeheartedly.[5]

It was a disappointment to a boy who was needing a hero, to discover next day that his certificate had been delivered while they were all out. The general had asked for *la Citoyenne* Tascher Beauharnais. She heard this with regret. Next morning she ordered her carriage and told it to drive to General Buonaparte's headquarters.

IV

On the night of January 21, 1796, the family of the Citoyenne Tascher Beauharnais proceeded to a banquet. They had a long drive, for their new home was considerably north of the Tuileries and they had to cross the river. Inside the carriage there was an unhappy air of constraint. Both the children had been summoned from St. Germain. The banquet was being given in the Luxembourg Palace by Directeur Barras. The date was the third anniversary of the death of Louis XVI.

Hortense had erred. "What, Maman!" she had impetuously exclaimed. "You actually associate with such people? Have you forgotten our family misfortunes?" The words were hardly spoken when she regretted them. They had made her mother wince. But her mother never gave way to anger. "My child," she answered, with the angelic sweetness that never left her. "You must remember that since your father's death, I have done nothing but try to save the remains of his fortune which we feared lost. Must I not be grateful to those who have helped and protected me?" Hortense, always easily cowed, wept and begged pardon.

The Luxembourg, which had begun life as a royal palace, had been a prison during the Revolution. General Alexandre Beauharnais himself had been imprisoned there. But such things were all forgotten now and it was a palace again where gaiety reigned. It had been absolutely stripped of furniture and when the Directory had met for their first committee there they had been obliged to sit on kitchen chairs and send out for firewood.

It had now been splendidly re-furbished, but the guests were a motley crew. Some of their faces were enough to make a little girl's heart stand still. As Hortense had expected, she knew no one at the very large gathering except the Talliens and her host. Barras should have pleased her much better than he did. He was of the old noblesse—a comte—and had served in the army in the East Indies and seen the great world. He came from the south —Provence—where he kept his wife. He was tall and well-made, not yet stout. His voice was clear as a bell: but his dark eyes were glassy: his mouth closed like a trap. He was noisy, though his manners were assured: he seemed on the best of terms with men who looked dreadful. He had invited coming men, and for women mostly single ladies of the *ancien régime*. There was the Duchesse d'Aiguillon who now called herself by her maiden name, and the Marquise d'Achy who was now *Citoyenne* Carvoison. Both had been in prison.

Hortense was well punished as the long evening wore on. At dinner she found herself placed between her mother and a general. In order to speak to her mother he kept on leaning forward and talking across her. Her mother, in her lovely slow caressing voice, said something merely polite about France's admiration of his military successes. This seemed to make him quite mad. He forgot Hortense completely. He addressed her mother as if she was a goddess. Hortense sat right back. Nobody cared. She had opportunity to take a good look at him. She thought his face was handsome and very expressive but that he was sadly pale. She gradually realized that he was Eugène's hero, the general who had let them keep the sword. After dinner when people passed from room to room he attached himself to her mother as if magnetized, and never left them.[6]

The long drive home was no happier than the outward journey. It was a week-day, Thursday, but the streets of Paris were almost bare. There was grass growing in streets where *aristos* had lived. Some palaces had "For Sale, National Property" on them. Most were empty and had missing panes, and paint peeling off their façades, and sacks humped over leaks in their roofs. A few were government offices. The number of shops offering second-hand clothes and furniture was remarkable. Paris in the Directory seemed to have become the old-clothes mart of Europe. But few people wanted such things. Fashions had entirely changed. Affected young men in tight coats and long pantaloons minced about with eyeglasses, and in neckcloths which seemed to be strangling them; women were scantily clad in imitation of the antique. The neo-classic had arrived. It had not brought universal

cleanliness. The ragged troops of Revolutionary France were a
favourite subject of English caricature. But these pipe-smoking,
slouching sons of liberty were upon the whole good-humoured.
They loved shouting to one another by their noble new names.—
"Come on, Titus!" "Going to dinner, Brutus!" It was a new Paris,
and the entertainment this evening had been of New Paris. Old
times were gone. All the statues of Paris, once of brass and marble,
were now of plaster and wood.

As soon as they were alone the children conferred together.
"She won't love us so much!" said Hortense. She told her brother
what she had observed and found he had formed the same alarming impression. General Buonaparte meant to have her. Eugène
said he would speak to her. He did this with his usual courage. He
simply said that it seemed to him that a second marriage would
be for her a kind of profanation, a blow struck at the memory of
his father. She made no reply, and whenever they came to Paris
the general was in their home. He tried to make himself agreeable.
He told them ghost-stories, which he did very well. They decided
to treat him with hauteur. He said he admired their manners so
much, he was going to send his youngest brother Jerome to the
same school as Eugène, and his youngest sister Caroline to Madame Campan. They did not have to egg on Fortuné to growl at
him. The pug, who had always been plain and was now old, evidently meant to bite the intruder in his own good time.

They still had the villa at Croissy but they went there very
seldom. Her next door neighbour in the little riverside resort
noticed with amusement that the Citoyenne Beauharnais came
only about once a week and always to entertain *le Directeur*. They
could always guess when he was expected, for Paris *confiseurs*
began to arrive with hampers. All was of the best, ices from
Velloni, turkeys, wine, fruits out of season. He thought the widow
a typical Créole, for in the midst of this luxury she nearly always
sent round to him for casseroles, extra glasses and plates. Finally
le Directeur himself would arrive, a fine figure on horse-back
attended by gay Paris friends.

Her neighbours at Croissy did not know that the widow was
entertaining for him also at his two houses in Paris. She sent out
the invitations in her own name. She was useful to him. She had
been living on her wits for some years now, while her youth slipped
past, and she had learned to be a hostess. Her graceful step, her
concerned airs which seemed prompted by genuine kindness,

were irresistible. Her taste in dress, too, was just correct for her situation, classic simplicity. But simplicity can mean expense. General Buonaparte, like a sensible man, managed to ask M. Emmery if it was not true that his client was very rich? The young soldier had been dazzled by the carriage and black horses, the lovely little home. She was of the old *noblesse* a *ci-devant* vicomtesse. When he was told that the estates had been in the West Indies and she was not now rich, he said it no longer mattered to him. A rich wife would have been a help in his profession.

The affairs of the Beauharnais family seemed to be going from bad to worse. Just before Christmas, Renaudin had died. It was too late. The old marquis could now, and apparently was going to, marry Mme. Renaudin at last; but he was no longer a grand old man. He was failing and testy and his title had been abolished and he had very little money left; and with Renaudin had died the separation allowance made to Madame. They were not able to look after the young Émilie whose mother had re-married. M. Castaing had been a deputy to the Convention and a lodger in her house. He was a mulatto from San Domingo, a widower with four children. Émilie was sent to live with a governess.

On March 2 the appointment of General Buonaparte to command the Army of Italy was announced and it seemed to Hortense when she arrived at the Rue Chantereine that he was the life and soul of a little group of friends all congratulating her mother. The appointment had been made, as it must be, by Directeur General Carnot, but Directeur General Barras had brought the news to the Rue Chantereine. Hortense summoned all her courage and begged her mother with tears not to marry again, or at least not to marry someone who would remove her so far from her children. She noticed with hope that her mother seemed to hesitate; but already she feared the general had more influence with her than her children. "She loved him."

The days went by and the *Moniteur* announced that General Buonaparte had left Paris yesterday—March 11. Next day Madame Campan sent for Eugène and Hortense to come to her study. She told them that their mother had asked her to break to them news which she feared would distress them. She had married General Buonaparte on Tuesday night, two days before he left. No family on either side had been present, only the general's aide de camp, Captain Lemarrus. M. Calmelet, M. Tallien, and Directeur Barras. Madame, their mother, had hesitated until the last, so now would have to follow her husband to Italy. Madame Campan then said that she must proceed to point out to the children the advantages of this marriage. Eugène, who wished to serve his country, could not do so better than under the protection of the general who was his stepfather. Moreover, the general had not been implicated in the horrors of the Revolution. On the contrary he had suffered by it. His family was an old one, honourably known in Corsica. Madame Campan closed the interview by saying it was in every way a suitable match.[7]

Not everyone agreed with her. There was a little notary who must surely be the smallest in Paris. M. Raguideau only just missed being a dwarf. He had been summoned to the widow's bedroom to look at the marriage contract and when he had done so he urgently begged her not to sign it. The husband-to-be had frankly declared he owned "neither lands nor goods beyond his personal wardrobe and his military accoutrements." "Though no doubt estimable," wailed the notary, "he is bringing you nothing but his cloak and his sword." She had laughed and called to a young man standing in the window "General! Have you heard what M. Raguideau has been saying?" The notary much disconcerted, found himself being warmly shaken by the hand. "I hope that M. Raguideau will continue to look after our affairs, for he has inclined me to put my trust in him."

When they signed the marriage register the bride took five years off her age, declaring herself twenty-eight and the bridegroom added two years to his twenty-six. This made them equal, but only thirteen when Eugène had been born.

There was a most unkind Paris rumour that when the general had appeared at the Tuileries to hear the citation naming him to the command of a division, the pair of fine buckskin breeches which he had worn had been lent to him by the actor Talma, who certainly often supplied him with complimentary tickets for the Théâtre de la Revolution where he was now the leading performer.

v

As the spring months of 1796 passed, the astonishing news from the Army of Italy filled the papers, and even streets outside taverns and coffee houses where bulletins were posted. General Buonaparte had defeated the Austrians at Montenotte, at Millesimo, at Dego. He had beaten the Sardinians at San Michele,

Ceva and Mondovi. On April 28 they signed an armistice with him which left him free to turn again upon the Austrians. He crossed the Po and the Adda. On May 14 he entered Milan.

Madame Campan read aloud to Hortense the accounts of the victories. "Do you not realize that your mother has united herself to a most remarkable man? What gifts! What valour!" "Madame, I will give him credit for all his other conquests but I will never forgive him for having conquered my mother!" Madame repeated in Paris drawing-rooms the *bon mot* of her little pupil, the step-daughter of General Buonaparte. Her school already had a waiting list.

Their mother had not hurried to Italy. Burning love-letters arrived to her almost daily, urging her to join her lover. She looked through them languidly. "*Il est drôle, Buonaparte!*" She wrote to him that she had been ill—a *méconception*. She had had one the year before Eugène. The thought of her suffering in such a cause provoked torrential letters of pitiful abasement. She was still far from well, she pleaded, when she set off at last in the end of June. She had a splendid escort, ranging from an Italian grandee, the Duca di Serbelloni, and young General Junot to Fortuné.

Her children felt very lost when holidays came and everyone else was collected. Madame Renaudin had now married the marquis but they had not yet moved into their St. Germain home (5 Rue de la Lorraine.) They were still in lodgings. Madame Tallien sent an invitation but Madame Campan said she could not advise acceptance.

The victories continued and the spoils of Italy were tersely heralded by General Buonaparte to his employers. "Tomorrow, Citoyens Directeurs, there will start for Paris twenty superb paintings, chief of these the famous St. Jerome of Correggio . . . I shall be sending more soon from Milan, amongst them works of Michael Angelo . . ."

No officer bringing despatches or captured flags failed to bring also messages and keepsakes for the stepchildren of General Buonaparte at St. Germain. Eugène got a splendid gold watch, and Hortense a tiny round one set with pearls, and Venetian chains and little boxes containing flacons of scent. Presently letters from their mother began to come. She was being incredibly fêted, and this country was beautiful but she could not accustom herself to being separated so long from her children. She had been

under fire, on the shores of Lake Garda, and her husband had
sworn that he would make the Austrian General Wurmser pay
dearly for her tears, a promise which he had fulfilled at the battles
of Castiglione (August), Bassano (September), Arcola (November)
and Rivoli (January).

Eugène had twenty months of boarding school at St. Germain,
Hortense four years. They both realized that great sacrifices had
been made to give them these opportunities, and worked hard,
winning every possible prize. Eugène excelled in mathematics,
history, geography and foreign tongues—English! At Easter 1797
they both made their first communion. On a July day of that year,
at last, Eugène held in his hand his reward—a letter ordering him
to join the Army of Italy at Milan. With it came his commission
as a second lieutenant of the first regiment of hussars—cavalry!
It had always been his hope. He was almost sixteen and well
grown for his age. The only grief was in parting from his sister.
Though she now had a companion in Émilie, her first cousin,
this girl was naturally rather melancholy.

VI

To arrive at the Villa Cerutti, at Bovisio Mombello, in the
summer of 1797 was even for seasoned travellers a surprising
experience. Two poets from Paris, both authors of classical
tragedies, a career diplomatist M. Miot de Melito, and Captain
Antoine Lavalette, fresh from delivering instructions on the
establishment of a Ligurian Republic at Genoa, all wrote down
their impressions of the most remarkable man of their age, happy
with his family in his summer residence.[8]

By mid-May the weather in the capital had become a little
oppressive. The Palazzo Serbelloni, lent to him by the owner, was
kept open, but he visited it only occasionally and on business.
The Villa Cerutti stood about seven kilometres outside Milan on
the Como road.[9] It was spacious, but even so not nearly large
enough to accommodate the thousands who flocked to see, if not
actually meet, the hero who had delivered Lombardy from the
Austrian yoke, the protector of the Holy See. A big tent was
attached to the house for receptions and gaieties. These were
unceasing. Principal singers came from the Scala to give performances; there were boar hunts, balls, expeditions to the lakes,
under the velvety Italian night sky and stars. The villa even as

such villas went was romantic. It had two carriage drives, one for ascent, the other for descent. It stood four-square mounted on a terrace on high ground, overlooking the Lombardy plain. There was the original nucleus, in the usual shape of a square feudal tower, with smaller towers at the four corners, but there were also much more comfortable suites of apartments, and galleries and colonnades of white marble, rising out of a background of dark cypresses and magnolias. The park was immense, and the general sometimes walked in it for a couple of hours talking without cease to a knowledgeable guest. The garden had fountains, statues, rockeries, ilex groves and sharp drainage; there were cascading flowers in urns, and many picturesque stairways.

M. Miot de Melito thought that the General in Chief of the Army of Italy had a court already. He dined, so to speak, in public, with a queue of inhabitants of the country kept on the move along the side of the room in which he was eating. His waiting rooms were filled with a crowd of high-ranking officers, contractors, members of the haughtiest nobility, and the most eminent scholars. The severe etiquette surrounding the diplomatist's own introduction gave him the idea he was being received by royalty rather than at an army headquarters. Buonaparte's Chief of Staff came from the old monarchist army and a military family. He had been born at Versailles. His record was impressive. He had served in America, and had been Chief of Staff to Marshal Lückner, with the Army of the North. He had distinguished himself in Dumouriez's Argonne campaign and in the Vendéan wars. He was not young—forty-four, and not handsome, rough-haired and weatherbeaten, but had experience, diligence, accuracy, complete mastery of detail. If anything was deputed to Major-General Alexandre Berthier it was as good as done. His seven aides de camp no longer had meals with Buonaparte. Captain Lavalette noted them carefully. He himself had filled one of the vacancies occasioned by the late victories. Colonel Junot had been a sergeant when he had saved the General's life at the siege of Toulon. He was rumbustious, handsome. Colonel Marmont was if possible even less repressed, and also a Burgundian, but of ancient family. Colonel Duroc, much the least showy, looked at first sight rather calculating. His eyes were set too high in his head. He had short slightly bandy legs. But he had quality, heart. He was, in fact, a charming character. The youngest aide, except for the young Beauharnais, was Captain Lemarrus, who had witnessed the general's wedding—"Scarcely seventeen years old and covered with wounds." Colonel Sulkowski was a decorative and valiant Pole, fluent and restless. One of the most effective things about the establishment at Mombello was the guard of three hundred Polish lancers in blue and purple uniforms.

The general had dropped the "u" from his name, and was now Bonaparte. Madame Bonaparte wore with grace and charm a necklace of cameos sent her by the Pope. She went for expeditions sometimes with her husband. They were still a honeymoon pair and had lovers' quarrels. They had been to the Borromean islands together and stayed on Isola Bella for two days. Madame Bonaparte was having herself, her husband and her son painted by a struggling young artist called Gros, once a pupil of David, who had come up from Genoa in hopes of getting her custom. She had a terrible tussle to get the general to stand, even for a few minutes in the mornings after his breakfast. He was being represented at a crucial moment in his career, that in which he had seized a flag and led the troops across the bridge at Arcola. Her own portrait was a head and shoulders, not flattered, but her husband kept it thereafter in his bedroom. Her son was painted in his new uniform as a second lieutenant, adjutant, and aide de camp to his stepfather, with the distinctive aide's scarlet and white sash tied round his left arm. "Put on the sash!" That had been a proud moment. All the pictures had Italian backgrounds.

There were nine of the Bonaparte family staying in the villa. Neither of the children of Josephine ever suffered from the delusion that they were loved by the Bonapartes, and their mother very soon complained to them of her ill-treatment by her brothers and sisters in law. But it could not be denied that *en masse* the Bonapartes were good looking and intelligent.

Madame Letizia, the matriarch, was not yet fifty, but her noble features were lined and worn. She had been a mother at fourteen, a widow at thirty-four. But she had never been one of those to complain of the blows of fate. She was extremely economical. She had been living in two rooms in Marseilles until her soldier son had begun to send her money. When the general had come out to greet her at the head of a fine mounted company and had folded her in his arms, she had said, "Today I am the happiest woman in the world." He was her second son. The eldest, Joseph, had gone down to Rome as ambassador. The third, Lucien, was not at present mentioned. He had disgraced himself by marrying, when he was under age, an inn-keeper's pretty daughter. Louis was another soldier. He was nineteen. He was much the tallest and perhaps would be the best-looking son. He had been the first man to cross the Po at Piacenza and was a great favourite with the general. But he said disconcerting things. Just before Arcola, which admittedly had been a close-run thing, he had actually written—"The troops are no longer the same, and shout loudly for peace."

The first meeting between the general's bride and her mother in law had been a nervous business, for he had only informed his family of his marriage when it was a *fait accompli*. However, Madame Letizia could not complain over much, for she had herself allowed her eldest daughter, Elisa, to marry a young Corsican, Felix Baciocchi, who probably would make her very happy and never do anything unpredictable. A church marriage at Mombello had followed the civil wedding at Marseilles as soon as the general had heard what had happened, and he had not seemed very angry, at least he had provided a dowry. Elisa had reached a serious age—twenty. She was a product of the pre-revolutionary school for officers' daughters at St. Cyr and slightly priggish. The remaining two daughters, Pauline and Caroline, far outshone her in looks. Pauline at seventeen was perfectly beautiful. She had curling black hair, sapphire-blue eyes, classical features and a sylph-like shape. She had been prepared to dislike her sister in law before she had set eyes upon her because she believed that the influence of Josephine had caused the general to forbid her to marry a man with whom she was madly in love. He had been a *mauvais sujet*, old enough to be her father, and with a mistress and two illegitimate children. The general had found her instead little Leclerc, who was intellectual, and had always been in love with her. He was known at headquarters as "*Le Bonaparte blond*" as he was very fair and imitated his Commander in Chief in every possible way. They were going to be married in September after which Madame Letizia would return in triumph to her native Corsica. This was perhaps as well, for although her new daughter in law had excelled herself in delicate attentions it was clear to all the Bonaparte family that their most valuable member had been entrapped by a woman much his senior (though the ravages of time were excellently disguised), a fashionable woman, an ex-vicomtesse, wildly extravagant. The poet Arnault had hardly known where to look when he had noticed Pauline, after Madame

Bonaparte had swept on, playing the gracious hostess to perfection, sticking out her tongue at that elegant back.

Caroline, youngest daughter of the family, had a rose and lily complexion but was too plump at present. She was only fifteen, but disliked exceedingly the prospect of being sent to Madame Campan's school, where Hortense Beauharnais was the best and most lovely pupil. Eugène had already met Jerome, Benjamin of the Bonapartes, at the Irish college, St. Germain. He had spent a few months there in 1796 before the general had moved him to the College of Juilly, near Meaux. He was destined for the Navy, which might mean great unhappiness for him, for he was, at thirteen, extremely undisciplined. He had the same curling dark hair and blue eyes as Pauline. There was only one other member of the Bonaparte family visible at Mombello in the late summer of 1797, Madame Letizia's half brother, Joseph Fesch, a helpful rather noisy talkative person who had been in the church but was at present an army contractor.

Pauline did worse things than mock at her sister in law. She told her mother that she thought the general ought to know that he had imposed upon the family a woman who had lovers. There was one here, under his very nose. Captain Hippolyte Charles had been one of the party of eleven who had travelled with the general's wife from Paris to Milan. He was a beautiful little pocket-Hercules, a dashing hussar, a natural mime. He never left off clowning from the moment he woke in the morning. To see him after a pompous social occasion imitating all who had been present, some of whom were still present, left ladies at a loss whether to laugh or cry. But they generally laughed. He kept them in fits of laughter. He poured a libation of glue inside the scabbard of Junot's sabre. He was brilliant as a languorous lisping Créole, in a turban. Directly he poked his head in at a door, his black eyebrows arched, pretending he was not quite sure of his welcome, an entertainment was made. He sometimes entered standing on his hands.

Madame Letizia refused to interfere, but presently headquarters were startled by the news that M. Charles had been arrested and was to be shot. He was not shot; he had been detected in speculations in army stores. He was ordered first to Rome, then to Paris.[10] But he did not leave Italy for several months, not until after Headquarters had moved to Passariano above Udine.

VII

Now that the young Beauharnais had paid his respects and had his portrait painted, his stepfather did not intend to keep him hanging on to his mother's apron strings. He sent the boy up into the mountains, to learn his profession, in charge of Captain Lavalette. The stepfather took the trouble to draw up a plan of studies and observations of which they were to give an account. Earlier this year the general had been faced with the choice of advancing over the Brenner pass into the Tyrol or over the river Tagliamento towards Trieste. He had chosen the second route and had not halted until he was almost at the gates of Vienna. He told his stepson now to reconnoitre the passes which separated the Isonzo from the Drave and Tagliamento. It seemed incredible that this innocent empty landscape had been the scene of a battle (though not quite a conclusive one) as recently as a few months ago.

On October 17 the Treaty of Camp Formio was solemnly signed at the imposing enormous Manin Villa near Udine, and next day Eugène de Beauharnais set out on his first independent exercise as a soldier. His orders were to report to General Serrurier, Commandant at Venice, and to Colonel Robeau of the Marine who would furnish him with transport to Corfu. Here he would present the letters enclosed to General Gentili and remain several days. He would inspect the fortress and city and then proceed to Otranto, where he would be provided with transport to Naples. From Naples he would travel by road to Rome where he would wait upon His Excellency the Ambassador of the French Republic, *le citoyen* Joseph Bonaparte.

At Venice everything went like clockwork. The brig *Alerte* was ready for him: he embarked for the first time in his life upon the waves. He had an extremely stormy passage lasting twenty-four days before he came in sight of the snow-capped mountains of Albania towering above an unexpectedly lush green isle of white-washed villages, steep cobbled streets with minarets in the native quarters, and many large olive and cypress trees.

The history of this charming place was bloodstained. Octavius had here assembled his first fleet for the Battle of Actium. Since then it had been ruled by Greeks, Normans and Angevins. The islanders had finally invited the Serene Republic to protect them from their neighbours the Turks. It had now passed by the terms of the Treaty of Campo Formio to Republican France.

General Gentili was delighted to see the stepson of General Bonaparte and so were the civic authorities when they had digested the copy of the terms of the Treaty which had been provided for their information. (General Bonaparte had told the Directory in August, "The islands of Corfu, Zante and Cephalonia are more important to us than the whole of Italy. If we had to chose, I believe it would be better to give back Italy to the Emperor and keep these four islands. They are a source of wealth and prosperity for our trade".) After consultation, the municipality of Corfu decided to mark the occasion by the gift of an inscribed sabre.

The aide de camp had a fortnight at Corfu, living in the Governor's palace. He made all his observations and enjoyed himself thoroughly. He was much fêted. The entrance to the palace was a cul-de-sac. One night, when he had told his servant Lefebvre not to wait up, and had gone off to an entertainment alone, he was surprised on his return to find the man very wide awake and in mortal terror. Three characters who were armed with daggers, and must have gained admission by forged keys, had passed through the outer room in which the servant was in bed and gone on in a purposeful manner towards the second. Finding it empty they had retreated as silently and swiftly as they had entered. Next morning Eugène told General Salicetti about the strange occurence and the Governor said these men were probably convicts and had meant to assassinate a French officer who had occupied that room last week. The officer had now left Corfu. Despite this incident Eugène treasured golden memories of the scene of his first military duty, and many years later, when he was looking for a home for his family, seriously considered Corfu.

The brig *Alerte* was waiting for him at Otranto and presently the son of General de Beauharnais was following in his father's footsteps, standing awe-struck in winter sunshine, enchanted by the beauties and antiquities of Herculaneum. He gave Naples and environs six days and then set off for a fortnight in Rome, prepared to spend his time there in the same manner. The French Embassy in Rome was delightfully established in the historic Palazzo Corsini overlooking the river. It was in the Trastevere district "across the Tiber," always famous for inhabitants who claimed to be descendants of the original Romans and to have inherited their unconquerable pride and love of liberty.

He found at the Embassy Joseph Bonaparte, who was unmistakably a brother of the general though much drier in manner, the youngest sister Caroline, Joseph's wife Julie, and Desirée, younger sister of Julie. Madame Joseph Bonaparte had been a bride approved by all the family. Her father, François Clary, had been a principal silk merchant of Marseilles. Julie was not pretty but had brought a redoubtable portion. Her sister, who would have been very pretty but for a retroussé nose, was just going to be married to an officer recently arrived from Bonaparte's staff, General Duphot. Eugène was begged to put off his departure for a few days, so that he could assist at the festivity. He agreed to do this, but something dreadful happened.

In Rome, the French Revolution had been followed with much interest and there were some enthusiasts who dreamed of a revolution in their own domain—the Papal States—and a return to the days of the ancient Roman Republic. It did not, in fact, suit France at present to depose the Pope. Bonaparte had written to Paris, "This archaic machine will disintegrate voluntarily." The hot-heads of the Trastevere movement had interviews with Duphot, who was in Eugène's opinion a brave man, but excitable. After talks with him it was permissible for them to believe, without being absolutely assured, that what they had in mind would be supported by the French government.

On the morning of December 27, a boy who had grown up in the French Revolution began to hear sounds resembling but not quite identical with those with which he had become horribly familiar during the Terror. A noisy crowd arrived rather suddenly in front of the Palazzo Corsini. The design of their leaders, apparently, was to announce a Roman Republic. They believed fondly that the Vatican was entirely unaware of their intentions and would be taken by surprise. In this they were much mistaken. A detachment of infantry and a cavalry piquet were soon on the scene. The cavalry ordered to disperse the mob, by force if necessary, were greeted by shouts of *"Vive la République!"* The piquet charged and cut down all within reach: about forty people. The mob, which was swelling, backed into the Embassy courtyard for refuge. The Ambassador and his staff and guests had been just about to sit down to dinner. Duphot interpreted the action of the Papal cavalry as an insult to his nation. He rushed out of the palace, sabre in hand, calling on all behind him to follow him. Every one of them, including the Ambassador, was convinced that it was not part of their duty to do anything but attempt to quell this trouble and conciliate the parties.

Eugène's account was full. "But the papal infantry which had been posted at the Trastevere gate took a different view of the situation, and seeing five French officers advancing towards them with drawn swords (followed, it is true by some of the crowd which had been swept into Embassy territory), they received us with a volley which killed Duphot and wounded about twenty people behind us. Seeing that he had no chance of making himself heard, the Ambassador withdrew with us into the palazzo, making use of a small alley which led into the garden, to effect his retreat.

"The Palazzo Corsini was barricaded as if for a siege. All doors were barricaded and arms were given out. However, the premises were respected and no damage was sustained except for a few windows broken by pistol shots. During the night the Ambassador asked the Roman government for his passports, which were granted, not without objections, and we all prepared to leave before daylight. A curious circumstance about the affair is that, while trying to calm down the republican zealots who had taken refuge in the French Embassy I struck several times, with the flat of my sabre, one of the most excited and angry of them." His name was Ceracchi. He reappeared three years later as the crazy sculptor of Trastevere who suffered on the scaffold after an attempt upon the life of Bonaparte.[11]

VIII

He would hardly have recognized his home. Josephine had sent messages from Italy that it was to be redecorated in a style suitable to a victorious general. Her order had been obeyed regardless of cost. Roman fasces, the ensigns of authority and power, greeted the visitor in the vestibule; Pompeian frescoes military trophies and curule chairs abounded. In the salon the theme was "Peace and War." The rising architect to whom she had given *carte blanche* seemed to have believed that striped fabrics had been especially beloved of the noble Romans. In the principal bedroom he had surpassed himself. The general's bed was of tent design; the mural paintings represented a procession following Venus: Music and Dance preceded the Triumph of Love. There were some well-liking swans waiting to be attached to a chariot. Josephine admired the swan as a motif and thereafter it became for ever recognized as her emblem. The loot which she had brought back from Italy had been poured into the little house —presents from grateful cities, from the Pope, from individual owners—statues, pictures, furniture. There was only one familiar face and voice missing. Fortuné had met in an Italian garden the big dog belonging to the army headquarters cook, and that character had decided that a pampered pet had lived long enough.

Even the name of the street in which his home stood had been altered in compliment to the returning hero. The Rue Chantereine was now the Rue de la Victoire. When Bonaparte saw the bills for redecorating a house of which he had only a lease, he pondered. He bought it outright in March 1798. There can be no doubt that Eugène and Hortense admired their metamorphosed home. When they had homes of their own they copied leading features, and they treasured classical furniture and bibelots left to them by their mother.

Her mother had begun to take Hortense out into society. Another girl of fifteen, who was to become the wife of one of Bonaparte's marshals, remembered seeing them at a ball in the Faubourg St. Honoré that winter.

"Madame de D. who was not of an absolutely timid character looked about on all sides to see if she could at least discover one seat, when her eyes encountered a young and charming face with a pair of dark-blue eyes, surrounded by a profusion of light hair. This, most graceful of sylphs, was conducted back to her seat by M. de Trénis, which proved that she danced well; for M. de Trénis invited none to have the honour of being his partners but such as deserved the character of good dancers. The graceful creature, after curtesying with a blush to the Vestris of the ballroom, sat down by the side of a female who appeared to be her elder sister, and whose elegant dress had excited the notice and envy of all. 'Who are those persons?' enquired Madame de D. of the old Marquis d'Hautefort. 'What! is it possible that you do not know the Viscomtesse de Beauharnais? It is she and her daughter. She is now Madame Bonaparte.' "[12]

CHAPTER FOUR

Egypt
1798 : 1799

I

THE INSTRUCTIONS which he received on April 18, 1798, with additions on the 22nd, told him that he would leave Paris at four a.m. on Monday 23rd, in a travelling carriage in which he would find three companions, one of them Louis Bonaparte. They would wear civilian clothes, were forbidden to mention that they were all aides de camp, and if asked their destination would let it be believed to be Brest.

They would arrange so that their grooms and luggage would be waiting for them at Lyons, on the afternoon of the 24th. They would travel by Auxerre and Chalon, and at Lyons would take rooms at the inn in the Place Bellecour (*ci-devant*, Palais Royal), if it still existed. From there they would report to Duroc and Lavigne at the Hôtel de Provence and see if the boats were ready for their passage down the Rhône. They would embark there with their effects and two carriages, and must take sufficient food for two days.

They were going to Toulon to embark in a Grand Fleet for the conquest of Egypt; but the instructions said nothing of that. All over France during those spring weeks officers fetched from barracks and camps and home-fires, and from Italy and Switzerland and Germany, were inconspicuously speeding towards Toulon and a great adventure.

The idea of exploiting the riches of the East and perhaps founding a colony in Egypt was not new to French diplomacy. It had been considered in the palmy days of the monarchy. On his return from Italy Bonaparte had received a hero's welcome which was a little too much for what was left of the Directory. He was suspected of aiming at supreme power, and although he behaved himself very quietly, he was given the command of the Army for

the Invasion of England and sent to cool off for the winter on the
coasts of Picardy and Artois. By March, the new Minister for
Foreign Affairs had been pressing an expedition into the Levant
which would threaten the commerce of India, and the Minister of
Marine confirmed General Bonaparte's gloomy opinion that to
carry out a descent on England, with the present fleet assembled
near Boulogne, and without naval supremacy, would be disastrous.
The Toulon fleet, on the other hand was ready and General
Bonaparte asked no more than twenty-five thousand troops.

He arrived at Toulon, early on May 9 in a post-chaise. Quarter
of an hour later, in a large *berline*, came a party which included
his wife, her son, and his private secretary, the *Citoyen* Bourrienne,
who had been at the military school at Brienne with the general
but had deserted the profession of arms for law and diplomacy.
Bonaparte had summoned him when he had been engaged in
negotiations for peace with Italy. Bourrienne was a managing
character, proud of his employment, and of a fine green morocco
portfolio which he carried, inscribed in gold lettering "Bonaparte,
General in Chief of the Army of the East".

Josephine had left Paris in the end so hurriedly that she had
not been able to get down to St. Germain to say farewell to
Hortense and Caroline and Émilie. But she had been down quite
recently, for the important business of showing Émilie to her future
husband. Before Bonaparte left France a husband must be provided
for poor Émilie. Hortense loyally wrote in her memoirs that she
was lovely, and as sweet as an angel, and that a thousand charms,
added to her connections, made her a most desirable match. But
although both her parents had been Beauharnais, they were divorced and had re-married most inconsiderately. Bonaparte had approached Marmont who had said he could not marry the daughter
of an *émigré*. After getting the same reply from Junot and Rewbell,
son of *Directeur* Rewbell, Bonaparte had thought of Lavalette.

His appearance was distressing, for he resembled Bacchus, but
that was an affliction, not an indication. He was the son of a
well-to-do tradesman and was rising thirty. He had seen Émilie
twice but was not sure if he would recognize her again. A family
party drove down to St. Germain and General Bonaparte inspected the school, and then Hortense, Caroline and Émilie were
taken for a drive and cold repast in the forest. They all sat on the
grass. It was beautifully warm, and Colonel Lavalette made
himself agreeable to Émilie. When they got up, he asked Eugène

to conduct his cousin into a solitary walk, and then leave them alone. Lavalette then made his proposal, without any attempt to conceal his origins and want of fortune. Émilie was too shy to answer, but gave him her nosegay, whereupon Lavalette kissed her. They then rejoined the others and she was told that the wedding would take place next week at the home of the old Marquis Beauharnais. This was duly effected.

After the ceremony at which Caroline and Hortense attended her, Émilie whispered to Hortense that she had been in love with Louis Bonaparte who had been down to the school sometimes. Hortense, feeling she was in the presence of tragedy, could only say why had her cousin not told her this before? She believed she could have persuaded her mother to stop the marriage. But now it was too late—Bonaparte, mother, brother, Louis all had suddenly left Paris.

Bonaparte had kept the secret of his departure well. On the night of May 3 he had dined with Barras at the Luxembourg before a performance of *Macbeth*, after which he had set out for Toulon. He had nearly come to grief when almost in sight of the coast for he had ordered his coachman to take a short cut he knew which avoided Marseilles. Everyone in the *berline* had been asleep when the vehicle came to a halt on the bank of a torrent spanned by what was now a broken bridge. The mountain of luggage on the top of the vehicle had caught in an overhanging tree and pulled up the horses within ten feet of the ravine. After all this hurry they were detained at Toulon for over a week by contrary winds. Josephine wrote to Hortense from Toulon to say that she was not going to Egypt with Bonaparte. He wished her to take a course of waters at Plombières. (This was a spa in the Vosges of high reputation for curing sterility.) He was going to send to fetch her in two months.

The Army of the East sailed on Saturday, May 19, in brilliant sunshine. Spectators said it was the grandest sight since the Crusades. There were thirty-five thousand troops, nearly four hundred transports and an escort of thirteen ships of the line. Josephine went on board Admiral Brueys' flagship *L'Orient* the largest warship in the world, and then returned to a balcony reserved for important wives. Bands struck up, warships and forts exchanged salutes. Eugène thought the spectacle magnificent as the fleet got under way, and swiftly left the coast of France, bound for the glory and hazards of a distant expedition.

II

Admiral Brueys was sailing with a ship's company cut down to nearly half of the usual complement. He had to accommodate two thousand one hundred and forty five persons. Military officers who had been on board the enormous ship during the weeks before the embarkation had been awed by the size, and on the lower decks the cavernous darkness and silence, of a man of war mounting a hundred and thirty guns. They had felt as if they were entering Notre Dame. As *L'Orient* made sail on the afternoon of May 19 a solemn party gathered in the Admiral's great cabin and introductions were made. Bonaparte had asked for, and got, a team of over a hundred and fifty scientists, artists, historians dietetians and other experts, to examine and report on the possibilities of Egypt as a colony. All were men of high reputation from the Institute and École Polytechnique. For the first few days the fleet had a strong wind, which was going to carry it at a great speed past the east coast of Corsica. There were many sufferers. By degrees passengers began to recover and the General in Chief held conference with his scientists. One of them, Monge, the famous mathematician, had been a guest at Passeriano; for the eastern expedition was no new idea to Bonaparte.

Berthollet, a leading chemist, was another favourite companion. Before dinner marine bands played, but only between decks. The general did not care for music in his cabin. The library embarked was subdivided under seven headings—Arts, Science, Travel, History, Poetry, Romance, Politics. The Commission had brought seeds and roots to be planted in the new colony. The general's intention was to found in Cairo an *Institut* on the same lines as that in Paris. The graceless young aides de camp who observed Bonaparte's educational sessions with his *savants* treasured the sight of General Junot fast asleep, with his mouth open, snoring loudly. When woken, he cried with his usual good cheer "That *sacré Institut* of yours sends everyone to sleep, General, including yourself!"

At last on the 10th of June they arrived in sight of Malta. Junot was sent in to Valetta to summon the Grand Master to open the gates. He brought back the answer that the Government was resolved to defend the isle. Squadrons of troops were landed to the west and east of the city and a third column was sent off to

the isle of Gozo. On the morning of the 11th Eugène was close to
Marmont at the moments when the garrison made a sortie. It was
repulsed with loss, leaving four flags. Eugène captured one. In the
evening Marmont ordered him to take all four to Bonaparte on
board *L'Orient*. Next morning negotiations for peace opened:
Malta was taken over on June 13. The scene could not be divested
of drama.[1]

Bonaparte began at once to transform the administration. He
abolished slavery, armorial bearings and titles. He inspected the
Mint. He arranged for sixty Maltese youths to be educated in
France. For several days, heavy packages and boxes were carried
down the many steep steps of Valetta to be consigned to the hold
of de Brueys' flagship. The conquerors were removing the historic
treasures of the Most Venerable Order of the Hospital of St.
John of Jerusalem. Inspection of the defences proved that these
were extremely decayed though the natural advantages were
great. Eugène heard General Du Falga say to the General in
Chief, with a knowing look, that it was most fortunate that there
had been people inside to open the gates. If this fortress had
been deserted the army would never have got in. It appeared
that Malta had long been "prepared" by propaganda for the
French arrival. The single day of resistance had been just a
harlequinade.

On June 15 Bonaparte was off again, leaving the flag of the
Republic standing out bravely in a north-west wind. It fell to
Lavalette (back to duty after his honeymoon) to escort the dispossessed Grand Master and his officers to the extremity of the
Adriatic Gulf, lest they fell into the hands of Barbary corsairs.
When they were two days out from Valetta they spoke a Ragusan
vessel and learned that she had seen that morning an English
fleet steering towards Malta. This was an unpleasant surprise. The
English had not had a fleet in the Mediterranean since September
'96. This must be something new. Lavalette was horrorstruck as
he thought of the slow-moving Armada from which he had just
parted. The captains of very few of the four hundred transports
were Frenchmen. He feared that if they encountered English
frigates they would soon be dispersed. Losses must in a fleet action
at sea be heavy.

But *L'Orient* was making her last passage happily with no
interference. On the night of June 22 the weather was thick.
Brueys heard signal guns and steered for the security of Crete.

Next morning there was no enemy sail to be seen and on the 24th the high lands of Candia came in sight, beautiful, snow-covered. A look-out frigate reported the Barbary coast at dawn five days later, and on the same day everyone in the fleet had a first sight of it. The Egyptian coast, their promised land, was low and sandy, resembling in every respect the ground between Calais and Gravelines. The time had come for a first stirring message from the General in Chief to be distributed. It was dated,

> "On board *L'Orient*
> "June 22, 1798

"SOLDIERS!

"You are going to undertake a conquest, the effects of which upon commerce and civilization will be incalculable.

"You will give the English a blow which will be followed up by their destruction.

"We shall have some fatiguing marches—we shall fight several battles—we shall succeed in all our enterprises. The Destinies are in our favour.

"The Mameluke Beys, who support English commerce exclusively, to the injury of our merchants, and who tyrannize over the unhappy natives on the banks of the Nile, will cease to exist within a few days of our arrival.

"The people amongst whom you are going to live are Mahomedans. The first article of their faith is 'There is no other God but God and Mahomet is his Prophet.' Do not contradict them. Act towards them as you did with the Jews and Italians. Treat their Muftis and the Imams with respect, as you did the Rabbis and Bishops. You must act with the same spirit of toleration towards the ceremonies prescribed by the Koran that you did to the Synagogues and Convents and the religions of Moses and Jesus Christ.

"The Roman Legions protected all religions. You will find here customs which differ from those of Europe; you must accustom yourselves to them.

"The people amongst whom we are going treat women differently from us; but in every country he who violates them is a monster!

"Pillage enriches very few; it dishonours us; it destroys our resources, and it makes enemies of those we need as friends.

"The first city at which we shall arrive was built by Alexander the Great and with every step we take we shall meet with objects capable of exciting emulation.

"BONAPARTE"[2]

Orders were given for landing in a bay about six miles east of Alexandria and disembarkation went on all night in spite of a very heavy sea and a howling wind. Eugène thought that he was not likely to forget this night in which he performed the duties of an aide de camp in a somewhat novel manner. He had to take orders to all ships, tossing in a tiny craft which seemed likely at every moment to be either waterlogged or squeezed to death between the towering sides of the men of war up which he had to climb. The French consul who had come on board *L'Orient* had brought the news that an English Fleet under Admiral Nelson had left Alexandria that very morning. They must have missed him twice by a few hours, the first occasion being when he had actually crossed their route in thick weather of the 22nd.

The advance to Alexandria began without delay. At day-break General Kléber's division, marching in the centre, saw a few horsemen who, observing that they had no cavalry, rode up close and discharged carbines. Some French riflemen gained possession of sandhills on their flank and put a stop to that. Outside the city walls the troops found a mosque with a cistern. They drank of its water with delight, for they were parched with thirst. It seemed the sweetest they had ever tasted.

The walls of Alexandria were lined with turbaned figures, and with women and children who cast down showers of stones. The General in Chief ordered the charge to be beat and an attack to be made at all points. The troops flew over the ramparts amidst a hail of bullets and stones. Generals Kléber and Menou were wounded, Kléber, who was immensely tall, by a musket-ball in the head, Menou by a fall of masonry. Both were removed to an open space below a landmark known as Pompey's Pillar, visible from the sea, and the glad word went round that they were likely to recover. The principal fort had been carried. The Turkish garrison, seeing the number of troops arriving, made signs of surrender by grounding their arms and uttering ghastly yells.

Bonaparte ordered the *générale* to be beat, and the troops who were proceeding to engage the inhabitants in the city to evacuate it, and range themselves under an eminence on which he stood. Eugène had been surprised, when he had finally burst open the door of a house from which firing had been coming, to find it empty except for one old man, with ten or twelve rifles which were being charged and handed to him by his wife and children.

Before noon Alexandria had capitulated. The main body of the army stayed there only five days. As a town it was universally voted a bitter disappointment. Here it was, of considerable size still, and once one of the most famous cities in the world, and it was absolutely nothing except a collection of filthy mud houses, with flat roofs, a few holes for windows, covered with a clumsy wooden lattice, and doors so low that you must break your back entering. The streets were all crooked and so narrow you had to flatten yourself against the walls to let a cart pass.

They had got the plague here. On the way up from the bay they had met stretchers on which lay bright-eyed writhing wretches. But it was announced that these came from foreign ships and the plague was never bad in Egypt for the five or six months of hottest weather.

Everything was extremely dear, and there was not a Cleopatra left in Egypt, or if there was she was kept indoors. The women they did see wrapped themselves up in a bit of cloth which passed over the head and descended in front to the eyebrows. The poorer sort covered their whole faces with linen leaving two eye-holes. Of the poorer men, and this meant most of the men, the costume was a blue shirt reaching half way down the thighs, but generally tucked up into a girdle, and a turban in rags.

The only traces left of ancient grandeur were Pompey's pillar, the obelisks of Cleopatra, her baths, a subterraneous temple, some catacombs, mosques and a few churches. The corps of the Arts and Sciences were being left in Alexandria for the present to enjoy these. Pompey's column was one hundred and four feet high. One of Cleopatra's so-called needles was lying on its side. It was covered with lettering: all were of red granite. The only beautiful thing about Alexandria was the two bays, separated by a causeway leading to the Pharos—ruined, of course. Nobody was sorry to leave Alexandria and prepare to march on Grand Cairo, the largest city in the world, the mart for the caravans coming from Mecca and India.

III

The march on Cairo was unforgettable. Nobody who had been with the Army of Egypt and experienced that ever forgot or

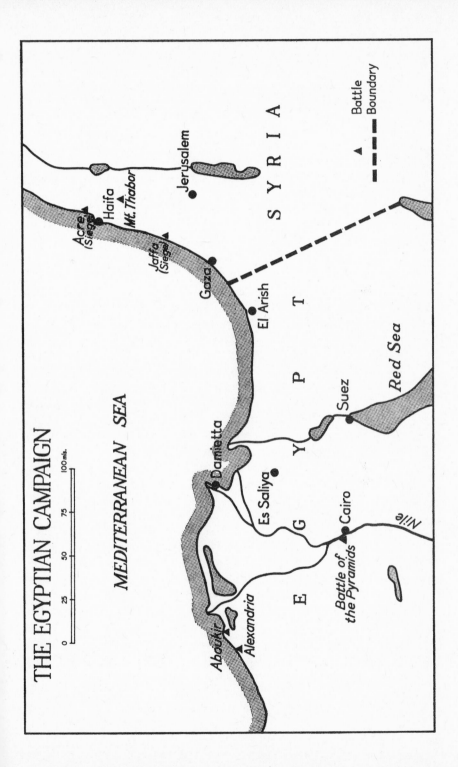

THE EGYPTIAN CAMPAIGN

MEDITERRANEAN SEA

SYRIA

Jerusalem

Acre (Siege)
Haifa
Mt. Thabor
Jaffa (Siege)
Gaza

El Arish

E G Y P T

Damietta

Es Saliya

Suez

Red Sea

Aboukir
Alexandria

Cairo
Battle of
the Pyramids

Nile

▲ Battle
━ ━ Boundary

0 25 50 75 100 mls.

forgave the Libyan desert. They marched by day under a sky and over sands equally burning hot. The cisterns were sometimes ten or twelve leagues apart and the advance columns were selfish. The troops were harassed incessantly by hordes of mounted robbers called Bedouins who killed not only men but officers, and that within five paces from the main body. General Dugua's aide de camp was murdered while he was carrying an order to a file of grenadiers not a musket-shot from their camp. The advance always had to be made in close order because the slightest confusion in the ranks caused the Bedouin to dash in, and every imaginable cruelty was exercised upon the unhappy stragglers who fell into their hands. The seasoned troops who had served under Hoche heard of noses and ears cut off and swore, "It is a more destructive war, by my faith, than that of La Vendée!" They marched for seventeen days without bread, wine or brandy. They foraged for meat and got nothing but skinny poultry and a few vegetables. They suffered from a diet of water-melons. Where there was no decent food for men, it was not surprising that there was no hay or oats for horses. The poor animals got a few beans and a meagre ration of chopped straw. By the time that the army came in sight of the Nile a few unhappy Frenchmen had blown their brains out, and several flung themselves in the muddy waters to drown. They had lost their reason. They had been tortured by visions of sheets of water, glittering through the heat haze. These were a familiar phenomenon—the mirage.

It was confusing even for educated men to be told that they had not yet met the real enemy. They had come to Egypt to deliver the Egyptians from the Mamelukes, and reinstate the Sultan of Turkey. The Mamelukes were a race of warriors, a governing caste. The word mameluke meant, in Arabic, a slave, and they had originally, in the days of Saladin, been a bodyguard of the Sultan, recruited from the Caucasus, Circassia and Georgia. They had seized power in a palace revolution and now they were princes in the land. There were at present two outstanding Mameluke leaders, the Beys Murad and Ibrahim. On the morning of June 21, it became clear to the advancing French that they were going to experience their first large-scale encounter with the Mamelukes. (There had been a skirmish near Shubra Khit a week earlier in which the Mamelukes had attacked violently, been repulsed and had retired, their favourite tactics.)

The scene set for one of the famous battles of history was

dramatic, the desert between Gizeh and Embaba on the left bank of the Nile. To the north-east, across the river, the towers and minarets of Grand Cairo were visible; to the south, much closer, arose the unmistakable shapes of pyramids. The Mameluke camp was believed to contain six thousand splendid cavalry and twelve thousand infantry, in first class condition. As far as numbers went the French probably surpassed them, but the troops had marched far and had been poorly fed.

Eugène's recollections of a crowd scene were surprisingly clear. At the moment before the "Marseillaise" was played and the French went into action, General Bonaparte made one of his short energetic speeches to inspire his troops. "I recollect that I heard him say, pointing to the Pyramids, 'Soldiers! remember that the monuments of forty centuries look down on you.'

"This was a dangerous day for the aides (or those who were doing their work), for each of the French divisions formed a square, and as these formations were placed in *échelon* and within a cannon's range of each other, the enemy cavalry was practically always to be found in the area between, so that it was very difficult to take orders to subordinate units. One was always in danger of being either beheaded by a Mameluke scimitar or hit by our own fire."

Nothing could have been more picturesque than the approach of the Mamelukes under the bright blue sky in the shimmering midday heat. Their Arabian horses, splendidly harnessed, snorted, neighed and pranced, gracefully and lightly, under their accomplished riders whose armour was inlaid with gold and gems. Their tunics were brilliant in every oriental dye, their turbans were surmounted by aigret feathers. Some wore gilded helmets as well as breast plates. They charged with wild cries in a cloud of dust, trying to break the French squares from several sides. The French played the waiting game, and then poured in at close range their fire of ball, grapeshot and musketry. It was a noisy and violent action but not long drawn out or costly for France. There were Mameluke casualties, but they could hardly be said to have been annihilated, as when they found they were making no impression they galloped off as swiftly as they had charged, leaving their wretched Albanian infantry to be destroyed. Ibrahim Bey's troops, drawn up on the right bank of the river never came into the battle. Bonaparte made an attempt to follow the flying warriors of Murad Bey. Several hundred of them holding a redoubt above the Nile found themselves cut off, and were drowned in the river in an undisciplined attempt to escape. The camp was found to contain four hundred camels loaded with valuable baggage. That night Bonaparte slept in Murad Bey's country palace in Gizeh. Here he and his staff found gorgeous silken divans and delicious grapes, but all the servants had fled.

On June 24 he entered Grand Cairo in triumph. He called his victory the Battle of the Pyramids.

It seemed incredible, but Grand Cairo, the largest city in the world, was the worst disappointment yet. It was larger than Paris: that could be believed. One could lose oneself in it for a day. But except for the quarter belonging to the Mamelukes it was without a handsome habitation. The troops began to be witty about their experience. "Well, I expect it will be delightful when we get to Rosetta." "Not at all. Those who are stationed there say it is only a shade less wretched than Alexandria." "Really! but then there is the Delta, that surely is rich and prosperous." "You get tired of palm trees and sycamores and there is only a little wheat, rice and lentils grown there. They have cattle, but no fine houses, only homes for fleas, bugs, mosquitos and gnats." "Ah! but then there is Cairo, the wealthiest, the most prosperous city in the world." A thousand voices in concert will tell you, "It is the vilest and most miserable dog-hole on the face of the earth!"

Egypt seemed to excel in packs of savage dogs, who roamed the streets, and in people of all ages with eye-trouble. The liberators of Cairo watched glumly while strings of camels fastened to one another, heavily loaded and led by a single man, manoeuvred precariously down narrow streets. The inhabitants, with pipes in their mouths, passed apathetically through the small vacant places. A few austere looking Mussulmans, seated on mules, had stick-bearers going before them who struck the crowds out of their way. Beggars, hiding their faces, pestered the troops for alms. Their singular cries seemed to be angry imprecations. A shocking dust and dreadful stinks assailed the foreign victors. They believed the smell came from mummies. But they made the best of Cairo, and galloped cheerfully on donkeys, sliding between the camels with roars of laughter. There was a restaurant, club and sort of public garden, "Le Tivoli", where there were lamps of coloured glass strung among lemon and orange trees, and a band played after dark for dancing. Organized visits to the Pyramids were announced, and the troops cut their names on the walls inside the King's Chamber and raced one another up the exterior. The General in Chief had written home for a troupe of actors, some dealers in toys, a hundred women and all the wives of the corps, fifty gardeners, brandy, uniform cloth, blue and scarlet, soap, oil, twenty surgeons, ten physicians and thirty apothecaries . . . He himself lodged in the palace of Mohammed Bey el Elfi on Esbekiya Square. From its windows he could see skins of every colour from Nubian ebony to Circassian ivory.

He ordered due celebrations for the anniversary of the birth o Mahomet, lasting three days from August 20. One morning he appeared for breakfast in a turban and *caftan*, but finding it un-comfortable and unimpressive never repeated the experiment. General Bonaparte proceeded to organize Egypt as a French pro-tectorate. He established his Arts and Science Corps in a pleasant suburb from which they could radiate all over Egypt. There was an installation of the new Divan or Council—an assembly of nine bearded automatons in long robes and turbans who reminded Adjutant-General Boyer of nothing but the twelve apostles. The poor husbandmen of the Nile valley appeared to the French the most laborious and broken-spirited fellows in the world. They lived in a state of filth and degradation that excited pity and horror. If they had a promising looking child of either sex it was demanded by the Mamelukes. Adjutant-General Lacuée, writing to an uncle, who was a member of the Convention, thoughtfully concluded, "This country is nothing at present. It merely offers magnificent recollections of the past, and vast but distant hopes of the future. It is not worth conquering in its present condition. If able statesmen and administrators should undertake to manage it for ten years, it might become the most valuable colony in Europe. But where are such administrators?"

The wife of Murad Bey had thrown open her palace as sanctuary to all Europeans in Cairo. General Bonaparte instructed his stepson to wait upon the lady. Several French officers, in-cluding Rapp, had been stabbed in the streets of Cairo by assailants whom nobody could trace. The suspicion was that Madame Murad Bey was sheltering also some Mamelukes. Eugène's instructions were to assure her that her house would be respected by the troops, but that if she wished for French pro-tection she must engage to abstain from communication with their enemies.

He was received with great distinction and offered a cup of coffee from the hands of the hostess. It afterwards appeared in print that he had been given a diamond ring of great value. That was untrue.[3] Madame Murad Bey said that in order to convince her guest that she was harbouring no unauthorized persons she would herself lead him round her house. They walked all round the ground floor through vast halls where there were enough piles of cushions and couches to hide any number of Mamelukes —warriors said to be adept in cutting off your head with a single wave of their scimitar. They could sever a scarf floating in the air. Eugène had an impression they were being watched by many unseen eyes. The floor above was occupied by the harem. The most grotesque scene followed. At the sight of a French hussar these mad women flew upon the defenceless warrior like a pack of hounds about to kill. In vain Madame Murad Bey screamed to them to retire. In vain he attempted to disentangle himself and throw them off, rather rudely in the end. Only the entry of the eunuchs with ox-hide whips ended an experience more terrifying than the Battle of the Pyramids.

He had to visit one more harem. There had been a complaint that French troops had invaded one near the Mameluke quarter. On this occasion he was one of several officers, sent to call the Hola! "We found the house easily as it had a large and ugly-looking crowd outside it, shouting that profanation was being committed. Inside there were men of many regiments abandoning themselves with an excess of brutality which their long deprivation explained if it did not excuse. The officers were reduced to using the same methods as the eunuchs, but upon the soldiers. They beat them, however, only with the flats of their sabres."

Eugène was not without employment in Cairo. The general sent him out on reconnaissance into the desert and this nearly always meant an encounter of some sort with stray Arabs or Mamelukes. He went out on an ambush twice at night, but got no prey. He always volunteered for longer expeditions. "I had the desire, natural to all Frenchmen to distinguish myself." "Young man," said the general, "realize that it is not your duty to run into danger. If you perform your duty it will, when it pleases God, come to you." It was about this time that he began to realize that his stepfather was under great strain. This was occasioned partly by the low *morale* of a section of his troops. Kléber, whom he had left behind with six thousand men at

Alexandria, was jealous of him. The burly Alsatian always felt that he had been passed over when the command had been given to a general fifteen years junior to him. This increased a trouble which was normal—and not really unhealthy—competitive jealousy of old Army of the Rhine troops, of Army of Italy men. But the General in Chief had another and personal reason for misery.

"News had reached him from France, where someone was trying hard to upset his domestic happiness. Although I was very young at the time, he trusted me enough to confide in me. Usually it was in the evening that he told me of his worries, while he was striding up and down his tent. I was the only person upon whom he could unburden himself freely. I tried to calm him down and do my best to console him (so far as my youth and the awe with which I regarded him would let me).

"I have recorded this in some detail because it explains why the General in Chief (after he had become Emperor) described me in such flattering terms when he announced to the Senate that I had been given the rank of Imperial Prince."

The officers with whom he had seen Bonaparte discussing the situation were all men of probity and with his stepfather's welfare at heart. It was his duty to warn his mother.

On July 27 from camp at Gizeh he took the plunge:
"My dear *Maman*,

"I have so many things to say that I don't know where to begin. Bonaparte has been very sad for five days, and it comes from an interview he had with Julien, Junot and Berthier. It has upset him more than I would have believed possible.

"What I have heard amounts to the following—that Charles travelled in your carriage until you were within three posts of Paris—that you saw him in Paris—that you have been to the Theatre of the Italians with him, in one of the private boxes—that it was he who gave you your little dog—that even now he is with you.

"This in scattered words is all I heard.

"You will know that I don't believe it, but what is certain is that the General is very upset.

"All the same, he redoubles his kindness to me. It seems as if, by his actions, he would say that children are not to be held responsible for the faults of their mother. But your son chooses to believe that all this gossip is fabricated by your enemies.

"He loves you as much as ever and longs to embrace you, I hope when you arrive here all will be forgotten."

By the same post-bag there travelled a letter from the General in Chief addressed to *Citoyen* Joseph Bonaparte, Deputy to the Council of Five Hundred, Paris.

"You will have seen in the press accounts of the conquest of Egypt. There was enough resistance to add another page to the military annals of this army. Egypt is the richest country in the world in wheat, rice, vegetables, meat; but it is entirely barbaric. There is no money, no, not even to pay the troops. I think of being in France in two months. I have great grief in my domestic life. The veil has been entirely torn away. You alone remain faithful to me in the world.

"Please arrange so that I may have a country house on my arrival, either close to Paris or in Burgundy. I reckon on passing the winter there. I am sick of society. I need solitude! I am tired of glory. At twenty-nine it has lost its attraction. There is nothing left for me but complete egoism. I mean to keep my Paris house. I shall never give that up to anyone. I have no other resource. Good-bye my one and only friend. I have never treated you unfairly, have I?"

Neither of these letters reached their destination. French captains had standing orders, in view of capture at sea, to have lead attached to their despatches and cast them overboard before they surrendered. But expert British tars of Nelson's fleet plunged after such rich booty.

In the winter of 1798 a glorious *cache* of captured letters from the Army of Egypt arrived in London and newspaper extracts from them were so popular that eventually two volumes, with translations, a map and some facsimile documents and autographs, were published. Eugène's letter appeared in the *Morning Chronicle* for November 24, 1798. The letter from Bonaparte to his brother eventually came to rest as a valuable exhibit of the British Museum.[4]

iv

On August 13 in camp at Es Saliya, on the edge of the Sinai desert, Lavalette was handed by an Egyptian peasant, an open letter. This had been entrusted to the man by an aide de camp of General Kléber whose horse had been unable to go any further.

Lavalette read it, and advancing towards the General in Chief begged him to withdraw from the groups of staff officers who were laughing around him. They were in high spirits for they had just re-taken the spoils of the legendary Mecca caravan intercepted by the Mamelukes on its way into Cairo. Presently, the general said to them, "It seems you like this country. That is very lucky. For we now have no Fleet to carry us back to Europe."

Kléber's news had been that on August 1 Admiral Nelson had attacked and defeated the fleet of the Republic off the mouth of the Nile. Of France's thirteen ships-of-the-line, nine had been captured and two burnt. Only two had escaped—and not for long. *L'Orient* had taken fire and had blown up. With her had descended into the depths of Aboukir Bay, the body of Admiral Brueys, dead on his quarter-deck, the historic treasures of the Order of St. John of Jerusalem so recently collected from Malta, and what was more immediately serious, the six hundred thousand pounds in ingots of gold and diamonds extracted from the Swiss Republic and Roman state, to finance the Army of Egypt and the Eastern Expedition.

Amongst junior officers of high spirit it was not considered correct to complain of disasters. Eugène never mentioned the Battle of the Nile in his memoirs.[5] There was a domestic repercussion which affected him closely, and to that he did refer. It was now clear that Madame Bonaparte would never join her husband in Egypt. There had been a plan that she should come with the bride of Marmont. But she had sent word from Plombières that she was not well. She had fallen from a rotten balcony. Her place was now being filled in the general's carriage by Madame Fourès, the blonde nineteen-year-old wife of a Lieutenant of *chasseurs* who had been sent to Paris with despatches. She had been installed in a villa adjoining Bonaparte's headquarters in the Elfi-Bey Palace. The aide de camp on duty always had to ride beside the open *calèche* when the general drove out. Eugène went to Berthier, Chief of Staff, and asked to be sent to a regiment. He could not endure the humiliation of his present position. He had a brief, alarming interview with his stepfather, but the drives with Madame Fourès ceased, he continued as aide de camp, and the general "did not treat me badly."[6]

On October 21 a violent insurrection broke out in Cairo, mainly on account of the taxation hastily imposed to replace the bullion lost in *L'Orient*. It was headed by fanatic students in the university quarter of El Azhar, but spread like wildfire. General Dupuis, commander of the garrison, was assassinated with several of his staff. Two army surgeons were cut down defending the entrance to the hospital. It was clear that strong and immediate measures must be taken. The rebel headquarters in the mosque of El Azhar was bombarded and carried. Berthier received orders that all prisoners taken in the citadel must be decapitated and their bodies cast into the Nile. Colonel Sulkowski, with an escort, reconnoitring the stretch of desert separating the town from the citadel, was ambushed and slain by Arabs. He had been wounded at Alexandria and at the Battle of the Pyramids and should not have been on this duty, but had insisted that he was entirely recovered. The aide de camp who would have gone if he had not intervened was Beauharnais.[7]

The Cairo insurrection was put down in less than three days and Bonaparte announced a General Pardon except for six ringleaders. Cairo appeared as perfectly peaceful as it had been before the uprising, and he prepared to set out for Suez. Eugène, who preceded him with the advance guard, remembered for ever that terrible march. It was now very hot during the day, but cold at night. This desert was the route for caravans from Suez to Tor and all countries north of Arabia. It was part of a nightmarish experience that they kept on kicking up bones, and not only of animals—human skulls. He had trouble over water-stealing which he had to quench, sabre in hand. It struck him, as he laid about him, a beardless boy, that there was something ludicrous in his having to deal so many blows on old soldiers of the Rhine and Italy—indeed *vieilles moustaches*. They bore him no malice and all was forgotten when they entered Suez where they found no resistance. He reported to Bonaparte, who was going to follow in ten days, and received little notes which he kept all his life.

"December 11, Cairo.

"I see with pleasure from your letter that you have arrived at Suez at the head of the advance-guard. Always march with the infantry, never trust the Arabs and always sleep in your tent. Keep me informed.

"I have received, *citoyen*, the sketch which you sent with your letter. It is very well done. By the number of your last letter I see I have received three. Be careful never to sleep outside and with eyes uncovered. I embrace you."

The General in Chief arrived, and announced a great desire to cross the Red Sea to visit the Fountains of Moses, some natural springs near the coast of the Sinai peninsula. The distance was not great, and the party had no difficulty in finding the ford at low tide, guided by Eugène who had already made the excursion. They identified the springs and tasted them, and found them brackish, even when disguised with coffee. Some Arabian chiefs who had perceived them came down to thank the French General in Chief for the protection he gave their caravans. They pointed out some distant heights which they said were Mount Sinai. The return journey was not so prosperous. They had lingered too long and darkness followed sunset in the usual swift Egyptian style. The guides whom they had engaged made off and they were threatened by the fate of Pharaoh when pursuing Moses. The tide was coming up, and they were crossing the Red Sea lower down than in the morning. They had to dismount and lead their horses, testing every foothold. Bourrienne said later that they had waded in waist-deep water, but denied that a guide had carried Bonaparte pick-a-back, or that they got utterly lost in the marshes. Eugène said the water was up to their armpits, but not one of the party of sixty was the worse of the wetting. The only person who seemed likely to drown was General Du Falga Cafarelli who had a wooden leg. The troops had an extraordinary fixed fallacious belief that this officer, a veteran of the Rhine army, had invented the Egyptian campaign for his own aggrandisement. "It's all right for him. He has always one foot in France."

Junior officers at this time got some unhallowed amusement out of their Chief of Staff. It was well known that Berthier, who was forty-six, was in the throes of a love affair as violent as if he was a boy of nineteen. It was said that he set up every night in his tent a sort of altar, covered with rare cashmeres, on which reposed a portrait of Madame Visconti. He had first met her in Italy, as wife of François Visconti, brother of Ennius-Quirinus Visconti, Antiquarian at the Vatican, who had taken political refuge in France in 1799. Madame Visconti (born Josephine Carcano) had already been the widow of a Signor Sopronsi. Berthier was said to have asked Bonaparte for leave to go home to visit her and the general had told him to go if he must; but he had not gone. He was nothing to look at. Only intelligence made his irregular features interesting.

At Suez Eugène received a notification from Berthier that the General in Chief had been very favourably impressed by his services since the opening of the campaign. He was promoted lieutenant. It was now nine months since he had left Paris.

The landmark known as the Gates of Syria was no more than two columns of granite. These indicated the separation of Africa from Asia. Next day they were told they were in Palestine. The General in Chief sent from Suez a flowery epistle to the Sultan, explaining that he had liberated Egypt. It was obvious to the Army of Egypt that the annihilation of the French fleet might incline the Port to alliance with England. In fearing this the general was right, but he did not know that Turkey had already declared war on the Republic, and that Talleyrand whom he reckoned should already have reached Constantinople as Ambassador, had never started. He foresaw resistance from the few concentrations of Turkish troops in Syria and was determined to forestall them and the English fleet by gaining command of the chain of seaports of the Syrian coast.

He had written to Tipoo Sahib of Mysore announcing his arrival on the Red Sea with an invincible host. "Filled with the desire to rescue you from the iron yoke of England." The dream of changing the face of the world by conquering India had not yet quite faded from his brain, but Syria was the first step. He had other reasons for anxiety. Plague was reported from Alexandria where he had left a garrison of five thousand under Marmont. Murad Bey had retired into Upper Egypt but Ibrahim Bey was at large in Syria where the Pasha Djezzar did not desire him and hoped the English would at least subsidize his removal.

The advance began with the familiar pattern of successes. It was wonderful to be in a green and fertile land. El Arish, which had fine encircling walls, held out three days. The articles of surrender stipulated that the defenders should go to Damascus but they mostly threw themselves into the next strong place on Bonaparte's list, Jaffa. Eugène was much struck by the romantic aspect of sea-girt El Arish, especially by moonlight. Returning from a night reconnaissance at top speed under sudden fire, he caught his leg in a trailing plant, as thick as your wrist, and knocked himself out. When he arrived at headquarters he found they had just decided he had been killed.

They had unreliable guides for their march to Gaza. Khan-Yonus had been given by the General in Chief the rendezvous, and as usual he followed after the last columns. He was attended only by fifteen horsemen and some dromedaries. The first four guides to enter Khan-Yonus found Mamelukes. When the general arrived, instead of the camp which he had expected, a detachment of enemy cavalry was waiting for him. There was nothing for it but to retreat as best they could, under cover of darkness, and they were already exhausted. Eugène's horse failed and he had to march nine miles on foot.

It was at this point that he formed a friendship with Duroc which ended only with death. Duroc was nine years his senior, first aide de camp to the General in Chief, of an old military family, and had already distinguished himself on the Isonzo and Brenta and at Gradisca. On the night before they entered Gaza Eugène was ordered at a moment's notice to set out with directions for Kléber who was some miles off, near Ramleh. He had just come in after a most exhausting day and was sleeping like the dead, or the very young. The officer who was responsible for delivering the order did not fail to wake him but he did not wait to make sure that he understood. Eugène heard the order but it failed to penetrate to his brain. He fell asleep again, deeper and deeper. He was awoken in earnest by someone shaking him, trying to get him off his couch and on to his legs. He told the intruder to go away; he could do no more. Duroc redoubled his efforts and shouted, getting angry, "You'll disgrace yourself!" This word did rouse him and adding his own efforts to those of his helper, who was much smaller, he got up. He went off without an escort, as he was already so late, and he lost himself. After about five hours he came up with Kléber, just in time. The general was in the act of putting his division into movement.

Gaza seemed at first sight well garrisoned, but it offered no resistance. Eugène looked up, fascinated, at the heights from which according to tradition, Samson had carried away the gates. They had a Samson's Tomb in Gaza, which even if it was not quite old enough, was several hundreds of years old and was good for trade. He was lucky in arriving early at Ramleh and being sent out to reconnoitre. In early spring Palestine was full of wild flowers and had a peaceful biblical look. He took twenty-five men and rode down the valley which led to Jerusalem. He was afire at the thought of seeing a city so famous, so venerated. But he was not to get there. Troops of Arabs and Syrians, all armed, hung about, without daring to attack him. However, he had got far enough to have a good distant view, and as things fell out he was the only officer of the Army of Egypt ever to see Jerusalem.[8]

At the same night at Ramleh there was a terrific thunder storm. The rain came down in torrents. The troops, to dry themselves, set fire to a whole grove of olives. The olives were full of oil, and the effect of such a conflagration lighting up such forms and faces, all in a steamy haze, was recognized by him as the very picture of the romantic side of a soldier's life.

They arrived outside Jaffa on March 4 and after three days preparation took it by assault. He was ordered to come in on the side looking seawards. It was a difficult passage for cavalry, precipitous narrow streets, full of holes and sharp turnings. The troops had a tough time getting up into Jaffa and wreaked their vengeance. The massacre and pillage following that capture went on all night. Next morning he was sent to try to restore some order and to stop the excesses. "It was the first time I had seen a town taken by assault and it filled me with horror. Almost all the people of Jaffa had been butchered, regardless of age and sex. The ground was heaped with corpses and blood was still running down the steep streets." It had been a lovely place, encircled by gardens abounding in orange trees, cedars, and a remarkable number of European fruit-trees.

The massacre at Jaffa was to become infamous. Unfortunately there was another incident connected with this operation which he could not pass over in silence. Tired of carnage, on the day after the assault, the troops took a great number of prisoners. These were a terrible embarrassment, as eight hundred had already capitulated with the fort, and the Army of Egypt had not enough food for itself. The General in Chief, after consultation with his senior officers, gave the command for the prisoners to be shot. Some colonels, and Adjutant-General Boyer, refused to execute such an order. Colonel d'Armagnac of the 30th regiment who did eventually undertake it, did so much against his will. It did appear revolting, but hunger is an imperious necessity and many critics did not know that a large number of these prisoners were the garrison from El Arish who had broken their parole. Were they spared, they would do so again. Still Eugène thought the event deplorable, unlike France at war, renowned for her honour and generosity. He must state that he knew the General in Chief had not given the order without much grief, and the troops had not executed it without murmurs.[9]

It was a relief to arrive at St. Jean d'Acre, a most beautiful fortress, known as "The Key to Palestine." Cleopatra had conquered it. St. Paul had slept there. The Crusaders had taken and re-taken it again and again. Its harbour was spacious and it did great trade, shipping the caravans from the far East. Its history had always been chequered and calamitous. The place was surrounded by a double rampart and fortified by towers at intervals. It was almost an island: three-fourths of its ramparts were bathed by the ocean; the remainder was protected by a double ditch. Trenches were at once opened.

Eugène was sent to reconnoitre Haifa, a little town on the south of the bay of Acre. It was apparently occupied, and by considerable numbers of people, but not troops. When they saw him coming, some of the many inhabitants crowding the walls descended to open the gate. They had hardly got it open when, acting on impulse, he galloped into the town and straight down to the harbour, followed by his escort of four troopers. An English cutter carrying a senior officer had at that moment left the shore and was rowing along. He and his escort gave it five shots from their carbines and several pistol shots, but with no success, and the returning fire was equally ineffective. He afterwards discovered that he had encountered for the first time in his life, one of the most dashing and eccentric of British sea-officers, Commodore Sir Sidney Smith. It was generally believed in the Army of Egypt that Sir Sidney was at least partially responsible for the Battle of the Nile and the loss of their Fleet. He had escaped from Paris, where he had been in prison in the Temple, in time to reach London and give warning to the First Lord of the Admiralty that Bonaparte was bound for Egypt.

The British squadron had got to Acre first and had made a success of instilling some discipline and knowledge into a Turkish garrison. The siege of Acre began. It was to last sixty-two days and include forty assaults by the French and twenty-six sorties by the garrison. Colonel Lavalette was witness on the day that the enemy perceiving Bonaparte and his staff standing on an eminence, placed their shells so well that one fell three paces from the general, between his aides de camp Merlin and Beauharnais, and the other, two feet distant, descended on a party of eleven getting breakfast, not one of whom survived. It was a curious coincidence that Turkish gunnery was so exact because they had been trained by a French *émigré* officer who had been at the military school at Brienne as a lad with the General in Chief.

Before the first assault, on April 1, aide de camp Duroc was sent into the ditch below the infamous "Damnable" Tower which had been mined by a party of engineers. He was to discover and report the depth of the breach. A howitzer wounded him deeply in the right thigh. On the same day, aide de camp Beauharnais was severely wounded in the head, and the blast of the shell which hit him brought down the bastion, so he was for some time buried alive, and when released was taken up for dead. Duroc was slightly lame for life and not able to take any further part in the siege, but Beauharnais, who said his wound was in comparison slight, was on duty again in nineteen days, just in time for the second assault.

While the friends lay *hors de combat* they heard the gruesome story of the deaths on the same day of the gallant young Mailly de Château Renard brothers. The elder was hit in the moat below the walls of Acre at the head of the first column in the first attack. He lay in the ditch under a heap of bodies all night and at dawn was discovered and decapitated by the enemy. The younger had been sent into Syria six months ago with peace proposals. He had been captured and locked up in the lighthouse at Acre with about four hundred Christians whom he had collected on the coast of Syria. The day after the failure of the first attempt to storm Acre some French troops who were out in the trenches mentioned to General Vial that a lot of bundles which looked as if they might be bales of rice or coffee were drifting in on the shore. He went to look at them and recognised the young Château Renard, who had been strangled during the night. The other bundles were his four hundred companions in captivity. Such was the vengeance of Pasha Djezzar, "the Butcher", for the first assault on the Damnable Tower.

On April 9 General Du Falga Cafarelli died of his wounds. He had fought well with one leg, but had not been able to survive the amputation of an arm. On April 16 Bonaparte deserted the siege of Acre for something more to his taste, a spectacular victory which he called the Battle of Mount Thabor. Ibrahim Bey had spirited up the Arabs of the Nablus mountains and his fellow Pashas of Damascus and Aleppo. Kléber had been sent to support Junot who had been attacked by a superior force near Nazareth, and had succeeded in that, but Bonaparte had to rescue him when Kléber was about to fight a defensive action, much outnumbered, in the Plains of Esdraelon. The General in Chief had not much trouble. The Ottomans panicked and ran when they heard the first shot from a French cannon.[10]

V

The retreat of the Army of Egypt from Syria was a humiliating experience but the troops always held that it was not the enemy who had prevented them from taking Acre, it was the plague. It had been brought up by the Second Light Brigade from Damietta. The army had also found it at Jaffa. When the day came for the army to march, no officer or man rode on a horse except for a few forming a rearguard of each column. Three of Eugène's five horses carried wounded, two plague cases. He was one of the last to leave the scene. He had to arrange the dismantling of the last guns. The enemy, who had guessed what was happening, had kept up a desultory fire during the night. He thought that, considering how he had escaped in such a murderous affair, it would be a pity if he was hit now, for there would not be anyone to remove him. He would just have to lie in a trench until day, when a Turk would save him the trouble by cutting off his head.

The scenes at Tentoura, a little town on the sea-shore, were enough to make the least imaginative open their eyes. The place was a shambles of wounded and plague-victims, over whom the vultures were already hovering. The ground was littered by cast-away stores and weapons waiting to be burned or dumped in the sea. Larrey, the Principal Medical Officer of the expedition, was resolute and splendid. He had all the calm and courage of a son of the High Pyrenees. He was by no means a stranger to Eugène. General Beauharnais when with the Army of the Rhine at Strasbourg had commended the flying ambulances invented by a very young surgeon-major. They were light two-and four-wheeled carriages with hoods and springs. Desgenettes, Chief Physician, who had a theory that this plague was not the bubonic variety dramatically injected himself with it in sight of a hospital ward. Some patients recovered. For the rest of his life, and after his death, the reputation of Bonaparte was attacked by people who said that he had poisoned his plague-stricken troops in Egypt. His stepson wrote that he did not propose to enlarge on an accusation which he knew was slanderous. The following had been his own experience.

When he had himself been sent to the hospital at Jaffa to report on the number of patients left there, he had found Larrey who told him that the place was cleared except for fifteen moribund cases who would not survive removal. Larrey had let the aide de camp see them, and they had been heart-rending, for they were not unconscious. They were in burning fever, crying for water. They had enough sense to realize that they were being abandoned.

In the year 1809 a glowing canvas by Gros was exhibited in the Paris Salon. It represented Bonaparte visiting and even touching the plague victims at Jaffa. Hortense, who had suggested the subject to the painter, was much dashed when her brother came in from seeing it very angry. "I know what took place at Jaffa, because I was there, with the other aides de camp. We certainly did not feel very comfortable, but we did not hold our handkerchiefs in front of our mouths. How could we have dared, when the general in order to reassure the patients was exposing himself as he did?"[11]

The homecoming to Cairo of the Army of Egypt was swifter but worse than the journey into Syria. Thirst was a terrible problem for on this return passage they found the wells blocked by corpses and poisoned. Their ration was a little rice and biscuit and a sip of water bottle every four hours. Eugène had a tiny vinegar bottle in an osier case with which he moistened his lips and nostrils.

Behind them the scene was garishly lit by roaring flames, for fields and villages were being burned to frustrate the pursuing enemy. They trod over the Egyptian border with shouts of joy, as if they were home again. At El Arish they left, under guard, some of the wounded who could go no further. Others were shipped for Damietta. Officers got back their horses. On the day before their arrival at Cairo the eagle eye of Bonaparte perceived a convoy of some size on the horizon. Eugène was ordered with a troop of twenty-five to investigate it. It proved to be a tribe of two hundred Arabs with a flock of four hundred camels and cattle. Some of the troopers' horses were so tired that they could not come up with the procession at speed. Eugène took on four of the best mounted, told the rest to follow, and charged for the centre of the convoy. Seeing the remainder of his men coming up, the Arabs abandoned it and fled into the desert. Eugène was embarrassed when he was joined by two piquets sent by Bonaparte to see what had happened to him. But they served to help to bring the convoy into Cairo. It was the hottest day he had ever known. Nevertheless they came into Cairo as if from a victory, with palm fronds in their hats, captured banners aloft, and bands playing.

Before they left Acre the General in Chief had heard that there was an army from Constantinople at sea, bound for Alexandria. To allay anxiety he went twice to Gizeh camp to see how the Corps of the Arts and Sciences were getting on with their research into the Pyramids, the Sphinx etc. The *savants* had also been up to General Desaix's headquarters and visited Thebes, Tentyra, Karnak and Luxor. The most beautiful result of their labours began to appear in 1809 and continued doing so until 1828. *Description de l'Égypte* was issued in ten volumes of text, accompanied by fourteen volumes of plates. It was responsible for a revolution in French, and eventually European, interior decoration and female costume.

The General in Chief also visited Madame Fourès. She was as pretty as ever, but had become something of a liability. Her husband, sent to Paris with despatches, had been captured at sea by the English and returned under parole to Alexandria. He had arrived in Cairo in fury, and she had obtained a civil divorce on the grounds of his cruelty.[12]

The landing season was fast approaching. General Desaix, the untidiest but one of the bravest of commanders, was believed to be doggedly pursuing Murad Bey to his last entrenchment, the oasis near the Pyramids. Bonaparte, who had posted himself with cavalry near by, was just coming out from his second visit to the Great Pyramid, with Duroc limping behind, when he received an express from Marmont. A Turkish army had landed at Aboukir and made itself master of the great redoubt and the fort, after massacring the garrison. He set off at once for Aboukir, a distance of over two hundred and forty miles. Because of what he called "a disagreeable accident" Eugène had to drop out at Ramanieh. He was sick to death. Larrey was summoned. "Lieutenant! what have you been eating?" The agonized patient replied that he had been so tired when he had got in last night that he had eaten nothing, except some water-melons—with avidity, and in profusion. Larrey gave him something that caused him to wake up the next day to find himself in hospital. He was not going to die of poison or plague, but he must lie up a bit. He tormented Larrey into giving him another powerful draught which he could take with him, and he was in the saddle by one a.m. He reached the army on July 24 opposite Aboukir.[13]

Bonaparte had concentrated ten thousand men at Alexandria

and attacked the next day. The Turkish army was believed to be about twice the size of the French, and was evidently expecting reinforcements with Murad Bey. Although he was not an artillery officer Eugène found himself ordered by Bonaparte to direct the first two guns captured from the Turks, against the English gunboats which at the moment were on his left, and drawing away. Eugène noticed that one of his shells fell close enough to a launch to drench the men in it. By a curious chance Sir Sidney Smith was still with them. Fifteen years later, in Vienna, the English sea-officer assured Bonaparte's stepson that he recollected the incident perfectly.

The Battle of Aboukir was another of Bonaparte's lightning successes. General Lannes anticipated an order to make himself master of the great redoubt and thereafter the issue of the day was decided. The Turks fled towards Aboukir village pursued by Murat's cavalry which sabred and drove them into the sea. Eugène thought he had never seen a battle-scene so astonishing. There were ten thousand turbans bobbing about amongst the waves. Very few of the men reached the English ships, anchored at more than a mile and a half from the shore.

Next day, in attendance upon Lannes, he went for an inspection of outposts, and in a last sortie of Turkish troops the unfortunate Lannes got a bullet in the leg. The wounds he had received at Acre were not yet healed. Lannes was thirty, and looked more. He was every young officer's hero, a lion-heart. He had been a sergeant-major and was blunt and outspoken. He had hardly any education, but was as tough as his boots. (He was going home to divorce an unfaithful wife.)

Fortunately the Turks had no water in Aboukir fort so they capitulated in four days. Kléber arrived to discover that Bonaparte had secured one more brilliant tactical victory in Egypt. His surprise and admiration superseded for the moment the carping criticism he had always voiced of his General in Chief, especially outside Acre. "Bonaparte," he would declare, "is the kind of general who needs a monthly dividend of ten thousand men." He was not to be deprived much longer of the command which he had always felt should have been his.

Some French officers had been on board Sir Sidney Smith's ship to arrange about an exchange of prisoners. The English commodore suggested that General Bonaparte might like to see some French newspapers. Eugène never forgot the long night in which he and his stepfather sat reading the news of the past eight months. Italy was lost! The Russian Field-Marshal Suvàrov, in alliance with the Austrians, had routed Schérer. Cossacks had entered Milan. On the Rhine, the Archduke Charles had defeated Jourdan. In Switzerland, Massena was still fighting like a lion. There was unrest in Paris, and a financial crisis—and no wonder. Now and then, as the small hours passed, he heard his stepfather groan and ejaculate brokenly. "Miserable creatures! Is it possible? Poor France! What are they going to do?" He was afterwards convinced that in that night Bonaparte had decided that he was more needed in France than in Egypt; but he had received no confidences when they returned to Cairo.

On August 23 he was back at Alexandria, and in sight of the sea. There were two French frigates attended by two smaller craft waiting in a cove, three miles west of the city—provisioned and armed to run the English blockade. It was 10 p.m. and he was one of a party all given the same rendezvous and all, he believed, no further information. There was one Admiral, and Generals Berthier, Marmont, Lannes and Murat (the last two severely wounded). There were three leading members of the Arts and Sciences Corps—Monge, Denon and Berthollet. Eugène was unattended by his servant. He had been obliged to leave Lefebvre behind in hospital in Cairo. The General in Chief, however, had a picturesque new personal attendant, who was to become a familiar figure sitting with folded arms on the box of his carriage, and waiting impassive by his door, for the rest of his active life. Roustam Raza was an Armenian who had been stolen when he was seven years old. He was supposed to be now about nineteen. His fourth owner, Sheik El-Bekri, had presented him, and another young Mameluke to Bonaparte three months ago, on his return from Syria. He was richly dressed and armed.

The General in Chief had taken with him to Egypt eight aides de camp. Of these, Julien and Sulkowsky had been murdered by the Arabs, Croisier had been killed at Acre, Guibert at Aboukir. Duroc and Eugène had both been severely wounded at Acre. Only Lavalette who had been in every encounter had escaped entirely. There was also a casualty which nobody yet realized. Louis Bonaparte who had been invalided home last November was never to be the same man again.

Bonaparte noticed his stepson and said, "Eugène, you are going to see your mother again!" They sailed with dawn.

CHAPTER FIVE

From the Orangery To Marengo
1799 : 1800

I

THEY FULLY expected to find the English Commodore in their way. In that case the frigate *Carrère* had been told to engage the enemy while the *Muiron* ran. The General in Chief was in the *Muiron*. But both frigates were Venetian-built and very bad sailers. They stole along the coast of Africa for thirty days without ever standing far out to sea. The passengers dared not show a light at night so had to go to bed with the sun. Still, they buoyed themselves up with the reflection that some French ships did get through the blockade. Eugène had in his pocket now a letter brought by one recently, which he had picked up in Cairo.

"St. Germain.
"Pension de Madame Campan.
"How I have cried on getting your letters, my dear Eugène. What! you have been wounded and I did not know for four months. Luckily for your Hortense perhaps, for she would have been inconsolable at the thought that you were suffering and she was not near you. I do beg, my Eugène, if you still love me, look after yourself, don't expose yourself unnecessarily. Remember that you are the protector of your mother and sister and if anything should befall you they would be in despair. They are sad to be so far from you and their only consolation is to know you are happy and still keep a big place in your heart for them.

"Except for the letters which Louis brought, the only ones I have had from you are dated April 22 and July 7. As for me, I have written whenever I could, but I fear that they have never reached you. I hope this one will be luckier, because it is being sent with those of the Directors, secretly. As *Maman* writes to

Bonaparte, and as we are only allowed two letters, she can't write to you. So do not be surprised, and remember always that our happiest moments are the ones when we are chatting about you, darling, and Bonaparte.

"*Maman* has bought La Malmaison, which is near St. Germain. I go there nearly every week. She is living there very quietly and seeing nobody except Madame Campan and her nieces Mlles. Auguiés, who often go with me. She has only given two big dinners. She asked the Directors and the whole Bonaparte family, but the latter always refuse. Of them all, only Madame Bonaparte, the mother, is amiable to us, and we of course show her every attention; but I believe she is soon going back to Corsica. *Maman* is, I assure you, very upset that the family won't live on friendly terms with her, which must vex her husband whom she loves greatly. I am sure that if she could have gone out to him she would have, but now you know it is impossible.

"Before I close my letter I must add a little grumble. Yours are so short. It is true that you have written to me when you could, and often, but I wish you would send me a long letter, and send it in duplicate, then I might get at least one, and I should have some detailed news of our poor friends of the Army of Egypt. Say to them all, I beg, everything that is kind, embrace Bonaparte heartily for me. I hope he still has a little affection for me."

He could almost smell, see, and hear, Madame Campan's seminary on a Sunday afternoon, as he read this most innocent of letters—the polished beeswaxed parquet, the drawing boards, the practising of scales ... Hortense had composed words and music for a marching song for the Egyptian Army. "*Partant pour la Syrie*" it was called, and it was to be sung by generations of French soldiers who never knew it had been written for them by Bonaparte's stepchild.

There was a postscript to Hortense's letter, in his mother's hand. "I love you with all my heart, my dear Eugène; I think of you without ceasing. I await the moment which will reunite me with all I love. I should have nothing more to wish for if only I could have Bonaparte back, as he was when he left me, and as he should have continued to be for me. Think, my dear Eugène, of all I have suffered by the absence of both of you. Take care of yourself for the sake of your mother and your sister, both of whom adore you."[1]

At last the east wind began to blow in a determined way. They arrived at Bonaparte's birthplace, Ajaccio in Corsica. They had come from Egypt where there was plague so they could not enter the port, but the townsfolk hearing who was on board came flocking out in boats. As the frigate had been forty-four days at sea and had not one sick person on board there was no danger. Bonaparte's old nurse came out, and he cried "*Madre!*" and folded her in his arms.

They had an anxious hour when they were well in sight of the lovely hills of Provence. The topmast look-out saw two large ships. They could only be English, and they soon discharged cannon. There was a council of war and opinion was unanimous that the general ought to go back to Ajaccio in the post boat which was in company. But he utterly refused. "My destiny is not to be taken and die here." So they proceeded for Fréjus and were not molested.

Their experience at Fréjus was a fair sample of what they were to get all the way to Paris, "a triumphal march," wrote Eugène. The pressing crowds cried "Welcome our Liberator!" "Save France!" and "We perish but for you!" From Lyons, where the enthusiasm was delirious, the general and his stepson went by post-chaise. It was painful that the one place in which Bonaparte got no welcome was his own home. At 6 a.m. on October 16 the house in the Rue de la Victoire was empty. The bird had flown. The general's mother was soon on the scene and her looks spoke volumes. During the day most of the rest of his family came to bear testimony against his wife. In vain the trembling Agathe Rible stammered that Madame had left to meet the general the moment she got the news he was in France. It was just possible that this was true and that she had taken the eastern road through Burgundy. Louis Bonaparte, who had certainly done this, but separately, was also missing. Whatever the reason, her disappearance was most unfortunate. From her point of view it might be fatal. Her son wrote dismally, "Thus we arrived in Paris forty-eight hours before her, and her enemies had a clear field for that length of time in which to prejudice her husband against her." With feelings of despair he saw all the reconciliatory efforts which he had made in Egypt frustrated. A collection of his unhappy mother's belongings was humped in the hall for her to take away or send for. It had indeed been essential for her that she should see her husband before his family poured their poison into his ears. For she had, despite her son's hopes, been seeing much of

M. Charles. The merry little Charles was nine years junior to her and had recently given clear indications that he was not a marrying man.

There had already been a terrible scene between her and her husband before he sailed, when Joseph had reported, quite accurately, that she had been disgracefully involved with Charles in getting contracts to supply the army of Italy for a firm called Bodin. Everyone knew it. Louis Gohier, who was President of the new Directory, had suggested to her that she should divorce Bonaparte and marry Charles. The suggestion was futile.

Her last cause for nervousness was one chronic with her—her debts. These were quite beyond her reckoning, but she was sure, probably rightly, that people had asked what they liked from the wife of France's most successful general. Joseph had been put in charge of her allowance by her husband before he went abroad and it was to him that she had to apply for money to buy Malmaison—which she had already done.

After midnight on October 18 a carriage with jaded horses drew into the courtyard of the house in the Rue de la Victoire. It contained the errant Josephine, and her daughter, whom she had called for at St. Germain to accompany her on their unlucky journey. But when he heard the unmistakable commotion below Bonaparte removed to his upstairs study and locked the door. In vain the weary and weeping pair hammered and cried for him to hear them. Hours passed, daylight broadened. It was the faithful Agathe Rible who at last suggested an appeal from both children. The general used to be fond of the children. They came to him together, and said "Do not abandon our mother. It will break her heart." "Do not let us lose again our natural protector, our father, sent to us to replace him slain on the scaffold." "You shall not bear the burden of your mother's faults" said Bonaparte to Eugène. "You shall always be my son. I will keep you with me." "No, no, sir," said Eugène. "I must share my mother's ill fortune, and shall say farewell to you." This was the right note. At last, but most unwillingly Bonaparte allowed them to bring their mother to him, so that he could at least hear her story before he condemned her. The wretched woman had been lying at last, almost full-length and half-frozen, on the back stairs. Her children placed her in her husband's arms.

Next morning when Lucien Bonaparte was announced, he was asked to go up and found them in bed together.[2]

II

His mother who loved doing such kindnesses had found just the servant for Eugène to replace Lefebvre. Even the name of poor Constant sounded promising. He was the most superior young man; anyone could see at a glance that he had been born to better things. He was three years older than Eugène and a child-victim of the Revolution. His father had owned a select hotel called Le Petit Château, near Jemappes, where noble families stayed when taking the waters at the spa of St. Amand. Constant had been intended for the church, but when the Comte and Comtesse de Lure had asked to take him to Touraine to be educated with their own son, the proud parents had not been able to resist the offer. The de Lure family had disappeared in the Revolution and the boy could not get home. After various viscissitudes he had found a home at another spa—Plombières, and there a slightly odd but brilliant ladies' hairdresser whom she was taking back to Paris had recommended him to Josephine.

Constant took to Lieutenant Beauharnais at first sight and the approval was evidently mutual for the lieutenant engaged him on the spot, and his new *valet de chambre de confiance* dashed off to collect his modest luggage as happy a man as there could be in Paris. He had been given to understand by Carrat, the hairdresser, that he was replacing, only temporarily, an old servant, "totally devoted to his master as everyone who knew Lieutenant Beauharnais must be." Still, Cairo was a long way away.

Constant misjudged his new young master to be about his own age. Lieutenant Beauharnais' features were not exactly to be called handsome, they lacked classical perfection, but all the same they produced a good impression. He was well enough made, but did not as yet show it to advantage; his walk was gangling, a thing often noticeable amongst young men who spend much time on horseback. He looked frank, gay, amiable, generous and as if his countenance was the mirror of his soul.[3] He was very well mannered towards his parents and they evidently put every confidence in him. They allowed him to give little bachelor breakfast parties at the house in the Rue de la Victoire, to which he invited his brother officers and actors from the Théâtre Français. In spite of their recent experiences in Egypt all the young officers had remarkably high spirits. Constant remembered a merry party when Thiémet, the ventriloquist, had baffled them all, and another when two performers had pretended to be a man who stuttered and a man with an ear-trumpet. That, of course, had ended in a fight. But the best had been the one on the morning of the famous 18 Brumaire when the guests had all been officers and one of them had taken off two of the poor old Directors, to the life. The ex-Abbé Sieyès was to be seen taking riding lessons in the garden of the Luxembourg every morning nowadays. It was easy to guess who was being imitated when someone took a toss from an imaginary steed. Director Barras *à la grecque* was a little more sinister.

They were tight packed in the Rue de la Victoire in the three weeks after the general's return. His private secretary had appropriated the little lobby-room on the ground floor from which he could see everyone who came and went. The general went out to private parties very seldom and not much at all for entertainment, but there was a constant influx of people calling to see him, sometimes rather peculiar ones. There was a newspaper proprietor, the *Citoyen* Roederer, and *Citoyen* Réal, from the office of the *Citoyen* Fouché (Minister of Police) and General Bernadotte, out of temper out of uniform, but unmistakable with his short black curls and hook nose and long lank legs. He had married Desirée Clary and was now Joseph's brother in law. The three Bonaparte brothers called every day.

All the way up from the coast the crowds had called upon Bonaparte to save France. That was no secret. Something must be going to happen; but at the end of three weeks nothing had been offered to him except the command of any of France's armies that he might choose. He had asked to be allowed time to consider this proposal. On 16 Brumaire (the foggy month) the two young ladies of the family, Mademoiselle Hortense and Mademoiselle Caroline were sent back to boarding school at St. Germain. They had pleaded hard to be allowed a few days more but Madame had been adamant. That looked as if affairs might be about to move. The lieutenant was sent out several times. He called at the houses of General Moreau and the *Citoyen* Garat. But then suddenly Colonel Lavalette called for him and they went off to a ball together. The colonel who had to be on duty at midnight left before that, but the lieutenant, who was very fond of dancing and an excellent dancer, stayed on late.

III

The admiring Constant thought that his master was fully in the confidence of the general and his mother about the forthcoming *coup d'état*, but when Eugène came to write his memoirs, he said that he had been too young and too little initiated into public affairs to be able to follow in detail all that preceded and occasioned the overthrowing of the Directory. He remembered that on the night of 17 Brumaire, very late, after midnight, he was sent by his mother with an invitation to Gohier, President of the Directory, and Madame Gohier, to come to breakfast. Bonaparte was to have dined with them that night.

November 9 (18 Brumaire) was the most beautiful sunny day after a misty dawn. Eugène had his own breakfast party for his officer friends. He gave them a rendezvous at the swivel bridge the nearest route to the Carrousel parade ground. He had first to go on alone to the Tuileries. Bonaparte had entrusted him with a message for the Council of Ancients which would be in session there. It was not a difficult message—merely that the general wished to call upon them to receive their commands; but Eugène had never spoken in public before and the assembly was a large one. When he got back to the Rue de la Victoire he had difficulty in getting in. There were about eighty officers of regiments in the Paris area, all in full uniform, in and outside the house. Some were saying they did not know what their summons meant. General Lefebvre, who had risen from the ranks and was much loved by the troops, was an old Republican with an ominously large chin. He must be talked round. Luckily he abhorred lawyers and politicians. All the officers who had come to the house followed their host, with the exception of Bernadotte. Joseph took his brother in law by the arm and led him to his own home. Bernadotte was the only general who had appeared out of uniform. He had no intention of collaborating at this stage of affairs. He too was an old Republican.[4] Bonaparte was looking out for his stepson and as soon as he got the message from the Ancients he went out into the courtyard and made a short speech about the situation, after which he rode to the Tuileries and spoke there again.

"What have you done with this France which I left so glorious? I left you in peace. I return and find war. I left you victories. I find defeats. I left you the millions of Italy. I find despoiling laws and misery everywhere." Eugène nervously considered his step-father's address rather long. It ended with a suggestion that in view of a Jacobin conspiracy the two chambers of legislation—the Ancients and the Five Hundred—should remove to the old royal palace of St. Cloud. It was about nine miles west of Paris on the Versailles road, and a place where they could create a new provisional government at leisure and undisturbed. The Ancients were not present in force. They had been inhumanely summoned for five a.m. to pass three decrees which they had meekly accepted. The first was that changing the site of government. The second required that they should meet at St. Cloud the next day, and the third appointed General Bonaparte commander of all the armed forces of the capital and empowered him to arrange the removal of the legislature to the suburbs. He had been sent for to take the oath of loyalty to the Republic. When he had done this and got outside, he reviewed about ten thousand troops assembled in the Tuileries gardens. He read the decree, addressed them rousingly pointing out that the country was in a miserable condition under a corrupt government, and was wildly cheered. That was all that happened as far as the man in the street could see on the famous 18 Brumaire, and nothing had gone amiss, but then, some people said, Bonaparte had had to deal today only with soldiers. At the Rue de la Victoire painful repercussions went on till midnight when heavy rain began to fall. There was a long session for Josephine of poor Madame Gohier in tears, for Gohier had never come to breakfast and a detachment of troops under General Moreau had been to the Luxembourg to expel any remaining of the five Directors who refused to resign. Josephine had seen a great deal of the Gohiers during her husband's absence, and Madame Gohier who had been her husband's cook was a simple soul and devoted to him. Eventually she went off, told to do all she could to get him to follow the example of the other members of his government, for he would certainly get high office in the next. (He refused, but eventually was glad of a small post abroad.) Barras, who had been another old friend, also got some special treatment. He was suspected of having intrigued to bring back the exiled royal family. Talleyrand and Admiral Bruix were sent to see him at the Luxembourg, to get his resignation, and if necessary gild the parting handshake. But this was not necessary. Barras knew his time had come. He had made an enormous fortune while in the service of his unhappy country. He retired smiling, to write the most scurrilous and vindictive memoirs of the period, especially about Josephine. He could not endure that a couple whom he considered that he had brought to power should kick away the rotten ladder by which they had risen.

On the morning of 19 Brumaire everyone set off for St. Cloud. The palace had been built by the artistic Duke of Orleans, brother of Louis XIV, and was of surpassing beauty. It stood high above the river and was approached by a narrow bridge and a long avenue of fine chestnut trees. The park and gardens covered many acres. It had been a favourite residence of the unhappy Marie Antoinette. As they passed through the old Place Louis XVI, site of the guillotine, Lavalette asked Bourrienne what he thought was going to happen today. "*Mon ami,*" said the Bonapartes' secretary, "either we shall sleep tomorrow at the Luxembourg or there will be an end of us."

The Council of the Ancients was not very numerous, so it had not been difficult to find a hall in the palace capable of accommodating it. The great gallery of Apollo with decorations by Mignard had been chosen. It occupied nearly the whole length of the first floor in the right wing of the building. But the Council of Five Hundred was another matter. Workmen were still hammering in the old Orangery, in the opposite wing of the palace, an hour after noon.

The two assemblies came into action very slowly. The Ancients opened their session after two p.m. after listening to an orchestra playing the "Marseillaise." Several delegates rose instantly to ask the reason for the move to St. Cloud, and after an hour it was ruled that it could not be considered legal until both bodies had officially informed the Directory. The session was then suspended while notices were issued to the Five Hundred and the Directory.

The news of the Battle of Aboukir had reached Paris a few days before Bonaparte's return from Egypt, and as a mark of respect his brother Lucien had been elected to the Presidency of the Five Hundred. Lucien, who had only recently been gathered back into the family fold after his unsuitable marriage, was to win his spurs that day. While the general strode up and down a reception room outside the council chamber, furnished by just two chairs, and Sieyès sat in one of them and poked a smouldering fire with a stick, Lavalette and others brought in news as to how matters were proceeding. In the Orangery, the majority of members evidently wished that no decisions should be reached that day. The Five Hundred included many Jacobin and ex-terrorist deputies. When it was announced to him that they had entered upon a ceremony of individual oath-taking calculated to occupy at least an hour, Bonaparte's patience gave out. There had been about thirty officers of his staff in attendance in the next reception room and they all followed him when he strode out saying, "This must have an end!"

He mounted a horse and rode across the façade of the palace. A regiment of infantry just arrived from Paris was ranged in the courtyard. He called up the officers and harangued them. He then dismounted at the foot of the great staircase leading to the Gallery of Apollo and mounted it at speed. Disregarding all etiquette he presented himself at the bar of the Council of the Ancients. They were just rising for a break of quarter of an hour. Until Berthier, unusually pale, begged him to desist, he uttered brokenly a long confused tirade of accusation. He spoke of "a plot against Liberty." He appealed to "brothers in arms" with "the frankness of a soldier." He left the hall as violently as he had arrived, with the words "Let those who love me follow me!" He was followed by cries of "Dictator!" "Cromwell!" "Caesar!" and "Tyrant!"

As he came down the stairs, he received a message from Paris. It was from Fouché of the Police, urging him to hurry. Outside shouts of "Vive Bonaparte!" resounded, but these came from the troops and were, in the words of his secretary, merely a sunbeam between the storms. Bourrienne had been sent on a message, so missed the strange affair in the Orangery, destined to be the subject of many dramatic paintings under the misleading title of 18 Brumaire. Eugène did not record the humiliating call upon the Ancients. Distances at St. Cloud were great. But he was in attendance when Bonaparte, for the second time that day, pushed his way into a Council in session, and the stepson recorded his evidence probably as clearly as any eyewitness of such a strange tumultuous crowd-scene could hope to do.

Bonaparte took on the Five Hundred single-handed. They were furious at his intrusion and several deputies closed in on him. He never got a chance to speak because they began at once to belabour him. He was cut off from his followers by a file of grenadiers whose duty it was to protect the council. To his horror, Eugène heard cries of "Out of the house! Get out!" and worst of all "Outlaw General Bonaparte!" That last dangerous cry had preceded the murder of Robespierre. Eugène did not himself see any daggers pointed at the general, but that was not to say it had not happened. He was several paces behind, and had been able to see his stepfather's entrance very imperfectly. (Afterwards, a grenadier was found to have received a thrust from a stiletto which cut through his coat. It might have been meant for the general.) Bonaparte was certainly rescued from the hall by grenadiers, but it was Lucien who eventually saved the day. Lucien joined his brother and announced to the guard that the Council was being intimidated by certain deputies, possibly in the pay of England, "I went to speak to them," affirmed the general, "and they answered me with daggers." Eugène saw a changed man. "General Bonaparte retired from the hall in a great state of agitation. His features were altered, and this was well explained by the situation in which he found himself. He must now exert himself to succeed, or perish ignominiously on the scaffold. Re-entering the courtyard he mounted his horse and addressed the troops with vehemence, and gave the order for the hall to be cleared by them."

The infantry outside had begun to understand that an attempt had been made on the life of Bonaparte. Drummers were ordered to sound the charge. Generals Leclerc and Murat led a column of grenadiers with fixed bayonets through the corridors into the Orangery.

From that moment a scene which had threatened a tragedy became broad farce. Deputies made their way out of the hall by every exit possible, even the windows. As darkness fell, the improvised council chamber and the garden outside were pathetically littered with the noble Roman togas of fine scarlet cloth and square classical caps of office of five hundred legislators all running away from nothing.

Her son was back in the Rue de la Victoire before midnight to give the anxious chief lady of France an account of the day's happenings. Bonaparte did not follow until between three and four a.m. He had, amongst many things, to get out his manifesto referring not only to daggers but to firearms presented in the Orangery. It was essential that a cloak of legality be cast over the day's proceedings. Before they all departed Lucien had brought the Ancients to agree to nominate a provisional government of three Consuls. (Originally Bonaparte was the third and the others were Sieyès and Roger Ducos, but by December 13 Bonaparte was

First Consul assisted by Cambacérès and Lebrun, reassuring names, men who had taken no part in the intrigues that had preceded 18 Brumaire.) Lucien finally collected a sufficient number of the Five Hundred—less than a hundred—to ratify the action of the Ancients.

The gentle voice of Hortense told the end of the story of a crucial day: "General Murat, a true knight-errant, sent us four grenadiers of the Guard, of which he was the commander, to tell us what had taken place at St. Cloud, and the appointment of General Bonaparte to the Consulate. Imagine the effect of four grenadiers knocking on the doors of a convent in the middle of the night! Everyone got a terrible shock and Madame Campan blamed this military method of sending news. But Caroline read it as a proof of love."[5]

IV

Before he slept, on the dawn after his *coup d'état* Bonaparte had told his secretary that he would move into the Luxembourg that day. He was not quite able to do this, as Gohier had to be assisted to move out, but he was in by the evening of November 20. He immediately set about forming a new council of state, a legislative body and finally a new constitution. Bourrienne noticed that the Consul when looking through the notes on persons suggested for posts was most influenced by a record of inflexible integrity. He liked talent, and generally rejected a man who was said to be safe but mediocre. He did not like men of the Revolution, but was aware he could not at present get on without them. He equally resisted, except for social occasions, the members of the old nobility pressed upon his notice by Josephine. He had to make exceptions for two devious men—Fouché had been a Terrorist, and Talleyrand had been a Bishop and a nobleman.

He never slept again in the little house in the Rue de la Victoire. At the Petit Luxembourg he took over the suite of apartments on the ground floor, to the right of the palace when entering from the Rue de Vaugirard. His cabinet was close to a private staircase to the first floor where he had established his wife and step-daughter. His stepson and his secretary had bedrooms on the second floor and spent their days in ante-chambers of his cabinet. The days were remarkably similar. Bonaparte did not like new faces or irregular hours except when unavoidable. He met his secretary at seven a.m. He breakfasted at ten, with his family, staff and a few guests. They generally sat down twenty. He had long morning sessions with Monge, Cambacérès, and other ministers. He saw his brothers often. Three or four times in the week he went to the council. To get to the great hall he had to cross the courtyard from the little palace to the main building and as December was very wet he hurried on arrangements for a move to the Tuileries palace. On council days he waited until afternoon to sign documents and see letters and glance at what was recommended to his attention in newspapers. That meant he got no exercise at all on those days. At five o'clock his *maître d'hôtel* appeared to announce "*Le Général est servi*". He had no luxury at his table and seldom sat at a meal more than twenty minutes. He was served by both his Mamelukes. Ibrahim Ali, the Arabian one, had turned up from Egypt. He proved dreadfully unsatisfactory, was jealous of Roustam and quarrelled with every-one in the household. He was ugly, which seemed to fit his character. When Constant threw him into the ornamental water at Malmaison, because he had drawn his dagger on the valet, he screamed such blue murder that Josephine took his part. But eventually even she saw through him, and he was sent to perform duties at the palace of Fontainebleau.

After dinner Bonaparte went upstairs for receptions in Josephine's apartments. At midnight, at latest, he gave the signal, "*Allons nous coucher*" and according to Constant went to bed with Madame Bonaparte like a *bon bourgeois*. He much disliked the extremely scanty costumes of fashionable women and the *Moniteur* reported him at a gathering in the Luxembourg in December, as having given repeated orders to make up the fires which were already blazing, until he had to be told there was no more fuel in the palace. He said pointedly, "Well, it will have to do; but I wanted a good fire, for the cold is intense and these ladies are nearly naked." For recreation and exercise he depended much on Saturdays and Sundays and sometimes Mondays at Malmaison.

Another problem figure had turned up from Africa, Eugène's servant Lefebvre, restored to health and burning with zeal. Eugène suggested to him that he might like to go in to service with Madame Bonaparte. He thought it might be quieter for him. Alas! a simple soldier servant, a veteran of the Armies of Italy and Egypt addressed himself to Madame Bonaparte, whose heart was tender. A tear trickled down a rugged check. Next morning Lieutenant Beauharnais had to speak sadly to his *valet de chambre de confiance* "Constant! I am extremely sorry but we shall have to part. Lefebvre is an old servant. I shall have to take him back." He added that he hoped still to see Constant often; Madame Bonaparte was going to speak to him. Constant, who had known deep waters, applied to her at once, and passed into a service which he found rather soft for his age. Three months later he was suddenly asked by the First Consul if he would like to go on a campaign. He was, for the next fifteen years, first valet to Bonaparte and eventually wrote memoirs to tell posterity how Bonaparte could not shave himself, and was a demon to shave, liked a chicken every day, drank very sparingly, and many other fascinating details. He was an absolutely first class valet and his new master began at once to look more tidy. His young master, "the brave, modest and good Lieutenant," back in the care of the veteran became a little less highly polished but possibly this was all for the best, as ladies of the *ancien régime* were already remarking that he was clearly of their world. "His figure was graceful, he was skilled in all bodily exercises, and he inherited from his father those fine manners of the gentleman of the *vieille cour* in which perhaps the Vicomte de Beauharnais had himself given him his earliest lessons. To these advantages he added simplicity and kindheartedness; he was neither vain or presumptuous; he was sincere without being indiscreet, and could be silent when silence was necessary."[6]

This was all very fine, but as aide de camp to a general who had become a statesman he was absolutely bored to death. "The service was very disagreeable to me who had always been in the army, and was passionately anxious to get experience in my profession. We passed our days in a waiting room, with a flunkey always on duty to open the door and honestly we performed much the same functions. I wanted to get out. The creation of a Guard for the Consuls soon furnished me with an opportunity."

On November 28 an announcement was made of the function of a Consular Guard—an *élite* corps. Bonaparte was using as nucleus the old Guards of the Directory and Legislature. He was purging these of Robespierrists, over-age officers and undesirables. (Grenadier Thomé, who had "preserved him from the daggers of the 19 Brumaire," was asked to breakfast by Josephine and got a diamond ring and a bonus of 600 francs.) On December 2,

Citizen-Lieutenant-General Murat was named commander is chief and inspector general of the Guard. His recruiting posters were stirring. "The First Consul intends that the Guard shall be a model for the army. Admission will be restricted to men who have performed heroic actions, have been wounded, or have otherwise given proofs . . . in several campaigns of their courage, patriotism, discipline and exemplary conduct. They must not be less than twenty-five, must be between five foot ten and six feet, of robust constitution . . . able to read and write . . ."

The First Consul's stepson was not nearly twenty-five yet, but far from taking his application amiss Bonaparte applauded it. The new Guard was reviewed by Murat in the Luxembourg Gardens on February 18, 1800. The corps provided a general staff, two battalions of grenadiers, a company of light infantry, two squadrons of light cavalry, a company of *chasseurs* and one of horse artillery; Captain Eugène Beauharnais led the *chasseurs à cheval*. These were the old *Guides*, a hundred and twelve sun-burned veterans of the armies of Italy and Egypt. The band played "*Dans la rue Chiffonnière*" and "*On va leur percer le flanc*". The men of the Consular Guard wore blue coats with white revers and scarlet cuffs, white waistcoats and breeches, red epaulets, and bearskins. The two squadrons of cavalry were distinguished by orange shoulder knots and orange cords on their fur caps. Their horse-furniture was blue with orange braid trimmings. They wore green dolmans and dark red pelisses. (Green had always been the prerogative of the *Guides*, and Bonaparte's favourite attire was the undress uniform of the *Guides*, the *chasseurs à cheval* of the Guard. He wore their dark green coat with dark red cuffs and collar, white waistcoat and breeches, but his famous grey *surtout* was entirely his own idea.)

Newspapers recorded the new Guard as "impeccable," but light was thrown on their discipline by a request from Bessières, colonel in charge of the cavalry, that *chasseurs à cheval* should refrain from smoking their pipes while escorting the Council of State, and should remember to salute generals and other officers. They were tactfully reminded that although they were going to serve as a model to all troops they were not to be haughty. The regiments of the Line were their comrades in arms.

Bessières looked Dutch, for he had a smooth dish-face and flat fair hair, but he was not in the least. He came from Cahors in the Limousin. When he had enlisted in the army of Louis XVI he had entered his profession as wig-maker. He also had experience as a barber-surgeon. He had repeatedly distinguished himself in Bonaparte's Italian campaign and had been a *chef de brigade* in Syria. He was thirty-two and very popular with the troops. He was quite imperturbable.

On the day after the Luxembourg parade, which was in some sort a dress-rehearsal, Bonaparte reviewed the new corps in the Place du Carrousel. He was on his way to take up residence at the Tuileries. He arrived in a coach drawn by six white horses given to him by the Emperor on the conclusion of the Treaty of Campo Formio. The royal palace was to be re-named Palais du Gouvernement. Josephine, with Hortense, Stéphanie and Émilie sat in a window of the Pavillon de Flore (the Third Consul's residence in the Tuileries) to watch the procession, attended by ministers and generals' wives. One of these was Caroline Bonaparte now Murat. The signing of her wedding contract had been the last festivity in the Luxembourg. Bonaparte had not been keen on the love match, but Josephine and Hortense had used diplomacy, and at last he had decided that at any rate no one could say that he had sought for an *aristo* as brother in law. Murat had been born the child of an inn-keeper. In appearance he was a true son of the south. He was tall, swarthy, dashing, with thick lips and black curls. His courage was unquestioned. He loved attiring himself in the most *bizarre* uniforms. Caroline, at eighteen, had a brilliant pink and white complexion, decidedly pretty features, golden hair and a slightly thick figure. The couple seemed ideally suited. Both were highly ambitious and passionate. In later life, they gave the impression of being a little more highly-coloured and larger than life-size. Caroline had some brains but had arrived at Madame Campan's, as Bonaparte had warned her headmistress, knowing absolutely nothing and with no desire to apply herself. In vain gentle Hortense had tried to help her at lessons, and with friendship. They had not become friends until Caroline had informed Hortense in a burst of dramatic school-girl confidence that she had never wanted to come to school. She was in love with Colonel Murat.

All the ladies watching the parade on this fine sunny day were dressed in what were believed to be Grecian costumes, muslin gowns and light shawls. Bonaparte reviewed the troops on horse-back amidst deafening applause. He then walked up the steps into the palace. When he had shown his friend Roederer the suites he meant to occupy, the journalist had remarked "This is a gloomy spot, General." "Yes," replied the First Consul, "as gloomy as grandeur."

Josephine had the same impression, and told Hortense she knew she was not going to be happy there. "I see poor Queen Marie Antoinette everywhere . . . I felt forebodings from the first moment I entered." She was to sleep in the late queen's bedroom, on the ground floor facing west, overlooking the garden, and Hortense had a bedroom and boudoir opening out of it. Contrary to the arrangement at the Luxembourg, Bonaparte now had his rooms above them. The reason was that these were the apartments which had belonged to Louis XIV, XV and XVI. His study communicated with a small private staircase through a dressing room which had been the oratory of Marie de Medici. He had a huge gilded brocade royal bedstead in one of his state rooms, but only for show. He nearly always slept next door in a small single bed. To the right of his study was a little closet for Duroc. This room, and that in which Bourrienne worked with the Consul, were lovely on a May day with the chestnuts outside the windows in flower. But the whole arrangement was extremely inconvenient. The cabinet gave on to an echoing grand staircase, a grand Presentation Saloon and the Hall of the Guards. As the Grand Saloon was between his study and the room with the state bed in which he usually gave audiences, should he want a fact, or a date, or a name, a confidential servant had to be summoned by a bell and sent skating over hundreds of yards of polished parquet to fetch the secretary.

A few days after the great remove, a reception was given for the diplomatic corps. All the ancient ceremonials of a court of France had been what the secretary called "raked up" and after the representatives had been received by the Consuls they were conducted to the apartments of Josephine, in imitation of the old custom of waiting on the queen after presentation to the king. By eight o'clock Josephine's drawing room was crowded by guests in formal costume making what Constant called "a splendid display of dresses, feathers, diamonds." There was a murmur of universal admiration when Madame Bonaparte was announced, and she was led in by Talleyrand. She wore a simple white India muslin gown, high waisted and short sleeved, a tortoiseshell comb in her hair and a pearl necklace. She looked her most winning, but in truth her simple attire might have infuriated her husband. He

The house in the Rue Chantereine
after a lithograph by G. Engelmann
By permission of the Bibliothèque Nationale, Paris

The Villa Bonaparte, Milan
from a contemporary engraving

It was built in 1790, near the Porta Orientale, and presented to Napoleon, who made it a residence for Eugène as Viceroy of Italy. It is now the Milan Municipal Gallery for Modern Art.

knew that India muslins came via Britain. He was capable of tearing in two a dress which he had convicted of issuing from that source. In vain Josephine and her daughter used to tell him that this was not India muslin; it was lawn of St. Quentin. Her new necklace, too, had already aroused his suspicion. It had in fact belonged to Marie Antoinette and was not yet paid for. But she had told him, and got Bourrienne to back her up, that it was the pearl necklace presented to her by the Cisalpine Republic, actually a much smaller affair.

Hortense had hoped to return to St. Germain once her mother was installed in the new and most unhomely home but she soon found this was not to be. Both her brother and her stepfather were leaving shortly for Dijon, headquarters of the new Army of Reserve. She had rather above average talent as an amateur artist. She had a little painting room in her new Paris quarters and here she diligently copied Gros's portrait of Eugène. Unfortunately it, and all her equipment, were destroyed by fire, owing, she admitted, to her own incompetence in dealing with stoves.

Eugène said his farewell on April 1, when Colonel Bessières led his cavalry, equipped for action, out of Paris. Their first halt was Corbeil, their next Noyon. The First Consul was going to win back Italy.[7] The young officer was thoroughly glad to be off on a campaign at last, but to the end of his days Paris was a word which held magic for him. "I spent the whole of that winter of 1799 in perfecting myself in the details of my profession, and to tell the truth I must add those of the pleasures of the capital, which was beginning to have many attractions for a young man of my age and position. But they never for a moment withheld me from my duties."

v

Bonaparte's choice of Dijon as a rendezvous for his Army of the Reserve was the result of long calculation. There were in the field already, Massena's fragment of the old Army of Italy, now hard-pressed in Piedmont, and Moreau's much larger Army of the Rhine lying between Strasbourg and Constance. He could not himself as First Consul assume command of the Army of the Reserve. He appointed Berthier to the post, intending to direct the whole French force available, using Berthier as his Chief of

Staff. The Austrian army which he hoped to take by surprise far outnumbered him, but its commander Baron Mélas, although experienced, was no longer young. Bonaparte hoped to get the Army of the Reserve over the Great and Little St. Bernard passes to take Mélas in the rear, while Moreau advanced to join him by the Gotthard, and Massena held down opposition in Piedmont.

Most of the famous illustrations depicting Bonaparte crossing the Alps in May 1800 were in detail incorrect, but they left an indelible impression of a still young hawk-faced general urging on heroic troops in impossible weather. Bonaparte did not ride over the frozen precipices on a spirited horse. He sat on a sure-footed mule, like a sensible man, led by a strong young peasant who afterwards received a tip sufficient to set him up in a little farm of his own. The grenadiers of the Guard did not volunteer impromptu to harness themselves to the guns and drag the artillery up to the hospice of St. Bernard. Mules and sledges had been ordered to Dijon as long ago as March. Still, the general picture left on the public mind of the forcing of the St. Bernard was essentially founded on fact. The snow was deep; icicles as long as a man hung from the eaves of rude wooden dwellings. The blessed crosses on the roof of the *hospice* stood out black against the white world. The enormous dogs kept by the monks for such rescues brought in several frozen French soldiers.

The passage began on May 15 and took five days. Bonaparte who had posted from Geneva by Martigny stayed for three of the days in the *hospice*. A large store of provisions for his army had been collected there. Each soldier received from the monks as he marched past, a generous slice of bread and cheese and a tumbler of wine. The community was handsomely rewarded. An attempt to bestow a bonus on the gunners who had brought up fifty pieces of cannon with caissons was according to the popular press refused. They had merely done their duty. But this had included cutting down fir trees to act as sledges and hollowing out the trunks to receive the guns. The mules had carried only ammunition and baggage. The Army of the Reserve was up! It was over! It went down into Italy sliding and singing. It marched into the ancient mountain city of Aosta heads up, as implacable as a Roman Legion. Bonaparte in all his bulletins had compared his crossing of the St. Bernard with that of Hannibal. All the country hereabouts spoke of Rome. Aosta was encircled by a Roman wall, and had a Pretorian gate and a Triumphal entry named after Augustus and a huge fragment, seventy feet high, of a Roman theatre, through the arches of which could be seen the snow-capped Alps. There were Roman columns even in the cloisters of St. Ours, which was a by-way in the centre of the town. Bonaparte and his staff lodged in the Bishop's palace in the dark cathedral square, which was to record the fact on a solemn plaque. His troops who felt themselves already heroes, though they had yet to see a white Austrian uniform, swaggered a little, fed well and slept heavily before taking the road again. The hardy people of the old town who had strange accents and the high speech and direct gaze of a mountain race, watched them go silently. Eugène decided not to attempt a description of the celebrated passage of the St. Bernard. "But it did make me realize how much can be accomplished by a leader who has perseverance and knows his own mind."

His mind's eye was filled by unforgettable pictures of awful mountain tops which seemed almost to incline above the little hamlets beneath them, of early mist moving off the heights, grim moraines and gushing pale blue and green rivers, and glaciers as bright as jewels. And now it was May in the valleys and suddenly hot, with nightingales singing in broad daylight, and grasshoppers chirping in meadows thick with wild flowers. In France it was now Prairial, the meadow month.

He came up with his stepfather for the first time when he was jingling with his *chasseurs* down the incredibly romantic Val d'Aosta. This valley was as rich in antique castles as the Rhine. There seemed to be one on every craggy hill-top. Not all were ruined, unfortunately. Bonaparte mounted a strategic knoll to look through his glasses at another—inhabited. The Army of the Reserve had to leave some valuable heavy guns to deal with the fortress of Bard in which Mélas had left a garrison of four hundred. It looked like a castle in a child's fairy-tale by Perrault, but it commanded the valley south of Aosta. The cavalry and infantry had to file off to the north over Monte Albaredo by rude lateral paths hardly accessible to goats. There was a foaming river below dashing over glistening black rocks, the Dora Baltea, the colour of *café au lait*. Engineers began to cut a new stretch of road, but luckily the fort could not fire directly downwards, and a number of the artillery got through the steep little town below the fort in darkness. Marmont had wrapped straw round his horse's hooves and the wheels of his guns.

Ivrea, which Bonaparte had given as his headquarters after

Aosta, was another old Roman town. He wrote home: "At last, here we are in the heart of Italy. In the next ten days a great many things will have been settled. All goes well and I shall be in Paris before the end of Prairial."

It was at a little place called Buffalore that the *chasseurs* of the Guard came into action for the first time. They received in earnest the order, *"Escadrons ... en avant ... marche! Au trot! Au galop! Chargez!"* With cloaks slung diagonally and sabres raised they came on. "General Murat was in command. He was very active at this crossing of the Ticino river by force of arms, and chased the enemy back to Milan which we entered pell mell with his advanced troops. I made a pretty enough charge with my company to force those enemy elements still in the field up into the citadel."

Murat's troops entered Milan with sunset and the Austrian garrison surrendered, as it must. Eugène spent three days up in the old castello overlooking the city. It had been built by the Visconti and rebuilt by the Sforzas and had two castles and several courtyards inside a curtain wall above the Roman Porta Giova. Bonaparte was going to have the fortifications destroyed again and a new and modern stronghold erected. It had always been the focus of the struggle for the possession of Lombardy. He stayed in Milan a week. On his first night he read happily the two-way captured correspondence between Mélas and Vienna. Mélas hardly believed the Army of the Reserve to exist and in any case said it had not yet left Dijon. Strong reinforcements were nevertheless being sent to him. The Army of the Reserve was also gathering strength. Detachments from the Army of the Rhine had got over the Mont Cenis, the Simplon and Gotthard. With a heavy cold in the head Bonaparte attended a performance at La Scala, by the beautiful Grassini.

Lannes had forced the passage of the great and famous river Po a mile below Pavia, where he had found welcome stores of food, equipment and ammunition. The scene was one of bustling activity. Bonaparte had just passed through, in a typical Italian early summer downpour. Eugène unexpectedly ran into an old hero of his Egyptian days. General Desaix had this moment arrived from Cairo. He had jumped at the offer of employment with the Army of the Reserve. He was as good as ever, gentle, courteous, composed. He remembered a very junior officer perfectly, and they had several hours together during which he did not disdain to give his views on the campaign which was just opening, and his hopes for his new command. (He was to be given two infantry divisions.) He seemed quite unchanged, entirely unconcerned as to such trifles as food and dress. Bonaparte had once said of him that he was happiest sleeping under a gun, wrapped in an old cloak. Before they parted he said something which Eugène found strange. "In the old days the Austrian bullets respected me. I'm only so afraid they may have forgotten me!"

But he had no time to ponder. The *chasseurs* had been ordered to cross the Po under cover of darkness and make south for Piacenza by way of Stradella to meet Murat who was collecting material for the passage of troops there. The pontoon had been cut by the retreating garrison of the bridgehead. Bonaparte was going to establish across the plain of Lombardy a complete barrage between Mélas and his old headquarters at Mantua. He had heard, again from captured despatches, that Genoa had fallen and that Mélas had reached Turin. The heavy guns of the Reserve Army had at last reduced Bard and had got away from that murderous defile, but Bonaparte would not wait for them to come up. He had told Lannes, "Attack and overthrow whatever is in front of you," and on June 9 Lannes had won the battle of Montebello, from which hitherto obscure but picturesque hamlet he was later to take a ducal title. "The affair of Montebello" as Eugène styled it, had been, he heard, sanguinary, but had taken place a day too soon for him to have been on the spot. On the following night, pushing due west for Alessandria he came into action again himself—a skirmish. Murat's cavalry ran into an enemy column which they obliged to repass the Bormida, one of the two tributaries of the Po flowing parallel to one another through the flat land between Tortona and Alessandria. Canals and lesser streams, bordered by pollarded willows, also separated these fields, blushing brilliant green with rich cereal crops. There were orchards and farmhouses, village churches and vineyards. This was the plain of Marengo, one of the few natural cavalry battlegrounds in northern Italy.

June 13 was very oppressive, with inky skies, rolling thunder and sudden storms. The *chasseurs* had a difficult time getting over the Scrivia, generally a slow-running sluggish stream but now overflowing its banks and turbulent. They bivouacked near Bonaparte's headquarters, the Castello di Garofoli, a long building with a campanile, about eight miles from the village of Marengo. At dawn they were awakened by the sound of gunfire. By seven a.m. the word passed round of a general Austrian attack in force. Bonaparte had sent out repeatedly last night to assure himself that all three bridges over the Bormida were cut, and in his anxiety to find out where the enemy were he had deprived himself of two divisions, which he had sent out to reconnoitre north and south and delay the enemy if possible. It now appeared clear that his information had been faulty and that Mélas was advancing from Alessandria over the Bormida with an army compactly massed and amounting to thirty thousand men with over ninety guns. To oppose them on the open plain, Bonaparte had left about twenty thousand men and fifteen guns. A great battle was about to take place. He sent messengers to recall the missing divisions. "In the name of God come back!"

The first half of the Battle of Marengo, the French defeat, followed inevitably, although the new army fought as gallantly as the veterans of the Rhine and Italy and Egypt. The French disputed every yard of ground and two hours passed before the Austrians reached the Fontanone brook and took the village of Marengo. Eugène could affirm from his own observation that criticisms of the First Consul for having been taken by surprise were unjustifiable. He had himself during the previous night witnessed the constant activity around Bonaparte's bivouac, the coming and going of officers all of whom had assured him that the Austrians were leaving Alessandria and all bridges were cut. The French retirement went on for about four hours from noon. A message had come that Desaix was half-a-day's march on the Novi road to Genoa so he could not be on the scene for five hours. Bonaparte was observed here, there and everywhere, standing at the Marengo crossroads to the last possible moment, flicking his boots with his riding whip and shouting "Courage! the reserves are coming!"

"It was during this interval that the cavalry of the Guard began to take a more active part. The infantry were tired and their morale was low: the First Consul sent us to support them. We moved from the left wing to the right wherever the need was greatest. General Lannes being rather heavily pressed, wanted us to make a charge, but it was not a success. He had, facing him, two battalions of infantry and two guns, behind which was a mass of cavalry in close column. His men were retiring in some disorder, so, in order to have a breathing space in which to rally them, he ordered Colonel Bessières, our commanding officer, to charge the enemy column. The ground did not favour us, for we had to pass through some vineyards; however we managed this, and arrived within range of the two battalions who held their fire while waiting for us and seemed at their ease. Colonel Bessières having formed us up, went forward to lead our charge when he noticed that the enemy cavalry was deploying on our left wing and was going to outflank us. He ordered us at once to make a half turn to the left and we had to negotiate the vineyards again under fire of grape and ball. However, when we had done this we were able to take on the enemy cavalry. General Lannes was very much displeased about this operation and complained furiously. But it is likely that if we had carried out his orders few of us would have lived to tell the tale. During the retreat my *chasseurs* were told to destroy armaments which we were being obliged to abandon and they did this with great intrepidity, sometimes waiting until the enemy was actually upon them before blowing up the ammunition wagons, and then jumping on their own horses."

Desaix appeared on the scene none too soon but much sooner than it had been possible to hope. He had heard the thunder of guns and turned about on his own initiative. Bonaparte held a hasty conference with him and Marmont, and asked Desaix what he saw. "The battle is completely lost," said Desaix with his habitual calm, "but it is still only five o'clock. There is yet time to win the second battle."

The first stage of the battle of Marengo had been long drawn-out; the second was swift. When it became clear that the reserve division had indeed come, all arms combined full of fresh courage for a counter-attack. The new army had not wished to lose its first battle, the veterans were accustomed to regarding themselves as invincible. Desaix led at once against the Austrian main column. His fresh troops drove back the enemy upon their supports, and at this moment the dashing cavalry commander Kellermann (a contentious little man of an old Saxon army family) sallied out of the French line with four hundred sabres to make one of the most spectacular charges in military history. Mélas, deeming the day won, had gone home to Alessandria, leaving his second-in-command to do the tidying up. The unfortunate General Zach was captured together with his staff. Marmont had brought up two guns to assist the infantry, and as he fired his last round of case-shot the heavy cavalry of the Consular guard raced past him to the front, wheeled inward against the flank of the great Austrian column, and rode through it. Kellermann next threw himself upon the Austrian infantry. Towards evening the light cavalry of the Consular guard were called upon, and they performed in the opinion of Captain Beauharnais a charge, not less brilliant. The *terrain* was unfavourable, two enormous sticky ditches ahead, but the *chasseurs* got over in time to prevent a much more numerous squadron of enemy cavalry from deploying, and chased them to the first bridge over the Bormida. The *melée* lasted ten minutes, and he thought himself lucky to get away with no more than two sabre cuts on his chabraque (the handsome lambskin rug worn over the saddlecloth of a hussar). But the *chasseurs* had lost many horses. Of the hundred and fifteen which they had possessed in the morning, there were now only forty-five. A *piquet* of fifteen had always been in attendance on the First Consul, and several men only slightly wounded, but whose horses had been killed, had remounted.

On the morning after the battle an armistice was concluded with the shattered Austrian commander by which he evacuated all Italy up to the Mincio. The first Consul promoted Captain Beauharnais *chef d'escadron*. But in the midst of their triumph the whole army was in mourning. Nobody had seen Desaix fall but he had been hit leading the first charge. His aide de camp, Savary found him amongst a pile of corpses, all stripped naked. He recognized a very dark old-fashioned *queue* and turned the body over. Yes, it was Desaix, shot through the heart. He covered it with a soldier's cloak and had it removed to headquarters. Bonaparte was grief-stricken. He said at once that he had counted on Desaix as one of the great commanders of the future. He ranked him as equal to Kléber. Later he said, "I intended him for Hortense."[8]

CHAPTER SIX

Consulate

1800 : 1809

I

"YOUR SON" wrote Bonaparte to Josephine, "is advancing by giant strides towards immortality. He has covered himself with glory in every action. I look upon him as likely to become one of the first commanders of Europe."

In Milan there was now no doubt of the feelings of the inhabitants. Beautiful ladies cast down little baskets of flowers on to Bonaparte's carriage as he returned from Marengo. Only seven *chasseurs* of the Guard attended him. All the rest had fallen by the way after their late exertions. The distance which they had covered without a halt in sun and dust, at the trot, had been more than thirty miles.

The First Consul left Milan on June 28 but the *chasseurs* had gone on six days earlier. They had to be in Paris for July 14, the great Revolutionary anniversary. Eugène took his men over the Little St. Bernard to Geneva where they could best get their horses re-shod and their equipment mended. Their arrival caused a sensation in Switzerland and they were given a banquet at which "the celebrated Madame de Staël did the honours." Her notions of the duties of a hostess were rather embarrassing. Every officer and man found a laurel wreath round his table-napkin and inside it a copy of verses from the pen of the famous authoress. She adored Bonaparte but her passion was not reciprocated.

From Lyons Eugène wrote home in high spirits, prophesying that the Austrians were going to have to make very liberal terms. He was proud to say that his stepfather had observed and applauded his capture of an Austrian officer. "Adieu, my dear good *maman*! Eight days hence I shall clap spurs to my dapple-grey and hasten to throw myself at your feet."

At Nogent sur Seine the *chasseurs* arrived just in time for a christening. They were carried along with the procession to the Mairie, and the stepson of the First Consul, universally adopted as chief godparent, improvised gallantly and gave the infant the names of Alexandre Marengo.

The *chasseurs* had been assigned the honour of bringing the captured flags into Paris. They arrived at ten o'clock on the morning of July 14 and went first to the Tuileries. After this they were ordered on to the Invalides. They rode beside the carriage of the First Consul. The flags were deposited and there was a fully choral service: Grassini had come from Milan to perform. Then there was a Grande Fête on the Champ de Mars. The troops which had been garrisoning Paris looked wonderfully impressive and smart, but the loudest yells of the crowd came when the army which had won Marengo marched on the scene. They presented a startling contrast, lean, bronzed, weary, their uniforms stained with the dust of gunpowder. The crowd was the largest Eugène had ever beheld on this site, much larger than that when the fishwives of ten years ago had tried to put his poor old tutor in the shafts of a cart, and he had beaten them with an umbrella. He had been only nine then, and now he was nineteen and a major of the *chasseurs* of the Consular Guard and his command was going to be doubled in numbers. His figure was greeted with particularly loud cries of recognition, but he thought perhaps this was because he was the stepson, and again it might have been because an unfortunate rumour had reached Paris that the young Beauharnais had fallen gallantly on the field of Marengo as full of holes as a sieve.

Later there was a banquet at which the First Consul gave the toast, "The fourteenth of July and the People of France". The day was going to be known henceforth as the Festival of Peace. After dark, fireworks climbed into the night sky and crackled above the big open space on which the guillotine had stood. It was now beautifully renamed Place de la Concorde.

Eugène was happy.

"This was one of the most beautiful moments of my life. These generous testimonies of public recognition and remembrance seemed to me the sweetest and most beautiful reward for our hardships. They inspired in me a strong and noble feeling. Our army had, in less than two months, accomplished great things and saved *la Patrie*."[1]

II

As the weather was now very hot they went out to Malmaison nearly every Saturday. There was a legend that Josephine had first seen the little château on her first honeymoon. She had certainly visited it from her holiday riverside villa at Croissy. It was just opposite, across the Seine, and when she had come to drive her bargain she had enlisted the Mayor of Croissy, and of course her invaluable man of business the tiny little M. Raguideau. She had shown the place to Bonaparte before he had left for Egypt and he had considered buying it. The situation was good. The traveller left Paris as if for Marly or St. Germain by the Porte de Neuilly, and proceeded for eight miles west, through suburban country, very highly cultivated with many little orchards, vineyards and gardens. The name of Malmaison was really the only ugly thing about it, and even that had a euphonious sound. (Joseph Bonaparte had bought himself a much larger estate with a gloomier name—Mortefontaine.) Why Malmaison had been so called no one knew. There was a story that there had been a leprosaria on the site, perhaps in the very early days when it was a fief of the abbey of St. Denis. And then again perhaps it had been a brigand's haunt, or just very damp. A little stream, which could be groomed to a charming serpentine water and lake, ran through the green meadows that in spring were filled with innumerable cowslips. The soil was favourable for horticulture and aboriculture. There were some well grown fashionable trees —weeping willows, Lombardy poplars. A cedar of Lebanon was planted and called after Marengo. Josephine, but nobody else, called her house *La Malmaison*. In the course of time everyone came to forget that the words meant literally bad house and connected them only with a lovely carnation and a lovely woman.

The present house had been built early in the seventeenth century. It was a milk-white farmhouse with tall casement windows, and high-pitched grey slate roofs. There was a court-yard of entrance called the *Cour d'Honneur*, but that was as yet the most imposing thing about Malmaison. Nevertheless, with skilful additions and redecoration, it became in the opinion of every visitor a charming country château backed by a good square patch of woods, in which there were romantic rides. (When it became the property of Eugène, Hortense had a handsome "E" erected over the entrance.) It had known many owners, most of whom had moved in court circles. A steward of the Orleans family had bought it from a nobleman called de la Jonchère, War Treasurer. Shortly before the Revolution it had passed into the hands of the well-known financiers Lecoulteux du Moley. They, of course, had been ruined. Josephine had bought it with nineteen farms and a quantity of dilapidated furniture. It amused Bonaparte to calculate whether he could make the estate a paying proposition. He began by employing the well-known architects Percier and Fontaine. The entrance hall had excellent proportions and with the additions of a verandah and marble pillars, and with windows cut down to the ground, would serve for quite large receptions. Engaged piers had to be built to support the façades. The piers were topped by statues from the palace of Marly, and vases. Classical statues glimmered also in the park. A torrent of striped materials in shades supposedly beloved of the Greeks, Romans and Egyptians descended on the unsophisticated house. Bonaparte's council chamber had to be completed in ten days, "in the military style". It was a tent. Spears supported the draperies. The only portraits were of Henri IV and Frederick the Great. Malmaison was rich in pictures of merit, but Josephine had a continual tussle with Denon who wanted these for the Louvre.

New wings were added east and west of the Cour d'Honneur. On either side of the entrance were a bronze centaur and an Egyptian pyramid of red marble with gold hieroglyphics. The enlarged vestibule and the adjoining dining room were paved with black and white marble and had frescoed walls, and a ceiling enlivened by likenesses of Minerva, Homer, Virgil, Voltaire and Dante. There was a library with good mahogany furniture, and this gave on to a tent-like exit to a small private garden enclosed by trellisses and high hedges, used by Bonaparte for thoughtful pacings. To the left of the vestibule came a billiard room, ante-chamber, saloon and music room painted with arabesques. Upstairs Josephine's bedroom was a tent again, but luxurious. It had amaranth coloured kerseymere hangings and cashmere-covered furniture to correspond. The ceiling, too, was amaranth with golden stars, and had a Pompeian frieze. Her favourite cognizance of the swan appeared already in several places and was to do so more abundantly. There were black swans from New Holland and other curious aquatic birds on the rivulet and lake in the park. Amongst the unusual inhabitants of Malmaison were Euphemia, Eugène's old mulatto nurse safely back from Martinique, and two enormous Newfoundland dogs, suggested by Charvet, the concièrge, as a security measure. One of them once caught Constant by the throat when the valet ventured to set foot outside in the dark. The meadows nearest to the house were styled the park, and diversified by a ha-ha, to keep picturesque cattle at a respectful distance. A boundary wall ran all round the park, and it puzzled Bonaparte's private secretary that not only Madame Bonaparte but her young daughter liked to walk outside the wall, deafened by the noise and choked with the dust of the Marly or Nanterre high roads. Apparently they liked to see family parties bustling out of Paris with a clatter and glad cries, especially at week-ends, rather than wander through peaceful glades and charming shrubberies designed by Fontaine and Percier in the English style.

Both these artists had studied in Rome, and Fontaine had sheltered in London during the Revolution. They had also collaborated as authors, and for the next decade they never ceased to find employment at Malmaison. At the command of Josephine they added to its attractions a music room, chapel and *grande galerie*, a bathing room (hung with white cotton in the shape of a tent), a grotto, Temple d'Amour, pavilion, ruined mediaeval chapel (from Milan), several ornamental bridges, a pheasantry, a Zoo, a botanical garden (with a renowned hot house containing a perpetual fountain), more stables and an Orangery. Van loads of beautiful furniture arrived at intervals, and reception rooms were decorated with presentation plate and ceramics, trophies of victory in the field, and civic welcomes. The bedrooms were transformed by Beauvais and Savonnerie carpets, Gobelin tapestries, curtains of taffetas and muslin, and giltwood and inlaid furniture. On the walls hung watercolours of flowers, painted on vellum by Pierre Joseph Redouté.

The happy years at Malmaison were from 1800–1804, and of these the first two years were the best. There was still simplicity and gaiety, and the house was essentially a home in which an over-busy man could relax. A troupe of his family and staff amused him and themselves riding in the park and surrounding country, giving little concerts and performing very creditably in amateur theatricals. Josephine's talent for music had been inherited by both her children; Eugène's voice was a pleasant baritone. Curiously enough, on the parade ground it was considered one of the most resonant. Hortense, a shy girl, displayed unexpected talent as an actress. They had first-class instructors. Talma himself came from the Comédie Française to rehearse them, sometimes together, sometimes separately.

France's first actor, who became a familiar stock figure in the life of Bonaparte's stepson, was admirably suited by nature to his profession. The word Talma meant fearless in Arabic, and he encouraged a story that his family had come to Holland from Spain and had been Moors. His father had been a fashionable dentist in London, and the young Talma had himself practised dentistry for eighteen months. He had been an ardent revolutionary. But in conjunction with his bosom friend the artist David, he had won fame by his advocacy of realism in stage costume and scenery. It was said that when first Talma had stalked upon the stage with one hand stuck in his draperies and the other holding a scroll, he had brought Rome into the home. He used to study the attitudes of classical figures and copy them. He had a good figure, which was to thicken, a dark complexion for the descendant of a peasant family of northern France, mobile regular features, and a small pursed mouth. He also continually dropped in for a chat or a loan at the Tuileries. Two leading actresses, the queens of tragedy and comedy, came to Malmaison and dined with the family. Innocent Hortense found Mesdemoiselles Raucourt and Contat distinguished artistes with excellent manners. The best performers at Malmaison were Isabey the artist (a remarkable voice), Colonel Lauriston (safe but rather heavy), Jerome Bonaparte, the sailor brother, and his sister Caroline (both middling but lively), Eugène and Hortense (both very good, Eugène particularly in elderly character parts), two nieces of Madame Campan, and Didelot (who was to become French Ambassador to Copenhagen). Such was the verdict of Secretary Bourrienne, who thought himself not at all bad. The pieces which the First Consul liked best were *Le Barbier de Seville*, *Défiance et Malice*, *Projets de Marriage*, *La Gageure dépit Amoureux*, and *L'Impromptu de Campagne*. In *Le Barbier* Didelot was *Figaro*, Hortense *Rosina*, Eugène *Basil*, Lauriston *Almaviva*. When *Figaro*, *Basil* and *Almaviva* had to attend a conference or join their regiments, Isabey and Bourrienne stepped in. In *La Gageure Imprévue* Hortense made a charming old lady as Madame Leblanc, and Eugène was astonishingly convincing as Monsieur Lenoir.

The First Consul also enjoyed playing outdoor games, and in

Malmaison
after a contemporary engraving

these he did take part. Prisoner's base was his favourite. A new face appeared in this—Rapp, aide de camp to the lamented Desaix and to Bonaparte. He was large, solemn and Alsatian. Isabey, Hortense and Eugène were the fleetest of foot. Bonaparte fell down often but arose laughing like a boy.

Some graver figures came from Paris for the day. M. de Talleyrand generally limped in for dinner and sometimes stayed until two or three a.m. Josephine liked entertaining *savants*, artists, authors, philosophers. Monge and Denon, de Volney and Lemercier came often. A swarm of younger men, mostly mothers' darlings, hovered around Hortense. She rode with the Prince de Poix and the Comte de Mun. Companions for a ride were also always to be had in Generals Murat, Lannes and Berthier, Duroc, Rapp, Savary, Lauriston, Lebrun, Lacuse. These were happy days.[2]

III

At six p.m. on the evening of October 10, when he entered his mother's apartments in the Tuileries, Eugène detected an air of tension. He had already dined with Bessières. They had been told nothing except to be there at six. They were a little surprised to find every aide de camp on his staff already with the First Consul. Josephine had gone to get her shawl. Bonaparte broke the silence by announcing with a short laugh *"Eh bien!* haven't you heard they are going to assassinate me at the Opera?"

It was an almost incredible tale. A dismissed officer called Harrel had gone to the First Consul's secretary some weeks ago to say that he knew about a plot to murder Bonaparte. Bourrienne wanted to send the affair on to Fouché of the police but Bonaparte had said no, we could manage this ourselves. It grew odder and odder. First of all Bourrienne had to supply some money to foster the plot, then for the conspirators to buy their weapons. Then it turned out they had to have a permit to show to a gunsmith; so Fouché had to know. Bonaparte said he had consulted his fellow consuls and they had agreed with him that they would never catch the men if he deviated from his usual routine. So he had better keep his engagement and go to the Opera as usual. Eugène was horrified, but Bonaparte was not to be moved. He would only tell Bessières to do his best as to anything he judged necessary as an extra precaution. Accordingly, Bessières told Eugène to take a piquet of *chasseurs* and go to the Opera house. He was just about to do so when Hortense entered. Her brother gave her in an undertone a hasty sketch of what was afoot. "Eugène begged me not to say a word to anyone, especially not to our mother whose fears would interfere with the Consul's plans. Imagine my alarm when up to the moment we entered the Opera house I saw everything as quiet as usual."

Eugène's timing had been just right. Having placed most of his men at strategic points, he led the rest up, double file, to the box, at exactly the right moment, halted them and turned them face to face. Less than a moment later the First Consul passed between their ranks, perfectly calmly, and into his box. His party followed. He was wearing his unmistakable grey greatcoat and dark green uniform, and was followed by Bessières and Bourrienne. He walked to the front of the box and acknowledged the applause of the audience. There was also noise from the entrance hall. Bourrienne was sent down to find out the cause and soon returned to murmur that all was well. All the conspirators had been picked up. They were Jacobins armed with daggers and pistols and all declared their murderous intention. Two of them were quite well known men, Ceracchi, the sculptor from Naples, and Arena, also a Corsican an ex-deputy, who had been violent in the Orangery on the day of Brumaire. They were all found guilty and executed.[3]

Junot had married. Bonaparte had ordered him to do this, now that he was Governor of Paris. Junot told his bride that the first thing she must do was to pay her visit of ceremony at the Tuileries. He would arrange all. She was doubtful of this. Junot's parents were of humble origin, and although Junot had great good looks and address the etiquette of the Faubourg St. Germain was to him a closed book. His bride came of a very old imperial Greek family. Bonaparte liked his generals to marry decorative young women of birth provided they did not give themselves airs. Laure Permon arrived at the Tuileries feeling quite ill with nervousness. Junot had to leave her at the bottom of the great staircase of the Pavillon de Flore. It was a very large staircase and she was rather small. She was just sixteen and pretty, in a wax-doll style which deceptively masked a very sharp eye and tongue. It was past ten o'clock. Junot said he had arranged she was to pay her call after they had been to the Opera. She had insisted on their leaving in the middle, but even so the hour seemed astonishing. Outside the entrance to the Pavillon they met Duroc and Rapp. "How late you are!" exclaimed Duroc. Laure would have liked to turn back but Junot stuck to it that Madame Bonaparte had said "after the Opera".

A pair of folding doors clicked upstairs and a young man in a dark green uniform came running down the great staircase, quite at home. He said his mother had heard a carriage arrive and that as nobody had come up she feared that Madame Junot might by mistake have been denied admittance. "I was very sensible of this attention, and the more so as the messenger himself was very fit to dispel apprehensions of a doubtful reception. Monsieur de Beauharnais gave me his arm and we entered the salon together. This fine apartment was so dimly lighted that at first I thought it was empty. There were just two branch candlesticks placed on a mantelpiece with gauze to soften the glare. Eugène de Beauharnais contributed wonderfully to restoring my composure. 'You have nothing to fear!' he assured me gently. 'My mother and sister are so kind.' "

In the same moment Laure detected a regular family group having a quiet evening at home—Madame Bonaparte, superb with a tapestry frame in front of her, Mademoiselle de Beauharnais, a mild agreeable girl with a nymph-like figure and a profusion of beautiful light hair, and last and most alarming, the First Consul himself standing in front of the fire with his hands behind him, his piercing eyes fixed upon the incoming guest.

The call went off wonderfully well.[4]

A few days later Eugène left Paris with his regiment for the mountains of Savoy. Austria had not accepted any peace-terms yet. She was bound to England. The armistice had expired and Bonaparte was going to cross the Alps again himself. He said he regretted he had not insisted on the acceptance of the old Campo Formio terms on the day after Marengo. Eugène's station for the winter was St. Jean de Maurienne. This was a very small antique place, notable only from its situation on the road from France over the Mont Cenis into Italy. He spent Christmas there, and still negotiations were going on, and Bonaparte had not yet left Paris.

In the last days of 1800 he heard of another and much more alarming attempt on the life of his stepfather. It had been frustrated because Josephine had been late starting for the Opera, (a new shawl had just arrived from Constantinople), and because the

First Consul's coachman had been so drunk he had taken a wrong turning. The Infernal Machine, ingeniously placed in a water cart on the route, had gone off just after his carriage should have passed and just before the arrival of the one which had contained Josephine, Hortense, and Caroline Murat. Josephine had fainted. Caroline had displayed great courage, although she was seven months advanced in pregnancy. Hortense had been slightly cut by glass from their carriage window. But eight innocent people had been killed, and twenty-eight men, women and children injured in the street. Gradually it became known that the plot this time had been a Royalist one—conspirators from La Vendée. The First Consul and Madame Bonaparte had shown themselves in their box at the Opera House and had received a tumultuous welcome; his popularity seemed to have been enhanced and secured. Eugène was ordered back to Paris.[5] On December 3 General Moreau's army had won a decisive victory at Hohenlinden against that of the Archduke Charles. Joseph Bonaparte had gone off to arrange a separate peace with Austria at Lunéville.

In July 1801 the First Consul made peace with the Pope, and France returned officially to the Roman Catholic belief. An impressive service was held at Notre Dame on the following Easter Sunday. In October 1801 came peace with England, Spain and Holland. Its official name when the treaty was signed was the Peace of Amiens. But old King George III himself said, "I call it the Experimental Peace."

IV

In his Memoirs Eugène explained, "I shall pass rapidly over the years from 1801 to 1804 because during them nothing very interesting happened to me personally. I was promoted Colonel in 1802. I worked hard to increase my knowledge of military science, by attending lectures, and holding conversations with experienced officers. I gave myself up to studying the details of my profession."

One of the reasons why it had been possible to give him command of a regiment was painful. General Kléber had been murdered by a fanatic in Cairo on the same day that Desaix had fallen at Marengo. With Kléber went Bonaparte's last real hopes of his Egyptian colony. General Menou, the successor, had been thoroughly beaten by an English expeditionary force at the Battle of Alexandria. He had capitulated and agreed to evacuate. In the summer of 1802 the last of the Army of Egypt returned to France. The *Guides* from Egypt were now incorporated in the Consular Guard. The horse *chasseurs* were reinforced by a hundred and twenty *chasseurs* and hussars from the Line and the mounted *Guides* from Egypt. Colonel Rapp was put in charge of another detachment from Egypt—the squadron of Mamelukes of the First Consul. They numbered a hundred and twenty and were a picturesque addition to every state occasion. Their presence also gave the impression that the Egyptian adventure had not perhaps been after all such a *gaffe*.

Colonel Beauharnais now had a little house of his own, where he could give the bachelor parties to his brother officers which were his favourite form of entertainment. His stepfather had given him, in April 1801, a little hunting lodge at Bougival. It was part of the old Malmaison estate and called the Pavillon de la Jonchère after the seventeenth-century Treasurer for War who had built it. Bonaparte had bought it but left repairs to the new owner. It was charmingly situated on a hill, with a fine view and had a little park of its own, in the English style, ten acres in extent. It was on the left bank of the Seine, south of Malmaison and exactly opposite Croissy which was so well known to him from his school holidays. (Later in the nineteenth century it was to become the haunt of many painters.) A place was still always laid for him at the First Consul's table in the Tuileries when the family were in residence there "but I availed myself of this favour with discretion. Nevertheless I went every day to receive my orders and salute my mother."[6]

Josephine still believed or pretended to believe that she might bring Bonaparte an heir. "After all," she told a party of ladies including her eldest sister in law, "I know I can have children. See! I have had Eugène, Hortense." "You were younger then, sister," suggested Elisa. I· was cruelly said and the poor painted ageing woman burst into tears. Bonaparte looked at his sister furiously. "I only spoke the truth," muttered Elisa. "It is not always good to speak the truth," her brother told her.

Josephine went off to take the waters at Plombières again in July 1801. She took Hortense with her and Émilie Lavalette joined them. The story of poor Émilie was still rather sad. On the return of Bonaparte and Lavalette from Egypt she had plucked up courage to tell Bonaparte that she had always loved his brother Louis and could hardly face returning to her husband. Bonaparte had gone to Louis and asked him, if Émilie got a divorce, whether he would still like to marry her. But the reply of Louis had been humiliating. "She is a kind good woman, but even if she were free I would not want to marry her now. She is too much changed since she had smallpox.⁷ Josephine had repeated this to Émilie who had returned to Lavalette, found he was a perfect treasure and started a family.

During the past year Eugène had been able to see a good deal of all the Bonapartes at close quarters. They did not grow upon him. Joseph's wife after six years of sterile marriage had taken a course of Plombières waters and produced two little girls. They had a splendid estate on the other side of Paris from Malmaison. Madame Joseph Bonaparte was always kind, but not really an interesting woman; her only topics were her family and her domestic arrangements. Joseph himself had never forgiven Josephine for marrying Bonaparte, and extended his coldness to her children. Lucien had got into trouble again and had been banished to Madrid on a special embassy. He had been occupying the post of Minister of the Interior and had published, anonymously (with Joseph's co-operation) a pamphlet entitled *A parallel between Caesar, Cromwell and Bonaparte*. Some of the ideas he suggested were already in the mind of Bonaparte, but the time to test public opinion on the subject of a return to monarchy was not yet here. With Lucien to Madrid had gone Elisa Baciocchi and her husband. Poor Lucien's unsuitable consumptive wife, of whom they had all become quite fond, had died in childbed. He also had two daughters, no son. He had made an offer for the hand of Hortense which Josephine had repulsed with hauteur. In the opinion of Laure Junot, Lucien had limbs like those of a field-spider. He was the tallest of the Bonapartes and had a remarkably small head, but you could see from his features that he was one of the brothers. He was very short-sighted and went about stooping and smiling with his eyes half closed. Curiously enough, he had considerable success with women. He was probably the cleverest of the brothers, and his courage had been evinced on the day of Brumaire, but he really lacked common sense. He had done very well for himself in his important office and had a fine château near Senlis. He got into trouble again in Madrid quite soon. He wrote to Paris that, in conjunction with

Prince Godoy, the Spanish chief minister, he had successfully concluded a treaty of peace with Portugal. Bonaparte had been just about to partition Portugal with Spain, and Spanish troops had actually crossed the border; but Godoy had been heavily bribed from Lisbon. In view of peace with Portugal, Lucien hastened to add, it would be now a valuable move if his brother would divorce Josephine and marry an available Infanta who was young enough to bear him an heir. When he was reproved, he threw up his appointment and returned home. His proceedings during the next two years completed the breach between him and Bonaparte and he faded from the life of Eugène. He refused to make an alliance with the widow of the King of Etruria, and secretly married his mistress, Madame Jouberthon who had already brought him the first son of a fine family of ten. He was ordered to leave French territory and settled in Rome, always supported by his mother. In 1807 he attempted to sail for America but was captured by a British ship and stayed in England till 1814. He returned to his brother's side during the Hundred Days, after which he returned to Rome again, and took the papal title of Prince of Canino, from an estate which he had bought during his first spell of exile.

Louis, the fourth of the Bonaparte brothers, had never been a friend of any of the Beauharnais family. Although he had been in Paris, invalided from Egypt, while Josephine and Hortense had been always to be found in the little house in the Rue de la Victoire he had hardly ever called upon them. He was three years older than Eugène with whom he had not one taste in common. Louis was in the army, but unwillingly. He had never wanted to take up a profession for which indeed he was most unsuited. He was nine years younger than Bonaparte and was treated by him rather as a son than a little brother. He had shared Bonaparte's years of struggle and poverty and had been tenderly looked after by him. At twenty-three he was perhaps the handsomest of Madame Letizia's remarkable sons but recently he had become such a hypochondriac, and took so many nostrums, that his appearance was not attractive. He had very heavy-lidded eyes, and anything but a military carriage. He loathed discipline of any kind and had his head stuffed, said Bonaparte, with the theories of Jean Jacques Rousseau. In October 1800 he had come to say farewell at Malmaison before setting out on a year's tour of Germany and Northern Europe in search of health.

He had given Hortense an unpleasant surprise by suddenly kissing her passionately.[8] If she had ever thought about him at all it had been as a sort of utterly inferior brother and she had been accustomed to mock at him a little. She hoped he was not trying to tell her that he too had a tender feeling for her. The idea dismayed her. She, or rather her mother and stepfather on her behalf, had refused a good many suitors by now. Duroc, who was her brother's great friend, had offered for her. It could not really be regarded by Bonaparte as presumption, for Bonaparte had himself offered Duroc the hand of Pauline before she married Leclerc. However, Josephine had been withering. She complained that Bonaparte had always promised her that he would make brilliant matches for both her children. "I could never get used to hearing you called Madame Duroc. Are you in love with him? I should be in despair if you were." Hortense, always shy, reassured her mother, and in truth, although she liked Duroc, he was not quite her young girl's dream of a husband. (He went off bitterly and married the plain, disagreeable daughter of a Spanish banker with whom he was unhappy.)

Hortense left for Plombières with her mother, nervously aware that on their return a marriage would be arranged for her. Louis, of course, had not stuck to his programme of a year's tour. After three months he had reappeared in Paris, and taken a country house, where he lived apparently the life of an invalid. Then he had said he must join his regiment in Portugal and accepted to stay for a fortnight's farewell visit at Malmaison. But this time he had left in the middle of one night without explanation.

Jerome, the youngest Bonaparte, was almost a relief after Louis. He was now seventeen and completely uninhibited. He was plump, rosy, with black curly hair, cheerful breezy manners, and no notion at all of the value of money. He was in the Navy, at present stationed at Brest. Eugène had known him best of the family, for Jerome had shared a dormitory with him and one of Madame Tallien's sons at their academy at St. Germain. It must be said for Directeur Barras that whatever his motives he had come regularly to take the three hungry boys out for a fête.

Those St. Germain days now seemed a very long time ago and what proved a final link had been severed last year when Eugène's old grandfather, the Marquis de Beauharnais, had died in the Rue de Lorraine at the age of eighty-six. For *Tante* Renaudin, the Marquise, had remained a disconsolate widow only a few months.

She had re-married in January 1801 *"un simple particulier"* M. Pierre Danès de Montardat. She survived until March 1803 complaining that her niece Josephine, who owed everything to her, was too grand to come to see her any more.

Bonaparte continued to look after the interests of his step-children. He presently bought and presented to Eugène a Beauharnais property in Domingo called Lacul. It had belonged to François, the father of Émilie, Madame Lavalette, who was taking the waters at Plombières with Josephine and Hortense. It soon did not look like being a very remunerative investment, for the blacks had taken command during the Revolution. But Bonaparte was sending an expedition to recover the island, under the command of his sister Pauline's husband, Leclerc. Pauline was in despair at the thought of having to leave Paris, where she reigned as a queen of fashion, but Bonaparte insisted that she must accompany Leclerc. The expedition was very popular generally and few people doubted of its success.

v

The city of Lyons had suffered dreadful things in the Revolution and the noise of hammering and sawing made it rather an undesirable military station in the autumn and winter of 1801–2. Bonaparte was expected early in the New Year. He had summoned the Consulta of Milan to meet there. The Place Belcour completely rebuilt, was now the Place Bonaparte. The Hotel des Celestins was transformed. Good old times had returned to Lyons. Mountains of furnishing silks and rolls of rich carpets were unpacked. A Triumphal Pyramid was erected in the new square. It was decorated with trophies of arms, bearing medallions representing the victories of Arcola and Marengo. Talma arrived, to appear at the Grand Theatre in four classical tragedies.

When Bonaparte himself drove in on January 8 Eugène already knew that Hortense had been married to Louis Bonaparte five days earlier. Josephine had come with her husband to Lyons, so her son might hope to hear more details. These sounded reassuring. The first person to enter Hortense's bedroom on the dark, snowy morning of January 3 had been old Mère Rousseau. The Beauharnais family wet-nurse had hurried to Paris from her village on hearing her darling was to be a bride. During the day Hortense had gone through the usual touching duty of distributing various pieces of her maiden jewellery to the palace servants, who received them with moist eyes and regrets that they would no longer wait on her. Josephine had proposed that the young couple should live near her, in the Tuileries, but the First Consul had made the decision, astonishing for a Frenchman, that it would be better for them to have a house of their own. He had given them the romantic little *nid* in the Rue Chantereine, now Rue de la Victoire, and that was where they had become man and wife. Hortense had been presented with a magnificent set of diamonds by her stepfather, and her mother had ordered a white satin gown garlanded with hot-house flowers; but when the hour had come Hortense had worn only her usual little pearl necklace and a white crepe dress, and had carried a simple bouquet of orange blossom. Another couple had received the blessing of the church at the same time—Caroline and Murat. At the time of their marriage only a civil contract had been possible. They were still madly in love. The civil marriage of Louis and Hortense had taken place at the Tuileries at nine p.m. before the Mayor of the First Arrondissement, and many dignatories, in the state apartments. The bridegroom had seemed annoyed that his brother had insisted that he arrived by the grand staircase while the bride with her stepfather and mother came up the little private stairs from the First Consul's suite. The civil ceremony so largely attended took two hours, and it was past eleven o'clock by the time the family party reached the house in the Rue de la Victoire where a priest was awaiting them. This was Cardinal Caprara from Rome who had come to Paris to arrange the Concordat. He was assisted by the stepbrother of Madame Letizia Bonaparte, the Abbé Joseph Fesch. This inoffensive character who had gone into business (army contracting) during the Terror, but had now gladly returned to his old profession, was being very helpful over the Concordat. He was going to become Archbishop of Lyons and receive a Cardinal's hat. A temporary altar had been fitted up in the drawing room, and in the dining room there was a show of wedding presents. Hortense had gone through the whole day like a marble statue. Her poor mother had shed many tears. The happy couple were now at Malmaison.[9]

It was not possible for her brother to discover much more about Hortense's wedding, for a perfect orgy of balls, concerts and theatrical gala performances occupied the evenings of the First Consul's eighteen days in Lyons, and on the first morning after his arrival he called upon his stepson to attend him at an early hour on horseback, in plain uniform, seeing troops and public buildings. This was the pattern for every morning. The afternoons were mostly given up to meetings. A bewildering troop of Italians had come over the Alps to arrange the transformation of the Cisalpine Republic into the Republic of Italy. Eugène met for the first time a number of politicians with whom he was to become very familiar. Actually four hundred and fifty interested inhabitants of Lombardia and Piedmont had been invited. They were lavishly entertained while Talleyrand, Minister for Foreign Affairs, from Paris, and Marescalchi, his opposite number from Milan, dropped hints as to what the First Consul wished. Count Francesco Melzi d'Eril, most outstanding of three brothers of that family, had certainly expected to be elected President of the new Republic. But it transpired that the First Consul himself would like the post. He accepted office for ten years and told the Consulta with characteristic firmness that he only did so after having searched in vain for someone "who for his services to his country, authority with the people, and freedom from party politics, had earned the appointment." Some of the more democratic deputies were very angry, but they could do nothing. Melzi found himself vice-president with a few honorary functions.

A good many people, including his own family, had expected that Bonaparte would choose to become King of Italy. But he laughed off the suggestion. He still had no obvious heir, though the marriage of Hortense to Louis had greatly improved the position of Josephine. If her daughter were to bring a son to Bonaparte's brother, the Beauharnais were established for ever.

Hortense herself afterwards recorded that Bourrienne had asked for an audience with her, to tell her that both her mother and the First Consul ardently desired to unite her with Louis, who was a most amiable character. Her mother did not wish her to marry a foreign prince and leave France. "Her misfortune as you know is that she can no longer hope for children. You can remedy this and perhaps ward off a still greater misfortune. I can assure you that intrigues are constantly on foot to persuade the Consul to a divorce. Only your marriage can tighten and strengthen these bonds on which depend your mother's happiness. Can you hesitate?" She had hesitated very much, horror-struck.

She had asked for a week in which to consider this proposal. "My brother had just gone to Lyons with his regiment. He had preceded the Consul. I could not have the advantage of his advice, and moreover, I felt it was for me to make my own decision . . ."

At the end of a week, during which she had been very wretched and disturbed, she had given Bourrienne her answer and thereafter had become strangely calm, as if moving in a dream. Josephine, however, had wept continually. "Her glances seemed to say 'You are sacrificing yourself for me.' I realized that in order to console her I must appear well content." Every time the First Consul had asked them to fix the date of the wedding, Josephine dissolved in fresh tears. In the end he had been obliged to put off his departure for Lyons for two days.

"I was glad of my brother's absence. From him I could conceal nothing. I should have pitied myself when I met his eyes."[10] And she knew that if Eugène had wrested from her the secret that she was sacrificing herself for their mother he would not have allowed her to do so, at any rate in a hurry. He had never lacked moral courage. While still in his teens he had sought a dreadful interview with their mother to beg her not to marry Bonaparte. In Egypt he had faced up to his stepfather on the subject of Madame Fourès. But he had not been available to observe his sister, and she had been rushed into a marriage which from the very first was a failure. It was a perfect tragedy that he had just gone to Lyons.

VI

1802 was a splendid year! There was the signing of the Peace of Amiens in March, the Concordat on Easter Sunday; and on April 26 Bonaparte pronounced an amnesty covering nearly every class of *émigré*. Already a large number had returned to France and were in his employ.

Malmaison had for some time been too small for official entertaining. He had St. Cloud put in order as his principal country home. Already Josephine had four ladies in waiting, all with resounding patrician names. Etiquette was now modelled on that of the old *régime*. The Consular liveries were green and gold. Spiteful people said that Bonaparte's household was not quite a court but at any rate it was no longer a camp.

In May he inaugurated an Order which was to become famous. The Legion of Honour was designed to reward not only personnel of the army and navy for services to the state, but also civilians.

What was to prove the last Republican celebration of July 14 was particularly gay. There was a grand parade at the Carrousel, at the close of which Bonaparte was presented with a matchless steed. A reception of the diplomatic corps was followed by a banquet, illuminations and fireworks. On August 2 Bonaparte was elected Consul for life. Henceforward he signed himself by his christian name only, or the initial "N".

In October he engaged a new private secretary, but M. de Méneval was not to be so described. Bourrienne had found the title too valuable. That gentleman's style of living had ceased too glaringly to correspond with the possibilities of his salary. He had also become a little authoritative. He disappeared rather suddenly. M. de Méneval would never so offend. He was an industrious, quiet young man of twenty-four, with round blue eyes and a look of childish innocence; but he had been educated at the Collège Mazarin, served in a Dragoon regiment as a conscript, and trained under Joseph Bonaparte's eye in the Embassy at Rome. After he had been four years in his post some of the palace chamberlains still did not know him by sight.[11]

He thought his employer liked St. Cloud because he could relax there better than at the Tuileries. The palace though not one of the largest was easily made beautiful and comfortable, and the gardens were magnificent. "His workroom was very large and its walls were literally covered with books from floor to ceiling. He had himself designed his writing table. Papers were spread out on its wings. His usual seat was a settee covered with green taffeta, which stood near the mantelpiece on which were fine busts of Scipio and Hannibal . . . Beyond the workroom was a small drawing room in which he used to receive M. de Talleyrand . . ."

On October 10 Eugène arrived at St. Cloud to pay a call on his sister. Hortense had been to a reception at the Tuileries the night before, and her baby was not expected for a month, but during her brother's visit she was seized with such intense pains that he hurried off to fetch their mother. Josephine arrived on the wings of love, and Louis did not leave her bedside for a moment until nine p.m. when the child was born. She heard her nurse and waiting-woman exclaim in triumph, *"Voilà notre Dauphin"!* and in that moment she felt that her sacrifice had not been made in vain, though the dynastic suggestion did not please her and seemed to make Louis furious. He had been particularly touchy and tiresome during her pregnancy, full of his own aches and pains, wanting to go off to take a cure in the Pyrenees and wishing her to accompany him. He frightened her, waking her up in the middle of the night to make her swear that she would follow him everywhere even though he might declare he did not want her. They had moved house twice.[12]

Eugène now had a Paris house of his own, one of the most beautiful palaces in the capital. The First Consul had made him a present of it as long ago as last November when there had been no question of his occupying it. The Hôtel de Villeroy had been built in 1714 by the architect Boffrand for himself, and occupied by a Colbert, the Marquis de Torcey, and then by the Duc de Villeroy. It stood on the left bank of the Seine alongside the palace in the Rue de Bourbon in which the Princess Hohenzollern had been so good to the children of Josephine in the days of the Terror. Its principal entrance was in the Rue de Lille. It was built of greyish-yellow sandstone and had a mansard roof, a massive centre block with a pediment full of classical figures, and on either side heavy flanking wings. From the courtyard it was possible to see light glinting through a long range of big tall windows on the first floor—reception rooms overlooking the river. The stables were ample. There were Lombardy poplars in the entrance court, and on the other side a garden in the English style with some fine exotic trees. Beyond this came a terrace on the quayside. Within, the house had a noble grand staircase and there were glorious views across the river to the Tuileries, over the Place de la Concorde, and the Champs Elysées. But it was clear even to an inexperienced owner that the place needed extensive repairs. Eugène engaged as architect a M. Bataille, and his major-domo, Calmelet, presented bills for 1,800,000 francs. The result was generally acknowledged to be one of the most desirable houses in the capital. The furniture was, of course, modern—that is to say in the classical style after Egyptian or Greek models, of mahogany, marble and bronze.[13]

All he needed now was a wife. He was quite popular with elegant women, though it was thought that his amusing stories sometimes smacked a little of the camp and brought blushes to the cheeks of the prudish. His stepfather, at this stage in his career, sought alliances for his relatives and generals amongst the old aristocratic families of France. Bonaparte made enquiries about a Mlle. de Talleyrand Périgord. The match would have been very agreeable to her uncle M. de Talleyrand, but alas! it appeared that the young lady was engaged, no! had actually married, rather suddenly, Comte Just de Noailles, one of the survivors of a family who had gone to the guillotine almost *en bloc* with great courage. Berthier now had their palace in the Rue St. Honoré. Mademoiselle de Rohan was also unavailable for the First Consul's stepson—a very long-standing promise elsewhere. But there was no hurry. The young man had not formed any glaringly unsuitable connection. The only stage favourite with whom his name had been linked was the Italian *danseuse* Bigottini. She was not only beautiful: she was extremely rapacious.[14]

He perfectly understood that his marriage would be arranged for him. The situation would have been just the same if it had been his father the Vicomte settling the affair, instead of a stepfather who was First Consul. He never had the slightest hope of choosing for himself. Hortense's marriage must be recognized as a failure. But it really need not have been, had Louis been amiable.

VII

One of the most striking results of the Peace of Amiens was that it brought English tourists to France in huge numbers. It was reckoned by the Paris police that during the eighteen months from November 1801, when the Dover and Calais mail packets began to run again, no less than ten thousand British arrived in Paris. They all wanted to see the First Consul, and the Venetian horses looted from the Church of St. Mark's, and many of them desired also to see the Apollo Belvedere and the Venus de Milo in the Louvre. There were two dozen theatres in Paris, offering varied fare, and innumerable public and private ballrooms where English families hoped that they might behold nymphs dressed *à la sauvage* or *à la Grecque* dancing the *valse*. A number of houses belonging to the old aristocracy had been bought by enterprising confectioners and opened as *glaciers* to provide light refreshments. Restaurants abounded. The best for a bottomless purse served marvels of confectionery in the classical style—Grecian ruins, ships at sea, groves of dates and palms—all made of sugar, nougat, and marzipan. Fireworks began at 10 p.m. every evening in Paris during the season, as if some victory was being celebrated. The visitor entering by the Neuilly bridge saw the lights of Bagatelle glancing through green leaves, and the façades of the Idalia and Elysium positively blazing. Parties bound for Frascati and Tivoli clattered past. These places were "a sort of Vauxhall of the first order".

Anyone could find their way to Notre Dame especially after dark. Between its lofty twin towers was an illuminated star, thirty feet in diameter. Paris was a fairyland, incredibly gay, wonderful! There was an outbreak of *grippe* in the bitter New Year of 1802 but the British did not seem to succumb. It was believed that they were habituated to every variety of unpleasant weather. There was a new shade worn in Paris this year, not very kindly named *fumée de Londres*. There were other topical colours more appropriate to France—*Terre d'Egypte, Gris Antique, Mameluke, Point de Jour*. Fashions seemed to English ladies very extreme. Hats were nearly out; cashmere shawls were still in, and still hideously expensive. The most exclusive dressmakers were Leroy, a young man, and Mlle. Despeaux, a woman, no longer young, whom the First Consul was said to have thrown out of his wife's dressing-room, bandboxes and all, for persuading her to overspend.

With 1803 the flood of English became a torrent. A leading statesman arrived—Charles James Fox. With his heavy jowl and drayman's shoulders he seemed to Laure Junot the picture of an English farmer. Two gay young officers rode up when Madame Récamier was having a reception for him after a luncheon party at Clichy—Philippe de Ségur and Eugène de Beauharnais. The First Consul's stepson brought an invitation from his mother, to inspect her greenhouses.

The Duchess of Gordon's arrival was dreaded by the British Embassy. She was an impossible woman. At an official dinner she said to Berthier, Minister of War, who sat on her right, "I always feel frightened when I look at you." To Decrès, who represented the Navy, a service which never seemed to have quite recovered from the Revolution, she added with a loud laugh, "But when I look at you I feel reassured!" She had a daughter, Lady Georgiana, for whom she had bought some fine new Paris outfits. Unfortunately the girl was one of the few English who had been very ill with *grippe*. The duchess had marked down the eligible young men of Paris, and the First Consul's stepson came high on her list. He danced beautifully with Lady Georgiana and the broken English of a handsome young Frenchman who owned one of the finest houses in Paris was considered almost irresistible. Low-class English journals credited the duchess with designs upon the First Consul himself. French society accepted her with good humour as "a burlesque figure". She was not a whit more foolish in her conversation than the wife of their own foreign minister, who had come from nowhere, had many protectors, and had only been married by M. de Talleyrand, just before the Concordat, at the insistence of Bonaparte. (When a bold companion ventured many years later to ask him why he had bestowed his name and a fortune on a character so amazing as Madame Grand, he had replied imperturbably, "The time was a very disturbed one!").

Many of the visiting British kept journals of their Paris stay. There was a Warwickshire squire, Bertie Greatheed who arrived with his wife and beloved artist son late in 1802 and wrote down everything he noticed and heard. On January 5, 1803, he attended Bonaparte's audience and parade. The parade, which came first, took place on the Carrousel, which, with the surrounding buildings, was very fine. Bonaparte rode in at about noon mounted on a grey, in the plainest possible uniform. He halted to receive petitions from about twenty people and conversed with them in an affable manner. "As the General passed Beauharnais, at the head of his Hussars, he nodded familiarly." He reviewed about six thousand troops.

At two p.m. father and son Greatheed, in court dress but without powder, joined Lord Whitworth, British Ambassador, in an audience chamber in the Tuileries, where coffee, chocolate, wines and liqueurs were being handed round with much difficulty. There were so many people. Bonaparte appeared an hour later in the third of three reception rooms and proceeded round a crowded circle. Greatheed took a good look. Bonaparte was more cheerful than he had expected, and less sallow. His celebrated eyes were lighter and smaller. His hair was unpowdered and in disorder. His voice was musical and deep. He leant forward as he spoke, and his person, which was meagre, did not perhaps look its best in the gold embroidered carnation velvet Consular uniform in which artists loved to depict him. He rather won Greatheed's heart by the kind way in which he asked young Bertie if he had been to Paris before, etc. "His apprehension is quick and he frequently repeats your answer. He spoke much of hunting and asked which was the best county for it."

Next month, in horrible weather of frost and snow, Greatheed went to a ball given by Lady Cholmondeley. "Moreau was there and a good many of the old *régime*. If Beauharnais had not been there the room would have had an opposition look. We supped at 3.30 and had bad wine as I knew we should beforehand. It was good taste in the Duchess of Gordon, to be sure, to tell Beauharnais that Pitt and Dundas are the two greatest men that the world contains, and the English the first Nation. He said he did not think so, and that according to the nature of things he considered the English as enemies and must always do so."

The duchess evidently had her claws in fast, for when Greatheed went by appointment with an English party on an April morning to witness another parade, from Madame Bonaparte's apartments, "that foolish woman the Duchess of Gordon came too and we had a great abundance of her nonsense in the worst French and most illiterate Scotch I ever heard. Before we had been long in the room Madame Louis Bonaparte came in with her child and not very civilly turned us out. We then went to Madame de Lucey's apartment close by, where we had an excellent view. Beauharnais stayed some time with us, and Madame Louis again appearing, I supposed we should be again dismissed; but it was only to pay a visit. There was no cavalry, and all the infantry drawn up within the iron railing with their knapsacks ready for marching. Beauharnais told me there were twenty-one battalions . . .

"Madame Bonaparte's name was Pagerie, her family was good, for she used to go to court. She was mistress to Barras who, when tired of her, made her over to Bonaparte, and the Italian army as her portion." Greatheed's first efforts to see her were frustrated. Bad news had come in from Domingo. The expedition had failed and General Leclerc had died of yellow fever. The beautiful Pauline Bonaparte, a widow at twenty-three, had cut off her raven tresses in accordance with Corsican tradition, and strewed them on her husband's bier. The frigate *Swiftsure* had come into Toulon bringing the coffin, the widow and her infant child. She was too ill to accompany the funeral procession to their country home, Mongobert. She was going to live with the Joseph Bonapartes. But it would be most inadvisable to draw public attention to the fact that France had now almost certainly lost her richest colony. Bonaparte continued to hold reviews and give audiences.

When Greatheed did at last succeed in being presented to Madame Bonaparte she made a very favourable impression. "Her person is good and her manners elegant and pleasing. He was more easy than he is at his own audience, and looks far better in his blue and white uniform than in the ugly red consular coat. The whole business was very fine and princely." The English tourist had been to the Invalides. "The colours taken by the French in their wars have a fine effect in the church, which is a beautiful building, but the frost was so sharp that we were forced to hurry through. Bonaparte has given a library, where there is his picture by David, crossing the Alps on a furious horse, in a great wind. It is very like, and has much spirit." He was certainly still handsome. Lady Oxford said he represented her ideal of manly beauty.

Nothing escaped Greatheed—Madame Récamier's bedchamber and bath "in the highest degree of fairy like beauty"; "the spot where the Bastille stood, now a wood-yard"; Vestris, dancing at the Opera, wonderfully, when you considered his age, Talma over-acting laughably with his new leading lady, beautiful statuesque Mademoiselle George, in a very poor thing of Molière's *Le Médecin malgré lui*. He saw the Bibliothèque Nationale, and shops overflowing with old books, and the guillotining of a murderer, and the Panorama from the top of the Pantheon and —almost best of all—General Junot sitting snug with his wife on a cold Saturday afternoon very unaffected and pleasant, though they gave the most select elegant balls and their house was superb. "Modern furniture of the highest price is very beautiful and in admirable taste. Marble is much used, and blended well with wood and bronze . . . In the shops the women beat ours in manners and dress."

He walked all around the outer wall of Paris which took four hours ten minutes. He was even present at the historic Sunday reception when Bonaparte was suddenly so rude to Lord Whitworth that it appeared the Experimental Peace was drawing to an end.[15]

On the morning of May 2, Bonaparte sent for Junot, Governor of Paris, and delivered to him an order. "All Englishmen from the age of eighteen to sixty or holding any commission from His Britannic Majesty, who are at present in France shall immediately be constituted prisoners of war." He said that the measure must be executed by seven that evening. "I am resolved that tonight not an Englishman shall be visible in the obscurest theatre or restaurant in Paris." Most of the British cast into captivity that night stayed prisoners of war in various fortresses for nine years.

The Duchess of Gordon as usual was lucky. Although many tourists could not get a vehicle, or even a seat in one, she got away on May 14. Britain declared war on France forty-eight hours later. Lady Georgiana married the Duke of Bedford at the end of June. He was much older than Eugène de Beauharnais, nearing forty, bald and a widower.

There was no parade to celebrate the Fall of the Bastille in Paris that year. The Consul was absent on a tour of Northern France and Belgium, and his stepson's regiment formed part of his escort. Josephine went too. She shed tears of joy and pride when the inhabitants of Amiens took the horses out of the splendid Consular equipage and insisted on drawing it into their city themselves. She was so happy, with her famous husband sitting by her and her handsome son trotting alongside their carriage, through the dust and sun. The Consul had given her almost *carte blanche* so that she could appear with elegance.

Madame de Rémusat, one of Josephine's aristocratic ladies in waiting, thought that she noticed a distinct lowering of temperature in their welcome when they entered territory beyond the former boundaries of France, particularly at Ghent. At Antwerp the Consul gave orders for extending the harbour in view of his intentions of invading England. Brussels was brilliant. There was a memorable service at St. Gudule. At the theatre, Talma performed.

CHAPTER SEVEN

Paris Days
1804 : 1805

I

WHEN Eugène reached the year 1804 in his memoir he wrote somewhat heavily that he could not pass over in silence three events of which he had been an eyewitness.

The first was the conspiracy of Georges Cadoudal, the Breton peasant leader, and General Pichegru. Cadoudal had inspired the Chouans during the Revolution, so Eugène's opinion of him was inevitably low. He had known the Chouans in his days under the command of Hoche and although he had been very young then, he had not forgotten horrors. Cadoudal had certainly been indirectly concerned in the attempt on the life of the First Consul in 1800. After that he had fled to England. In June 1803 he had returned to France and although the Paris police had been on the look-out for him he had succeeded in eluding them until February 1804. When brought to trial he refused to ask for pardon. He was executed in June.

Pichegru was his senior by ten years, and had served with distinction in the Army of the Rhine during the Revolution. There he had been an enemy of Hoche. His conquest of Holland had been justly applauded. He was a strong disciplinarian. But then he had taken to plotting for the return of the Bourbons, and retired in disgrace. He had been deported to Cayenne, escaped and reappeared in London, and then in Paris, with Cadoudal. Here he had been betrayed by a man whom he said he had trusted. After two months in prison he was found dead in his cell one morning—strangled. He was an incorrigible intriguer, of great physical strength with a dangerous power of captivating upright fellow-soldiers. His removal was obviously so agreeable to the First Consul that many people dismissed the suggestion that he had died by his own hand. He had been liquidated. Nothing could be proved, and he had always been an egoist and highly temperamental. Doctors thought he could have managed it.

That General Jean Victor Moreau, the victor of Hohenlinden, had been plotting with this pair for the assassination of his step-father, Eugène could not bring himself to believe. "I was still very young, and with the candour natural to my years, versed in all the principles of military honour; it seemed to me impossible that a French officer, covered with honours won in the field, could have so degraded himself as to have a hand in a conspiracy, and to associate with people whom I regarded as vile murderers. In every discussion while the trials were pending I stood up for him. I was sure he was being calumniated. I was furious at the idea he could have acted dishonourably." The young colonel was only a little shaken when he had conversed on the subject with "a person much more versed in the secrets of government" who gently begged him not to plead in a bad cause. So he decided to attend some of the sittings of the Tribunal to convince himself of the innocence of Moreau. Alas! within quarter of an hour he was perfectly convinced to the contrary. Moreau on trial for his life had anything but the appearance of a man of courage. He fumbled, he prevaricated. He could not deny that he had been secretly to see Pichegru—and not for the first time either. He had denounced Pichegru for traitorous correspondence with the *émigré* Prince de Condé as long as six years before. It had been hushed up and forgotten. Bonaparte had given him a second chance and he had won Hohenlinden. He now pleaded that he had wished merely to kidnap the Consul and restore the Republic, but never Louis XVIII. He was found guilty, and a sentence of two years' imprisonment was commuted to one of banishment.

Moreau, always in powder, with a *queue*, erect, dapper, one of the old school, impossible to alarm, very courteous, had been every aspiring officer's model. He went to America. Bonaparte was said to have brought pressure to bear to get him convicted, and to have considered the sentence too lenient. During the trials, Josephine, and even her son and daughter, were pestered with applications for mercy by relations and friends of the accused. Most of these were high-ranking old royalists. Her son said that Josephine was glad to be able to assist MM. de Rivière and de Polignac, both aides de camp to the Comte d'Artois. They had been sent over from England to judge of the situation, but according to their own testimony had decided to do nothing, and were arrested when they were just about to leave again. The alteration in Moreau's character was said to have been effected by his marriage to an ambitious wife, a Créole with an even more determined mother. He was arrested at the château of Grosbois where he had been living in style. It was a dozen miles or so outside Paris, and had a long history of royal owners and visitors. Josephine knew it well. She had acted as hostess there for Barras. Bonaparte now presented it to Berthier, in whose family it was to remain.

It was well for Eugène at this season that he was filled with indignation at the thought of attempts on the life of his step-father. The third notable event of early 1804 which he had to relate left him with an abiding sorrow. This was what he called "the unhappy affair of the Duc d'Enghien".

While the trials of Cadoudal, Pichegru and Moreau were still pending, he was on duty with his regiment guarding the barriers of the outer defences of Paris. It was an exacting service. He was on the watch day and night, and was able to thank heaven at the end of it that owing to the vigilance of his men not one conspirator had contrived to escape from Paris. Fifty had been picked up. On the morning of March 21 he arrived at Malmaison to find his mother in tears, bitterly reproaching his stepfather who was receiving her strictures in unusual silence. Eugène learned at the same moment of the arrest, the court-martialling and the execution of the Duc d'Enghien. He had never seen this prince, who was two-and-thirty and had been in exile since he was sixteen. But he knew enough to be aware that the young bachelor duke was the white hope of the house of Bourbon. He bore a very high character and had never taken part in plots. A dreadful malediction seemed to surround the story of his last days. Everything possible went wrong for him.

During their investigations of the Cadoudal-Pichegru-Moreau plot, Paris police had received disturbing accounts of the expected arrival of a French royal prince in France, timed to coincide with the disappearance of Bonaparte. The only person whom the accounts fitted was the Duc d'Enghien who was living in retirement just over the frontier in Baden. He had been paying mysterious visits to Strasbourg. He had been seen over the frontier. One of his visitors had been the renegade General Dumouriez, another a Colonel Smith, from England. (It turned out, too late, that General Dumouriez had been a mistake for General Thumery, and Colonel Smith was a Captain Schmidt.) After calling a council at which Berthier, Caulaincourt, Réal, Cambacérès, Talleyrand and Savary were present, Bonaparte decided to strike first. A party of three hundred mounted gendarmes crossed the Rhine secretly, surrounded the prince's dwelling and hurried him to the fortress of Vincennes on the outskirts of Paris. Next morning at two thirty a.m. he was led into the moat, shot so clumsily by a firing party that his face was rendered unrecognizable, and buried on the spot in a grave which had been ready before he stood trial. Méneval believed a letter sent to Bonaparte asking for an interview had not been delivered in time. He knew that Bonaparte had sent Maret, Secretary of State, expressly from Malmaison to tell Councillor Réal to report to him after interviewing the prisoner. But Réal, after a hard day, had told his valet not to call him before five a.m. and a letter which looked like a routine communication from the Secretary of State's office was put amongst his mail. On reading it he dashed to Vincennes but was met *en route* by Savary who told him the execution had taken place. The prince's nocturnal ramblings had a normal explanation. He had been visiting a lady. He was perfectly innocent.

The effect throughout Europe was terrible. The Czar ordered court mourning and broke off diplomatic relations. In England all the bad old stories were revived of Bonaparte poisoning his plague victims and murdering his prisoners. But the Duke of Baden and the King of Prussia took no action. And, if an example had been needed to show that it was inadvisable to try to remove Bonaparte, the dreadful deed was efficacious. There never was another attempt by a Bourbon prince to plot against him.

He took the blame for what had been done in his name. He could do nothing else. Sometimes he applauded the act as high policy. But to the days of their deaths his counsellors passed the responsibility on from one to the other, like a marked card. Méneval said Talleyrand had managed to destroy all but one document which damned him. Hortense said that Josephine had told her that Talleyrand had been the prime mover, but Murat had also been involved. Talleyrand convinced Louis XVIII that Savary was the man, and got him forbidden the court. Réal, Prefect of Police, Junot, Governor of Paris, Caulaincourt who had been sent to Baden, Ordener who had brought the prince thence, Hullin, President of the court-martial, all got their mead of suspicion and abuse. The last word was softly spoken by Talleyrand. "It was worse than a crime. It was a blunder."

A few days after the tragedy Josephine told her son that she was glad that she had been able to collect a few souvenirs of the unfortunate prince to send to a lady whom he had loved. These had included a last letter, and a little dog, who had performed the traditional canine act of refusing to leave the grave. Eugène did not mention the lady's name but it was well known—"*la belle Charlotte*," Madame de Rohan. Eugène said that, writing twenty years after the tragedy, he well remembered plenty of people now horrified, who at the time had not only spoken of it as a very good thing, but had even highly praised it. "For my own part I was deeply grieved, because of the respect and attachment which I bore to the First Consul. It appeared to me that his glory was tarnished."[1]

II

The third important event of 1804 which Eugène approached with diffidence could not be called horrible. On the morning of May 18 Cambacérès, Second Consul, came to St. Cloud accompanied by many troops. He made a set speech. It had all, of course been planned for weeks, but Méneval and everyone around him received, he said, the sensation as of an electric shock when a flunkey drooped before him and announced, "Sir, the Emperor wishes to see you." "All looked at one another at first with glances of surprise, but then with smiles, as if to say 'It is no dream! We are wide awake.'"

At the reception which followed, Madame de Rémusat thought that Bonaparte took the novelty of being addressed as "Your Majesty" very coolly, and when the Senate proceeded to the apartments of the Empress she replied to the proclamation of her new title with the natural grace which always raised her to the level of any position, however lofty, in which she might find herself.

Duroc, now Grand Marshal of the Palace, appeared before a family dinner party to announce that the titles of Imperial Prince and Princess had been bestowed upon Joseph and Louis Bonaparte and their wives. The day had been very hot and thunder was rumbling. It was a painful party. When the Emperor gaily addressed Hortense as "Princess" which he did more than once, the rage of Bonaparte's sisters Elisa and Caroline was unconcealed. Madame Murat sat with large tears rolling down her scarlet cheeks. Murat glowered in sullen silence. Joseph and Louis looked pleased with themselves, Madame Joseph apprehensive, Madame Louis submissive, "and Eugène Beauharnais, whom I cannot praise too highly in comparison with the others, was simple and natural, evidently free from any ambition or repining."

Next day, after a tiring ceremony of creating Marshals of France, the Emperor had to face a second family dinner during which Caroline openly attacked him, and he shouted back furiously, "Really Madame, to hear you, one would think we had succeeded to the crown of our late father!" Madame de Rémusat, seated next door in Josephine's boudoir, heard the raised voices and screeching worthy of a fishwife. Caroline contrived a faint. A few days later she and Elisa were gazetted Imperial Highnesses.

As far as Eugène was concerned, the change from Republic to Empire was principally for the worse. "Several months passed between the election and the coronation. During this time the Emperor, wishing to surround his throne with every dignity necessary for a monarchy, re-established the strictest conventional etiquette and saw that it was observed. From that moment I ceased to have intimate relations with him, and during this period I found myself relegated by my rank and functions to a waiting room, the most distant from his apartments. I made no complaint.

"But there were not lacking courtiers who, under the mask of attention, attempted to irritate me by expressing their astonishment that the stepson of the Emperor, after such long and happy intimacy found himself suddenly so far off. I kept my mouth shut to these lackeys, telling them that I was quite content wherever my duty happened to take me—which was in fact the truth.

"A little time after, the Emperor made me the offer, through my mother, of the post of Grand Chamberlain. But I refused the honour saying that it did not suit my tastes or character. My vocation was military and I really did not know much of any profession except that of arms. I must confess that if the Emperor had offered me the appointment of Master of the Horse I might have accepted, because I should have had to deal with horses which I loved passionately, and an establishment which resembled that of a regiment."

Other members of his family found that their new elevation brought trials as well as triumphs. The position of Hortense was pitiable. When her son was six months old, her mother and Bonaparte came to see her and her husband with a proposition. Bonaparte wanted to adopt little Napoleon Charles. During her pregnancy Hortense had often tried to keep up her spirits by drawing little pictures of an angel child. When he arrived, he did seem to her to resemble them. She loved him passionately. The idea of having him adopted was terrible to her. She need not have worried. Louis, transported with jealousy, absolutely refused to allow his baby son to be set above him in the line of succession. He wrote a letter of which Hortense was ashamed, advising Bonaparte to get a divorce and a child of his own. This made Josephine very upset and downhearted. Eventually the succession of the Empire was arranged to descend first to Joseph (who had only two big daughters) and next to Louis and his male children.

But the Emperor still toyed with the idea of adoption, and had inserted a clause giving him a pre-emptive right to do so. He had excluded his brother Lucien, because of Madame Jouberthon, and his youngest brother Jerome, for the present, at any rate. This ebullient midshipman, weary of being blockaded by a British cruiser in the West Indies, had taken a passage in a neutral ship for an exploratory tour of the United States. At Baltimore he had fallen in love with the daughter of the President of the local bank, Miss Betsy Patterson, and on Christmas Eve, 1803, he had married her. Bonaparte heard the news from the English press, and from his mother whose consent should have been asked to make the union legal, as Jerome was still in his teens. The bridegroom had not dared to address himself to his brother, but he was sure that when Bonaparte saw the bride he would be pleased. He was mistaken. The Emperor never meant to see her.

Hortense found herself breeding again. Louis wanted them all to spend the winter in Italy. In the end he went off alone, to Montpelier. Before he left, he told her, with one of his dreadful looks, never to go to stay at St. Cloud, never even to spend a night there. An occasion arrived when it was difficult for her to refuse—a slight carriage accident. All the same she said she must go home. Josephine began to say her daughter no longer loved them. She threatened tears. Hortense had to confess that her husband had forbidden her to stay under her stepfather's roof. She did not know why. The Emperor looked terrible. "Does he get his information from the English slander sheets?" Even then she had not understood. She only saw that she had made her stepfather very angry with her husband; and now Louis would be angry with her for having broken her promise not to say he had forbidden her to stay at St. Cloud. Amongst his threats before he left had been to separate her from her son, and shut her up in some out of the way place from which no power on earth should deliver her.

Madame de Rémusat believed that Louis opened all his wife's letters, and told her she was the true daughter of an unprincipled woman. "She found her only comfort in the affection of her brother, whose conduct, though jealously watched by the Bonapartes, was unassailable. Eugène who was simple and frank, lighthearted and open in all his dealings, displaying no ambition, holding himself aloof from every intrigue, doing his duty wherever he was placed, disarmed calumny before it could reach him. He knew nothing of what happened in the palace. His sister loved him tenderly, and confided her sorrows to him only during the few moments that the suspicious jealousy of Louis allowed them to be together."

One June day that summer Eugène gave one of his luncheon parties at his country hunting-box, la Jonchère. It was a large party. Amongst the guests was a Polish countess who was fashionably "in despair" because she was having to leave France next day, and one of the attentive young officers whom Louis had forbidden Hortense to receive. M. de Flahaut was supposed to be the son of an elderly Comte de Flahaut who had been guillotined, and a fascinating woman, now wife of the Portuguese Ambassador, the Marquise de Souza. But he was fairly widely believed to be in fact a son of Talleyrand. Up to this moment Hortense had dismissed him as rather a light-weight. But when she saw his countenance as he prepared to say farewell to the lovely Pole, she said to herself, "He is indeed capable of love. He suffers. He interests me. He has shown his friendship for me: he shall have mine. He deserves it, and I can give it; for as he loves another woman he is harmless to me."

On Sunday July 15 there was a touching ceremonial of the distribution of stars of the Legion of Honour. It was staged at the Invalides after a Mass in the chapel. Madame de Rémusat was proud of her mistress on this pompous occasion. "Her costume was admirably selected and in perfect taste. The investiture took place under a burning sun. She appeared in broad daylight in a robe of rose-coloured gauze, spangled with silver stars, and cut very low, in the prevailing fashion. Her head-dress was a tiara of diamond wheat-ears, and this brilliant attire, the grace of her carriage, the charm of her smile, the sweetness of her countenance, produced such an effect that I heard many persons present say 'The Empress of the French outshines all the ladies of her court.' "

This was Josephine's last public appearance in Paris during the summer season. She went off to take a cure at Aix la Chapelle where her husband and son were to join her after some weeks in the camp at Boulogne. It was reckoned that there would soon be no less than a hundred thousand troops concentrated along the coast getting ready for the Invasion of England.[2]

III

It was said that the Emperor was always present, if only in the spirit, on the Iron Coast. Ever since the declaration of war last spring he had been visiting the Grande Armée and invasion ports. Even in the depths of winter he liked paying flying surprise visits. Middle-aged members of his staff did not greatly appreciate a schedule which entailed leaving Paris after dark, breakfast at Chantilly, supper at Abbeville, and then eight or ten hours in the saddle, inspecting ports and troops, or rocking in a boat watching embarkation and disembarkation exercises.

Last year, on his road to Brussels, he had said he would dine at Compiègne. The palace had been taken over by an establishment called The School of Arts and Trades. It was amazing how soon a place could become run down. All the mirrors, marble, chimney pieces, floors, doors and panelling had simply vanished —where? Splendid saloons were now filled with anvils, bellows, forges and the tables of joiners, cobblers and tailors. The only part of the building not devastated was the landing at the top of the grand staircase, and there his dinner had been served. He had written the same night to the Minister of the Interior to tell him to put the palace in repair. He was going to live there. The School of Arts and Trades was sent to Châlons. This year he dined at Fontainebleau, a much larger establishment, and one which was to become indissolubly linked with his name. He inspected the repairs and the rooms being got ready for the Pope.

At the Tuileries fifty-six rooms had been redecorated. The Pope was coming for the coronation in October. This news had caused such a sensation, not only in France, that it was necessary to put up with some annoyance sooner than recede from the scheme. For Pius VII was being a little difficult.

The Emperor settled down to three weeks amongst his troops, busy and happy and at his best. He had as headquarters a small château in the village of Pont de Briques about two and a half miles from Boulogne, and also on the cliffs a pavilion, built in forty-eight hours, on a site from which he could survey with a sweeping glance, his four principal camps, the town and the quays. His Imperial Majesty's *baraque* did not at all look as if all the timbers and glass had been brought to this salty grazing land ready cut and numbered. It was pearl-grey without. Inside there was a fine lofty Council Chamber, with a ceiling painted with an eagle speeding through gilded clouds in a cerulean sky. There was an enormous map of the Channel and coasts, on the wall. There was only one chair—of green morocco. Officers had to prop themselves on their sword hilts if conferences lasted long. His bedroom presented the same combination of simplicity and luxury—an iron bedstead, a splendid dressing-case, a telescope adjacent which had cost twelve thousand francs, and through which could be seen very clearly the walls of Dover Castle. A fence lighted after dark by reflector lamps railed off the *baraque* from the rest of the cliff top. Marines of the Imperial Guard and Grenadiers of the old Consular Guard were on sentry duty night and day. Engineers had arranged in the foreground an ornamental sheet of water on which floated two black swans surrounded by flower beds and shrubs.

The Grande Armée had settled in on the Iron Coast, and there were broad highways, with signs set at intervals labelled "Avenue de Marengo", "Rue de St. Bernard" etc. The veterans of Italy and Egypt had made themselves homes with rockeries, pyramids, vegetable gardens, aviaries and poultry yards. They were well exercised, well fed, bronzed and expectant. They were building fine new roads and bridges. They drilled and marched and sang soldiers' songs:

> *"From England we'll bring back a treasure*
> *That won't have cost us a sou!"*

The Emperor was said to have murmured as he directed his

telescope on the hated white cliffs, "Yes—a favourable wind and thirty-six hours."

He had chosen his birthday, August 15, for the grand Fête at which he was to review the Army of Invasion and present crosses of the Legion. He had ordered to be erected on the spot (but it would not be ready) a colossal Column of the Grande Armée, to be topped by a figure. Everyone coming in from the sea would be able to see him.

He wrote to Josephine frequently, lover's letters to a jealous mate. In nearly every one he remembered to say that he longed to cover her with kisses and was in fine health and spirits, except for missing her, which made him work too hard. He was very pleased with the troops, the flotilla—at last he was coming to her! "Tomorrow I shall be in St. Omer, on the 28th at Arras, on the 30th at Mons, and on the 31st or September 1st at Aix la Chapelle. Eugène is courting all the ladies of Boulogne, and has nothing but success."[3]

IV

He arrived at Aix only one day late. In view of the coronation he had expressed a wish to be shown the relics of Charlemagne, which were part of the famous treasure of the old Imperial city. The Emperor's tomb had been opened but left intact by Otho III in the year one thousand. Barbarossa had removed from it the sword, the crown and the marble seat in which the body had been found seated. The Emperor Napoleon could not hope for the diadem, but he got the promise of a loan of the sword, and the dean and chapter begged him also to accept a talisman which had been discovered attached to the collar of Charlemagne. His great predecessor had always worn this when going into battle.

He had already adopted from the relics of another Emperor a cognizance which was to be renowned—the Imperial bees. This idea came from Tournai. When the tomb of Childeric, King of the Franks, who had died in 480, had been opened in 1653, there had been discovered upwards of three hundred small objects in gold, in the shape of bees. It was believed that the royal robes had been decorated with bees. He liked the notion exceedingly and adopted it forthwith. Wherever the Emperor Napoleon appeared hereafter in state, his garments, the decoration of his apartments and even his personal belongings were lavishly powdered with

Imperial bees. They completely superseded the fleur de lys.

He proceeded with Josephine on an enjoyable trip up the Rhine in perfect early autumn weather. There were to be manoeuvres at Mainz and Eugène had been ordered to command them. "The public therefore," wrote Hortense, "jumped to the conclusion that an alliance was about to take place between my brother and one of these royal families of Germany who had hastened to present their respects to the Emperor." Constant heard the rumours and was deeply interested. The duke and duchess Leopold of Bavaria represented the Birkenfeld branch of the ancient house of Wittelsbach. They had brought their heir, who was at the awkward age, neither child nor man, and their daughter, the Princess Elizabeth. The Parisian valet thought she was not pretty, but was well made and might look much better if well dressed. No doubt at the small courts of her father and the Elector of Bavaria manners were simple. At dinner, when she was placed between the Emperor and Eugène, she was extremely talkative. The Emperor, perhaps to snub her, left her to her own devices, and to his stepson. Eugène, Constant noticed, whose manners were always dictated by the heart, was, as ever, beautifully polite. But it was much to be hoped that this princess was not to be chosen. The Emperor's manners, alas! could not be said to be perfect. Madame Junot had been startled, at his wife's receptions to hear ladies addressed with the remarks "Your arms, Madame, are very red", and "Madame, I think I have seen that dress before."

The valet's spirits drooped in Cologne. He heard—for he counted—sixty-five different clocks sounding the hours from the enormous quantity of churches and convents with which the city was overweighted. Bonn was much better. The Empress had a house with a garden filled with fairy-lights and moonlight, running down to the banks of the broad and lovely river, on which had been stationed a boatload of musicians. At Coblentz, the Prince of Nassau-Weilbourg came to offer two yachts in which the Empress and her suite might ascend to Mainz while the Emperor took the new riverside highway. The ladies had their first thunderstorm of the tour when nearing Bingen, but they arrived at Mainz on the minute. It appeared that the whole population of the town had turned out on the quay. They were said to have been waiting for eleven hours, headed by maidens in white robes with baskets of flowers. The Emperor had not been very pleased to find the streets on his road to the palace dumb and empty. The Empress had been upset by the storm. The Princes of Baden, of Issembourg and of Nassau-Usingen, and the Electoral Archchancellor were now added to the throng, and the matter of presentations to all these royalties caused a dispute. Josephine had taken for granted that Eugène would be amongst those presented. Most unfortunately, when she found this opposed, she had added, that for the late Vicomte de Beauharnais, when he had travelled in Germany, there had been no such question. In the end it was arranged that the son of the Empress should happen to be standing beside her when the assembled royalties arrived.

He was perfectly indifferent; all that troubled him was that the review of four regiments of cavalry on the afternoon of September 30 went off to perfection. The Princess of Hesse-Darmstadt was the next arrival, and Josephine was particularly interested because with her were coming her son, the hereditary prince, and his fiancée, the Princess Wilhelmine of Baden. The Empress was aware that this young princess, said to be the most beautiful girl in Europe, had been suggested as her successor should the Emperor consider a divorce. The suggestion, like the difficulty over Eugène's status, she attributed to the malevolence of Talleyrand. She had always feared him. Had not the negress soothsayer in Martinique told her she would wear a crown but should beware of a priest? He had been a Bishop. Her fears were soon banished. The princess was not admired by anybody from the Emperor to his valet. Constant found her quite inferior, much too thin, with a long pale face and no expression. If she filled out later she might become a beauty. Luckily there was no question of her for his young master.[4]

Eugène had become a Member of the Legion of Honour last December and a Commandant in June. On October 17 he was gazetted Colonel-General of the mounted *chasseurs*. "This gave me great pleasure, because the Emperor in giving me this promotion was leaving me in the profession which was my element."

V

One of the many disagreeable side-effects of the impending coronation was that it raised the dynastic question again. Hortense gave birth to a second son on October 11 but this, far from causing the Bonaparte family to give up hope, seemed rather to increase their animosity. They did not think Josephine should be crowned. The Emperor complained, particularly of Joseph and Caroline, to a very old friend, the Comte de Roederer, Secretary of State. "They are jealous of my wife, of Eugène, of Hortense, of everyone close to me. Well, my wife has her diamonds and her debts . . . that's all. Eugène has no more than 20,000 livres a year. I love these children because they always try to please me . . . If a shot is fired, it is Eugène who discovers from whence it came. If I have to leap a ditch, it is he who gives me his hand. I love Hortense, yes, I love her. She and her brother always take my part even against their mother when she produces some grievance . . . My family tell me that my wife is false, that the attentions of her children are studied. My wife is a good woman who does them no harm. She is willing to play the Empress as well as she can, and have diamonds and finery, the miserable solaces of her age. If I had been thrown into prison instead of mounting a throne she would have shared my misfortune. It is right for her to share my success. I know her children treat me as an old uncle. This makes the sweetness of my home. I grow old at only thirty-six! I need a little comfort. They say I am going to give Italy to Eugène. I am not such a fool. I trust I am still capable myself of looking after my Kingdom of Italy and of Venice . . ."[5]

Unfortunately Josephine provoked one of the scenes he detested soon after their return to Paris. The dreadful familiar words were heard: "Send for Colonel Beauharnais." Eugène arrived to find his stepfather saying this was the end. His patience was exhausted. It appeared that Josephine had attempted to surprise him with a lady. "You must make arrangements for your mother's departure. I must be allowed my freedom." For two days after this no move was made by either parent. Josephine had told Madame de Rémusat to hurry to Paris to fetch Princess Louis. "She had just seen her brother who had come from St. Cloud. The Emperor had signified to him his resolution to divorce his wife, and Eugène had received the news with his accustomed submission, but refused all the personal favours which were offered to him as a consolation, declaring that from the moment that such a misfortune should befall his mother he would accept nothing, but accompany her to any retreat which might be assigned to her, were it even to Martinique. He was resolved to sacrifice everything to her great need of support."

Bonaparte had listened to him in unbroken silence. Madame de Rémusat thought Hortense weakish. She said, with meaning, that there were other wives more unhappy than her mother. She believed the best thing to do was nothing. Her mother's tears had worked the miracle before and would again. She proved to be quite right. Next time Eugène called, a tender reconciliation had taken place, but Josephine said dramatically that it had been different this time. The Emperor had begged her not to make it impossible for them to continue to live together. Her son seconded this, and like a child she promised to be good.[6]

A few days later the Emperor, with a smile, told her that the Pope's arrival was imminent and he had decided that she should be crowned. So she had better set her mind to making her arrangements. She did this with great good will. Many dusty tomes were being lifted down from obscure shelves by learned men, to be searched for precedents. There had not been the coronation of a consort since Marie de Medici. Soon after the formation of the Empire, Madame Campan had been summoned by the Empress to tell her exactly what had been the etiquette in the household of Marie Antoinette. Her aristocratic ladies of the palace had developed genuine fondness for their Empress. Her impulsive generosity, her thrilling and entirely uninhibited revelations of her private life disarmed criticism. But the Emperor did not relish that ladies of the first families of France should be invited by his partner to believe that he was a perfect monster.

Twenty years after the coronation Eugène wrote that he did not propose to speak of it at all. It had already been written about in great detail. He had never been much struck by display. He really did not now remember which of the regalia he had carried in the procession. (It was the Emperor's ring.)[7] Providentially he could appear in uniform. But he had to order one of the Court dresses prescribed for every rank of attendant gentlemen. There were in addition to the ceremony in Notre Dame to be many concerts and receptions. The Marshals of the Empire were giving a ball at the Opera for which the entire auditorium was being boarded over. The Senate, the City and the Legislative Assembly were all offering fêtes. At the last-named there was to be an unveiling, after a banquet, of a marble statue representing the author of the Code Napoléon—the Emperor as Law-giver. The galleries of Lucrece and La Réunion in the Tuileries were being transformed into an immense garden, filled with oleanders, lilacs, jonquils, lilies and jasmine—all these in full bloom while snow was falling outside. The new court dress was enthusiastically but confusingly described as "Spanish," "Henri IV" and "the Troubadour style." Bonaparte himself was going to wear a variant of it for his arrival at the cathedral. It consisted of a white satin or velvet doublet embroidered with bees, a very high cravat and a large jabot, worn with skin-tight knee breeches, silk stockings and shoes with rosettes, all white. A silly jaunty little cape with a huge upstanding collar, and an upturned black hat crowded with ostrich feathers, completed the costume. It needed a good figure and complexion to carry it off. Persons not quite young, weather-beaten or bandy-legged, such as Duroc, looked like actors or prosperous dancing-masters. Isabey had designed the décor and dresses. Leading theatrical characters were being employed to drill the performers.

Talma was again a frequent visitor at the Tuileries. But he had waited after the formation of the Empire for a summons, and had then presented himself in court dress. There was going to be a coronation (but of Cyrus) in his gala free production at the Français on coronation night. His two leading ladies were Duchesnois, a great actress, but hideously ugly, patronized by the Empress, and Mademoiselle George, whose dazzling blonde statuesque beauty had so much captured the audience when she first stepped upon the Paris stages as Clytemnestra that there had been a dead hush followed by an outburst of applause. She was believed to have been the Emperor's mistress for about two years. Wicked old Mlle. Raucourt had spotted her at the Amiens theatre where she had been the fourteen-year-old daughter of the *chef d'orchestre* ... At the coronation there were going to be three orchestras and four hundred and fifty musicians ... A hundred and forty Spanish horses had been bought for the royal procession of thirty carriages. It would take an hour passing from the Tuileries to Notre Dame, where some insanitary dwellings had been swept away (the Choir School and the Chapel of the Ancient Chapter), but not, to the regret of the Clerk of the Works, the complete *Hospice* of the Rue du Parvis. There simply had not been time.

The sad fact was that long before it took place the very word coronation seemed to have made many persons of the new court a little mad. The Emperor's own family took the lead in being difficult. His sisters, represented by their husbands, said they refused to carry Josephine's tail. It was represented that there was a *mystique* here. The princesses would be supporting the Imperial mantle. In the end on the condition that they obliged Josephine, each lady was allowed a chamberlain, a grown man, to carry her own tail. The effect was ridiculous. The Emperor's mother, whom he had much wished to attend, would not arrive in time. She was soothing Lucien in Rome. Pauline, on the other hand, rather against his will, was coming from Rome. She had remained a widow less than ten months. Joseph had suggested her second husband, but the Emperor could not disapprove. Prince Camillo Borghese was five years her senior, twenty-eight, and had been a *francophil* since Bonaparte's first Italian campaign. He was head of one of the noblest families in Italy and owned vast properties and famous collections, notably of statuary and jewellery. He was perfectly amiable and the darling of his widowed mother. Pauline took every opportunity of reminding her sisters that she was "a real princess", but in a remarkably short time she had been disillusioned in her prince. His fiercely curling dark hair, his large and liquid eyes did not betoken a passionate disposition. Roman society, in which she had expected to shine, was a desert compared to Paris, where she had bought, on the death of the Duc de Charost, a lovely home, the Hôtel de Charost, Rue du Faubourg St. Honoré. She had never been well since her disastrous residence in the West Indies (where she had admittedly behaved with great courage). Her new marriage was childless. She had lost her son by Leclerc, at the attractive age of six, and had cut off her hair again . . . She could not be repulsed . . .

Others of the essential characters were raising problems. David, who was commissioned as Painter in Chief, said he had been promised a box in which he would be undisturbed. The Grand Master of the Ceremonies had sent him two tickets for a stand. There was talk of a duel. He needed a whole stand for himself and his impedimenta and it must be above the high altar. He had to be pacified with a compromise. The dilatoriness of the Pope had caused two postponements. "I am willing to wait until December 2," wrote the Emperor. "If the Pope has not come by then the coronation will take place without him." The weather would not be good, but the Emperor never allowed the weather to interfere with his social arrangements. At last, on November 25, the Pope was here. His carriage was met "by accident" in the forest of Fontainebleau by one containing the Emperor. The Empress awaited the Holy Father on the steps of the palace. Her son dined to meet Pius VII on the night of his arrival. Next day Josephine quietly disclosed the tragic fact that she was united to the Emperor by only a civil contract. A religious service of marriage was performed by Fesch in the palace chapel forty-eight hours before the coronation. It was private, but for the Emperor to divorce her now would be, if not impossible, much more difficult. She had triumphed.

The provenance of the regalia had caused a vast correspondence. Eventually the Emperor decided to order a complete new set from various Paris goldsmiths. Biennais, at the sign of "The Violet Monkey" had provided his own gold laurel wreath and Imperial crown. Marguerette received the order for the Empress's lighter crown. They were on exhibition at Fonciers.

Paris drawing-rooms echoed to stories of tussles for medals, precedence or even seats, and names and addresses of tradesmen —Levacher for velvets (Tyrian purple, ruby, sapphire, *gris antique*, Imperial green); Picot for embroideries (silver and gold and silk); Veuve Toulet for Russian ermines, astrakhan, leopard and bearskins; L'Olive and Beuvry and Demoiselle Fournet for laces and gauzes and gloves; Jacques for boots and slippers; Poupard for plumes. Leroy and Raimbaud had made the gowns of the Empress. The fashions dictated for the coronation were to rule Europe for a decade.

Work had gone on by torchlight as well as by daylight but when the doors of the cathedral opened at seven a.m. on the morning of December 2 for the first ticket-holders, carpenters were still nailing crimson draperies on tiers of timber platforms and galleries in the dark blue gloom. When a thousand candles were lighted in twenty-four crystal chandeliers it would get warmer. It was a most unpleasant morning with scurries of snow, and the Paris mob who had been on the street all night, even before the military came on duty, waxed humorous over gentlemen clanking with decorations, escorting shivering ladies, clad in low cut, high-waisted gowns with puff sleeves, through the slush and sand from the distant places where they had been obliged to leave their carriages. The crowd was inclined to be ribald when a single figure pattered on to the scene mounted on a mule and carrying a large wooden cross. But it was the papal chamberlain traditionally heralding the Holy Father, and the simple and dignified white-robed figure of Pius VII was greeted by awed silence. He was received by a hundred bishops and archbishops and the orchestra struck up; but he had a two hours' wait. It was quarter to twelve before the loudest cheering yet was heard outside, and the Emperor and Empress arrived in their new Imperial glass coach drawn by eight dapple-greys. Over the west entrance had been superimposed a temporary timber gothic four-arched porch decorated with many lifesize gilded eagles and crowned letters "N". At this moment to the relief of all and the delight of the superstitious the sun broke through.

Darkness was falling by the time the ceremony was over. It had been a great success although both the Emperor and Empress had tottered ascending to their thrones, owing to the weight of their robes. Several spectators agreed that the Empress's train had been unkindly tugged. She had trembled when she had found, on arrival, that she had lost the ring given her by the Pope and blessed by him. But her son had found it for her later. It was not true that the Emperor had snatched the crown from the Pope to put it on his own head. All that had been settled by letter weeks before.

Three years passed before David's enormous crowd-scene picture of the coronation was on show at the Louvre. It was a little untruthful. Madame Mère had not been there... The Imperial princesses, not two adoring ladies in waiting, had carried Josephine's tail... But the Emperor, after a long look solemnly removed his hat. "David, I salute you!" "In the shade of my hero," replied the deeply-bowing Court Painter, "I shall glide to posterity." Actually, to the thousands who were to behold it in future years, the picture was Josephine's coronation. Her son was sympathetically presented, standing in a graceful attitude with his left hand on the hilt of his sabre behind the figures of the clergy and just above two choir boys. It was impossible to pretend that he had occupied an important position. He had been allotted his place, fifth in the Emperor's procession, simply as Colonel-General of mounted *chasseurs* of the Guard, after the Marshals. Murat, carrying her crown, had led the Empress's procession.[8]

The coronation had come at a most unfortunate date for Eugène. He left Paris six weeks later, at rather short notice. On Sunday, January 13 he took the usual parade. He was just able to attend a large ball in his fine new house. It was in some sense a gesture of farewell to his youth. For he had been in love and now he was out of love. Madame de Rémusat had much sympathy for him. "Eugène was sore at heart, but his outward composure laid him little open to attack. Suddenly, towards the end of January, in very severe weather, he received orders to proceed with his regiment to Italy within four-and-twenty hours. He was convinced he was in complete disgrace. The Empress, believing this to be the doing of Madame X. wept bitterly, but her son strictly forbade her to make any appeal. He took leave of the Emperor who received him with coldness, and on the following morning, we learned that the Guard's Regiment of *Guides* was on the road, their colonel marching at their head despite the bitter weather."

"Madame X." was Madame Duchâtel and she was about his own age, nearly twenty-four, but her husband was thirty years older. She had not been quite qualified, either by birth or background, for the post of a Dame du Palais, but the Empress had accepted someone of whom her son spoke ardently. He was quite at a loss to explain what had followed her appointment. The ungrateful lady no longer showed the slightest interest in him, even avoided his glances. Duroc, best of old friends, soon opened his eyes. The Emperor was starting a new *affaire*; there were all the bad old signs. It was the new Dame du Palais, Madame Duchâtel. It was not true that Murat was her lover, though to throw people off the scent he had danced with her all night at the last ball. (Madame Duchâtel danced beautifully.) She had been planted by the Murats to detach the Emperor from the Empress. But it seemed possible that she aspired high, and saw herself as a second Louise de la Vallière. (She had a quantity of very fair hair, and large blue eyes. Madame de Rémusat afterwards said they could wear any expression except candour.) Madame Murat had told Duroc that when she had given the lady a miniature of the Emperor set in diamonds—a present from him—she had kept the portrait but given back the setting, saying she was insulted. Presently Duroc said that he had been out with the Emperor several times, in the evenings to visit Madame Duchâtel. On one occasion, in the park on Murat's estate at Villiers, when they had heard a noise, the Emperor had jumped over a high wall. "I, who was cooler," said Duroc, slapping his lame leg "dared not imitate him." Duroc added seriously that he was constantly terrified at the risks which the Emperor ran and would be delighted when this *liaison* ended.[9]

CHAPTER EIGHT

Viceroy of Italy
1805 : 1806

I

HE WROTE to Bessières when he was ten days on his road, at St. Pierre le Moûtier.

"For my own part, old chap, I am travelling with a light heart, thinking often of Paris—not that I would wish to be back there, but sometimes I wish I knew how my dear mother is. I have no recent news of her. I don't think that she is ill, but I am afraid she is worried. I should like to know that all is well at home; that is the news that would give me the greatest pleasure."[1]

He never forgot the name of the obscure hamlet between Roanne and Lyons where he was overtaken by a courier with a letter from the Emperor, dated February 1. It was at little Tarare that he learned he had been appointed an Arch-Chancellor of State and of the Empire, a rank which gave him the entry to the Privy Council, the Grand Council of the Legion of Honour, of the Senate and the Council of State. "My cousin," wrote the Emperor, "this change offers no obstacle to your military career. Your title is The Prince Eugène, Arch-Chancellor of State, and you are also Serene Highness. You will no longer be colonel-general of *chasseurs*. You will be brigadier-general commanding the mounted *chasseurs* of my Guard."

The Emperor's message to the Senate which accompanied this sudden elevation was carefully and typically worded.

"Senators, we have appointed our stepson Eugène Beauharnais Vice-Arch-Chancellor of State to the Empire. Among all the acts of our sovereignty there is not one more gratifying to our heart. Brought up by us, and from his childhood amongst us, he has proved himself worthy of imitating and with the help of God of one day surpassing, the examples and lessons we have given him.

Although he is still young, we shall from this day forward consider him, on account of the experience we have of his conduct in the most momentous circumstances, as one of the pillars of our throne. In the midst of the cares and trials of the high rank to which we have been called, our heart has sought for affection in the tenderness and consoling friendship of this child of our adoption, a consolation which is no doubt necessary to all men, but pre-eminently so to us, whose every moment is devoted to the affairs of nations. Our paternal blessing will follow this young Prince throughout his whole career and with the help of Providence he will one day be worthy of the approbation of posterity."[2]

More letters than he had ever in his life received reached the new prince at Lyons. Some of them were very gushing, and came from the very people who had previously annoyed him by pointing out that nothing had ever been done for him. He decided that he could honestly say that he was not in the least elevated by his change of fortune. He could continue to live with his officers and men exactly as he had done before. The thing that pleased him best was the wording of his stepfather's citation. He tried to explain this when replying to the good wishes of Bessières.

"You know me well and can easily imagine what I feel. I will admit that, knowing the Emperor had good intentions towards me, I had dared to hope for something, but nothing so wonderful or so complimentary as this. I will admit to you that I have been quite taken aback by what has happened."[3]

The troops struggled into Lans le Bourg laboriously. They had been caught in a blizzard near Modane. They lost horses and men owing to landslides and falling rocks. They had a detestable passage of the Mont Cenis and very slow—eight days. But they had to get through at all costs for they were running out of forage. At last they were at Verceil and he could begin to tackle more of the correspondence which was swelling his valises. His line to Madame Campan must be elegant. "Be so good as to be the friend of Prince Eugène. Your kindness to him in the old days is one of his dearest memories."

He got in to Milan on March 16. He had left Paris with nearly nine hundred *chasseurs*, grenadiers, mamelukes and artillery. He arrived in Milan short of thirty-four men and thirty-six horses. Some, of course, would reappear. It might have been much worse, for they had encountered as well as blizzards and landslides, drenching rain, floods, broken bridges, roads icebound and blocked by fallen trees, and finally deep snow.

A few days after his departure a deputation headed by Count Melzi had invited the Emperor to become king of Italy. It had all been most carefully arranged beforehand, but the inhabitants of Milan did not at first welcome what they mistook for another French army of occupation. But most knowledgeable people, since they could not have a United Italy, preferred the domination of France to that of Austria, and gradually it became known to all that the Emperor, who was coming to Milan for his coronation, was bringing no more troops, only a court. When it was realized that a succession of splendid pageants was being planned, resignation gave place to interest.

The cathedral (after St. Peter's the largest in Europe), stood in the most ancient quarter of the old Lombardic capital. It had an elaborate exterior but was in a sad state, and only half finished. The streets leading to it were demonstrably insanitary. Yet, the Emperor had said he would stay (for the coronation at least) in the royal palace in the cathedral square. Eugène superintended the erection of a temporary gallery connecting the palace with the cathedral which was being decorated in the Italian style with hangings of silk and gauze. He himself, was, with his staff, up in the barracks, the Castello, almost equally uncomfortable, but at least at a distance from the teeming cathedral area. He organized a succession of rooms for the Imperial pair. His mother's chief lady (and connection by marriage) Madame de la Rochefoucauld would have to get a much better bedroom than her mistress—most unfortunate. But it was essential that the Emperor's bedroom had a bathroom adjoining.

The Palazzo Reale had been originally the dwelling of the Visconti and Sforza, and the Palazzo di Corte, but had been entirely transformed about thirty years ago by the architect Piermarini for the Austrian Archduke Ferdinand, Governor of Lombardy. There were many sumptuous apartments and one really magnificent salon, the Hall of the Caryatids. Nobody would be able to sleep, because of the noise of traffic and the cathedral bells. After a month of Milan in torrential rain alternating with strong sunshine, Eugène wrote to Bessières. "Between ourselves the atmosphere is very bad in this bitch of a town. The country is most beautiful but there is no public spirit, no leadership, nothing unanimous except utter aversion from everything that is not Italian."

He went up to meet the Emperor and Empress at the old hunting lodge of Stupinigi six miles out of Turin. It had indeed begun life as a hunting box, but the kings of Sardinia (now vanished to Sardinia) had enlarged it until it was stupendous. It easily swallowed, as well as the Emperor's cortège from Paris, that of the Pope on his way back to Rome. Pius VII was attended by sixteen cardinals and bishops, and upwards of a hundred lesser clerics who had struck the French as exceedingly excitable and noisy. Covers for four persons were laid when a family party dined with His Holiness—the Emperor, the Empress and her son.

The arrival of the Emperor coincided with that of wonderful weather. On a perfect May day he made an expedition to Marengo. He wore the same coat and hat as on the day of the battle and when the troops caught sight of him there was a thunderous roar. Rapp noticed in the strong sunshine that the coat was very much motheaten.

A wretched figure crept out of the Emperor's presence after an audience at Alessandria. The ship bringing Jerome Bonaparte and his wife to Europe had docked at Oporto. The Emperor who had annulled his brother's American escapade in March, had sent orders for him to come up to Italy. Miss Betsy Patterson and a brother whom she had prudently brought with her were not allowed to land. The marriage had been legal in America and the bridegroom's mother and eldest brother had given their consent, but from Stupinigi the Emperor had sent a cruel letter to his mother telling her to warn Jerome he would give him only one interview. "If he persists in his *liaison* I shall show him no mercy." Jerome went off to win his spurs in charge of a small squadron ordered to Algiers to demand the return of two hundred Genoese seamen being kept there as slaves.[4]

His family were infuriating the Emperor at this moment. He had needed a King for Italy. Joseph had refused. If he should outlive Bonaparte he would be Emperor. He did not wish to jeopardize his prospects. In France, Louis, offered the kingdom for his son Napoleon Charles, had actually written that he would do nothing to seem to give colour to the unpleasant rumours about that child's paternity. Not only what the Emperor called 'the English slander sheets' declared that Bonaparte was indeed the father of Hortense's first born. Lucien had made the suggestion to Louis. Lucien was the Emperor's last hope. If he would give up Madame Jouberthon he might have Italy. He had not yet replied. This was very inconvenient.

M. de Rémusat had come to Milan in advance of the Emperor but his wife was not coming. He wrote to her that Prince Eugène had received him with his usual cordiality. The prince had asked eagerly for Paris news. Rémusat had to tell him that the affair of Madame Duchatel seemed to be still going on. This made the prince look sad. Perhaps Milan would brighten up when the court arrived. The inhabitants showed little affection for the French. The nobility shut themselves up in their palaces and regretted they were too poor to do the honours in fitting style. Prince Eugène was trying to collect them about him, but succeeding imperfectly. There was no doubt that he longed for the moment when the coronation was over and he could return to France and his profession. The Italians seemed in a sort of suspense, not quite sure whether to regret or repine at their new destiny. The new kingdom was called the kingdom of Italy but it comprised, as yet, only Lombardy, the duchies of Parma and Modena and the old Papal legations of Bologna and Ferrara. The dream of the patriotic Italian was of a united Italy. The kingdom of Naples was naturally wholly Austrian in sympathy, since the rulers were Habsburgs.

Three days before the coronation, a mounted detachment of the National Guard fetched the iron crown of Lombardy from its resting place in the sacristy of Monza. This cathedral city, where there was another large Piermarini palace, stood nine miles outside Milan. It had been the coronation town of the kings of Lombardy since the eleventh century. The iron crown was not really made of iron. It was a circle of faded gold about three inches wide, with decoration of deep-sunk flawed irregular jewels and enamel-work. But inside could be discerned a silvery slender band of metal traditionally brought by the Empress Helena from Jerusalem, and a nail of the True Cross.

The coronation took place on a day mentioned by the Emperor as superb. The ceremony was basically the same as that performed in Notre Dame, and Cardinal Caprara, Archbishop of Milan, had been present there, so knew all that should be done. There was no coronation of Josephine. She sat in a gallery attended by the Emperor's eldest sister Elisa, who had tormented him into giving her a small Italian principality—Piombino, commanding the straits between Tuscany and Elba. He had held out hopes that he would soon add that of Lucca which would be much more valuable. As he placed the iron crown on his head the Emperor loudly announced in Italian, "God gives it to me; woe to him who touches it." It was noted as symbolic that after he had received such insignia as the ring and the mantle he handed them to his stepson.

Next day he began a succession of public appearances at one of which he instituted the Order of the Iron Crown. He gave instructions that the works at the cathedral should be immediately resumed and that the statues on the pinnacles should include one of himself. The Doge of Genoa arrived to beg that his Republic might be united to the Empire. This would be yet another glaring breach of the Treaty of Lunéville, but the Emperor graciously acceded.

Everything possible must be done to recall the days of Imperial Rome. But although Milan had undoubtedly possessed a wealth of classical buildings, various invaders, notably Barbarossa, had demolished them. Only a few could be seen clearly beneath the débris of the centuries. Sant' Ambrogio still preserved the shape of a basilica and had in front of it a fine atrium. St. Ambrose had baptized St. Augustine here and afterwards closed the gates of the church against the Emperor Theodosius. Prince Eugène commanded the mounted escort when the new King of Italy attended a Te Deum at Sant' Ambrogio. Afterwards in the arena up by the Castello there were games and chariot races, supposed to resemble those of Roman days, and a balloon ascent by a female aeronaut. Josephine aroused enthusiasm by her gracious act in assisting an octogenarian who got knocked over by the crowd pressing to see the Imperial couple arriving for the exhibition at the Brera. Talma had refused to come to Italy, although heavily in debt, but there were admired performances by a French company in which Raucourt scored a great success. There were rumours that Bigottini was coming to her native land. Two of the most famous singers of Italy, Banti and Marchesi, appeared, not only at the Scala. There was no need to warn Prince Eugène when there was a concert at the palace. Music drew him like a magnet. Mademoiselle d'Avrillon wrote him down "music-mad". It must be admitted that this correct spinster gloried in rumours of his supposed successes with the fair sex. So did his lamentably melancholy sister, Hortense.[5]

The Emperor was due to leave Milan on June 10. On the 7th he summoned the Legislative Assembly and announced that he had appointed his stepson Viceroy to govern Italy in the absence of its king. The prince immediately took the oath of fidelity. The surprise was great for his mother and sister. Hortense got a letter from the Viceroy himself expressing his regret at being separated from his family and country. She said, in her slightly affected way, that news of his death could hardly have hurt her more. "My unhappiness made his love more than ever necessary to me. He alone really knew and believed in me. Without him I should remain utterly exposed to my husband's persecution."

Josephine wept as the hour of her departure approached. Mademoiselle d'Avrillon said that when the Emperor came upon her mistress in tears he spoke harshly. "You are crying, Josephine. That is not sensible of you. You cry because you must part with your son. If the absence of your children causes you so much pain, guess what I must always feel. The affection which you display for them makes me feel bitterly the unhappiness of having none myself."[6] This checked her tears and left her staring, horror-struck.

The jewellers of Milan had heard with regret that so lavish a customer was about to leave them, and she rallied to buy a necklace of amethysts engraved with classical figures which she thought would look well on the white skin of her blonde daughter. Eugène chose a malachite necklace, decorated in the same style, to be taken to his sister.

His mother had tried to comfort a very young Viceroy who seemed indeed taken aback by his splendid appointment. With coy smiles and whispers she bade him not to lose hope—be patient. A lovely companion would soon be coming to share his splendour. Her son knew which princess she meant—a daughter of the Elector of Bavaria. She was now sixteen and had deposed her relative of Baden from the position of being the most beautiful princess in Europe. But like all the other lustrous matches proposed for him she was already engaged to someone else—Prince Karl of Baden.

II

The Emperor had not left his stepson stranded. He had provided him with a carefully chosen personal staff and a letter of instructions resembling a booklet.[7] Colonel Etienne Méjean appeared a model of tact as well as being a most agreeable man. His recommendation had come from M. Maret, Counsellor of State (afterwards Duke of Bassano). He had been trained as a lawyer. Mirabeau had thought well of him. He was married, with a young family. Captain Auguste Bataille de Tancarville seemed to be able to converse in any tongue, but was a model of discretion. Colonel d'Anthouard, like Bataille, came from the artillery, and was highly qualified. He looked, and was to prove, a difficult man. There was not a cavalryman in the Emperor's selection, and only in the appointment of his private secretary had the Viceroy been allowed to express a preference. M. Antoine Darnay de Nevers, fetched from Paris, was soon written off by the court at Milan as grave and cold, with little influence. They were mistaken.

Three of these original members of the Viceroy's household were to be found under his roof twenty years later. His biographer had arrived. This was fortunate, for with his elevation to the rank of Serene Highness his own memoir came to an abrupt close. But now that he had a first-class personal secretary, his papers were to be preserved and kept in order. Darnay could only find three from the Emperor to the prince in youth. After the secretary took up office enough was kept to fill ten printed volumes. These were almost without exception, from the Emperor, with the Viceroy's replies.[8]

The Viceroy studied a list of the principal Italians whom he must try to remember and recognize. *Melzi*, Grand Chancellor; *Codronchi*, Archbishop of Ravenna, Grand Almoner; *Litta*, High Chamberlain; *Caprara*, Grand Equerry; *Feneroli*, Chief Major-Domo; *Luosi*, Minister for Justice; *Bovara*, Ecclesiastic concerns; *Venori*, Treasury; *Prina*, Finance; *Pino*, Defence. (Unfortunately Pino and Prina could not pull together.) *Aldini* was Secretary of State and would reside in Paris and act as liason officer between the Emperor and the Viceroy. *Testi* was in charge of foreign relations, *Abrial* would supply legal advice. Painter in Chief was *Appiani*. He must also learn the names of his officers in charge of Finance, Taxation, Gendarmerie, Customs, Police, Roads and Bridges.

The Emperor's letter of farewell instructions for his stepson gave the impression, at first sight, of being an extraordinary rag-bag of entirely uncoordinated information and exhortation. It seemed to have been dictated, as no doubt it had, at top-speed and with impatience. Sorted out under headings it was a startling document.

"*Personal behaviour*

"You are young and inexperienced. Be very prudent and circumspect. Never give anyone your complete confidence. Never discuss your principal officials with anyone. If you ever find yourself speaking unnecessarily, from the heart, say to yourself 'I have made a mistake!' and remember not to err again. The less you talk the better. You are not well educated and lack experience. Learn to listen, and remember silence is often as impressive as knowledge. But never mind asking questions. You are only twenty-three, and however people flatter you, they are perfectly aware of your limitations.

"Do not attempt to imitate me. You must be more reserved.

"At public ceremonies, wherever you have Frenchmen and foreigners together, have a programme prepared to which you will adhere. Do not show too much regard for foreigners. There is nothing to be gained by it. Take greatest care never to expose yourself to any affront. If anything of the kind happens, nevertheless, do not hesitate. Whoever the offender, have him arrested on the spot . . . even if he is the Austrian or Russian Ambassador.

"*Italians*

"Cultivate the younger Italians. The older ones are all futile. Italians are naturally more deceitful than French. Show respect for them, and all the more as you become more disillusioned. (There really is not much difference between one nation and another. You will realize this gradually.) Your duty is to make my Italian subjects happy. Your first sacrifice will be to adopt some of their customs which you instinctively dislike. As Viceroy of Italy, but only then, forget you have the glory of being a Frenchman. Count yourself a failure if you do not succeed in convincing the Italians that you love them. They know there is no love without respect. Learn to speak good Italian. Go about. Show yourself. Single out valuable characters. Admire what they admire. Get to know them and their families.

"*Your Staff*

"Never form a clique. There is only one man here in Milan who really matters—the Minister of Finance (Prina). He knows his duty and is a worker. The rest, although they will know that I will support you, will be trying to get your measure. See that your orders are carried out; especially with regard to the army; never allow them to be disobeyed.

"The decree which I have issued explains the powers I have delegated to you; I have reserved to myself the most important—to direct your operations.

"You will find M. Méjean useful, so long as he does not attempt to make money, which he will not do if he realizes that you are keeping an eye on him, and that the least attempt will ruin him in my regard as well as yours. Pay him well, and see that he has hopes of promotion. But make it clear that you expect him to be available at all times. He will be no good if he comes on duty for stated hours only. You will have to scold him for a typically French failing—nostalgia for France.

"Never show my letters to a soul. It ought not even to be known that I wrote to you, or when. Keep one room sacrosanct—even from your secretaries.

"*Finance*
"Keep my house and stables in order. Make up accounts at least once a week.

"This is essential as they have no idea how to adminster such things in Italy.

"*Culture*
"Attempt to know the historical backgrounds of all the principal towns in my kingdom. Visit the fortresses and all the famous battlefields. It is probable that you will see fighting before you are thirty and it is a great asset to be familiar with the *terrain*.

"*Army*
"This is the one thing you can deal with directly and with knowledge. Hold a review in Milan once a month.

"*Spies*
"These are generally more trouble than they are worth. Never trust one. Military police will take care of the army. Milan is not an explosive centre. Most foreign ministers are, to put it bluntly, a sort of accredited spy. Keep them at arm's length. They always think more of those they see seldom than those who offer friendship and protection.

"*State Council*

"Do not preside often; you have not the experience to do this with success. I do not see why you should not attend while an Assessor presides, but from his ordinary seat. Your slight knowledge of legal affairs and the Italian tongue provide an adequate excuse for infrequent attendance. Never address the Council; you would be heard in silence, unquestioned, but they would see in a moment that you are not competent to enter into a discussion. No one can calculate the power of a prince so long as he keeps quiet; if he talks it must be with the knowledge that he is the greatest expert present.

"Work with your ministers twice a week, once with each separately, once in Council . . .

"You have an important assignment and will find it hard work. By degrees you will come to understand my outlook. I expect a daily report."

The Emperor ended this remarkable discourse with the words "Punish dishonesty ruthlessly. And don't allow smuggling in the French army." But these were far from being, as he declared, his last words of guidance. While he proceeded slowly towards France during the last three weeks of June, he sent his stepson no less than thirty-two further letters. His energy was colossal. During his Italian trip he had written nearly every day to his Minister for War, Admiral Decrès, and to Fouché. The Viceroy's mail did not escape Fouché's surveillance. The Emperor had to send his stepson a stinging rebuke for having written to a lady in Paris, who was known to the police and was mud in the gutter. This acquaintance must cease.[9]

His directions for the reorganizing of the Palazzo Reale were enough to make even a devoted reader's head swim. "When the Legislative Assembly has finished its session, stay for a month at Monza and have the repairs done at the palace in Milan. I think I told you what I wanted—to be able to walk through the present Great Apartments and reach through them those which face the cathedral. In this way, the bedroom originally given to the Empress will be the King's Bedroom. The room which used to be that unfortunate boudoir will be the King's Salon; the preceding room will be the Throne Room, and the Ladies in Waiting's Room will be the first salon. The room which Madame de la Rochefoucauld occupied will be the bedroom of the Empress, and of suitable size. My own apartments will be the small ones. The library will be there, also the archives, the map room and a little bedroom with bathroom leading straight to the room I use as office or study, in other words the last of the present series."

III

On June 11, 1805 the Viceroy of Italy sent his stepfather his first report.

"Sire,

"I have the honour to announce to Your Majesty what I have done since your departure. Yesterday morning, following your instructions, I assembled the Ministers. I reproached them for not having yet furnished me with the budget, for the lack of activity and order in their offices, and finally for their much too compliant attitude towards their subordinates. They were convinced of the truth of this and promised to redouble their efforts to please Your Majesty.

"I went on to work with the Secretary of State, M. Aldini . . ."

"Sire,

"I come this moment from the Council of State. According to Your Majesty's orders, I made a Consulting Counsellor preside. It was, today, Paradisi, (Director-General of Roads and Bridges) . . ."

He had received a complimentary deputation from the Legislative Assembly, headed by their President, and had replied in Italian.

"Called while yet young, by the heroes who preside over the destinies of France and of Italy, to live amongst you and represent you, I can to-day offer you no more than my hopes . . . Trust me, gentlemen, and the feelings which inspire me. Your hopes will not be disappointed. From this moment I am entirely at the disposal of the people whom I have the honour to govern, with the assistance of all the local authorities, and particularly the enthusiastic and enlightened legislative assembly, under the direction and guidance of our mighty sovereign. Mindful of the lessons I have learned from him and the example he has set me, I wish to emphasize that I have only one aim, which is the glory of the Kingdom of Italy and happiness of its people." He added that the words had been composed by Méjean, but he had told the colonel what he wanted to say. It was disappointing that the Emperor's reply, headed, "Brescia, June 12, 1805," opened, "My cousin, I have received your letter without date." Presently he was told to state not only the place and date, but the day of the week. There had been a letter from which the Emperor had been unable to make out whether the prince had been at Piacenza today or yesterday. He took this lesson so much to heart that he began to state even the hours at which he wrote—sometimes those dedicated by the native of Italy to the siesta, but more often after the palace had retired for the night.

The Emperor's letters ranged over an amazing field—the Budget (repeatedly), the Simplon Pass, the Code Napoléon, and the National Colleges at Pavia, Ferrara, Bologna and Modena (to be organized on the same lines as the Royal College, Fontainebleau). When he reached Mantua he found that both the ducal palace in the town and the hunting lodge called Palazzo del Te were in very poor condition. He said that it was his intention to appropriate them and the repairs must be charged to the civil list. Mantua was in a key-position "the bulwark of the kingdom". The Viceroy had better spend a month there every winter, say in November. Then he would be able to superintend the planting of many trees. It should not be difficult to discover where there was a nursery, and what were the best trees for this marshy country. There must be a big plantation round the Forum Bonaparte. The gardens at Milan also needed to be much enlarged. Mantua needed something else important—sanitation. With Bologna and Brescia the Emperor was pleased. They had energy. The foundry at Pavia was said to be very indifferent. "Let me know what jewels there are in the Treasury, suitable to be given as presents."[10]

It was while the Emperor stayed at Mantua that his last Bonaparte candidate for the throne of Italy backed out. M. Lucien arrived from Rome at six o'clock one evening. Duroc told Constant to stay in the room adjoining and see that nobody disturbed the brothers. The valet could not help hearing. M. Lucien violently refused to abandon the mother of his children. The Emperor shouted. "You are a fool to refuse a crown on account of a trollop." "At least my one is young and pretty," replied M. Lucien. Constant was very shocked at his master; but Prince Eugène had always been his hero. "To be sure nobody better deserved such an elevated position, by reason of his inherent nobility, generosity, courage and skill in administration. No prince was ever more sincere in wishing for the prosperity of the people over whom he was set to rule. I often saw how happy he was, how his natural gaiety lit up his features when he was succeeding in making those around him also happy."[11]

The sad misunderstanding over the taxation of the Legislative Assembly was the Viceroy's first serious mistake. The Emperor, as was often his custom when he was angry, told Duroc to send a letter expressing his deep displeasure. The miserable beginner could see at a glance that the Emperor was right and he was quite wrong. He had manifestly exceeded his authority. It was not for him to alter even details. "Your system of government is simple. The Emperor wills it thus." It was unfortunate that this was the moment when he was told with great *empressement* to prepare to receive his first royal guest. The eldest son and heir of the Elector of Bavaria was coming to Milan. He perfectly knew why he was instructed to show so much attention to this young man. Prince Ludwig was the brother of the Princess Auguste Amélie.

"Milan, August 5, 1805
"Sire,

"The Prince of Bavaria arrived here on Friday evening. He called on me on Saturday morning and I returned his visit on Sunday at noon. He dined with me the same day. I had thirty-five guests—ministers, counsellors of state, some ladies, generals etc. I have sent him a mounted escort, saddle-horses, and a box at the theatre. In fact I have been as civil as I could. He told me he much wanted to see the French cuirassiers, so I am taking him this week to Lodi.

"He is a young man of nineteen who seems more lively than most German princes. He has the misfortune to be deaf and to stammer which makes conversation difficult. He has been travelling for eight months, it appears with profit. He is attended by General Comte de Reuss and two chamberlains. The first-named has been with him only six weeks, and was a replacement. A previous mentor, who had perhaps been a little too strict, had got into disgrace with the prince, who had sent him away. The prince appears to be going on to France and hopes to be in Paris this autumn. He has spoken to me much about Your Majesty and much wishes to be presented. In accordance with your wishes I went out on Thursday to reside at Monza."

The travelling prince, who had been giving his keepers trouble, was unusual. He was a poet. He was not blind to female beauty, far from it, but the expenditure which was terrifying them was on antique statues. He had lost his heart to Ancient Rome. He would like to build neo-classic palaces, streets, cities, and fill them with objets d'art. With his wild red hair, luminous gaze, and tumbling speech he certainly had quality. There were strong signs, disguised by good manners, that he was anti-French. Queen Marie Antoinette had been his godmother, for he had been born when his father had been an officer in a French regiment stationed at Strasbourg. He attributed his deafness to French cannon-fire. The Viceroy had been incorrectly informed as to his date of arrival. He was staying in a hotel and had been to see Italian infantry drilling in the Forum Bonaparte, and Milan cathedral in detail, before he bestirred himself to pay his respects at the *parvenu* court. The attention shown to him had been impressive—many saloons filled with splendid uniforms, decoration in the latest French style, all as smart as paint.

At the dinner party he had sat between his host and the first lady of the Italian court, the famous beauty, the Marchesa Litta Visconti Arese, born Belgiojoso. Her husband was High Chamberlain and her family had once owned the palace on the Corso given by the Cisalpine Republic to the First Consul and now known as the Villa Bonaparte. The architect had been a Viennese appointed by the ubiquitous Piermarini. It stood on the outskirts of Milan near the famous Porta Orientale. The Bavarian prince wrote to his father after a further day of entertainment at Monza that this palace also was handsome, but the interior arrangements were very out of date. The establishment was in full swing, but there were no ladies. Before dinner he had walked with his host in the English garden. Afterwards the Viceroy had taken him for a drive to a little villa in the park, Mirabello. There was a maze at Monza and, after an ample meal on an August day, French gentlemen in embroidered coats and uniforms had played in it like children. It was explained that there was a maze at Malmaison. The French were simply loathed in Italy.[12]

Prince Ludwig returned to Milan after a tour of the lakes and saw the Brera, Sant' Ambrogio, Sant' Eustorgio, and the Last Supper, masterpiece of Leonardo in the refectory of Santa Maria delle Grazie.

It might be a coincidence, but on the very day that he first came in contact with a prince of very lofty family, renowned for their patronage of the arts, Eugène de Beauharnais ventured to suggest to his stepfather that the summer palace of the Dukes of Modena, some ten miles south-west of that city, would be a valuable acquisition. Sassuolo had struck him as the most beautiful spot on the other side of the Po.[13] Every room and staircase had mural decoration of a high order. There was a gallery of Fortune, of Justice, of the Seasons, of Jove, of Phaeton, of Music . . .

He was glad to say that he had at last established a nursery-garden at Monza from which he hoped to supply all the kingdom, notably with fruit trees which could perfectly well be grown, but had never been known. He was hard at work on the new town-planning for Milan. He was going to include a museum. There were hundreds of fine pictures available from the suppressed monasteries and churches. He wrote gravely of a library, a natural history museum, a medical museum, a school of design, sculpture and engraving . . .

At last, having made his mark, the Prince of Bavaria was gone. He had stayed on two days later than he had intended in order to see the celebrations for the Emperor's birthday. It gave his deputy true pleasure to be able to say that he had never witnessed such spontaneous enthusiasm as that shown on this occasion by the Milanese. There were cries of *"Vive l'Empereur"* before the fireworks. The Bavarian prince was coming to Paris by Geneva, Lyons, Marseilles and Bordeaux.

He had gone and he had done his duty, which was to obey orders from home to inspect what his sister scornfully called "le Boharnet." As long ago as last April she had sent him a gay little note headed "Eight o'clock" and opening "Good morning dear brother!" In it she had spoken most disrespectfully of her suitor, the stepson of the Emperor Napoleon. "What a disgrace that would be for our house!"[14]

IV

The Emperor's letters began to be dated from the Camp at Boulogne again. He had hurried to Paris after receiving serious news. His acquisition of Genoa and Lucca had accelerated something inevitable, a formal third Coalition against him by England, Russia and Austria. But after a fortnight at St. Cloud and Fontainebleau he went up, as he had always planned, to the Iron Coast.

"My fleets," he told Eugène "have arrived at Martinique whence they have drawn Nelson and the English squadrons. They have left for another destination." It seemed probable that the invasion of England, following the annihilation of Nelson, might be the next news received in Milan.

August peace and warmth settled down upon a waiting Europe. Josephine had gone for her usual cure in the Vosges. She wrote to her son from Plombières.

"No, my dear Eugène, I have not forgotten you, I think of you all the time—what you are doing, your pleasures, your pains. As to the last, I can assure you that in spite of appearances to the contrary I am more upset than you." (The explosion over his wretched *gaffe* about the taxation was still running its course). "The Emperor seems to me always pleased with you." (But she had to admit that there had been one more complaint of his behaviour—minor, of course.) "For the rest he is convinced of your devotion to him and loves you tenderly. It is not the same in his own family. They have heard of your appointment with great grief. Murat keeps on fawning. His wife has been ill and appears to have undergone a change in disposition. She has adopted an attitude which she calls dignity (which to me entails composure). This effort does not prosper. Everyone knows her jealousy of us. If only they would behave themselves properly they could not have better friends than us.

"The Emperor is always amiable towards me, and I for my part do all that I can to please him. No more jealousy, my dear Eugène. This is absolutely true. This makes him happy and me even happier.

"I can't give you any up to date political news. The situation is a mystery which the Emperor allows no one to penetrate. He is at the moment still at Boulogne. All I know is that he kept a courier waiting eight days before he sent him off to me. You have no doubt heard that the marriage of the Prince of Baden is broken off, which gives me great hopes of the lady (you will know whom I mean). I have seen her portrait. She could not be more beautiful.

Your sister is well, also her children. I had the second one at St. Cloud. He is absolutely sweet. Louis is the same as ever. I long to see you, my dear Eugène, although it may not be till the middle of the winter. That was the date when you held out hopes of coming to visit me. How happy that will make your mother! You know my dear son how I grudge every day separated from you and how my eyes fill with tears whenever I think of you, or someone talks of you. I have not been able to write before since my arrival because I was exhausted and tormented by visitors. Besides, I had no news, and now shall be writing every week. I have arranged with Lavalette to take my letters. Good-bye, my good Eugène, the best of sons. Your mother embraces you with all her heart and loves you dearly. Say everything polite to Madame Litta and to Méjean."[15]

Despite her promises it was a month before he heard from her again. Hortense was a much better correspondent. Her gentle letters purled on, like a village brook. She had been down with her darling elder son to stay at Boulogne Camp. The Emperor had asked them and Louis had actually said she might go for eight days. They had stayed at Pont de Briques with the Murats. It had not been very comfortable, to be sure, two or three in a bedroom and in such hot weather. She had dropped asleep after dinner one night playing chess with the Emperor. The strong sun and sea air had made her feel perfectly stupid. But she could not have enjoyed herself more or have been more fêted.

She had been to call upon M. Emmery, the kind Dunkirk banker who had helped Maman in their saddest days, getting her rents from Martinique. Madame Ney had given a fête in her honour—so pretty, all the floral decorations arranged in her initials. But they had had to leave the ballroom in haste. "The Emperor has embarked for England!" Everyone had dashed along the highway to Boulogne. It was a false alarm, another exercise. The Emperor had superintended the embarkation and returned home at dawn. He had been annoyed at her departure. "Very well, madame, go, since you fear to vex your husband more than to please me." She had joined Louis at St. Amand on the borders of Hainault. He was taking another cure. For her own part she believed that the shock of hearing of Eugène's appointment had really done her good. She had forced herself to admit that his fate was perhaps worse than hers, because he was far from all his family and with nobody to whom he could open his heart. Like her mother, she had been listening to gossip. "For the moment, dear Eugène, you must live in hopes. If the project which the Emperor has in mind comes to pass, you can perhaps look forward to a happy home. If she is, as people say, a being created to capture a heart, you may look forward to great happiness."[16]

He was to become, however, even more unhappy, for when news did arrive from the Iron Coast it was of a campaign in which he would not take part. A letter from the Emperor dated August 27 told him that in view of the vast preparations being made by Austria he was sending Marshal Massena down to Italy in command. There were two French generals already there, but neither St. Cyr in Naples nor Jourdan had anything like the prestige of Massena. He told his stepson to get off at once in "a sort of incognito" to visit all the fortresses in which warlike stores and rations should have been accumulating steadily for three months. There should now also be armed brigs on the three lakes of Garda, Lugano and Maggiore. The Emperor's address to his Army of England was to be more colourful.

"Brave Soldiers of the Boulogne Camp, you are not going to England. The Emperor of Austria, bribed with English gold, has declared war on us. His army has crossed prohibited frontiers. Bavaria is invaded! Soldiers! new laurels await you beyond the Rhine!"

He did not mention that Admiral Villeneuve's fleet had retired to Cadiz at the moment when his presence had been essential to escort the Boulogne flotilla to England. His last line on August 31 was that the Grande Armée was in full march. They should be on the Rhine by September 1.

Both his mother and his sister did what they could for the Viceroy. The Emperor only teased Hortense when she ventured to mention the name of Eugène. He had formed rather a habit of teasing her. When she had tried to pump him about the prospects of getting the Princess Auguste, not daring, of course to mention the name, just suggesting Eugène needed a wife, he had been intolerable. He had seemed to be struck with the idea as a novelty, and said if Eugène was coming to Paris this winter, they must begin to try to find a little Parisienne for him. He now said, "And does she want her little brother to go to be killed?" She stiffly said that she was sure he would have been glad to serve under Massena. Josephine wrote one of her nervous letters. The Emperor would not allow her to go with him on this campaign. She was to stay in Strasbourg. She was terrified of something happening to him and foresaw an awful fate for her beloved children left to the mercy of the Bonapartes. Murat had marched with the Grande Armée. Louis had succeeded him as Governor of Paris. If Italy was to be the principal theatre of war as everyone said, her son might be in great danger. She remembered dramatically that when she had said farewell to him she had had one of her presentiments. "Write to me soon my dearest son ... With what feelings do I trace the horrible word 'Good-bye' "

Italy was not to be the principal theatre of the new war. Marshal Massena drooped, smiling dreadfully, over the hand of a young Viceroy and professed himself the most attached servant of His Imperial Majesty and of his Serene Highness, the Emperor's stepson. He had got Josephine to write a letter on his behalf commending him to her son's hospitality. He made, at their first long interview, a very safe pressing offer. He invited the Viceroy to visit his headquarters. "The chosen son of Victory" was now fifty and looked much more for he was spare and gnarled. He had begun life as the son of a small wine merchant on the Côte d'Azur, and his first employment was said to have been as cabinboy, but he had soon deserted the sea for land. He had coal-black eyes and hair, and a yellow skin stretched tight over high cheekbones. His nose had a hook in it. He had been Bonaparte's most trusted divisional general in his first Italian campaign. In those days Italy had belonged to Austria and he had just taken all he needed. Now it belonged to the Emperor and the inhabitants wailed on a piercing note when they found their possessions commandeered. He also asked the Viceroy for large and immediate financial assistance. The rapacity of Marshal Massena was notorious. The Viceroy wrote in anxiety to his stepfather, and the Emperor who knew his Marshals to a hair, replied that Massena must be sent a fine coach and six, also four fine saddle horses and a subsidy of 50,000 francs. ("Charge this to my civil list.") He must be told these were a gift from the Emperor in view of his great services, past and to come. The Archduke Charles was at Padua with eighty thousand troops, and the Archduke John was said to be on his way through the Tyrol with reinforcements. "Encourage Massena."[17]

Massena departed for Mantua and concluded an armistice with the Archduke Charles, for which the Emperor had given him powers. He then waited for nine days until a despatch arrived telling him that the Emperor had cut off and surrounded Marshal Mack at Ulm. Austria had fatally decided that sixty thousand troops would suffice for Mack in Germany until he was joined by the Russian advance guard. But the Emperor had moved like lightning. He had counted on Prussia lingering until Austria showed signs of victory. He had called up Bernadotte who was in Hanover with an army of occupation. He had been joined by allied troops from Bavaria, Württemberg and Hesse. Mack capitulated on October 2 with fifty thousand men. Kutosov, in charge of the Prussian and Austrian forces gave severe punishment to one French division (Mortier's) but had to leave Vienna unguarded.

The Grande Armée entered it, ragged and footsore but triumphant, on November 14. As soon as he heard the good news from Ulm, Massena broke off the armistice and attacked at Caldiero on the Adige. The engagement was claimed as a French victory; in any case the Archduke Charles withdrew into the Tyrol. The troops coming to meet him there had been called back to the Iller.

The Viceroy, who had been told to show activity, found plenty to occupy him. He sent his own surgeon, in the grand manner of ancient wars, to attend the wounds of the Prince de Rohan, an Austrian divisional general. He continued to send off daily newsletters to the Emperor. After October 18 these included bulletins from the Army of Italy. He wrote that he had sent Colonel Méjean up to Massena's headquarters to report and he enclosed the result. With the Emperor's approval he had empowered an experienced and high-ranking Piedmontese, the Marchese Luigi Arborio di Gattinara di Breme, to deal with the whole problem of commandeered and requisitioned material and payments. The Marchese had been Ambassador from the King of Sardinia to the courts of Naples and Vienna, and was to be promoted Italian Minister for Home Affairs.

Eugène kept in close touch as he had been instructed, and also sent on all news, to the Emperor's eldest sister in Lucca and Cardinal Fesch in Rome. He inspected and ordered fifty thousand shoes for the new Italian conscripts. He ordered the bells of the cathedrals of the kingdom to be rung in joy for the surrender of Ulm. He formed camps at Bologna, Modena and Reggio for a newly-raised National Guard. The Emperor had impressed upon him the necessity of keeping open the Simplon and Gotthard passes so that couriers could get through, and if possible vehicles and artillery. He had heard from the Emperor from Strasbourg on October 1 ("Very fine weather!") from Elchingen next day, from Louisbourg on the 4th. After that silence fell for a fortnight, and during this anxious time he took the opportunity for a three days' expedition up to the top of Lake Maggiore, the foot of the Simplon. It was mid-October, the loveliest date in the year for autumn colour. There was dazzling fresh snow on towering heights outlined against cloudless blue skies. The Emperor had suggested with unusual mildness, that if he was not too busy, it would be a good thing to get, while he was still young, a picture of this *terrain* which would remain imprinted on his memory for life. The Gotthard would mean going on foot. The Simplon new works could be surveyed now (the Emperor hoped) from horseback. The young man drew rein entranced when he saw the new road ordered by the Emperor, and thought again how great a man he had for stepfather. "Sire, I have the honour to report that I have returned this morning from the trip I made up to the Simplon. The road is as fine as I expected: artillery will be able to use it very soon. I doubt, however, if it will be passable during the period of heavy snow. Apart from that, the whole piece of work is an admirable monument, worthy to be classed with the other works of Your Majesty." His own regiment had marched with the Grande Armée. Colonel Morland would look after it well. It had almost certainly been in action by now.

He inspected and evacuated hospitals. He issued a proclamation ending dramatically, "People of Italy! Your King counts upon you; trust him. Think of his record as a military commander, as the scourge of double-dealers, remember his brilliance as a general, the loyalty and bravery and success which he inspires, and finally the cause for which he fights."

M. de Talleyrand most civilly sent him news of a first French victory at a small place called Dertingen (five thousand prisoners) followed by the surrender of Ulm. The Emperor added a friendly informal postscript in his own hand to the official bulletin dated October 18. This arrived in the middle of the night at Monza twenty-four hours later. After that came another dreadful silence, this time for five weeks. Hortense believed that the Emperor had written to Josephine that he had never known a quicker or more brilliant campaign. He had only the Russians now to defeat. "The moment I am at ease in my mind about Italy, I shall be giving Eugène employment."

Hortense was not, like her brother, a rock of strength in time of trouble. Eugène never failed to repeat to his stepfather, in nearly every letter, that the people of His Majesty's kingdom of Italy continued in perfect spirits and loyalty. Hortense wailed that

Paris was so *triste*—almost empty—no friends left. Jerome Bonaparte came to see her and wept about having been made to put away his wife. The poor woman had not gone back to America as the Emperor believed. She had gone to enemy England and given birth to a son, Jerome Napoleon Bonaparte, in an obscure hamlet called Camberwell. Jerome sailed with a squadron to destroy British commerce in the West Indies . . . Louis had orders what to do when the English landed in France . . .

Her brother sent his portrait to Hortense, and she replied in one of her sudden gusts of short-lived high spirits that everyone in Paris expected he was going to become King of Italy when this campaign was over, and make a splendid match. The Baronne de Cetto, who was a Wittelsbach connection, and wife of the Bavarian minister in Paris, had told her that when the name of the French prince was mentioned in the presence of the Princess Auguste she changed colour. Her brother, Prince Ludwig, who had visited Eugène in Milan had been enchanted by him. (The Viceroy would never have guessed it.)

She wrote this on November 21 and enclosed an account of the battle at Cadiz—it was to be called Trafalgar in England.

Josephine showed more courage. She congratulated her son on the exploits of the Army of Italy. She had no doubt that the moment was drawing near when the Emperor would send for her. She heard that the Elector of Bavaria was giving orders for great fêtes to be prepared for her in Munich. M. de Talleyrand had sent her such a sweet letter telling her how highly the Emperor spoke of her son. "It is astonishing what progress this young man is making. He is already more capable of governing than the Imperial Arch-Treasurer Le Brun." M. de Talleyrand had instructed her to burn his letter because it spoke also of a marriage which was interesting to her as a loving mother. She had met the Bavarian prince Ludwig, and he had spoken much of his admiration of her son and sent polite messages.

How times had changed! With his mother's letter came a neat little note saying that M. de Choiseul ardently desired to place his son with the Viceroy as an aide de camp, or if that was impossible, as a second lieutenant in an Italian regiment. The young man was a very good subject and the Empress had promised her protection. It was from her chief lady in waiting, Madame de la Rochefoucauld. People had been astonished that this appointment had gone to a lady no longer young and almost deformed.

But her manners like her name were very distinguished, and she was perfectly entitled to address the Viceroy as "my dear Eugène." For when he had been a shabby little boy, pushed from pillar to post, his gay father and he had almost lived upon the de la Rochefoucaulds in their second town palace on the quayside on the Seine. Madame de la Rochefoucauld *née* Pyvard de Chastulle had been his father's first cousin.

Her husband, in his later years said reminiscently that Josephine could not speak the truth. But she always lied with elegance, and sometimes from kindness. She replied dreadfully untruthfully, a fortnight later, to an enquiry from Hortense whom she loved but had always thought a fool. No silly gossip must be allowed at this eleventh hour to upset a most desirable match for her even-more loved Eugène.

"I am extremely surprised at the rumours of which you speak. Surely, if there had really been a question of your brother's marriage you are the first person whom I should have told. Of course I did hear when I was at Strasbourg that German newspapers were talking about it. I remember that at that time everybody believed it. I found myself the only person not in the secret. You know very well, my dear, that the Emperor, who has never said a word to me on the subject, would not marry off Eugène without telling me. However, I accept the public rumours. I should much like her as a daughter in law. She has a charming character and is as lovely as an angel; she combines a beautiful face with as beautiful a shape as I have ever beheld."[18]

The Emperor had told her to come on by way of Karlsruhe and Stuttgart to Munich where he would join her, and she had left Strasbourg on November 28. Her last duties there had been delightful. Her husband had given her almost *carte blanche* to buy presents for the Bavarian royal ladies—stepmother aged thirty, two girls, eighteen and fourteen. She had been in her element.

But the Emperor had still to fight his great battle and he now had a very long line of communication. He had sent for Bernadotte to march through supposedly still-neutral Prussia. On the morning of December 2 the young Czar, who had just arrived on the scene, received optimistic reports that Bonaparte's forces were exhausted and wavering. The Allied army advanced on Austerlitz in Moravia some fifteen miles outside Brno, and there, as the sun rose after a foggy morning, the Grande Armée cut it in two.[19]

The Bridegroom
His Imperial Highness the Prince Eugène-Napoleon,
Arch-Chancellor of State of the French Empire, Viceroy
of Italy, aged twenty five, engraved by P. M. Alix after
the portrait by C. Schule in the collection of Her
Imperial Majesty the Empress Josephine
By permission of the Bibliothèque Nationale, Paris

CHAPTER NINE

The Princess Auguste
1806

I

HE GOT his first news of the Battle of Austerlitz from Mortier. The Marshal's aide de camp arrived in Milan on December 9. There had been cavalry charges which would be celebrated in history. Morland, commanding the *Chasseurs* of the Guard, had been fatally wounded. His body was being brought back to lie in his native soil and an avenue in Paris was to be named after him. The engagement had been an affair of sixty-five thousand French against eighty-two thousand Austrians and Russians. About a fifth of the Grande Armée who had marched from Boulogne had perished, but compared to the Allied losses in that battle their ten per cent had been very light. The *Chasseurs* had lost two officers, and eleven non-commissioned officers and troopers killed. Seventeen officers and fifty men had been wounded. The regiment had a hundred and fifty-three horses put out of action.

Once communications were re-established letters from the Emperor began to come in regularly again. It was a relief, for a fortnight earlier the Russians and English, encouraged by Trafalgar, had landed an expeditionary force of twenty thousand in Naples, and King Ferdinand, who had been hesitating, had abandoned his neutrality. His timing meant that he went into exile, and was succeeded by Joseph Bonaparte as monarch. Massena went to establish him. The Czar, staggered and humiliated, was retiring to his own country. He had agreed to the Emperor Francis asking for an armistice and a separate peace. The terms of the Peace of Pressburg were bitter for Austria. She lost Venetia, Istria, Dalmatia, the Tyrol and Vorarlberg. Bavaria, Württemberg and Baden were to be independent; so she had been pushed out of Germany as well as Italy. Prussia, by the Treaty of Schönbrunn got Hanover in exchange for Anspach and Neuchâtel. Berthier became Sovereign Prince of Neuchâtel.

As he had always promised, the Emperor relieved his stepson of Massena at the earliest possible moment. On Christmas Eve the Viceroy received official confirmation that he was appointed Commander in Chief in Italy, including the new provinces relinquished by Austria which would need much attention. He had gone down to Padua to inspect the Italian troops there—seventy thousand men, three divisions. Comte de Bellegarde, Austria's vaunted cavalry general, had retired by sea to Trieste. The Archduke Charles had left some warlike stores in his haste, but a ruined countryside. Marshal Massena had left nothing that could be turned into money, not a gold piece, not a sequin.

The year 1805 passed out quietly. The Emperor had promised that it would be one of great events and he had kept his word. M. de Rémusat, toiling up from Strasbourg to Vienna, was horrified by the condition of the countries through which he passed. "The land still reeked of slaughter. Devastated villages, roads encumbered by corpses brought before my eyes all the horrors of war. The distress of the vanquished added an element of danger to the discomfort of this journey so late in the season ... In the accounts of victories only the bright side was shown to the public."

Amongst the things to vanish with 1805 was the Republican calendar. It had hung on long enough. "Sire," reported the Viceroy on January 1, 1806, "This morning I went to the basilica of St. Antony, the most beautiful church in Padua. I heard Mass and a Te Deum sung to thank *le bon Dieu* for your victories and the peace which your genius and valour has given to Europe. I was accompanied by the ministers for war and finance and all the officers of my household who happened to be with me, in fact by all the generals in Padua. The service was devout, noble, much the finest I have ever attended."

The rejoicing crowds in the narrow old streets had been great, and this evening he had gone to a little ball given by his officers for the ladies of Padua, but had left after two hours so as to write to the Emperor. He reckoned that his stepfather should have joined his mother in Munich. On January 2 he got a document which took him aback. The shock, although the news was not entirely unexpected, was great. He had sent a messenger with New Year good wishes to his mother. The man now returned without a reply from her, but with a communication from someone called Boulanger, Inspector of Posts at Munich.

"Monseigneur,
"Her Majesty the Empress has commanded me to write a second time to Your Highness to acknowledge the message from Your Highness, and to confirm my first despatch in which Her Majesty commanded me to make the official announcement of your marriage to the Princess Auguste of Bavaria."

This turned out to be one of Josephine's not quite truthful excuses. She had not written to anyone for three weeks and then had been conscience-stricken lest her son should not hear the great good news first from anyone but her. It was typical that she should have taken this extraordinary means, when as he pointed out to her gently: "There are ten thousand people around you who would have been pleased to bring it personally." Her well-meant effort was closely followed by a confirmation in a familiar hand brought by an Imperial courier. Prince Eugène turned in his hands, in his dark Paduan palace, a porcelain coffee cup of fine German manufacture (the Royal Nymphenburg factory). It was decorated with the picture of a girl, who if the artist had not lied, was as beautiful as any he had ever seen.

The Emperor's letter was curt.

"December 31st 1805.
"My Cousin,
"I am arrived in Munich. I have arranged your marriage with the Princess Auguste; it has been announced. This morning the princess paid me a visit and we had quite a long conversation. She is very pretty. I am enclosing a coffee cup with her portrait but it does not do her justice."

The future bridegroom's reply was prompt.[1]

"Sire,
"I have the honour to inform your Majesty that I have received the coffee cup and have written to the Prince Ludwig of Bavaria, the only member of my future family with whom I am acquainted. The picture on the cup is wonderfully beautiful. I shall do my best to make the original happy. I have begged the Prince to lay me at the feet of his sister, the Princess."

By the next courier from Munich he got his marching orders.

"2 a.m. Jan. 3rd.

"My Cousin,

"Twelve hours at latest after the receipt of this letter you will set off for Munich in all possible haste. Take care to arrive as soon as possible, then you may still find me there. Leave your command with whichever of your divisional generals you consider most capable and honest. It will be useless for you to bring a large suite. Leave at once, incognito, as much to avoid danger as to avoid delays. Send me a courier to announce to me that you will be arriving twenty-four hours after him."

The Emperor seemed to be in one of his dictatorial rushes. He added a P.S. "One hour after you get this send me a courier with the day of your arrival."

The bridegroom's reply was suitably prompt.

"Sire,

"I have the honour to announce to your Majesty that I have this instant received your letter which leads me to believe I shall have the pleasure of seeing you. It is now 8 a.m. I leave this evening at 8 p.m. I expect to arrive on Friday at latest. I must once again thank you Majesty for all your goodness to me.

"I have pitched upon General Miollis to command in my absence, but as he is still at Mantua I must at once busy myself to supply him with detailed instructions on the situation here, military and administrative."[2]

It was Monday, January 6, 1806, and long before eight p.m. it would be pitch dark. The Tyrolean passes had a bad name both for brigands and road surface, and directly after a war were likely to be worse than usual in both respects. One of M. de Talleyrand's messengers carrying secret despatches had been set upon by a typical band of post-war desperadoes recently, and General Lemarois, while asleep at an inn, had been robbed of all the army pay he was carrying. But this last event was considered rather careless and disgraceful, and the weather was still open.

The bridegroom took with him on his wild ride only one officer, his senior aide de camp Colonel d'Anthouard, who might reasonably hope for promotion if he delivered his young master safely at the altar. The faithful secretary Darnay, and two Italian noblemen, the Conti Bentivoglio and Mereningo, were to follow next day, accompanied by a chamberlain and groom, and had orders to bring the Viceroy's full uniform. For he had very little doubt that he would return to Italy a married man.

II

Maximilian Joseph, first King of Bavaria, was an enlightened prince of a cheerful aspect. He was taller, burly and more robust than his artistic heir, and of a ruddy complexion. He liked to walk about his capital on foot, and in the country, to visit startled cottagers in their hamlets. He had known his ups and downs. He had married late, a princess of Hesse-Darmstadt, who had died prematurely leaving him with two sons and two daughters, Ludwig, Auguste, Caroline and Karl-Theodor, all under ten. He had naturally re-married as soon as possible. In those days he had been Duke of Deux Ponts, a prince of the house of Wittelsbach which had given two Emperors to Europe. But he had been a representative of a younger (Birkenfeld) branch and though the blood of Charlemagne flowed in his veins, no more than a colonel in the French army.

Prince Max, as he had been affectionately known, had been exceedingly popular with his troops. He had not at birth had expectations of any more resounding title. When nearly forty he had succeeded an elder brother. During the French Revolution he had transferred to the Austrian service: his duchy was overrun by French revolutionary troops. He was on the move for five years. During this time, on the extinction of the Sulzbach line of his renowned family, he had become Elector Palatine. But here again his properties were a battleground. His own sympathies had always been rather French than Austrian and he had an extremely able opportunist first minister who was a French *émigré* — the Comte de Montgelas. Acting on the advice of this character, somewhat against his will, he had signed a treaty of peace and alliance with Napoleon Bonaparte, First Consul. When Bavaria had been invaded in September 1805, her troops had joined themselves to those of the Emperor Napoleon. The promised reward for this was to be that on the day after the signing of the Treaty of Pressburg, the Elector of Bavaria was raised to the rank of king.

But this was not entirely a mark of gratitude. There was a price to be paid—a princess to be given in exchange for a crown. In this direction, however, there was a hitch.

His second marriage had been to a lady with illustrious connections. Princess Caroline of Baden had not been a beauty, she was slightly hard-featured, but her sisters had married the Czar, Alexander I and King Gustavus IV of Sweden. She had an only and much younger beloved brother, Karl. It had been her dream that he should marry her elder stepdaughter, Auguste. The young people were of perfectly suitable age and had long known and liked one another. By January 1806, he was twenty and she was just eighteen. But mentally and physically they were not at all fairly matched, as Prince Karl was very slow and pathetically overweight. His good natured face was cherubic; with his staring pale blue eyes and chubby red cheeks he was said to resemble a baby-boy-doll.

As long ago as April 1804 Count Thiard, Imperial Chamberlain, had been searching the courts of Germany, looking for marriageable princesses for the Bonapartes—royal brides for the Emperor's stepson, and presently also for his brother Jerome. It was hardly possible for anyone not familiar with the hidebound etiquette of these establishments to realize how interlocked they were by dynastic marriages and with what disdain they looked down upon the *parvenu* French Imperial régime. The lovely Queen Louise of Prussia, who was a niece of Max Joseph, called Napoleon "Moppel" which in German slang meant a looney. (She was to rue it.) English cartoons and newspapers had always been violently vulgar and abusive, and gave the impression that the Emperor was a sort of filibustering scarecrow and Josephine a daughter of joy. French was the language of the Bavarian court and the king's eldest daughter was always called "Auguste" in the family circle, but both the elder royal children were full of enthusiasm for Germany as a coming first-rate power. They wrote little notes to one another in that language. When his sister's fate seemed settled Ludwig could still bring himself to say no more in praise of "*le Boharnet*" than that he was "unquestionably much the best of those French."

The fame of the beauty of the Princess Auguste of Bavaria had of course brought other suitors. There had been the Crown Prince George of Mecklenburg, brother of the Queen of Prussia. The princess, at sixteen, had quite liked him. He was a first cousin;

but he had turned out to have a ballet-dancer gaining rapid possession of his fortunes, and was said to have been a lover of Bonaparte's sister, Pauline. A French nobleman in the Dutch service, Prince Charles de Croy, had been so much struck that he had disguised himself as a coachman and had hoped to persuade the young princess to elope in his carriage. Prince Ludwig, though romantic, had declined forwarding this proposal and Princess Auguste knew nothing of it.

There were three powerful adversaries of the Beauharnais match and all were very close to her. The widowed mother of Prince Karl was understandably furious at the thought of her son being slighted. His sister, the stepmother of the princess, had a double reason for disapproval of Bonaparte and all his works. While the Condé regiment had been stationed at her father's court at Karlsruhe she had formed a romantic attachment for the last of the house of Condé, the young Duc d'Enghien. To her, the Emperor Napoleon would never be anything but a murderer.

The third opponent of the French suitor was curiously enough always addressed by the princess by a French *petit nom*. The Baronin von Wurmb was simply *"ma chére."* Frederika von Wurmb, originally governess and now first lady in waiting of the princess, came of an aristocratic stock from Hesse. Her story was unusual. Her mother had followed General Count Clement Maupeou (cousin of Louis XV's chancellor) to France, after the Seven Years War, and upon the death of her first husband had married him. Frederika had become a Catholic and lived in the household of the Princesse de Rohan, niece of the Cardinal. The princess Auguste also was a devout Catholic, although her mother had been Protestant. On her death-bed Max Joseph's first wife delivered her children to a spiritual counsellor whom she knew to be sage and honest—Joseph Anton Sambuga. His father had been an Italian who had wandered into Bavaria and stuck there.

Against these three ladies were ranged Count Otto (born a German, but the Imperial Minister in Munich), a skilful diplomatist who had performed the almost impossible task of getting England to accept the Peace of Amiens, and Baron von Gravenreuth, a Bavarian diplomatist, second-in-command of the Comte de Montgelas, who was an extraordinary-looking old man with the slyest smile and longest nose ever seen outside the pages of a children's fairy book. They consulted Paris, tussled with the Elector and Electress and saw to it that whispers of someone much more adventurous than poor Karl of Baden reached the ears of the princess. Still she seemed unconvinced, and with reason. Baden was so near to her old home, so familiar, such lovely country, and Karl had a heart of gold. His mother brought him up to stay at Munich again. The suit of the Beauharnais seemed hopeless. But at this point M. de Talleyrand also moved. He annihilated a feeble effort to fob off the Emperor Napoleon with the second Bavarian princess, Charlotte, a gentle girl of fourteen. She was not pretty, and like her brother Ludwig was badly marked by the smallpox.

The Empress Josephine arrived in Munich, and a French-woman who understood perfectly the art of pleasing let it be known that the Viceroy of Italy was the best and tenderest of sons and brothers, adored by his little nephews, courageous, talented, generous to a fault . . . His portraits seemed to bear her out that he was at any rate handsome. Her chief lady, Madame de la Rochefoucauld, spoke equally adoringly of her dear cousin. The Beauharnais, it must be remembered, were of the old French nobility. Talleyrand had been rewarded for his efforts in negoti-ating the Peace of Pressburg by the principality of Benevento, a small enclave which had previously been a papal state in the kingdom of Naples. He never went there, but henceforward he was officially styled the Prince of Benevento, though everyone still thought of him as Talleyrand. The Prince of Benevento had heard from General Graf Gyula in Vienna that a daughter of the Emperor Francis, a Habsburg princess, had been actually sug-gested for Prince Eugène by the Austrian Foreign Minister, Baron Thugut. But the Archduchess Marie Louise was only just fifteen and also showed signs of having survived smallpox.

The arrival of the Empress Josephine heightened the tension in the Residenz at Munich, which was really more of a little city than a palace, and seemed to have recovered with great resilience from Austrian occupation. Max Joseph had most amiable manners. He always took care to remember and commend himself to the leading domestic attendants of other crowned heads. While Mademoiselle d'Avrillon, chief *femme de chambre* to the Empress, was superintending the unpacking of her employer's enormous and fascinating wardrobe, an elderly Bavarian person came rambling in to ask her in perfect French if the Empress had everything to which she was accustomed. Was there nothing further the Empress needed? Were the staff happy? Mademoiselle d'Avrillon wrote him down as a very superior confidential steward, and was astonished when she saw him next day visiting her mistress. (When the Emperor came in, the King of Bavaria shook hands warmly with his valet, which gave Constant a fine anecdote for his memoirs.)

Princess Murat was the next arrival and was lodged in the Palais Herzog Wilhelm to await her husband and father. But the Emperor did not appear, and on Christmas Day came an intimation that the Grand Marshal of the Household, General Duroc, old comrade in arms of the Beauharnais, was about to present himself, bearing seasonal wishes and the official proposal for the hand of the Princess Auguste.

Montgelas and Gravenreuth sorted out the preliminaries with Maret and Otto. The prince was to be adopted by the Emperor as a son, and as heir-presumptive to the throne of Italy. He was to be raised to the rank of Imperial Highness and known henceforward as Eugène Napoléon de France. He would receive meanwhile an independent principality in Italy—the duchy of Parma, Piacenza or some such—and continue to act as Viceroy with an establishment suitable to this office (six palaces).[3] The suggested marriage portion amounted to the enormous sum of three hundred thousand florins, and the dowry to four thousand million florins. The marriage was to take place within the next few weeks. Sadly but nobly, Max Joseph approached his desk. Up to December 17 he had been telling Talleyrand that he knew nothing of his daughter breaking off her engagement.

"If there was the slightest glimmer of hope, my darling and dearly beloved Auguste, that you could ever marry Karl, I would not come to you on my knees begging you to relinquish him. Still less, dearest child, would I ask you to marry the future King of Italy if it were not that when peace comes that particular kingdom will be guaranteed by all the powers, that I know the sterling qualities of Prince Eugène, and that I am sure he could make you happy.

"Consider, dearest child, that if you marry him you will not only help your father, but bring happiness to your brothers and your country, since they wish nothing so much as to see this union. To show you that the match is a good one, I should mention that Baron de Thugut, who unfortunately for us has taken the helm again, has already offered the elder daughter of the Emperor. It cuts me to the heart, my dearest child, to see you so unhappy, but

I rely on the affection and the attachment which you have always shown for your father, and I know that you would not wish to disappoint him in his declining years. Consider, dear Auguste, that a refusal by you would turn the Emperor Napoleon from a firm friend into an equally constant enemy. Spare me the anguish of having to attempt an explanation to him which could prove fatal to me in my decrepit state of health.

"Send me a letter with your answer, or give your brother a message. God well knows that I long only for your welfare and that no one loves you more than your faithful father who is also your best friend."

His duty done, Max Joseph took to his bed and announced he was not able to see anyone. He really did feel extremely ill, especially since his spouse on returning from her Christmas service had flopped down beside him and wailed that the heart of Auguste would be broken.

The letter of the Princess was a model.

"My dear sweet Father,

"I must break off my engagement to Prince Karl of Baden. I will do this, however much it costs me, if the peace of mind of my beloved parent and the happiness of a people demands it. But I cannot give my hand to Prince Eugène if peace has not been made and if he is not recognized as King of Italy.

"I put my future in your hands, dear papa. However hard it is to do so, the blow is softened when I realize that the sacrifice I am making is for my father and my country.

"Your child comes to you on her knees to ask for your blessing. It will help me to bear my future with resignation."

She also wrote very kindly to poor Prince Karl.

"Good Prince,

"This is the first bad thing I have ever had to say to you, and it will be the last; for our lives must be henceforward for ever apart. My grief is inexpressible. But I must obey the command of my father and listen to the voice of my country."

She had been told that Prince Karl had vowed that if he could not have her he would hereafter live solitary. This must not be. She wished him well, for ever, and his beloved country. She

suggested that he should think now, as of a wife who had died, of
"Your unlucky friend
Auguste, Princess of Bavaria."[4]

III

The Emperor arrived in Munich at last towards midnight on
December 30 and was given a tumultuous welcome. He was accompanied by a torchlight procession to the Residenz where
military and royalty had been at attention since eight p.m.

Late though the hour was he tackled his host at once on the
subject of the marriage. He had been furious when he learned that
the contract was not yet signed. He was perhaps chilled and
weary. He certainly said some unforgiveable things. When
Max Joseph expressed his satisfaction that his troops had been able
to come to his aid, the Emperor said "If they had not, I should
have put in Murat as king." Max Joseph's manners were simple
but he was a Wittelsbach, and proud of it and he loved Bavaria.
He did not forget the unfortunate boast. The Emperor had the
Baronin von Wurmb presented to him. He must have heard that
she had great influence with the princess, for to her too he said
something unforgiveable. He stared at her and asked "Has the
Princess Auguste been to bed with the Prince of Baden?" The
recoil of the middle-aged aristocratic spinster, the look that could
have killed him, told him all he needed to know. He had always
considered that the princess's attachment to her cousin existed
only in the imaginations of her governess and her Baden relations.
He had seen Prince Karl—a guest at the Paris coronation.

Now that he had seen the girl too, he was the more determined
to have her. It was eagerly noted that after he had kissed her hand,
the Conqueror of Europe had stood silent for a long moment as
though struck dumb by her beauty and her majestic carriage. The
Princess Auguste was tall with the figure of a sylph. She had fine
features with a very sweet expression, curling chestnut hair and
jewel-blue eyes. Her colouring was brilliant and at the moment
additionally so, for she was very angry with the Emperor. For his
part he was perfectly enchanted with her. He wrote to Eugène the
next day to tell him that the engagement was announced, and to
Berthier that the young people would make a very handsome
couple. By the light of day he found the princess decidedly not
pretty. She was absolutely beautiful and what was more, obviously

as good as she was beautiful. He emerged from a long interview
with her, chuckling. Nobody knew exactly what had passed, but
it appeared that the martyred princess had tried to strike her
little bargain with him—no crown of Italy for her husband, no
bride. He had probably promised all she asked. It would be
simpler. He had said to her father, "If you had not given me the
Princess Auguste I would have had her abducted by a regiment
of cuirassiers." It was said with a laugh, but there was a nasty ring
of truth in it.

Other horrible things were being said during these dark New
Year days in the old Residenz. Caroline Murat afterwards told
Hortense that seeing her brother so enthusiastic over Eugène's
bride she had suggested, "Divorce Josephine and marry her
yourself." "Auguste," wrote her stepmother to the old grandmother in Baden, "was broken-hearted for one day. Hers is,
however, a happy nature. All is now forgotten." The poor queen
felt that her palace was a hot-bed of intrigue. The Empress was
sugary, but she could never like her. The Emperor, surprisingly,
she found truly charming. She doubted if any woman had ever
really understood him. They became real friends.

In the town enthusiasm grew. Heralds, escorting horsemen and
preceded by a band of trumpets, drums, fifes and cymbals,
announced at every important street-corner the accession of Max
Joseph the First, King of Bavaria. Next day there was a service of
thanksgiving at the Frauenkirche, the church with two towers
capped by onion-shaped domes which was almost the most outstanding architectural feature of the old electoral city. The
Emperor Napoleon had brought back to Bavaria fifty-nine guns
and fifty-one standards captured by the Austrians. The guns were
decorated with flowers and ribbons and mounted on waggons
pulled by richly caparisoned horses. They were slowly dragged
through the snowy streets, accompanied by cadets from the military college bearing the recaptured colours. The blue and white
Bavarian flag flew from every possible place of vantage. The
royal wedding day was announced and the new King and Queen
received congratulations. It was noted that the Queen was civil to
the Emperor, but spoke little. They met every day at a succession
of stately entertainments—banquets, parades, concerts. The
Emperor was taken out wild-boar hunting in sleet and snow at
Forstenried. Bavarian generals were decorated with the Legion of
Honour. On January 7 the Emperor wrote to M. Cambacérès that

he would have to be a few hours late arriving in Paris. He must personally assist at the wedding of the Princess Auguste, who was perfection, with a bridegroom whom everyone knew was tenderly loved by him. He thought the Prince might arrive on the 8th, but it was snowing hard again now.

The Prince arrived exactly when he had said that he would. About ten o'clock on the morning of Friday, January 10, two cavaliers rode quietly under the entrance of the Residenz leading into the Konigsbauhof. Of course they were observed by many pairs of eyes which had been watching from many windows since first light. Inside the palace there were discreetly flying footsteps and whispers. The scene came to life. He had arrived. He was here. He was led at once to the Emperor, who received him with glee and hardly gave him time to take off his boots. They must go immediately to see the King and Queen—just a family affair, no etiquette. Perceiving as he hurried him down a succession of corridors that the young man was holding himself as if on parade, quite rigid with nervousness, the Emperor slipped his arm into that of his stepson to reassure him.

The King and Queen were ready for them, and the King adopted his favourite role of gay Prince Max, an officer in the Royal Duponts. He greeted his future son in law as a comrade in arms. The Prince was presented to the Queen, who had been visibly thawing since the engagement had been announced and become inevitable. There were rumours that the splendid cashmere shawl presented to her by the Empress had been the first in her wardrobe. The Prince was last triumphantly presented to the Princess *"Ma fille! Mon fils!"* She advanced mechanically. She held herself well, but she still looked down. The hand over which he bent trembled in that of *"le Boharnet."* With a nod and a smile the monarchs and Queen withdrew. It had been agreed that they were to leave the young people for a few minutes to get acquainted with one another.

There were no witnesses of the first words spoken by Prince Eugène to the Princess Auguste, but whatever had happened, it seemed to the large and interested audience to which they presently appeared, hand in hand, as if they had known one another all their lives. They advanced together, entranced, radiant. They had all the appearance of "a pair of lovers, greatly attracted to one another." There was a theory that the amiable and courageous Prince, horrified by the spectacle of beauty in distress, had instantly offered, if this marriage was so entirely distasteful to her, to take upon himself the whole responsibility for a rupture. Whatever words had passed, the atmosphere had changed as if by magic. Everyone was suddenly smiling.[5]

There was only one person in the palace who did not share in the general joy. The Emperor felt a slight pang of conscience as he carried his stepson off to greet the Empress. As the hour was not yet noon she was still in bed. She was also in tears. She had heard that her son had arrived and had hardly been able to believe that he had not come to see her. The Emperor pushed the young man in first, crying "Well, Madame, here's your great lout of a son!" At the sight of him she screamed and wept the more. He looked terrible! Had they wanted to frighten the Princess? The fact was that he was shaggy. But there had been disturbances at two places, Parma and Piacenza, caused by the new conscripts, and he had only just had time to take measures and inform General Miollis.

The barber was sent for, and a mother who had counted upon her handsome son making a favourable first appearance was mollified by the entire sacrifice of his cavalry moustache.[6] She had wanted him to shine, and during the three days that followed she was not disappointed. He was universally approved. Even the poor Queen wrote to Baden that Prince Eugène had a good figure and carriage; he seemed considerate, sensitive and anxious to be friendly. The wedding which had been arranged for January 15 was put forward one day. He was given twenty-four hours of comparative peace in which to sleep off his journey and welcome his secretary and fine clothes, and then the festivities began. Christmas had been rather sad, a time of tension. Now there was a lovely Christmas-like air of happy expectation, bustle, secrets, general goodwill.

The Residenz, venerable palace of the Wittelsbachs, possessed seven courtyards and suites of apartments of every date—Renaissance, Baroque, Rococo. It boasted the first museum known north of the Alps, and eight galleries of priceless porcelain. The Electors had been tireless collectors of art-treasures. The present King had not been able to afford great additions. The rooms redecorated by him for his second wife were in the style of the last French Court he had seen—that of Marie Antoinette.

On January 11 he took his future son in law to the palace of Schleissheim for pheasant shooting. This country residence of the Electors of Bavaria was one of their two Versailles, and had sprouted in its grounds charming lesser palaces. There had been a thaw and the day was one of rain and wind. Next day the bridegroom was formally adopted by the Emperor and a letter was sent to the Senate announcing that Prince Eugène Napoléon de France was heir to the throne of Italy, failing the birth of male heirs to the Emperor, and that his male descendants would inherit his crown.[7] He would at once take precedence of their Imperial Highnesses Joseph and Louis. It must be understood, however, that in no case or circumstances would this adoption authorize him or his descendants to claim the throne of France.

A court ball followed. The Parisian court jeweller, Nitot, had come up to Munich in hopes of custom and was not disappointed. The bridegroom had been brought to realize that he had no wedding gift for the bride. The Empress came to the rescue. Nitot had fortunately brought with him a superb diadem. It had been copied at the request of the Empress from a tiara of costume jewellery worn in a classical drama by Mlle. George. It was deflected to the innocent Princess Auguste. She was said to be already a little overcome by the "*corbeille de noces*" ordered by the Emperor, which had also arrived from Paris. She had been brought up very simply. Nobody in Munich had ever seen such luxury.

It was considered that at the civil marriage which took place on January 13 her beauty was enhanced by one of her Paris trousseau gowns. Her stepmother wrote off to Baden that they had shed some hot tears together in the morning, but the arrival of Prince Eugène had soon banished those of Auguste, and at the dinner after the betrothal ceremony she had been in the best spirits in the world.

The protocol for this ceremony had been extremely strict. Caroline Murat had taken to her bed when she heard of the inferior position allotted to her. She might be the sister of the Emperor, but she had to give place to the bride of his adopted son. This was worse than having to hold up old Josephine's tail in Notre Dame. She utterly refused to appear. There was one more important absentee. Louis Bonaparte had made one of his scenes and said he could not come, and that he would be disgraced for life if Hortense appeared without him. As things turned out she could not have got there in time, but her grief was enormous. She had been personally invited by the Emperor to bring her darling Napoleon Charles to see his uncle Tété married to Tante Auguste.

Plenty of the people who knew him well and wished him well, however, assembled on the first floor of the Green Gallery—Duroc, Bessières, Berthier, Junot, Maret. The Prince of Benevento was also there. The Green Gallery had been designed by the court dwarf of the Elector Karl Albrecht, afterwards Emperor Charles VII. This sounded an eccentric appointment but the Cuvilliés, father and son, had been Paris-trained and masters of their craft. The gallery was a two storey building of seven bays on both floors, illuminated by as many round-headed windows and crystal chandeliers. The bridegroom passed to his wedding down a corridor decorated by the portraits of a hundred and twenty of his wife's ancestors. He would become by this marriage cousin of the Queens of Prussia and Sweden and the Czarina, of the Grand Dukes of Baden, and Hesse-Darmstadt, nephew of the Queen of England and cousin of the Princess Royal of England, Queen of Württemberg.

In the gallery, the Emperor and Empress and the Queen sat on a dias under canopies. The only other persons to be allowed seats were five ladies, including the Princess Charlotte, sister of the bride, and three princes, Ludwig, Murat, and the Prince-Primate of Germany, who sat beside a sort of temporary altar wearing his mitre and cope. For, although this ceremony was entirely civil, an altar had been introduced, and Eugène and Auguste met at it, accompanied by their official witnesses, four apiece. The bridegroom wore full dress uniform with decorations, the bride a severely simple Empire gown of white satin embroidered with silver foliage, a fresh bouquet of white flowers pinned to her left shoulder, a double necklace of diamonds and her wedding-gift tiara.

The religious wedding was performed at nine p.m. next evening in the chapel of the Residenz, a large and light structure. As soon as the couple had received the blessing of the church all the bells in the city pealed and salutes were fired. There was a wedding supper on the ground floor of the Green Gallery. In the largest courtyard of the palace there was an illuminated pyramid. The much-loved first parish church of Munich, "Old Peter," and all public buildings of size, were also illuminated, and many private houses had put up transparencies. Even humble dwellings had produced tallow candles. Throughout the night the Bavarian

The civil wedding ceremony of Prince Eugène and Princess Auguste-Amélie of Bavaria,
in the Green Gallery at the Residenz, Munich,
January 13 1806, by F. G. Menageot

By permission of the Stadtmuseum, Munich

capital danced and sang although snow was falling again. The wedding ball was to take place in the Hercules Gallery on the 15th, and a performance of "Castor and Pollux" followed in the Residenz Theatre on the 16th. This little building (another masterpiece of German rococo and Cuvilliés) was almost a horseshoe in shape. Eugène and Auguste sat in a royal box lined with crimson damask, surmounted by the crowned monogram of the Emperor Maximilian III, and a life-size figure of Fame blowing a trumpet. Carved and painted red draperies hung in front of the box, and on either side it was flanked by golden palm trees supported by Titans. The whole audience rose and joined in the refrain when Munich's *prima donna*, Madame Renner, came forward on the stage to sing the wedding hymn of welcome to the bridal couple.

Next morning their royal hosts and the bride and bridegroom attended the Emperor and Empress personally to their carriage at ten a.m. They were bound for Paris by Stuttgart and Karlsruhe. That night there was a masked ball with performances by country dancers. It went on till four a.m. The atmosphere was relaxed. The Emperor had departed entirely satisfied with his first effort at a grand dynastic marriage for his family. He had exerted himself with complete success to win over the bride's stepmother. She had not liked Josephine, but that was understandable and did not matter a fig as her stepdaughter clearly did. (His attentions to the Queen had been so marked that it was said that the Empress had been jealous.) He had given the old governess a good diamond necklace from Nitot (50,000 florins) thanked her for having produced a princess who was perfection, and told Eugène to get rid of her if she became a nuisance.

The Viceroy and Vicereine left for Milan on January 21, and again there was a roar of royal salutes and the sound of trotting hooves accompanying a string of carriages. All the joy bells rang for the last time. There were four degrees of frost. The New Year of 1806 was to be remembered for its excessive and prolonged cold. Max Joseph returned to his palace wiping his eyes. Auguste's tears had been profuse. But nothing could exceed her father's relief that unlike many members of the old *noblesse* who had attached themselves to Bonaparte, Eugène de Beauharnais was not at all slippery. He was yet to discover that he had got a son in law who would be a friend for life.[8]

CHAPTER TEN

Prince of Venice
1806 : 1808

I

THEY were so happy, they laughed and sang, on and off, all the way down to Italy. The journey had taken Eugène four days, but he had come on the wings of love. For the return journey the Emperor had ordered full ceremonies. It took them three weeks. Whatever the hour that they arrived at a place, even if it was at three a.m., the guard had to be turned out and salutes fired. Civil dignitaries and military greeted them with sweet music and speeches, to which they had to smile and bow and reply, even if it was through a snowstorm. There was nothing to do but laugh it off as soon as they were alone again.

They had a strong cavalry escort and no trouble on the roads except from the weather. The Emperor had left behind a high official of his stables, the Comte de Villoutreys, with orders never to lose sight of the carriage containing the Vicereine, until she stepped out of it at the Villa Napoleon, Milan. The poor unnecessary gentleman had to ride alongside the honeymoon couple, day and night. The King of Bavaria paid expenses until the Italian frontier, when the troops under the command of the Viceroy took over all duties. In the second carriage rode the Gräfin Sophie von Sandizell, Chief Lady, the Baronin von Wurmb and the Italian Contessa Paro who had come up to Munich for the wedding. Their first stop for more than a few hours was the Palazzo degli Emilie, near Sant' Anastasia, Verona, a place which was very well known to Eugène, as one of his stepfather's first instructions to him had been that he saw to the repairs of the Roman Arena. This town had been half Austrian until a few weeks ago. The river Adige, now much swollen by the snows from the Brenner, torrential and lion-coloured, had been the boundary.

They were received by all the local grand officers of the crown, principal ladies, chamberlains and ministers. It was Eugène's first experience of assuming possession of the territories conceded by the Treaty of Pressburg.

Before she left home Auguste had sent one of her model letters to the Emperor. She was not really afraid of him. In a business despatch to Eugène he had added a postcript "Two kisses to the Princess Auguste, one from myself and one from the Empress." She now got a letter to herself.

"Stuttgart 19 January 1806
"My daughter,
"Your letter is as charming as yourself. My feelings for you will but increase every day. I realize this by the pleasure which I feel in recalling all your good qualities, and by the desire I feel to receive frequent assurances from you that you are pleased with everybody and happy with your husband. Amongst all my cares there will be none dearer to me than those which may ensure the happiness of my children. Believe me Auguste, I feel a father's affection for you and I count on you for the love of a daughter. Look after yourself well on your journey, and also in the new climate to which you are travelling, by taking all necessary repose. You have had much to try you for a month past. Remember I cannot have you ill.[1] I close, my daughter, by giving you my paternal benediction."

In her first letters home she confessed that she was tingling from the cold of Italian palaces. These picturesque and spacious buildings had no fireplaces. Little tiny braziers were brought into cavernous apartments and dumped here and there. She longed for a good German stove.

They stayed ten days in Verona. During the first two, Eugène struggled to start his labours again from the point at which he had broken off when summoned to Munich. He now had instructions to proceed as Governor General with the rehabilitation of the newly-joined provinces. The Emperor had arrived in Paris, he reckoned, at the same moment that the bridal pair had reached Verona. Letters from St. Cloud began to shower in remorselessly. General Lauriston, who was to be Commissioner in Dalmatia and Istria, reported for instructions. He was a very old acquaintance, a fellow aide de camp of the Egyptian campaign, of

Scottish extraction, very handsome. The Viceroy got off to Paris his budget for the expenses of his establishment in Italy for the coming year, with the exception of the stables, which he promised to forward from Milan. He sent to Berthier his recommendations for the promotions of d'Anthouard to Brigadier-General and Bataille to full captain. His Paris palace was still proving a source of annoyance. The Emperor wrote that the sums demanded by Calmelet for repairs both there, and at the country box la Jonchère were ridiculous. Almost for the first time a firmer note entered the stepson's reply. He was persuaded Calmelet was honest. Eventually the Emperor decided to take over the palace himself and install Eugène and Auguste in the Pavillon de Flore in the Tuileries when they paid their promised visit to Paris. It turned out that the Empress had told M. Calmelet to go ahead and spare no expense.

The Emperor was surprised that he had not had a word from his son about his passage through the Tyrol. "Your wife is more amiable than you." He wanted the fullest information about everything that befell. This was a tall order, for the festivities in Venice, where they arrived on February 3, quite eclipsed those of Verona which had been unceasing. The Viceregal couple were received by twelve dignitaries of the late Republic and conducted to a canopied barge upholstered in gold and silver brocade, with rare eastern carpets, and filled by sweet-smelling spring flowers. On either side of the state barge were handsome smaller craft, decorated with dyed plumes, and containing lesser officials. Beyond them came a swarm of gondolas manned by gondoliers fantastically attired in rich antique costumes. Music sounded from orchestras, drums rattled; there were loud cries of welcome, and artillery salutes. The scene was considered so historic that an artist performed a vast picture of it, much in the style of Canaletto, which Eugène and Auguste treasured in their various homes in after-life.

The Viceregal couple, so young, so smiling and so in love touched the imagination of a romantic people. The bride never forgot their welcome. "One could see it came from the heart. The people shouted 'Vivas,' clapped their hands and threw up their hats. There were ladies in every balcony waving handkerchiefs and blowing kisses. There was a fête every one of the five nights we stayed there and I enjoyed everything except perhaps the Opera."[2] She still preferred the German style. Two important ladies from Milan had come up to join her train—the Marchesa

Litta Visconti Arese and the Countessa Calini. Part of what was to become Bonaparte's Palazzo Reale (at the cost of sweeping away the ancient church of San Geminiano) had been the residence of the nine procurators of the Republic, and occupied the south side of the renowned Piazza of St. Mark. This square was paved with marble and trachyte from the Euganean hills, a hundred and ninety yards long and from sixty to ninety feet broad. The Emperor on his first sight of it had dubbed it "the best ballroom in Europe." It was haunted by pigeons, and from the pedestals of the three decorated flagstaffs in front of the basilica, flags of the various rulers had fluttered since the year 1505. In fact Venice was at the moment pitifully run down and only what they were shown was brilliant. The proud Republic had been going to seed long before it had been cynically handed over to Austria by the Peace of Campo Formio, and even that had been six years ago. Only the Grand Canal was still vocal and brilliant with colour and life. The side canals were in a demonstrably unhygienic condition. The trade of the port of Venice had all been snatched by Trieste. This would have to be altered.

II

"At last I have reached Milan," wrote Auguste to her father, "and high time too, as I fell ill the same day and was feverish all night. But nothing bad followed." She had begun to think that she was pregnant.

Milan, always jealous of Venice, had prepared a welcome which was to last a fortnight. They drove in under a succession of triumphal arches, and all buildings on their route were decorated. Glowing Italian materials hung from every window. They enjoyed the last day of the carnival so much that they stayed up till four a.m., Auguste on a balcony of the palace overlooking the gay scene, and Eugène sauntering with some of his aides de camp amongst the revellers, up and down the Corso, and being pelted with bon-bons and confetti. At the performance at the Scala in honour of his wedding his natural modesty asserted itself. There was a grande finale in which a couple representing him and Auguste descended from Olympus and adoring crowds prostrated themselves and worshipped them as if they were divine. Eugène flushed, rose, and said in high embarrassment "They must let down the curtain."[3]

He went with his bride to Sant' Ambrogio to attend a Te Deum. Auguste wrote home complacently that with their large military cortège they must have presented a fine spectacle. She gave audience to a deputation of the ladies of Milan and spoke personally to seventy-five. Society in Italy had most peculiar habits. Mlle. d'Avrillon had been staggered by the discovery that every lady had a sort of lover who went with her to every entertainment and seemed to perform every duty except that of being the father of her children. In Milan ladies seemed to go out little except to balls, theatres and for the routine evening drive up and down the Corso. On all of these occasions the *patito* was invariably on duty. It was difficult to realize who was married to who, for husbands were also *patitos* and waited upon ladies who were not their wives. In every rank of life, wives seemed to hold rather an inferior position compared to those of Paris or Munich. Even if they had been married for their money they were left hardly any for themselves, and men looked after many domestic details. *Menus* differed much from those of France and Germany. There was a great deal of shell-fish, pasta and, of course, ices.

The Villa Bonaparte, which would now be the Vicereine's home in Milan was absolutely up-to-date in its internal arrangements and had some fine rooms,[4] all neo-classical. The spacious dining-room had pillars painted to resemble marble, and Eugène was going to order a central picture by Appiani—Apollo and the Muses—for the ceiling. There was hardly a mythological character unrepresented in the Viceroy's villa—Vesta, Saturn, Pluto, Diana, Silenus, Bacchus, all were there, in mural decoration of some variety. There were two floors of large, cool and lofty saloons, opening out of one another, providing vistas very suitable for the effective placing of statues and busts. There was an enormous bust of the Emperor by Canova in the pillared ante-sala of the ballroom, which was not so much impressive as elegant. Its only furniture was marble vases, classical tripods for four branches of candles, and gesso tables, couches and chairs, all set against the walls. The villa was pleasantly situated and looked out, in front, over its courtyard of entry (and eternal attendant sentinels) to the Corso with beautifully planted avenues, a lake and stream. The windows at the back overlooked its own garden, also with lake and stream (but much smaller) and various grottoes, artificial ruins and little temples. The viceregal couple would never use the *palazzo* opposite the cathedral except for large public occasions, and very soon they began to show a preference for Monza. The palace there was huge and not up to date, but for Auguste it possessed a rare attraction. She could go out in the park there without the military escort which had to be ordered whenever she wanted to make an expedition in the town. And Eugène was having a little garden-house rearranged for her, in which she could give informal parties, "Villa Augusta".

"I have everything to make me happy," she assured her father. "I have been given a wonderful welcome, and the prince is to me— *charmant*." To her brother Ludwig who was now in Paris, she was a little more outspoken. "I am wonderfully fortunate. Eugène is so good and kind. Forgive me for saying this, but I do not believe you could be so indulgent to a wife as he is. In this he exactly resembles our dear father. That is why I love him so much . . . I lead a very quiet life. I almost always have meals with Eugène alone. We have parties only on Sundays—ladies and gentlemen. But I am very busy . . ."⁵ The Emperor had mentioned in one of his affectionate notes that he was sure that her interest would be warm, and her purse always open, in support of schemes for the welfare of the wives and children of Italian soldiers.

Eugène meanwhile was writing to thank the Emperor humbly for "the companion with whom your paternal bounty has provided me. She is sweet, lovable and good."

Early in March arrived two valuable additions for the household of the Vicereine, a *femme de chambre* chosen by the Empress, and a hairdresser-valet recommended by no less a character than Duplan, the first ladies' hairdresser of Paris.

Her fabulous *corbeille* from Paris had begun to arrive—more shawls, gowns, hats, shoes, accessories of every description. The Emperor wrote that the Empress would keep her advised as to the fashions. He was sending her something more solid, a carefully chosen little library. She certainly had not told him that she was a little lonely. But the Viceroy's dry-looking secretary had soon informed the Vicereine's ladies that his young master, before marriage, had been accustomed to work on an average ten hours a day. The Emperor had his own secret sources of information. He kept on asking Eugène and Auguste if the Baronin von Wurmb was still there. She was, and Eugène had not any inclination to dismiss her. It would be most unkind to Auguste, and he counted upon the old governess to look after his wife when he went on campaigns. For the life of an administrative prince, although he was beginning to show aptitude, would never be his choice. The Baronin was herself innocently writing to her brother in Munich. "I am the Vicereine's lady in waiting. I live in the palace and everyone shows me the greatest respect. The admiration that my dear and beautiful Princess receives affects me much, and people thank me for her excellent upbringing. The Emperor wished me to attend her, the King equally so, the Prince and Princess longed for it. The Emperor has given me, voluntarily, a pension for life of fifteen thousand francs. It says in my patent of appointment that it is in gratitude for the education I gave the Princess. That is what this great man is like. My Princess is blissful. How could she be otherwise? The Prince possesses distinguished and heroic qualities. He loves the Princess and treats her with the tenderest attention."⁶

Their programme had become very regular. They went to Mass in the palace chapel with a full attendance every Sunday. Afterwards Eugène received gentlemen—mostly his Ministers. They had their first military review in front of the palace, a very fine natural parade ground, and Auguste watched from a balcony. Afterwards every officer was presented to her—very tiring. It was all very formal compared with life in her old home. She never saw Eugène on a weekday morning, and he was often still working when dinner was waiting. But she begged her brother not to get the impression that she was not lucky. She said she had the perfect peace of mind which means true happiness.

Their Paris news in March was that the most extraordinary marriage had been arranged. Poor Prince Karl, who was going mourning to his grave a broken-hearted bachelor, had been offered and accepted Eugène's first cousin, Mademoiselle Stéphanie de Beauharnais. It was years since Eugène had seen her. She was the motherless child of the *émigré* Comte Claude and had been brought up by her grandmother, Comtesse Fanny, whose only keen interest was in her literary salon. The girl had been fetched from Madame Campan's boarding school and told she was to be adopted by the Emperor and have the dowry and establishment of a Daughter of France and marry little, fat, blue-eyed, rosy-cheeked Prince Karl who would, when his grandfather died, become Grand Duke of Baden. Actually, the Emperor had spoken earnestly and secretly in Munich to Auguste's stepmother about his concern to find a suitable bride for her poor brother who must be feeling his broken engagement so much, so to the Queen of Bavaria "the little Beauharnais" was no surprise.

But nobody had told Eugène or Auguste a word. The Emperor's letter to Eugène said that he was to tell Auguste whom he was sure would be pleased, and that at their first interview Stéphanie had been extremely shy of her bridegroom. Everyone still spoke of her as a child, but she was now seventeen. She bore a superficial resemblance to Hortense—a fairy-like little creature, silver-blonde and laughing. Auguste wrote to her brother wondering why the Emperor had sent her this message. "Was he making fun of me? Tell me what you think of the prince and how he behaves. Will they still be there when we come to Paris?" Since the Emperor had adopted Stéphanie as his daughter, Auguste realized that they were now sisters in law and, what was odder, Karl was her brother in law. It could not be imagined that these adoptions of Beauharnais, male and female, could be pleasing to the family of Bonaparte. Hortense had told her brother that when Prince Murat had heard of Eugène's appointment to be Viceroy of Italy he had broken a sword across his knee!

The people in Paris who could have answered all Auguste's questions were Mme. de Rémusat and Constant, both of whom recorded their first-hand impression with delight. Stéphanie was very quick, and when patronizing people told her how pleased she must be to be going to be married to the Hereditary Grand Duke of Baden, she said that she considered she was doing him a great honour. "The daughter of the Emperor might have expected a king." The Emperor heard this and laughed, but Madame Murat's jealousy was hideous, for Stéphanie now took precedence of her, and the child's trousseau was of unimaginable luxury. Mlle. de Beauharnais had been pettish about Prince Karl's looks and in hopes of pleasing her he had cut off his military *queue* and appeared suddenly before her in a fashionable classical hair-style, the "Brutus". But she had burst into tears and said she liked him worse. Constant believed that poor Prince Karl spent his wedding night seated in an armchair. His bride had screamed at the sight of him and called in to share her bed another silly little school-girl.[7] But Prince Karl, although his sister had complained of his apathy when she was trying to prod him into marriage to Auguste, had remarkable staying power, and Stéphanie resembled Hortense in colouring only. They slowly became a devoted couple and in dark days were most kind to their Beauharnais kin.

Hortense's letters excelled in self-pity as she wrote to congratulate her brother on his "arranged" marriage which was such a success. She did not think she had been so disappointed in her life as she had been over her failure to attend his wedding. She had given a little fête in his honour on the happy day, in his own house, and asked everyone of whom she could think amongst his old comrades. Lavalette would have written him an account. His portrait had been set up surrounded by myrtles, and she had danced with one of his *chasseurs* who had a wounded nose. He had been a captain. "Speak of me to your wife, tell her how I love her and how chagrined I have been. How I feel for her having to leave her family so suddenly. I know you will replace them, but I know also there is nothing so sad as being separated from one's dear ones. Show her my letter. I hope she will realize my sorrows and love me a little. Do write. Tell me all you think. Are you coming to Paris? Oh Heavens! how sad I am not to be near you. Perhaps you will not love me as much now and will not think so much of me." She sent a portrait of herself, her own work. Her elder son was independent and had sent a letter of his composition to "Nonnoque et Ta-Ta". "His style as you will observe" said Hortense, "is laconic." (He was four.)

A week later the Emperor had written very handsomely telling her she had a sister in law who would be worthy of her. Was it too much to hope that the princess would send her a little line? Perhaps it might be a good thing if Eugène sent also a little line to Louis . . . Her hopes of seeing the couple in Paris rose when the Emperor returned and told her he was making alterations at the Tuileries to provide a permanent residence for visiting royalties.[8] But Hortense truly seemed to be one of those unhappy people who attract misfortune. It soon began to dawn upon her that even if Eugène and Auguste came to Paris she would not be there. The Emperor had offered Louis the Crown of Holland, and to her horror and surprise Louis seemed disposed to accept.

III

The Emperor loved sending admonitory letters to his adopted Beauharnais children.

"To Her Imperial Highness the Princess Stéphanie of Baden.
"My daughter,
"I have received your letter and am glad to hear you are well. Love your husband; he deserves it for the love he bears to you.

Be agreeable to the Elector; this is your first duty; he is your father now. Moreover he is a prince whom I have always esteemed. Treat your subjects well; sovereigns are only made for the welfare of their people. Accommodate yourself to the customs of your new home; nothing is more impertinent than to be always prating of the pleasures of Paris which you no longer enjoy. This is a common French error; do not fall into it. Karlsruhe is a most lovely place, but you will not be loved and esteemed unless you show love and esteem for the country in which you dwell; this is something of which people cannot be too much aware."

"NAPOLEON"[9]

"To His Imperial Highness, the Prince Eugène, Viceroy of Italy.
"St. Cloud. April 14, 1806.

"My son,
"You are working too hard; your life is too monotonous. This is all right for you, because your work should be your recreation, but you have a young wife who is pregnant. I think you should contrive to pass your evenings with her and gather some company around you. Why not go to the theatre once a week, use the royal box? I think you ought also to have a small hunting establishment and go hunting at least once a week. I will willingly make you a grant for this. There ought to be more gaiety in your house; it is necessary for your wife's happiness and your health. One can get through a great deal of work in a short time. I am leading the same life as you, but I have an old wife who does not need me for her amusements; I also have more work to do than you, yet I can honestly say I get more time for pleasure and diversion than you do. You used to like enjoying yourself in the old days; you must return to those tastes. What you might not choose to do for yourself, you must do out of duty to the princess.

"I have just established myself at St. Cloud. Stéphanie and the Prince of Baden get on pretty well together. I spent the last two days at Marshal Bessières'; we behaved like boys of fifteen.

"You used to get up early in the mornings. You should re-establish that custom. This would not disturb the princess if you retired with her in the evenings at 11 p.m. And if you left off working at 6 p.m. you would still have ten working hours, if you rise at 7 or 8.

"The Cattaro business has obliged me to postpone our fêtes arranged for May here, but I think not for more than a month. I hope that you and the princess will come to Paris then. I have had the Pavillon de Flore prepared for you; the Prince of Baden will have the second floor; you get the first. Tell the princess how pleased people will be to see her in Paris. By that time her condition need not prevent her from travelling, if she takes it gently. Indeed, provided the weather is fine it can do her nothing but good.

NAPOLEON"

Unhappily, by the time that the month of May arrived Auguste knew that she was no longer pregnant, and to add to her misery her husband had just been preparing to leave her for the first time since their marriage. She wrote to him every day while he was away and reported something extraordinary. Her brother Ludwig had asked the Emperor when they were coming and had been told that she was going to stay on in Paris for her confinement. She would have better treatment in Paris than Milan! "What do you say to that?" she asked Eugène. "Don't be angry, but it made me burst into tears. Never shall the Emperor achieve that with me." To Ludwig she expanded on her determination. "Eugène was absent ten days, never have I felt so forsaken. I could never endure a longer parting. And if the Emperor believes that I would ever decide to lie-in in Paris, there he is mistaken! Eugène can never leave Italy for long, and I will never part from my husband."[10]

The Emperor's reply to her letter telling him of her disappointment was kind and gentle.

"I understand how lonely you must feel alone in the middle of Lombardy. But Eugène will soon be back, and you only realise how much you love someone when you see him again, or when he is away from you. You only appreciate good health when you have a touch of migraine or when you are out of sorts. It is often beneficial for all kinds of different reasons to get out a bit, and amuse yourself. Everything that I can remember about Italy tells me that you are leading too sensible a life. I have heard nothing about Mme. de Wurmb. I imagine that she is still with you and that you still like her. I always enjoy hearing from you, and enquire about you from everyone who has come from Italy and am delighted to find everyone thinks you are perfection itself.

"Your affectionate father
"NAPOLEON"[11]

IV

Eugène had heard what was to be his new title. He was Prince of Venice, a fine sound and bringing happy memories of his honeymoon welcome in a uniquely beautiful place. Nothing further had been heard about the Emperor resigning the crown of Italy to him; but there had always been an understanding that this would not take place until peace was established, and Russia had not yet signed the definitive treaty. Far from it, Russian and British flotillas based on Corfu were attacking the Dalmatian coast. Somewhat to Eugène's disappointment, the Emperor ordered General Marmont down in command to settle what he called "the Cattaro business". This business was the subject of innummerable letters from and to the Viceroy for the next twelve months and was eventually only settled after the signature of quite another treaty with Russia. Cattaro occupied a ledge between the mountains of Montenegro and the Bocche de Cattaro, a romantic winding inlet of the Adriatic. Five hundred years ago its trade had rivalled that of Ragusa and even made Venice jealous. It had survived devastation by the Turks, fire, plague and earthquake, and a Russian admiral had now settled in with a collection of wild Montenegrins, Croats and some Greeks. In vain the Viceroy sent across an aide de camp with a copy of the treaty of peace with Russia signed in Paris on July 20. Admiral Siniavin preferred to wait to get his orders from St. Petersburg.

Ragusa was another source of anxiety. Lauriston had captured it but had been blockaded in it by Montenegrins and Russians. General Molitor had to be sent to relieve him. Marmont had arrived to his command in a bad mood. He had never been able to get on with Lauriston and he was disappointed that he was not yet a marshal. Ragusa, episcopal city and garrison town, once the chief port of southern Europe and eternally the haven of refugees of every nation, had been left by the Treaty of Campo Formio neutral, and a republic. Marmont occupied it after defeating the Montenegrins at Castelnuovo in September 1806. In the following year it was formally assigned to Italy and Marmont became a beneficent military and civil governor. But the Duke of Ragusa never forgave the Viceroy who had sturdily backed up Lauriston.

The Emperor's pen was as active as ever. He sent no less than nine letters on various topics from St. Cloud to Milan on May 6, and his stepson replied gravely that roads did not really exist in Dalmatia. Most of them were mere goat-tracks and difficult even for goats. They were strewn with a particularly vicious type of pointed stone which was death to the footwear of the troops. He was sending three more pairs of shoes apiece to every soldier going there under Molitor. The Turkish frontier was covered with footpaths into the mountains all debouching upon the capital of Bosnia. (He enclosed a good map by General d'Anthouard.) Dalmatians upon the whole were prepared to be loyal subjects. It was not true that they had blockaded Lauriston. The Emperor instantly enquired if they should not then be employed in the wasting duty of coast defence.

The kingdom of Italy had two new fortresses in the neighbourhood of Udine, and Eugène had received instructions to enlarge those at Mantua and Peschiera. Early in May his plans were made for a trip to Istria. He was horrified by reports of dysentery in the camp at Palmanova. It sounded like Egypt over again. He sent off the First Physician to the Italian army, and two sage men whom the Emperor would remember, one the famous Vailly who had got himself so much talked about in Constantinople, the other Cimba, Chief Surgeon to the Italian Guards.

On May 20, having postponed his departure twice, he took Auguste out to Monza. It would not have been a possible expedition for her even if she had been well enough. He cheered her by pointing out that now nothing need detain them from their Paris visit. He wrote to ask the Emperor what suite they should bring. Auguste wanted to bring one Italian lady, her two Munich ladies, and a chamberlain. For himself he thought two aides de camp would suffice. All the high officials of their court wanted to come. Auguste longed to see Paris. Her father's tales of his days as a young officer at Versailles had always fascinated his children. But she wondered how she would be received. "You can't imagine how frightened I am," she wrote to her brother. "I am so shy. I shall behave awkwardly and people will laugh at me." Her mirror and her husband told her otherwise. Eugène himself longed to see his birthplace again.

So much was happening. St. Denis was being repaired, and the Vendôme column, and the new triumphal arch at the Carrousel was being built. He would soon hardly know his home. There were plans for embanking the Seine with new quays and altering the whole neighbourhood between the Tuileries and the Boulevards. The Rue de Rivoli was nearly ready and the colonnade of the Louvre and the bridge to be called after Austerlitz, near the Jardin des Plantes where the conservatories had been enriched with spoils from the hot-houses of Schönbrunn. The Viceroy had inherited his mother's tastes and already there were rare new shrubs and trees in the gardens of the Villa Bonaparte and in the park at Monza, where fortunately there was plenty of room, for a hundred and fifty years later his specimen conifers were to be majestic—Ginkgo Biloba (the Maidenhair tree), Cedrus Atlantica glauca (a blue-grey pyramid), and aura (golden), and argentea (silver), Cedrus Libani (the wide-spreading cedar of Lebanon) and Cedrus deodora (from the Himalayas).

He reviewed the Dalmatian battalion at Bergamo where he was joined by the Minister for War. At Palmanova he scolded the authorities for being so backward with the new fort, and at the hospital at Capo d'Istria he fairly roused about the chief medical officer who seemed to him the poorest type possible—terrifying the troops by talking in front of them about contagion. The Viceroy agreed to General Séras's suggestion of the establishment of a second hospital eight miles away.

It was quite like old days, to be setting off at two a.m. for Monfalcone and Udine. He rode up the right bank of the Isonzo to reconnoitre, as far as Caporetto. He got back to Monza on June 3 and it soon became clear that Auguste and he were not going to Paris this summer. By July 15 Josephine was confiding in Hortense that Auguste was certainly expecting again. The Emperor simply said again that she would lie-in in Paris—next March. But meanwhile he had to warn Eugène that Prussia was rattling the sabre. When he heard that the Emperor was going to take the field again, Eugène wrote at once to ask to be employed in the forthcoming campaign against Prussia. The answer was as usual. His duty was to stay in his present appointment and pay particular attention to the provinces newly acquired from Austria, to the strengthening of his fortresses at Verona, Mantua etc., and to the improvement and encouragement of Venice. A palace on the Brenta canal between Padua and Venice was being acquired so that he and his wife could stay there in the hot months occasionally. His faithful secretary wrote down in pride that in the presence of Duroc, and Bessières, and on the field of Austerlitz, the Emperor had said with satisfaction "See into what hands I have entrusted my sword of Italy."

The Emperor's campaign against Prussia curiously resembled in design that against Austria. He wrote to Eugène from St. Cloud on September 24 that he was leaving for Mainz that night, from Bamberg on October 7 that hostilities would begin that day, and on October 31 from Berlin, "The army of the King of Prussia no longer exists." He ordered a grand service of thanksgiving to be held in the cathedral at Milan for the victory of Jena. To a cavalry officer, to witness France taking the field against Prussia was particularly interesting. The prestige of Frederick the Great was still high. He was believed to have set his stamp irrevocably on the Prussian army, notably the mounted regiments. Prussian officers of the high command were probably the most highly trained in Europe. But there never was a more exploded legend than of the invincibility of modern Prussia. There had been incredibly short-sighted economies. The unfortunate troops went into the field in October without greatcoats, and with muskets many of which had seen service in the Seven Years War. A number of intelligent officers were to be found on the executive staff, but they had no leader. King Frederick William III was a pathetic figure, a long-faced indecisive young man, thought to receive far too much instruction from his beautiful wife, Louisa of Mecklenburg-Strelitz. She was believed to have engineered in November 1805 a dramatic secret oath of alliance with the Czar at the tomb of Frederick the Great. As her husband's country was invaded and defeated her language became intemperate. She wrote to her unfortunate mate that she wished the Czar would shoot the abominable General Bennigsen. When General Zastrow's ship, lying in the roadstead at Memel, was saved by a frigate, she said that she would willingly have spared him to the fishes. Bonaparte was usually just "the Monster", but she gave him a new name when she heard that her husband was going to meet him and Talleyrand, rightly prophesying "You are no match for the wiliness of that subtle diabolical Dr. Faustus and his familiar spirit."

After his triumphs at Jena and Auerstadt the Emperor entered Berlin in triumph, as he had done Vienna. One of his last letters before he left France was so voluminous it resembled a pamphlet. It contained minutest instructions as to measures to be taken against possible enemy action by Austria, by Russia, by England. It must be remembered that brigands would take advantage of the absence of the ruler of Italy. (Why had the Emperor been

The Italian Homes
"Beloved Monza"
The Palazzo Reale built by Giuseppe Piermarini in
1777, summer palace of Eugène as Viceroy, 1805-1814

The Villa Pisani, Strà
The palace presented to Eugène on his marriage, built
about 1740. "Too big for a private person and much
too small for a Court" (comment of the Vicereine, 1811).
Photographs by the author

left to hear from another source that a courier had been murdered in broad daylight on the frequented Modena-Reggio road?)

Eugène went down to Venice for a week in July as he had been directed, and paid close attention to its fortifications, harbour and hospitals. He wrote to the Emperor that Auguste was melancholy. The Emperor replied that this was natural in her situation. Seeing her brother would cheer her. He asked if the Baronin von Wurmb was a good Italian yet. He thought Auguste should cultivate the society of the wife of the Minister for War, Caffarelli. She was a valuable woman, virtuous, intelligent and handsome.

In the nick of time Prince Ludwig arrived in Milan. They took him out to Monza next day, and his sister entertained him while Eugène went down to Mantua for some inspections lasting forty-eight hours. Ludwig had not been very happy during his seven months in Paris. The Emperor failed to understand a young man who did not care for hunting or military parades and preferred to spend his days writing poetry and looking at pictures. (The Emperor had recently enquired how Eugène was getting on with his hunting establishment. He hoped that Italian noblemen would take kindly to long days in the saddle. It would do them much more good than sitting about in the company of ladies.) Hortense had tried to be kind to Ludwig because, although he looked odd, he was witty and he was Eugène's brother in law. But she really had no common sense. She lent him some of her best jewellery so that he could appear with éclat in a royal quadrille, but she had not been able to resist joining with Stéphanie in one of their high-spirited Malmaison-style practical jokes directed against him. He had become an ardent admirer of that classical beauty Mlle. George and had been in correspondence with her. They sent him a letter supposed to be written by her, and watched eagerly while he read it. He compared the handwriting with one which he drew from his pocket and asked Hortense if she thought they both came from the same person. He was devoured with anxiety to see the lady who said that she was waiting in his apartments, but almost equally nervous as to what the Emperor might say. So Hortense and Stéphanie and their suites all took candles and escorted him to his rooms down many long corridors. Karl of Baden led the solemn procession. The lady lying in his bed, wearing a pretty nightcap on her curls, and a nightgown, was a large doll. "He seemed very much upset."

He was astonished and repelled by the glitter and glare in

which his sister was living. She took him for the day out to Villa Mirabello in the park, but a piquet of horse accompanied them to the very gates. The same thing happened when he went to inspect Monza cathedral. This ancient building interested him profoundly. It had been founded by a Wittelsbach princess, Theodolinda, wife of two successive kings of Lombardy. He was shown the Iron Crown and Theodolinda's crown, and her fan and comb, and a little array of a hen and seven chicks, silver-gilt, supposed to represent Lombardy and its seven provinces, made to her order—all sixth century. He saw a curious relief representing her, above the portal, and in the chapel where she was buried, frescoes of rare beauty telling the story of her life. He would have preferred that a peal of joy bells had not greeted him. Eugène came back from Mantua in high spirits and they were perfectly happy. They had meals out of doors in the scented Italian heat, and under the stars the Viceroy and Vicereine sang duets. Sunday was very formal. They went in state to mass, and they sat down forty to supper. Games of chance and cards, were played in the Viceregal court, but not for money. Ludwig had to discuss with Eugène the possibilities of two marriages in his family. It had been suggested that he might marry the elder sister of the Czar, and Charlotte the Prince of the Asturias. The Empress had been quite pleased at the thought of her son's sister in law being Queen of Spain but Auguste believed her father did not fancy the bridegroom. Could Eugène find out what the Emperor really thought? (Neither of these marriages took place owing to the march of events in the next year.)

Prince Ludwig departed on his further travels[12] and Auguste passed the dreaded third month of her pregnancy without disaster. She had written to her spiritual adviser Sambuga to ask him to baptize her child. He had replied saying wonderful things about how much the honour of becoming a mother surpassed that of wearing any earthly crown. The Emperor wrote that it made him laugh to see how frightened she seemed that she might not produce the little prince they needed. He said he would be happy to see a daughter as amiable and good as herself. The Empress had ordered for the confinement, in March, Madame Frangeau, the most experienced *sage-femme* of Paris, accustomed to work with M. Baudelocque, *accoucher* to the Queen of Holland. The important couple had directions to be over the Alps in good time.

Life at the Villa Bonaparte and Monza continued smoothly,

on the surface. Italian conscripts, sent up in increasing numbers
to join the Grande Armée in Strasbourg, continued their disconcerting habit of disappearing into the mountains. Eugène duly
mentioned such accidents but as before in difficult times, did not
cease to affirm that the kingdom of Italy enjoyed perfect tranquillity. He recommended buying the Caprara palace in Bologna,
where the Emperor was proposing to found a female seminary
—the Maison Josephine. Count Melzi appeared to announce that
his gout required a month in the country. He was asked to dinner.
He had a villa on the borders of Como at which he hoped the
Vicereine would honour him by a visit. He wondered if the
Emperor had got his letter. Eugène wrote that he guessed the
Emperor would at the moment be more interested in the retreat
of the King of Prussia than the retreat of Melzi!

A secret agent, a Dalmatian, whom the chief of the Italian
Police had sent in, had been hearing things in Carniola, Carinthia,
Croatia. He had actually arrived in Laybach on the fête day of
the Austrian Emperor and had been astonished by the number of
carriages carrying ammunitions and food, on the road to Agram.
He travelled in the character of a cattle dealer which gave him
opportunities to notice the movement of supplies. He had a helpful compatriot who had fought against the French at Ragusa
but had been disillusioned by Russian barbarity and had lost a
brother, and had a hand fractured, so was now peacefully engaged
in the coasting trade from Trieste to the Greek isles, selling
cheese and oil . . . The Emperor had refused to hear of the Viceroy engaging a clever man who was Austrian. He said he made
a rule never to see spies himself. This rule he hardly ever broke.

There was alarm in Venice in the end of October when a
British frigate and bark were sighted. The Viceroy was off to
Venice directly, but the enemy sail had passed on towards Corfu.
In Berlin, the Emperor was about to issue decrees announcing
that the British Isles were in a state of blockade, prohibiting all
commerce with them or their colonies, and declaring that all
goods coming to or from them were to be seized. He had changed
his mind about accepting the King of Prussia's peace proposals.
Information which had come into his hands at Potsdam had
shown him that Frederick William had been intriguing for
Russian support so successfully that the Czar was preparing to
fight the Grande Armée in Poland. The Emperor had himself
raised a Polish contingent of thirty thousand men, whom he had

led to believe would be fighting for the independence of their country. His first brush with Russian troops came in Christmas week, at Putulsk, in seas of mud, and was indecisive. Eugène spent Christmas in Verona where he had a grand parade service and gradually inspected the third Italian division. He had been on a twelve day tour of inspection—Udine, Palmanova, Treviso, Verona. He was having great trouble in getting horses for ambulances. Palmanova had been damaged in a terrible storm. He was sending off reinforcements to the Grande Armée to report at Magdebourg, according to his latest orders. He was back with his wife for New Year and their first wedding anniversary and now hoped not to have to leave again before the great event of the arrival of the little prince.

They heard with relief that Auguste's father was sending Ludwig up to the Emperor's headquarters, and Eugène wrote him an elder-brother letter of advice telling him that he would find he had gone to the best school in the world. Bavarian troops had been fighting bravely. Ludwig had taken the opportunity when passing through Weimar to lay flowers on the grave of the immortal Schiller. Auguste had been grieved and shocked to hear of the death in action of the young Russian prince Louis Ferdinand. She remembered him well. He had been a guest at her father's country palace Nymphenburg only a year ago. Her father took the loss of their cousin more philosophically. He said Louis Ferdinand had been clever and plucky, but a hot-head.

The Emperor arrived in the capital of Poland on New Year's day, after dark, on horseback. He had been obliged to leave his carriage and escort in the marshes. He took up residence in the Stanislas Augustus palace on the Place de Saxe. At the end of the month he began a move towards Willenberg, but was obliged to order a counter-march. General Bennigsen whom he had known to be in Königsberg, had broken out and was advancing on Ney's corps, which was holding the left wing of the Grande Armée. The Emperor attempted to encircle the Russians but Bennigsen fell back on a position outside an obscure hamlet called Eylau. The Battle of Eylau, fought in a snowstorm, was a French victory only in name, against superior numbers. The slaughter on both sides was terrible. When an aide de camp from Soult came to tell the Emperor at three a.m. on the morning of February 9 that the Russians had retreated, no order was given for pursuit.

"My son," wrote the Emperor five days later, "Your aide de camp Lacroix will have told you what has happened here. He himself charged with the *chasseurs* of the Guard who covered themselves with glory . . ." General Dahlmann had died of his wounds. The casualties of the regiment were twenty-one officers, two hundred and twenty-four men and two hundred horses. The Emperor was heard to say as he rode over the field of carnage, "This scene was devised to inspire princes with a love of peace."

The incredibly wonderful *layette* from Paris was safe in Milan, and the *sage-femme* and *accoucheur*. "I have said my prayers," wrote Auguste to her brother on February 23, "so now I am ready for anything." It was well that her courage was high for she had another three weeks to wait, and then, as Saturday, March 14 dragged past agonizingly, it became clear that delivery was going to be difficult if not dangerous. At last the guns sounded, the joy bells of Milan rang and the carefully chosen messengers were sent off on their long journeys—important Italian noblemen to the Residenz and to Malmaison, and to Polish headquarters General d'Anthouard (whom the Emperor rewarded by sending him down to besiege Dantzig). The Emperor presently wrote to the young mother herself:

"My daughter,

"What you say of the Prince gives me great pleasure. I enjoy very much hearing of your perfect happiness. I know that you have suffered much and that you showed great courage.

"Your affectionate father"[13]

On March 27 from Osterode the Emperor wrote—

"My son,

"I congratulate you on the accouchement of the Princess. I am anxious to hear that she is well and out of all danger. I hope that your daughter will be as good and as amiable as her mother. Perhaps next year you will have a son." In a postscript in his own hand he added "Call your daughter Josephine."

The Empress sent the good news from Paris to the Queen of Holland at the Hague. "Eugène is enchanted with his daughter. He complains only that she sleeps too much. He has not really been able to see her properly as yet."[14] He had sent a little lock of his daughter's hair—twelve days old! What a charming idea!

One could see that the child had inherited the wonderful chestnut shade of the Vicereine's tresses.

The infant was christened Joséphine Maximilienne Eugénie Napoléone after her father's mother, and her mother's father, and of course her own father and the Emperor. Though not the little prince so much desired she was destined to be the ancestress of many royal houses of Europe.

V

The nightingales sang so loud in Italy in May that they woke the Vicereine, lying in her bed in the Villa Bonaparte.[15] On her nineteenth birthday, June 21, her husband presented her with the Villa Augusta in Monza park. It was quite close to Mirabello. She wrote to Sambuga that it was her little kingdom. She had stables and cow-sheds and already two cows. "Eugène is being so kind," she told her brother in July. "He is teaching me to ride. The garden is my riding school."

A French cavalry officer, Comte Stanislas Girardin, was wished upon her son by Josephine and arrived at Monza to be entertained. His connection with the Beauharnais family was irregular but very long-standing. Madame de Longpré, whose elderly husband had obligingly absorbed into his family an infant Alexandre, of whom Eugène's father, the young Vicomte de Beauharnais, had in fact been the parent, had been born a Girardin.

The Paris guest was suitably impressed by the Viceroy's stud— the most beautiful Persian stallion upon which he had ever set eyes. Eugène drove him in a light Neapolitan vehicle behind a string of four horses. The Viceroy still seemed to like playing ball games like a boy. Comte Stanislas wrote everything down. He had long serious talks with his host. "I was never ambitious," explained the Viceroy with obvious sincerity. He gazed around the glittering Italian scene. "My present position," he said "sometimes seems to me like a dream. In the midst of all my splendours I sometimes long to return to my independence in Paris—the days when I was with my regiment. But, as regards the Emperor, I have only one course—obedience. He ordered me to feel no longer myself a Frenchman, and I obey . . . Yet how often do I seek consolation in memories of my country . . . But I have another consolation. I have married a princess. I adore her, not for her birth and beauty but for her heart and virtue."[16]

He had every reason to feel some anxiety. It seemed clear that the Emperor's present campaign was going to follow that of 1805 in detail. After his victories of Jena-Auerstadt and his occupation of Berlin, he had been in quite as hazardous a situation as after Ulm before Austerlitz. Eugène had scarcely a flicker of hope that he would be allowed to go to Poland, and by June 14 the utter defeat of Bennigsen at the Battle of Friedland showed him that the summer campaign of 1807 was over. The Czar sued for an armistice at once, and had prolonged discussions with the Emperor against an unusual background. The bridge over the river Niemen at Tilsit had been blown up, but French engineers constructed a raft on which was erected a fairy-tale pavilion decorated with enormous crowned intitials "A" and "N".

Here was framed the Treaty by which Frederick William of Prussia lost half his kingdom. Everything west of the Elbe went to form a new kingdom, Westphalia, to be given to Jerome Bonaparte. The King of Saxony got Prussia's Polish territory. There were also secret clauses directed against England and Turkey.

Another member of his family had been longing to join the Emperor. Josephine had been allowed to accompany him no further than Mainz where she had sat disconsolate from September till January, when she had returned in despair to Paris. Her husband's letters assured her that it would be quite impossible for him to have her in Poland. In April he was established in a château which he described as really beautiful—Finkenstein; but still it was out of the question that she should come there. The spring floods were something that had to be seen to be believed. The unfortunate Queen of Prussia, on her road from Memel to Königsberg, very nearly came to a horrible end. The two leading horses in the team of six tugging her coach through the mud simply disappeared from view. Duroc's coach crossing the marshes between the Oder and the Vistula had overturned and he had his right clavicle broken.

Josephine knew that she had no reason to be jealous of the Queen of Prussia. The Emperor had only met her three times, and had refused every single thing for which the poor proud woman had humbled herself to plead. She had driven away from their last interview weeping bitterly. But Josephine listened to gossip, and Polish ladies at Strasbourg and in Paris were boasting that the Emperor had taken a new mistress in their country, eighteen years old, aristocratic, blonde and passionate Marie Lontschinska,

Countess Walewska. But if a promise that Poland should again be an independent kingdom had been the price of her virtue, the sacrifice had been vain. The new Grand-Duchy of Warsaw had gone to swell the King of Saxony's domains.

Josephine wrote repeatedly to her son in the early autumn of 1807. The Emperor had returned to her in July. He had been ten months away from Paris, his longest absence yet in a career which now seemed to have reached its highest pinnacle of success. She told Eugène that it had been a relief to find his affection still warm. She had been tormented while he was in Poland by tales that Murat, always inimical to the Beauharnais, had been urging him on to divorce. "It is clear that he wishes to succeed him." She was forty-five and in poor health. Eugène agreed unhappily that he heard much, both from Munich and Paris, of divorce. But he was reassured by her description of the Emperor's attitude. "If it was such as you describe," he had to add. He urged her always to speak the simple truth to His Majesty. If the worst came to the worst, and the Emperor believed that for his own happiness and that of France he should re-marry, there could be no question as to what must happen to Josephine. She must settle in Italy, with her children. The Emperor must be asked to make suitable provision for her. Her "truly affectionate son" told her not to look ahead and make herself miserable by dwelling upon things that might never come to pass, not to annoy the Emperor by scenes and by debts. He suggested more prudence in her confidences to those about her. "Pardon me, mother dear, I am so ready to speak reason to you and offer sage advice because I myself need it."[17]

The Beauharnais family had another reason to feel anxiety about the future. Although Louis had always refused to allow the Emperor to adopt his eldest son there had been little doubt in any quarter that this child would most probably succeed him in France. Suddenly, in May 1807, after six days' illness, the beloved little boy, who had reached the attractive age of four and a half, died at the Hague. When Hortense was brought to realize that her darling was no more she seemed likely to lose her reason. She gave up hope and only asked to be allowed to die too. She lay for several hours apparently paralysed with grief. She could not weep or take nourishment. The Emperor was still in Poland. Louis brought his wife to the Palace of Laeken near Brussels where Josephine took charge of her. After a suitable interval in Paris

Hortense went for convalescence in the Pyrenees. The Emperor offered a prize of ten thousand francs for research into diphtheria, but none of the eighty-three memoranda received at the Institute seemed to offer much help. He became exasperated by Hortense's self-reproach and self-pity. The disease which had carried off her son was a killer. No known remedy could have saved the child. Hundreds of children died of it every year. Louis had also been deeply moved by the death of his first-born and when husband and wife met again a reconciliation took place. It was doomed to be short-lived, but it produced the third son of Hortense. He was an eight months' child and weakly. Her second son had always been fragile. It appeared to everyone that the Emperor would have to think again on the question of a successor within his family.

He wrote to Eugène's wife who had sent him a letter of condolence "I thank you for what you say relating to the death of the little Napoleon. His mother is not being reasonable, and is afflicting herself too much. One has to summon courage to resign oneself to blows of fate which it is beyond our power to avert. I want very much to see the little Josephine and I hope she resembles her mother."

Eugène and Auguste had written at once to Hortense asking her to come to Monza. Hortense sent her brother painful detailed descriptions of her symptoms and her loss. Unfortunately, she had been asleep, after five nights of agonized watching, at the moment that the little boy had drawn his last breath. She said Eugène was, and always had been, her only protector in this world, and that but for her remaining children she would come to live in Italy for ever, with him and his family. She would like to send her love to Eugène's baby, but the very mention of a child made her tears flow again. She said—and this rang perfectly true—that she would never be the same as before the death of her first-born.

The summer of 1807 passed otherwise very happily at the Viceregal court. The Treaty of Tilsit had solved the Dalmatian trouble. Except that the Emperor continued to fire contentious letters at the Pope, which Eugène had to forward as if from himself, no major difficulty seemed to threaten their peace. Eugène had met Pius VII and, like everyone sensitive to such impressions, had realized that he was in the presence of a saint-like character. Auguste had the deepest veneration for his office, and was horrified when the Emperor threatened that if the Holy Father did not close his ports against British merchandize he would reduce him to the status of simply the ruler of Rome.

In August the Emperor effected another of his dynastic marriages, this time for a Bonaparte. There was an enormously stout, rather horrible, old Grand Duke of Württemberg whom the Emperor had turned into a king in recognition of the services of his troops during the last war against Austria. Constant thought the King of Württemberg must have been invented to show how much strain the skin could bear. He had a half moon cut out of his dinner table, specially built chairs to bear his weight, and a ferocious temper. He was said to lay about him in all directions; everyone agreed he beat his staff; Constant heard that even his second wife, who had been the Princess Royal of England did not escape. He had two weakish sons, one of whom had fought against the Emperor in the late campaign and got himself taken prisoner, whereupon the Emperor had treated him with nothing but contempt. There was also one daughter, the Princess Catherine, dark and rosy, plump and good humoured. Jerome Bonaparte who had served well in command of the Bavarian corps in Prussia was told by his brother that he was to be King of Westphalia and marry the Princess Catherine of Württemberg. There was a great summoning of royalties to the Imperial Court to witness the marriage, which was, surprisingly, to turn out quite a success, although it was not in the nature of Jerome to be a faithful husband.

When the festivities were over the Emperor seemed disappointed that in spite of all he had expended in time and money, there had been little real gaiety, a noticeable lack of spontaneity. Perhaps the crack of the ring-master's whip had been heard too audibly. He decided to go down to Italy before Christmas. The weather would not be good, so he would not be taking Josephine. She was told she might send a very handsome present to Eugène's wife, and decided upon a garland of flowers, in diamonds. The flower she chose was the Hortensia, which sounded as if the recipient should have been Eugène's sister. However, Auguste was to get it, and as she would never know, Eugène was told to sound the jewellers of Milan as to the probable cost of such an ornament. The Emperor believed that the jewellers in Paris who had shown one to the Empress were all robbers.

The Emperor's wishes for his visit were ascertained and a schedule was drawn up. Auguste's family were to be invited to come from Munich, in force, King, Queen, Crown Prince, Princess Charlotte and the Comte Montgelas in attendance. The young King of Etruria was coming, and his mother who had been born an Infanta of Spain. Two Bonaparte sisters would be present—the Baciocchis from Lucca, the Murats from Paris. Talleyrand and Berthier would be with the Emperor. The difficulty would be to fit them all in. Monza could swallow any amount of royalties with their suites, but such exalted people could hardly be asked to drive ten miles in to Milan and out again daily. Auguste decided her father would have to come to the Villa Bonaparte.

The Emperor was expected about November 20 and would not require the Viceroy to meet him at Stupinigi. Eugène would receive him in Milan. There would be a grand evening reception on the first night, with music provided by military bands, and a display of fireworks and illuminations throughout the city, part-icularly in the cathedral square. There would be a presentation of leading Italian poets—Monte and Cesaretti, of painters—Appiani, of course, and Rossi, and of savants—Moscati, Lamberti, Ciognano. The next morning (Sunday) the Emperor and Viceroy would ride in procession to the cathedral for a Te Deum before a parade of troops. There would be a gala performance at the Scala that night.

The Bavarian royal family who would be coming over the Brenner would join the progress at Verona. The Emperor had said he would need a fortnight based on Venice where he would be meeting the King of Naples. Venice proposed a regatta, gondola races, launching of a frigate and corvette, a masked ball and a performance at the Fenice Theatre. The Emperor would inspect the harbours and fortifications. The guests would be shown the manufactures of glass and marble, famous churches and palaces and galleries.

The Emperor's instructions about the disposal of the art treasures of Venice were detailed. He had never himself visited the place since it had become part of his Kingdom of Italy and he realized that perhaps the lesson he had taught the Venetians at the time of the Peace of Camp Formio had been too severe. They had never got over having their beloved copper-gilt horses re-moved from above the entrance to St. Mark's basilica. "It is my wish that all the masterpieces should stay in Venice in order not to make the city feel too humiliated. I see no reason why you should not use those which were the property of the Republic, in the royal palace at Venice, and in the same way in the Brenta palace or Monza. It is fair to treat Venice in the same way as Brescia or Bologna. But don't start trouble, particularly at a time when the commercial life of Venice is suffering owing to the blockade. Hand over any masterpieces which are not the personal property of the Crown to the royal Intendant-General; in that way you can have them transported wherever your wish."

The palace on the Brenta was at Strà and had been built by the fashionable architects Frigimelica and Preti for a member of the Pisani family who had been elected Doge of Venice in 1735. The stables were particularly likely to please the Viceroy as there was a beautiful model of a spirited horse, mounted on a pillar, guarding every stall. The palace itself was decidedly grandiose. It was now to be renamed Villa Imperiale. It was noted for its huge ballroom with ceiling paintings by Tiepolo. The Emperor had bought it, and was presenting it to the Viceroy as a summer residence to use from Venice or Padua. Its gardens were also famous. The night to be spent at Strà when their superb new home would be presented to the young couple was one of the leading features of the visit and would take place on the road to Venice. To be exact, the Emperor would leave Strà by barge as the palace was so close to the Brenta canal that its pillared façade was reflected in those still waters.

During early December the Emperor intended to visit Treviso, Palmanova, Udine and Osoppo. Another single night for which a palace would have to be hastily put in modern working order would be that spent at Mantua in the historic but not cheerful Reggia dei Gonzaga. They must be back in Milan by the middle of the month for various public ceremonies including sittings of the Corporations of the Possidenti, the Dotti and the Commercianti, and the formal adoption of Eugène as Prince of Venice and heir-presumptive to the throne of Italy. At the same session his daughter, the little Josephine, would receive the title of Contessa of Bologna, with a rich endowment, and Melzi would become Duke of Lodi. The second bout of entertainments in Milan was calculated to put those of Venice in the shade. The Viceroy would attend the Emperor to Turin on his homeward road, and their last engagement together would be an inspection of the immense new fortifications at Alessandria.

At last all the oceans of redolent white paint and gilding had been applied and the classical furniture of the Emperor's various bedrooms had been set in position. His baths gushed hot water. His canopied four-posters with bottle-green silk curtains, adorned with eagles and laurels and his initials, were waiting for him at Strà and Milan and Venice and Vicenza and Mantua.[18] In every kitchen were abundant supplies of his favourite Parmesan cheese.

He never allowed the weather to interfere with his social arrangements, so he got caught in a blizzard on the Mont Cenis and had to struggle on foot to a cave for shelter. Nevertheless he was at Milan on November 21 where the Viceroy alone received him. The Vicereine had suffered a miscarriage. Luckily, she had still been out at Monza. She had been three and half months pregnant.

VI

The full programme was carried out, though lacking the chief lady. The Emperor went out to see her in her bed at Monza on his first Sunday, between the service and parade at Milan cathedral and the evening performance at the Scala. The presentation to Eugène alone of Strà was rather a deflated occasion, and nature seemed to appreciate this, for the rain came down in torrents on a scene which needed brilliant sunshine, and his triumphal barge arrived to bear the Emperor to Venice in a steady downpour. This continued for the first days in Venice, but there was plenty for the foreign visitors to enjoy indoors. The Queen of Bavaria went for delightful incognito shopping expeditions and bought largely of very pretty Venetian glass beads and ear-rings, produced, she was told for the export market—the Levant and India. The Emperor presented her with a marble statue of Psyche by Canova. He toured the harbour and forts deep in discourse with his brother Joseph. He took the Bavarians out on the lagoon for a very rough cruise in a gunboat, and during the firing of royal salutes a sailor fell from a mast-head in full view of the queen, who covered her eyes while the people of Venice raised a dramatic howl. The man, however, was rescued.

From Mantua the Bavarians returned to Monza. Mantua had presented less difficulties than other places as regarded accommodation, for Eugène had been staying there at intervals during the past two years and had occupied a fine suite of apartments redecorated for another fleeting royal visit—that of the Empress

Maria Theresa . . . They were on the first floor with a view of the Piazza Sordello, oblong in shape, and a side view of the red brick Duomo with a particularly picturesque campanile. The Emperor was accommodated in a splendid saloon with signs of the Zodiac all over the ceiling.

On the night of their arrival, about nine o'clock, Méneval slipped out, to go across the piazza to the most considerable inn of Mantua. Here his instructions were to say he had called for the Secretary to the King of Naples. This was the errant Lucien Bonaparte, who was brought in to his brother's presence by a secret entry. Eugène waited and wondered, in the uncongenial company of Murat, in a painted gallery for three long hours that night. The Sala dei Fiumi was embellished with allegorical figures of the rivers near Mantua. Each was represented by a large nude river-deity. In front of the gallery was a hanging garden. It was not a cheerful scene on a December night. Later, in Milan, the Emperor burst out to Max Joseph in complaints of Lucien, whom he described as quite wrong-headed, still mad about an impossible woman and mad enough to insist that the Emperor should recognize their eldest son. "How can I do that, when he was born two years before their marriage, and everyone in Paris knows he was not the father?" The only agreement reached had been that Lucien's eldest daughter should be sent to live with her grand-mother in Paris as a preparatory for a possible match with the Prince of the Austurias. For himself Lucien still rejected any principality or power.

Méneval noted at the session of the three Corporations, when Eugène's adoption and new title were announced, that the Emperor had to poke his self-effacing deputy. "Get up! Bow! It is you they are applauding."[19]

On more than one night of the Emperor's stay in Milan, candles were still burning in his apartments looking out on the cathedral square until the small hours. He was working with his secretaries. His interests were now no longer only European. There had been emissaries from the Shah of Persia at Finkenstein, come to arrange an anti-British, anti-Russian alliance. His thoughts still sometimes seemed to return to India—to Egypt. But England was the enemy who always evaded him. The English had collected the Danish Fleet and the Portuguese Fleet. Just before he had left home he had signed a secret treaty with Spain, providing for the carving up of Portugal. Junot had crossed into Spain to march on Portugal before it had been signed. The Portuguese royal family had been evacuated to Brazil by Eugène's old acquaintance, Admiral Sir Sidney Smith. The Milan Decree, which the Emperor issued on December 17 declared that any neutral ship submitting to the British Orders in Council was subject to seizure by France.

The Bavarian royal family stayed on in Milan for Christmas and the New Year, but the Emperor arrived back in Paris on January 1. He was satisfied with his visit to his kingdom of Italy. The new fortifications should be perfectly adequate to deter Austria from any attempt at invasion while he went to Spain. Amongst the good strokes of business which he had managed on this trip had been urging the Queen of Etruria to join her parents in Spain. He would be needing Tuscany, but her son was to be given ample territory in conquered Portugal. It was to be known as Lusitania.

CHAPTER ELEVEN

Commander in Chief

1808 : 1809

I

ON JANUARY 11, 1808 the 1809 class of conscripts was called up. In February, in accordance with instructions from the Emperor, Eugène sent General Miollis down to occupy Rome. A month later the provinces of Ancona, Macerate, Fermo and Urbino were united to the kingdom over which he bore rule. The Vatican broke off diplomatic relations with France, but nothing further happened yet in that direction. Pius VII had enclosed himself in the Quirinal.

The Emperor left Paris in March, avowedly for the south of France: his letters to Milan continued. Throughout the year they were occupied with three main topics—the necessity for establishing the new order in the newly-acquired states, the necessity for reorganizing the army of Italy, the necessity of watching Austria. There was very little about Spain in the Emperor's letters but occasionally he added a scribble of a few explanatory lines in his own hand to a letter dictated to a secretary. These were generally prefaced by the words, "For your eye alone," and Eugène thanked him with great gratitude for such confidences.

By the middle of April the Emperor had established himself in a castle called Marrac about a mile outside Bayonne. Here he waited patiently for the royal family of Spain to walk into the trap. They did this with uncommon docility, but not without mutual recrimination. They had recently been the subject of a famous family group by their renowned artist Goya, and it was clear from the Emperor's description of them that they had not been libelled. It would hardly have been possible to represent them as more unattractive and disreputable than they were in fact. Carlos IV, who was a very bad sixty, was stout, stupid,

Her Imperial Highness the Princess Auguste-Amélie of Bavaria,
Vicereine of Italy, aged twenty, from an engraving by Paolo Caroni after a portrait by Antonio Locatelli
By permission of the Stadtmuseum, Munich

placid, crippled with gout. He pleased the Emperor most. He had not abdicated quite voluntarily. He had been entirely ruled by a favourite, born Manuel Godoy, who had received the title of Prince of Peace in recognition of the part he had played in concluding the Peace of Basle in 1759. Godoy, whom nobody doubted was the Queen's principal permanent lover, had been very nearly torn in pieces by the inhabitants of Aranjuez when a rumour had gone round that he was removing the King and Queen to Seville or America. The country had endured him for fifteen years. He was now forty and losing his looks. The Emperor said he reminded him of a prize bull. The character of Queen Maria Luisa was written in her face, though she too was not as young as she had been. She looked like an angry witch. The fourth important Spanish royalty was the first to arrive. He was the heir to the throne, the Prince of the Asturias. He had been intriguing secretly with France for some months, asking for a bride of the Emperor's choosing. Unfortunately for him, he had announced his accession as Ferdinand VII on his father's abdication, and it had been received with applause. This did not suit the Emperor's plans at all. He was a degenerate-looking young man of twenty-four, thick-set, swarthy, low-statured. The Emperor was hardest on him. He said he had thought he had seen royalty at its lowest in the King of Prussia, but compared to the Prince of the Asturias, Frederick William now appeared a hero. Ferdinand did not speak for several hours after his arrival. (He was hardly to be blamed. He had heard what had happened to the Duc d'Enghien. Moreover loyal Spaniards had tried to take the horses out of his carriage to prevent him leaving Spanish soil.) "He is indifferent to everything, entirely materialistic, eats four times a day and has not one idea in his head." He would have to be disposed of, for the Emperor's schemes had been long-laid and were exact. Before he had left France he had written to his brother Louis. "The Dutch climate disagrees with you. Besides, the country is too thoroughly ruined to rise again . . . Give me a categorical answer. If I nominate you King of Spain will you accept the offer; can I count on you?" Louis had said no, quickly. Joseph, who mistakenly believed that Spain would be less exacting than Naples, had accepted. This meant that Murat, who was now in Madrid as Commander in Chief of the French troops, would have to be succeeded in that position by Soult and take the crown of Naples left vacant by Joseph. He would not like this. He was counting on

Spain. He, and particularly his wife, had always asked for a king-dom. The Grand-Duchy of Berg was too small for them. It could now go to Hortense's son.

Hortense always regretted that she had not been present at an astonishing interview when the Emperor confronted Charles IV of Spain and his queen with their heir in the Château de Marrac. "My mother has often told me how the parents gave vent to their fury, with a vivacity and show of hatred such as our Northern and more controlled natures find difficult to understand."[1] This description was indeed controlled. It was generally believed that when the prince had been ushered in, the king, although he could hardly hobble, had gone for him with cane upraised, while Queen Maria Luisa had to be deterred from plunging her talons in her son's visage. The prince had stood immobile with downcast eyes. He had to be hurried out. It was represented to him that his father's abdication had been irregular, and therefore if he per-sisted in calling himself Ferdinand VII he would be guilty of high treason.

On April 18 the Emperor had written to Eugène that he was immensely occupied. The Spanish royalties had begun to arrive (a younger prince with measles). "There is plenty of movement in Spain. The Grand Duke is at Madrid, Bessières at Burgos, Duhesme at Barcelona. King Carlos has protested against his abdication and begged for my support. Time will decide what shall happen." By May 6 he was able to announce, "We approach a settlement. King Carlos has ceded to me all his rights to the throne. He will retire to Compiègne. The Grand Duke of Berg is nominated Lieutenant-General of the realm and President of all its juntas." There had been an insurrection in Madrid, but not serious, and really advantageous, as it had been possible to profit by the circumstance to disarm the city. Ten days later the Emperor thought that the blood-letting in Madrid had cooled all heads. "Here the *affaire* is finished. The house of Bourbon has ceased to reign in Spain."[2] Joseph was coming from Naples. The Emperor could return to St. Cloud, for a few weeks rest.

The fate of the Prince of the Asturias became rather comedy than tragedy. Talleyrand had been very difficult about the Spanish adventure. He disapproved of it. He was no longer foreign minister but had been awarded a rich plum—the office of Vice-Grand-Elector. He was now told that he was going to play host to three Spanish princes, the Prince of the Asturias, a younger brother and an uncle, at his country seat the Château de Valençay. He could not refuse. He had them for six years. When he was further told, early in September, that he was now expected to attend a second meeting between the Emperor and the Czar at an outlandish place called Erfurt in Thuringia, he was displeased. Much had been left unsettled by the Treaty of Tilsit. It had been suggested that the Emperor should send for the Viceroy to help to negotiate. The young prince was popular with the German princes with whom he was now allied by marriage, and who would be coming to Erfurt in strength. But the Emperor had dismissed the idea. "Eugène is not clever enough. He will carry out instructions to the letter, but he is no good at insinuating. Talleyrand will do it better. Besides, he will tell them as a sneer at me, how much they will please me by coming, and then I can show them that I don't care a fig whether they came or not." When Talleyrand produced the draft treaty which he had been told to prepare the Emperor could hardly believe his eyes. "How can you have forgotten Austria? It is the essential article. Are you still pro-Austrian?" "A little, sir," replied Talleyrand. "But I think it would be more correct to say that I am never pro-Russian and always pro-French."

II

1808 passed peacefully at Milan and Monza. Both Eugène and Auguste sat to Italian artists—Locatelli, Calliano, Bosio . . . The Viceroy was depicted in full-dress Henri IV costume. Behind him on a table lay two volumes of the Code Napoléon. He was also represented on a snorting steed. In the background of one portrait of Auguste, a gentle Italian scene of mountain and lake showed through an open window: in another she walked in a garden with sentries at a distance: her gown was patterned with the fruitful vine. In February, the Palazzo of the Brera was promoted Palazzo Reale of Science and Art. There was a new Conservatoire of Music in Milan, a new girls' school, a new lying-in hospital. At Venice the Viceroy had re-established the Accademia. His name should surely descend as a Patron of the Arts. He had ordered the artist Joseph Bossi to restore the "Last Supper" of Leonardo.

His wife had become quite accustomed to being left while he went on short tours of his domain. She said they had at Monza a little shady walk, *"Allée des larmes,"* where someone sad could walk and weep a little, unobserved.

In the beginning of June Eugène made an expedition to Ancona and rode up the line of the Piave. He returned by Venice and Mantua which he had already visited in March. The Emperor had written that he thought Lauriston should be the only governor of a province assigned a royal residence. He had better take part of the Palazzo Reale in Venice, or Strà. He had a wife whom everyone liked. The Lauristons were a decorative couple.

The Prince of the Asturias was obviously no longer valuable in the marriage market. In June, Auguste's sister Charlotte made a match which sounded in every way more suitable. The Emperor had sounded her parents upon it when she had been brought to Italy, and they had approved. Prince William of Württemberg was the elder son, and would succeed his enormous father as King. The wedding took place in the same setting and with almost identical festivities as that of Auguste and Eugène—Green Gallery, Chapel wedding (but with inferior rites, as the bridegroom was a Protestant), gala performance at the Residenz theatre. The church of "Old Peter" was illuminated; there were peals of bells, bonfires and salutes. There was no question of Auguste attending. She was again three months pregnant.

The Emperor had at last worn down Berthier to consider marriage. He had pointed out that the marshal's gout and migraine were depressing, and to continue single for the sake of Madame Visconti was ludicrous. They were both now between fifty and sixty, and although Madame was remarkably well-preserved she had a son by her first marriage, the Conte Sopronsi, who was by no means the youngest of the marshal's aides de camp, and a son by her marriage to Visconti, also of full age. Berthier shed tears before he agreed to marry the Princess Elizabeth, daughter of Duke William of Bavaria, of the Birkenfeld branch of the Wittelsbach family. She was the excessively talkative plain princess whom Eugène had attempted to entertain politely at a banquet in Cologne in 1804. She was now twenty-five and although she had to put up with Madame Visconti, and indeed accepted her as her best friend, she maintained stoutly to the last that she had made a very advantageous match. Berthier became the father of two sons and a daughter, and they all lived together with every appearance of concord in his beautiful country château of Grosbois outside Paris. But there were soon surprising stories that

Berthier, hitherto open-handed, had on his marriage to a royal princess become ludicrously mean. When out riding in the park he had actually stopped the baker's delivery of a certain fine bread ordered by his wife, and sacked his long-established majordomo for furthering the order. The marshal felt that Fate had dealt him a mean trick. Three months after he had married Princess Elizabeth, Madame Visconti's husband had died.[3]

But Berthier's marriage was a brilliant success compared with those of Rapp, and Eugène's cousin Stéphanie de Tascher. This girl had been suggested for the Prince of the Asturias or William of Württemberg, but had lost her head over Rapp. Josephine had spoken to her very sharply about considering such a mésalliance and she had given way and accepted the Duc d'Arenberg. She was raised to the rank of princess and her family were delighted, but although she had not had sufficient force of character to refuse to marry him, she was quite steadfast in refusing to live with him. At the end of ten years the marriage was annulled. Rapp took, at the Emperor's command a beautiful and rich wife, the daughter of a banker, but she was so flighty that even the Emperor had to agree Rapp must seek a divorce.

It was almost a relief that Lucien Bonaparte's daughter need not be found a husband. The young lady had, according to the arrangement made at Mantua, been sent to live in Paris with her grandmother Madame Mère to be groomed for a throne. Nobody had warned her that the Emperor saw private letters. Her letters home were so witty about the Bonapartes *en masse* that the Emperor could not resist reading them aloud to the victims one summer's day after a Sunday dinner at St. Cloud. But there could be no question but that such a clever girl had better be returned to her father without delay.[4]

Eugène saw a fine frigate launched at Ancona, *La Princesse Auguste*. He came up by Forlì and Ravenna, once the capital of the Byzantine exarchs. The Emperor Napoleon's stepson, handsome in his Guards uniform, stared at Emperors and Empresses depicted life-size in tiny little brilliant bricks. Their forms were elongated. They had haloes and almond eyes. Ravenna was the most unusual place. He stayed at the palace of the Archbishop, Condronchi and visited the basilica of San Vitale and the tomb of Galla Placida, a royal lady of the fifth century, and the tomb of Dante. He gave orders for the repair of the mausoleum of Theodoric. Ravenna was now dead-alive, deserted by the sea, breathing nothing but malaria and melancholy, but the mosaics in its famous monuments were still touching in their simple and austere beauty. His visit ended with a call at the University Library and a horse-race.

He had only two letters from the Emperor from Erfurt. The first was about the King of Naples and his horses, and the second about a Greek spy from the Seven Isles called Claudans who was said to be in Venetia and had better be rounded up and relieved of his passport. The Conference had been brilliantly mounted. Talma had performed before what he called "a parterre of Kings and Princes"—Saxony, Bavaria, Württemberg, Baden ... The Czar was so deaf that he had to be given a chair on a platform close to the stage, and that meant that the Emperor must have one too ...

Suddenly in November, it appeared that the Emperor must go to Spain again. He got back from Erfurt on October 20. On November 4 he was at Bayonne. He was in Vittoria, in Burgos. He had forced the Somosierra pass in a snowstorm and was in Madrid. Two days before Christmas, in Milan, Auguste gave birth to her second child. "The little prince, how does he get on?" had been the Emperor's jocular enquiry before leaving for Erfurt. The parents asked Hortense to be godmother to Eugénie Hortense, and the Queen of Holland replied typically that if the name of someone so unlucky should not be considered of evil omen she would be much pleased to be sponsor to an infant so dear to her already. There had been a little unpleasantness in September when Eugène had ventured to suggest that as her baby was now six months old she should return to her husband in Holland. She told Eugène that the Emperor was thinking of giving his hunting box la Jonchère to a young married couple—General Bertrand who had been an Imperial aide de camp since Austerlitz, and Fanny Dillon, whose mother had been a Girardin and had been first married to M. Vasse de la Touche, so was a relation. Hortense said if these horrible affairs in Spain finished this winter would not Eugène and his family be coming to Paris?

But the horrible affairs in Spain had barely begun. The Emperor had entirely mistaken the character of the Spanish resistance. Eugène, who had been trained in the wars of La Vendée, would have found the pattern familiar. A patriot army of nobility and peasants, urged on by priests, was arising spontaneously all over the country to throw out the French. Moreover, they had called in the English to help them. They had originally been quiet because they had thought that the Emperor was getting rid of Godoy and would support Ferdinand VII, but Joseph on his arrival in Madrid had found it necessary to warn his brother, "Your name is absolutely hated here." In August, while the Emperor was planning to go to Erfurt to ensure that Russia should at least pronounce herself neutral should Austria try to come in to Italy by the back door, Junot had suffered an undeniable defeat at the Battle of Vimiero. He had been obliged by the Convention of Cintra to evacuate Portugal—a treaty agreeable neither to France nor England. Bessières had routed the main Spanish army at Medina del Rio Seco, but Dupont had been fairly caught at Baylen. The Emperor realized that he had not been able to bargain as satisfactorily as he had hoped at Erfurt. The Czar knew that a great part of the Grande Armée was locked up in Spain. The Emperor's wrath was particularly roused by Spanish claims that the veterans of the Grande Armée had been defeated by their guerillas.

On December 20, he set out for Salamanca with Ney's army corps, to take General John Moore in the rear while Soult kept him pinned down in Burgos. He had yet to learn that insufficiently escorted French officers ordered to ride in haste across unfrequented districts in Spain did not arrive. A French despatch rider murdered by the peasants at the post-house of Valdestillas, near Segovia, had been carrying a letter from the Emperor in the hand of Berthier directed to Soult . . . On the night that this document reached the hands of John Moore, the English march on Valladolid was cancelled and the troops were put through a half left-wheel and turned north "for a wipe at Soult." At Sahagún, the furthest point of his advance, Moore made the difficult decision to retreat. But his attempt to threaten Bonaparte's long line of communications had succeeded beyond his wildest expectations. At Astorga on New Year's night 1809 the Emperor found that he had missed Moore. It was claimed that he also found letters portending trouble in Germany and even in Paris.

On New Year's Day the Viceroy sent his customary letter repeating his great wish to serve again under the Emperor in arms. But the Emperor had left Spain, never to return. He had failed in Spain, and although the British Expeditionary Force had suffered terrible things, including the death of Moore on the field of Corunna, another army would be sent out from England within the year. Spain was to become an ulcer, a running sore.

III

The spring of 1809 seemed on the surface just as peaceful as that of 1808. Eugène believed that war with Austria must come and very soon, but the Emperor seemed to think it was not coming yet and that the great thing was to pretend one had no idea of such a possibility. He sent instructions to Eugène and Auguste to go down to Strà in early April. No explanation was ever offered of his sudden and dramatic return from Spain, leaving a campaign which had hopelessly miscarried to be dealt with by his marshals. He had also left a great part of the Grande Armée, two hundred thousand veteran soldiers, ten thousand cavalry, five hundred guns—Soult, who was very unpopular in Spain, Mortier, liked everywhere, Ney and Victor whose very names were trumpet calls. His available troops, should Austria attack him, were the Army of the Rhine, under Davout, spread over Franconia and Saxony, and Bernadotte's Hanseatic corps, about a hundred thousand men in all. He could also reckon on about a hundred thousand allied and vassal contingents—Saxons, Bavarians, Württembergers, some of them very good fighting material. Reports from Austria were that whereas in 1805 only the Government had wanted war, now the government, the people and the army all wanted it. And in the army there had been a complete reorganization. It now had three able commanders, the experienced Archduke Charles, the Archduke John, and the Archduke Joseph (Palatine of Hungary). The Emperor of Austria was blessed with no less than seven brothers.

In Paris the Emperor Napoleon had decided to form a Young Guard, drawn from selected conscripts of the Guard and trained by the Old Guard. He said that if the word conscript continued to be found depressing they could be called *tirailleurs*—skirmishers or sharp-shooters. No more was heard of a plot between Talleyrand and Fouché, possibly in conjunction with Murat, to overthrow his authority while he was on the far side of the Pyrenees. If such trouble had been brewing he had arrived home in time to stop it.

Eugène could not get him to consent to putting the Kingdom of Italy in a state of defence by concentrating its forces on the frontiers. Either the Emperor thought he was dealing with a young Commander in Chief longing to show his mettle, or else his long

248

experience of lethargy in the Austrian cabinet led him to believe he had time in hand. In the end Eugène got his permission to depart on another of his tours—inspections and parades which should take him about the usual three weeks. By early April Auguste had entirely recovered from her confinement and both his children were flourishing. (Like a good French papa he usually alluded to them as his *"petits choux"*. Sometimes they were even his *"marmosets"*.) Princess Josephine, Countess of Bologna, was now two years old, running and talking, perfectly able to realize that her papa was going to the army. The children of the Viceroy, like children in comfortable homes all over Europe, wore almost a uniform costume—full length white muslin gown with puff sleeves and high waist, a necklace of beads (in Italy often corals) hair cropped so that they looked like little boys, morocco slippers. For cold weather their Aunt Hortense sent them from Paris little knitted woollen jackets with long sleeves called after an English peeress who rode to hounds "spencers".[5] During her husband's absence Auguste would have her nursery and her ladies, her music and her library and her sewing-bag. German princesses were trained to arrive for the day with their sewing. At Württemberg the violent old king had shown the Emperor whole rooms entirely covered, so he said, by needlework performed by the females of his family.

The Viceroy departed from the Villa Bonaparte in Milan on the morning of April 1, inconspicuously. But on the box of a carriage containing an officer who had been on the Egyptian campaign and was the son of the Emperor, sat an impassive Mameluke with folded arms—Petrus. Eugène began at once to prove himself a good correspondent.

"April 5, 1809
"(seven o'clock at night.)

"I arrived at the gates of Verona, my beloved Auguste, at two o'clock in the afternoon and at once got on a horse to review the troops. I then visited the Artillery park and the château, and on getting back received all the authorities awaiting my arrival. By seven o'clock I had a good appetite for my dinner. After dinner I remounted, but into a carriage, to go up to Trent and Lavis (on the Avisio). I don't know whether tomorrow will be sufficient for me to see all this part of the country.

"We had a very cold night. Charpentier and d'Anthouard were luckier than I. I did not sleep a wink. Would you believe it, we found snow at Brescia, and today, during my review, we were chilled to the marrow. There are three inches now of snow—truly extraordinary.

"I hope, my dear Auguste that you are well, and our little darlings. I have only just left them, and yet I am longing to be with them again. Adieu my beloved Auguste, my sweet friend. You know, I hope my feelings for you; they will never change."

"April 7, 1809
"(ten o'clock at night.)

"Here I am back from my long trip up into the Tyrol, my beloved and very dear Auguste. I have not been able to write before because the day before yesterday I covered two hundred and fifty miles in a carriage, on a horse and on foot. We have seen plenty of snow in the mountains. It has not been possible for me to preserve my incognito. At Trent I was recognized by Trinzle, Poiro, and the Chevalier Seinsheim who is working there. I dined with three principal Bavarians of the district, whom as you can imagine wanted to hear all about you. This, as you already know is a subject for conversation which I much enjoy. So talking to them I forgot the hour, and midnight sounded before we rose from the table. I go on tonight to Mestre for the night and shall stop only to review troops for two hours at Vicenza.

"My Paris letters tell me that the Emperor is about to start for Strasbourg. He is sending three or four general officers who are bound to pass through Milan. If they ask for an audience, do receive them the same day. I am hard at work on a report of my tour for the Emperor."

He did not tell his wife that it appeared he had had a narrow escape. Luckily, when he had gone up the valley of the Adige, four hours march on foot, he had left a piquet at Salurn. Colonel Vaudoucourt had found it and hastened to warn him that there was a plot to capture him and deliver him to the Austrians.

"Mestre.

"I have only time for two words, my beloved Auguste. I reviewed a division this morning at Vicenza, got in here at four, got on a horse again and went round the fortifications. On getting in I dined, but then had to work without ceasing until this moment. Next door there is much snoring from the gentry asleep in their chairs who await my signal to get on the road again. I shall get to Udine to-night. There, as always, you will be continually in my thoughts and in possession of my heart. My time really is divided between my work and the joy of occupying myself with my little family. I embrace you with all my strength, also our little loves."

"Udine, April 10

"I can't send as long a letter as I should wish, my very dear Auguste. I have been absolutely beset with business since the moment that I arrived here after dinner. The weather has been awful and if these rains continue I should not be surprised if we were several days late in getting back to Milan. Anyway it depends on what happens. Last night, I saw all my spies, and all maintain that the Austrians are going to attack soon. But nothing is reliable, and I don't believe it. For the rest, I have seen a great part of my army and as you will believe found them in good shape and well placed.

"Adieu, my good and tender friend. I end with regret, but not without repeating my unalterable devotion. A thousand kisses, to be divided between you and my little darlings. You shall tell me how you distributed them."

"April 11
"Udine.

"Set your mind perfectly at rest, my dear and best beloved Auguste. War was declared yesterday morning and at the moment that I write most of our advanced posts are being attacked. I am joining the troops. Do not worry, and I hope we may come well out of the affair. I press you to my heart, and our two little darlings."[6]

IV

In his first pitched battle as Commander in Chief of the Army of Italy Eugène had the mortification of seeing his troops flying like sheep upon the mountains. He could hardly believe his eyes. He had thought he had chosen his position well—marshy ground where the Archduke John's superior force of cavalry could not manoeuvre to advantage. He knew he had taken a risk in offering battle before General Lamarque brought up his cavalry; but they should have arrived on the scene in time. (Lamarque was an old general, not co-operative with a young Commander in Chief . . .) It could not be said that the decision to fight at Sacile after his retirement from the Isonzo had been ill-advised or hurried.

He sent a short letter to his wife on the night of the 12th, saying that he was afraid she must have been anxious, since he had not been able to write to her for thirty-six hours. But really there was no cause for anxiety. The enemy had attacked his positions in great force at many points, but he was getting together his reply. His troops were on the march from Padua, Treviso and Vicenza. Broussier's, the only division to have come into anything like a serious action so far, had acquitted itself with some measure of success. "Good luck, my dearest love; take good care of yourself and my children, and be at ease in your mind about me. A thousand kisses!"

The name Sacile, appeared for the first time next day in a little note with no date or address. He hoped to arrive at Sacile that night. It was a walled mediaeval town on the river Livenza with a redoubtable ditch and a fine gothic cathedral. It might have formed an incident in the background for the figures of a Virgin and Child or Holy Family in any work of an Early Italian Master. It was some five and thirty miles south west of Udine, where on the outbreak of hostilities the division of General Séras had been concentrated. Grenier's division had been on the Tagliamento, between Sacile and Udine, those of Barbou, Lamarque and Severoli at Treviso, Vicenza and Padua. Fontanelli's camp had been above Verona—Monte-Chiaro. The enemy had attacked at Ospedaletto on the 11th, and near Palmanova forty-eight hours later. After the Viceroy had decided to reply at Sacile, General Sahuc at Pordenone, eight miles east, given orders to perform a reconnaissance with dawn, had run into serious trouble. The Archduke had arrived at Cividale after dark on the 10th. His force was reckoned at about sixty-five thousand to the Italian forty-five thousand. By the 14th the Viceroy's first line was occupying the heights of Sacile, his second was based on the little village of Fratta behind. In reserve at Pordenone he had light cavalry and three good regiments of light infantry, and at Fontane Fredde more light cavalry and one infantry regiment. He had the same at Motta, on the right bank of the river. This last force had received orders as to the destruction of bridges. He slept well to the sound of rain coming down. He got off a long letter to the Emperor.

On April 16 the armies were in position, the Austrians on the heights of Palze, drawn up in three lines. Séras opened the attack at eight a.m. Weather conditions were bad, and the Viceroy who had been over the ground yesterday in detail knew it was in poor condition. But the affair opened perfectly according to plan. Before nine, Palze village was in French hands. Thereafter the Viceroy was observed always where his presence was most needed. There was a brilliant charge of Italian Napoleon dragoons, but the Austrian advance guard held out stoutly, giving their main body time to re-form. The Archduke appeared puzzled that Prince Eugène was not going to engage him on the nearby plain of Roveredo. He did not know that Lamarque's cavalry had not yet arrived. He saw the little village of Porcia becoming a key-point, taken and re-taken. He decided to launch a cavalry charge on the centre of Eugène's left wing, menacing his retreat on Sacile. At three p.m. the fate of the day still hung in the balance, while Broussier laboured to re-take Fontane Fredde. An hour later, since he still had no news of his reserve cavalry, the Viceroy sadly gave the order for retreat. The left of the Franco-Italian army arrived in Sacile in pouring rain and full flight about eight o'clock. There was no choice for their Commander in Chief but to retreat to the Piave.

His next letter to the Emperor was dated "April 17: Banks of the Piave", and was sad. He said he had three reasons for offering battle to the Archduke John—firstly that he was being pressed by the invader, secondly that he could not bear the thought of retiring from the new provinces without striking a blow, thirdly the bad news from the Tyrol.

"I offered battle yesterday and I have the sorrow to report to Your Majesty that I lost it.

"The action opened at nine a.m. and until three p.m. the success lay in our hands, but in the evening the enemy deployed a large superior force of cavalry which gained them the day. Our troops left the field in the greatest disorder.

"I am the more distressed by this lost battle because I realize the serious consequences. However, today I have rallied my forces, and tomorrow I shall be taking them in two columns to the

Adige, having left a sizeable garrison for Venice. I shall have the honour to send to Your Majesty a detailed account. It may seem extraordinary, but it is none the less true that several incidents in this action were very creditably performed by our troops. The losses of the enemy were very large. In these circumstances I need above all else the indulgence and fatherly understanding of Your Majesty."

(His letter to his wife of the same date is missing.)

"Yesterday, my dearest Auguste, I wrote to you in despair, because I had seen with my own eyes my army completely routed. When these idiots take to their heels there is no stopping them. Today I am calmer, and have taken fresh courage. The enemy has not profited by our folly and I am taking advantage of their folly to rally my people.

"If the news from the Tyrol is good, there is still hope for us. Good-bye for the moment, my dearest Auguste; be calm. If, in spite of all precautions, the enemy come down upon us from the Tyrol, through Verona or Brescia, you know your programme—to leave Milan for Turin, and if necessary Turin for Lyons. But this need not be considered except under extraordinary circumstances. My *valet de chambre* who is carrying this has been told by me to collect my confidential papers and personal belongings to go along with you.

"Adieu, my dearest Auguste, I tremble for your peace of mind. I fear that the news I send must seem to you bad. I long to hear from you."

He need not have concerned himself over the mental health of the Princess Auguste. This daughter of a warrior race was a most resilient character. After the campaign was over the Emperor sent her a letter of congratulation on her admirable conduct during her dark days in Milan. This was the more creditable to her, as letters to her brother Ludwig, to whom she was always very close, expressed her extreme misery at being separated from her husband in his time of trial, and her dread of the Emperor's wrath being inflamed by people of the anti-Beauharnais faction who would have his ear. She attended religious services as usual, with a full suite; she showed herself and the two Italian-born children rather more than usual, driving in the Corso. She busied herself with her charities for the families of the army and the wounded. By his valet Lacroix she sent her husband miniatures of herself and his children.

"Your letter of the 19th brought tears to my eyes, my good, my tender Auguste. I know I was wrong to afflict you with my ills, but at the moment that I wrote it seemed there was scarcely a ray of hope. It appeared that Chasteler had come down from the Tyrol, had possibly already passed Trent. This made me retire to the Adige. The army will be there in two days. I can't get over your letter. What courage and composure I find in you, and how you deserve the love I bear you."

He could not, of course, expect such understanding and sympathy from the Emperor, but when a letter dated Ratisbon, April 25, reached him it was not quite as unsparing as his worst fears had led him to expect. By some mischance, a letter from Duroc (always a bad sign) telling him that the Emperor was too busy to write personally, was dated April 26. The Emperor himself scolded his stepson for offering battle without his cavalry, and supposed that an officer bringing him a full account of the action would be arriving tomorrow. Duroc disclosed that Eugène's two letters had been found unsatisfactory. The Emperor had said "One can always find a remedy for a lost battle" but demanded how was he to offer advice when he had no information? After this he gradually lost his temper. He had always indulged in calculated outbursts, but according to stories from France his temper had recently become much worse—beyond his control.

There had been an embarrassing scene after his return from Erfurt when he had heaped insults upon Talleyrand at a special meeting of the privy council. He had seemed on the point of striking his impassive Vice-Grand-Elector. Talleyrand had shrugged it off with the remark, "What a pity that such a great man should be so ill-bred." Since Erfurt, the Czar had in fact possessed two employees in Paris Count Nesselrode, his Ambassador, and Talleyrand, Prince of Benevento. It would certainly have been wiser to send Eugène, who was not so clever, to negotiate at Erfurt.

It was not Eugène's fault that their communications were halted. He had been obliged to take possession of the bridge over the Piave, so that the enemy could not cross the river nor could Venice be blockaded. He had sent word of his losses—five General officers wounded, three thousand dead, three thousand five hundred taken prisoners. He had sent as soon as possible from Vicenza a full account of the present position of his troops. Between April 17 and 30, when he was able to report a brilliant cavalry skirmish, he wrote seven times. But the Emperor, left in the dark, began to upbraid him. Why was he concerning himself with affairs in the Tyrol? At the news of the first success of the Grande Armée these troubles had begun to evaporate. General Chasteler had occupied Innsbruck and defeated the Bavarians in a battle at Sterzing, but he was not coming down upon Italy. The so-called army doing that was only a force of six thousand infantry of the line and a swarm of armed peasants, led by the Prince de Rohan.

"I can't make out anything from your letters of the 17th and 19th," raged the Emperor from Landshut. "Your conduct is very strange. Instead of sending me reliable officers you employ couriers and bad ones, who know nothing and say nothing. You have fixed your attention on the Tyrol from which direction you have nothing to fear . . . It must have been a terrible defeat to cause you to abandon the Piave line . . . It is now nine in the morning of the 27th and I still have no news of my Army of Italy. I sent off Calvaletti to you yesterday. I keep on hoping that you have not evacuated the Piave, and abandoned to Austrian pillage the beautiful country between that river and the Adige . . . Tomorrow I shall probably arrive at Salzburg. But for the incredible disasters which seem to be overtaking my Army of Italy the destiny of the royal house of Austria would be entirely settled. My son, it is now the 30th, thirteen days since you lost your battle and I still know nothing . . . Your conduct is unheard of . . . Just think, instead of reports day by day from you, and visits from officers who could give me the details of what happened on that wretched day, I know only what the Austrians publish, and the only details I have are from their newspapers. Whatever can have made you behave in this strange way? What orders do you think I can give to my Army of Italy? Don't you see that by leaving me in ignorance you are seriously compromising my operations?

"Why do I hear nothing? Have you lost your head? It is possible to lose a battle and yet not forget all sense of duty and of what is fitting. The more I think about it, the more I am persuaded that my affairs in Italy are in such a bad way that you dare not tell me . . . War is a serious occupation in which you can lose both your reputation and your country's cause. When you are in rational mood you should consider your position and see whether you are cut out for this occupation or not. I know that in

Italy you claim to despise Massena; if I had sent him, this disaster could not have taken place. Massena has such military genius that we should all bow down before him. You must forget his faults, for we all have them. I made a mistake in giving you command of the army. I ought to have sent Massena and given you command of the cavalry under him."

He drew to a close with the suggestion that if the situation was really desperate the Commander in Chief had better write and ask Murat, King of Naples, to come up to take command.[7] But on the very night that he made this wounding proposition, the Archduke after eight days of comparative inaction had moved—eastwards. He had heard uncomfortable news from home.

By the time that the Emperor's full blast of fury reached his stepson, Eugène had collected and rehabilitated his wet and disspirited troops. "You have no idea what a job this has been," he told Auguste. The threat from the Tyrol seemed to have passed. An Austrian manoeuvre to dislodge him from his present excellent position had not succeeded. There had been a dramatic minor incident. The Austrian Intendant-General, Baron de Goes had been captured in his carriage by Italian dragoons, in the streets of Padua. His documents had included proclamations to the Italian people to cast off the yoke of France . . . Reconnaissances began to disclose advance enemy positions very lightly piqueted. "I watch them, and they watch me," wrote Eugène, "and I shan't lose a good chance. I long to do something worthy of you." His sister and even his mother had gloomily supposed, on hearing the bad news of Sacile, that now Eugène would go off and get himself killed trying to repair his lost battle. Josephine had written from Strasbourg begging him not to expose himself.[8] They were sure the Emperor would realize he had been outnumbered. But either he had been long accustomed to violent outbursts from his stepfather or he did not allow himself to be worried by them so long as he felt he had done his best. He sent punctilious apologies for his enormous error in failing to despatch a responsible officer to give a detailed eyewitness's account of the battle of Sacile. To Auguste he said "The Emperor is very annoyed with me, not for having lost a battle but for having failed to send him details by word of mouth. However, I hope that when d'Anthouard arrives he will have a calming effect. I shall be anxious until he does; still, things are going well here which is a little less worrying for me."

Not only his stepson had been receiving letters from the Emperor calculated to wound. Berthier had erred. He had disobeyed orders, leaving a gap of nearly eighty miles between the corps of Davout and Lefebvre.[9] The Emperor had been determined to show the world that in spite of old prophecies he could fight on two fronts. He had sent for the Guard from Spain and rushed them up to Strasbourg in wagons. He had issued a masterly set of march orders by which his whole army was to be concentrated for manoeuvres between Regensburg, Augsburg and Donauwörth. The Austrian offensive had taken him by surprise. But when he had arrived to take over the command he had swiftly corrected Berthier's faulty dispositions and won the battles of Abensberg, Landshut and Eckmühl, afterwards reckoned by him to have been amongst his most remarkable. At Eckmühl he had stopped the pursuit and allowed the Archduke Charles to cross the Danube. But the Emperor had been able to enter Vienna. As to the battles of Aspern-Essling on the banks of the Danube there was considerable doubt. Each side claimed victory; each seemed to have lost about twenty thousand men, and amongst the soldiers of France Marshal Lannes had died of his wounds. After this engagement the Emperor was believed to have said that he would need a month to prepare for his final battle against Archduke Charles.

The news which turned the scales in Italy was that of the fall of Ratisbon. The Viceroy ordered salvos to be fired up and down his lines outside Verona. In the nick of time his army had received a valuable addition from Paris—General Macdonald. His orders had been issued three weeks before the disaster at Sacile. Eugène had indeed asked for him, at the suggestion of Josephine and Hortense. His young army of Italy had five old generals. Macdonald was, like Lauriston, of Scottish descent, but his story was far more romantic. His father had sailed over the sea to Skye with Flora Macdonald (a cousin) and Bonnie Prince Charlie. Afterwards, this West Highlander had settled in Paris, married a Frenchwoman and founded a family. General Macdonald had experience, but was not too young—forty-four. He had served with distinction in both the army of the Rhine and the Army of Italy. He was a gallant and courtly figure—had been Governor of Rome and Versailles, and Commander in Chief in Switzerland. He came prepared to serve under Eugène as a Divisional Commander and was given charge of the corps of

Broussier and Lamarque. He was very anxious to please. He had been in disgrace since the trial of his old leader Moreau.

The Viceroy was now ready to attack. He engaged the Austrians on the last day of April at Monte Bastia, "not a battle, but a brilliant affair of outposts. Our troops behaved admirably." Throughout the first fortnight of May he moved steadily east-north-east while the Austrians fought delaying actions. He lost General Sorbier, of wounds. General Broc was slightly hit and had two horses slain. They came in sight of the Piave which they must expect to be hotly disputed. At Castelfranco they took eleven hundred prisoners and the enemy dead were reckoned at three hundred against an Italian loss of a hundred and twenty. The Viceroy rode at the head of the cavalry. At St. Artien near Lovadina they found that the enemy had destroyed all bridges. The passage of the Piave was costly but effected with wonderful speed. The Viceroy personally supervised the construction of rafts. Strong swimmers were stationed near the two fords to save heavily equipped men being swept away by the strong current; but not all were saved. Between two and three thousand prisoners were taken —very hungry and dejected. The weather was still terrible. Eugène's despatch to the Emperor from Conegliano was cheerful. "The Army of Italy has well avenged the affront of Sacile; the rout of the enemy was complete." General Caffarelli sent a glowing description to Duroc, ending "The Prince has conducted himself like a worthy son of the Emperor. I admire his *sang froid* and decision. One cannot reproach him except with too much courage. The day ended with the troops shouting *"Vive l'Empereur*.[10]

They repeated that cry as they ascended the Julian Alps. The weather, as they got up into the mountains became typical of the season, sharp in the early morning and after sunset, but suddenly burning hot at midday. They caught up with the Austrians at St. Daniel and had a sharp action. The Archduke, who was with his rearguard had been resting some of his infantry and artillery before beginning the long ascent of the Fella. Eugène with his advance guard made them hurry. The Army of Italy collected a further one thousand five hundred prisoners. The Austrians were truly exhausted but Eugène thought his own men only a little tired. The passage by fords of three consecutive major rivers in flood had naturally told on their feet. Now they had the Brenta, the Piave and the Tagliamento behind them. His plan was to reunite with Macdonald and his reserve who had come over the Isonzo at Klagenfurt. The bridges were gone on the Fella, and his engineers asked for four days to collect material and build replacements. He ordered light bridges to be made for the infantry, and said that the cavalry could swim; but the artillery he would have to send round by Cividale and Caporetto to Tarvis. At Venzone they had run into some Austrian stragglers, and taken an officer with a famous name, Colloredo, wounded in the thigh. At last they were at La Pontebba and it was twelve noon on the afternoon May 15. "Behold me, my very dear Auguste, on the frontier of our kingdom. Our advance guard is over it . . . Keep on loving me. Kiss my two little angels and say polite things to your ladies, especially Madame de Wurmb. How is the Duchess of Litta? I shall be interested to hear who in your circle put a good face on things when they were going badly and whose faces were long . . ."

He had given Caffarelli orders to occupy Trieste in the name of the Emperor. From Tarvis, in Carinthia, he had to beg the Emperor's indulgence on behalf of the writing paper he was obliged to use. He had got so much ahead of his baggage that this was all he would muster to report the very satisfactory capture of the forts of Marborghetto and Predel and the combat of Tarvis. He wrote to Auguste at midnight to tell her this had been one of the most beautiful days in the history of the Army of Italy. "I hope that the Emperor will be satisfied. I am."

At Klagenfurt in Styria he began to experience the disadvantage of having so much outrun his wagon train. "It has poured all day, and I can't change, because my baggage is two days behind me, and I suppose I can't hope to see it till tomorrow. I am like a little St. John with a single garment on my body, for I have lost my greatcoat."

The union of the Army of Italy with the Grande Armée began to be effected on the wooded hills overlooking Vienna from the south on May 26. According to Méneval the scene was romantic. "The appearance of the runners of the Army of Italy on the Semmering was quite an event. The Emperor, who expected it, had sent his aide de camp Lauriston to meet it. A *chasseur* of the 9th regiment of the Italian army met a *chasseur* of the 20th, sent to reconnoitre by General Lauriston. The pair, after inspecting one another cautiously for some moments, fell into one another's arms."[11]

Eugène gave aide de camp Bataille the enjoyable task of riding ahead to the Emperor, whose opinion of d'Anthouard was already very good (though he still complained of the brevity of Eugène's description of the battle of Sacile). The Army of Italy had captured seven enemy standards. A young cousin, Louis Tascher de la Pagerie, was allowed to carry the first three into Vienna. In his letter of thanks the Emperor mentioned *en passant* that the Papal states were now part of France. He had told Murat to take possession of them. He sent a splendid congratulatory proclamation to be issued to the troops under the command of the Viceroy. He asked for the names of officers and men who had distinguished themselves. Even Darnay was satisfied the next day when the Emperor came forth to meet his master at the entry of his headquarters in the palace of Ebersdorf outside Vienna and clasp him in his arms, having announced loudly "It is not only for his courage that I have sent for Eugène. It is for his heart."

It was half an hour after midnight when Eugène reported to Milan. "I am on the crest of the wave, my tender Auguste. The Emperor has sent me a charming letter in reply to mine telling him of our junction. He is very pleased with us and orders me to issue to my army the proclamation of which I enclose a copy for you.

"We have really achieved some incredible marches, despite the running fights and other innumerable obstacles with which the enemy presented us. I hope that this good news will give pleasure in Milan. The king, your father will be glad to hear that we have destroyed the army which behaved so badly to him . . ."

V

One of the difficulties in finding out to what quarter the Archduke John had retired was that in Hungary distances were immense, place-names were fantastic and the peasantry were of primitive intelligence. On June 5, Eugène began to move towards a fortified town called Raab on the banks of a river of the same name, a large tributary of the Danube. It was about eighty miles south-east of Vienna, equidistant from Pressburg and Budapest to which, according to first accounts, the Archduke had been wending his way.

Eugène's army had been reinforced by three thousand Baden foot and five hundred *chasseurs* under the command of Lauriston.

Some of Grouchy's dragoons acting as advance guard came up with Austrians near Kormend which they took on the 8th, and next day Sachuc's division pursued them to a village called Goganyfa. Montbrun's horse, part of the valuable loan under Lauriston, occupied a place called Karaco, guarding a strategic bridge over another Danubian tributary, the Marczal, and went on to a cavalry action at Papa, a town on the marshes of the lower Raab valley above the Bakony Wald. The Archduke John, driven out of his positions at Tuskevar and Papa, retired to unite his troops (about thirty-five thousand, of which four thousand were cavalry), with those of his brother the Archduke Palatine (about eight thousand) on the right bank of the Raab. By June 14 he had taken up a new position on ground known as Szanbadhegy. His van occupied the heights of Czanack and his cavalry Kis-Barati. This was Moravia, a country rich in vineyards, corn and cattle, but treeless and sparsely populated. Eugène reported slightly sadly. "It's no use my cudgelling my brains in an attempt to master the German language, for I can't remember more than three or four sentences . . . Furthermore, although I am in the midst of proud and splendid-looking Hungarians I have no desire to speak their tongue. I stick to my own, and to Italian, and that's good enough . . . Your loving husband."

To the Emperor he reported, "From the little that I have seen of Hungary, the people appear tranquil and in the most profound ignorance of what is happening in the outer world." He had been soberly informed, when he asked where he should find the Archduke John's headquarters, that these were in Mantua. "I stopped to have a long conversation with a country magistrate who seemed to have been upset by some excesses committed by the troops of the advance guard. He told me that we were not at war with Hungary, and that conduct which was proper in Austria is not in their country. He knew all about Your Majesty's victories and when I gave him a double napoleon to wear as a medal he kissed my hand and was apparently deeply touched." (In spite of having given the strictest orders as to behaviour he had to report that there had been some undesirable incidents.) The Emperor had told him that this part of the country was famous for horses. He must get some; but though requisitioned they must be paid for. He heard daily from the Emperor and had received instructions to keep Macdonald's corps in reserve. They had been occupying Gratz awaiting Marmont, but were now making forced marches

towards Kormend.[12] The troops were expecting something
splendid for the anniversary of Marengo and Friedland.

At four a.m. on June 14 Eugène took a last look at the enemy
positions and then gave his generals their orders. He moved off
with Montbrun's cavalry at eleven, but the rest of his army did
not advance until noon. Daylight lasted long at this time of year.
All had received a ration of broth. The battle which was to be
fought was to be known as Raab, but actually that was just the
name of the nearest town. The disputed ground centred around
the heights of Szanbadhegy and a village called Kismegyer, of
which the outstanding feature was a group of picturesque farm
buildings. A rivulet of the Raab lapped the crenellated double
walls of Kismegyer farm, which arose on a grassy plateau and
was very strongly held. After several sorties its great doors were
battered down with hatchets, and Séras's and Roussel's infantry
poured in to slaughter the garrison; but it was taken and re-taken
no less than seven times.[13]

Eugène, in his first account to the Emperor gave Austrian
casualties as two thousand killed and wounded; one thousand
five hundred prisoners. He reckoned the Army of Italy had one
thousand five hundred dead or wounded. He sent General
Caffarelli to report, and since the general had not been present
during the whole action, a Colonel Rambough, who had, was
told to accompany him. The enemy had been forced to re-cross
the river. Darkness only had ended the pursuit. Eugène said that
he had been interested to discover that the Archduke John had
certainly been reinforced much beyond their expectations. He
had been engaging a force which exceeded his by fifteen thousand.

He did not have time to write to his wife for two days, but the
Emperor was considerate.

"Schönbrunn, June 15.
"My daughter,
"I have this moment heard that Eugène has obtained, on the
14th, anniversary of Marengo, a battle at Raab in Hungary,
against the Archduke John and the Archduke Palatine. They
have taken three thousand men, several guns and four
standards . . ."

"Schönbrunn, June 18.
"My daughter,
"You will have heard from Caffarelli news of Eugène and the
battle of Raab. I have heard from him himself today. He is before

Comorn. The armies of the archdukes, after their defeat fled over the Danube to Comorn. The alarm has extended to Buda, and the Empress (of Austria) has already evacuated that town. If you are now several days without news you have no cause for anxiety."

"Schönbrunn, June 21.
"My daughter,
"I write, in case you have nothing from Eugène, to assure you that there is no reason for you to worry. He is between Raab and Comorn, quite well. Give no faith to any wicked rumours which may reach you. Everything here goes on well."

After midday on June 15 Eugène sent off young Tascher to Milan. He explained that for several days he had been for as much as twenty hours, daily on horseback. He had gained a complete victory, but the engagement had been one of the hottest of his life, and his losses, without approaching those of the enemy, had been considerable. He had d'Anthouard, Triaire, Delacroix and young de Brême (the Italian Foreign Minister's son) all slightly wounded, and his Mameluke Petrus had been hit in the head when riding just behind him. "I am a little tired because I have not slept more than six hours during the last eight days." He had been delighted to hear that the Emperor had ordered the guns of the Grande Armée to fire salvos in honour of the victory gained by the Army of Italy, "a granddaughter of Marengo."

He had told the Emperor in his first despatch that he intended to summon the town of Raab the next day and he did so, but Raab stood siege from Lauriston until June 22. It had a garrison of two thousand five hundred. Eugène took up residence in a comical little house on the borders of the river, down among the mills and heavily laden barges. His wife would have been twenty-one on the twenty-first of June, and he recurred to the subject with French elegance.

"My darling Auguste,
"I calculate that my letter should reach you on your anniversary, and to be sure of it I am sending this by the hand of my courier, Fortis. I cannot send you an officer, for all of mine are stretched on beds of sickness. For your twenty-first birthday I am sending you just the same as I send you every day—my love, which is sincere and passionate, and far more lasting than any oaths which I might take could ever express."

(His horses were still near to his heart.) In a skirmish yesterday the Austrians had lost three guns and two horses. "I had three of my grenadiers killed, one horse from the dragoons, and my parade horse wounded in the stable. This poor beast was unlucky, for he was the first to be hit of the sixty which were there. It's true that the enemy sent more than a hundred shells and cannon-balls at my billet . . .

"We have now left the beautiful part of Hungary and as far as eye can see there is nothing but an enormous plain of sandy waste, the only buildings a few wooden huts belonging to peasants."

However he had every hope that they would not be here much longer. He moved into Raab after the town had surrendered, but it was rather horrible. Most of the town had been pounded down and he was haunted by memories of pitiful screams and lamentations which had reached him across the river as walls fell in and homes were set ablaze. Blackened walls were still falling, and glass from sightless windows crunched under the feet of the retiring garrison. He sent them to Vienna, but most of the wounded no further than Papa where hospital facilities were good. He sent a handsome donation to the curé of Baraty, a small village which had distinguished itself in works of charity. He asked that it should be distributed amongst the poorest refugee families. He had stuck up the portraits of his three darlings on the walls of his lodging, and very early on the morning of June 29 as he lay in bed, he got one of her best "pretty little notes" from the Vicereine. She had heard of his victory.[14]

CHAPTER TWELVE

Campaign against Austria and the Divorce
1809 : 1810

I

ON THE evening of July 4 the Viceroy sent a line to his wife, dated from Ebersdorf Camp.

"I am in a great hurry. I got in from Hungary this morning with my whole corps, and I believe that the Emperor is preparing to give the Austrians a bit of his mind. Adieu! don't worry. I am all right."

He was going to experience something which had been his ambition for the past nine years, ever since Marengo. He had been summoned to take part in one of the Emperor's great battles. The weather was dreadful. Méneval watching from a window in the Emperor's lodgings, where he was what he called shut up with M. de Champagny, Minister of External Relations, was struck dumb with horror. Peals of thunder shook the ground, lightning crackled and rain was coming down in torrents as the army assembled in the island of Lobau marched off in perfect order over ten temporary bridges and many rafts.

Amongst the letters received by Eugène while he was besieging Raab had been one from his stepfather asking for two hundred anchors and large supplies of cable. They had run out of these in the near vicinity of the fortress now rechristened Isle Napoleon. During the storm a heavy bombardment of the western shore was kept up. It was difficult to distinguish between thunder and gunfire. Savary afterwards remembered as typical of his master that after the operation had been set in motion, the Emperor, who had been on horseback all night, retired to take a little rest. "He had only with him the Viceroy of Italy, the Prince of Neufchâtel and myself." Towards five o'clock in the morning he reappeared and the troops took up their positions—Massena on the left, Bernadotte with the Saxons on the right, beyond them Oudinot and Davout. In the second line came the Viceroy with his four divisions of the Army of Italy, and to his right Marmont with two Dalmatian divisions. In the third line Bessières commanded four cavalry divisions; the Reserve was composed of six regiments of the Imperial footguards.

A beautiful dawn disclosed the wooded heights of the Kahlenberg behind Vienna. The battle of Wagram, which was going to cover some daylight hours of July 5 and 6, was to centre around a small village of that name in the plain of Marchfeld twelve miles north-east of the capital. The Emperor who had calculated on the enemy having heard of his advance, was surprised to see nothing of them until four p.m. The Archduke Charles had been waiting for his brother John bringing his troops from Pressburg. Nevertheless, the action of the evening of July 5 could hardly be called satisfactory from the Emperor's point of view.

The Army of Italy went into action after a bombardment of the enemy centre at six p.m. over a rivulet called the Russbach. They had been preceded on their right by Oudinot and on their left by Bernadotte. The stream was crossed under a sharp fire and the enemy were pushed back as far as the first houses of Wagram village, but the Archduke launched a heavy counter-attack. The Viceroy's and Bernadotte's troops were obliged to retreat over the river and as darkness fell there was some disorder in the Saxon ranks. The atmosphere was still very sultry in spite of last night's storm and the battle smoke hanging motionless enveloped the field. The plain was so barren that not a single light from a building pierced the dark blue gloom. There was difficulty in finding some trusses of straw and bits of old doors with which to kindle a fire for the Emperor's use. His generals came for conference. Davout stayed longest. The Emperor slept for a short time behind an embrasure composed of stacked grenadier drums, wrapped in his cloak.

With dawn of July 6 both armies took the offensive. Afterwards, in Paris, when he heard a Minister speaking disparagingly of Austrian troops, the Emperor said, "Evidently, you were not at Wagram." The Archduke Charles, having reflected upon the success of his left wing yesterday, ordered three corps to advance upon Massena and a fourth upon Davout. Bernadotte, who had been driven from his advanced posts earlier came to the support of Massena, but the Grand Armée did not seem to have the dash and spirit which had secured its former victories. There were some contretemps. The Marshal had had a fall on the Isle of Lobau. His horse had put its foot in a rabbit-hole. But he had insisted on taking his place on the field of battle, driving in a carriage and four with his doctor beside him. The Emperor, having tried in vain to give him a successor, had directed General Reille, an old aide de camp of the Marshal, to ride by the side of the calash.

Having sent Berthier to rally his shattered right wing, the Emperor, mounted on a conspicuous Arabian steed, proceeded to ride past his whole army formed in battle array. "Euphrates", white as snow, had been sent to him by the Sultan of Persia. At every moment Savary dreaded to see him hit, and falling on his horse's neck. Shots flew around the small figure in dark green uniform with red facings and plain black hat, but he passed back from his inspection at a slow pace unharmed. His mere appearance at this critical stage in the struggle produced a great effect. He next ordered Lauriston's artillery to concentrate a tremendous fire upon the Archduke's centre. The artillery consisted of seventy-two guns of the Guard and forty from Italy. Two divisions of the Viceroy's army were then ordered to advance under Macdonald, followed by the Bavarians and the cavalry of the Imperial Guard. The force which the Emperor was flinging into action in this great *coup* numbered thirty-five thousand.

But there had been another unforeseeable accident. Bessières was hit, thrown from his horse and apparently killed, in full view of the Emperor. He had been struck in the thigh, which was completely paralysed. The Emperor averted his gaze, and stretcher bearers removed the body. Lauriston's bombardment and Macdonald's heroic advance made the desired opening, and the Viceroy himself directed and led several charges by Italian royal dragoons, but the cavalry of the Imperial Guard lacked leadership to take full advantage of the situation. Comte de Nansouty failed to gather his men after a loss of twelve hundred horses, and Comte Walther awaited orders. Massena had performed his masterly flank march to Leopoldau but, when about five p.m. advanced patrols of the Archduke John's force appeared suddenly, Davout's corps, renowned for their imperturbability, communicated something of their alarm to the whole French right wing. Oudinot had reached and held the village of Wagram since noon, and two divisions of the army of Italy had joined him, but at this stage the Archduke Charles, unaware of his brother being so close, gave up hopes of his arrival before dark and ordered a retreat. His army withdrew gradually towards the town of Znaim in Hungary.

The action had been a murderous one. Both sides were calculated to have lost around twenty-two thousand men. The Austrians had to mourn three generals, France one of her best-loved cavalry commanders, the gay and dashing Lasalle. Méneval arrived at the Emperor's bivouac to hear the shocking cry "*Sauve qui peut.*" Some French marauders had run into patrols of the Archduke Ferdinand's army and fled in disgraceful panic. The Emperor rode over the battlefield, halting and ordering silence whenever he thought he heard groans. As it was harvest time, the corn was high. Wounded men had attached white rags to their muskets and waved them desperately in hopes of attracting attention. Later, his stepson visited the Emperor in his tent. He had been pursuing scattered parties of the enemy through the villages of Gerusdorf and Sedlersdorf. The Emperor had handsome compliments to make on the conduct of the Army of Italy, and next morning was repeating them before eight a.m. as he rode through their lines. Macdonald, who was generally accepted as having turned the fortunes of the day at the battle, he took in his arms and promoted Marshal on the spot. Only Bernadotte held that he and his Saxons had really won the Battle of Wagram. The Emperor issued a withering contradiction.

The Viceroy wrote in good spirits to his wife on the morning of July 7.

"Victory was granted to us, my good Auguste! I am very well and very tired. We were in action forty-eight hours. The Army of Italy has covered itself with glory. The Queen's Dragoons particularly distinguished themselves."[1]

II

The Emperor was disappointed by the number of prisoners taken. He said that the shot that had felled Bessières had cost him twenty thousand prisoners. The Archduke Charles had been able to remove a force of eighty thousand intact. But on July 11 he asked for an armistice and resigned his command when the Emperor Francis and the war party refused to accept the fact that peace must be sought. Eugène had been given an additional force of Württembergers and Saxons and sent off into Hungary again. He wrote to Auguste from a castle called Hof near Marchegg on the borders of Austria and Hungary which he said was large and beautiful. It made him feel terribly homesick because in some respects it reminded him of Monza . . . Now that it seemed certain that peace was coming, everyone was longing to get home to their families. But he was afraid he might have some months yet to wait.

His next halt was at Pressburg, an historic city, the old Hungarian capital and scene of many coronations. Davout had bombarded it earlier in the campaign and there were nearly two hundred burnt-out blackened houses. Eugène's instructions were to get the bridge over the Danube back into operation. The sport in this district was said to be first class, and the town to rejoice in a distinguished society. "But I have not seen a cat and have been passably bored for three nights." He wished he could dare to take a day off to go shooting with his young gentlemen, the aides de camp. He had been terribly short of them. He had started with seven, but one had been killed in action, two were sick and two were with their regiments fighting the English in Spain. He was being obliged to send his letters home by courier, and by Strasbourg since the Tyrol had blown up again. He believed either General Chasteler or the brigands of the Tyrol had enjoyed a good many of his letters to his wife. However, he had asked the Emperor for three more young gentlemen—his cousin Tascher, Captain Labédoyère who had been aide de camp to the lamented Marshal Lannes, and Lieutenant Desève, aide de camp to Caffarelli. It was a relief when he found that Adjutant Triaire played chess. He got so little news now being so far from the Emperor. The probability seemed to be that his next camp would be near a château of Prince Esterhazy—Eisenstadt, "where, I think I shall do very well. They say it has a superb park full of game. I shall shoot every morning, work and think of my little family all the day." But his next call, on July 22, was to Vienna. The Emperor told him to come and stay at Schönbrunn for a few days. This was wonderful. Amongst other amenities he collected on arrival a *cache* of no less than fourteen letters from Auguste.

The Emperor was established in the palace of Schönbrunn. The entrance to this favourite residence of Maria Theresa, half a league outside the capital, was imposing. His stepson rode in over a bridge crossing a rivulet, guarded by four stone sphinxes. A massive gate opened on to a courtyard in which eight thousand troops could manoeuvre. It was at present occupied by an encampment of men of the Imperial Guard. On either side of the gateway were huge obelisks surmounted by gilt eagles. The Emperor was occupying the same study with adjoining bedroom which he had chosen in 1805. Both rooms were decorated with Chinese lacquer of great antiquity yet the colour and gilding were still quite fresh. His windows looked out over fine wrought-iron balcony railings and a formal garden to the classical colonnade on the skyline known as the Gloriette. He had begun to look older. He was pallid and seemed to have put on weight. As a young man he had been as thin as a rail, but now he was within a few weeks of his fortieth birthday. Still he appeared in the best of spirits. Eugène soon discovered, as most people who were in close touch with headquarters must, that there was a reason for the Emperor's cheerfulness. Nearly every night Constant went with a closed carriage to a villa in the park to fetch a lady who was admitted by a private entrance. It was the Countess Walewska, from Paris. The days were past when Eugène had refused to ride beside a carriage which contained his stepfather and a mistress. Besides, Madame Walewska was perfectly discreet, never appeared in public with the Emperor, and was, according to all accounts, genuinely devoted to him. She was beautiful, well-born, quite devoid of personal ambition. While she satisfied the Emperor there was not likely to be any more talk of divorce from Josephine. It might have been much worse. This *liaison* had now lasted, though with interruptions, almost three years and there was no sign of any resultant family, though the Countess had borne a son to her elderly husband before meeting the Emperor.

Eugène wrote home diligently, the letters of a young man in love. He assured Auguste, "*Je ne changerai jamais.*" He was "*Ton fidèle époux et ami.*" "My first thought this morning, as every day, was for you and my pretty family." He remembered her name-day and supposed that his little Josephine would now be old enough to make her mother her own little compliment on the anniversary. He was able to give his wife news of her brother. Ludwig had been asked to breakfast with the Emperor. He had been serving with a Bavarian martial hero, Baron Wrede, in Lefebvre's corps. The choice seemed considerate, for Lefebvre was an old rough diamond who would annoy no one by Paris airs and graces. However, it did not seem to have been much of a success. The fact was that Ludwig really seemed to dislike all French for their own sakes and made only a grudging exception in favour of his brother in law. The Emperor, in one of his exasperated moods, had been heard to ask what was to prevent him from having the Crown Prince of Bavaria shot for an intriguer. Yet he had fallen on his neck and kissed him after the Battle of Eckmühl. Ludwig was going back to the Tyrol. It was much to be hoped that the news of the armistice would have quietened down the troubles there, and also stabilized the situation in Italy. A very awkward thing had happened about the Papal states. In May the Emperor had issued a decree from Schönbrunn announcing their annexation to France. Pius VII had retaliated by a bull excommunicating, not the Emperor by name, but "aggressors against the Holy See." General Miollis, acting on his own responsibility, had ordered General Radet to go and arrest the Pope at the Quirinal and this had been done with the maximum disturbance in the middle of the night. His Holiness had been carried off to Grenoble. The Emperor could do nothing but back up his overzealous deputies; but it was awkward. He thought the Pope had better be removed to Savona on the Riviera coast, near Genoa. Eugène wrote to tell Auguste to have a Te Deum in the court chapel on the Emperor's birthday, August 15, a large audience after the mass and in the evening a concert at the Villa Bonaparte. She would have all the reception rooms open and pass from one to another followed by her suite making a "grand circle", saying a few charming words to everyone suitable. This was the kind of thing that his born princess did to perfection. When he forwarded the decoration of the Legion of Honour awarded to General Pino, he suggested that it would be agreeable to the officer to be formally invested by the Vicereine.

He had not been able to see much of Vienna as yet. He had dined one evening with Duroc and Bessières (marvellously recovered from his wound). It was five years since the trio had met, and after dinner they had thought they would go for a walk on the ramparts. But it was still daylight, and although they were in overcoats such a party was instantly recognized. Sentries stiffened, words of command rang out. They had soon collected such a crowd of gaping women, and children running alongside, that there was nothing for it but an ignominious retreat. The Emperor was giving Eugène a marvellous array of rewards and promotions

for the Army of Italy. The announcement would be on the Birthday, when there was to be a large new creation of dukes and
marshals etc., with appropriate pensions. Berthier, already Prince
of Neufchâtel, was to add the title of Wagram. Davout would
become Prince of Eckmühl. Macdonald, Oudinot and Clarke
were being given the dukedoms of Taranto, Reggio and Feltre.
Five generals of the Army of Italy were becoming Counts—
d'Anthouard, Broussier, Charpentier, Grenier, Lamarque and
two colonels Barons—Delacroix and Bataille. He was particularly
pleased over Charpentier's award, as he had written some weeks
past to beg the Emperor that this worthy man who had worn
himself out in the service of his country might, if he were to be
retired in favour of General Vignolles as His Majesty intended,
be given a comfortable arm-chair. He had suggested the post of
Inspector General of the Infantry of the Army of Italy, and as a
second favour, an appropriate pension.[2] The Birthday passed off
with celebrations as brilliant as any at Milan—Te Deum, parade,
fireworks, illuminations, all very well attended by the pleasure-
loving Viennese. Eugène was asked to dine with the Emperor, and
they went out afterwards in an open carriage to call in at several
barracks where the troops were having their gala repast. Later
—was it to be believed?—they set out together on foot and
mingled with the crowd: nothing unsuitable happened: it was
dark by now; very few people seemed to recognize them.

Eugène's three days in Vienna stretched to three months. He
visited the Army of Italy in their quarters outside the capital. He
was himself splendidly lodged in a palace built in 1801 for the
Archduke Frederick. It was in the south-west part of the inner
city between the Augustinerstrasse and the Burggarten.[3] Vienna
was magnificent. If he could have had his wife and children here
he would have been happy. The weather became very hot. He
went bathing at Schönbrunn, and to the Opera. He went out
shooting with Berthier. This could be a painful experience.
Marshal Massena, now Prince of Essling, had never been fond of
Marshal Berthier, now the Prince of Neufchâtel and Wagram,
even before he had suffered the loss of his right eye owing to an
unlucky aim of his fellow guest on a day's sport at Fontainebleau.
Some people said that it was really the Emperor who had hit
Massena. It never ceased to amaze Eugène how brave men who
had no idea of shooting accepted invitations to do so. He had been
lucky. He had been taught his manners for *la chasse* by the Army

of the Rhine when staying with his elegant father at Strasbourg.

"Vienna, September 20, 1809.

"My very dear Auguste,

"I have just had this morning the most beautiful day's sport that I have ever experienced. There were six of us, three very unskilful; and our bag was fifty-four pheasants and twenty-two wild-boar. My share was twenty-three pheasants and six boar. I was very pleased with my troops yesterday ... I have a multitude of letters here to read and so far have only answered two. You can guess whose. Adieu, therefore!"

Not surprisingly, perhaps, he received three more invitations to shoot on the estate called Laxenburg which was Berthier's headquarters. He went up to Baron Larrey's hospital on the Rennweg to visit two *chasseurs* who had lost legs at Wagram —Daumesnil and Corbineau. The peace negotiations were going on so slowly. The Emperor Francis and the war party were still hoping that England, or Prussia or Russia would intervene on their behalf. Eugène could still, by the middle of September, only tell his wife ("for your ear alone") that he thought that in November he might again clasp her in his arms. Bets were being laid in Vienna on peace or war. He betted on peace because he knew that was what his stepfather wanted. His hopes rose when three Austrian generals were announced at Schönbrunn. One of them was Prince John of Liechtenstein who had got the command on the disgrace of the Archduke Charles. The Emperor's plans were to start for Paris as soon as the peace was signed. He had ordered Eugène to take charge of a review of the whole of the cavalry of his army. "As I am in perpetual motion," Eugène felt well, but now that the fear that he might be killed in action had been removed, Auguste had other trials. Some of the people who had counted on Austria winning and had behaved very badly during the anxious weeks, were either trying to crawl back into favour or having violent quarrels with the old faithfuls—Vaccari, Caffarelli, Prina, Caprara, Madame de Litta ... Despite the Emperor's warning never to listen to mischievous gossip, a story had reached her ears that the Viceroy was not coming back to Milan. Eugène wrote firmly.

"Clerici brought me your letter, but my delight in receiving it has been slightly clouded, my darling Auguste, for I have seen in it some unhappy notions which, I swear to you, should not be in your little head. Trust me, and trust our Star (which is a lucky one) and remember that we can always rely on the Emperor dealing fairly, and on those links that bind us together."

He began to buy presents from Vienna to bring home—toys for the children, large and small; for their mother a pearl necklace and a good piano; for their father and mother horses, more pianos, engravings, porcelain. [4]

By October 8 the Emperor seemed in such good humour there could be no doubt they were getting near the end of their time of waiting. He had bestowed the title of count upon the Viceroy's official artist, Signor Annoni. Another painter had been engaged by Eugène in Vienna. Albrecht Adam, a young member of an artistic Bavarian family from Augsbourg, had not known who had visited him one September evening when two French officers in uniform had appeared to ask to see his sketches. He had noticed that one was a general. He was much startled to find himself appointed war-artist to the Viceroy with a commission to produce oil paintings of the action at St. Michael on the Mur in Styria on May 25, and the battle of Raab. [5]

On October 14 Eugène sent off a courier to say that peace was going to be signed in two hours. Three days later his spirits were not so high. The Emperor was leaving for Paris tomorrow but had given him new instructions. He was to wait on in Vienna for the ratification. That meant only a few days: but there was also the pacification of the Tyrol to be effected. Still, that should not take long now that the peace was signed; and he could not possibly object. It was obviously part of his duty to lock the back door on Italy. It would be something to be so much nearer home.

On the night of October 15 he drove out of Vienna with the Emperor as far as the first stage on the road to Paris. The Emperor could not have been kinder. He said he hoped to see both his children from Milan in Paris for a month this winter. He urged Eugène to hurry home as soon as his mission in the Tyrol was accomplished. "That I shall do with all my heart . . . Today I have been walking round the fortifications of Vienna. It is a wonderful spectacle . . ." He had begun to pack.

The Emperor had indeed had every reason to appear satisfied. The Peace of Schönbrunn had been brutal. Austria had lost Salzburg to Bavaria, western Galicia to the Grand Duchy of Warsaw, and eastern Galicia to Russia. France's portion was tracts of Carniola, Carinthia and Croatia, Friuli, Trieste—"the Illyrian Provinces". The Austrian army was to be cut down to a hundred and fifty thousand men; she was to pay an indemnity of eighty-five millions, and hasten to rejoin the Continental System directed against England.

There had been an attempt to assassinate the Emperor on October 12. A German student while presenting a petition at a review had tried to murder him with a kitchen knife. The Emperor had given the young man a long interview, but he had refused to apologize, so he was going to be shot tomorrow.

Hortense, back at Malmaison, heard the Paris comment. "The generals and other officers, alarmed at the idea of what might have happened thought again about the necessity for a direct heir to the Empire. They asked themselves who could possibly have been chosen had the attempt succeeded, and their choice was unanimous for Eugène de Beauharnais. Public opinion in France agreed." Savary was amongst the officers. "The Viceroy was a prince well qualified for business; of a lofty mind and deeply impressed with the extent of his duties towards the Emperor. He would have imposed upon himself the obligation of consolidating the whole system of government handed over to him. I know that the Emperor was always pleased with his obedience and sometimes said that he had never given him the smallest cause for displeasure. He dismissed the idea of appointing him his heir, however, because he had nearer relations."[6]

III

The story of the Tyrol, since he had left home in April, was extremely vexed and indeed disturbing. Since the district had been transferred from Austria to Bavaria by the Treaty of Pressburg, it could hardly have been said to have been at peace. The name of Andreas Hofer first appeared in a letter from Eugène to his wife on November 2, 1809. He had reached Villach on his homeward road and had received that night some good news for which he had been waiting. His proclamation to the rebel insurgents had been issued on October 25, and he had just heard from General Baraguay-d'Hilliers that he hoped to enter Linz without striking a blow. The Viceroy's volatile young gentlemen, with whom he had spent half-an-hour this evening in this dullest of headquarters, had rushed off instantly to pack! His war-artist

Adam had performed on their journey a sketch of the Army of Italy bivouacking in a wood, which was destined for the Queen of Holland. Eugène wrote to Auguste, "I send you a portrait of André Hofer; people say Time has struck a blow at him since this likeness was taken."[7] Hitherto, if he had mentioned this character at all in despatches it was as a commandant of the rebels, or a brigand chief.

In Italian Tyrol no persons of fortune or family had joined or raised private armies, and the unfortunate irregulars had followed such characters as Garbino, a tradesman from Verona wanted for murder, and Dalpoute, a forger from Brescia. Generally speaking in German Tyrol, rebels had been of every class.

Andreas Hofer was the outstanding figure. He was a perfectly honest inn-keeper and horse-coper. He had inherited his inn, in the Passeier valley, from his father, and was sometimes known by its name, "Sandwirth". He had fought against France for nine years before the Treaty of Pressburg, first as a sharpshooter and then as a captain of militia. He was not, like the prominent Austrian rebel leader, the Baron von Hormayr, fanatically devoted to the House of Habsburg. He really dreamt of the day when the Tyrol should gain independence. He had been invited to Vienna to concert about a rising with the Archduke John and had taken a distinguished part in the defeat of King Max's troops at Sterzing, after which the Tyrolese had entered Innsbruck in triumph. The French advance to the campaign of the Danube had enabled the Bavarians to reoccupy Innsbruck, but only for a few weeks. The Emperor Francis himself had sent Hofer a letter assuring him that the Tyrol would never again be separated from Austria, and the inn-keeper had gone home, satisfied that for the present he could do no more. He had been fetched out of blameless retirement by the news that the Tyrol and Vorarlberg had been surrendered to French vengeance. Innsbruck was reoccupied. After a painful period of searching his soul he once more entered the field. He was a devout man; his secretary was a Franciscan friar named Arckinger. When he had re-entered Innsbruck, having routed Marshal Lefebvre, Baron Wrede and Crown Prince Ludwig, he was at pains to prevent his irregulars from sacking the town. He took up quarters in the Hofburg and was elected Oberkommandant of the Tyrol. He had a simplicity of character which led him to believe that the Emperor of Austria who had sent him a chain and a medal of honour (which he wore in his portrait), would not again desert him. The Treaty of Schönbrunn had almost broken his heart. He realized that he could not possibly hope to win against the overwhelming French armies now released to subdue the Tyrol.

His portrait showed a sturdy man of middle age—he was now forty-two—with gnarled features, a full head and beard of fiercely curling black hair, and unusually large luminous brown eyes, reminiscent of those of a faithful hound. He looked what he was, typical of his race and country. From the point of view of France he was all the more a menace since he was universally recognized as of entirely virtuous life. A price had been set upon his head.

On November 5 Eugène experienced a day of shadow and shine. Reports coming in could hardly allow him to claim that all rebels had taken note of his proclamation and were handing in their arms; but he thought it quite likely that in the places where advanced posts complained that they were still being attacked, his offer simply had not yet penetrated. Also, with a touch of humour, he explained to the Emperor, he thought it was probably not easy to give up being a brigand, especially if it was really your only profession. He had received what he imagined was a preliminary letter from Hofer, enquiring as to terms. He had been much surprised to get an extremely intemperate one from a most unexpected quarter to which he had sent copies of both documents. King Max was angry with him.

"I really had not said anything in my proclamation," explained Eugène to the Emperor, "except what Your Majesty ordered —that I would nominate commissioners to hear the complaints of the people when they had laid down their arms. Your Majesty would soon solve these difficulties if you decided promptly to make Tyrol an independent state. Or, alternatively, it could be divided between Bavaria and the Kingdom of Italy. But I am certain from my own observation that all the Tyrolese detest Bavarians."

To Auguste he poured out his misery. She had been asking, since he was now only two days' journey from Milan, if she might join him, but he had been obliged to tell her not to think of such a thing. He might be coming any day now. "I am so unhappy tonight, my good and dear Auguste, and you know I never keep anything from you. You remember my proclamation to the Tyroleans? I dared believe it was good even before I began to see the effects . . . But it contained phrases which have displeased your father, the king . . . I am dreadfully hurt . . . Don't attempt to do anything, but I must say I am bitterly surprised that the king does so little justice to my character. He is being deceived when people tell him that it is possible to bring this country to heel by force of arms. He would merely lose the bravest of his soldiers. I myself have had to employ the velvet glove, and I don't think the dignity of a sovereign is compromised in any way by hearing and making a list of the complaints of the people. After all, as I have pointed out to him, order has been restored and the people have laid down their arms. I curse, a thousand times, this horrible mission! There will be no praise if one succeeds and if things turn out badly it will be my fault. Farewell, my beloved Auguste, you and my children are my only consolation in this world. It is a century since I have written to the Empress, or to my sister. Honestly I have not had the time. Do, please send them my news."

He was at ease in his mind about both his mother and Hortense. After staying at Strasbourg for many months they had both gone off for cures at spas, which was what they enjoyed, and by now they were back in Paris and had got the Emperor home. It was fortunate that he had not yet despatched his letter to the Emperor, for as he wrote a deputation from Hofer was announced. The Leader had sent a letter signed by a dozen of his chief officers. It was not nearly as long as his first effort, which must have been composed to his orders by his capuchin secretary—so full of "Imperial Highnesses" and "Monseigneurs". His second had been to the point.

"My Lord,

"The Tyrolese people, relying on the benevolence, the wisdom and the justice of your Imperial Highness, entrusts by our spokesmen its fate into your hands. The people are prepared to lay down their arms, if, by this means, they can obtain the benefit of your benevolent protection. They have suffered much from the Austrian rule, which by its cowardly insinuations (only too recent, which is more) have made them rebel."

The Leader remembered even such details as the Viceroy's humane treatment of a rebel officer taken prisoner. He had also sent two draft proclamations addressed to his followers. The second opened in terms of complete submission. "We cannot make war against the invincible Napoleon. Entirely deserted by the Austrians our situation is miserable ...." The deputies were to ask for a safe-conduct from the Viceroy in his own hand.

He gave them that the same night, a dozen passports for Hofer and his staff to come to him for conference. He foresaw that they might be going to ask to send a deputation to Paris. As to this he asked the Emperor for instructions. Things were going better. His father in law was coming round. Eugène had sent the angry king a very long reasonable reply to his outburst. Within the week Max Joseph had cooled down sufficiently to write "My affairs are in good hands and I leave them entirely to you." He signed himself "Your faithful father and best friend."

Eugène filled in one of his days of waiting by going down a lead-mine at Bleyberg. "I put on a miner's outfit and was shown everything. It was most curious." He dearly hoped soon to be able to send his date of return. The troops were coming past on their homeward journey with perfect regularity, and every hour he heard of more rebel arms being handed in. He could not help congratulating himself that with care and patience he believed he was averting a war which, in a country such as this, must be long, difficult and murderous. Both King Max and Prince Ludwig had gloomily spoken of the possibility of a second Vendée.

On November 9 he heard from General Drouet d'Erlon at Linz that Hofer had applied for *laissez-passer* for all his troops, accepting the condition that they gave in their weapons. They would not, Eugène knew, like doing this, for the Tyrolean was born a sharpshooter. There was a set-back when General Rusca was sharply opposed entering Brixen. The trouble went on for two hours, but Eugène did not really think this affair was going to light again the flames which he had almost extinguished. "It is," he repeated to Auguste, "terribly disagreeable to have to wage this disgusting sort of war."

He had twice heard from the Emperor now, suggesting to him that he had better go home. He said that he hoped tomorrow, the 11th, to hear news which would decide this. He was waiting for Hofer. He had sent young Tascher de la Pagerie up to the head-quarters of General Baraguay-d'Hilliers asking the General to forward the aide de camp for an interview with Hofer. At the end of six days, having heard nothing, he left instructions for Tascher, if he had got the man, to bring him on to Milan.

"I am getting into my carriage this moment, my good Auguste, to come to you. I send this by a courier who will see to my horses. I can promise you I am following him as fast as I can."[5]

IV

Auguste had prepared a beautiful surprise for him. It was a picture of the wife and family of the Victor of Raab. She was portrayed in a splendid Empire velvet gown powdered with gold embroidered flowers and sprays, sitting on the edge of an Empire chair pointing at a map framed in a sort of fire-screen. At her knee stood the little Josephine, also with her finger on the word Raab. Eugénie, a lovely blonde curly-headed Beauharnais infant, sat precariously perched on her mother's left arm. In her hands the younger princess held a medal.[8]

The homecoming had surpassed even expectation. He would be here for Christmas, and before that they had a full programme of celebrations to fulfil. There would have to be a triumphal entry of the Army of Italy. The city was offering a ball at the Scala. Another in the public gardens of the Riconoscenza was arranged for December 2. On December 3, a Te Deum at the Cathedral, would be followed by at least two investitures and receptions . . . There were many officials to be congratulated who had done well during the crisis. An enormous correspondence awaited attention. The presents bought in Vienna had begun to arrive. There was only one cloud, as the late November days passed. Tascher had come back without Andreas Hofer. He had gone up to Head-quarters at Villach and there met, in dead secrecy, the capuchin secretary and two other delegates. They had said that their leader had had to go to ground "because of the implacable enemies of the French". Their plans were suspected. There was no more to be done for the moment. But the General would like to follow the Viceroy to Milan as soon as possible. Tascher had been surprised by the degree of unrest he had noticed in the Tyrol. As soon as he had got beyond the last village which had a French outpost, he had found armed peasants who said no orders had reached them from Austria. Eventually he had gone off alone except for a native guide, to a hut in the mountains near Bruneck where, he was told, Hofer would meet him at nine p.m. After two hours of wait-ing only the figure of the capuchin had emerged out of the eerie gloom. "Hofer was still too closely watched by the enemies of

France." It was impossible to judge whether he was frightened or trying to gain time. After witnessing several sharp clashes between the peasants and French troops, Tascher had returned. There had been a sensational victory for the rebels near St. Leonhard, above Meran, Hofer's birthplace. It had included some of the worst features of guerilla warfare. The bandits had maimed and slaughtered French troops by hurling down upon them, in a narrow mountain pass, enormous rocks and boulders. The Viceroy's disappointment and surprise were great when he saw the leader's next proclamation, dated November 22.

"Beloved Brethren!

"Behold another example of divine assistance! We are now in the valley of Passeier ... We have taken nearly a thousand prisoners. Behold! my beloved brethren, we have been manifestly chosen by the Almighty as His darling instrument. For we are engaging the strongest foreign nation in the world. We shall fight like the heroes of the days of chivalry, and God and the Blessed Virgin will give us Their benediction. And after the war we shall hope to live undisturbed, and not as the forsaken orphans of the Emperor of Austria, who, doubtless will return to us as master of our country. Above all, do not lose courage. Reinforcements are coming from Carinthia."

There was obviously nothing to be done but to renew hostilities. The end was certain, but the time and lives that must be lost in this most horrible of warfare was a sad prospect. On the last day of November Eugène was able to report that Hofer's chief emissaries had given themselves up, and he had indirect intimations that Hofer himself was asking General Baraguay-d'Hilliers for a safe-conduct. If this should be the truth, he strongly advised the Emperor that for the benefit of the Tyrol his request should be favourably considered, and that Hofer's life should be spared. But he must unquestionably be asked to revoke his last proclamation.[10]

On December 1 an express from Paris banished all thoughts of the Tyrol from his mind. The Emperor's message was curiously worded.

"My son,

"It is my wish that if no other engagement prevents you, you should leave Milan so as to arrive in Paris on December 5 or 6.

Come by yourself with just three carriages and only four or five members of your personal staff. Come by Fontainebleau. This is always supposing no major engagement holds you in Milan."[11]

Eugène did not pretend to understand it, but Auguste had no doubt. Their star was in the ascendant. At last her husband was to be declared the Emperor's heir. Disappointing though it was to lose him so soon, there was a thrilling atmosphere of expectation and secrecy at the Villa Bonaparte as orders were sent to the stables, and the few companions of this sudden journey were chosen and warned—Comte Caprara, Baron Bataille . . .

Eugène said he must start that very night. It was a tragedy that he must miss the ball offered by the City of Milan—the Te Deum . . . It would be too late to cancel them, but Auguste he knew, would play her part bravely. He would probably be absent only a few days. They parted with much emotion but Auguste bore up well. She was sure that her husband would return to her a king and heir to an Empire.

He wrote to her at four o'clock on the afternoon of December 3 from the hospice on the Mont Cenis. It was quite dark outside and the roads so far had been horrible but he hoped to press on to-night on horseback as far as Lanslebourg. He heard up here that the Queen of Naples had been stuck for three days. The snows which could detain Caroline Murat must indeed be heavy. He reckoned his carriages would not be catching him up for another twelve hours.

Three days later he was safe and happy in his native land, bowling down the celebrated Paris highroad from Lyons. In the town of Nemours, about twelve miles short of Fontainebleau, it was necessary to slow down to cross the bridge over the Loing. It was here that his outriders perceived a coach and six with Imperial liveries drawn up, and footmen stationed at intervals watching the traffic coming up from the south. The Viceroy's unmistakable three strong fast emblazoned travelling carriages were flagged to a halt. There was a beautiful lady, much dressed, sitting in the coach. It was Hortense, Queen of Holland, his sister. Almost before the steps of her equipage could be let down he was seated beside her, taking her in his arms. But her expression had struck him as tragic. She began to weep. He asked, "Is the news that brings you to meet me good or bad?" She answered, "Bad! Bad! The worst."[12]

V

The story which Hortense had to unfold as they drove on together to Fontainebleau really began five years ago when the Murats had presented the Emperor with a mistress to attract him from Madame Duchâtel. Eléanore Denuelle de la Plaigne, a beautiful brunette of eighteen, had been recommended to the Murats by Madame Campan. She had been a pupil at the famous school, and had a hard-luck story to tell. She had been married to a scamp who had claimed to be a captain in the 15th Dragoons. When he had been arrested for forgery two months after the wedding he had left his wife destitute. The Emperor had met her at the Murats' country house and been attracted to her, though she was not at all clever. A child had been born in December 1806, and the Emperor had provided for mother and son, But the girl was not straightforward and Murat had also been visiting her. The Emperor had ceased to do so though the little Léon, a bright child, was brought to be shown to him at due intervals. He would have liked to believe that he had a son. Suddenly, this autumn in Vienna, he was left with no further doubts as to his capacity. Countess Walewska, who was a person of complete integrity, had become pregnant. Her child would be here in May 1810. The Emperor had decided to re-marry and as soon as possible "for the sake of France."

Eugène's first thoughts were, his sister noticed, for another. He asked at once, "Our mother! has she the courage to face it?" Hortense said, "Yes." "Very well," he announced, "We will all disappear quietly and end our days more peaceably than we began them." Hortense laid her head on his shoulder and wept tears of relief. "I had once more found a protector and friend; so, forgetting for a moment the sad reason that had brought him, I began to pour out all my own troubles. He knew a good deal already, and confessed that he would hardly have known me; I was so changed by suffering." He began to tell her of his own happy home, but with grief she watched his handsome features clouding, his bright grey eyes grown sad. He exclaimed "But why did they marry me to a princess! My poor wife is the one of us who is to be pitied. She had hoped that our children would wear crowns. She has been brought up to consider that important. She thinks I have been sent for to be named heir to the throne of

France!" But his smile was tender as he added "But I know she will be brave. She loves me dearly and is so fine a character that she will accept that, if one behaves well one need never be really unhappy."

Everything possible seemed to have been arranged to make his homecoming painful. He could not go to his own expensive palace on the banks of the Seine. The Emperor had taken it over for visiting royalties and the egregious Jerome, King of Westphalia, and his queen, were established there awaiting the peace celebration festivities. Rooms had been hastily found for him in the Hôtel de Marboeuf, the Paris house of Joseph Bonaparte, now in Spain.

Hortense said that the Emperor had arrived at Fontainebleau from Vienna before Josephine. She had hastened from Malmaison but he had greeted her very roughly. "So Madame, you have come! I was just leaving for Saint Cloud." He had been persuaded to stay, and Josephine had arrayed herself in a most elegant new confection for dinner, but that night she had found that orders had been given for the doors communicating between their apartments to be sealed up. She had made a scene and fainted, and Corvisart, the Emperor's first personal medical assistant, had to be summoned in the middle of the night. (Hortense did not know that as they carried the Empress down the awkward stair to her own bedroom she had recovered sufficiently to whisper, though with closed eyes, to Comte Bausset, Prefect of Police, "Don't hold me so tight!") Hortense said that when she was fetched, the Emperor was explaining apologetically to quite a large audience, "Divorce has become a necessity for me!" When she had proudly said that Eugène would provide a home for his mother and sister, he had seemed appalled and cried, "You will all leave me!" They had argued long, in private. He had said that his action was entirely political, that Josephine should always be his dearest friend, Eugène his son. But he could not make Eugène his heir because the same blood did not flow in their veins. There was also the consideration that Eugène was in his thirtieth year and had himself no heir. His wife's record was two miscarriages and two daughters.

Hortense had one more very disagreeable anecdote. The Viceroy, hoping to give a promising young aide de camp, who was a cousin, his chance, had sent Louis Tascher to Paris to tell the Emperor the latest news of Hofer. To his amazement, when the poor young man had presented himself at the Tuileries the Emperor had snapped at him. "Has Eugène sent you to spy upon me? Have you not been with the Empress?" The astonished youth had replied that he had this moment alighted from a post-chaise in the courtyard and had seen no one. He had then been allowed to make his report and at the end of it the Emperor had snapped again, "Go down to your cousin."

Tascher had found the Empress in a pitiable condition. "The Emperor is going to abandon me! He is going to divorce me! Where is Eugène? When does he arrive?" "I don't know, Madame. When I left him he did not tell me of anything bad happening to you. He did not tell me he was coming. Perhaps he thought I knew. I can only assure you he was perfectly well."

The Empress had sent him on to another weeping lady, Queen Hortense, who was very anxious about her brother's future. She had at any rate given the young man something to do for his master. She had sent him to watch the Orleans road for Paris, and Comte de Lavalette to watch the third possible route. She herself had taken the likeliest, which had proved successful.

On the morning of his arrival in Paris, Eugène called first upon the Emperor then upon the Empress. Both wept. He decided that the present situation was intolerable. They ought to meet, and in his presence. Hortense had said that Princess Pauline was behaving like a devil. She had entirely taken charge of the Emperor's amusement and was giving parties for him every night, was even said to have got ready another mistress—Piedmontese.

It was very late when Eugène sat down to his last unpleasant task for that day, the letter which was to wipe the smile of proud expectation from the face of his wife.

"I could not tell you, my love, before we parted, the reason for my journey because I did not myself know it . . ."

He thought, upon the whole that he had succeeded today in getting affairs upon a reasonable basis. It was obvious that for the sake of the Emperor they should be settled as soon as possible and becomingly. He was glad to say that all parties had been calm. The Emperor had said at once that Josephine must lose neither her position nor his affection. Eugène had said at once that he thought they had better all disappear.

"Sire, allow me to leave your service."

"What is that?"

"Yes, sire. The son of her who is no longer Empress cannot

remain a Viceroy. I will join my mother in her seclusion and help
to comfort her. I shall resign my post."

"Never! you cannot so desert me!"

"I must, sire, otherwise people might say that our family had
been dismissed. And you might find my mother in the way. Our
simplest actions would be misinterpreted. Even your enemies
would injure our good name by offering us friendship, and so
leading you to distrust us. It will be much more seemly for us to
vanish. Choose a place for us all, far from your Court and its
intrigues where we can help our poor mother to bear her load of
misfortune."

The Emperor had listened looking very serious and begun to
reply slowly. He said that he had been useful to Eugène in his
career. He now needed him, and Hortense, who should remember
she had children who were his nephews. Nor did the Empress
really want what her son asked. "With your exaggerated ideas
you increase her sorrow. You must think of the future. If you all
go off, you must realize it could be said that the Empress was dismissed, and perhaps rightly."

He then began to mention his terms—extremely generous—
Malmaison for herself and her heirs, the Elysée palace for a
Paris residence, all her debts paid, her rank and title to remain
unchanged. She brightened sufficiently to cry out, "But once we
are separated my children will be forgotten. Make Eugène King
of Italy. You will ensure the peace of mind of a loving mother and
all foreign powers will applaud your policy." Eugène had interrupted to say hotly that his name must not enter into the affair.
"Your son will not have it said that he has won a crown at such a
price. If you bow to the Emperor's wishes it is of you alone he
must think."[13]

The Emperor agreed quickly. "There speaks my Eugène's
true heart. He does well to trust to my affection."

"You know me well enough," continued Eugène to Auguste,
"to appreciate how I feel. The one thing that makes it bearable
is the idea that I possess your heart, and that your feelings for me
will be unchanged by these disasters. I saw the King of Saxony at
the Tuileries tonight and we spoke long about you. Tomorrow I
must begin to pay my calls of etiquette upon my arrival, and I don't
know when I shall end them. Farewell, my good friend! I love you
and I shall do so all my life and our two dear children. Perhaps
I shall get back to Milan sooner than we thought possible."

The first ceremony in connection with the divorce, the only one which Josephine need attend in person, was fixed for December 15. In the morning Mlle. Avrillon noticed as the Empress sat at her dressing table that her eyes were very red, as if she had wept much and slept little; yet she read again and again a sheet which rattled in her hand. It was her speech of renunciation; the Emperor had desired that she should get it by heart. Mlle. Avrillon, like all Josephine's staff, was lost in admiration of the bearing of Prince Eugène—"What a soul was his! Excellent son of an excellent mother!"

It had been an amiable habit of the Empress to read aloud to her attendants the letters of her son. "One of her chief pleasures was in writing to him in Italy, and unlike all young men, he always replied, giving her the wisest counsels, urging resignation, resolution, avoidance of complaint or self-pity; in a word, letters which were a perfect model of filial piety, without once speaking of the Emperor in terms other than the most respectful." From the moment of his arrival in Paris he had devoted himself to his mother. He sat by her for hours together; he did all he could to protect her from herself—violent scenes and indiscreet confidences. On the fatal evening he appeared to escort her to the Emperor's principal study adjoining the throne room, a little before nine p.m. The whole family was assembled in full court costume— Murat, King of Naples and Queen Caroline, Jerome, King of Westphalia and Queen Catherine, Louis, King of Holland and Queen Hortense, Pauline, Princess Borghese, Julie, Queen of Spain, Madame Mère. Josephine's ladies had done their best for her, and in a simple white muslin gown absolutely devoid of ornament she looked still a desirable woman. Her children led her in, and Constant thought that of the three his old master, the Viceroy, looked the most tragic. He stood with his arms folded, trembling so violently that it seemed as if at any moment he might fall.

The Emperor opened proceedings by reading a statement about the necessity for his providing France with an heir. He announced that the name of Josephine, the companion who had adorned fifteen years of his life, would always be engraven on his heart. Her speech was handed to her by Talleyrand and she made a gallant effort. She got past the worst passage, about her being too old to hope for children, but her voice failed as she passed on to offer in the interest of France the greatest proof of attachment and devotion in her power. She handed the sheet to the Secretary of State to the Imperial family, but before he had finished it he too was weeping openly. The official report of the proceedings having been signed by all present, the Emperor embraced her and led her out. Her children followed her. Only Constant noticed that in an ante-chamber Prince Eugène reeled and fell unconscious. An aide de camp hastened to his assistance.

Next morning the Senate met, and unluckily for Eugène the Emperor had decided that, to make it clear that her family agreed with the divorce, the son of the Empress, who had been since 1805 Arch-Chancellor of State, should give the Senate an explanation of his mother's desire to end a marriage which had become an obstacle to the welfare of the Empire. He had to ask for the ratification of a document already in their possession, giving legal sanction to the dissolution of the civil marriage which had taken place in 1796. (The question of her religious marriage in 1804 did not arise. It was hopeless for the Emperor to approach the Pope, who was his prisoner at Savona, and had excommunicated him. But Cardinal Fesch, who had performed the ceremony, was finding loopholes, in conjunction with Cambacérès, Arch-Chancellor. The parish priest had not been present; the consent of the Emperor had not been formally obtained.)

The second ceremony dissolving the civil marriage, unlike the first, was long drawn out. It was long past the dinner hour before Eugène arrived to his mother to tell her all was satisfactorily concluded. In order to keep up her mother's courage, Hortense had been reminding her that another queen—Marie Antoinette —had left the Tuileries only to mount the scaffold. "I did succeed." Eugène, who tried a lighter vein, was not so fortunate. The Empress had asked, as they sat in dreadful silence, what had happened to a young lady of her court who had married and gone to serve Auguste in Italy. Eugène seized the opportunity to tell one of his gay stories. It happened that this lady had accompanied Auguste in full Court dress to a *grande soirée*. During the festivity she had been seized by the first pains of labour, and so violently that she had only time to fly from the ballroom, fling herself into her coach and tell the driver to whip up his horses. To save time, her next frantic instruction was that she should call on the way home to pick up the midwife. But alas! when the footman had aroused the *sage-femme* and brought her down and opened the door of the waiting coach, it was at once evident that Nature had forestalled her. She was greeted by the sound of despairing groans and the cry of an infant. "Laugh, dear madame! Laugh! It was really amusing!" But Mademoiselle d'Avrillon could see that as he attempted gaiety, his beautiful heart was riven.

A unique equipage was to take the Empress into retirement —l'Opale, the latest design in court carriages in Paris, that is to say in the world. Unfortunately the day had developed into a thoroughly wet, cold, December Saturday evening. She embarked, heavily veiled, with the weeping Hortense, in torrents of rain, as if Nature was in sympathy with her plight. All was untidy, noisy and confused. Bandboxes galore, and even furniture were being embarked. Constant thought indignantly that many recipients of past favours who should have been present had kept away. The scene which ought to have been a tragedy became almost a farce. There were the Empress's cage-birds to be packed in one of the string of vehicles. Mlle. Avrillon was unlucky, she got in with them and the brace of Alsatian dogs which had been bought at Strasbourg. The female had just pupped.

Late that night Eugène reported to Auguste.

"Everything has passed off quietly. The Empress displayed the greatest courage and resignation. Tomorrow or the next day the newspapers will publish everything and you shall have copies. The Emperor has gone to the Trianon, the Empress to Malmaison where I am this moment leaving to join her. Adieu, my darling Auguste, I love you and my children beyond all expression. P.S. The King and Queen of Bavaria arrive on Tuesday. They are coming to the palace where I am now and I am moving to a little apartment in the Tuileries."

Next evening he wrote again.

"I have been at Malmaison since last night, my very dear Auguste. If the weather could have been better we might have passed a less sad day but it has never ceased to rain. The Empress is well. Her sorrow revived this morning going through the rooms where she had so long lived with the Emperor, but she recovered her courage and is resigned to her new position. Personally, I think she will become in time calmer and more settled. We had several visitors this morning . . ."

He gradually found it answered best not to live at Malmaison solidly, but to go out there daily. This gave the Empress some variety, and the Paris news, and he got some exercise. He took two days off going down to meet the King and Queen of Bavaria at Meaux, to explain the situation to them before they entered Paris. As he had expected, Auguste's father was not pleased at the news; he also considered that he had been tricked into seeming to approve of the divorce which wrecked his son in law's future. He had not been warned that he was going to assist at anything except the celebrations on the signature of the Peace of Schön-brunn. Auguste's stepmother entered in her day-book all the festivities they attended. There was an expedition to lunch at a country seat, or to a concert, or a ball, or a famous sight every single day and night. The Berthiers had a shooting-party at Grosbois, which Eugène was asked to join, and a masked ball in Paris. The Queen saw the Louvre collection (twice), *The Marriage of Figaro, The Barber of Seville,* the Jardin des Plantes, the Sèvres porcelain factory and Notre Dame. Josephine had them to Malmaison, and Eugène and Hortense and Stéphanie to entertain them. Eugène wrote home that Stéphanie was as usual in high good looks and on bad terms with her poor husband.

The Emperor called at Malmaison and invited Josephine and her children to return his call and stay to dine at the Trianon on December 25. Hortense had never sat through a more dismal meal. Her mother could eat scarcely anything and the Emperor kept on wiping his eyes. They left as soon as possible. On January 3 Eugène rode over to Saint Germain and had a look at his old school. The scene brought back happy memories. He was asked to shoot at Marly and Versailles. January passed into February and he could still hardly take a day off without a summons to say that the Empress had been very poorly ever since he left. Good King Max had spoken his mind about some provision for his daughter, and Eugéne was allowed to tell his wife what seemed likely. "It seems we are to have a Grand-Duchy in Germany, and a very beautiful town as our principal residence. You will be in the middle of your family, with a husband who adores you and will do all he can to make you happy. As for me, if I can do that, I shall be well content." Next day he was able to tell her that the Emperor had said they might make a stay of up to twelve days in Munich this summer for her brother's wedding. Ludwig was marrying a German girl, the Princess Thérèse of Sachsen-Hild-burghausen. It was not a great match from the worldly point of view, but she was fair, placid and virtuous and he seemed very happy. On February 9, at last Eugène was able to say that he was starting for home after dark the day after tomorrow, "despite all the tears of my sister and the Empress." Josephine had a distraction. She had moved up to the Elysée for a few weeks and was busy arranging her possessions there.

The matter which had been holding up everything was at last decided. The Czar had returned a prevaricating answer to the request for a Russian Grand-Duchess to succeed Josephine. Eugène and Hortense had both spoken in favour of a Grand-Duchess from Austria. Russia was distant, and there did not seem the slightest chance of hostilities arising in that direction; there was also the religous question. A Russian Grand-Duchess would remain in the Greek church. Austria, on the other hand needed an alliance with France. Eugène had one more unpleasant duty before he mounted into his carriage. He had to go off in full uniform to Prince Karl Schwarzenberg, Austrian Ambassador, to ask on behalf of his stepfather for the hand of the Archduchess Marie Louise.

As he had expected, nothing could have exceeded the nobility of Auguste since she had heard all the bad news. He had received letters which he was to treasure all his life.

"Milan, December 13.

"I can't remember what I said yesterday, my tender and well beloved husband. The news of the divorce had so overwhelmed me. My grief is still strong, but it is for you that I grieve. I picture to myself your sad situation, and though so far away I can also picture the glee on the faces of those who wish us ill. You have not deserved these misfortunes. I speak in the plural for I imagine that we must prepare for more. I am ready for anything, and I regret nothing so long as you continue to love me. More! I rejoice in being able to prove to you that I love you for nothing but yourself. Wiped off the list of the mighty, we will write our names in that of the happy, and what could be better? I have not written to your poor mother. What can I say to her? Assure her of my respect and love. You tell me that you may be home soon; this comforts me in my grief and I long for the hour of your return with impatience. Do not think that I am downhearted. No, my Eugène, my courage is as high as yours and I shall prove that I am worthy to be called your wife. Adieu! beloved friend."

"Milan, December 16.

"I am resigned to all, and submit myself to the will of God. Your grandeur of soul may astonish much of the world, but not your wife who loves you, were it possible, the more."

Eugène's valet, Belanger, the most discreet person in the world, had told Constant that his master had sent the Vicereine a very sad letter, when he had to announce to her that he was not going to succeed the Emperor. She had tenderly replied, "It is not the heir of the Emperor whom I married, and whom I love. It is Eugène de Beauharnais." Belanger said that he had come in and found Eugène weeping. Such a princess, the valet agreed, deserved a crown.[14]

He had one last communication from the Emperor, on the very day that he left for home, and it was a fitting end to a horrible expedition. On January 27 Hofer had been captured on the top of the Brenner. A neighbour, a Judas, had betrayed him. He had been taken in chains to a dungeon in the Castello San Giorgio, Mantua. He had refused to revoke his second call to arms.

"My son,
"I did order you to have Hofer brought to Paris, but since he is at Mantua, give the order to appoint immediately a military court to judge him, and have him shot at whichever place your order is sent to. Get all this done in twenty-four hours."

The execution took place on February 18. When King Max heard, he exclaimed, "The French have shot my Hofer for me!" But he was shocked. Crown Prince Ludwig took up residence in Innsbruck on his marriage. He had always hated fighting the Tyrolese. Under his rule the beautiful northern part of the country became peaceful. It had been divided as Eugène had suggested between Bavaria and Italy.

When Prince Metternich arrived in Paris for the Emperor's wedding he had instructions to complain on behalf of his country about the fate of Hofer. The Emperor regretted the impetuosity of his generals; and Austria was demonstrably in no position to press the affair. But the Emperor had presented the Tyrol with a national hero.[15]

CHAPTER THIRTEEN

"Send for Prince Eugène"
1810 : 1811

I

THE VICEROY and Vicereine of Italy arrived in Paris on March 20, 1810. Eugène had been home eight days when he had received the Emperor's commands to set out again. The Archduchess Marie Louise was due to leave Vienna on March 11. The wedding was fixed for April 1. The party from Milan had taken eight days on the road, for they were travelling in some state. The Duchess of Litta and two other ladies of her household attended the Vicereine—all had brought attendants. The Viceroy, fortunately for his biographers, was taking Secretary Baron Darnay in his train this time. Now was to be seen the wisdom of having retained all these years the services of the Baronin von Wurmb and Gräfin Sandizell. The parents had been able to leave the two little princesses behind, confident that they were in reasonable loving hands. But this was about the only happy feature of the situation. They were going on their long-promised visit to Paris, the capital of the world, and they would much rather have stayed at home. Nor were they as happy at home as they had been. Eugène's loss of prestige on the divorce of his mother had been great. His appointment as Grand Duke of Frankfort had been announced. It only made people in Italy think the Imperial couple were leaving. The crown of Italy was reserved for the second son of the Emperor who now hoped for heirs. Some politicians, such as Melzi, still dreamt of an independent kingdom of Italy.

The occasion for which they had been summoned was bound to be full of extremely awkward, if not absolutely painful, encounters for both of them. The Bonaparte family, highly elated at the fall of Josephine, were mustered for a series of the spectacular fêtes and pompous public appearances in which they rejoiced.

Auguste had longed for more than four years to be shown his country by her beloved French husband. They would scarcely be given the opportunity; they would not see much of one another. Even their journey had seemed ill-fated. Before they left Milan Eugène had written to warn Hortense that General de Broc, husband of one of her best loved ladies, who had served under himself in the late campaign, was still lying dangerously ill at Milan. At Chambéry the Viceregal train had met the poor wife hastening to nurse her husband, and it had fallen to Auguste to tell her that she was too late. They had brought the widow home. Hortense had taken charge of her at Fontainebleau.

Their Paris home was to be the Elysée palace. That had been given to Josephine, so was an appropriate residence for them, but as soon as their visits of etiquette were paid they went out to Malmaison, and there Auguste stayed, having chosen a suite adjacent to that of what she indignantly called "the poor Empress". The ladies were as happy as possible considering the circumstances, even if their conversation had to be a little insipid. Half the time the Empress seemed to be telling Auguste how grateful she was that her beloved son had found such a wonderful wife, and for the other half Auguste expanded on the utter perfection of Eugène as husband and father.[1]

The Créole Empress knew what comfort was; she kept her country palace warm and had a redoubtable *chef*. A Neapolitan *artiste* in her kitchen, Signor Rouchese, devoted himself entirely to the production of ices. She herself ate sparingly, but amongst her guests from the world of art, letters, law, the church and finance were some of the first gastronomes of Paris. Though the spring rains came down on the park the ladies were cosy, with their sewing and music. There was plenty to admire indoors of great value and beauty. And the mother in law was able, as is the habit of ladies of increasing years, to refer darkly to her intention of leaving Malmaison to Eugène. Here was a place in France which Auguste could admire with a full heart, picturing her children living there some day.

Hortense arrived to stay. The first thing about herself that she had told Eugène on his last arrival had been that she wanted a separation. He had begged her to give Louis another chance. The Emperor could not have his family riddled with divorces at this moment. One at a time was enough. Hortense did not aspire to a divorce. A legal separation was her ideal. Louis had come from

Holland for the wedding. They would be under the same roof in the palace of Compiègne, but nowadays they hardly spoke. The King of Holland was in disgrace with the Emperor for letting English goods flow into his country. Hortense said there had been a luncheon staged by Jerome, after which she had been left alone with her husband. He had agreed with her that they ought to part, but told her that the Emperor forbade it. She must return with him to Holland. She had entreated him to leave her to end her days in peace with her mother. "Imagine that I have died." "That is quite different," he had answered quickly. "Look at the Emperor of Austria. He remarried immediately." His expression absolutely frightened her. She believed he would like to kill her. She had written a despairing letter to the Emperor; he had not answered.

The sisters in law were never to find one another truly congenial. Eugène, despite his sad and unsettled boyhood had retained boyish high spirits. He had a keen sense of the ridiculous. It was disappointing to find the Queen of Holland a Queen of Grief, without a laugh in her. Auguste was a stranger to self-pity, and it irritated her that her husband must be continually the audience for his sister's complaints. Between his mother (who had just cause), and his sister (who perhaps had), the poor man seemed to be never without a female relative collapsing on his shoulder crying that he was their sole tower of strength. "Send for Prince Eugène." Hortense, for her part, recorded her own first impressions.

"I had never met my sister in law before, but had heard much about her. The happiness that she had brought my brother endeared her to me. I went to meet her on the road to Fontainebleau. I found her much as she had been described, of a remarkable beauty and freshness. Although very tall and slight, her figure was so well proportioned that she did not look extraordinary. Her manners were simple and considerate. In fact she was the perfect princess, as I have often heard said, even by the Emperor. We became as close to one another as two people can be who have common interests and ideas but who have had totally different experience of life. How can a girl who has never known anything but happiness begin to enter into the feelings of one doomed early to misfortune?"

Josephine asked eagerly for the Paris gossip about her successor. Personally, she was well pleased with all she had heard so far.

The Archduchess Marie Louise had been one of the princesses discussed for Eugène. She had been considered too young then, and far inferior to Auguste in beauty. She was now eighteen, but evidently had not improved greatly. Hortense had heard she was very shy and gauche and that Prince Metternich had advised that she should take some dancing lessons before she faced Paris, and should not attempt to perform in public at present. There was something very droll in this, as the Emperor also was taking dancing lessons. He had made Hortense teach him to waltz. But after two evenings trial he had decided, "Each to their own taste. I am too old. Moreover, it was not as a dancer that I was ever meant to excel." He had ordered some very uncomfortable new suits at the suggestion of the Princess Pauline—pale satins with upstanding collars, big cravats and much gold embroidery. Murat, King of Naples, whose figure was still superb, had ventured to recommend his own tailor. He was a great dresser. Even from Warsaw he had written to Paris ordering ostrich feathers to the value of 27,000 francs. But the Emperor's new clothes were not to be much worn. Méneval noticed during the next few months, his master dropping quietly back into his usual uniforms—the green coat of the *chasseurs* for daily use, and the blue turned up with white for Sundays and feast days.

He could not hear enough about his new bride. He looked long at her portraits: "Ah! that is indeed the Habsburg lip." No artist had attempted to disguise that her underlip was heavy. Now she was on her way, in a coach and eight, attended by Caroline Murat. The cortège from Vienna numbered over a hundred persons, in nineteen coaches, travelling in three convoys. The Emperor wrote to his bride every day and she replied prettily. Méneval noticed that so great was the curiosity and excitement at court, that when the envelope from one of her little notes fluttered to the floor, people hastened to pick it up and try to prophesy her character from her handwriting.

She was the eldest of the thirteen motherless children of the Emperor Francis, and had a jealous neurotic Este step-mother. Her own mother had been a Habsburg princess of Naples. The Emperor closely questioned the aides de camp who brought her letters. "Be frank. How did the Archduchess impress you?" "Oh! very favourably, sire." "That does not give me any information. Come now, how tall is she?" "Sire—she is—she is about the same height as the Queen of Holland." "Ah! very nice. And what colour is her hair?" "Blonde. Much the same as the Queen of Holland." "Good, And her complexion." "Very pink and white, like that of the Queen of Holland." "Ha! then she resembles the Queen of Holland." "Not in the least, sire; yet I have answered every question absolutely truthfully." The Emperor dismissed the youth before saying "I see my wife is ugly; for not one of these confounded young fellows will say she is pretty. Never mind; so long as she is kind and brings me healthy sons I will love her as much as if she was the most beautiful woman on earth."[2]

By mid-March Eugène was extremely uneasy. The Emperor had given his mother a château near Evreux, more than a hundred kilometres north-west of Paris, and had asked her to take possession by quarter-day. It had been built in the end of the fourteenth century by the Kings of Navarre and continued to bear their name, although much altered. The Emperor had sent in an army of workmen. He could not have two wives in, or even near, Paris on his wedding day. But on the 27th when Eugène and Auguste left for Compiègne to join the family assembled there to greet the new Empress, the old Empress had not yet moved. She got on the road, in the end, on the same dark, wet, cold night that the procession bringing Marie Louise approached Compiègne. There was an elaborate programme involving thousands of people, planned for Soissons, but the Emperor's impatience and sense of the dramatic got the better of him. He set off with Murat in a calèche and came up with the incoming procession in the village of Courcelles. The coach with eight snow-white horses was unmistakeable. He leapt in and embraced his bride. Marie Louise screamed. Equerry Audenarde cried in the same moment "The Emperor!" Caroline Murat was sent to complete the journey with her husband. The first speech of Marie Louise showed that she had not forgotten her instructions to make herself agreeable. "Sire! Your portrait had not flattered you." Hortense took up the story from Compiègne.

"At seven o'clock in the evening we all took our places in full court dress at the foot of the grand staircase." (They had a two hours' wait.) "We kissed the newcomer but scarcely saw her. She passed through a gallery where all the town and the Court were gathered, disappeared, and was no more seen till next morning. She received us amiably. Her air was gentle and sweet, although a little embarrassed. We were all satisfied with her appearance."

Hortense suppressed an incident which was recorded with amusement by the Emperor's secretary and many other people present. A suite had been made ready for the Emperor at the Chancellor's residence, but having hastily confirmed with Cardinal Fesch that the proxy marriage which had taken place in Vienna was valid, he did not use it. The waiting court heard, soon after the Queen of Naples had reappeared from supping briefly with the bridal couple, that they were dismissed. The whisper passed from mouth to mouth *"Ils sont couchés!"*[3] Four years later, ill-wishers intent on separating Marie Louise from her husband, did not hesitate to remind her how terrible had been the insult offered to a Habsburg archduchess by a *parvenu* bridegroom.

The civil wedding took place four days later, at St. Cloud, in spring sunshine, though in Paris the pavements were swept by hail. By daylight, onlookers were able to see that the new Empress was rather plain than pretty, plump, and fair, with a docile expression. Her complexion was somewhat disordered, most likely from nervous exhaustion. Her nose and lips were thick. With extraordinary ineptitude, all the ceremonies had been arranged to follow as far as possible those at the wedding of her murdered aunt, Marie Antoinette. The opera performed on the night of her proxy wedding in Vienna had been *Iphigenia in Aulis* and the same strange choice was followed on the night of her civil wedding at St. Cloud. In London, Lord Castlereagh remarked pityingly that he supposed a virgin must be sacrificed occasionally to the Minotaur.

Eugène and his princess got good places at the civil wedding; he signed the register sixth, after the Emperor's mother, brothers and brothers in law. Nobody could guess from her expression what Madame Mère thought of her famous son's latest exploit. It was well known that when called upon to admire his magnificent style of living, this grand simple old lady commented merely, "So long as it lasts." Public rejoicings took place in the beautiful park as soon as the guns announced that the knot was tied. There was a general illumination and the fountains played under torchlight; unfortunately heavy rain never ceased to fall.

The religious wedding took place the next day from the Tuileries in fitful sunshine. A chapel had been arranged in the Salon Carrée of the Musée Napoléon, the Louvre. Marie Louise entered Paris in a gilt and glass coach through the Arc de Triomphe which had been temporarily finished, in wood covered with painted canvas. Four ladies had placed the coronation crown, made for Josephine, on her head. One had been Italian, the magnificent Duchess of Litta. The Emperor was having another crown made for her to wear at her wedding receptions. Despite all the careful preparations there were some unfortunate incidents. Hortense thought the crowds through which they passed towards the Tuileries were unusually cold. A full muster of cardinals had turned up at the civil wedding, but the Emperor's brow darkened when he saw how few awaited him at the altar. Thirteen were missing. He asked loudly, "Where are the cardinals?" Marie Louise heard and looked frightened, and as if she would like to cry.

The Queens of Spain, Holland and Westphalia and the Princesses Elisa and Pauline carried her train. Pauline had complained of the weight and begged to be excused; her health was so delicate. But her request had been refused. Caroline, Auguste and Stéphanie walked in front, carrying tapers and various insignia on cushions. The ubiquitous Fesch performed the nuptial rites, which Hortense found rather brief. She noted spectators looking closely at her and Eugène as if to decide what were their inner feelings.[4]

II

After their two marriages and a short stay at St. Cloud the Emperor and his bride returned to Compiègne, where they arrived on April 5. A few days later the Emperor, after glancing through his letters, said to his secretary, "Send for Prince Eugène."

The Empress Josephine wanted to come back to Malmaison. She said that her thoughts were with the Emperor night and day, and the château of Navarre had not one window or door which would close. She feared she might die of exposure if she had to remain there. She must not do that! Her son, with his usual good humour agreed to set out at once to inspect an architectural phenomenon, and in record time his carriage was to be seen hastening into Normandy in stormy spring weather.

The château of Navarre certainly had an unusual appearance. It had been largely rebuilt in 1686 by an admiring nephew of the famous Turenne, and was designed in the shape of a cube of two stories, on the top of which was a dome still awaiting a colossal statue of the martial hero. It reminded the villagers of nothing but an inverted cooking-pot and was locally known as "*la marmite*". Inside it was even more remarkable, for four elaborate entrances gave access to a vast central hall which rose to the top of the building and was only dimly illuminated by windows in the dome. The Empress, with simple pathos, drew her son's attention to small rooms of very odd shape, and insecurely fastened panelling. She agreed that the situation was magnificent —a valley between two hillsides covered with woods of the greatest beauty. Much might be made of the park. But there was too much water.[5] She had been very well received by the inhabitants of Evreux, on the morning of her arrival—the Mayor and Prefect with speeches of welcome, the National Guard and a band which had included choristers from the cathedral. It might have been her fancy that all the visitors appeared to have come to pay calls of condolence. Her principal neighbour, the Bishop, had been assiduous in waiting upon her in the evenings to play tric-trac. He was a very pleasant man; seventy-five.

But she was utterly miserable, cast-off, quite forgotten! Worse! she had heard horrible Paris rumours that she was never to be allowed to return there; that Malmaison was to be given to another; she was to lose her rank and become Grand Duchess of Berg or Navarre doomed to eternal banishment. For the first time the Emperor had not answered a letter from her. It was impossible to go out in the rain . . . Her son listened to all she had to say and then began to comfort and explain. He had seen the Emperor and received instructions. First of all, she might dismiss the wicked rumours with which she was tormenting herself. They must be nonsense. The Emperor had asked her to stay a month at Navarre. She would be wise to try to do this. After that he consented that she should return to Malmaison. He would by then be on a tour of inspection of the ports of the north coast and Low Countries on which he had asked Eugène to accompany him. He wanted her to discuss with her son a programme for her summer. He had sent her a letter.

Her relief was almost more painful than her expressed anxiety. She was with difficulty restrained from answering at once. But that would have meant sending away her best visitor who had hardly arrived, bringing all the latest Paris papers with the wedding in them. Although he never said anything approaching the disloyal to the Emperor, Prince Eugène's lively anecdotes of the various *contretemps* at the recent ceremonies were truly amusing.

The exiled Spanish royalties, for instance, had vied with one another in adulation. At the banquet given by them to the Imperial couple, ex-King Ferdinand, who had loudly cheered every mention of the Emperor's name, had suddenly begged His Majesty to adopt him.

By April 19 Josephine had been persuaded to agree to stay out her month. The Emperor had said that he would advance much more money to make Navarre habitable and even for large structural alterations to suit her taste. Eugène set out for St. Cloud with a letter couched in the most stately style: "Let your Majesty rest assured that I shall always respect your new situation. I shall do so in silence, confiding in the feelings you once bore me. I shall trust in your justice and benevolence."

He was back again in three days bringing a short but almost jocular reply from the Emperor beginning, "My dear!" He asked what on earth had Eugène been saying to her to make her write to him like this? "I am always the same; my feelings do not change." He ended his scribble "Adieu, my dear. Be fair to yourself and to me." She could not now be held back from answering instantly in high emotion. "A thousand thousand tender thanks for not having forgotten me. My son has just delivered your letter. How eagerly I read it, and yet how slowly! for there was not a single word but provoked tears . . ."

The weather was getting better every day, and she would be a good girl and accustom herself to the life of the country-dweller, little drives, little walks, cards and local company. She had begun another large piece of needlework—tapestry. Her son was having all the journals sent regularly from Paris. He had told her that with the generous assistance of the Emperor he had arranged advantageous marriages for both Louis Tascher and his cousin Maurice. His father was going to bring Maurice to call upon her. She would stay a very short time at Malmaison and then go on to take her cure wherever advised by Corvisart. She would spend the winter with Eugène and Auguste in Milan, return by Malmaison for the early spring, and then make her home at Navarre from May till August.[6]

So it seemed the problem of the poor *Maman* was settled, for the moment at any rate, but Eugène had observed many more reasons for complaint which she had not entered in her letter. Her devoted staff, understandably, were not devoted to one another. Already there were defections—Madame Ney, school-friend of Hortense, sister of Madame de Broc, asked for permission to obey her husband who had written from Spain ordering her to join him in Paris. Comte André de Beaumont and Comte de Montholon had urgent private affairs demanding their attendance in the capital. Everyone scorned the new Intendant. When he sent in furniture, the progress of the vans up the long drive was watched from the upper windows, and after the vehicles drew to a halt it was only a question of who had the best legs. The exiled courtiers fell upon the stuff like vultures. Amongst other pinpricks had been the fact that the Empress's hairdresser, the great Duplan, who had attended her for twenty years, had taken service with her successor. But Duplan had found himself in a quandary. It was true that the Emperor had offered him a greatly increased fee, but he was to attend the new Empress exclusively. Now, the Empress Josephine, the soul of kindness, had never cared (or perhaps known) that he had made a very large outside income attending her ladies. Queen Hortense made the supreme sacrifice and presented her own hairdresser to her dispossessed mother.

Getting his sister off for Holland had been Eugène's greatest success. He had managed to secure most favourable terms from Louis. She was to reside under the same roof as her husband, but have her own apartments and staff, chosen by her. She was to take her elder son, but leave with suitable guardians, such as her mother, the younger one who would be killed by the climate of the Low Countries. She was to be allowed to take her cure in the summer wherever she chose.

Her first letters from her kingdom did not sound reassuring. She had been so hurried by Eugène that there had been no welcome awaiting her at Utrecht. The King had seemed overjoyed when he saw his son again but had taken hardly any notice of her. Her description of her new premises was striking. "The Palace of Amsterdam, formerly the town-hall, was very handsome. My *salon*, previously the criminal court, was decorated with a frieze of skulls in black and white marble. Nobody had thought of removing this ornament which was highly thought of. The galleries were very dark and my rooms looked out on the blank walls of a church. They smelt awful, and when windows were opened it was worse, for from the canal arose a heavy air and odour of sulphur . . . My brother, anxious still about me, sent me one of his aides de camp. I told him to reassure the Viceroy. I was too much touched by Eugène's kindness to wish to increase his uneasiness."

On May 22 the Vicereine wrote to her brother Ludwig, "The Empress Marie Louise behaves very well towards me. She is cold, and does not appear to have much sensibility; but perhaps that is for reasons of policy. People think she is very much in love with the Emperor and he with her. As far as she can, she singles out Eugène, and yesterday, to my great astonishment, I got an outstandingly civil letter from her . . .

"The rest of the family are also kind to me. The Queen of Naples particularly pays me much attention. But when one has known them at close quarters one can only despise them. I could never have conceived anything so abominable as their ill-breeding. It is torture to me to have to go about with such people. They dissemble in front of me as much as they are able."[7]

She was not alone in disliking the Queen of Naples. Marie Louise had written to her father on her journey that she did not trust this lady. She had good reason. Her governess, the Countess Leczinska, had been dismissed by the Queen of Naples before they had left Munich. Things had been arranged so that she simply vanished, but indignant well-wishers had smuggled her in for a farewell scene. In fact, the Emperor had told his sister to get rid of the governess quickly if she seemed to have influence, which she certainly had; but Marie Louise had understood that Madame Leczinska was to stay for at least a year.

Gentlemen tended to admire Madame Murat. Prince Ludwig had been alarmed by the admiration expressed by his father. Gay Prince Max had been much amused by a very fine woman. It was generally taken for granted in France that the Murats had each gone their own way for some years. The Queen's *affaire* with Junot had been so paraded by her that the Emperor had taken measures. Afterwards there had been talk of Prince Metternich, and she herself had said quite openly to Queen Hortense before capturing young Charles de Flahaut, "You were the only person I feared." Both the Murats, however, had good points. Their four children were the best behaved in Europe. This was an extraordinary story. Mrs. Pulsford and Miss Catherine Davies (whose father had thirty-two other children) were impecunious

English governesses who had found themselves caught in Paris by the rupture of the Peace of Amiens. They had taken service with the Emperor's sister. He kept on telling her to send them packing, but she said they were so honest and taught her children such beautiful manners, she only wished she could get some more. She tried to keep them out of his way but the children performed an introduction one day. "You English are not good!" said the Emperor to Miss Davies. "Sir, there are some good and some bad as in France." "Do you like the French as well as the English?" "If I were to say that, sire, I should be a hyprocrite. I like those of all nations who are kind to me." "Bravo! Bravo!" Miss Davies, who was thirty-seven, found her mistress an excellent manager, and firm but considerate employer. The King of Naples was really her idol. "In person, Murat was the most princely man I ever saw."[8]

A reconciliation resulting in a pregnancy had taken place shortly before the Imperial wedding. It was five years since their last child had been born. Princess Louisa Murat recollected years later: "Each time they saw one another after many months of absence, Murat executed some equestrian movement at the head of his cavalry, which recalled the old paladins. All their resentments against one another disappeared and they were more closely attached than ever."

The Duchess of Tuscany, the Emperor's blue-stocking sister who annoyed him by behaving so pompously in her Florentine court, might have been considered too plain and serious for lovers, but the Paris gossips knew better.

Princess Pauline was famed for her romantic amatory excursions, but the truth seemed to be that she really loved deeply only two persons—herself and her brother, the Emperor. The Baciocchis, like the Murats, each went their own way, with the difference that their amours were short-lived and tepid. There was no question but that the child expected now would be a Baciocchi. The princess considered a train of admirers her due as a leader of an artistic salon and a royal lady, and her husband amused himself with inferior members of her staff. The poor Baciocchis were not at all admired in Paris. Nobody could help admiring Princess Pauline, whose Hôtel de Charost in the capital, and palace at Neuilly just outside, were, like herself, marvels of modern classical taste. She was far the most beautiful of the sisters and the Emperor's favourite. Her fête in honour of his wedding with an Austrian archduchess was acknowledged the best of an ambitious season. She had ordered in the grounds of her country estate at Neuilly a replica of the palace of Schönbrunn. The courtyards were filled by figures from Vienna—in carriages, on horseback, strolling, singing. There were dairymaids in their traditional golden bonnets, running footmen in Imperial Austrian livery, Tyroleans engaged in their local dances. The Emperor was so pleased that he asked for a repeat performance a week hence.

The Vicereine had her hair arranged in the latest style and sat to the fashionable painter Gérard. A version of this full-length portrait hung on the walls of the Viceroy's bedroom thereafter, in whatever palace he was living. As soon as her husband had returned from his tour with the honeymoon couple, and the poor mother in law had got back to Malmaison from Navarre, she gladly left the Elysée. It had been disappointing that her Paris sightseeing must be mostly undertaken without her husband's guidance. She was not feeling very well, and had little heart for a succession of formal public occasions—especially banquets and balls—at all of which she met the Bonapartes. She saw the Bibliothèque Nationale and the Jardin des Plantes with Eugène, but on one exhausting day, attending the bridal pair.

Marie Louise had talents. Her husband had been a little surprised at the solemnity of her reading. But it appeared that she read from a sense of duty, not for enjoyment. He was teaching her to ride and she loved that. She painted in oils, and the Emperor was sitting to her; but the smell of the equipment for this accomplishment was so unpleassant to her that she was unlikely to persevere. Already it was whispered that her court was much less amusing than that of the "old" empress. Laure Junot recollected sadly: "One of its greatest attractions, equalled by no other court in Europe was the collection of beautiful women with which it was graced. Almost all the French generals and the superior officers of the Imperial Guard had married for love, either in France or other countries . . . The Emperor's wish was that his court should be brilliant, and this wish being agreeable to everyone was implicitly followed . . . I well remember the truly fantastic appearance of the *Salle des Maréchaux* on the night of a grand concert when it was lined with three rows of ladies on either side, radiant in youth and beauty, decked with flowers, jewels and waving plumes. Behind them came officers of the household, and then generals, senators, counsellors of State and foreign diplomats, all clothed in rich costumes and wearing the decorations and orders which Europe offered us on bended knee."

The Emperor's choice of chief lady to attend his wife had been a stroke of genius. He had appointed Madame Lannes, Duchess of Montebello, widow of the hero who had died of wounds after Essling. "I am giving the Empress a true lady of honour."

An odd incident in the history of Eugène took place that summer in Paris. Marshal Duroc, Duke of Friuli, presented himself one morning, evidently on business. His old friend saw that some proposal was to be made to him and took him aside. The Swedes were asking for a king. The Emperor had empowered his Grand Marshal of the Palace to sound Prince Eugène. The situation was complicated. The last king of the ancient house of Vasa had been deposed in 1809, and his uncle, the Regent, had been proclaimed Charles XIII. But he was childless and old. All hopes had been pinned on the young Prince Charles of Augustenberg who had been elected as a successor to the throne. But he had now died suddenly in somewhat mysterious circumstances. There had been stories of poison, and riots had taken place at his funeral. A deputation had arrived in Paris and addressed themselves to Bernadotte, Marshal-Prince of Ponte Corvo. He was remembered as having behaved with courtesy to Swedish prisoners. But what an exhausted nation really required was a candidate agreeable to the Emperor Napoleon, under whom they might enjoy peace and prosperity. They knew that Madame Bernadotte was sister in law to Joseph Bonaparte.

Eugène asked Duroc to give him twenty-four hours, and next day regretted that he could not consider the crown of Sweden. He had discussed the matter with Princess Auguste and they had come to the conclusion that they must content themselves with their present situation. He added that the obligation to abjure the Catholic faith was exceedingly distasteful to the Vicereine. They sent their most grateful thanks to the Emperor. Eugène did not mention several other consideration. The first was a family one. The wife of the deposed king of Sweden was a princess of Baden, sister to Auguste's stepmother the Queen of Bavaria. Gustavus IV had been insane, but no valid explanation had ever been offered for the exclusion of his whole family from the succession. Difficulties might arise from that quarter. What was far more important was that if the Viceroy gave up Italy and accepted Sweden, it would be the end of possibilities of his ever succeeding to the kingdom of Italy and the Empire. The new bride might bring the Emperor daughters only; they might not have a family. (The Queen of Naples, who watched like a hawk, said that there was already anxiety that Marie Louise had not shown instant signs of providing one.) Duroc bowed himself out, and on the same day the Emperor, said to Eugène *en passant*, "I am so sorry. I should have been much pleased. But I daresay you were right." Bernadotte, of whom the Emperor had never felt quite sure, had agents in Sweden who used the Emperor's name and large funds skilfully to bring over hesitant electors. He received the homage of the estates six months later as Crown Prince, and soon became extremely popular in his adopted country.[9]

By mid-June Eugène knew with relief that his mother had arrived at Aix les Bains and his sister at Plombières; but now he had to add Auguste to his list of suffering females. She wrote a little sadly to tell her brother that now there could be no question of her coming to his wedding. Eugène tried to raise her spirits by telling her that their lucky star was in the ascendant. He was convinced that the child begotten in his native land would be a son.[10] Privately he was horrified at the thought of their journey home to Milan.

The last outstanding entertainment of the wedding festivities was fixed for Sunday, July 1. This was the ball given by the Austrian Ambassador, Prince Schwarzenberg. One thousand five hundred guests had been invited. The Emperor had been angry at an attempt by all three of his sisters to escape before this culminating social event. Princess Pauline had appropriated Schönbrunn for her fête, so the Schwarzenbergs had to fall back on a re-creation of the Austrian Imperial country palace of Laxenburg. Eugène was well able to appreciate the correctness of the replica, as it had been Berthier's headquarters and he had shot there three times. The Schwarzenbergs were less lucky than Princess Pauline in another direction. Her ball had taken place in her park on a balmy night. By early July the weather was uncertain. No room in the Embassy in the Rue de la Chaussée d'Antin was large enough to accommodate so many people if there was a sudden downpour. They ordered an enormous circular wooden pavilion, a Rotunda. It was built in four days. It was hung with gold and silver brocade, and the bouquets fastened to draperies of spangled gauze were said, despite the fact that flowers were at this season plentiful, to be so rare and perfectly grown that the money spent on them would have bought another palace. The pavilion had a surprise in every room. There was a concert hall, a hall with a stage and tableaux. In the centre came the ballroom, the greatest surprise of all—Laxenburg.

As darkness fell, a light breeze swayed layer upon layer of tulle and gauze draperies, and scenery painted to resemble the pillars, entrance gates and façade of an Austrian hunting box. The ballroom containing this piece of make-believe, lit by a succession of cut glass chandeliers and innumerable candles, was of fairytale beauty. Eugène escorted his wife up to the dais at the very top of the ballroom to take her seat amongst the assembled royalty, and prepared to do his duty by leading out Princess Pauline Schwarzenberg, sister in law of the Ambassador.

Afterwards, nobody could tell exactly where or how the fire had started. There was a story that a candle had fallen against a curtain, out of sight in an angle of the little wooden gallery above the dais. A tall attendant had torn it down, but too late, the roof was ablaze. The ball had been going on for some time and the Emperor was preparing to leave. He was passing round the ballroom conversing with some ladies who were not dancing. Marie Louise was stationary standing near the dais, also conversing. The flames spread with nightmarish rapidity and soon the scene was an inferno. Blinding smoke was seen issuing from the end of the structure attached to the house, so nobody thought of trying to escape that way. There was a sudden ugly rush for the only visible large exit, that into the garden. Afterwards it was claimed that there had been plenty of side doors, but they were all masked by draperies. As the roof collapsed, most of the chandeliers crashed upon the floor. Several people were injured and the floor gave way beneath them. They descended five feet amidst burning planks into the grotto which had been drained of water.

Auguste was as far as possible from the garden exit, but her husband found her. He had happened to observe while refreshments were being served on the dais, that servants had been passing in from behind. He found a door hidden by a curtain, but either it had now been locked from security reasons, or it had swelled with the heat. A *chasseur* of the Imperial Guard told his wife to stand right back and took a running leap at a stage scenery door. A few kicks demolished the fragments, and taking his wife's hand he led her into darkness. They were in an outer service passage of the old Hôtel de Montesson. They were saved. He put her in a carriage for return to the Elysée and hurried back towards the red glow in the sky. Here he met the Emperor who had also returned from setting his wife on her homeward road. Marie Louise had remounted the dais and waited, seated like a brave doll, until Metternich had found her.

But without fire-fighting appliances, particularly water, there was very little that volunteers could do. General Lauriston charged about like a mad bull until he found his wife. Catherine of West-phalia was very nearly trampled to death. She had fallen on the floor in a faint on hearing that Jerome was missing. He turned up and valiantly tried to be useful. An uncle of Marie Louise, the Duke of Würzburg, carried out Caroline of Naples, apparently lifeless. She recovered but later had a severe and dangerous mis-carriage. One of Queen Hortense's bosom-friends, the wife of General Comte Durosnel, and one of Madame Mère's ladies in waiting, the Baroness de Bressieux, were so badly burned that they were disfigured for life. And they were among the lucky ones. The beautiful sister in law of Prince Schwarzenberg, with whom the Viceroy had opened the ball, returned to the ballroom to search for a daughter and was felled by a chandelier under which she fell through the floor boards. Her body was recognizable only by family jewellery. Another mother searching for a beloved child was rescued by a Swedish officer, charred beyond recogni-tion but still able to speak. Her tiara had melted on her head. She died within twenty-four hours. She was the Princesse de la Leyen with whom the Viceroy had been so merrily discussing dowries for the marriage of her little Amélie with Louis Tascher only a few weeks ago.

After the fatal ball there were absurd rumours and scandals. It was whispered that there had been an Austrian plot to demolish the whole Imperial French family at a single blow. It was re-membered that at the marriage festivities of Marie Antoinette there had been a spectacular tragedy by fire. Austrian arch-duchesses brought ill-luck to France.[11]

IV

His mother's letters made Eugène decide that he had better try to soothe her on his homeward journey. He left Auguste at Geneva and Josephine came down to meet him at the excellent inn in the pretty little village of La Sécheron in the parish of

310

Petit Sacconeux. They had a happy day together. That is to say, Josephine was delighted to have her best audience for her complaints, and very much interested to hear about the fatal ball and that Marie Louise had fainted at a reception. This had, apparently, meant nothing, but she had been a wife barely three months. Josephine still hoped that the expected son of Auguste might inherit Italy if not the Empire. All she had to impart was melancholy. She had the worst of news from Malmaison. Her favourite parrot was dead. He was the one who would speak only Spanish and knew several songs and would accompany himself as he danced. She was anxious about having bought a little villa on the Lake of Geneva at Prègny, but it was really a necessity. Aix les Bains was a sad hole, not nearly as good as Plombières. There was hardly any society and her lodgings were inferior; so were the shops. The Lac du Bourget was dangerous, so she could not make expeditions except on the finest days and even then had been nearly drowned. Hortense wrote that she was most unwell. Josephine had asked her daughter to join her. Eugène expressed hopes that he would have the pleasure of entertaining his mother for the whole winter in Milan. She must come as soon as she liked. They parted with much emotion.

The latest bombshell from Hortense did not explode until he reached Milan. On the very night of the Schwarzenberg ball Louis had resigned the Crown of Holland, in favour of his elder son, leaving Hortense as Regent. He had simply disappeared with three attendants, "leaving the Crown Prince," wrote the Emperor in fury, "absolutely destitute." General Lauriston was sent to collect Napoleon Louis, who was not quite six years old. The Emperor announced his intention of uniting Holland with France. Hortense expected to hear that her husband had sailed for America so it was rather an anticlimax when he reappeared in Bohemia. He was at Toeplitz taking the waters and was never coming home. "Freed by the act of the King," wrote the Emperor to Hortense, "you can live undisturbed in Paris." Eugène and Auguste wrote to invite her to Milan.

The homecoming of the Viceregal couple was the beginning of a happier period. Auguste was none the worse of her varied experiences and long journey. The children were in high beauty. The young parents realized as they had begun to do when there had been the question of Sweden, that they had become devoted to Italy and its people. Monza was now always "dear Monza".

They had been welcomed home. They were popular. Milan had greatly improved under Eugène's direction. The new trees in the parks were beginning to look beautiful. The cathedral was nearly finished. The only thing about which he was not yet happy was the Palazzo Reale, down opposite the Duomo. The Emperor spoke of visiting Italy again, perhaps for the next christening. The Viceroy sent off a collection of architects' plans for yet another set of alterations, with the suggestions very clearly marked in yellow ink.

The Emperor wrote that he had decided to annex the Valais. "The wretched inhabitants of this district make the Simplon route almost useless."

Eugène got a sharp rebuke in August for putting Italy first. All her raw silk must be going to accursed England, for there were no silk factories in Germany. It must be diverted to France. "You must not lose sight of the fact that if English commerce triumphs at sea, it is due to her sea power. It is therefore suitable that as France is the first land power, she should appropriate commercial supremacy on the continent . . . If I were to lose a great battle, a million soldiers of my old France, two million, would hasten to my colours, and every purse in the country would be open to me. But my Kingdom of Italy would desert me. I find it very strange that there should be repugnance about helping the French manufacturers in what is practically the only way of damaging the English." The Emperor's opinion of Italy and her people had always been low. This was curious, for as a family the Bonapartes showed very strong signs, physically and mentally, of their Italian origin.

His inferiority at sea was a very sore point with the Emperor. Eugène spent many weeks this autumn in visiting the French fleet in Venice and the Italian in Ancona. The trade of Venice was being ruined but the people seemed calm and patient. The appearance of English ships was still a continual menace. Corfu and Ragusa must be provisioned. There were three frigates and a corvette wasping about the Adriatic this season. They had made a base in the tiny island of Lissa. An experienced sea-officer was sent up from the Toulon fleet and Eugène organized an expedition which planted the tricolour on Lissa. Three British frigates and a corvette sailed away to fight another day, and next February reappeared. The captain from Toulon was killed in action, and it turned out, wrote the Viceroy to Paris, that he had left a widow in Martinique with four children, one still in the cradle. The Viceroy gravely read the despatches of Admiral Sir Charles Cotton in the *London Morning Chronicle*. He inspected shipyards and sea-defences and hospitals. He stayed for a fortnight with the Marchese di Triumphi, who had a very fine palace outside Ancona. The Governor gave a ball and everyone danced lustily till a late hour. There were five Italian frigates and four brigs in the harbour now, and he went for a cruise taking his little war-artist Adam, whom he thought might do some marine studies. But it was blowing weather and nearly everyone of his staff suffered. Labédoyère on the Lissa expedition, had been as sea-sick as a young man ever could be. Petrus, the Mameluke, was still ill when they got to Bologna on their homeward journey. d'Anthou-ard and Darnay seemed to have picked up fever in Ravenna.

Auguste had received glowing accounts of Ludwig's wedding. The festivities had been such a success that an October Feast was going to become an annual fixture in Munich.

On November 20, by command of the Emperor, the Viceroy announced to the Senate the pregnancy of the Empress Marie Louise. The family had heard of this weeks before from the delighted Emperor. On December 9 Auguste bore her third child. It was at last "the little prince"—Augustus Charles Eugène Napoléon. If he could have timed his arrival two years earlier the history of Europe might have been different. Baron Bataille was sent off to Munich. King Max wrote that he was so happy he could not sleep, picturing his daughter with her son. Josephine, always the best at turning a phrase, said she knew how Auguste had longed for a son, though Eugène was perfectly happy with his daughters. The thought of their joy had made the Château of Navarre a happy house. She was spending the winter there. She had not made up her mind until November, which was very late to be hanging about a watering place. But it appeared that she had been hearing stories that she was being sent to Milan as the thin end of the wedge. She was never to return to France.

The Emperor had always said that she might, if she preferred, winter at Navarre; but he was not pleased when she stopped for twenty-four hours, which expanded to three weeks, at Malmaison and at the Elysée palace on her way through Paris. It was her last stay there. Next year he took it away and gave her instead the palace of Laeken ten miles outside Brussels. So she was left with no Paris house. It was whispered that once, on a drive, the

Empress Marie Louise had enquired what was this estate within a long brick wall. When she was told Malmaison, her colour changed, and she turned away from looking at it.

Her child was expected in mid March 1811, almost a year from her wedding day. A letter from Duroc on behalf of his imperial master required the attendance of the Viceroy and Vicereine to witness the event. Auguste had a good excuse. About a fortnight after the arrival of her son she had suddenly begun to suffer agonies from her right arm. She seemed almost paralysed. The Italian doctors said her affliction was rheumatic. They recommended the mud bath treatment of Abano near Padua, famous since Roman days.

v

The Viceroy was summoned to the Tuileries, together with all the other necessary witnesses, at ten o'clock on the night of March 19, and there they sat in full court dress the long night through, drowsing in chairs, interrupted often by appearances of the Emperor, to bring them the latest news.

Servitors offered trays of refreshments at which dishevelled ladies, with shiny noses, hair coming out of curl, and tiaras askew, cast eyes of increasing interest. Most gentlemen showed no delicacy in sustaining nature, but the Bonaparte ladies needed nothing except to have windows opened or shut again, and constant attention. With every sound from the birthchamber they shuddered and shook in sympathetic agony. They loved their sister in law so much. They were so sensitive. At four a.m. the company received a message that the pains had subsided; the patient was asleep. Several ladies, including the Queen of Holland, accepted offers of beds belonging to the staff. Queen Hortense was woken at eight a.m. by terrible news. The infant was in an abnormal position and the Empress was screaming horribly. Dubois, the *accoucheur*, had quite lost his head, and begged the Emperor for another opinion. He feared he could not save mother and son—for he knew by now that the child was the desired boy. The Emperor, who had shouted angrily on seeing the man's white face, "Well? If she is dead we will have a funeral!" at once took command of himself and the shattered expert. He told him to get on with his work as if he was attending the humblest woman in a slum. "Save the mother. It is her right!"

By a chance which Dubois declared to be one in a thousand, the Empress was having the same experience as the Vicereine in her first confinement. It was a case of breech presentation. But the Habsburg princess lacked the stamina of the Wittelsbach. When she caught sight of the delivery forceps she sobbed that she was being sacrificed for a dynasty. Dubois disengaged the head and the child was laid upon the floor, apparently lifeless. Seven minutes passed before the Emperor, who had left the room unable to bear the sight of his wife's ordeal, heard the first cry of his son —a perfect nine pound child.[12]

A salute of twenty-one guns was to have been fired to announce the birth of a girl, a hundred and one for a boy. When the twenty second salvo was heard Paris rejoiced with their Emperor. Successful in everything, he now had an heir. The bells of Notre Dame sounded the first carillon which was gradually taken up by every church in the country.

His letter for Josephine gave an idea of his triumph and emotion. "My son is big and healthy. I hope that he will do well. He has my chest, my mouth, and my eyes. I hope he will fulfil his destiny. I am always quite satisfied with Eugène. He has never caused me the slightest sorrow."

Now that the child was here there was no reason why the Viceroy should not leave Paris and visit Navarre. His mother's ladies found that it was quite wonderful how the gloomy place seemed to spring into life the moment his carriage was seen coming up the long drive. His naughty imitations of the Bonaparte ladies were enough to make a cat laugh. He organized concerts in which he took part, ladies' races in the park, and fishing competitions. Nobody could have guessed that although he loyally rejoiced with the Emperor his letters home were sad.

He had noticed from the first that on this visit to Paris no effort was being spared to make him happy. His own palace in the Rue de Lille was waiting for him. He had splendid days shooting at Marly and hunting at Fontainebleau and St. Cloud. The Empress on his arrival, had at once asked for news of the Vicereine's poor arm. But the best thing about this time was that he had long confidential hours alone with the Emperor and his military and political advisers, especially with Clarke, sharp-featured companion of his first Italian days, now Duc de Feltre and Minister for War. The Emperor got very impatient with his minister, and with Caulaincourt, Duc de Vicence, just recalled from Russia.

The Russian court had given the cold shoulder to an ambassador carefully chosen for his looks, birth and address. A story had got about that he had been responsible for the murder of the Duc d'Enghien. This was the more unfair because Savary, on whose name a smear had always rested, had been found charming in Russia.

Caulaincourt was entirely discouraging about opening a campaign in that far country. "Sire, I am ready to lay down my life for you on the battlefield, but my conscience, my honour are mine alone. I should be a wretch if in order to please Your Majesty I should betray my country." The Emperor asked angrily what the man was trying to say. "I say that this war will be disastrous for France. You are ruining yourself sire, and you will bring down France with you. All Europe will rise against you."

The Emperor could not be brought to admit that the Czar had good reasons for refusing to fulfil the obligations into which he had entered at Tilsit. The Continental System was infuriating many of his largest landowners, who relied upon sales of their timber to England. Russia had few factories. In December he had defiantly imposed high tariffs on French goods and opened his ports to neutral shipping.

The Emperor was hesitating between another appearance in Spain and a decisive swift Russian campaign first. He had swept a porcelain bust of Alexander off his wife's desk, and could hardly find words disparaging enough for the man who had failed to provide him with a Russian bride. It was well known that the Czar had hardly been to blame. The Dowager Empress had said that she would sooner throw her daughter in the Neva than give her to Napoleon Bonaparte. The Grand Duchess Catherine had been married off in haste to a vastly inferior and unattractive mate, merely heir to the Duchy of Oldenburg; there had been a half-hearted suggestion of the Grand Duchess Anna, not yet nubile.

It was wonderful to be once more the son of the house, hearing what happened inside the charmed circle of high politics, sitting early and late in the Tuileries again, with all the traffic of Paris in the gay season trotting by outside under the budding chestnuts and blue skies. Towards the end of April he was able to write home that the political horizon seemed clearer. General Suchet had taken Tortosa and was marching on Tarragona—to get his Marshal's baton, said the Emperor. Berthier reported that Lord

Wellington's army had twenty thousand sick and barely as many able-bodied men with the colours. It did not seem likely that England could attempt any offensive in Spain at present.

"Be quite calm, and above all put confidence in the real concern that the Emperor has for our well-being. Love me always. Believe that there could be no happiness for me without you, that we are both born for happiness and will put further trust in our good star, which has never forsaken us."

He departed for a tour with the Emperor and Empress to Cherbourg. There the tremendous works at the harbour situated opposite England were nearing completion. With his step father, the Viceroy visited the fortifications, the dockyards, the roads and the fleet. Marie Louise lunched with them on the dyke from which they had the annoying view of English ships cruising in the distance. She was taken on board a ship of the line. She was spared a descent into the vast basin cut out of the granite which was almost ready to accommodate fifty men-of-war. The Imperial pair returned by Alençon and Chartres to St. Cloud, where Eugène left them for Malmaison.

The birth of the King of Rome had slightly eased the position of Josephine. The Emperor had told both her son and her daughter that the ideal thing now would be for her to reside in Italy. He was willing to appoint her Governor of Rome. He thought that if she would only settle at the Palace of Laeken ten miles outside Brussels, she might create a brilliant court there. However, if she would not do any of these things, she might divide her year between Navarre and Malmaison. Eugène promised to press an invitation to Milan for the winter.

She was pathetic about her yearning, as each spring came round, to be at Malmaison to see her Dutch double tulips and double hyacinths. "Bonaparte always summoned me to him just at this moment." This year she had given a fine ball at Navarre in honour of the birth of the Imperial child and then hurried to her favourite home. The weather that spring was so perfect that her son mentioned it in his letters to Milan.

His mother had almost as many callers as in the old days. Perhaps some came from curiosity; but she gave them good fare. The first artists of Paris came out to perform at her concerts. Eugène said that he worked for three hours only, most mornings, and then after his ride and his walk or drive with his mother, and helping to entertain her guests with music and billiards, the day was gone. But although his letters painted a picture of perfect peace he had much which he dared scarcely write, even when he had seen his letter go into the breast pocket of aide de camp Gifflinga, bound for his native Milan. He felt much for Auguste whose long-awaited son had now been completely cut out. He had to tell her to hold a service of thanksgiving in the Duomo, and give a grand reception, "making the circle" and receiving congratulations from everyone. She had done all that, but she said that she could not help wondering now what was to become of their three children. If the Emperor had a second son he would inherit Italy. Eugène had not told her, for he did not himself know, that after the difficult delivery of the King of Rome, Dubois had told the Emperor something which had left him pale and staring. The Empress Marie Louise should not be asked to attempt any further pregnancies . . .

In Paris, the life of Prince Eugène was quite the reverse of that at Malmaison. He lived in a whirl the whole day. It was almost a relief to have to attend a meeting of the Senate. Towards the end of his stay he had to tell his wife, in strictest confidence, that there was a disturbing possibility that he might be appointed Governor or Regent (the exact title was immaterial). She and all the children would have to come to Paris of course. Nothing had been said to him directly but several friends had told him that the Emperor employed him as the only member of his family he could really trust, and that he had drawn up a decree entrusting the government of France to him for the period of every future absence.

The situation of Hortense was so awful that he could not enter upon it until he saw his wife face to face again. He wrote that she had a very bad cold in the head, nothing dangerous. She was going to Aix again this year and then coming to them in Milan. He had arrived in Paris unusually at ease in his mind about her. Her husband had taken a house for five years in Gratz, in Styria. She had their very fine Paris palace in the Rue de Cerutti and the château of St. Leu with two beautiful parks, easily available from the capital and Malmaison. She had both her sons under her roof and the Emperor on her side at last. Her *salon* was said to be the most fashionable in Paris. She had introduced a novelty at her evening parties—a round table at which ladies sat and sewed or drew, while gentlemen promenaded around it making conversation which was brilliant.

But what she had to tell her brother now was her most dreadful news yet in all their lives. Fouché, Chief of Police, had been dismissed, and she was in mortal terror of his successor. Savary, she whispered in wild alarm, was much more adept in ferreting out indiscretions. She had been indiscreet . . . She had been in love with Charles de Flahaut for ten years, and last autumn when he had been on sick leave at Aix he had become her lover. He was now on garrison duty in Paris. The Emperor insisted that she should represent the Queen of Naples at the christening at Notre Dame on June 9, and she was having Flahaut's child in the middle of September.

"Yesterday evening," wrote Eugène to Auguste, "I saw my poor Hortense. She is very low and will need a whole year of peace in which to recover her health and spirits." He added that in about ten days she would be starting for Savoy to take the waters at Aix again.

As usual he had quietly shouldered the responsibility thrust upon him. He had asked a very few necessary questions. He had pondered, and then spoken words of comfort. He would provide a suitable haven for her in Italy, perhaps on Lake Maggiore. He would bring Auguste and the children to visit her and this could be announced and would check any possible curiosity. He said he would call in upon her on his own road home now, and make arrangements. He kept his word.

VI

The mud baths of Abano had once more effected a cure. Auguste had never so much enjoyed her name-day fête. Villa Augusta in the park at Monza had been illuminated, the band of the Royal Guard had performed, and after the most beautiful fireworks, a party of peasants, male and female, in native costume had performed country dances in the *salon*. A month later she reported again to her brother. "Tomorrow very early I leave Monza with my husband to meet Queen Hortense on Lake Maggiore. She wishes to stay on there because she is so unwell, but we hope to persuade her to come here . . . You can imagine how delighted Eugène will be to see her."[13]

At last, in October, they took up residence in the palace given to them as a wedding-gift—the Villa Imperiale at Strà. It was very beautiful in its autumn dress but Auguste gave it only moderate praise. "The place is too big for a private residence but not large enough for a court. Also, my apartments are fine and well appointed but I have to go through every antechamber to reach my husband, which is most inconvenient. The garden is fairly large, but damp, as it is so close to the Brenta." She stayed there alone in growing melancholy while Eugène performed inspections at Venice, at Udine and Brescia. He visited his huge camp at Montechiaro. The fact was that ever since he had come home a dark cloud had shadowed their happiness. It was the Russian campaign. He could not deny that he thought the Emperor was determined upon it. This very choice of Strà for a holiday had been dictated by him. The place was so conveniently situated for the Viceroy to look to his troops and defences in every key point without attracting undue attention. And soon it would be impossible to pretend that the sound of men on the move was not audible throughout the Empire. 1812 was going to see the greatest victories yet.

In February, Eugène was instructed not to communicate with his wife's father about the passage of eighty thousand troops from his Lombardy camps, in nine columns, through Bavaria. Berthier had written personally and secretly to King Max, desiring him to have the Brenner cleared of snow so that their march might not be interrupted. Their destination was Northern Silesia.

During Eugène's absence, as before, Melzi, Duke of Lodi, would act as his deputy. There were still rumours of a kingdom being provided for the dispossessed son of Josephine. General Vaudoncourt had believed in Paris, in May, that he was to be offered the crown of Greece, with Salonica as capital. The prince had to write half-humorously to tell his old friend Lavalette that it was not true he was going to take his meagre form to ascend the throne of Poland. The suggestion was not so improbable as it sounded. Polish political leaders who longed for the re-establishment of a kingdom had intimated to the Emperor that the choice of His Imperial Highness the Viceroy would be most acceptable. But he still clung to the hopes of getting Italy some day. He told Lavalette, for his ear alone, that he was getting something much better. For the approaching campaign he had been given the fourth Corps—"a superb command". On April 17 the Emperor said to Méneval, "Send for Prince Eugène."[14]

Her Imperial Highness the Princess Auguste-Amélie of Bavaria,
Vicereine of Italy, aged twenty two, by François, Baron Gérard. A version of this portrait, painted during the Vicereine's sole visit to Paris in 1810, hung in her husband's bedchamber in the Palais Leuchtenberg, Munich.
Cliché des Musées Nationaux

CHAPTER FOURTEEN

Russia

1812

I

HE ARRIVED in Paris on the afternoon of April 22 and went at once to see his sister who gave him a carriage to take him on to St. Cloud. Here the Emperor received him affectionately and asked him to dine, which meant that he must return there after calling upon his mother at Malmaison. He had to admit that he was dog-weary by the time he sought his bed in the Rue de Lille. But everyone seemed to be in good health and spirits, and both the Empresses professed themselves enchanted with the miniatures of his children with which his wife had supplied him. He was amazed to find that there was far less talk of war in Paris than there had been at Milan.

He told Hortense that he had not disguised from the Emperor the state of public opinion, and the exasperation of the countries through which he had passed. The Emperor had not replied: he allowed such discussions only in Council. Fixing the stepson with a steady eye he had explained to him without delay the reason why he had been ordered to Paris. It was so that he could act as Regent. Eugène, horror-struck, had pleaded to be allowed to join his army corps. Junot had been given the temporary command and Eugène had received a letter from Germany which had annoyed him enormously. It seemed that Junot had met the Army of Italy near Dresden and immediately put them through man-oeuvres in heavy rain. "My brother who loved his troops as if they were his children, said to me, 'Did Junot imagine he was handling a lot of raw recruits? He shall see them in action. But why must he tire them out for nothing?'" The Emperor had not pressed his proposal. There had always been the disadvantage that the appointment of Eugène would be so popular that the

Bonaparte family, especially the Murats, would be transported with fury.[1]

Eugène heard that a Russian officer on his way from St. Petersburg was reported to have reached Metz. Everything might yet arrange itself. Marie Louise made herself particularly agreeable, asking him to play whist at her table and making detailed enquiries about his family routine. He thought it would be well if Auguste wrote to thank her.

On Sunday, April 26 at six in the evening Eugène sat down to a good long letter.[2]

"I am writing from St. Cloud my dear and tender Auguste. I have been here all day, attending various councils at which I had to be present. There was a Mass before, and directly after, a family dinner.

"The day before yesterday I saw the King of Rome. He is strong and bonny and has already twelve teeth. I thought him a little pale, but perhaps that can be put down to the teething. He is not as advanced, either in walking or talking, as our son was at thirteen months. Nevertheless, it is a very fine child." Eugène had been in the saddle all day and at the gallop for twenty leagues. He had perhaps, been a little tired by the time he had been taken to see the fair, fat, white little boy stumbling about his nursery. The young Napoleon's apartments were padded up to the height of a child of eight years, so that if he fell down he could not possibly hurt himself.

Auguste was having another child in July—begotten at Strà. It had been hard to leave her at such a time, and he could not really, after what he had listened to in council, hold out much hope that he would be home at all soon. They had spent hours talking about what was being said in the English Parliament. But the dear *Maman* was going to make the effort. She was absolutely leaving Malmaison on May 10. He had made all arrangements for her journey—post-horses, carriages, couriers. He sent a list of the Italian attendants, male and female, whom he thought might be the best choice for appointment to her household during her stay. She wanted to come *incognita* and to the Villa in Milan, not to the big palace on the square. So she could have the Viceroy's vacant rooms which would adjoin the birth-chamber. For a stay at Monza she could have either the *suite* they had always planned for her, or again the Viceroy's—not so gay.

The dear *Maman* was having six new dresses made for Auguste.

They would be on the road in four days. He enclosed patterns of the materials. The latest in Paris was that Jerome Bonaparte was to be King of Poland. He only mentioned it so that he could repeat how charmed he was that it was not he, and he prayed Heaven, which had assigned him so much more desirable a post, that he and his wife might be allowed to stay in Italy for the rest of their days. How happy it made him that, perhaps partly thanks to his labours, its finances, its agriculture, its arts, had attained a prosperity which put it in the first rank of European countries.

His expectation was that the Emperor would be leaving Paris in the middle of May. He did not know whether he would precede or accompany him. He described himself as waiting like a bird on a bough. Marie Louise continued her attentions. She had taken him in her carriage for a day at Versailles and Trianon. Suddenly, on May 1 he had to send one of his emotional letters. He was off tomorrow morning. He had a wonderful command —nearly eighty thousand men—fifty-five thousand Army of Italy, two French divisions, the Bavarians under Wrede, and the cavalry reserve. He was delighted that he had been given the Bavarians. He begged his wife not to be too sad yet. A peace might yet be arranged. Officers were still passing between the French and Russian capitals. The Emperors might have another meeting. "My lucky star won't leave me and all is for the best." He took the opportunity of sending a private note by the Marchese Litta; but he could only say that he had been as astonished as his wife would be to hear he was to be gone so soon; and really it was much for the best. It would break his heart if she thought that he had been keeping anything from her . . .

He expected to be eight days in a carriage now with no opportunity of writing, and would in future send letters by Munich. The place he was going to was called Glogau. It was "in the middle of the sandy wastes of Poland". He was a little better than his word as he was able to send her a line from Mainz at six o'clock in the morning, to say that his carriage had broken down in the streets of Paris, and that the best proof of love she could give him would be to look after her own health. He managed to write again, from Pillnitz, where he had a delightful night with the Saxon royal family in their summer residence outside Dresden. The good queen was laughably like her brother, Auguste's dear father. Their style of living was equally patriarchal.[3]

II

The Emperor's intention had been that his Grande Armée amounting to six hundred thousand men should assemble on the banks of the Vistula without Russia at all appreciating the enormous size of the armament mustered to invade her territory. He wished to spare the Grand Duchy of Warsaw from being over-run by Russia, as Bavaria had been in the last two wars by Austria. He was aware that Russia too could put large numbers into the field, but she was harassed by anxiety about her northern and southern flanks—Sweden and Turkey. She had been at war with the Turks for six years and a valuable corps under one of her leading generals, Tschitschagov, was tied down at Kiev. It was true that France was hampered by commitments in Spain, but the vassal states and allies had all agreed to send auxiliary corps to join the Grand Armée. The list of the commanders summoned from the shores of Calabria and the banks of the Guadalquivir was impressive.

Berthier, Prince of Wagram and Neufchâtel
Bessières, Duke of Istria
Davout, Duke of Auerstadt, Prince of Eckmühl
Macdonald, Duke of Taranto
Mortier, Duke of Treviso
Ney, Duke of Elchingen
Oudinot, Duke of Reggio
Victor, Duke of Belluno.

The Viceroy of Italy, commander of the Fourth Corps, was the only one not a marshal.

He had three weeks at a place called Plock, waiting for orders. It was not Glogau, where he had been instructed to report and where he had found and inspected his Bavarians. It was a little town, simple and obscure, seventy-three miles north-west of Warsaw, on the right bank of the Vistula. He had been right in saying he would be in a sandy desert. When he had stepped out of his carriage on the day of his arrival he had been as white as an angel. Sometimes, as the long daylight hours dragged past, he was struck by a sort of horror, as if he was waiting for something terrible to happen.

"My God! what a long way I am from you! Do you know, it is not yet a month since I left you, and yet to me it has been a century?" He kept himself and his troops on the go, as far as he could, but he soon had to report that his house was a hospital. His young gentlemen were dreadfully sickly or prone to accident. One of the Tascher boys, Louis, actually had gout. Soulange and Desève had both had falls, and Desève had broken a toe; Bataille had a high temperature, so had Soulange and Méjean. Only Gifflinga and d'Anthouard (just returned from Spain) seemed imperturbable. Two hundred guns had been allotted to the Fourth Corps. The Viceroy's baggage and horses arrived and he was thankful to be able to ride long distances to make himself known to regiments which he could only describe as "superb". "As for me I have a good appetite, good courage, a good heart and am yours for life. Adieu."

The prefect of the small town asked all the general officers of the Fourth Corps to spend a musical evening and it turned out that the ladies of Plock were "very strong performers on the piano and harp. But the mistress of the house took it into her head to give us a little song which was not quite so successful."

Once he was settled in his Polish home letters began to catch him up. As usual he got his best haul when he presented himself at the Emperor's headquarters at Thorn, which he did on June 4. This place was about sixty miles north-west of Plock, also on the Vistula. The Emperor, who had arrived from Dresden the day before, was in good health and as usual full of enquiries in detail about his troops. Nature had played the Grande Armée a scurvy trick. Spring 1812 was a fortnight late in Upper Silesia. There was still such frost that the courtyard outside the prince's house was covered with ice when he rode out at four a.m. on May 27. There were no green vegetables for the troops and no hay or oats for their horses. He was told to take charge of a supply of requisit-tioned corn which he must have ground into flour. He had also been allotted, from Thorn, three hundred bullocks and thirty thousand bushels of oats. But already much mischief had been done. Horses had been fed with green corn not nearly ready to be cut, and men had eaten largely of a sour black bread. There was already dysentery in the Grande Armée as it prepared to march into Russia.

Amongst the letters received from Milan had been one in a youthful hand. The Princess Josephine was now five and did credit to her Italian governess, "Mia" (to whom the Viceroy sent a message that he was hoping soon to see her uncle, a colonel in the 1st Regiment.) His normal handwriting was small, slanting and neat but, he gravely explained, he wrote a little larger than usual when replying to his daughter.

There was a friend of his earliest days now attached to the Emperor's staff, Philippe de Ségur who came of a highly distinguished royalist family and had also lost a father to the guillotine. He had originally wished to become an author. The Revolution had left him no choice but the army, in which he had prospered. He was a deceptively gentle-looking young man with liquid dark eyes. He had performed dashing feats in Spain and had been promoted general. He was going to write the history of the Russian campaign of 1812.

The Grande Armée began to move on the day after the Viceroy's call at Thorn. He was at Soldau, last town of old East Prussia, at Neidenburg, at Villenberg, at Ortelsburg . . . Some of the villages were so wretched that he had to order his tent to be pitched. At Rastenburg he lay awake remembering that he had eighty thousand men to feed and sometimes was not able to procure ten sacks of corn. He hardly dared think of what autumn and winter must be in such country. He wrote that he dearly hoped to pass this winter with his family. He was receiving the most incredible advances from highly-placed Poles who wished he could be their king—Prince Poniatowsky, General Rosniwky . . . But it did not at all suit the Emperor at present to affront his Austrian allies by re-establishing a kingdom in Poland. Eugène thought the problem would arrange itself.

His little official war artist had arrived and began to make very pretty sketches of thatched cottages, and presently noble ones of the Viceroy characteristically mounted on a dapple-grey steed. "This little villa is an ideal subject for a sketch, as it is situated on a narrow isthmus of land between two lakes. But don't run away with the idea that it is as attractive as Lake Como or even Lecco. In my opinion the most agreeable of all lakes is the tiny one at Monza!"[4]

He wrote to his wife "from my tent on the banks of the Niemen" on the penultimate day of June. He was watching his troops crossing the bridges which he had been told to throw over the river. "So here we are in Russia at last!" Actually they were still in Lithuania which the Emperor was going to liberate. This country had been absorbed in Poland for four hundred years and then collected by Russia in 1795. The Emperor's secretary, Baron

Fain, was a little disappointed to find that Russia was so dull; nothing but trees and sand still. However, some of the trees were birches, planted alongside good wide roads in an orderly manner. They had heard that Prince Bagration was marching on Vilna, once the capital of Lithuania. But in spite of sending out spies of several varieties, they had little news of the enemy. It was quite extraordinary, almost uncanny, how invisible they were in this silent featureless country, where it was daylight so that you could read the newspaper at ten p.m. and dawn came at two a.m.

Place names began to become strange, too—Berthier wrote to the Viceroy about movements on Bol-Solchniki, Oschmiana. He himself dated a letter to his wife from Novoi-Trocky to tell her that the Emperor had entered Vilna with Polish lancers on either side. He had ridden over to headquarters and asked His Majesty if he would stand godparent to the expected infant. "Yes, gladly." The Emperor approved of Eugène Napoléon for a boy, and Auguste Amélie if it was a girl. Amélie was after the Queen of Saxony and that was what the little puss would be called. He had collected four letters from Milan. Neither the Empress Josephine nor the baby had arrived there yet when his wife wrote. His dear mother was only a month late in starting. He thought he must be the father of four by now, and sent his tenderest regards to his wife, so far from him, and ten big kisses to the little stranger. "I love you and shall go on loving you all the days of my life."

It had been very much expected in the Grande Armée that a battle would take place on the anniversary of Wagram but it was impossible to engage a foe who continued to retreat. The Fourth Corps was soon off again hot-foot after Prince Bagration. The only consolation was that the Emperor in the last eight days had become master of all the country between the Dnieper and Dwina. Prince Murat had engaged light infantry outposts with his usual dash. He thought the enemy was retiring on St. Petersburg. Eugène's spies had contradictory tales. A man came in from over the Dwina and said that he had not seen a soul in uniform; the peasants had told him there had been parties of Cossacks near Ouchatsch. A Jew pedlar from Polotsk said that when General Barclay de Tolly had quitted that city he had left only a small weak garrison. This Russian commander was of Scottish origin, born at Riga in Livonia. His reputation was high. He had fought against the Turks, the Swedes and the Poles, and against the

Emperor Napoleon at Eylau where his conduct had won him promotion to Lieutenant-General.

It was with his vanguard that Murat and the Viceroy fought stiff minor actions in the last days of July, near Vitebsk. "The King of Naples and I form the advance guard. He commands the cavalry and I the infantry. We co-operate to serve the Emperor to the best of our ability and have caused considerable Russian casualties . . ." (Jerome Bonaparte had quarrelled so violently with Davout that he had returned to Westphalia). "I have written this letter in two bits as the Emperor arrived at my bivouac to establish his camp."

On the night that he wrote that, a conference was held and he joined with Murat and Berthier in begging the Emperor to halt the campaign in view of their enormous wastage and shortage of supplies. In ten days the army had lost upwards of one-third of its strength. Ten thousand horses had perished since they crossed the Niemen. The weather was what they could only describe as bizarre, a pewter sky and torrid heat by day, and nights during which they caught chills. Eugène wanted to know what he was to do with three hundred sick, and was told to find and put them in a convent. Men were dying of sunstroke, and straggling had become serious. A halt was called from July 29 to August 9. The Viceroy had such good maps that the Emperor borrowed some. He had also provided his wife with a set. He was afraid now that when she looked at them, and saw how far away he was, she must tremble. But the Emperor was determined to date letters from Smolensk, as he did, ten days later from a heap of smoking ruins; and at Smolensk he pointed out that Moscow was now only two hundred miles away.

It was encamped outside dreadful shattered Smolensk on August 17, that Eugène learned from the Emperor that the Vicereine had been safely delivered on July 3 of a daughter. When letters began to catch him up, that of his mother was typical in its charm and tact. She had only just arrived in time. On her first day she had dined with Auguste and they had gone for a drive. After that the pains had come on fast, and within five hours the little girl had made her appearance. Melzi, Duke of Lodi, summoned as witness, did not get there until all was safely over. Doctors Locatelli and Scarpa had performed their functions and Auguste had been very brave, but had cried for Eugène. She had no fever and was sleeping well.

"Your new daughter is so lovely! when you see her, you can no longer regret that she is not another boy."[5]

The Baronin von Wurmb wrote to the Viceroy every day for nine days until his wife could take up her story. "Nothing that is good, from her," he wrote in thanks, "can surprise me."[6]

III

On the night of September 5 the Emperor camped in a wood behind the Army of Italy at the right of the main road to Moscow, with the Old Guard drawn up in a square round his tents. The Russian army had come to a stop at last on the plateau of Borodino where the Kalatscha tributary joined the Moskva river. The French columns had straggled so badly that it was taking four days to concentrate them for the first great battle of the campaign. The Emperor knew now why he had received no reply to his overtures. Russia had made peace with the Turks, and Bernadotte, Crown Prince of Sweden, had receded from the Continental System which was ruinous for his new country. (The Czar had promised him Norway, at the expense of Denmark.) Freed to devote his forces entirely to demolishing the French invader, the Czar had appointed a new Commander in Chief. Barclay de Tolly had always been unpopular as a foreigner. Both he and Bagration had been by Grande Armée standards rather old—fifty-one and forty-seven . . . It was startling then, to learn that Kutozov was sixty-seven. A deserter who said he was of French origin, though in Russian uniform, spoke of the new Generalissimo in fear and trembling. Moscow had been illuminated in honour of his appointment and the Russian troops had stuck green boughs in their shakos. He was an old fellow with white curls, black brows, a big moustache and terrible eyes. He wore very shabby clothes, from choice. When he was angry he growled like a lion. He never went into action without saying his prayers and he crossed himself frequently during the day.

Some Cossack prisoners had been captured in a skirmish. The Emperor had them in for questioning. Both de Ségur and Constant wrote down their impressions of these extraordinary savages who seemed as if they had been made glued to a horse.[7] Their legs were perfectly bandy and once their feet were out of stirrups they seemed like stranded fish; nevertheless they gave themselves great airs. By spirited gestures, convulsive movements and war-like posturing they brought the Emperor to understand that there would soon be a great battle. He ordered brandy and they gulped it down as if it was water and held out their glasses for more. There was a local brandy of which some had been found at Smolensk. It was made of grain containing narcotic plants. It had absolutely the appearance of water, and young soldiers weakened by hunger and fatigue had a mistaken idea that it would restore their energy. After a single draught they fell completely inert. Wretches who drank deeply of vodka were overcome by dizziness and dropped in the ditches or on the road. They died dully without a whimper.

The horses of the Cossacks were nothing to look at, stumpy little animals with long tails. The men were all much taken by Murat who on one occasion had pursued them unaccompanied with drawn sword, and halting only a few paces from their front line, had ordered them to withdraw with such an imperious gesture that they had instinctively obeyed. As they were now going to fight with the Grande Armée they asked if they might have this king as their Hetman. The Cossack leader, Platov, went into action accompanied by his sorcerer, and had caused this unfortunate character to be flogged in the presence of his horde of four thousand when a bullet had struck an officer of his staff.

The Emperor was on tenterhooks lest the Russians should escape him again, though there was every evidence that they intended to defend Moscow, now only seventy miles to the southwest. Scouts reported that they were at work over the whole plain, throwing up breastworks and digging in. The Emperor warned the detachments sent out to gather supplies: "If you haven't returned by tomorrow you'll be depriving yourselves of the honour of fighting."

There had been some fighting already that day, for the foremost redoubt straddling the Moscow road, the Shevardino, had been captured, by the 61st regiment supported by the batteries of the Guard. General Caulaincourt, brother of the Minister, returned from the captured redoubt to say, "No prisoners." The Russians were accustomed to fighting the Turks: they had also been spurred into a fanatic state by their priests and officers. During the hours of darkness one of Davout's regiments, trying to find their place in the first line, blundered into a company of Russian cuirassiers. On the Russian side, camp fires blazed in a regular semicircle, but those of the Grande Armée burned with a faint and irregular light. Troops arriving late and in haste on unknown ground were having difficulty to find wood. A cold light rain was falling. The Emperor rode up between the battle lines and inspected the Russian front. His voice could be heard giving orders. "Eugène will be the pivot . . . The right will bring on the action . . . They will advance under cover of the copse, and from the redoubt will march on the Russian flank."

He retired to his headquarters to dictate to his secretaries. During the course of that steamy and boding day an extraordinary activity was noticed in the enemy lines. Kutozov was making an appearance surrounded by the dignitaries of the Greek Orthodox church in glittering vestments, accompanied by chanting choirs bearing religious symbols, jewelled icons and crosses. The Generalissimo made an oration telling his troops that they were consecrated to the defence of their faith and the sacred soil of Russia.

It chanced that on that same day the Emperor received from Paris a portrait of the King of Rome. He caused it to be set up outside his tent and called his officers, and even the rank and file of the Old Guard to behold his symbol of hope at this critical moment. He had received something else not so welcome, news from an aide de camp of Marshal Marmont fresh from the battlefields of Spain. Lord Wellington had obtained a brilliant victory at the battle of Salamanca on July 22 and was advancing on Madrid.

Night fell again and with it all the Emperor's fears that the Russians were about to escape him now that he was ready for them. In his anxiety to avoid another withdrawal he had quashed Davout's advice to turn their left wing. He slept hardly at all and kept on calling out to ask the hour, the reason for a noise, and if the enemy was still there. At dawn de Ségur found him sitting with his head in his hands. He asked General Jean Rapp if he expected a victory. "Without any doubt," replied Rapp, "but a bloody one." At five a.m. the Emperor left his tent shouting, "At last we have them! Forward march. We go to open the gates of Moscow." The sun was getting up in a cloudless sky and he pointed and cried, "Look! the sun of Austerlitz!" but his staff noticed silently that it was against them, making easy targets of their men. By seven, one of the Viceroy's regiments had taken the village and bridge of Borodino. Carried away by their success the 106th regiment pursued Barclay's troops over it and attacked the

Gorki heights. They were mowed down and brought back within the lines with heavy loss, by the 92nd regiment. When three generals had fallen wounded, moving against the central Russian fortifications under Kutozov, Rapp told the Emperor that the Guard would be necessary to end the encounter in that quarter; but the Emperor was sullen. He answered that he was not going to have the Guard knocked to bits, "I can win the battle without them."

Ségur knew what very few people had detected, that the Emperor was unwell. Anyone could see that he had a roaring cold in the head and had almost lost his voice; but there were worse troubles.[8] At noon after a terrific bombardment he sent Murat in to complete his victory but he had difficulty. The West-phalians sent to help the Poles, who were in flight amongst clouds of dust and smoke, opened fire upon them believing them to be Bagration's corps. Murat broke the Russian line and entered the gorge of the great Semenovsk redoubt as the Viceroy's infantry climbed up its faces. In the fearful mêlée that followed the Russian garrison perished almost to a man. The first line of fortifications on the ridge fell into French hands, but Eugène had to conceal his men, now winded, weary and few in number, on their knees, bent double in the shelter of shattered breastworks, and they were shelled down the second line.

This was the beginning of the end. Kutozov used a battery on the ruined village of Semenovsk, on the left of his centre, to sweep the plain of Ney's three gallant divisions, now reduced to six thousand, but they in their turn were saved when some of Davout's troops, lacking their commander who had been wounded, came to their rescue. Ney took the position. The Viceroy had gone from division to division reminding his troops of their previous victories. He was rallying his forces when he heard a shouting which meant that two regiments of Russian cavalry and several thousand Cossacks had fallen upon his reserve. He galloped back to put himself at the head of the decisive counter attack. In exile, the Emperor referred to this as the most terrible of his battles.

Eugène, like Murat, had asked in vain for reinforcements. The Emperor believed that he had imposed his will on the enemy and the road to Moscow lay clear before him. The battle of Borodino was claimed by both sides as a victory and was principally remarkable for the appalling loss of life on both sides. When the death of General Caulaincourt was announced to the Emperor, his brother, the Duke of Vicenza, was in attendance. The Emperor with a sympathetic gesture asked, "You have heard? Would you like to withdraw?" but the duke, with tears running down his cheeks neither spoke or moved; he simply touched his hat as a sign of thanks and refusal. Amongst the Russian casualties had been Prince Bagration, dead of his wounds. At ten o'clock Murat galloped in to announce that Kutozov was in full retreat over the Moskva in great confusion. He asked for permission to make a surprise attack to finish them off. But the Grande Armée had lost about thirty-two thousand men, a number later believed to be exceeded by ten thousand by the Russians.[9]

IV

De Ségur said that when the first scouts of the Grande Armée came in sight of Moscow from Poklonny Hill on the Smolensk road they quickened their pace to a run. It was two o'clock on the fine afternoon of September 14 and the sun made the city twinkle and shine with all the colours of the rainbow. They broke into a disorderly scamper, and the army following them clapped their hands and echoed the delirious cry "Moscow! Moscow!" The wild shout reminded de Ségur of sailors shouting "Land! Land!" after a long and dangerous passage.

The old capital of Russia was like nothing the Grande Armée had ever seen on earth before. Méneval wrote down Moscow as decidedly Asiatic rather than European. It was a revelation, suddenly discovered spread out beneath you like an Eastern carpet at the end of a desert and naked plain. There were twelve hundred spires and onion-shaped domes, painted sky blue and strewn with stars, linked to one another by gilded chains. There were hundreds of magnificent palaces painted coral red, jade green, amaranth and amber. The Kremlin, on Borovitsky hill, enclosed within its walls a hundred acres thickly covered with buildings of surpassing beauty, many of great antiquity. It was by itself, a Museum city. One of its gates might have made the Viceroy feel at home. The entrance of The Saviour had been built by a Milanese architect in the fifteenth century. The Gothic Tower surmounting it was English in design. The Kitay Gorod, the Chinese market, east of the river, at the meeting place of six great highways, was the storehouse and exchange of Moscow, an immense bazaar covering an even larger area than the Kremlin.

It was surrounded by porticos in which were heaped up, in large shops or in endless cellars which could be entered from the street, precious goods of every kind—shawls and furs of the first quality, Indian and Chinese textiles, drugs, wines, spirits, tea, sugar, sweet-smelling rare wooden wares . . . It was an Aladdin's cave.

Moscow was guarded by walls of stone and brick and palisaded earth but nobody was defending it. The Russian army had just evacuated the town. The Emperor's eye glistened as he beheld his capture. He said "So! here at last is this famous place!" and then "It was high time."

He spent the night in a wooden house on the outskirts of the city in the Dorogomilov suburb. It was not a hostelry; it was quite a decent-looking private house, but next morning Constant was disgusted to find not only his own bed and clothing but that of his master infested with vermin. Their entry, after dark, had been rather awe-inspiring. "No night was ever gloomier. There was something weird and dreadful about the army's silent march, halted now and then as messages were delivered from the interior of the town. No inhabitants were visible except a few ragged beggars who watched our arrival with lacklustre faces. Some seemed inclined to beg and the troops threw them a few silver coins . . . There was not a single face looking out from the windows on either side. Here and there a light shone, but it was soon gone. These scanty signs of life inspired us with a sense of horror."

The bridge over the river in this quarter was gone but the stream was fordable—only about two feet deep. During the night there were several alarms of fire, a thing very usual, but to be dreaded in a newly invested city. In the morning the Emperor sent for Marshal Mortier and threatened to punish him and the Young Guard. Mortier's only reply was to point at iron-roofed houses which were seemingly untouched. But the Emperor, very angry, told him to look at the volumes of black smoke issuing from them.

He had given orders that a suitable headquarters was to be found for him, and Berthier and his aide de camp Narbonne came to say that the Slobada palace, built and decorated with every luxury by the Empress Catherine the Great, seemed suitable and ready even to thousands of wax candles in the chandeliers. Its gates, to be sure, had been closed, but they had got in through a window. The Viceroy was established in the palace of Prince Momonoff near the St. Petersburg gate, and his staff in the nearby Jerananoff palace. It was perfectly uncanny that as dawn broadened to the daylight of noon, there was still not a soul to be seen in the street. The only sounds were those made by cannon and artillery caissons rumbling in. Inside the deserted palaces, hundreds of elaborate clocks of every size and shape, chiming in as many voices to record the hours, startled the billeting officers.

Méneval thought Moscow seemed sunk into a deep sleep as if an Arab enchanter had waved his wand. Like the Viceroy, he was struck by the fact that small mean houses and even mud-walled thatched cottages were interspersed amongst colonnaded palaces, large churches and government premises with really beautiful façades. "Everything spoke of the ease and wealth of a great city enriched by trade and inhabited by many wealthy aristocratic and merchant families."

The Emperor rode into the Kremlin with an overcast brow. He had made a diversion to the Chinese city, as rumour persisted that this had been on fire since two a.m. He had left strictest orders that every effort must be made to extinguish some visible outbreaks before they took a firm hold. His spirits revived as he exclaimed, "At last! Here I am in Moscow in the ancient place of the Czars, in the Kremlin." He eagerly examined some of its many treasures. Flushed with hope, he sent off a peace offer to Alexander I. But even as he signed it, in failing light, lurid flames were leaping into the skies, driven by a stiff north wind towards the Kremlin. He had to spend the night there. When Narbonne had gone to take possession of the Slobada palace he had found it ablaze and next day it was completely gutted. Fires had broken out in at least twenty places and were raging.

Duroc, Caulaincourt, Murat and Eugène came severally to beg the Emperor to leave the Kremlin before it was too late. He was persuaded to move only when word came that it had been mined, and they had some difficulty in descending through a postern gate into narrow old streets which were tunnels of flame. At one point they were held up by a convoy of powder wagons. Some soldiers of the first corps, engaged in looting, guided the Emperor towards the smoking ruins of a quarter which had been burnt out that morning. It was there that he met Marshal Davout who, although wounded, had insisted on being carried back into the inferno to rescue or perish with his master.

Moscow burned for three days and nights. During the afternoon of September 18 heavy rain set in, followed by a dull red sunset.

There was an awful acrid smell to which the invaders had to become accustomed. Headquarters had been moved to the Petrovsky palace three miles out on the St. Petersburg road. Stories as to the origin of the fire were various. The Russians naturally attributed it to drunken and careless French troops. The Grande Armée believed that not only had it been deliberately started by the Governor of Moscow, but that Count Rostopchin himself had let loose the galley-slaves from the gaols of Moscow and provided them with tarred staves and torches. De Ségur, whose evidence had authority, since his nephew afterwards married Rostopchin's daughter, said that the Governor had given orders for the city to be destroyed sooner than see the Czar forced into a shameful peace, or what was worse, the Czar deposed and Russia goaded into a revolution by French diplomats. Eugène's brother in law, Ludwig of Bavaria, said that Rostopchin admitted to him, during the Congress of Vienna, that he had given orders for the removal of all fire-fighting equipment. He denied that he had actually started the conflagration.

Eugène wrote home that a barbarous people, devoid of all honour, had with their own hands, destroyed the most beautiful city in Europe in order to leave a hundred thousand inhabitants without nourishment. He believed thirty wretches found feeding the blaze had been arrested. Caulaincourt heard there had been a violent quarrel between Kutozov and Rostopchin.

On the morning of September 17 the Emperor, straining his eyes with first light towards Moscow, beheld a fantastic sight. A column of flame towering into the dawn was dyeing the clouds blood red. He was heard to mutter, "This is going to mean something very bad for us."

When it was all over, and before it was safe, for buildings were still crashing down in the equinoctial gales, he returned to the Kremlin, and an extraordinary month followed.[10]

V

A fiction was kept up that the victors had settled satisfactorily in Moscow. The Paris mail came in every day at two p.m. It took a fortnight and came by Erfurt. It sometimes failed to arrive punctually. This was because the couriers had been attacked by bands of Cossacks. Eugène heard from Milan that his mother's visit was being an unqualified success. She had always enjoyed the rôle of grandmother. Auguste wrote in horror of the quantity and beauty of the Paris toys brought for her nursery, the children's outfits, the *layette* for little Amélie. They must have cost a fortune. Ladies in waiting told her that the Empress had herself chosen every one and seen them packed. Josephine wrote that she had been to see the Luinis in the Brera. Auguste was looking splendid again. As for the children, their grandmother loved them all to lunacy. The elder daughter, the little Josephine, promised to be a true beauty. She had her mother's brow. The younger was lively, *spirituelle*, very pretty. But the grandchild who made mincemeat of her heart was her dear little future Duke of Navarre, the boy of the family, "an infant Hercules." Directly Augustus Charles was set down at the entrance to her apartments he ran to get on her knee. "We are the best friends in the world." He was only a little puzzled as to what she was to be called. His mother had told him that this lady was *maman* too, but the *maman* of *papa*. He was heard voluntarily introducing into his prayers "The other *maman*." The Empress was going to economize so that this dear little boy should inherit her fine estate in Normandy.[11]

Eugène wrote back that there were no toys for children in Russia, only bears. So he could not send his little darlings any Moscow presents. But he was able to get off a typically Russian gift for his wife, which he knew was what ladies liked. The Czar, after Tilsit, had presented the Emperor with two Russian sable pelisses. The Emperor had given one to Princess Pauline, and she had impulsively passed it on to a handsome officer in whom she had been at the moment interested. Unfortunately he had worn it on parade, and in an astonishingly short time he had found himself on active service. A sending of scented tea from China accompanied Auguste's pelisse. Eugène told her to get out Graingmann's big map of Russia if she had not already done so. He was playing cards (vingt-et-un) with the Emperor in the evenings. There were no billiard tables.[12] Only the state apartments in the Kremlin had been kept furnished since Petersburg had become the official capital. The Emperor had installed his little iron camp bed.

The view from his windows included the famous cross on the belfry tower of Ivan the Terrible. The tower was three hundred and twenty feet high and the wooden cross covered with silver gilt plates was thirty two feet long. It glittered splendidly against the bright blue early autumn Russian sky. The Emperor said he was going to take it to decorate the dome of the Invalides in Paris. The Russians put superstitious faith in its protective powers. It was extremely difficult to detach, but some Sappers of the Guard succeeded. As they toiled flocks of ravens circled about, cawing loudly. The Emperor said impatiently, "It appears that these birds of ill omen want to keep it." In the end it came down with a rush owing to the breaking of one of the cables of the crane, and with it came part of the tower. The sacred cross was broken in three pieces. The wood inside it must have been rotten.

As days passed, to the gloomy peace of a dead city was added that of the surrounding wastes and the even more menacing dead silence of the Czar. M. de Lesseps, French Consul-General, arrived from Petersburg, but had nothing helpful to impart. He was appointed chairman of a municipal organization to restore order and bring some measure of relief to the inhabitants rendered homeless by the fire. The outskirts of Moscow in the first days after the tragedy had presented a disgraceful appearance. Huge bonfires had been kindled in the fields, on the cold thick mud, and were being fed with rich mahogany furniture and gilded doors and windows. Around them, on damp straw and a few boards, soldiers and even some officers, muddy and smoke-blackened, were taking their ease in brocade and embroidered armchairs and couches. Around them lay cashmere shawls, the rarest of Siberian furs, cloth of gold from Persia and silver plate from which they were eating coarse black bread and half cooked horse-flesh. The fire had forced back into the open about twenty thousand inhabitants, some of them of wealthy merchant class, who had gone to ground during the arrival of the Grande Armée. A few of them still had something to sell. The troops had also found untouched cellars packed with liquor, meal, biscuits, potatoes, sugar, coffee and tea. Starving natives led them to these hiding places and proceeded to share the spoil. The Emperor was obliged to place sentries in all shops which still had stocks, but the decision was taken too late and a vast quantity of provisions were pillaged and wasted.

The Principal Medical Officer in charge of the Foundling Hospital had stayed at his post. The Emperor learned that this establishment was under the patronage of the Czar's mother, and put General Tutolmine in touch with his own Chief Surgeon, the redoubtable Larrey. Tutolmine was ordered to write to Petersburg to tell his royal employer of the Emperor's clemency and longing

Crossing the Beresina
sketch by an unknown artist. (Baron Larrey's *ambulances volantes* are prominent in the foreground.)

By permission of the Musée de l'Armée, Hotel des Invalides
Photograph: Flammarion, Paris

for peace. The Emperor ordered the churches to be cleared of refugees and troops, and reopened for service. Having done all he could for the moment to provide for the material wants of his army, he devoted his attention to their entertainment. A troupe of French comedians under the management of an elderly Parisienne gave performances. An Italian tenor, Tarquinio, who had been teaching singing in Moscow was told to get up concerts. Prince Eugène was instructed to enquire about a supply of Italian musicians from Milan.

Like everyone else who saw much of the Emperor at this date he was becoming increasingly worried. Duroc and Berthier believed he meant to winter in Moscow. Caulaincourt doubted it. There were known to be three Russian armies wandering about, nobody exactly knew where, but lines of communication were sometimes attacked. Murat twice reported coming up with Kutozov. Eugène broke off a letter on September 22 when he heard gunfire. It turned out to be Bessières having a skirmish at Podolsk with a Russian rear-guard. At the end of the month the weather grew colder. There were even a few beautiful snowflakes which did not lie. His thoughts turned to his new plantations at Monza. Had the hares eaten all the little trees? Auguste had sent him a watch-chain, too good to be worn on horseback, and that was how he was spending his time, getting round his troops in the camps outside the city.

It was a dreadfully depressing landscape. There were immense plantations of vegetables, predominantly cabbage, in the sticky, misty, fields, and famished wretches were trying to eat them raw before the army got them. Some Russians had flung themselves into the river to recover the wheat which had been cast in there by Rostopchin before his retreat. Nowadays Eugène's home was not a comfortable one—a wooden house in a suburb. He rode up to see the Emperor generally twice a day. His staff were not very healthy. He was having to send Desève down to Vilna. His little war-artist said he was sick too. He had better be sent home. It was a relief when the Emperor summoned his marshals on October 3. He had conceived a new plan. He said that having received no reply from the Czar was intolerable. "Read, Prince Eugène". They listened in absolute horror while Eugène read. "We shall have to burn the rest of Moscow. We shall march by Tver to Petersburg where we shall be joined by Macdonald; Murat and Davout will form the rear-guard."

In the dead silence which followed the Emperor exclaimed, "What! Do you mean to say you are not inspired? Has there ever been a greater military exploit? Henceforward nothing short of this conquest will be worthy of us. We shall be over- whelmed with admiration. What will the whole world say when it learns that in three months we have conquered the two greatest northern capitals?"

Hesitantly but doggedly Davout began to voice the fears of nearly all present—the lateness of the season, the shortage of food the long lines of communication across barren and deserted country. Nobody except Murat believed the Russians were in a complete state of disorganization and that the Cossacks were ready to quit and join the Grande Armée. If the Emperor meant to winter in Russia, Smolensk was the same distance from Moscow as Petersburg. He seemed disappointed and closed the consulta- tion. Constant noticed that he, who had always eaten and drunk so sparingly, now lingered over his meals and often fell asleep in his chair after dinner. Sometimes he flung himself on a sofa with a novel; but he did not read it. He devoted three evenings to scrutinizing the accounts of the Comédie Française.

Caulaincourt believed that only Prince Eugène, Berthier and himself held the view that it suited the Czar to keep the Emperor waiting. Caulaincourt's constant references to the Russian winter were laughed at by the Emperor during those golden early October days. "Autumn and winter at Moscow are finer and even warmer than at Fontainebleau." He spoke of telling the Empress Marie Louise to come and winter in Poland with him.

Caulaincourt was out of favour for having begged to be excused from heading another deputation to Petersburg or even to Kutozov's headquarters. Lauriston had gone. He did not seem to be getting on very fast. Kutuzov could not forward him until he received permission from Petersburg. Berthier had got a letter from Prince Schwarzenberg which he carried round to show to his closest friends. The Austrian general-diplomatist said that the situation, already embarrassing, might become worse; he wished to record his personal affection for the Marshal. The Emperor saw at a glance what it meant. "This gives warning of defection at the first opportunity. The Austrians and Prussians are our enemies in the rear . . . ." Berthier begged him to give the order for the move back to winter in Poland. "You want to get to

Grosbois to see the Visconti," mocked the Emperor. But he gave an order for the evacuation to France *via* Vilna of twelve thousand sick and wounded. He kept on saying that he wanted only peace, and that the Czar would reply, or at least that Kutuzov would conclude a long-term armistice. On the night of October 17 Lauriston finally returned empty-handed. Next morning during a parade, gunfire was heard and an aide de camp galloped up with news that Murat had suffered a defeat at Vinkovo in a surprise attack by Platov's Cossacks from Kutozov's army. Murat's vanguard had been cut to pieces and the French position forced.

Suddenly, the Emperor seemed to be his old self again. Orders issued in a flood from him, some bearing on large matters, others on small. By nightfall on October 18 the Grande Armée was in motion. The Emperor himself left with the Guard before noon next morning. "Forward towards Kalouga!" he cried "And woe to anyone who crosses my path!"

Thereafter, for nearly two months, until December 8, absolutely no reliable news from Russia reached a most interested party—enemy England. It was as if the Emperor Napoleon and the Grande Armée had simply vanished.[13]

V

Outside the principal south gate of Moscow a wide avenue divided into two main highways, both leading to Kalouga. The one on the left was called the Old Road, the one on the right the New. The Emperor took the Old Road which ran through the country in which Kutozov had just defeated Murat. The morning was brilliant but during it his expression grew increasingly thoughtful. He complained that both the artillery and cavalry seemed to be rather crawling than marching. The departure of the Grande Armée from Moscow was, in truth, a sorry spectacle. A hundred and fifty thousand troops marching smartly with knapsacks and arms, with five hundred cannon and two thousand artillery wagons, were accompanied by forty thousand beings who appeared to be non-combatants. The procession looked like a Tartar horde returning from a successful raid. There was an inextricable jumble of light carriages, big emblazoned coaches with six horses, tradesmen's and market carts of every description. They filled the road, four and five abreast. Nobody questioned the wagons with the trophies—Russian, Persian and Turkish flags, and the immense cross of Ivan the Terrible. Indeed there had been a row between the Polish cavalry and the French artillery because some of the cannon captured from Poland, and recognized in the Kremlin, had not been put on the road for return home.

But it was difficult to defend some of the other equipages. Strings of long-bearded Russian peasants were driving sledges piled with plunder, urged on by soldiers, themselves wheeling barrows loaded beyond capacity. A good deal of value dropped off on the road on the first day. Straining after the army, came men of all nations without uniforms or weapons, and lackeys swearing in every tongue, in charge of elegant carriages to which were harnessed, with rope, pathetically tiny ponies. These contained either food and *objets d'art*, or women and children, mostly French. They had been residents of Moscow but dared not stay there; nor could a number of Russian prostitutes who had fraternized with the Grande Armée. The Emperor had trouble getting through this undignified mob and his staff looked grave. All that was needed to get rid of this rabble was two or three forced marches or a skirmish with the Cossacks. Eugène wrote to Darnay in Milan that he had been quite unable to get away from Petrovski in the morning, according to his instructions, owing to the disorder on the road.

After midday the Emperor decided to cross to the New Road by the fields. Heavy rain succeeded the early sun, the side roads became impassable and columns were obliged to halt. The cannon were stuck in the mud. This was a calamity, for Kutozov was evidently waiting on the Old Road and if the Grande Armée could get past without his knowledge on the New, they would reach Kalouga before him. The little town of Malo Jaroslawetz was only seventy-odd miles from Moscow, a distance which should have been covered in four days; but the slow-moving Grande Armée took six. On the morning of October 24 the Emperor was startled by the sound of gunfire. The Viceroy had run into trouble. He had been sent ahead from Borowsk with three infantry divisions, the Italian Royal Guard and Grouchy's cavalry. Malo Jaroslawetz stood on heights at the foot of which the river ran through marshes. The French coming from Moscow had to cross the Luja below a wrecked bridge, then climb the slope and hold the fort. The Russians on the other side of the river had merely to march into the place. By the time that Davout with the Guard arrived in support, all was over. The Viceroy's troops had taken and re-taken Malo Jaroslawetz seven times. A valuable general, Alexis Delzons, had been killed. The cry of "*Vive l'Empereur*" had been heard at intervals from the morning of the 24th until dawn of the 25th, when a final charge by Pino's division and the Italian Royal Guards had driven the Russians back into the plain from which they had appeared. There had been four thousand French and Italian casualties. The Emperor, after surveying the field announced, "The glory of this wonderful day belongs altogether to Prince Eugène;" but the spectacle was hideous. The town which had been of wood had entirely disappeared; the streets could be traced only by the heaps of dead men lying along them, many with their skulls crushed by cannon wheels. The sound of repeated volleys startled the foggy autumn mists as the fourth corps fired last salutes in honour of their lost generals and colonels. The Viceroy wrote to Malmaison, "I can only send two words to let you know I am all right. My corps has had a brilliant day. We were attacked by eight enemy divisions from morning till night but held our ground. The Emperor is pleased, so you may guess that I am." To Auguste he described the day as "very glorious for my corps, and a little for me."

He had recommended Generals Pino and Bertrand, and aides de camp Gifflinga, Labédoyère, Louis Tascher and Méjean. Charles de Flahaut wrote home to his mother. "We had a glorious affair at Malo Jaroslawetz (I hope you will be able to read and pronounce the word). It was the Viceroy only, with his corps, who was engaged, and he did not spare himself. There was only one opinion as to what he had done, and admiration was unstinted. What a brave man!"

But the Emperor had been disappointed when his staff, headed by Berthier, advised him that he could not afford a big battle the next day. During that night he was nearly captured by a band of Cossacks. Rapp had only just time to shout "Turn back!" Daylight showed that even if he wanted to fight, Kutozov had vanished again. "Things are getting serious," he said. "I beat these Russians every time and yet we never reach an end." Nevertheless he wrote to Marie Louise "Let the Vicereine know that the Viceroy has had a fine fight in which he has distinguished himself, and that he is in good health."[14]

Three days later the Grande Armée came upon the battlefield of Borodino, and anyone who had thought that Malo Jaroslawetz had excelled in horror had to revise his opinion. The ground looked like an extinct volcano. A cloud of birds rose into the air. Every tree was shorn off at the height of a few feet. All around, the earth was littered with battered helmets, breastplates, drums, shreds of blood-stained uniforms and flags. There were thirty thousand half-devoured unburied bodies and they had been lying there for six weeks. The stench was over-powering. The Emperor hurried by and after one or two glances, nobody else looked up.

A whisper ran through the lines, "The scene of the great battle." Almost before they had passed, the flock of ravens re-settled. The abbey in which the wounded had been left was close by, and people who visited it said it was worse than the battle-field because these poor wretches were still alive and knew they were going to be left for ever now. The Emperor took an officer who had suffered the amputation of a leg in his own landau, and as many as possible in all his carriages and those of his staff. A horrible thing happened to some wounded who had been put on sutlers' carts. These rascals slowed down to let the columns pass and the moment they were unobserved, cast off their load in the ditch. Only one man, a general officer, survived to be collected by the first wagon of the next division.

De Ségur thought that the Emperor had begun to lose hope of a sensational victory over Kutozov. He had given up the idea of forcing his way south by Kalouga into what he called the rich country, the Ukraine, and was now only bent on retreat to Smolensk. His troops seemed to share his regret and marched with downcast eyes as if humiliated. There had been an embarrassing moment for the Emperor's staff on the night of the 27th when Lieutenant-General Count Wintzingerode had been brought in, a prisoner.[15] The General, a tall, balding martial man of forty-odd and of German birth, was a naturalized Russian and an aide de camp to the Czar. The Emperor had upbraided him with extraordinary passion as a traitor and a spy and told him that he deserved to be shot. Berthier and even Murat had been shocked and distressed. However, it was possible that the outburst had been calculated and intended as a warning to German troops of doubtful loyalty.

On the night of October 29 the Viceroy confessed in his brief letter home that he was longing for Smolensk. He was lodged in the same château that he had occupied on the night before the battle of Borodino. Ouspinskoe was in the oriental style. But now the weather had suddenly turned winter-cold. Luckily he had bought a bearskin in Moscow. On the advice of Caulaincourt, who claimed to be the only person who had thought of having horses shod for frozen roads, he had provided himself and his corps, as far as possible by September 28. "I am clad in fur from top to toe." The troops had gaily thrown away even their overcoats in the hot weather ... Caulaincourt ordered for the household sheepskins, fur-lined mitts, caps with ear-flaps, boot-socks, heavy boots. He knew this country. A little more snow fell the next day. According to the Russians, winter was uncommonly late this year. On November 1 the troops woke to a white world and there were horrible sounds as horses who had broken their legs were put out of their misery. Men cut them up while they were still warm and fell upon the meat. Food was getting scarce and already orders had been issued for the abandonment and destruction of provisions for which there was no transport. Mortier who had been left behind in Moscow with orders to blow up the Kremlin, had arrived and added eight thousand men to the retreating army of which only two thousand were fighting fit.

On November 3 Eugène was drawing near to Viazma, where the Emperor had made a halt to wait for him and Davout. The baggage trains and artillery of the Army of Italy had preceded him. Daylight displayed to him a plain covered with stragglers flying from a charge of Cossacks. He could not retreat for he knew he had an enemy army behind, and in the same moment he heard firing which told him that Ney, who should have advanced from Viazma to support him, was fighting for his own life. De Ségur was enthusiastic about this incident of the retreat. "This prince was not one of those generals who owed their position to favouritism, who foresaw nothing and was always being taken by surprise on account of inexperience. He realized in a moment the danger and the remedy. He halted, turned about and deployed his divisions at the right of the high road and engaged the Russian columns that were trying to close the road. Their advance troops had already outflanked his right on the highway and were holding their positions when Ney sent up a regiment."

The Russians, attacked from behind, fell back. But Eugène and Davout were not able to continue the retreat, and there was tragic disorder in the 1st corps. While the guns of the Army of Italy came back laboriously from Viazma, Russian artillery came up, and opening an oblique fire, began to mow down Davout's ranks. Once again, however, although urged to come into action, Kutozov refused to move. Still, the engagement lasted seven hours and General Miloradovich's cavalry pursued the Fourth corps to the gates of the town, and through it. The First corps, which followed much encumbered with eighty guns, was attacked in narrow winding streets. Casualties were heavy.

On November 5 orders were issued to dispose of the wagons with trophies. The waters of Lake Semlevo, on which the ice was not yet thick, closed over the cannon, mediaeval armour and works of art looted from the Kremlin and the historic cross of Ivan the Terrible. The retreat was now often harassed by bands of Cossacks who charged with lances at rest, uttering cries more like those of wild beasts than human beings.

November 6 was memorable for two events. All the blue went out of the sky and the army began to march in freezing fog. Enormous snowflakes floated down. It was unbelievable how soon snow, driven by wind, piled up so that it was impossible to trace where the road ran. Men who fell into hollows and went off down side roads were never seen again. Those who slipped and fell and were too weak to rise, were soon no more than little white mounds. The snow quickly covered them. The only features in the landscape were the tall dark conifers; graveyard trees, the troops called them.

The second event was that the mail came in. The first courier who had been able to reach the Grande Armée for ten days brought bad news. A rumour had been spread in Paris that the Emperor had perished in Moscow and an attempt had been made to upset the government. The Prime Minister, the Commissioner of Police and the Governor of Paris had all been arrested and put in prison by order of General de Malet. This fellow had escaped from a private lunatic asylum, but had been sane enough to forge a convincing decree of the Senate and the signature of Savary. By the same mail the Emperor heard that all concerned had been arrested, Malet had been court-martialled and shot and Paris was quiet again; but nobody could deny that there must have been mismanagement.

Milan letters, of course, took a fortnight longer than those from Paris. Eugène got one from Auguste dated October 1. She had just heard that he had covered himself with glory in the Battle of Borodino on September 7. The little Josephine was jumping about clapping her hands and crying "Now the war is over! Papa is coming home again."[16]

VI

During the next six weeks he began to realize that he was unlikely ever to see his family again. He was living in a continued nightmare, both mental and physical. The word had gone forth that the troops were not to mention movements in their letters home, as despatches were being captured. But in any case this campaign had reached such a stage of squalor that there was scarcely anything he could tell his princess.

He told Darnay when he had had two horses shot under him —narrow escapes. It was a mistake. Darnay was a hero-worshipper. The Viceroy's increasingly short and featureless letters still showed signs of his early training by his step-father. He never failed to date them exactly even if the hour was three a.m. As the Russian night endured sixteen hours and they generally marched about four a.m. this was quite usual. On November 11 he told his wife that this affair was a good school in which to judge men. He looked like a Capuchin. He had not been able to shave for ten days. He had been obliged to part with his artillery and all his heavy baggage, D'Anthouard was wounded. He was to recover. The man was indestructible. Méjean had lost all his effects. Eugène had one carriage left. He said the troops had not lost their courage. They were counting on their re-fit in Smolensk.

The losses to which he referred thus briefly had been nothing less than the virtual destruction of the Army of Italy in the dreadful ice-coated marshes of the Wop, a tributary of the Dnieper. Such of the army as had escaped from death by drowning had been set upon by Cossacks and cannon on the opposite bank as they tried to scramble into the village of Dukhovchtina. De Ségur wrote that only the coolness of the prince and the efforts of some of his officers had saved the remnant of his corps. Ranks had been re-established: the rear-guard was rescued. Caulaincourt also paid tribute. "Everything had been done that courage could do, when inspired by the example of a gallant and devoted commander; but in vain." It was at this place in their frantic haste and disarray, that the Army of Italy discharged into the flood the last of their Moscow loot—bronze vases, oriental carpets, porcelain, silver-plate, pictures ... The artillery was completely bogged. Overdriven and ill-fed horses were encouraged as long as possible to get some of it out, but nearly all had to be abandoned, Colonel Méjean, observing an officer lying full length in the snow, groaning faintly, could not pass by on the other side. He raised the hat of the fallen man. It was his youngest son. He carried the boy like a sack over his shoulders to the nearest village, assisted, when his own strength failed, by unknown friends.

One of the dreadful things about the retreat was how disaster seemed to beget disaster. Every place in which they put trust for succour vanished as they approached, like an oasis in a mirage. Smolensk could not take them. The troops hammered on the gates of the town in a frenzy. They must wait. Rations were being assigned. When the Emperor had discovered conditions in Smolensk his wrath had been so terrible that the commissary responsible had saved his life, it was said, only by falling on his knees. The fine German and Italian cattle driven in for the Grande Armée over the Lithuanian sands, had had to be slaughtered almost immediately they arrived. The many corpses in the town had poisoned the air. Several convoys had been intercepted . . . A thousand oxen had been sold to the Jews who had got a good price from the Russians.

The march of the Army of Italy from Smolensk to Krasnoye nearly saw the end of the Viceroy. Riding with his Chief of Staff General Guilleminot, in the darkness, he was stopped by a Russian with a white flag who cried that Napoleon and the Guard had surrendered. "You are surrounded by twenty thousand Russians." The Viceroy had with him only fifteen hundred men of all ranks. He was an hour's march ahead of the rest of his corps. "He hesitated only a moment. Then with the arrogance born of a crown and repeated victories, he refused to consider surrender." He rode back to bring up his division and take them into action. He was generally modest, but he used his superior rank at awful Orscha as his claim when the choice lay between him and Mortier as to whose corps should search for Marshal Ney and the missing rear-guard. A Polish trooper had come in to say that Ney was advancing along the right bank of the Dnieper and was asking for help. This was one of the few truly glorious incidents of the retreat. The Viceroy found four thousand volunteers, who had been just about to sit down to their best meal since Moscow, and they set off into the blanket of the night. There was thick mist. They might well be advancing into the arms of the victorious

Russians. The prince ordered some cannon to be fired. A signal of distress answered across the sea of snow. Ney and Eugène, ahead of their troops, were the first to meet: they rushed into one another's arms: tears of joy froze on the Viceroy's cheeks, but the Marshal was warm with wrath as he cursed Davout. Their troops broke their ranks to embrace one another. They all marched back to Orscha together and the story of Ney's heroic rear-guard action was told for the first time. "A Marshal of France does not surrender!"

It was a little warmer now, and nothing worse could have happened than the thaw, from the point of view of the Emperor's brave engineers. At the passage of the Studianka they worked up to their armpits amongst the rushing waters and ice-floes to drive in the first supports for the two bridges across which the Grande Armée must cross the Beresina out of Russia. The Viceroy's corps crossed in the night of November 27. The bridge for heavy vehicles had collapsed twice, causing panic and heavy loss. They knew they had three Russian armies now encircling them, gathering for the kill. There was their unfailing, generally invisible, enemy Kutozov. Count Wittgenstein was moving from the north with Swedish and Finnish reinforcements. Admiral Tschitschagov, coming from the south, had occupied Minsk, last month marked down as an ideal supply town for the Grande Armée. But the choice of the Studianka as the crossing place had been unexpected. All but twelve thousand, mostly stragglers, were on the Lithuanian bank by the time that the manoeuvre was discovered. The army had to face attack from both sides of the river. Baron Larrey, with his operating table on a fine tree trunk, went to and fro several times, sometimes carried on their shoulders through the mad mob by the troops who loved him.

On December 1 the Viceroy wrote to his wife that his nose was as red as a rose, but he still had it. The ladies of France and Italy had been horrified by stories of an army returning to them without noses, ears, fingers or toes. He had supped with the Emperor who had kindly told the Empress to send on all news to Milan. The Duke of Bassano, in Vilna, had also been told to reassure the Vicereine. He did not make much of a job of it. All he could say was that the Viceroy was reported to be well. Some Cossacks had temporarily severed communications. But then he had seen the Prince d'Arenberg brought in, unconscious, and Marshal Rapp who had arrived in high fever, fearing he must lose his nose, two fingers and two toes. (A skilful Polish barber had saved him.)

Josephine had been unusually fortunate. Eugène's aide de camp Bataille had a bosom friend in Paris, M. de Beaumont, who sent his daughter regularly to Malmaison with transcripts of Bataille's letters. But presently even these ceased.

On December 6 the Viceroy told his wife that the Emperor had left for Paris. It was necessary. His presence was now much more needed there than with what had been the Grande Armée. The Viceroy was furious with a young aide de camp whom he had sent off for Italy with a great collection of letters. He had been found four days later on the road, quite gone to pieces. He had lost his servant and his horses and his despatches. But the Cossacks did not really understand that letters might be valuable, and incredible though it might sound, all this lot had been found, thrown away.

The thaw which had been such a nuisance crossing the Beresina had suddenly ceased, and on December 6 began a period of frost which broke all records. Birds dropped off trees. Marching men, with staring eyes, starving, weaponless, staggered on. Their frozen hair and beards clanked like the lustres of chandeliers. Now and then, out of the bare woods, came sounds which made their blood run even colder. They had not left the Cossacks behind when they had passed out of Russia, and now the cold was making the wolves bolder.

The Viceroy told his wife that the Emperor had bestowed the vacant command on the King of Naples. Nobody on his staff had questioned that the Emperor had been right to return to Paris. His army, which would soon be in Prussia, was at present perfectly valueless, and he had stayed with it a month after he had heard the disturbing news of Malet's conspiracy. He had used his carriage very seldom and as far as possible shared every hardship. He had gone on foot for miles in the snow, walking with a staff, and sometimes the shoulder of Berthier, or an aide de camp. But he had been much harassed before he set out (with Caulaincourt as sole companion of any stature), by the frenzied pleas of Berthier to be allowed to go too, and the feeling entreaties of his stepson to be allowed to return to Italy. The Emperor had answered "Some day! Continue to do your duty and trust in me."

From Gumbinnen in Prussia the Viceroy thanked his mother, sister and wife for the comforts for the troops which he had distributed at Vilna. To Darnay he wrote more frankly. "You will realize how we have suffered these last months. The climate has destroyed us. The beautiful Grande Armée is no more. Our losses are immense. The sights we witness every day are heart-rending. Our friends and companions drop on the road and die of misery, fatigue and cold. The Italians are dying like flies. The Garde Royale has not saved a hundred men. How happy should we be to see our homes one day. It is my sole ambition now. I search no more for glory. It costs too dear."[17]

CHAPTER FIFTEEN

"Honour and Fidelity"

1812 : 1814

I

AT A QUARTER past twelve on the night of December 18, 1812, just as the clock on the Tuileries was striking, a heavy post-chaise which had driven through the Arc de Triomphe (the roadway reserved for the Imperial carriage) was halted by a sentry at the gate of the Carrousel. "You can't pass." The groom preceding the vehicle, swaying in his saddle stupid with fatigue, stammered, "But it's the Emperor." "That's a good one!" smiled the sentry. "Yesterday the *Moniteur* said he was in Smolensk." Caulaincourt, Duke of Vicenza, unbuttoned his overcoat so as to display his facings. The officer of the guard moved up, and looked into the carriage. The Emperor was wearing over his uniform of the Grenadier footguards, a green fur-lined Polish cloak, and on his head a cap of marten's fur. The officer bowed deeply, his eyebrows starting up into his hair, moved aside, and waved the post-chaise on to the garden entrance of the palace.

Next morning, the guns of the Invalides and their newspapers told the people of Paris that the Emperor was home again. They had been shocked on the 16th by the twenty ninth bulletin of the Grande Armée which it had been the duty of Prince Eugène to read aloud to his assembled marshals in the Emperor's presence on December 3. It admitted heavy losses, owing to the forces of Nature, not the Russians. Queen Hortense was at the Tuileries early. "I asked anxiously if the disasters to the army had been as cruel as the bulletin stated. The Emperor answered in tones of suppressed grief 'I have told all the truth.' 'But,' I exclaimed, 'We can't have been the only sufferers. The enemies must also have had great losses?' 'No doubt,' he replied, 'But that does not cheer me.' I asked for news of my brother. He answered rather coldly. I found out why."

During the campaign, Savary, Duke of Rovigo, had been short of news from the Russian front. He had been glad to receive material from Prince Eugène's secretary, Baron Darnay. Now this excellent man was a hero-worshipper. Josephine had been enchanted by an article in *Le Journal de L'Empire* affirming what she had always known, that her son was one of the heroes of his age. But Hortense had been puzzled that in the official bulletin published the day before, the part played by her brother's corps was described without mention of him as commander. Savary, had also noticed this and had written to the Emperor explaining that he had not been the author of the enthusiastic article. The Viceroy's secretary had been solely responsible.

Caulaincourt came to see Hortense on the morning after his return. She told him that she was miserable to think of her brother left under the command of the King of Naples. He gave her many details of the retreat and especially how the Viceroy and Marshal Ney had distinguished themselves. But he suggested that when discussing the campaign with the Emperor, she should speak only of the Marshal and should not refer to the Viceroy. He was far too much the diplomat to tell her what he was going to write in his memoirs. "The Emperor again asked me whether I thought he ought to give command of the army to the Viceroy or the King of Naples. I said, as I had before, that the Viceroy was the more popular with the army and enjoyed more of its confidence." The Emperor had seemed to find these observations sound but had objected that Murat's rank make it impossible for him to be placed under the orders of Eugène. Besides, Murat would not stay if asked to serve under the Viceroy, whereas Eugène would certainly do his best under Murat. Berthier had agreed and also said that the other Marshals would consider Murat's rank, age and reputation the more imposing; so would the Russians. Caulaincourt was left with the impression that the Emperor would prefer to leave to his brother in law rather than to his stepson the honour of rallying the army. "He did not care for his stepson having credit for this further achievement in the eyes of the army and of France." Officers of the Army of Italy had been indignant at all the admiration bestowed solely upon the indomitable courage of Ney. Prince Eugène also had marched carrying a musket.

Another admirer of the Viceroy had unfortunately poured fuel on the flames. Auguste of Bavaria, who feared no man, had written to express her grief that her husband should be left to

serve under Joachim Murat. "These young wives!" exclaimed
the Emperor. "If I took any notice of them they would be the
ruin of their husbands."

The problem was suddenly solved when on January 16, 1813
the following announcement signed by Berthier, Chief of Staff,
was published:

"His Majesty the King of Naples being ill, his Imperial Highness the Viceroy has taken provisional command of the army in
the absence of the Emperor." The *Moniteur* added "The Viceroy
is more accustomed to high administration, and enjoys the entire
confidence of the Emperor."

Murat had gone off from Posen, nobody knew where, though it
was probably back to Naples. He had arrived at Gumbinnen to
find the army had got there before him and had come all the way
from Kovno without a rear-guard. Fortunately, the Russian
pursuit seemed to have slowed up once they had won back their
own territory. Very few people knew that there had been a
disgraceful scene at Murat's headquarters when he had summoned
his general staff and announced, "It is no longer possible to serve
a madman!" He had said that if only he had accepted the proposals of the English, he would still be a powerful monarch like
the Emperor of Austria and the King of Prussia. Davout had
shouted him down, telling him these rulers were princes born.
"I swear, I will denounce your black ingratitude to Napoleon."
Murat had received some communication apparently telling him
that during his absence his queen had taken upon her undue
authority. He had gone off to have it out with her. They were a
horribly excitable couple.

Caulaincourt heard more when Berthier, "a chronic invalid",
arrived in Paris on sick leave. He confessed that he now regretted
having been partially responsible for the command having been
given to someone who had done nothing but run away from it.
Caulaincourt was delighted with reports of his successor. "The
Viceroy, on the other hand, was indefatigable. Always in the
midst of his troops, he encouraged them and succeeded in rallying
the scattered remnant of the army. Confidence began to be born
anew. Neither France nor the brave fellows who fought her
battles will ever forget that this young hero never despaired of his
country or the army that had been entrusted to him, or that he
stayed with it in the midst of contagion, and paved the way for
our victories in the spring."

Madame de Souza brought round to show to Queen Hortense a letter from her son Charles de Flahaut, who had been right through the campaign.

"Posen, January 20.

"Since the King's departure the Viceroy has taken the command ... During the short time that he has been in control he has put our affairs in good shape. He is a hard worker; so unlike his predecessor who did nothing at all. He has won esteem, respect and devotion on every side." Laure Junot added another Paris tribute: "The Viceroy performed prodigies during the time he was without aid, and almost without hope, surrounded only by dissatisfied troops and by allies ready to desert our cause." It was gradually accepted in Paris that no Russian commander in chief had vanquished the Grande Armée of the Emperor Napoleon. The victor had been 'General Frost'; the Russians themselves admitted it.

Baron Fain said the last word. "On returning from Fontainebleau Napoleon learned that the King of Prussia had left Potsdam; but the Viceroy showed decision in immediately taking command of the Army, and the devotion shown by that young prince reassured the Emperor as to what might happen on the banks of the Oder."[1]

II

He held his first review at Posen on January 25. It was of the Guard, and in the imposing Theatre Square, went off pretty well. He was going to form a new observation corps, of the Elbe this time—seven divisions, including a Guard Division under General Roguet. This old boy was a grand character, ten years his senior, a natural leader who had come up the hard way. Throughout the retreat, although his boots were held together by rags, he had worn a white stock and marched at the head of his orderly division existing on gruel and melted snow. He had lost every possession. The Viceroy gave him a pelisse. A sutler had advanced him a thousand francs. He was a believer in very strict discipline, and indeed it was clear that what was left of the Grande Armée needed careful and complete reorganization.

One of the chief difficulties during the first weeks was to discover who was physically ill and who was mentally sick. Engineer-General d'Eblé, pontoon commander, whose wonderful efforts had produced the bridges across the Beresina, had simply taken to his bed and died in hospital at Königsberg. So had General Lariboisière of the artillery of the Guard, who had never recovered his spirits after the death of his son at Borodino. Berthier was in a condition verging on nervous breakdown. Ney was in a very strange state—suspicious. Bessières seemed to have lost the ability to concentrate. Old Lefebvre talked incessantly—all complaint. He too had lost a beloved son. Junot was perhaps the most unbalanced . . . The only thing was to ask the Emperor to allow them all to go home. So the new Commander in Chief did that, and when his wife heard of all these heroes returning to their families she wrote again to the Emperor. Her husband had to explain to her that she had done wrong. This was not the moment. He could not think of deserting this ship, although it appeared to have no oars or sails. He added that a storm was blowing up. One of the saddest things was answering his wife's enquiries on behalf of relatives of the Army of Italy. The Giovia family was a typical case. The younger son had been taken prisoner on the retreat, together with his father and the son in law, both wounded. The elder son had died at Gumbinnen. The fate of the Mameluke Petrus worried his master for weeks. He had seen him on to a sledge, very ill, together with Bataille who had been wounded, and had left money for the care of the servant at Kovno. Astonishingly, both re-appeared and so did Soulange, whom an unmanageable horse had carried into the enemy lines, deep in Russia. But he knew he would never see again the elder Méjean and two of the Tascher boys. The third son, Eugène, who had been wounded in the foot had died in hospital at Königsberg; the second son, Maurice, in hospital in Berlin less than three weeks later.

The untouched corps who had been stationed in Vilna and Riga had hardly been able to believe their eyes when they had seen what had come out of Russia to join them. Young troops from Mainz and Milan were also being sent to the Posen headquarters. The Viceroy said that he was up to his eyes in paperwork and was having to be very severe to get his motley crew into some sort of order before spring. Pillage was a major problem. When they beheld the beautiful sight of a farmyard, with hens and pigs running about, it seemed impossible for the troops to remember that they were no longer in enemy country.

It was a terrible long winter. The hospitals at Gumbinnen, Insterburg, Königsberg, Marienberg and Thorn were packed tight and if possible to be avoided. Villages reported stories of men without ears and noses wandering distraught in the frontier woods. Women on Pomeranian farms were afraid to go to a back door after dark to spill a pail, lest they were set upon by horrible relics of the Grande Armée, faceless men, hungry as wolves. There were said to be whole coachloads of French stars of the Opera and ballet still on the road. They had followed young officers of the Imperial Guard to Moscow, lured by promises of emeralds and sables. They were sitting staring in their coaches, frozen stiff weeks ago, with a dead man on the box, and in the shafts the skeletons of horses.

The defiant high spirits of outpost troops, forgotten at home, nobody's children, began to be noticeable in Prince Eugène's letters. He said that if he could get hold of a piano he would sing all day. February passed into March. Shrove Tuesday came, "never a sadder one for us." From the 4th to the 19th he received a string of angry letters in cipher from the Emperor. The Viceroy had retired, slowly, painfully, beyond the Oder, behind the Elbe. He could not help it. Before the remnant of the Grande Armée had quitted Poland, Schwarzenberg and his Austrians had slipped away towards their own country. The Prussian contingent under Marshal Yorck von Wartenburg had entered into a convention with the Russians, and on March 17 the King of Prussia had declared war. The Emperor was furious with him. He told his stepson that if Prussian towns "behaved badly" they were to be burned. Berlin was not to be spared. His letters began to resemble those sent to Prince Eugène during his first weeks as Viceroy, and on his retreat after the battle of Sacile. "Your despatches tell me nothing . . . The information you send is inaccurate and insufficient . . . I do not know enough about the situation of my army to be able to direct it . . . I do not know what is happening to you except from English newspapers." The stepson, as ever, had to apologize. He regretted that neither his movements nor his dispositions satisfied the Emperor. He had tried to do the best possible in His Majesty's service. It might be that his zeal exceeded his skill. If so, he begged not to be left much longer in a position in which it appeared that he could not please. From his new headquarters near pleasant Magdebourg he told Darnay quite calmly that his command was "getting respectable"—sixty thousand men, a hundred and fifty guns, four thousand horses. He told Auguste that his Paris news was that France was humming like a single huge factory to get ready the new Grande Armée with which the Emperor had promised to return. The Senate had voted him three hundred and fifty thousand conscripts. (In fact, a hundred and fifty thousand of them had to be boys, still in their teens.) A hundred thousand of the National Guard were being made available for foreign service. There would probably have to be one more big battle before France could dictate peace terms. The Emperor had sent Flahaut to confer with him. "I hope you will be a sensible little girl and not worry about me. If the knowledge that I am in some danger alarms your tender heart, take comfort in the thought that I am doing my duty, and am happy to be of a little service to the Emperor, more especially as I have been given the chance at a time when so many are fainthearted. I like to think that if I were not doing this, you would have neither love nor use for me. This is a difficult time; but just have a little patience, and above all don't lose faith in my star."

On a reconnaissance across the Elbe, near the village of Möckern between Leipzig and Halle, he had very nearly lost his latest miniature of his wife with the four children. It had been in his red portfolio, strapped to the saddle of his Polish commander of artillery. Colonel Kliski had been in imminent danger of being run through by a Russian spear when Prince Eugène had charged up and shot the Cossack dead. The lance had gone through the leather of the portfolio. Auguste preserved the relic proudly and the Viceroy's war artist performed a sketch of the incident.[2]

It was one of several such brushes during those first days of April, and he was glad to say that his green troops were standing firm. His casualties had not been heavy. Enemy wounded prophesied enormous numbers for the Russian and Prussian troops coming up. Both the Czar and King Frederick William were with their armies. The Russians were at present commanded by Wittgenstein. There had been another victim of the Moscow retreat. Kutozov had died. The Czar was said to be glad. By April 10 the Viceroy had heard, under the rose, that Soult, from Spain, was likely to relieve him, so that he could return to Italy where his presence might be more valuable.

He told his wife that he hated these pottering defensive actions. He was not accustomed to them. He had rheumatism, too. But he thought that was merely because he had gone out, on a treacherously sunny morning, without his cloak. One evening he had come in so stiff that he could hardly dismount, and when he had, his legs had given way beneath him. He had entirely lost his voice; but only for two days. He heard with grief that Auguste too was unwell. She thought of going to take the baths at Padua again. He asked her whether she would make Strà her head-quarters, in which case she could take all the children, or whether she would hire a little villa at Abano as she had done before. He thought she ought to go in some state—take a chamberlain and master of the horse, and an Italian lady as well as Countess Sandizell. She had better give General Pino eight or ten days' notice so that he could provide an escort of a hundred infantry of the Guard and a dozen gendarmes.

It was awkward that the wounded d'Anthouard might be there for treatment. This was a tiresome old story. Years ago, the Viceroy's first aide de camp had been courting, quite openly, the Vicereine's young German lady in waiting. Nothing could have been more suitable. But months had passed and he had never declared himself. The little countess began to peak and pine. Quite suddenly, and while Eugène had been absent, d'Anthouard had demanded an audience with the Vicereine. He came, he said, to ask permission to marry Countess Sandizell. But he proceeded to furious abuse of the Baronin von Wurmb whom he declared, was spying upon him. His accusation was probably justified. The Baronin would have considered it her duty to make some enquiries, and the result had been rewarding. He already had a wife. "Because of my extreme youth," Auguste recollected "he had doubtless hoped to intimidate me." It had turned out that he was jealous of her because he had soon seen that her influence with her husband would be paramount. When Eugène had returned he had forbidden d'Anthouard to approach the salon of the Vicereine for a month. It had been noticed and caused more gossip. D'Anthouard, frustrated in his hopes of ruling through the Viceroy, had betaken himself to intrigue for the post of Minister for War, but unsuccessfully. It was useless to send him to Spain. He came back covered with glory. Eugène was needing some new aides de camp again now. He ruefully told Auguste he would look twice at the candidates.[3]

"The days are slipping by, without my losing any more ground. If I can make the end of the month without further trouble, I reckon myself saved." On April 19 (he was good at anniversaries) he remembered that it was exactly a year since he had left home. "Be assured that the peace will not be long a-making. Both the victors and the vanquished desire it. I should not be surprised if this campaign, so painfully entered into, ended quickly." On the 13th they were suddenly back to winter again—a heavy snow-storm. But the Emperor had left Paris on the 15th and arrived at Mainz on the 17th. He was marching with a force composed of officers and privates who had not seen one another forty-eight hours previously, and of non-commissioned officers who had been given their stripes the night before they had struck camp. The new Grande Armée which crossed the Rhine was hardly more than a disciplined mob. Detachments had been sent forward by the hundred as the depots sorted and clothed them.

It was advancing with giant strides. Already the Viceroy's army could hear its voice—some distant cannon fire, doubtless affairs of outposts. On the 26th he announced in triumph from Mansfeld, "Behold us, my dear Auguste, on the move to join the Grande Armée. I got in here today, and tomorrow I shall ride at the head of my troops through Halle." It was an anti-climax that he would have to retrace ground to Eisleben the next night, a manoeuvre which would mean about fifty miles in the saddle. But he was perfectly well. "Exercise never hurt me!"

The Viceroy's army met the new Grande Armée, in the end, at four o'clock in the afternoon of May 1, 1813 at the obelisk on the Weissenfels-Leipzig road marking the spot where Gustavus Adolphus of Sweden had been killed in 1652. They were on historic ground, the battlefield of Lützen. Next day the Emperor fought his Battle of Lützen. He was deficient in cavalry and had lost his most renowned cavalry commander the afternoon before. Bessières, leading a reconnaissance through the defile of Rippach on the banks of that pleasant salmon-river the Saale, had been struck on the breast by a ricocheting musket ball and had died instantly. It was an entirely unavoidable casualty, but he had been curiously gloomy ever since Moscow, and his staff repeated in horror his words before he had ridden out on his last fatal sortie. He had burned his wife's letters and had been persuaded with difficulty to take some breakfast. "Oh! very well. If a ball comes my way I had rather it did not find me empty."

As the Emperor advanced towards Leipzig the Allies concentrated south-west of the city and turned Ney's flank which was based on three small villages. The arrival on the scene of the Emperor produced the usual effect. Marshal Blücher's name appeared for the first time in the Viceroy's hasty line to his wife.

"We had a fine battle yesterday, my good Auguste, and as you will expect, it went entirely in our favour. The Czar and the King of Prussia were both present. Despite their superiority in cavalry we beat them." Casualties had been heavy but his corps had lost a low proportion on account of their being sent into action late against the Allied reserve. He believed that the Emperor had had the extreme kindness to send Auguste a direct report. At a critical moment the Young Guard led by Mortier had attacked the Allied centre. The Emperor had ordered forward a hundred guns which tore through the enemy line and had marched his reserve through the gap.

In accounts from other sources it appeared that the Emperor had gained a strategic but indecisive victory. Although the Allied retreat towards Bautzen had been almost a rout it had not been possible to pursue them. The Emperor's first letter to the Viceroy himself four days after the Battle of Lützen was not generous.

"My son! Yesterday would have been a beautiful day if you had brought me three thousand prisoners. Why, in country where the enemy could not employ his cavalry to advantage, were you not able to send me anyone? The Duke of Ragusa is marching at four a.m. on Waldheim. Take care to leave not later than five . . . Try to get a little order into your corps. It much needs it. The Italians are committing the worst atrocities, plundering and stealing. Have one or two shot."

The Viceroy's march on Dresden was applauded in Paris as having been "skilful and well executed; the last exploit of his splendid campaign." His advance was not undisputed. He wrote to King Max from Dresden to say that after a fine battle and five good advance-guard combats, he had arrived in good health except for extreme weariness. The Russians had burnt all the bridges so he was having to re-establish one under intermittent enemy fire. It would be ready in a few hours and then he would send his troops over the Elbe. His Majesty's sister would be able, to enter her kingdom again. He had already asked Auguste to apologize to the King of Saxony for having to fight over his country, and he apologized also to his father in law for having brought war so near to his domains. He ended as he always did when writing to his wife's father. "My respectful homage to the queen; I embrace brothers and sisters." These were the remaining nine children of King Max's two marriages.

The Emperor had seemed very pleased to see him when their

armies had first met at Lützen. Now that the big battle was won the Viceroy thought that he might venture to ask for fifteen or twenty days' leave. To his relief, the Emperor replied that he was not at all averse from granting him two months' absence from the army here, where he was not so necessary as at Milan. "You may be sure I did not contradict this." He wrote off next morning to tell Auguste to conceal her joy, as he must till he got his orders, which he expected would be in eight or ten days. He was much surprised to get them the next night. It was May 12, 1813.

He never saw his stepfather again.[4]

III

At the Residenz in Innsbruck on a perfect Sunday forenoon he found his brother in law Crown Prince Ludwig translating Thucydides. Ludwig was now the proud father of a little Prince Max, and the Crown Princess was expecting a second child in August.

The King of Bavaria did not encourage his heir (who detested the Emperor Napoleon) to take an active interest in politics. The Emperor had prophesied that this prince would never inherit his father's crown. He was not quite right. Ludwig was to wear it for twenty-three years and then throw it away.

Eugène had found King Max benign as ever, surrounded by his family, relaxing at Schloss Biederstein, Auguste's stepmother's favourite holiday home. King Max did not intend to lose his crown. Times were admittedly difficult. He could not fail to be aware that his brother in law of Saxony had been sitting on the fence, and had only come down again on the side of France after the Battle of Lützen. The Emperor had spoken his mind very intemperately to leading dignitaries of Dresden who had welcomed the Russians during the Regency. Eugène spent only a few hours with his wife's relatives and reached Milan with noon on May 18.

At the Villa Napoleon, Auguste, who had hurried there from Monza, was as happy as ever in her life. For she had got her husband back, not on a miserable two months' leave, but indefinitely. His orders from the Emperor were to raise and train a new army in Italy, of which, together with the Illyrian provinces, he was given supreme command. A handsome gift accompanied the appointment. He was presented with the Villa Napoleon, which had been given to the Emperor personally in 1796, on the foundation of the Cisalpine Republic. Moreover his daughter Josephine, was raised to the rank of Duchess of Gallieri, and became mistress of the Palazzo Gallieri in Bologna, and rich estates in Venetia. Both these large tokens of esteem were well calculated to please the Vicereine.

She wrote at once to tell her brother of the Emperor's generosity. She said that she had always loved the Villa and particularly its garden. This had its own little river and island and classical temples and statuary. The noise from the big road leading to Vienna sounded only as a gentle murmur in the green walks of the Villa Napoleon. The duchy for her eldest daughter naturally appealed to her, who destined her children for thrones. The little Josephine was an outstandingly lovely child, and seemed to be as tactful as she was graceful. She had spontaneously wept when waving good-bye to her namesake after the highly successful Milan visit.

It was as well that the Vicereine was pleased with the Emperor for she was to find soon that although she had got her husband back over the Alps, she was to see little of him during the next few months. His new duties would entail much absence from home. It was flattering for them both to find that his safe return was regarded in Milan with enthusiasm, but he refused all festivities to celebrate the event. Too many families in Italy were in mourning for soldiers who would not return. It was whispered that of twenty-seven thousand who had marched away to fight for the Emperor, only three hundred and thirty three had survived.

He had been deeply grieved by the death of Bessières. Within a fortnight of his homecoming he learnt that at the Battle of Bautzen, Duroc had been fatally wounded. He had now lost his two greatest and oldest army friends, and in the same campaign. The Emperor had brought the Allies to action again on May 20, but although they had been badly shaken, the engagement had really been indecisive. On June 4 he agreed to an armistice and a Peace Conference at Prague. He wrote to Clarke that he had decided on this because of his lack of cavalry and his doubts of the loyalty of Austria. He had every reason to fear that his vaunted marriage with an Austrian Archduchess was not going to prevent his father in law from attacking him.

At the end of a terrible interview with that arch-opportunist Count Metternich, he had shouted, "I may lose my throne but I shall bury the whole world in ruins! . . . You will never again make war against me." The Austrian diplomatist, according to his own account had answered softly, "Sire! you are a lost man." The Austrian marriage had, however, effected its first object. There was now the King of Rome to be considered. His father was passionately devoted to the child and seemed genuinely attached to his young docile wife. He had left her as Regent when he had set out on his last campaign, and Méneval to act as her secretary. A new chief secretary had gone to the wars with him, M. le Baron Agathon Fain, so well-mannered and inconspicuous that people hardly noticed he was in a room. He was taking notes for a historical work *Manuscrits de Mil Huit Cent Treize*. He had accomplished 1812. He had been secretary of the archives for eight years.

Eugène, alone in Milan, got the usual flood of letters from his stepfather, though from Dresden and in a strange handwriting. Sometimes he got three in a day. He was to raise a new observation corps on the Adige. He spent hours writing to secure, first horses, then supplies of food for horses and men, to be stored in his garrison towns, and much clothing needed at once for his conscripts. Shakos were a difficuly. He tried Milan, Verona, Venice. He could not send the boys to Germany bare-headed. Turin came to his rescue. Auguste had to depart for her cure at Abano in the middle of June without him. Baronin Wurmb took the children for a Como holiday where their father visited them for one night.

He seemed to have come home to every minor trouble— British ships reported cruising off Venice, Fiume, Ravenna; plague at Malta . . . On the top of these came the spectacular breakdown of Junot who was Governor General in Illyria. The Emperor wrote that he must be removed at once from a post where his painful affliction was noticed by foreigners. He had better not be sent to Paris. He must be escorted to his family home near Dijon; his wife could join him there. He was violent. Eugène visited him at Treviso and saw at a glance that he had lost another friend. Three weeks after he arrived home to his parents Junot destroyed himself.[5]

Several banks in Venice and Bologna had closed their doors and, what was much worse, five in Milan, including the most respected—Bignami. The Viceroy reported everything and never failed to assure His Majesty that his kingdom of Italy was in a condition of the utmost tranquillity. He sent off d'Anthouard to govern Illyria until the Emperor's pleasure was known. This turned out to be Fouché, Duke of Otranto. In Paris he was attempting to have too much influence with the young Empress.

There were rumours of a Croatian uprising in Illyria, incited by Austria. General Hiller had arrived at Agram. The Viceroy performed visits of inspection at all his old haunts—Padua, Udine, Bassano, Verona, Palmanova, Ancona, Vicenza. He collected Auguste from Abano and took her with him for some days in Venice while he saw troops and ships there. She was very much pleased by her reception in a favourite holiday town. While he was at Udine he had engaged some spies who had left for Leoben, Gratz and Marburg. One of them who had come from Vienna and was going back to Linz said that the Czar had entered Bohemia on the excuse of visiting his widowed sister the Grand Duchess of Oldenburg, and that the Archduke John had been at Gratz.

From Monza he sent the Emperor what he justly called a book —"The situation of the troops under my command July 15." It was beautifully sub-divided under five headings: (1) the six divisions in the kingdom; (2) troops detailed to form the observation corps; (3) garrison; (4) French troops; (5) troops in Illyria. He said he would be off again in a few days. From Udine again on August 11 he apologized to his wife for a short line. He had been seven hours at his desk. A despatch from the Emperor had warned him that Austria might declare war at any moment. The armistice expired next week. He had got his army in motion on to the line of the Isonzo and was going on to the Sava. The artillery would not be able to get up from Verona for some days but meanwhile, since he could do no more, he was going to the local opera. "They are giving 'Griselda'. It ought to be marvellous." Great preparations had been made in the town for the celebration of the Emperor's birthday four days hence and they had better continue—procession on horseback to the cathedral, inspection, Te Deum. He found he was giving a ball. He achieved all and set off to Carniola. From Gorizia on August 19 he wrote home that Austria had pulled off the mask. They were at war again. "Yours for life etc."

IV

He fought like a lion to save Italy for the Emperor, but it was hopeless almost from the first. The Emperor believed him to be fairly matched with the Austrians under General Hiller so far as numbers went, though his new army was green. He was mistaken. Operations opened with Hiller taking Villach. He was driven out, but by the end of September the Viceroy had retreated to take up his position on the Isonzo. Three years later, when it was past history, several officers of his army published in Paris their reminiscences of Prince Eugène's last campaign.[6]

His devoted chief of staff Vignolles pointed out that although the Viceroy only fought one battle of the first order—on the Mincio on April 8, 1814—he won it; and there had been many other actions, perhaps best termed combats, in which his army had signally distinguished themselves. There were unforgettable memories such as old Grenier's attack at Feistriz (one of the early ones) with a mediaeval castle and a ravine sweltering in September light as foreground, and the Austrians perched in the cemetery of St. Pedro below. "Our troops, supported by the presence of the Viceroy, seemed to charge with double the courage!" They had need to take courage, for the Emperor had fought the last successful battle of the Empire, in the suburbs of Dresden at the end of August, and now Oudinot had been defeated by Dulow and Bernadotte, and Ney at Tebbewitz, and in the three day slaughter ending on October 19 at Leipzig, the Grande Armée had been driven back across the Rhine.

Bavaria had gone over to the Allies. Austria could now send troops through the Tyrol upon Italy. The Franco-Italian army retired foot by foot over the Tagliamento and the Brenta to the Adige. At San Pietro near Caldiero on November 15 the 53rd regiment, under sharp fire, seemed likely to be cut off. "The Prince, perceiving their hesitation, called me up and in a loud voice ordered me to attack." Although it was difficult to hear anything, his gestures were unmistakable. The 53rd advanced and rescued Colonel Bonnemain's cavalry. The Viceroy seemed to be perfectly unconscious of the manner in which he had exposed himself.

On the evening after this action the gentle country outside Verona presented an extraordinary appearance. The inhabitants of the city brought out their carriages to carry in the wounded. The Vicereine was in Verona. She met her husband in the Palazzo Canossa under the shadow of the old castle, which had a fine *salone* frescoed by Tiepolo, and a good view of the Adige. Her grief and dismay at her father's desertion of the Emperor were much what might have been expected. She had been entirely taken by surprise. Her husband, replying to King Max's long reasonable letter stating his case for leaving a sinking ship, said that he trembled to think of the effect of this news on the princess. Their reunion after a year's absence had produced the almost inevitable result. She was with child again. She had toiled across Lombardy and the Veneto bringing all the children, in torrential rain, on the chance of a few hours with her husband. But she was one of those on whom bad news acted as a spur. She said she had wept much when she had read her husband's reply to her father, so generous so calm.

"I am going to write to him that this will be the last letter which he will receive from his daughter. After that I will forget that I was born a Bavarian and will think only of our children and of the best and most beloved husband in the world. You know me by now, so your mind can be at rest. I will put up with anything so long as we are linked on our journey through life. Even if we lose all our material possessions no one can take from us the love which we bear to one another. You must have seen, darling, from my recent letters that I am impatient to leave this place; if I had dared I would have had the pictures and valuables packed up ready to go. Good-bye, and I implore you not to be anxious for my sake. I promise not to lack courage and I shall love you all my life with all my heart."

Her letter to Crown Prince Ludwig was even less restrained, for she had no doubt, as she frankly said, that he would be pleased their father was now against them. "I have written to him to commend our children to him, as soon their fate will depend on the compassion of outsiders. My husband and I will have nothing to give them except our dearest love. That is what things have come to! To save Bavaria and my family I offered myself as a sacrifice. I shall never regret it; but what has been my reward? To be forgotten, to be forced to beg for mercy on my children! God gave me an angel as a husband. That is my sole happiness."[7]

King Max genially put himself in correspondence with his old friend the Baronin von Wurmb. He had known what it was to be a refugee royalty with a young family and he had not the slightest intention of going on his travels again in his old age. Besides, the Emperor Napoleon had once told him that he had thought of giving Bavaria to Murat, and good King Max was devoted to the picturesque kingdom which under his beneficent rule was becoming prosperous. He did not wish to send any more subjects to be slain in order that the Emperor Napoleon should increase his domains. He was for peace now. He assured the baroness of his constant devotion (despite what he delicately called "my new position") to the interests of Prince Eugène, his daughter and their children. He spoke no less than the truth.

On the afternoon of November 22 a young officer giving the name of Major Eberle delivered a letter from General Hiller to General Paflachner commanding the Austrian outposts. It asked that the major might be given a trumpeter to accompany him on a confidential mission to the French lines. The Viceroy's headquarters were in a little village called San Michele, two and a half miles along the Vicenza road to Verona. The place enjoyed some reputation as being the reputed birthplace of the renowned Michele Sanmicheli, and had a round church with a peristyle, Madonna di Campagna, said to have been built by him, from the dome of which the Alpine view was superb. It was appropriate that the background of the scene which was to follow was serene and dignified, for Eugène de Beauharnais was about to be called upon to make the most important decision of his career. The so-called Major Eberle was passed through the Austrian outposts, and after about ten minutes challenged by a French piquet to which he gave the usual signal employed by an agent sent to parley. An officer came up and passed him on to General Rouyer whom he presented with a letter, actually of his own composition, but signed by Hiller. It said that Major Eberle had a communication of the first importance which he could transmit to the Viceroy of Italy by word of mouth only. He was kept waiting three hours, at the end of which he was told that the prince would see him at his headquarters. His eyes were bandaged for a very short journey, and when the handkerchief was removed he found himself outside the church of Madonna di Campagna in St. Michele. About quarter of an hour later he heard the sound of hooves. The Viceroy, who had been on horseback going round his outposts, dismounted and strode towards him. It was clear that he instantly recognized, in the supposed Major Eberle in a white Austrian uniform, Prince Augustus Taxis and Thurn, an aide de camp of the King of Bavaria. The young man had been on Baron Wrede's staff under his own command in the last campaign. Eugène de Beauharnais perceived that some offer was to be made to him. He took into his hand the letter from his father in law. He said, "As this is a free country and we have nothing to hide from this gentleman I should prefer to go out into the open air." His suite stayed at a distance of about a hundred yards close to the columned porch of the church, while the Viceroy walked and talked with his unexpected guest.

It was not until he had expressed hopes that His Majesty was in good health that Prince Eugène opened the letter from him. There were really two documents. The short covering note was dated Frankfurt on Main November 16, and told him that he could put perfect confidence in Prince Taxis, who though young was deserving of it. "The accompanying paper gives you a general idea of the state of things. Burn when you have read. I embrace you and shall love you, my daughter and my grandchildren while I draw breath. It is not my fault that you are not as happy as you ought to be. All the world up in this corner love and respect you; I hear it every day. Your good father in law and best friend . . ."

The waiting aide de camp watched fascinated while Prince Eugène read carefully, twice, the offer forwarded from the Allies offering him the crown of Italy on the condition that he deserted the Emperor Napoleon. He then answered without the slightest hesitation, "It grieves me very much to have to say No to the King my father in law: but he demands the impossible."

He was very kind to the young messenger. He said that he must not disguise that he would have to tell the Emperor of the incident. He sadly said that if the Emperor's star was paling it was all the more reason for those who had shared his glories to remain faithful. The aide de camp, according to his instructions, slipped in a suggestion that the King of Naples had not hesitated to treat with the allied sovereigns. It was hopeless. The Viceroy would only say that he still hoped this was not true, but if it was, he would be the last to approve of such conduct. A mention of his children found him as resolute. "Certainly I do not know whether my son is destined one day to wear the Iron Crown of Lombardy. But in any event I should not wish him to reach that throne by any but an honourable route."

Night had fallen. He burned the dangerous documents as requested. He sent the guest to dine with General Rouyer and set off for Verona with his staff. About eight o'clock an artillery officer brought a letter which Major Eberle put next his heart, before riding off again to Hiller's headquarters to get out of his white uniform and into his blue, and on to the road for Germany.

His story was dramatic to the last, for King Max had told him to report at Karlsruhe, and when he arrived there he was told he must go on to the theatre. The King of Bavaria was sitting in the royal box there, together with the Czar of Russia and the beautiful Grand Duchess Stéphanie of Baden, born Beauharnais. Prince Eugène's reply to the allied proposition was quite short.

"My dear father, It is just two hours since I received the letter which you sent to me by the hand of the Prince Taxis, and which he brought to the outposts of our lines. I am deeply touched that you should have thought of me, and so kindly, but it is quite impossible for me to depart by an inch from the line of conduct which I have laid down for myself. I would much rather sacrifice my future happiness and that of my family than break the solemn vows which I have taken."

There were a couple of paragraphs about the desirability of an armistice and Auguste being an angel, then, "Farewell, my dear father believe me, for life, your affectionate son."

The Grand Duchess looked at the King mischievously. "Well?" she asked. "Eugène won't," said the king. "I told you so!" smiled his cousin. "The crown of Italy," said the Czar. "It is very tempting." Count Metternich regretfully said that Prince Eugène had the most lofty character.[8]

V

The Emperor Napoleon had returned to Paris and wrote to his stepson that he heard with dissatisfaction that he had retreated to the Adige. He asked for full details of the situation. He said he was himself come home to raise six hundred thousand men. Eugène, who for the past three months had been reporting in detail to Clarke, Duc de Feltre, warned Auguste that he now had to send twice as much to Paris. He did not tell his wife, though he mentioned it to Darnay, that out on a reconnaissance near Legnago on November 28 he had been hit. If the ball had been live he might have lost his right leg. Luckily it had been dead, so he had only a beautiful contusion which would not even make him lame. He would be on horseback tomorrow. "If anyone asks you about this slight event, assure them it will have no consequences and is nothing but a fillip."[9]

He had sent off d'Anthouard to report to the Emperor, with instructions to point out that owing to the defection of Bavaria the enemy was reinforced by fourteen thousand very good troops. He mentioned by letter that the army under his own command had distinguished itself at the "affairs" at Villach, at Feistriz on the Drave, Tschernutz on the Save, and Lippa, and in "combats" had inflicted considerable losses on the enemy at Ala, Caldiero and Bassano. He had just heard of a further enemy reinforcement. General Count Nugent, an officer of Irish origin in the Austrian service, who had been the first to suggest to them to incite the Croats and had taken Trieste, had been supplied by a British squadron with a motley force. He had two thousand Corsicans and Calabrians at Comacchio, obviously to blockade Venice. The Viceroy said he would hold the Adige line as long as possible. After that, as His Majesty would realize, there was still the Mincio. As well as being attacked by English seaborne detachments on what was left of his Adriatic coastline, he had recently been obliged to spare troops to the other side—the Mediterranean and the Gulf of Genoa. Fifty transports escorted by a British squadron had been sighted from Spezia.

The Emperor replied that he was sending Massena to Genoa with a small force from Toulon. Eugène must raise six more battalions in Italy . . . "One must make great efforts. At this moment there is much movement. Don't let yourself be got down by the bad spirit of the Italians. The fate of Italy does not depend on the Italians." He meant the fate of his Empire. He said he had sent Fouché down to Naples to clear up the situation there and get Murat on the move up towards the Po. Provided Murat was still loyal this must produce a great effect. He was clearly extremely loath to believe that his sister Caroline and her husband could betray him.

Eugène was much better informed. Ever since the retreat from Moscow he had mistrusted the man who must be regarded as one of his few enemies. After Murat's disgraceful outburts at Posen last year, in which he had declared in the hearing of a large audience that he considered the Emperor finished, he had decamped to Naples. But he had returned to fight for him at Leipzig. He had then made another of his harum-scarum flights home, and had arrived in Milan, to the horror of the Viceroy's correct secretary, in a very theatrical manner, having lost his hat and his transport. Baron Darnay had hastened to offer his own carriage, but Murat, who was staying at an hotel, said he had borrowed twelve hundred livres from the Consul General and was off to Rome. Darnay had since heard that he had talked openly all the way from Milan to Bologna of his intention to "let the English in." Prince Taxis had been told to inform Eugène that the King of Naples had been in communication with the Allies since the fatal field of Leipzig. He was trying to strike a bargain with them. Meanwhile, Eugène was receiving orders to give him every assistance and was having to open to thirty-three thousand Neapolitan troops, who might at any moment turn against him, his granaries and his strong-boxes.

The English with whom Murat had said he was going to collaborate were Count Nugent on Eugène's Adriatic coast and Lord William Bentinck who was coming up to the Genoese littoral. Lord William was a haughty, violent man with East India experience, who had not been much of a success in the Peninsula and had been sent to govern Sicily with instructions to see whether the King of Naples meant to invade it or was willing to join the Allies in return for having his throne assured to him. His report had been that Murat was not to be trusted. The Emperor said that he was sending back to Italy all his Italian troops from Bayonne, so Eugène could expect a reinforcement of four battalions by mid January.

In the first week of December the Viceroy had to apologize to his wife for having failed to write for three days. Prina, Minister of Finance, had arrived at his headquarters with all his paperwork which was far from nothing! The army had had "one of our little successes, at Rovigo. Our soldiers really are becoming big boys! It is a pity we can't give them a better chance. But I keep on hoping that all this will finish soon." He had hoped against hope that the diplomatic manoeuvres of which he heard much from Paris and Germany (though not from the Emperor) were going to result in peace before Christmas. Metternich had persuaded the Czar and the King of Prussia to state that the allies would leave to the Emperor the natural boundaries of France —the Rhine, the Alps, the Pyrenees and the Ocean. Unfortunately the Emperor seemed to be quite immovable. Sooner than give up Holland, he would cut her dykes and let her sink back into the sea. The offer known as the Frankfort terms was withdrawn. He said it had never been sincere. A fresh series of talks, in France, was going to be suggested.

It was miserable in this weather, waiting for good news which seemed to be rather receding. Eugène had heard from Paris that his mother was ill. He hoped it was nothing serious. He heard no more. His only comfort was that his troops were under better cover than those of the enemy. Auguste came up to the Palazzo Canossa to visit him again. With great tact he had managed to prevent her bringing the four little angels. If they settled to bring the two eldest children, that would not include his son; if they brought three, the infant princess Amélie would be left desolate. He was in action at an outpost on the very morning of her arrival. She heard gunfire as she entered Verona for a stay of thirty six hours. They had to discuss where she would go to have her next child. It was now too late for her to get to Josephine's villa near Geneva; the Simplon or Gotthard were now impossible. She might go to some French provincial town. Marseille, still accessible from Genoa, might serve if he was ordered to evacuate Italy. Unsatisfactory though it was, there seemed to be nothing to do but wait. They settled that she had better write to her father for the New Year, but it must be just to enquire for his health and send best wishes from all at the Villa Napoleon to all at Munich. The same would do for her uncle the King of Saxony, about whose family they were anxious. He thought that as the Villa Napoleon was his personal property now, she need not pack up all their belongings there, as even if Milan were occupied, it would be respected. But the same could not be hoped for belongings in his remaining five official royal residences.

General Hiller had gone off to command the Austrian troops in the Tyrol, and a new Commander in Chief had arrived to take his place. Comte Henri de Bellegarde was a member of one of the oldest noble families of Savoy. His military career had been distinguished. He had fought at Marengo, Wagram—but he had excelled rather as a diplomatist. After the Peace of Lunéville he had been Governor of the Venetian provinces. He knew Prince Eugène's Kingdom of Italy as well as the palm of his own hand.

January 1814 came, and misfortunes began to multiply.

There had been one of the King of Bavaria's suggestions which Eugène had considered a possibility, and had communicated to the Emperor—to ask for a two months' armistice. The Emperor had written that he saw nothing against this. To his horror, this request made Allied headquarters believe that the Viceroy was beginning to collaborate. The offer which Taxis had brought was repeated on January 17.[10] When it got the same answer, he was told that Marshal Bellegarde could not consider even a fortnight's cessation of hostilities.

He had been holding on to the Adige line for two months. He now saw that he might have to go back to Mantua—the boulevard of Italy. It was not so good a position he thought, and the Emperor agreed, but had told him to hold on until Murat had openly declared war against him. His new headquarters would be at Volta. Murat had not declared against him, but Neapolitan troops had superseded French troops under General Miollis in Rome and were blockading Civita Vecchia; they were advancing on Bologna, Modena, Ferrara.

He had written to Murat at length and got the most extraordinary prevaricating reply, after a week. Murat, to whom he was "Dear Nephew," believed that they both had the interests of Italy at heart. If, as he did not as yet envisage, events demanded that he separated his cause from that of the Empire, his feelings for the Emperor, Eugène and his family would never alter. He would never attack without warning. On January 24 Eugène got a letter in cypher repeating that if the King of Naples officially joined the enemy, the Viceroy with all his army must cross the Alps and join the Emperor in France.[11]

On the day after the Emperor had sent these orders, Hortense went to hear Mass at the Tuileries. The Duchess of Montebello, meeting her said, "Haven't you heard the news? The Allies have crossed the Rhine. Paris is panic-stricken. What can the Emperor be thinking of?" The poor Empress Marie Louise had said to her, "I bring misfortune wherever I go." When Hortense arrived for the usual Sunday evening family dinner party she found the Imperial couple alone. The Emperor asked her was it true people in Paris were so shocked? "Do they already see Cossacks in our streets? Well, they are not here yet, and we have not forgotten our trade as soldiers." He said to his wife, "You may rest assured we will go again to Vienna and beat Papa Francis." After dinner the King of Rome was brought in. He was now nearly three and an attractive child, but although artists tried to stress a resemblance to his father he was going to be a thorough golden-haired, long-faced Habsburg. "The Emperor said to him several times 'Come on and beat Papa Francis', and the little boy repeated the phrase so clearly and frequently that the Emperor seemed delighted and laughed heartily."

Then the Emperor sent for his Chief of Staff and said "Come

Berthier, we must begin the Campaign of Italy over again." He dictated steadily for an hour. He left Paris on January 25, after a touching scene in which he commended his heir to the officers of the National Guard.[12]

VI

On February 8 the Viceroy and Marshal de Bellegarde went into action simultaneously on the Mincio. Murat had entered Bologna in triumph on the last day of January, and Eugène had heard from Fouché that the King and Queen of Naples had beyond doubt made a treaty with Austria. A letter from Count Metternich to Queen Caroline had come into the hands of the Duke of Otranto. Eugène wrote to tell the Emperor that now he knew the intentions of the King of Naples he could no longer stay on the Adige. He would take up a position on the right bank of the Mincio, with his left resting on Peschiera and his right on Mantua, his centre on Borghetto. The line was about seventeen miles long, and he thought it a good position, difficult to force and advantageous for offensive action, with a wide choice of field.

He issued two proclamations, one to the people of the kingdom of Italy, the other to his troops. "For three months you have had the honour of withholding the greater part of your country from enemy invaders. For three months the Neapolitans have solemnly promised to come to our assistance ... It is useless to deny that their defection makes things worse for us. But our courage will increase with our difficulties."

"Soldiers of the Army of Italy! I trust in you, rely on me. By doing so you will add to your interest and to your reputation. Soldiers! my motto is 'Honour and Fidelity'. Take it for your own. Then with the grace of God we will triumph over our enemies."

A few days before his move he sent Bataille into the enemy lines with a request. Such communications were quite usual between civilized commanders. Bellegarde had readily agreed to allow firewood to pass into Verona for the benefit of freezing non-combatants. He was now asked permission for the Vicereine to stay in Milan until she had given birth to her child, and after that to re-join her husband. The reply was in the best style of the days of high chivalry. Should his troops occupy Milan, the Marshal thought perhaps Monza might suit the princess best.[13] All that he would require would be the names of her suite.

375

The morning of February 8 was cold and foggy. Bellegarde's scouts had served him ill. He had been told that the Viceroy was retiring rapidly on Cremona. His first troops to cross the Mincio at Pozzolo, bound for Borghetto, ran straight into a column from Goito led by the Viceroy in person. The last battle on the grand scale of Prince Eugène in command of the Army of Italy lasted from dawn till dark and was very expensive for the Austrians, who outnumbered him by more than two to one. Afterwards Bellegarde blamed the *terrain* and two of his generals, but most of all the failure of Murat to come to his assistance. He would never have taken the route he did had he not been assured of the support of the King of Naples, whom he knew to have reached Reggio.

The battlefield was typically Lombardic, a vast plain stretching to the Po, diversified by many canals with steep banks, vineyards, farms ... There were two major roads leading to Verona and Peschiera and a few spinneys and eminences—Monte Oliveto, Monzambano ...

The Viceroy's troops were depressed by their new ill-luck and dark rumours; desertions had been on the increase. But they had several resolute veteran commanders, such as old Grenier, Verdier, Desquerelles, Bonnemains, Palombini, Darnaud ... And throughout the long day their Commander in Chief was always on the scene when most needed.[14] He had an agonizing period of anxiety while the greater part of the enemy were on the right bank of the river, and until he had seen clearly where to disarray them. After he had cut off Wrede's cavalry brigade, Pozzolo changed hands three times. From Marengo, next day he sent off Louis Tascher to report personally to the Emperor at his headquarters in France, wherever that might be. In his despatch to Clarke, he affirmed that he had pushed back the enemy over the river to Valleggio and returned to his own old Mincio line and Volta headquarters. "The army has conducted itself with extreme valour." He had two thousand nine hundred prisoners and the enemy had also lost five thousand killed and wounded. The darkening field had been littered with abandoned guns and transport. He believed he would find he had not more than two thousand five hundred *hors de combat*.

He had sent Bataille to see Murat, who had heard of the result of the battle on the 8th, and was making overtures. He sent d'Anthouard to Piacenza where the Italian troops from Spain had now arrived. He attacked at Borghetto on February 10, and on the 15th set off for Salò at four a.m., a ride of seventy miles. He was well satisfied with the result of what he described as a little affair, though it had in fact included a bayonet charge. The enemy driven from Gardone and Ponte Zanano had taken to the mountains, and he hoped for peace on his left flank for several days. Spring in Italy sometimes comes early. When they got in sight of Lake Garda the midday weather was balmy. An enthusiastic junior member of his staff who was going to write a history of the last campaign of Eugène de Beauharnais, having made his preparations for the assault from a suitable eminence, had to pause fascinated by the prospect below him—vineyards on steep banks above dazzling blue waters, and plantations of fig trees, orange trees and lemons.[15] The very air seemed sweet and scented.

There were war-like vessels upon the waters. The Viceroy's fleet gained some successes against the Austrian fleet during these weeks of tension. They opened by capturing barges loaded with grain and other supplies. They went on to a regular engagement in view of Torri del Benaco, in which Captain Tempié in charge of the Viceroy's squadron was severely wounded, but put to flight Captain Accunti. The Austrian flotilla ordered to Ostiglia from Malcesine was bombarded in Brescello. Captain Tempié brought his victorious squadron back to harbour under picturesque crenellated walls at Sirmione. This peninsula was famous as having been the haunt of Catullus and was rich in olive groves and ancient ruins.

On the night of February 17 Mantua heard gunfire from the Viceroy's lines. Good news had come from France. The Emperor had met and defeated Blücher at Champaubert and at Montmirail. Murat had issued his declaration of war on February 15 though official notification did not come from Clarke for ten days. Eugène wrote to his wife that he thought the King of Naples had chosen his time very badly. It had also produced an odd side-effect. A number of French officers and men from Murat's army had come over begging to be admitted into the Army of Italy. They were violently attached to the Emperor. A grenadier of Riom's company produced a marching-song in praise of the Viceroy. Its refrain was his motto, "Honour and Fidelity." But on February 18 the prince, hymned as a second Bayard, got a sad shock.

Letters arrived for him from the Emperor, from his mother and from his sister. Despatches from Clarke repeating the order to retire came in triplicate on the 15th and 16th. Poor discarded Josephine pressed into a service she hardly understood, pathetically entreated her son not to delay a moment, however great the obstacles. "His wish is that you should march towards the Alps, leaving in Mantua and the Italian fortresses only the troops belonging to the Kingdom of Italy." The Emperor's words to her had been, "France first! France has need of all her children!" She added on her own account, "I know your wife is preparing to leave Milan. Let me know if I can be of any use. Adieu my beloved Eugène. I have no more time than to tell you that I love you and to repeat come quick."

Hortense said she did not understand the situation, but if peace came in a few days she supposed Paris would not be taken. She had certainly thought that Eugène had been told to come only when the King of Naples had declared war. She was sure that he was following his heart and therefore doing all he could for the good of the Empire. He told his wife that he thought Hortense's letter sensible. It was quite out of character for the Emperor, who had always inveighed against petticoat government, to have called in the ladies of his family to bring pressure to bear on his stepson. Eugène's reply to him was also unusual. For the first time, instead of saying that he was sorry, he had been wrong, he said that he was sorry, but he was quite sure he had been right.[16]

"Sire,

"I have learned from a letter which I have just received from the Empress Josephine that Your Majesty blames me for not having executed swiftly enough the orders which Your Majesty sent me in cypher and which were repeated on the 9th of this month by the Duc de Feltre.

"Your Majesty appears to have thought that it was necessary to prompt me to bind myself more closely to France in present circumstances, by ties other than my devotion to the person of Your Majesty and my love of my country. Your Majesty will forgive me, but I have deserved neither the reproaches nor the lack of confidence which you display in the feelings which will always be the strongest motives behind my actions.

"Your Majesty's order stated expressly that if the King of Naples declared war against France, I should retire to the Alps. This order was a conditional one, and I should have been *guilty*

if I had carried it out before the condition which was to give rise
to the execution. Nevertheless, by retiring to the Mincio and by
forming in *échelon* on Piacenza, I did put myself in readiness to
retire as Your Majesty had ordered as soon as the King of Naples
had emerged from his indecision and had at last formally declared
war. Up to the time of writing his troops have not committed any
hostile action against those of Your Majesty; the king has always
refused to co-operate actively with the movements of the Austrians,
and two days ago he gave out that his intention was not to take
sides against Your Majesty. At the same time he let me know that
it only required some propitious circumstance for him to declare
in favour of the colours under which he had always fought. Your
Majesty will, therefore have no difficulty in seeing that I never
had grounds for thinking that the time had come for executing
his CONDITIONAL order."

He did not let the matter rest here. He went on to ask what
would have been the result if he had acted as the Emperor now
appeared to wish. He had an army of thirty-six thousand. Twenty-
four thousand were French, twelve thousand Italian. But most of
the French were Italian-born, and had no desire to re-cross the
Alps. He had already had desertions from the men coming from
the area of Mont Blanc and the Lake of Geneva. Behind his
retreat would be an Austrian force of seventy thousand, not to
speak of the Neapolitans.

If it had been His Majesty's intention that he should attempt
this march without delay, why had his orders not been more
decided? Could not a confidential officer have been sent?

He closed more characteristically.

"However that may be, there is no reason for Your Majesty to
have such doubts about me. Such loyalty as I have shown has
undoubtedly aroused jealousy in others, and provided that it
does not cause Your Majesty to withdraw your favour from me,
your regard for me will always be my dearest reward. The one
aim of my life will be to justify the confidence you place in me, and
I shall be only too happy if I can give you proofs of my devotion
and my pride in being in your service."

Auguste wrote to Hortense very hotly, but refrained from
addressing the Emperor. She said she felt that Eugène might not
wish her to do so. To Eugène she said that she no longer wondered
people were deserting the Emperor. For her part she would sooner
fall into the hands of the Austrians. They could not treat her worse

than this most ungrateful man on earth, who had plunged a dagger into her heart. If she could accompany her husband to America she would go gladly, disgusted with the grandeurs of the Old World. It had horrified her that her husband's good faith and courage had been doubted at a time when he was risking his life daily to perform the impossible. It increased her bitterness to realize that the Emperor's doubts were probably founded and fostered by enemies of Eugène, who knew that her father was trying to persuade them to join the allies.

King Max had sent another messenger through the Austrian lines. General Pocci, travelling under the name of Major Elz, had been directed to deliver to the hands of the Vicereine letters from all her family. Her father told her "The Emperor's army is feeble ... I believe the time is drawing near when Eugène may be able to get out of the business without embarrassment ... Give him this message from me. He must remember that he has a wife and children."

Eugène returned to his wife a copy of her letter to Hortense and her father's letter. He too had seen Pocci. His reply was resolute. "There would have had to be the most exceptional circumstances for me to find myself at liberty to act as an individual, for myself and my family."

He was miserably waiting to see if he must leave Italy,[17] making tentative plans for retirement to the Oglio, the Adda. He was looking out hourly for Tascher who arrived at last on February 25, having left the Emperor at Guignes, thirty miles south of Paris on the morning of the 18th. At once the whole situation seemed relaxed, or at any rate the Viceroy was given the orders he needed. Tascher said he had been surprised to be admitted at once to the Emperor, who had received him kindly and asked him had he spread the news of the Viceroy's victory in the various towns and villages through which he had come. When the aide de camp said that indeed he had, His Majesty said, "Good," and proceeded to ask for details of the battle of the Mincio—casualties, spirits of the troops. Why had not the Viceroy pursued Bellegarde? Were the Italian soldiers fighting well? What was the feeling in Italy? Tascher gave him enthusiastic answers and explained the impossibility of chasing Bellegarde further, with Murat coming up to attack. The Army of Italy now numbered approximately thirty-six thousand. Opposed to them were Bellegarde with seventy thousand, the King of Naples with twenty-four thousand

and the Anglo-Sicilians with eight thousand. He said that the Army of Italy was devoted, but the population were tormented by Austrian secret agents. One or two victories gained by the Emperor would soon put all in the right frame of mind. The Emperor smiled and said "Ah! you put faith in them!"

He had added that tomorrow or the next day the aide de camp would be able to witness that the Grande Armée fought as well as the Army of Italy. Actually, his action against Schwarzenberg at Montereau on the 18th had been but an inconclusive victory. His orders to his stepson, however, were unmistakable.

"I have got your letter of February 9 and see with pleasure the advantages that you have obtained. Had they been a little more decisive, and had the enemy been more deeply involved, we should have been able to keep Italy. Tascher will tell you the story from here. I have destroyed the Army of Silesia (Russians and Prussians). Today I begin upon Schwarzenberg. In four days I have taken between thirty and forty thousand prisoners, a hundred and fifty to two hundred guns, and an enormous quantity of baggage. My losses have been negligible . . . It is therefore possible that if fortune continues to smile upon us, the enemy will be thrown back from our frontier in complete disorder; in that event we could hold on to Italy. In such a situation the King of Naples would probably change his coat again."

Eugène duly wrote to Clarke to tell him that his orders were to hold on. Afterwards, military experts including Lord Wellington ("Excellent! quite excellent!") agreed that in none of his campaigns had the Emperor displayed his genius to greater advantage from the technical point of view than in that of the spring of 1814. He was fighting with his back to the wall, on French soil. The inhabitants of Alsace and Lorraine were solidly behind him. Extraordinary though it might seem, during six weeks of this campaign a Conference was going on at Châtillon to arrange Armistice terms. Eugène kept on reporting hopefully to his wife the progress at this distant council table. His worst shock from the Emperor followed his relief at Tascher's news by a mere twenty-four hours. The Emperor must have sent it off directly the young man was gone.

"My son,

"The Vicereine should go to Paris without delay for her confinement. I intend that in no circumstances should she stay in enemy-occupied country; see therefore that she goes forthwith."[18]

VII

The news that the Vicereine, with all her children, was coming to have her fifth child at her husband's headquarters in Mantua caused a sensation in that picturesque city. Many had heard that the heroic decision had been hers alone. She was greeted with sonnets. There had been weepings and wailings when her cortège left Milan, where she had been well loved, but there had been a malicious rumour that she was going back to her father and that Prince Eugène was being kept in a fortress by Marshal Bellegarde. Of course the two Bavarian officers, passed through the Austrian lines under safe-conduct to the Viceroy, had been magnified by gossip to dozens. There had also been an aide de camp from the Emperor Francis in Vienna. General Count Neipperg had lost an eye in action, but was very handsome. He had brought a most courtly letter offering the Vicereine perfect security at her favourite palace of Monza and an Austrian body-guard. She had written her last angry letter to the Emperor Napoleon. It was sad that it was in fact to be her last letter to him. She had said that she would obey him so far as Monza was concerned, but that she was not coming to die in child-bed in France. She would seek shelter with her husband, on whose name no stain had ever rested, and if necessary they would perish together. In spite of the way the Emperor had behaved to them, she would continue to pray for him and his wife.

Eugène and she had both leapt to the conclusion that the peremptory summons meant that she and the children were to be handed over as hostages for his good faith. He had found it afflicting, as he stiffly told the Emperor, to be addressed in such a manner. He had said he would pass on the order and, if his wife's health allowed, she would obey. But he repeated, they had not merited such treatment.

He was immensely touched by her suggestion that she should come to him. At first it had made him only smile tenderly. If he had to evacuate Italy would she be able to travel to a quiet place in France—Valence or Aix? Would there be time? But after sleeping on the problem, he had seen everything in favour of Mantua. The palace was large enough to contain a full suite of visitors, and at least some of its extraordinary conglomeration of state apartments, modernized for the Emperor, were in good order. The bed of an Austrian Empress—Maria Theresa—awaited her. To have his children pattering about the painted galleries and large and little "rich rooms" of this dark and slightly sinister old residence of the Gonzagas would be delightful.

He began at once to make arrangements for her to get on the road. If she and the children left at a comfortable hour on Sunday morning March 27, having sent on ahead on Saturday a first relay of staff, they should arrive after midday on Tuesday afternoon.[19] The dreaded journey was safely accomplished and the Viceroy and Vicereine settled down to one of the strangest months in their Italian story. They had almost ceased to get news from France and were dependent on the Frankfort and Geneva papers.

On the very day that Auguste arrived, another cortège had to be met and forwarded through Murat's outposts. The Pope was travelling back to Rome after almost exactly two years' confinement in a suite of regal magnificence at Fontainebleau. The weather in Lombardy had been tempestuous. The bridge at Vicenza had been swept away and side roads were impassable. Nevertheless Bellegarde, who had made a reconnaissance all along the Mincio line on March 10, had been pushed back again, and seemed quiescent. The Viceroy had ridden out in a downpour to support old Grenier, who was holding the right bank of the Po brilliantly against Nugent. So much rain followed by hot sun was bringing out the flowers. The Viceroy checked his horse on the banks of the Mincio. As early as March 6, he had found "Would you believe it! Violets! I send them to you. They remind me of our happy hours when we gathered them together. Patience! they will soon return."[20]

On March 14 Lord William Bentinck, who had been instructed to take Genoa, had issued a proclamation calling upon all Italians to rise in defence of their liberties. This was the last thing the Allies desired and was to have terrible repercussions in Milan. The King of Naples had, as Eugène described it "at last raised the mask," and attacked Italian troops at Reggio.

The Emperor had replied to both the Viceroy and Vicereine separately very shortly, from Soissons on March 12. He told Auguste that knowing her temperament he was not surprised at her letter. He had been trying to help her. "I did not send my orders to you sooner, because Paris was then threatened, and I could not see that anything was to be gained by putting you in the midst of the alarms and excursions of Paris, rather than those of Milan. Recognize your injustice. I trust to your heart to rebuke you."

To Eugène he said that the Vicereine had sent him an extravaganza and they both seemed to have lost their heads. He could hardly credit that Eugène had been mad enough to scent a political issue in the order. He had always written in that style to him. Eugène's reply to the King of Bavaria had earned him the esteem of Europe. "I pay you no compliments because you only did your duty, and that in a simple matter." He said he would send further instructions in cypher. They were dated the same day. They were mostly about the King of Naples being mad. After that no more came from the Emperor.[21]

On April 8 Eugène sent off his Italian aide de camp General Gifflinga to report that the Mincio line was still being held, and to ask for orders. To this letter he never got any reply. Three days earlier he had despatched d'Anthouard to General Marchand at Grenoble. The General had written that Lyons had fallen and he had lost touch with Marshal Augereau. The Viceroy urged him to hold on; but a cryptic message from Melzi from Milan had told him that the sky was very dark and the public was alarmed.

The same bookish young French officer who had been struck by the beauty of Lake Garda at war, had time to appreciate headquarters at Mantua. Although Volta had limited resources, he was able to take long and agreeable walks in the neighbourhood. He admired the two palaces. That called 'Te' because it was built in the shape of the letter T had famous murals painted by a pupil of Raphael. Like every tourist he was struck by the Sala dei Giganti in which Titans were depicted rolling in hideous agony. There was a charming Camera dei Cavalli with portraits of the favourite horses of Duke Frederick Gonzaga, life-size and so life-like they seemed to be absolutely stepping out of the walls. He admired the Ducal residence in Mantua, with its mediaeval red-brick battlemented walls, and tilting yard, and the much older fortress of San Giorgio where Hofer had lain in chains in a dungeon. There was a horrible relic on a tower on the Piazza Sordello almost in view of the Viceroy's windows—the iron cage in which condemned prisoners were exposed. He took his Virgil with him on his outings, and grew sentimental in the spring sunsets, dreaming of the peace for which all Europe was waiting.[22]

The Vicereine gave birth to her fifth child in the Ducal Palace at Mantua on Wednesday, April 13, 1814. The father only just got in in time. He had been out until late on the night before on a reconnaissance at Governolo. The mother had been so constantly ailing and anxious during this pregnancy that the arrival of yet another beautiful and perfectly formed daughter was not allowed to be a disappointment. They had settled to call her Theodolinde after the Wittelsbach queen of Lombardy, whose life-size effigy on the façade, and many portraits in the mural paintings inside, decorated the Cathedral of Monza, their favourite home. Auguste's brother was so much taken with the idea of reviving the memory of this ancestress that he, too, called a child after her next year. While the Vicereine lay in child-bed, salvos from the enemy lines sounded repeatedly. They were to celebrate the entry of the Allies into Paris. General Count Neipperg had sent a message to General Vignolles. The Viennese Count, the ideal diplomatist, came personally to the palace on the Saturday, accompanied by General Count Ludwig Wartenburg Roth, aide de camp to the King of Bavaria. They came to discuss terms for a Convention and brought a letter from King Max to the Viceroy.

"Munich, April 11.

"My well-beloved son,

"Up to now I have not been able, my dear friend, to do anything but admire your loyal conduct. Now I can say more. It made me proud to have such a son.

"Now, all is altered as you will see from the accompanying newspapers. You can leave your party without dishonour.

"A courier who arrived to me tonight brought me the news that Marmont had joined us with six thousand infantry, two thousand horses, all veteran troops, and fifty pieces of artillery. The Marshals have obliged the Emperor, who is at Fontainebleau, to abdicate, telling him that the army will no longer obey him. It is declared that, on conditions, the Empress may be Regent for the King of Rome. Ney, Macdonald and Caulaincourt have come to Paris with this proposition in the name of the army. All waits upon the arrival of the Emperor of Austria for an answer. It will be I believe negative, seeing that he has already pronounced for the Bourbons.

"The Allies wish you well, my dear Eugène, profit by their good intentions and remember your family. A further holding-out would be unpardonable.

"Farewell, my dear boy, I embrace you, Auguste and your children. The queen does the same. Your good father,

"Max Joseph.

"Postscript. The Empress Josephine left on the 29th for Navarre."

A letter from the Empress Josephine was dated two days before King Max's from Munich.

"What a week I have had, my dear Eugène! How I have suffered at the way in which they have treated the Emperor. What attacks in the newspapers. What ingratitude from those upon whom he had showered favours! But there is nothing more to hope for. All is finished: he is abdicating.

"As for you, now you are free and absolved from any oath of fidelity. To try to do anything more for his cause would be useless. Act for your family."

Now that the end had come, it was remarkable how swiftly events moved. Eugène signed a convention of seventeen articles the same day. The French troops were to leave Italy under the command of Grenier, and go home, if possible, by the Mont Cenis. He endured heart-rending scenes of farewell and speech-making. It was pointed out by some critics that he said that henceforward his lot would be cast elsewhere. He simply meant that he believed his mandate as Viceroy still bound him to Italy. He had not yet seen the terms of the Treaty of Fontainebleau in which the Emperor Napoleon had renounced the Kingdom of Italy for himself and for his heirs.

But having refused that crown twice when offered by the Allies, the ex-Viceroy now had some reason to hope that he might be chosen ruler by general acclamation, in Milan. Melzi had written to him on the 15th suggesting the necessary machinery for pronouncing the Kingdom of Italy independent. Unfortunately Melzi's gout was so incapacitating that when the appointed day, April 20, came he was not present to engineer proceedings. What did happen was so horrible that tears poured down Eugène's face as Darnay recounted it.

Prina, Minister of Finance, a thoroughly reliable and honourable character, to whom it had fallen to make the suggestion, had been literally torn in pieces in Milan. There had been uproar in the Senate chamber. The portrait of the Emperor Napoleon by Appiani had been torn down, slashed and cast out of the window

Five of the children of Eugène de Beauharnais
The children, in order of age, are Josephine, Eugénie,
Augustus-Charles, Amélie and Theodolinde. The two
youngest children, Caroline and Max-Joseph, were not
yet born. A version of this picture hung in Eugène's
bedroom in his Munich palace. Water-colour by Lieder,
1815.

By permission of the Napoleon Museum, Arenenberg
Photograph: Willi Müller, Gottlieb T.G.

by Count Federico Gonfalonieri, always a crony of General Pino, deadliest enemy of Prina. Pino had been allowed to retire from the Mincio line by Eugène, before a thoroughly incompetent and dissatisfied general made more trouble. The young aristo-cratic revolutionaries of Italy wanted neither a Bonapartist nor a Habsburg nominee; they wanted what Melzi had always wanted, an independent kingdom. Austrian agents also did not want the Beauharnais. There were cries for Melzi, but in the end those for Prina were loudest, and a bloodthirsty gang, who had been waiting outside, pursued the unhappy minister from his house to a tradesman's booth on the Contrada del Marino where he had taken refuge. He had been beaten to death by umbrellas, a rope had been attached to his legs and the corpse had been dragged through the mirey cobbled streets by torchlight. Darnay had been an eye-witness, and also the Viceroy's war-artist. The faithful secretary had managed before he fled from the capital to collect all for which he had been sent—private valuables and cor-respondence.[23]

Eugène de Beauharnais learned on the same day that he was no longer Viceroy, and not the heir of the Emperor, according to the Treaty of Fontainebleau. There was nothing to keep him in a country where his presence might only increase scenes of disorder. He had to make another farewell speech:—

"Now I address you, heroic Army of Italy! Warriors, whose faces, whose sacrifices and whose deeds I shall carry to my grave inscribed on the tablets of my memory—whose wounds I have seen with my own eyes, and for whose heroism I have been able to obtain fitting rewards ... It is possible that never again will you see me, fighting at your head, and in your ranks, that I shall never again hear your acclamations ringing in my ears! But if your country should call you back to the colours, I have no doubt that in the thick of danger you will rejoice when you recall the name of Eugène."

Darnay was indignant when a rumour spread that Prince Eugène had escaped to Bavaria in an Austrian uniform because he had dreaded falling a victim to the Tyrolese, who looked upon him as the murderer of Hofer. The departure of the Viceroy and Vicereine and their family, wrote Darnay, had been perfectly organized. Marshal Bellegarde had offered an Austrian officer and twelve soldiers to accompany the cavalcade, more to honour than to protect it. As the princess was only nine days out of child-bed, they travelled by easy stages—the first night at Villafranca, the next at Verona, etc. Darnay went in the carriage with the children, and heroically declared that he found much to surprise and interest him on a very happy journey. They arrived in Munich on May 4 and Prince Eugène set off the same night for Paris. A letter from the Empress Josephine had been awaiting him. She was ill and begged him to hasten.

CHAPTER SIXTEEN

"*Cutting up the Cake*"
1814 : 1815

I

THE *Moniteur* under the new régime had changed sides but not policy. On the morning of May 31, 1814 it excelled itself.

"The death of Madame de Beauharnais excites widespread sympathy. This woman was unfailingly gentle and possessed much charm and attractiveness in manner and in mind. Extremely unhappy during her husband's reign, she sought refuge from his roughness and neglect in the study of Botany. The public is aware of the way in which she strove to rescue Bonaparte's victims, and is grateful to her for having thrown herself at his feet to beg for the life of the Duc d'Enghien."

It was useless for the *Moniteur* to pretend that the Empire had not existed. A weary looking middle-aged gentleman with long features and high cheek bones, found himself stopped in the Rue du Faubourg St. Honoré by a man of the people weeping audibly. "Oh! monsieur! Have you heard the sad news? We have lost the good Empress!" The stranger to Paris was the Emperor of Austria father of Marie Louise. He was shocked. There had been luncheon parties at Malmaison only last week. Josephine, who had been a famous hostess, held her largest receptions on the three days following her death. Malmaison was nineteen miles outside the capital, but twenty thousand people filed past her bier while she lay in state in her strange striped tent-like bedroom designed for the wife of a military hero. Her ladies in waiting noticed with awe that she seemed to be still smiling her little characteristic tight-lipped smile.

For the first twenty-four hours her staff only were admitted to behold her, lying in her bed, as if asleep. Many kissed her hand; all wept. Then the undertakers came in, and the room was draped with black and the coffin was surrounded by hundreds of steadily-burning candles. The weather was perfect, and outside her gardens and her park were in their highest beauty.

Her end had been rather sudden. When her son had arrived on May 9 he had written to Munich quite cheerfully that he had found both his mother and sister well. Throughout his stay she had entertained tirelessly, mostly people who might be of use to him in pushing his claims, though she was always glad to see anyone who had loved the Emperor. (Madame Walewska was welcomed.) Prince Eugène was sent off at once to the Tuileries to pay his respects. His Italian aide de camp, General Gifflinga, had produced a dramatic effect by arriving from Mantua after the abdication, with a letter from the Viceroy still asking for orders from the Emperor. When Gifflinga applied for an audience on behalf of his master with Louis XVIII, it was at once granted. It was a little awkward to know how the ex-Viceroy should be addressed. There was a new Minister of War who had no doubt. To General Dupont he was simply "Royal Highness." To the Czar he was always still "Imperial." Hortense read with fury that his aide de camp had announced him as "*le Marquis de Beauharnais.*" Anyway, she pointed out, visitors are not announced to royal personages, and Gifflinga himself had told her he had never known Eugène had succeeded to that title. The popular story went that Louis XVIII had leapt from his seat and come forward with outstretched hands crying, "Say the Prince Eugène, monsieur, and add Grand Constable of France if that is your good pleasure!" Eugène in his first letter home said that he had been perfectly well received, and later, "I do hope that you didn't think that the announcement in the papers that I had become a Marshal of France was true. It was false, of course. I would have told you first! It is not true."

The king had asked for news of the Princess Auguste with great benevolence. He was a very bad fifty-eight, a childless widower, enormously stout, gouty, and not quite scrupulous, but decidedly clever and could assume an easy grand manner. For upwards of twenty-three years he and his quarrelsome court had been passed like a marked card from Belgium to Germany, to Courland, to Poland, and finally for six seasons to Buckinghamshire. Now he had come home and could afford to make himself a little pleasant. With him were his brother "Monsieur," the Comte d'Artois, heir-presumptive, who recalled his friendship with Prince Eugène's father, and the two sons of "Monsieur," the Duc d'Angoulême, who paid little attention to the visitor, and the Duc de Berri, who told him that French troops were very fine-looking and asked him if he had seen any. Somebody tactful hastened to tell the startled ex-Viceroy that the Duc de Berri was his ardent admirer and had followed all his campaigns with admiration.[1] In the afternoon Eugène saw the King's cousin the Duke of Orleans. He came back to Malmaison saying he was well satisfied with his reception. He hoped he might not have to go to the Tuileries again, but it had not been quite as bad as he had been led to expect.

There had been stories of decorators' assistants at work all night tearing down Imperial eagles and sticking fleur de lys over the bees of Bonaparte. He had seen plenty of Imperial symbols about still, and familiar state rooms in all their old glory, and above all Paris, his birthplace, on a May day with spring sunshine theatrically lighting her noble façades of dry tertiary limestone quarried on the Left Bank, all pearl grey and snow white under lavender skies.

One famous landmark had gone. The first attempt by a mob of Bourbon agitators to pull down the Emperor's statue from the top of the triumphal column in the Place Vendôme had been unsuccessful. It had taken skilled artisans many hours. A battalion of Semenov's regiment had cleared the square and bivouacked there. Everyone had been terrified of the Cossacks coming to burn down Paris in revenge for Moscow, but they had now been adopted as natural curiosities. If they wanted to fetch a samovar from the other side of a tree in the Bois, they got on their horses to do it.

The Emperor had said good-bye to his Guard in the Cheval Blanc courtyard at Fontainebleau, before getting into his carriage on the morning of April 27 for his journey to St. Tropez. He had landed safely in Porto Ferrajo, in Elba, days before his stepson had arrived in Paris.

On his second day in Paris Prince Eugène sought out in their various palaces, the Emperor of Austria, the Czar and the other royal allies. (The King of Prussia had got Prince Eugène's palace.) He dined with his wife's elder brother, and found he had just missed her younger, who must have crossed him on the Munich road. He told her that when he had paid all his calls he thought he should be able to judge better how their affairs stood. He had found out already that there was nothing to be got on the Rhine. Genoa was a possibility, also Berg. "They wanted to give us

Genoa in order to avoid giving us anything on the Rhine. If anyone mentions Frankfort or Mainz it is needed on that side of the river, if Berg or Cologne it is claimed on the other." He enclosed a very satisfactory letter from the Czar.

As the days passed he learned a good many sad details of the abdication. He saw Caulaincourt who had to present him with a parting gift from the Emperor—his best dressing-case. Caulaincourt had spent the night of April 12-13 at Fontainebleau in close attendance on the Emperor. His Majesty had spoken much in praise of the Viceroy as a prince who had served him faithfully to the last. "Eugène is the only one of my family who never has given me a single cause for dissatisfaction. His mother made me very happy; these are the sweetest recollections of my life." The Emperor had spoken these valedictory-sounding words at two a.m. because he had by then taken poison. There had been an attempt at suicide, unsuccessful because the lethal dose given to him by his doctor, Yvan, at his request in Russia was eighteen months old.[2] Bertrand had been on duty as Grand Marshal of the palace, and Comte Turenne, chief surgeon, the *valets* Constant and Roustam, and Yvan, of course. But the doctor had taken fright and seized the nearest horse for a dawn escape. There had been no other eye-witnesses, and although there had been rumours which had reached Grosbois and Malmaison, nobody had talked . . .

Next morning the Emperor had put his signature to the ratification of the Treaty of Fontainebleau, his unconditional abdication. The suite to accompany him into exile had been very small. He had been disappointed that Berthier, the Mameluke Roustam and Constant had all failed him. Those three figures had been part of the picture of the Emperor known to the man in the street.

Caulaincourt had said good-bye to the Empress Marie Louise on April 23 at Berthier's château, Grosbois, where she had been staying. "Her situation was all the more painful because she retained little hope of rejoining the Emperor." (Hortense had said that the Empress had told her she dreaded the arrival of her father, the Emperor, in Paris lest he should say she ought to go to Elba.) She had told Caulaincourt that she hoped soon to be in her own Duchy of Parma "and that from thence she would be able to convey to her husband the consolation which, as she knew, he so badly needed."[3]

The provision assured to the Emperor's family by the Treaty of Fontainebleau looked handsome on paper.

To Madame Mère 300,000 francs
To King Joseph 300,000 francs
To King Louis 200,000 francs
To Queen Hortense and her children 400,000 francs
To King Jerome and his queen 500,000 francs
To Princess Elisa 300,000 francs
To Princess Pauline 300,000 francs.
   There shall be set aside for Prince Eugène, Viceroy of Italy, a suitable domain outside France.

Caulaincourt said that he and Macdonald had seen the Czar who assured him "that Prince Eugène's future had been settled and guaranteed in a splendid and fitting manner by arrangements already made with the King of Bavaria." They had insisted that they must have something more exact, upon which the Czar had said "he would second them with his whole weight should there ever be occasion." Josephine was sure that the Czar was the man upon whom they must depend, when it came to what Eugène called "cutting up the cake."

Talleyrand was not amongst the figures invited to Malmaison. Madame de Rémusat had brought a letter, drafted by Talleyrand and herself, for Josephine to send to the Tuileries. Hortense had seen to it that the very notion was repelled with hauteur. The mistake was to prove costly. Talleyrand had been well-disposed towards her. There could be little doubt that he knew, with most of Paris now, of her liaison with Flahaut. Savary had known. When the Emperor had suggested, on the death of Duroc, that Flahaut should succeed him as Grand Marshal, Savary had raised his brows and murmured, "The Queen of Holland?" General Bertrand had got that appointment.

The Czar agreed with the ladies of Malmaison that it would be most unseemly for them to approach the Bourbons. The Czar had been much struck by the story of Hortense. The thought of another being who attracted misfortune on the grand scale made him feel they might be twin souls. Alexander I was now thirty-six and not as slight as he had been at Tilsit. His slightly washy pale blue eyes beamed with mystic fervour. His guinea-gold curls were thinning on his brow; he tended to stoop. But he was still a very handsome, very tall man, and his prestige in Paris was enormous.

He was so grand, he said what he liked. He paid calls quite informally, and gave an appearance of intimacy to every interview, as owing to his deafness he had to sit rather close and incline towards his companion.

He told the widowed Madame Junot that Savary had been responsible for the murder of the Duc d'Enghien, and that bad advice given recently by this character had been largely responsible for the fall of the Emperor Napoleon ("How I loved that man!"). He came, or wrote, to Malmaison every day and said he had never really wanted the Bourbons. Why had not Prince Eugène been chosen? He asked Hortense about her mother's divorce and her own unhappy marriage, and told her that Louis XVIII had showed him the proclamation he intended to issue on his accession. It was dated, "In the nineteenth year of Our Reign". He had tried in vain to get that changed.

Hortense's younger son was now a very bright, blue-eyed child of six, with a great idea of occasion. He presented the Czar with his greatest treasure, a little ring given him by his Uncle Eugène. The Czar put it on his watch-chain and said he would keep it for ever. Hortense and Eugène took the Czar to see the famous waterworks at Marly. "En route we discussed friendship in general, and that between Eugène and me. The Czar said the same sort of thing existed in his family. He turned to Eugène and said 'I can't believe I have known your sister such a short time. She seems to me to be someone I have found again.' " He wanted to see Hortense's Paris home, so she asked him there, and then he wanted to see her country house, the château of St. Leu. There was a probability that she was to be allowed the title of Duchess of St. Leu and to keep such of the property as had not belonged to the Duc de Condé, who had now returned to claim it. She arranged a party. Looking back, Eugène decided that his mother's last illness began on May 20, but her closest attendants said she had been secretly ailing for some time and that on the day of the Czar's visit, May 14, she had caught a chill.

The Czar drove up before noon in a small barouche, accompanied only by his aide de camp General Prince Ivanovitch Tschernitscheff. Hortense had asked also the wife of Marshal Ney, and Caulaincourt. She, with her mother and brother had arrived the night before. During luncheon the Czar said, did they realize he had played truant from the solemn service being celebrated in Paris that day in honour of the murdered Louis XVI

and Queen Marie Antoinette? All the other monarchs had gone!
He said that on their drive here he had drawn Tschernitscheff's
attention to the curious fact that he had come to Paris filled with
animosity for the Emperor's family, and then he had found that
the only homes in which he had enjoyed himself were theirs.

A char-à-banc came round. This vehicle, which would take
ten people, had been imported by Hortense from Switzerland.
They all embarked for a beautiful drive in the forest of Mont-
morency, and she pointed out the rides she had cleared, and all
her improvements. The Emperor said, "None of this still belongs
to you." and looked guilty. She bravely replied, "I shall always be
able to enjoy it." The legal document ensuring her an income and
a title based on the estate had been sent back by her in dudgeon.
In it she had been styled "Mademoiselle de Beauharnais."

It was a curious day, cold and damp. When they returned,
Josephine flung herself on her bed in all her clothes. Her devoted
Mlle. Avrillon tried to persuade her not to go down to dine with
the company. She said she must, and made the effort, but she
ate nothing. She returned to her room rather early but she had
achieved her object while music was being played—a tête-à-tête
with the Czar on the subject of Eugène's future.

The Czar walked in the park quite late and Hortense told him
of her sorrows. Her young ladies played games under the trees.
Another unmerited grief had descended upon her last summer.
When she had gone to take the waters at Aix she had made a
little expedition one day to see a picturesque waterfall. Her lady
in waiting, Adèle de Broc, widow of the late General, had placed
her little foot on a plank which had turned beneath it on the hillside. In a moment she had disappeared into the cascade. Her
lifeless body had been recovered, and Hortense had brought it to
St. Leu for burial. Adèle, a niece of Madame Campan and sister
of Madame Ney, had been her oldest friend. The Czar said that
he always found prayer a great consolation. He had always
brought all his troubles to God. He spoke of his little daughter
who had died, and showed her the miniature of the woman he
had loved for eighteen years. He spoke of his wife. "Although any
reunion is impossible between us, she has no better friend than
I."[4]

The Czar left about nine and next day the family party returned to Malmaison. During the next week they all seemed to
have caught cold but the entertainment of famous figures con-

tinued. Crown Prince Ludwig came to dine. The King of Prussia came for the day, bringing his two sons. Prince Eugène took charge of the boys. They turned out to be just about the same ages as the Czar's two youngest brothers, but very small compared with them. The Grand Dukes Nicholas and Michael, who were sent with their tutor, were like the Czar remarkable for their inches. They were eighteen and sixteen. Eugène, feeling iller and iller, had business interviews with Baron Wrede and Count Metternich.

Montgelas had written that all that had arrived from Italy as yet to the Munich customs was four chests of books and linen for the Princess Auguste. Scandalous rumours had said that the Viceroy and Vicereine had got away with sixteen millions in ready money, in wagons escorted by eighteen Italian dragoons.

Josephine had not been well enough to show her royal guests her property, but she had appeared at table, and lain on a sofa while her son and daughter did the honours. She said she had a very sore throat but would not hear of calling in specialists who might hurt the feelings of her good Dr. Horeu, and Hortense's Messieurs Bourdois and Laserre. As these gentlemen all agreed she had nothing worse than a catarrh, her son and daughter went separately for the day to Paris. Eugène dined with his wife's brother, who like the Czar and most of the rest of the foreign royalties, was soon going on to England. He told Auguste that he really thought he had all their affairs in good train and hoped to leave for home as soon as the allied potentates left for London.

By May 25 he was not so cheerful. His mother, Hortense and he were now all feverish, and a new bogey had stepped upon the diplomatic scene. Even the optimistic Czar thought their arrangements for cutting up the cake could not be concluded until after the Congress, now beginning to be talked about for September in Vienna. After this the situation at Malmaison deteriorated rapidly. On May 27 the Czar's personal physician suddenly appeared. Josephine, although perfectly exhausted, managed to tell him how much she thanked his master. "I trust his sympathy will bring me good luck."

May 28 was a complete nightmare. The Czar was expected to dine, and Josephine had settled every detail of the entertainment, and expected to get up, as her doctors had repeated last night that her illness was only a cold. One of the sad things about her since the divorce was that since she no longer had to keep up to the pace set by the Emperor she had become very stout. She followed a rigorous diet and her doctor did not encourage her to lie in bed, which always made her melancholy. But when that Saturday morning came, they had to decide to put off the Czar. Nobody was fit to leave their room. Hortense had just settled this when the Czar arrived, much earlier than expected. She took him to the bedroom of Eugène, who was in a high fever, and returned to tell her mother that the guest had asked to be excused and would come another day. Unluckily this worried Josephine. She whispered hoarsely, "I am sure the reason he did not come is because he felt embarrassed at having nothing to report about Eugène's affairs . . . Hortense, you must speak to the Czar. He is our best hope. Are we going to let him leave for England, and nothing done?"

The Czar stayed by Eugène's bedside until dinner time when Hortense left her mother to take the meal with him. Directly after it she returned to her mother, and he to Eugène. The Czar had dined at the Tuileries on Monday, and had been much entertained by the length of the meal and how much all the good things had been appreciated by the Bourbons. "What a change . . .! A great man lived there not so very long ago . . ."

Hortense re-appeared repeatedly. By now she and her brother were in high alarm and had sent to Paris for further opinions. It was Saturday and traffic was pouring out of the capital into the country. At last the guest left and the specialists arrived. They would only say that the family must prepare for "a long illness". Josephine had refused to say goodnight to Hortense's children. She could scarcely speak now, but had got out something about "Air is not good in here. It might harm them." These were really her last rational words. As Hortense had been up all day, Dr. Horeau and a maid went on duty for the remaining hours of the night. Hortense came in several times and Eugène was at the bedside early. The maid said the Empress was quiet. She had uttered some unconnected words "Bonaparte . . . Isle of Elba . . . King of Rome." But when she saw both of her children who had been to early Mass together, she stretched out her arms and tried in vain to tell them something. Hortense fainted and had to be carried out of the room.

Eugène now saw that the time had come when he must take command. He feared there might not be time for the priest to be fetched from the village church. He arranged that Hortense's

Abbé Bertrand, her children's tutor, should administer the sacrament. It was Sunday morning, the Feast of Pentecost. His mother died in his arms about midday, that is to say he was kneeling by her bed with his left arm under her pillow and her right hand in his. He told Méjean to write to Munich to ask Baroness Wurmb to break the news gently to the Princess Auguste. At two o'clock the carriage he had ordered came round and he took his sister away to St. Leu.[5]

II

Even for a devoted French son, Eugène de Beauharnais mourned profoundly. Eight days after his mother's death, he assured his wife that not a day had passed without his finding tears streaming down his countenance, provoked by some memory or fresh instance of her loving-kindness. He said she had not left an enemy in the world, and that she had loved Auguste as if she had been her own daughter. He was very pleased to hear that the village church at Rueil had been packed tight for the funeral on Thursday, June 2, and that crowds who could not enter had covered the whole route from the château. This had also been lined by local National Guards. The military honours had been furnished by a detachment of Russian Imperial Guards. The Czar had offered to attend, but it had been explained to him that Imperial etiquette in France required that the nearest relatives of the deceased did not make an appearance. They were theoretically too grief-stricken. In the present case it happened to be true. Both Hortense and Eugène were still very unwell. Hortense's two little boys were the chief mourners, well supported by many more of Josephine's own kith and kin—Comte Louis Tascher, the Duchesse d'Arenberg (Stéphanie Tascher), the Marquis and Comte de la Ferté Beauharnais and the Comte and Comtesse de Lavalette (Émilie Beauharnais). Karl of Baden attended in person, as the husband of Stéphanie Beauharnais. The Czar sent Field-Marshal Sacken, and most of the visiting potentates were represented by aides de camp. The Archbishop of Tours expanded in his oration on the charity and mercy outstanding in the character of Josephine, and particularly her intercession for émigrés. Many present agreed that with her usual perfect grace she had chosen just the right moment for her swift retirement from a troubled scene. It was tearfully accepted that she had died of a broken heart, and there were pathetic anecdotes of her sitting for hours at an upper window of Malmaison, watching for a flash of the hunt as the Emperor passed by on one of his Marly or St. Cloud days. Her son and daughter arranged for masses for her soul and planned a monument to be erected above her grave on the right hand of the choir at Rueil. The inscription was to be simply "To Josephine; Hortense and Eugène," and the design eventually accepted was a life-size kneeling figure of the Empress, much resembling that in David's famous picture of her receiving her crown from the hands of her Emperor in Notre Dame.[6]

The Treaty of Fontainebleau had promised Eugène a domain outside France. He had now inherited two estates in France—the Duchy of Navarre and the Château of Malmaison. His days of convalescence were painfully spent with officials of his mother's and Hortense's households trying to sort out the Malmaison estate. Soon he had to ask his wife to send him an expert from Munich, M. Hennin who had served them in Italy, to confer with Josephine's staff. Auguste also sent him Baron Bataille, a rock of strength. It was useless to deny that the beloved *maman*, who had lived in debt, had left debts—"They exceed considerably two million francs. It is truly afflicting . . . But set your mind at rest, I can meet them all, and will not leave Paris without having paid or at least assured the payment of the whole." It was unfortunate that his other best man of business, the Comte de Ré, had gone down to Italy to confer about the property left there. They had to apply to Hortense's husband, the last person they wished to disturb, to get his signature to one document. Bataille told him that Auguste would like to come to Paris, if she would be welcome. There was no doubt of that, but her husband would be grateful if she would give up the idea. There would be difficulties of precedence. She could not come without having been presented to the new rulers and she would be in deepest mourning. He sent back by Bataille, Paris mourning costumes for all the children. His household at Munich must all, male and female, indoor and outdoor, have new black liveries. (Triaire would order them.) For Auguste herself, the etiquette would be six weeks in very deep mourning (black wool); six weeks in deep mourning (crepes and silks permitted), and three months half-mourning. He sent also six Paris embroidered dresses for Auguste's little half-sisters—not mourning, lovely. Mourning jewellery for his wife was sent by both him and Hortense—diamonds in black and white enamel, and of course pearls. Hortense's *parure* was gothic in design and had the name of Josephine on it.

The house at Malmaison had been left to him; the contents were to be divided between him and his sister. Hortense was never mean, and one of the alleviating features of the first sad days was that brother and sister pressed one another to take outstanding treasures of Josephine's collection. The lawyers told them that their mother's wardrobe was very valuable and they would get a good price for many objects, such as the cashmere and lace shawls, at a public auction. But they could not bear to consider such an idea, and after enormous trouble sorted out all for bestowal upon her many attendants and pensioners. Inevitably, not all were satisfied with their shares.

The results of the inventory in the end were cheering. It represented eighty-nine days work. It included sculpture, ancient and modern, bronzes, paintings, drawings and engravings, furniture, books, linen and plate, musical instruments, exotic plants and jewellery. It totalled eleven million francs; so when the debts had been settled there would still be over eight million to be divided between the son and daughter. Moreover, on his last call before embarking for England, the Czar had quietly left behind the documents creating the Duchy of St. Leu, so Hortense's future was assured. She heard later that Louis XVIII had stuck out to the last against signing the patent, as it referred to her as Queen, and that the Czar had been obliged to say that Russian troops would stay in Paris unless the letters had been sent after him, signed, to Malmaison. He had stayed there just before his departure and had presented himself attired in mourning. This, Hortense felt was typical of his almost feminine delicacy and tact. He had left saying he would meet Eugène at Vienna for the Congress. It was sad that her chief reason for wishing to settle near Malmaison had been removed by death, and her spirits sank as the day approached for her brother to return to Germany. But they had received so much sympathy that the government was said to be uneasy. Some workmen from the suburbs making a demonstration outside the Tuileries had been heard to mention the name of Prince Eugène.

"My brother, alarmed at my condition, had looked after me with a tenderness to which I was not accustomed. For the first time in my life I had found in the hour of trial a loving hand to ease me of my burdens. I appreciated this immeasurably, and my

Hortense Beauharnais, Queen of Holland, Duchess of Saint-Leu
by François, Baron Gérard

broken heart thanked Providence for not having left me without such a comforter. Sorrow shared is softened, and becomes bearable."

Amongst the business troubles which afflicted Eugène during his last stay at Malmaison was one connected with Lavalette. This stalwart Bonapartist and companion of his earliest campaigns, who had married his cousin Émilie de Beauharnais, had come to him in deepest secrecy with a tale so extraordinary it seemed drawn from the wildest pages of fiction. Lavalette had filled the office of Postmaster General with credit for many years. Before the Emperor had left for the fatal Russian campaign he had told him to go to the Grand Marshal (Duroc) and get Treasury drafts for 1,600,000 francs. The Minister of the Treasury would convert them into gold. Alarmed by being left in charge of so bulky a treasure, Lavalette had got the ingenious M. Regnier, Keeper of the Ordnance Department, to make him fifty-four strong-boxes which looked exactly like quarto volumes. Each took thirty thousand francs and they had on their spines the repellent title *Ancient and Modern History*. Lavalette had asked the Emperor for further instructions on his return from Russia, but he was now setting off for Leipzig. "We will speak of it when I get home." Before he left Paris for the third time, for the campaign in France itself, he had said, "Oh well then, hide it at your own country house." Lavalette had pointed out that La Verrière was a most unsuitable place in which to hide something so valuable. It was on the main road from Versailles to Rambouillet. But the Emperor had been adamant. Lavalette's steward, who was a resourceful person, had made, under his surveillance during the hours of darkness at La Verrière, under the inlaid floor of a closet, a cave large enough to swallow the seeming books. They were there still although three hundred Prussian troops of the army of occupation had been billeted at the château, and fifteen had slept in the very room in which the treasure was hidden. The guests had now marched off. Lavalette had the dreadful persuasiveness of the entirely uncomplicated character. He said he knew Eugène was, like himself, devoted to the Emperor, and he was about to return to Germany. He asked him, as a very old friend, to take charge of half of the treasure and send it to Elba. Before the Emperor had left he had told Marie Louise to send her letters to Prince Eugène. "Trust all to him." It was useless for Eugène to point out that now he had just as little chance as Lavalette of getting in touch with Elba. Eugène, said Lavalette, was not being haunted by the Paris police.[7]

III

Baden-Baden was so called to distinguish it from Baden in Switzerland and Baden just outside Vienna, to the south. It was one of the most fashionable health resorts in Germany, so Hortense was at first dubious when she got an invitation from her brother to meet him and his wife there. They had planned to take a holiday together at Aix but then they had been warned that Marie Louise was expected there, and the Secretary to the Russian Embassy advised Hortense against something which would appear suspect in the eyes of the Bourbons. So she had gone to Plombières. As she had just obtained permission to live in France with her sons she was advised by Caulaincourt not to remove them from that country. Anyway, Eugène would not be bringing his children to Baden. His invitation was seconded by a letter from Grand Duchess Stéphanie and the King and Queen of Bavaria. The waters there were said to resemble those of Plombières, which she was finding a very dull place. She sent back her brother's aide de camp with a joyful acceptance and a message that she would start in two or three days.

The procession which drew towards the vaunted holiday resort in the Black Mountains on the evening of August 10 was modest. The Duchess of St. Leu travelled with only two equipages. She had never really replaced Adèle de Broc as a companion. The girl who sat in the *berline* with her now was not a stranger. She had been promoted from the post of reader which she had held for some years. Louise Cochelet had also been a pupil at Madame Campan's school. She was already a little apt to be managing. Perhaps her head had been turned by calls and notes from the Czar, who had used her as a go-between when making arrangements with her employer in Paris. In the second vehicle, a *calèche*, came two maids.

Baden-Baden was set in scenery which was wildly romantic. At the end of a long alley of noble trees running alongside the rushing river Oosbach, the travellers perceived in the sunset light a solitary horseman galloping towards them. It was Prince Eugène. Louise Cochelet watched with edification the two children of Empress Josephine meeting with tears.

During the next fortnight the lady in waiting noted every detail with gratification. She had never found herself on holiday with so many royalties. Two of the queens were actually ex-queens, but that was never allowed to appear. They were still addressed as "Majesty" and got equally deep curtsies. Baden was heavenly. There was an ancient castle mouldering up on the hillside on the right bank of the river, and below it the one still in use by the Grand Duke. He came to Baden for only one day from Karlsruhe. He was very busy in preparation for going to the Congress. Etiquette at the castle was very strict but most of the royalties were not living there, they only went when asked to dine. They lived in charming villas scattered over the wooded hillsides, nearly all on the south east bank of the Schlossberg, grouped around the bath houses. Below the two castles came the old town which was delightfully quaint.

The oldest of the baths dated from Roman days. The Trinkhalle was the most popular rendezvous in the mornings; the Lichtentaler Allee on the left bank of the Oosbach was most frequented in the afternoons. It had enormous old trees surrounded by flower beds and carefully tended shrubberies. The avenue leading down to the bridge was renowned for its *boutiques*. Tradesmen from Strasbourg sent up goods of high quality, not only the *frivolités* in which all holiday-makers rejoice. Prince Eugène bought Queen Hortense a guitar, which she treasured. The best shopper was the dear old King of Bavaria, with his round hat and his cane, sauntering along looking at everything, even the ladies' hats. "Do you like it?" he would cry to his wife or his sister in law; and then to the bowing shopkeeper "We'll have it!"

It was brave of him to be in such spirits, for he was full of anxieties. His eldest daughter, the wife of Prince Eugène, adored her husband; but he had at present no home or occupation. His next daughter, the Princess Charlotte, had recently been removed by him from Stuttgart. Her husband, the Crown Prince of Württemberg, had made his bargain with the Allies in good time, and must succeed before long to the fine patrimony of his enormously stout old father. Unfortunately he refused to live with his wife. He had done so from the day of their wedding (which had been another of those engineered by the Emperor Napoleon). After eight years of martyred silence, the Princess Charlotte, who was very diffident and conscious of her lack of beauty compared to Princess Auguste, had agreed that she would

like to come home, and her father was sending the case down to
the Pope in Rome. It appeared there would not be the slightest
doubt of an annulment being granted.[8] The princess said she
would prefer to live alone in some smaller Bavarian town. She
was the favourite sister of Crown Prince Ludwig and even more
anti-French. She could live with her sister while Prince Eugène
was in Vienna. The King of Bavaria said that the Crown Prince
of Württemberg was a villain. Popular rumour said that he was
not really averse from females. He had two children in Frankfort
by the wife of a civil servant. The whole situation was painful, as
the Bavarian, Russian and Württemberg families must all meet
at the Congress. However, everyone expected wonders to be
worked there. The tragedies of his two daughters did not end the
anxieties of good King Max. His sister's husband, the King of
Saxony, was in a parlous position. He had panicked and returned
to the Emperor Napoleon after the battle of Lützen, and the
Allies had not forgiven him. He had presented himself, a lament-
able figure, bowing and smiling from the balcony of the Hotel de
Prusse, when the Allies had made their triumphal entry into
Dresden, but the Czar had shut him up in the castle of Friedri-
chsfelde, near Berlin, and his kingdom was being administered by
the Russian general Prince Repnin. His future would have to be
decided at the Congress.

The Princess Auguste was the first caller on the ex-Queen of
Holland. She was perfectly beautiful, as everyone had said, and
most sympathetic. She never ceased to explain, "Eugène has
done his duty. His fine reputation is still preferable to all the
thrones to which I might have aspired and I am proud of being
his wife." Louise thought it was quite touching to see the Prince
setting out from his humble domain with his wife on one arm and
his sister on the other. Grand Duchess Stéphanie, who had been
born a Beauharnais, was also prompt to call, and was beautiful
but in a different way, *blonde, petite, spirituelle*. She was a perfect
hostess when they went to the castle, and sang some of Queen
Hortense's songs in a lovely voice. Queen Hortense exchanged
visits with the Czarina, the Queen of Bavaria, the ex-Queen of
Sweden and the old Margravine of Baden who was their mother.
The Czarina was noble-looking and sad. Her complexion was
pallid, perhaps owing to the climate of her husband's country.
She gave a dinner-party, and they all sat down one side of a long
table and the meal started with a cold soup which was not ap-

preciated by the French ladies. The Queen of Sweden was the least distinguished looking of the sisters, but still very handsome and very gentle in manner. The Queen of Bavaria, while being the least handsome, was really the most pleasing. Dinner was announced at the Czarina's party by her Grand Marshal Prince Narischkine, and immediately the King of Bavaria offered one arm to his hostess and the other to his mother in law. The Queens of Bavaria, Sweden and Holland came next. Then came Prince Eugène with Grand-Duchess Sophie, and Princess Auguste with the Hereditary Princess of Hesse-Darmstadt and Princess Amélie of Baden. The rest of the company followed pell mell. A young Swedish prince, and the Russian Ambassador to Baden brought their numbers up to fourteen—nine ladies and five men.

They went for some enjoyable expeditions, mostly to viewpoints or churches and convents, on roads ascending at first between meadows and orchards and then through sweet-smelling forests of conifers. One afternoon they heard a rushing of stones and came upon a carriage-and-four overturned. Louise disentangled, and gave her arm to, the Queen of Sweden who had been out for a pleasure drive with the Czarina. The lady in waiting would have been happy to stay at Baden indefinitely but it was clear that her mistress found the German princesses, although not lacking in affability, somewhat formal and uniform. "When you have once met them you find them exactly the same." To be sure they were kind, flattering her sketches and music. She said that if she had not been in mourning she believed they would have asked her to dance. Their beaming arrivals for the day, with their sewing-bags, slightly depressed her.

Madame de Krüdener could not be accused of formality. She had been married to an elderly Russian Minister to Venice, Copenhagen and Berlin, but had been divorced and had led a very gay life until she had been converted to pietism by her shoemaker. She was now a prophetess, and an arresting figure, very tall and clad in flowing white garments. She was fifty, and as thin as a wraith, and her eyes burned under a wild head of faded ash-blonde hair. Louise, who had met her years before, at once recognized her when she called at their villa, and rose to embrace her, but the visitor waved her off majestically. She said she had come to see "your Queen" to warn her of a great danger. She must fly from it to Russia. When Queen Hortense came in with her brother and sister in law, Louise told them what they had missed and the Queen said she would like to meet the prophetess. Prince Eugène and Princess Auguste also said they would be interested. Next morning, Madame de Krüdener arrived early and came out from seeing Hortense, crying, "What an angel your Queen is!" but Louise saw her mistress had been weeping. Nevertheless she had made an appointment for the prophetess to come again to meet the ex-Viceroy and Vicereine. This occasion proved an anti-climax. Queen Hortense, having made the introduction, rushed out of the room in fits of laughter, signing to her lady to go on in. Louise entered nervously. The sight which greeted her eyes was indeed strange. Princess Auguste with her usual grace had begged the visitor to be seated, but Madame de Krüdener had exploded at once into one of her best bouts of prophecy. The princess was standing with her beautiful eyes and mouth forming three perfect round o's. Prince Eugène, accustomed to swift decision in the battlefield, had evidently already made up his mind. This poor woman was quite mad. Madame de Krüdener flung up both arms and began to repeat a favourite trumpet-call with which Louise was already familiar. She said that 1815 was going to be the most frightful year. "You think that the Congress at Vienna will succeed? Don't deceive yourselves! The Emperor Napoleon will come again from his island. He will be even more powerful than before. But those who take his side will be trapped, persecuted, punished! They will not know where to lay their heads."[9]

IV

The Congress which had been put off twice was now announced to open on October 1, but there would be useful preliminary meetings. Prince Eugène arrived on September 29, having intentionally missed the state entry of September 25, when the Emperor of Austria and all his court had gone to meet the visiting sovereigns. It might have been difficult to know where he was to be placed in the procession. He really represented nobody except himself and his family. He had called in at Salzburg upon his sister in law the Crown Princess of Bavaria. Everything had been charmingly arranged to suit his tastes. He was taken for a beautiful walk to a view-point where a collation had been prepared. In the evening, while he drank his tea, a band of Tyrolean singers arrived to entertain a musical guest. Ludwig had said that he was charmed by the French fashion of dining at small round or oval separate tables but his wife preferred in her house the old German style. She seemed able to manage a difficult young man, and had a lovely placid countenance. Eugène had to confess in his first letter home that the mountain roads had been terrible. He had come with only two attendants, but both first class—Darnay and Bataille. Tascher was to follow. He sent Bataille out at once to announce his arrival to Metternich (now promoted Prince) and Count Rechberg, Chamberlain to the King of Bavaria. He could not have been received with more politeness. He was summoned to the Hofburg the very next evening. The Emperor of Austria had a very large house-party staying for an unknown period of time—presumably until the Congress was satisfactorily concluded. Not only all the principal potentates of Europe had come to Vienna with their ministers and representatives. Several had brought their families to a city famous for its charm and hospitality. The Czar was accompanied by his wife and two sisters. The Queen of Bavaria was here, the Archduchess Beatrix, four monarchs, two hereditary princes and three Princes of the Blood. It had been decided by the Festival Committee, with the gracious connivance of the Czar, that precedence had better be by age. So the King of Württemberg took in to dinner every night the Empress of Austria, third wife of Francis II. She was a wilting and hysterical Italian, stone deaf in one ear. If she had been left to sit next to the Czar, who was deaf in the opposite ear, they would have been perfectly incapable of communicating. Special liveries and carriages had been provided, and the horses in the stables were said to number one thousand four hundred. Dinner was at two, supper at ten. As the weeks passed, some of the royalties found that they could hardly bear the sight of one another. They began taking meals in their own suites. This meant additional expense for their host.

Talleyrand had been very clever. He was quite alive to the fact that concern for the welfare of France—Bourbon or Bonapartist —was at a low ebb amongst the allies. He managed to secure a lease of one of the best houses in Vienna, the Kaunitz Palace, and invited the young wife of his nephew, Comte Édouard Talleyrand de Périgord, to act as his hostess. Her mother had been a Princess of Courland, wife of the last reigning Duke, before the Czar had absorbed that province. Her sister in law had been Bonaparte's first choice as a bride for Eugène de Beauharnais, but had been married off to Comte Just de Noailles, whose cousin Comte Alexis de Noailles now accompanied Talleyrand to Vienna. Much less to Eugène's taste was the French second in command the Duc Dalberg, an able, but obstinate and unreasonable man. However, Madame de Périgord was a born social leader, and Talleyrand himself had beautiful manners when he chose. There was a young Comte de la Garde Chambonas who had come to the Congress, nobody quite knew why. When he presented himself at the French Embassy, Talleyrand welcomed him with the words "I had to come to Vienna, Monsieur, in order to have the pleasure of seeing you in my home."[10]

He had not been so polite at the first Conference of the four great Powers to which he had been invited by Metternich, somewhat unwillingly. He had at once carried the war into the enemies' country. Taking the only vacant seat at the council table, between Metternich and the English representative, Lord Castlereagh, he asked why he had not been warned to bring his French colleagues. He was told that this meeting was only for the heads of Missions. He asked then where was Don Pedro Gomez Labrador, representing Spain? The Don had not yet arrived. Why had Prussia two representatives? This was painful. Prince Hardenberg, a most noble-looking character, was hard of hearing and must have Baron Humboldt to whisper in his ear.

The French representative next objected to the use of the word "Allies". Against whom were they allied? Surely not against the Emperor Napoleon who was in the Island of Elba, or against King Louis XVIII? He had imagined that after twenty years of war they were at last at peace. He won every point at his first appearance, though he nearly over-reached himself when on a mention of the claims of the King of Naples, he said he did not know who this person was. The situation in that quarter was very tricky as England had undoubtedly concluded a Treaty in form with Murat.

Prince Eugène had no claim to be summoned to conferences. Unkind gossips wondered why he had come to assist the Congress with his advice. Comte Fleury thought he looked very poorly in his deep mourning, physically exhausted and out of spirits. He was of course anxious all the time, as he hurried round paying his duty calls, thankful to be able to write home that everyone was being very attentive asking after the princess and his children. He told his wife that he was charmed she had not come amongst this enormous mob of royalties and politicians, all pushing for place. Would she believe it there had been a discussion about whether the Queen of Bavaria or the Duchess of Oldenburg, took precedence? He did not tell her that the Archduchess Beatrix, who was the mother of the Empress of Austria and the widow of the Archduke Ferdinand, had behaved with startling rudeness. He had succeeded her late husband in Italy, and innocently attempted conversation about the beauties and antiquities of Milan. She had turned her back on him and spoken exclusively to King Max.

Prince Metternich had assured him that once the Congress went into session serious matters would be settled quickly. He called upon Lord Castlereagh, who had the name for being very aloof, and he must have made a good impression for he was asked to dine and to sup several times, and to take Lady Castlereagh and her sister, Lady Matilda, and Lord Castlereagh's stepbrother, on a trip to Baden—the one outside Vienna.

He went out to Schönbrunn and paid his respects to Ex-Empress Marie Louise. He said he thought she had changed much in appearance, but he did not say whether this was for the worse or for the better.

The Emperor Francis had a President of Police and Censorship who sent secret reports to the Hofburg every morning. Baron Hager's staff included slightly besmirched aristocracy, embassy porters and coachmen and even the housemaids who emptied paper-baskets. For a gentleman to visit any lady after dark was enough for them to conclude the worst. Prince Eugène was paying inconspicuous visits to a leading court jeweller in order to raise some money on jewels belonging to him and his wife. He was being advised to exchange them for diamonds which would be easier to dispose of and less subject to loss on sale. On October 23 the Viennese Secret Police bulletin ran: "The Viceroy has bought jewellery to the value of 32,000 ducats through the jeweller Neuling, partly with money, partly with relinquishing a valuable cavalry sabre of Napoleon's, three diadems etc. His mistress, Madame Orondi whom he allowed to come from Karlsruhe, is thought to have caused him to do this."[11]

Everyone concerned said that Hager was in close touch with Fouché.

But if Hager's spies believed the worst, the little Comte de la Garde Chambonas, who had a countenance of touching innocence, bright curls and a turned-up nose, always saw everything and everyone through rose-coloured spectacles. He had been a little worried when first he arrived as to what was going to happen to Prince Eugène. He had the greatest veneration for this prince who had employed him diplomatically from Milan to Marmont in Illyria, to Joseph Bonaparte in Rome, and Lucien in Naples. Anyone could see that Prince Eugène had suffered. He looked ill and sad, and no wonder. But fortunately, while Society in Vienna was still hesitating, the Czar publicly gave him his arm. He went everywhere with the Czar. His situation was no longer in doubt. Chambonas himself had hastened to attach himself to the head of his family—the Prince de Ligne, most illustrious octogenarian in Vienna. The prince had a house up on the ramparts where his young connection was a constant visitor.

Not only people were all interesting and splendid in the world of Chambonas. Places interested him equally. He was going to write enough to fill a book (as indeed he eventually did) about social life at the Congress. He was able to open magnificently with a masked ball at the Hofburg. A Grande Redoute came next —all the furniture covered in white velvet and all the curtains white and silver silk, illuminated by eight thousand wax candles in crystal chandeliers. The Grand Staircase was embowered in spring flowers and shrubs. He thought Prince Eugène was relieved to find another old friend here—though very much on duty— Isabey.

The artist was performing not only a command conversation group, but individual portraits of delegates. The Czar went out to Schönbrunn with Prince Eugène, and the prince introduced to his all-powerful friend M. Méneval, who was quite without occupation since Marie Louise now did nothing without advice from her *major-domo* Count Neipperg. The Czar kindly offered the secretary work in Russia. Isabey, who was producing a likeness, much admired by the Queen of Bavaria, of the little King of Rome, found time to do also one for Prince Eugène to send to his sister—once a pupil of the painter.

Hager's informants told him that Prince Eugène had been invited to dine by Marie Louise once, twice, thrice. General Neipperg had played the piano and Prince Eugène had sung to amuse her. But they could not say what topics had been discussed. Certainly the prince had not seen her alone. The Poles, who idolized him, were a little irritated that Prince Eugène had refused them audience. The Czar had been heard to say, "Prince Eugène is not only an excellent soldier. He is a perfectly honest man. If he were to enter my service I should be enchanted."

The Duchess of St. Leu was causing her brother uneasiness again. He thought it admirable when her husband had come out of retirement in Styria to rally to the side of the Emperor, but the return of Louis to France meant fresh trouble for her. He wanted their elder son. Both her brother and the Czar begged her to temporize but she was determined to keep both her sons at all costs. "My case" became a leading feature of her letters. As weeks passed it gradually deteriorated into "my miserable lawsuit".

She had come out of mourning and went formally to thank Louis XVIII for allowing her and her children to reside in France. The Czar had advised against her having anything to do with the Tuileries, but she knew better. Her brother, in Vienna, had also come out of mourning. He said he had been asked to all the fêtes but so far had not been to any. They were said to be of great magnificence.

"I thank you," he wrote to his wife, "for your pleasantry on the fair ladies of Vienna. (1) I have not even seen a cat; (2) You know, my dearest, how much I love you, and I beg of you not to doubt that my love will be constant during this testing time. Adieu! be at peace in your mind and count on me. I will leave no stone unturned to secure the future of my children." He opened his letter to say that he had been interrupted by an arrival of the Czar.

By the middle of October he really thought he was getting on. He had seen Castlereagh and Metternich again. The Austrian had given his word that the question of the Viceroy's property left in Italy should be dealt with promptly. The Englishman, in whom he put more trust, said that he would certainly exert his interest the moment the question came up. The Congress had not even opened yet. But one could see that the big problems would have to come first. Russia wanted the whole of Poland, and Prussia wanted the whole of Saxony. Murat must be jettisoned, and the former rulers put back in Naples and Spain. Austria must be restrained as far as possible in Italy. It was disappointing that at the end of October the Czar, the Emperor Francis and the King of Prussia went for a state visit to Hungary.

The Congress opened at last in November. Eugène had now met all the archdukes and most of the other military leaders against whom he had fought. His younger brother in law, Karl Theodore, who was now eighteen and a charming lad, sat open-mouthed while Field Marshals and kings talked of famous battles. (He was also madly in love and had bribed the head gardener at Schönbrunn to provide him with an unending supply of mar-guerites—the name of his *inamorata*. He wore them in his button-hole and tore off their petals.) Prince Ludwig had to be restrained from calling out the Crown Prince of Württemberg, and it was said the Czar had threatened to call out Metternich because of the Polish settlement. Hortense, in Paris, heard that Eugène had called out the Grand Duke Constantine.

Eugène had been to see Cardinal Consalvi, the Pope's represen-tative, about such of his property as still remained in the reclaimed Papal States. He had been to his first court ball—truly mag-nificent. He re-opened a letter to say that he had been asked to dine at the Hofburg, which he thought a good thing, and with Count Stackelberg of the Russian delegation. (But of Russian support he had never been doubtful.) Princess Trautmannsdorff, a leading Viennese charmer, asked him to a Sunday supper—very select. At Prince Metternich's ball he had danced with the Czarina and both the Grand Duchesses. There had been con-siderable anxiety about this gaiety, as a wooden hall had been ordered and people remembered the fire at Prince von Schwarzen-berg's Paris ball. All passed off well, however, and it was actually gay—typically Viennese. Something which had been fashionable as long ago as the days of Louis XIV in France was revived by the Festival Committee—a lottery. The prizes were sometimes very valuable. At one given by Princess Bagration, a young actress from Paris, a pupil of Talma, recited speeches from classical drama. The Grand Duke Constantine came off best. He won two porcelain vases presented by the King of Prussia; he offered them to his hostess. The King of Bavaria won a mosaic box which he gave to Princess Marie Esterhazy. The Czar gave his two little bronze candlesticks to the fair *tragédienne*, Mlle. Séraphine Lambert. Soon Hager's spies were reporting that the Czar, the Grand Duke Karl of Baden and Prince Eugène were visiting her at her hotel "the Römischer Kaiser"—Prince Eugène nearly every day. But they had not quite got her name right. "Sophie" and "Lombard."

The King of Bavaria got such a cold he had to ask his son in law to write for him to Munich. His queen had been unwell

during most of her stay. "The racketty life of Vienna does not
suit either of them." It had soon ceased to fascinate him too.
Wrede had given a ball for ten thousand guests. It had made a
beautiful spectacle at first sight, but had not been really amusing
—heavy. He mentioned as a piece of good news that the French
Ambassador, Noailles, on being presented to King Max had
voluntarily confided in him that Louis XVIII had told him to
look after the interests of Prince Eugène. Wrede said that his
case had already come up in committee and not a voice had been
raised against it; the principle was admitted. They had nothing
now to settle except where the sovereign state was to be. It seemed
at first that something in Italy or possibly the old ecclesiastical
domain of Trèves might be offered.

It was quite like 1809 to be shooting on Prince Esterhazy's
estate again and at Laxenburg—both superb days of sport. The
Austrian Empress had her own fowling-piece and shot heron. He
was getting on with his efforts to raise some money on Josephine's
bequests. "You ask me, my dear, if it is true that Soulange has
gone to England. He thought it necessary to go there himself to
superintend the sale of the three great pieces of jewellery which I
left in Paris."

In the second week of December, when everyone important
seemed to be recovering from their various illnesses, his spirits
rose astonishingly and he wrote that he hoped within four days to
know their fate. The Emperor Francis had replied to applications
from King Max and the Czar, and the King of Prussia was understood to have no objections, but was still indisposed.

This was the moment chosen by the senior and most elegant
delegate to depart to a better world. The Prince de Ligne, eighty
but erect as a ramrod, said with a smile that he was glad to be abl'
to offer Congress yet another spectacle, the funeral of a Field
Marshal and a Knight of the Golden Fleece. But his fame was to
rest on his earlier remark. "The Congress does not take many
steps, but it dances." He was a wit of the first water. Eugène's old
adversary, Sir Sidney Smith, was making himself a figure of
fun, dashing about wearing an unusual buttercup-yellow Swedish
order and organizing a charity subscription picnic. At this he
had recounted his exploits at the siege of Acre at such length that
the old Prince had nicknamed him "Long Acre".

On Christmas Eve Eugène wrote, "A little patience and we shall
become, I hope, happy for the rest of our days." With the New

Year, as must be expected, the fêtes redoubled. The Festival Committee had wonderful ideas—a mediaeval tournament, musical rides in the winter riding school, ice-carnivals by torchlight. Even Eugène bought a little *traineau*, the sort of sledge shaped and painted like a bird or beast in which a lady sat wrapped up in furs while a cavalier skated, standing up behind her driving a gaily caparisoned steed. The noise of the little joybells suited his mood. It would do to take home. Not only famous white horses performed in the winter riding school. Beethoven himself, though now completely deaf, conducted at a gala concert his Seventh Symphony, and his most recent composition written in celebration of Lord Wellington's victory at Vittoria. Prince Eugène was also observed at the Opera where Bigottini performed. Ballerinas are indestructible. This one was said to have been the prince's mistress in his salad days. At her "benefit" on November 16, he was said to have given her a splendid ring. But he was never known to have visited her. She was getting to the end of her long *affaire* with Comte Ferdinand Palffy, patron of the arts and theatre-owner, who had given her a farewell subsidy welcomed by her as dowry for an adored daughter. Prince Eugène was much taken with the *tableaux vivants* produced by talented society amateurs, a form of entertainment new to him.

The Czar called for him on many sharp mornings and they walked fast round the ramparts. He knew that this intimacy was causing jealousy. He knew that the papers about his new domain were on the desk of the Emperor Francis. On February 3 he had to ask his wife to declare her preference. Italy now appeared to be out of the question "and frankly I am not sorry". What did she think of: "(1) Trèves with additional lands; (2) the old Duchy of Deux Ponts alias Zweibrücken; (3) Corfu—that is to say what they call 'The Seven Isles.' " In the last two cases and probably in the first also, they would get a subsidy from Italy. The Seven Isles was not nearly as valuable as Trèves and he supposed that was why it was placed third on the list. Against it, he realized, was its situation in the middle of the Aegean between Naples and Turkey. Perhaps she would miss her friends and relations. All the same it was a beautiful country, not really far from Sicily and far enough from continental disturbances (now perhaps settled!). Had he been single, he thought he would really have voted for the Isles. He refrained from asking her opinion on Deux Ponts. Both she and her brother Ludwig had been born there. It had been removed from her father by Bonaparte in the Peace of Lunéville. At Trèves you would be under the eye of France; in Italy under that of Austria. "Answer quick, but keep this to yourself." She must not forget that Russia wanted them to take Trèves, and if they did, France would want him in her army. "That could not happen, and as for serving against her, my character, my inclinations and my loyalty to my country would all stand in the way of my taking such a course."

Metternich smoothly promised him that his affairs would infallibly be signed and sealed within the week. Now that the major vexed problems had been settled by Congress everyone thought that the sovereigns and statesmen would be leaving at the end of the month. But one more famous figure had just arrived—Lord Wellington from the British Embassy in Paris. In England, the Opposition had been becoming so truculent that Castlereagh had been implored to return to lead the House of Commons in debate in the forthcoming session.

Hortense had met Lord Wellington and surprisingly thought he looked more the diplomat than the soldier. He had spoken in a typically cold obstinate English way of the Emperor Napoleon's great military gifts. But he had assured her that he would again call the attention of the French government to the fulfilment of the Treaty of Fontainebleau. Eugène had called at once at Minoritenplatz 30, but his lordship was at present battling with the prevalent feverish cold.

On the morning of February 13 he wrote that he had grounds for believing they would go to Germany. "But I will not hide the fact that there is a good deal of opposition from the Germans who do not want, so they say, a Frenchman in Germany. Only Russia supports us, but luckily she does so powerfully." He added a note that their fate was settled—"The Czar has collected on our side Prussia, England and France, and I believe the rest will fall into line and we shall get Deux Ponts with two hundred thousand inhabitants. A thousand kisses!" He said he would now send a courier into Italy to get all their effects sent up to Munich, with the exception of the pictures, which he thought would be best sent over the Mont Cenis to Paris to be forwarded to Deux Ponts, and not over the mountains of the Tyrol in March. He was appreciative of Wrede's efforts to get them something in Italy or the Isles, but the weight of Russia had been against him, and he believed Lord Wellington had supported the Czar. It was sad that there seemed to have been a good deal of bad blood about the orders sent to Bellegarde about sending their belongings from Milan. The French did not want Prince Eugène in Italy, the Germans had not wanted him on the Rhine. One could never please everyone. He had thanked the Emperor of Austria on behalf of himself and his wife, and knew Metternich had been told he would leave Vienna content. The Czar would be coming to stay with them in Munich.

On Thursday March 8 he still slightly regretted the Seven Isles. He had been sounded as to becoming governor of the new country west of the Rhine, given back to Bavaria to compensate her for losing the Tyrol. 'You can guess that I sent a clear refusal.' He went out of town to sup and got home after midnight. He found his house picketed by police. A message had come in from Genoa that morning that the Emperor Napoleon had escaped from Elba. Congress had been summoned and was still sitting.[12]

v

To find the cup dashed from his lips after such long waiting and hard work, much of it humiliating, so overwhelmed him that he sent off to Auguste a letter expressing almost despair. "Certainly nothing worse could have happened for us." She did not get it for three weeks. He had always been a subject of interest to Hager's police. There had been previous pin-pricks. He still wore Imperial French uniform. His liveried staff had the Iron Crown of Lombardy on their buttons, surmounted by a crowned E. This would be correct when he got his principality . . . He was now definitely a suspected man. The signs were unmistakable, and he sadly lowered his opinion of several companions.

He tried to see Wellington and Metternich and Talleyrand, but they had all gone off to Pressburg to insist that the King of Saxony signed his treaty. Some people thought that the Emperor would have gone to join Murat in Naples, others said he would land in France. "If it is correct that Napoleon has gone to France, that means civil war for my unhappy land. I groan to think of what will follow." French newspapers had ceased to appear in Vienna. Only from German ones could people learn what was happening there. Hortense had written to her brother on March 7 to say that she had lost her case. She enclosed a copy of the *Moniteur* which, she said, made her fear their poor country was to know more sorrow, and a book of riddles which she thought would amuse the Czar. The paper announced the landing of the Emperor at Golfe Juan on March 1.[13]

After five days Eugène began to look on the bright side of things. The Czar came to take him out for a long walk again and said Napoleon's army would be weak. But he was afraid Eugène would not be able to leave Vienna at present. The news coming in was astonishing. Napoleon had been received in Grenoble with wild enthusiasm by the inhabitants and, what was even better from his point of view, by the troops. Colonel de Labédoyère had taken over to him the whole of the Seventh regiment. Marshal Ney, who had promised that he would bring back the Emperor in an iron cage, had fallen on his neck in tears. Good King Max called on his son in law to say that Ludwig's Adjutant, Count Pappenheim, was off to Munich tomorrow and could take a letter. The King himself hoped to follow next week.

Auguste was sick with anxiety. Her husband reassured her as best he could. He begged her not to believe wild rumours that he was in danger. "I am taking no part in this struggle. I am staying neutral—arch-neutral!" Obviously nobody could go into the country on the other side of the Rhine at present, and it might perhaps never be possible for them to go there now. But she must keep up her hopes, and they would meet soon. The latest from Paris was that Louis XVIII had fled to the Low Countries, leaving the capital open for the advance of his rival.

The Emperor Napoleon was carried up the steps of the Tuileries on the night of March 20 by a rejoicing crowd which almost suffocated him. The carriage of Queen Hortense, arriving to welcome him home, had been recognized and greeted by cheers.

It was at this point that his sister indeed began to cost Prince Eugène dear. He had been irritated by finding that a necklace for the little Josephine's birthday had been stopped by Talleyrand's second in command, "that scoundrel Dalberg." He was under stricter surveillance. There were four police all day outside his house and at night they sat in a cab. On April 1 he merely thought it was polite of the Czar to send a message that he was too busy to walk. He was thunder-struck to discover that his most powerful friend seemed to have severed relations with him. He wrote "in the sharpest affliction" to ask what had been his offence and General Tschernitscheff delivered to him, without any covering note of explanation, copies of a *cache* of correspondence for him from Paris. The son of his steward at Malmaison had been on leave. The youth had told the Stuttgart police quite openly that he carried mail from Paris for his master, Prince Eugène. It had been sent up in hot haste to Vienna and read aloud to Congress. Lavalette's short note expressed uninhibited joy. There were two for Darnay. That from his brother dwelt rather upon the stupefaction than delight of the people of Paris. The other from Soulange Bodin at Malmaison was certainly on the same lines as that of Lavalette, rather more so. But it was the letter of Queen Hortense dated April 22, which had made members of the committee cry out that Prince Eugène and all his household must be sent off to a fortress in Hungary. Hortense herself, when she came to write her memoirs was hardly repentant.

"Just as I was going to bed I was told that my brother's man of business was sending a courier to Vienna to tell him about things, and I was asked if I had anything to send. I scribbled a few lines in haste. I wrote of the Emperor, of his cold reception of me, of his very warm reception by all Paris. Finally I said that I hoped to see my brother very soon. I was so innocent of politics that I believed he would come back with the Empress and the King of Rome. I did not forget to mention my earnest hope for peace. I urged my brother not to neglect any means of persuading the Emperor Alexander to sacrifice his personal animosity to the dread of war, which to judge from the enthusiasm of the French nation, would be long and bloody."[14]

VI

A letter from Napoleon, from Lyons, summoning Prince Eugène to France, together with one for the Empress Marie Louise, had been stopped and suppressed. The appearance of the Beauharnais in Italy had been even more dreaded by Metternich. High ranking officers of the Army of Italy had been deliberately sent, since his retirement from their command, to posts in Transylvania, and many had called on him *en route*. No proof that he had foreknowledge of the Emperor's escape was forthcoming. Metternich himself acknowledged this. The unhappy Beauharnais wrote hotly in reply to that most devious politician: "Your Highness, I hasten to have the honour to acknowledge receipt of the letter which your Highness was good enough to send to me by the hand of Baron Hruby.

"I read it with a keen sense of gratitude and with emotions which were a mixture of astonishment and pain—a man whose whole life has been foreign to intrigue and whose actions have been directed only by his doing his duty, might have hoped that he had the right to consider himself immune from any conspiracy against him, and still more from any attempts at revenge. But since it is a PARTY that is ranged against me, any excuses are possible. The spirit behind the party makes it wish to bring down anything which it cannot win over, and even loyalty itself is not a sufficient safeguard."15

He did not see the Czar again in Vienna but he knew that he had reason to be grateful to him. Hortense had gone on to write a letter offering to meet Marie Louise at Strasbourg. Afterwards she said that her letters had been opened and additions made throwing ridicule on the Czar. She said that the Emperor had asked to whom Josephine had left Malmaison. He wanted to stay there. She had replied, "Actually to Eugène. But it's the same thing."

Caulaincourt, a true patriot, who had most unwillingly accepted the office of Foreign Minister, had asked her to write to Vienna. He had sent other messengers. There was a crony of his tempestuous youth whom Talleyrand has sent to London *en poste* in 1801. "Who the devil is the Marquis de Montrond?" the Duke of York had asked. "Sir, they say he is the most agreeable scoundrel and greatest roué in France!" "Really! then we must immediately ask him to dinner." Of Caulaincourt's three emissaries to Vienna he was the only one to arrive. The Comte de Flahaut and the Baron de Stassard, who had stated their business at the frontiers, had after enormous difficulties not got beyond Linz; but Montrond had sailed through. He had adopted the character and papers of the Abbé Altieri, returning to Rome with Vatican Archives looted by Napoleon from Rome. He had terrified Méneval by turning up at Schönbrunn laughing, saying that he had a free hand to kidnap Marie Louise and carry her off to her husband, in boy's clothes if need be. Méneval suspected he had a private mission from Fouché, not Napoleon, to Talleyrand. He threw Hager's numerous spies off the scent by meeting Méneval by appointment in the famous hothouses at Schönbrunn where he appeared as "an amateur of horticulture." Hager's spies reported he had talked to Prince Eugène for two hours.

Méneval entrusted him with a very sad letter for Caulaincourt.

He said that troops were in motion against the Emperor in every direction, and the Czar particularly was vowing eternal vengeance against him. He could not say whether the Empress would be likely to return to France. The Cabinet here was against it and her mind had been so worked upon that she thought of the prospect with terror. He had not received an order from her mouth for six months. "General Neipperg has acquired great influence."

Prince Eugène had left that morning at three a.m. in the suite of his father in law the King of Bavaria for Munich. He had been received in Vienna with much suspicion and mistrust. Then, for three months he seemed to have won the confidence of the Czar. "Since the letters which were sent him from Paris of March 22 the Emperor Alexander has ceased seeing him. So that Congress might not separate without having done something for him, the principality of Ponte Corvo was proposed for him some days ago." (It was in Sicily and the title had once been borne first by Bernadotte, then by the second son of Murat.) "A condition imposed was that he should not reside there at present but go to live at Bayreuth with his family. On his refusal, Congress admitted that an establishment was due to him and that until it could be given to him he should be placed in the enjoyment of his estates and revenues in Italy; but up to today (April 7) no such orders have been given.

"Last night at half past twelve he had not received his passports. Since April 3 they have been deliberating whether to grant them or not. They wanted him to give his word of honour that he would not leave Bavaria, but he refused, saying he was not a prisoner of war. He intends to stay one or two weeks in Munich and then take the princess and her children to Bayreuth."[16]

VII

The palace which the King of Bavaria had assigned to his son in law and family was handsome and well appointed. It stood in the Schwabingergasse[17] and was of three storeys with a mansard roof and marble portal. It had two courtyards and was conveniently near the royal palace without being actually overlooked by it.

The Baron de Stassard, when repulsed at Linz, went on to Munich to wait for a reply from the Emperor Francis to whom he had forwarded his despatches. About a month after Prince Eugène had arrived in the Schwabingergasse he sent a message to the Baron asking him to call upon him on private business. Prince Wrede, who had come from Vienna the day before, had brought an offer from the Emperor Francis. If the Emperor Napoleon would consent to abdicate at once, not only would Austria consent to recognize his son as Emperor, she would even "in case of need support him." An un-named sovereignty would be assigned to the ex-Emperor, and whilst awaiting it he should go to live in one of the cities of the hereditary Austrian states. At the same date Metternich was sending almost identical overtures to Fouché by way of a M. Werner in Basle; an earlier offer had been entrusted to a M. Bresson. Baron Stassard got back to Paris, but the Emperor Napoleon, who was now reviewing the Guard before it marched on its last campaign, perhaps hesitated to accept proposals made to him from a quarter in which he had learnt to place no confidence.

These were the last efforts for peace known to have been made by his irreconcilable enemies as they were preparing to give him his death blow at Waterloo.[18]

CHAPTER SEVENTEEN

Duke of Leuchtenberg, Prince of Eichstätt

1815 : 1822

I

WHEN THE Allies occupied Paris for the second, and it was ardently hoped by the inhabitants for the last time, the problem of the future of Prince Eugène was still unsettled. It could not be denied that the Czar, the Emperor Francis, and the Kings of England and Prussia had personally or by proxy put their signatures to a treaty promising him a principality outside France. His stepfather's untimely re-appearance on the scene had jeopardized his prospects, but now the Emperor Napoleon was simply General Bonaparte, carefully looked after by the English in the island of St. Helena, and it could not be proved the prince had taken any steps to assist him during the Hundred Days. It was true that he had objected to a formal request that he should engage himself not to leave Germany, but he had stayed there and he had always said, since the first abdication, that what he wanted for France was peace. Europe was now at peace, but it was gradually and sadly discovered in Paris that when cutting up the cake was done, not a crumb had been left for Prince Eugène. Still there was the King of Bavaria to be reckoned with, and in a lesser degree, the Czar. The great sudden friendship extended by that potentate had been blighted in the bud by the conduct of ex-Queen Hortense, but although the Czar steadily refused to notice her existence while he was in Paris, he did reply to letters from Prince Eugène. He wrote to him a month after Waterloo giving him a bird's eye view of the situation in France.

The truth was that the Allies were vexed with the Bourbons for having failed to endear themselves to their native land and for having fled from it at the very name of Napoleon. While still in Vienna, the Czar had been heard to mention the name of Berna-

dotte as an alternative to their return. The King of Rome was
not put forward as a candidate even by his grandfather. The Duke
of Orleans was said by some French to be a disastrous prospect,
and a brother of the Czar as a very doubtful one. A Republic,
the Prince of Orange, the King of Saxony were all discussed. In
Vienna, Prince Karl Theodore of Bavaria had been in no doubt
that an excellent sovereign would be found in Prince Eugène.
This hero-worshipping and somewhat erratic young man was not
yet of age, but the same suggestion was presently made in Paris.
Ex-Queen Hortense heard from General Grenier, a member of
the Provisional Government, that her brother's name had come
up in the Chamber of Deputies. The General said that he had
felt that neither Prince Eugène nor she would approve. She sent
him her thanks and warm confirmation. Whenever such a
suggestion had been made in her hearing she had quashed it at
once. "I told them that my brother would never accept a throne
to the detriment of the son of his benefactor. I asked them to be
good enough not to speak again of the subject." Expediency
dictated the return of Louis XVIII, and Fouché promised to
speak to him very severely about improved conduct. He re-
entered Paris on July 5, preceded by the armies of Blücher and
Wellington. The Czar wrote to Prince Eugène hopefully as
regarded his prospects. Indeed, he ventured to say that he thought
they were better than after the first abdication. He was being
more consulted and would make every effort. With regard to ex-
Queen Hortense he was unbending. He would never forget those
letters read aloud to Congress. She had made him ridiculous.
And to the very last she had supported the vanquished Napoleon.
She had entertained him in her brother's house at Malmaison
after Waterloo up to the hour of his departure, when she had
pressed upon him her mother's best diamond necklace. Caulaincourt had pleaded in vain that she had followed her heart.

"It is painful for me to have to speak to you about your sister.
Unfortunately everyone is unanimous about the part she played
in the recent unhappy events. Even this unanimous opinion would
not have been sufficient proof for me if I did not have, unhappily,
other evidence about which I spoke to you in Vienna. That is the
fate of women who set out, with the highest intentions, to attempt
to play a part in public affairs. The majority of them make
mistakes of judgment, and then they find themselves out of their
depths."

On July 17[1] she was notified by the Prefect of Police that she must leave Paris within two hours. The Czar had a new spiritual adviser, Madame de Krüdener. She was installed in a house behind the Elysée and he visited her every day. He had accepted with grateful tears her announcement that God had sent her to him for his salvation. Her prophecies as to the dreadful fates of those who had aided Bonaparte were being strikingly fulfilled. In 1815 four more familiar figures disappeared tragically from the life of Prince Eugène. On June 1 the body of Berthier had been found on the pavement below his quarters at Bamberg. He had fallen out of the window. Some people thought he had been murdered—strangled and thrown out. The most popular story was that he had cast himself down in despair when he had heard Russian artillery rumbling over the cobbles on the way to invade France. He had been strange in manner since the Russian retreat.

Labédoyère was the next to quit the scene. His offence had been rank. A member of the old aristocracy, he had taken his whole regiment over to join the returned Emperor, and at a critical moment, five days after the landing. He was a cousin of Flahaut, and much of the same type, romantic, high-spirited, adventurous. He had been recognized travelling in a public conveyance to Paris and had been denounced by a valet, a former employee. The story sounded like the bad old days of the French Revolution come back again. He had returned in disguise to see his wife. Painful efforts were made by her and his family to secure a pardon. He faced a firing squad on August 19. The police had a Black List of all who had been in government employ during the Hundred Days. Flahaut had hardly left the side of Napoleon, but he got away, to England, in November. It was accepted that his arrest would have been unwelcome to his reputed parent, Talleyrand. The capture of Ney was believed to have vexed Louis XVIII. His had been the most important test case. He had been a popular military hero and had personally led several charges at Waterloo. He was tried by his peers, who brought in the unavoidable verdict, and was shot in the gardens of the Luxembourg on December 7.

The most spectacular victim of the year had shared his fate on October 13. Afterwards, in St. Helena, Napoleon reflected that if he had had Murat at Waterloo the day might have gone differently. At the end Murat had made a theatrical effort to copy the Imperial mystique. He had kept in touch with the exiled Emperor in Elba, and on hearing of his arrival in France, had advanced against the Austrians with his unreliable Neapolitan army. He had been completely vanquished at Tolentino on May 3 and had appeared in Naples pale and emaciated, his lancer's uniform white with dust. He had told his queen, "All is lost except Life and I was not fortunate enough to find Death." He had escaped to Cannes and entered into negotiations with Fouché, but his overtures were rejected by his old leader. There was now a price on his head. He fled to Corsica where he narrowly missed being murdered, and wandered in disguise almost famished. He received an offer from Metternich of asylum in Austria as a private person under the name of Lipona (an anagram of Napoli), but he could not resist a last throw by which if successful he might rule over a united Italy, his eternal dream of power. He landed near Salerno with a party of about thirty old officers, and being separated by storm from his little fleet, and treacherously deserted by supporters who were to have met him, was speedily captured, though not without a running fight in which, swimming to board a boat at anchor, he personally slew two of his many assailants. He was court-martialled on the spot and condemned to death. Theatrical to the last, he refused to allow his eyes to be bandaged and himself gave the order to fire.

The trial of Lavalette came on in Paris in November and lasted a month. He had been kept waiting for it since July. He was accused of having intrigued to assist the return of Bonaparte from Elba. He frankly said he would have liked to have accompanied the Emperor to St. Helena but could not, for family reasons. His wife, who had borne him only a daughter (Josephine, now aged fifteen) had been pregnant again for the first time since. He lay in the dreadful Concièrgerie prison for five months. Great efforts were made to get his sentence of death revoked. The wife had two audiences with Louis XVIII and was hopeful after the first one. She gave birth to a little Napoleon who survived only a matter of hours. Lavalette's death by guillotine was fixed for December 21. A few days later, editors throughout Europe were presented with an ideal opportunity for dramatic paragraphs. Madame Lavalette, whom her family had always believed to be too feeble to say boo to a goose, had herself initiated and organized his escape. She had arrived for a farewell interview attired in a conspicuous red merino cloak richly lined with fur, and a striking black velvet hat with upstanding coloured plumes. A figure in this attire had left

Lavalette's cell, weeping into a handkerchief. Madame Lavalette had walked up and down in the empty cell, leaving the gaolers to believe it was still inhabited. He had got away. When no trace of him was found after a fortnight, a rumour spread that he had sailed for America.[2] The witch hunt continued. Baron Darnay reckoned that in the first year after Waterloo his master had supplied funds amounting to a hundred thousand francs to help old companions on the run, and in the next, sixty thousand. They included Poles and Italians.

On a dark day in mid-January 1816, the secretary came with a shaken look to announce one more gentleman from France. After hearing his tale the prince immediately left for the Residenz to ask for a private audience with King Max. It was Lavalette. It was true that the King had exclaimed on hearing of his escape, "Let him come here! I will look after him," but since then he had become a world-famous refugee and the king did not desire worse relations with France. However, after dining with the king, his son in law saw his unexpected guest and told him that a lodging within twenty miles of Munich would be ready for him in three days. He would receive the papers and name of M. Cossar which he would find in order.

Lavalette's escape story was almost incredible. He had lain up in Paris for a fortnight while it was being combed for him. Friends and total strangers had helped him. The Comte de Chassenon had twice, in the guise of a cab-man, driven him across the capital. The three gentlemen who had accompanied him out of Paris in broad daylight had been English—Sir Robert Wilson of the British Intelligence, Captain Hutchinson of the Guards and Mr. Michael Bruce, the well known traveller. They had presented him with the uniform and instructions of Colonel Losack, "brother of the Admiral," travelling on a mission from the Duke of Wellington to Munich and Vienna. Before parting from him at Mons, Sir Robert had given him letters to the King of Prussia, and Mr. Lamb, English resident in Munich, and wished him luck. It was unfortunate that he could hardly speak a word of German. At Worms he was horrified to pick out of a German paper that his wife was still in prison, being treated with inhumanity, and that Sir Robert Wilson and his two friends had been arrested. He decided to strike for St. Petersburg and the Czar. At Mannheim he sent a letter to the Grand Duchess Stéphanie, first cousin to his wife. She was out of town, and he learned at his inn that the Grand Duke refused passage to any outlaws from France. He drove on over the frontier of Baden into Württemberg and narrowly escaped arrest at Stuttgart where the old king was known to be ardently anti-Bonapartist. He got through Ulm and could hardly believe his good fortune when he found himself in Bavarian territory.

His first hiding-place in Bavaria was in the old cathedral city of Freising. It was in the heart of a forest and deep in snow, but he could not resist going out of his room ten times a day for a stroll. Another French emigrant came to call upon him and slyly reported his presence to the Duc Dalberg in Munich. His friends moved him on to Starnberg. This was much better. It was a very poor little village, a summer lake-side resort, but it was less than twenty miles outside Munich, and twice a week Prince Eugène used to come to eat a hunter's meal at the house of a gamekeeper of the royal forest. He brought newspapers and books and delicacies. Lavalette learned that his wife had been released. He did not hear immediately that she had suffered a complete mental breakdown and no longer recognized even her own daughter. He was able to tell Eugène the history of the remaining volumes of *History Ancient and Modern*. The Emperor had asked what had happened to his secret hoard during the Hundred Days, and on hearing that Lavalette had given half of it to Prince Eugène who was now guarding it in Munich, he said, "It could not be in better hands." He had sent the other half to Messrs. Lafitte in Paris.

In May, suddenly the refugee heard he must be off again. The Crown Prince had heard of his presence. Prince Eugène saw to it that he got rooms in the house of a gardener down the opposite side of the lake. This was his best home yet, and when the whole family came for their summer holiday at the castle of Berg he would see his old friend every day. He would meet the children of Prince Eugène and Princess Auguste, and the King had sent a message that, when he came, he expected M. Cossar to dine.[3]

II

The decree of banishment issued against the family of the late Emperor had been very ferocious. It appeared in the *Moniteur* for January 16, 1816. "The forefathers and descendants of Napoleon Bonaparte, his uncles and his aunts, his nephews and nieces, his brothers, their wives and their descendants, his sisters and their husbands are banished from the Kingdom for ever and are bound to leave it within the period of one month under the penalty incurred by article 91 of the penal Code."

The Czar had loftily said that ex-Queen Hortense had received leave to go to Switzerland which was what she had asked. Louis XVIII had shown certain indulgence to her. She was allowed her title of Duchess of St. Leu and the property left her by her mother. But when she got to Switzerland, she found herself constantly annoyed by the police.

While she was in Geneva, Cardinal Fesch and his half-sister, the mother of Bonaparte, arrived there. Their passports were for Italy and despite the advanced age of Madame Mère and the severity of the weather the local authorities pushed them on. Hortense moved to Aix in Savoy, but still she was unlucky. The Austrians were withdrawing their troops and she would find herself at the mercy of the French or Piedmontese governments. Friends advised her not to stay. Dreadful excesses had been committed against Bonapartists in Southern France. She got permission to cross Switzerland again and with the snows reached Constance. This was in the domain of Karl of Baden. She wrote to him at once to announce her arrival, and a court chamberlain came from Karlsruhe with a letter from Grand Duchess Stéphanie regretting that politics should be allowed to supersede kinship. It was well known that his family had been trying to persuade Karl to put away a wife who had been born a Beauharnais and adopted as a daughter by Bonaparte. Karl was standing fast, but to refuse to receive one of his wife's undesirable relations would be a propitiatory gesture. Constance in the depths of winter had a horrible fascination for the broken-spirited wanderer. "The sight of its sad-looking houses, the silence of its empty streets, the calm which seemed to envelop it, made me feel I had arrived to a lost corner of the world." She was in constant touch by letter with her brother. Her passports were from the Russian minister, stating in the name of the Allies that she should be allowed to remain in Baden. She drew the attention of the authorities to this and they seemed likely to turn the blind eye to her presence, at least temporarily. She left the horrible Hotel de l'Aigle in a street running down to the lake-side, and took a little house on the shore. Gradually it appeared that Constance was not a town of the dead. It was full of French refugees needing assistance.

Prince Eugène came for Easter, April 14, 1816. "How many things I had to tell him; how much suffering can be banished by a moment of happiness! I was not, after all, alone in the world! Someone still loved me! Eugène listened without surprise to my tale of woe, and said that although he had taken no part in recent events, he too had experienced the hatred aroused by the word Frenchman all over Europe. He did not hide from me that libellous pamphlets against me were in circulation in Germany. He was very sore about it and though he did not for a moment distrust his sister, he spoke sadly of the charges brought against her. He had come out of the chaos as he deserved. Brave, loyal, frank, generous, incapable of breaking his word, preferring honour to place, a dignified retirement to ill-gotten gains and a career of duty to one of pleasure, his disposition was gay, indulgent, even and gentle. Easy-going in little matters, he was very firm on important ones. His understanding was more solid than brilliant, his feelings more deep than expansive, his judgment clear and far-sighted. Accustomed to serving a man who was jealous of his own power, my brother had formed the habit of effacing himself to some degree and standing in the shadow. And in this world the qualities which glitter are those which receive applause. In a word, I had left a super-man and found again a good man."[4]

The first thing she needed was some money. She still owned half of the contents of Malmaison, and the Czar was buying some of Josephine's art treasures. Her brother had got into touch on behalf of the Duchess of St. Leu with Mr. Nathan Rothschild of Frankfort. Everything was arranged. "Send for Prince Eugène."

He told her that Lavalette was in hiding near him, at home, with the approval of the King of Bavaria. He invited her to come to join them on a family holiday this year.

He stayed for a week. She had a favourite walk to a little wood called Lorette. The lofty mountains covered with snow, reflected in the lake, gave an imposing beauty to the scene. Close at hand leaves were in bud and violets began to appear ... "Of all the luxuries which I no longer had, I think I missed most the bouquets of roses and Parma violets which used to be brought to me every morning in season at St. Leu."[5]

The children of Josephine walked together on the borders of the lake of Constance and the Duchess showed her brother a picturesque cottage which she would like to buy. It would have a lovely view. She thought perhaps the Grand Duke would sell her some of the forest around it. She could see opportunities for fine avenues. But she had not yet got permission to live in his country. After her brother had gone, her sadness was increased by hearing from the Grand Duke that this property was not his to dispose of. It belonged to Prince Ludwig.

Louise Cochelet had told Prince Eugène how wonderfully the prospect of his visit had cheered her poor mistress, how she had chosen the furniture for his room, and run up a dozen times to see all was ready; how she had sat listening for his carriage wheels. When the summer came he repeated his invitation. In the end it was June before she arrived with Louise at Berg. This was a charming little antique castle on the Starnberger See. They had come at a sad moment. The youngest of Eugène's children, Caroline, called after the Queen of Bavaria, had just died. She had been only six months old but they were in deep grief. They had never before lost a child. Hortense was able to tell them how she was able to sympathize. The Queen of Bavaria was very polite, recalling how Hortense had entertained her in Paris. The children were an angel choir. Josephine was going to be the most beautiful princess in Europe; Eugénie had not such regular features but an expression both gentle and sweet. Augustus Charles was a very fine lad, advanced for his age, and of a happy disposition. Amélie was a rosebud. "And this is your one!" exclaimed Prince Eugène, placing Theodolinde on his sister's knee. Certainly, the resemblance was remarkable. Little Louis Napoleon was at first intimidated by finding himself amongst so many strange faces but soon happy as the day was long, running wild with young companions. Lavalette was sent up into the mountains on the one day when there was a large party but he came down in time to meet the Dalbergs. He had to move on again.

When Hortense got home she found a letter from her husband telling her that he was going to petition the Pope for the annulment of their marriage. It had been contracted against his will. He had been threatened with banishment by Napoleon unless he married the daughter of Josephine. She knew that this was not true, and when a deputation of the Chapter from the Cathedral of Constance came to take her testimony upon oath, she said so. She knew also that Louis was wanting to re-marry in Rome and wanted possession of both of their sons.

In October, an extraordinary wedding took place in Munich. Princess Charlotte had been told by her father that she was to become the Empress of Austria. The Emperor's third wife had died, and he must have a hostess and companion. He was forty-eight; she was twenty-four. She would be the step-mother of Marie Louise and the step-grandmother of the King of Rome. By an odd chance, on the very day that she became Empress of Austria her first husband, who had been no husband, became King of Württemberg. He had succeeded his enormous father at last. He had been for some months married to the Czar's widowed sister, the Grand Duchess of Oldenburg, who had fallen passionately in love with him. Last time the Emperor Francis had been a widower—for he had now lost three wives, and all by death—she had been taken with the idea of marrying him. She was dissuaded with difficulty. She was told he had fixed regular habits and childish tastes. He liked making seals, and coffee. He was rather untidy. "If he is dirty I can wash him!" she had cried. Auguste's younger sister went off meekly for her family's good to occupy a splendid position.

Better relations with Vienna were essential. With the collapse of France, all the old fear and jealousy of Austria had revived. In the cutting up of the cake the Tyrol and Voralberg had gone to her, followed by most of Salzburg, and Bavaria was not satisfied with getting in exchange Würzburg, Aschaffenburg and bits of the left bank of the Rhine and Fulda.

On December 20, 1816, Auguste began to keep a diary which was to prove a boon to biographers of her good husband.[6] Since they were almost always together now, no letters passed between them. Her diary was no mere chronicle of social engagements. She put in enlightening trifles, such as that her brother Ludwig called her his prickly sister, and that when the amazing Princess of Wales came on a visit from her villa on Como, she wore on her large legs little socks "like those worn by my little girls". And when the poor demented creature insisted on singing a duet with Eugène, although everybody else had been hardly able to contain their laughter, he had been so gentle. He had danced with her. He took her for a drive. She wore skirts above her knees and a man's hat with a forest of red feathers. She had been born a princess of Brunswick and was King Max's guest at the Residenz. She gave Eugène a book, her life-story in French, *Mémoires d'une Anglaise*.

In January, 1817, Eugène and his wife paid a visit to the Duchess of St. Leu at Constance. He still did not know what he was to call himself or what he was to get from Italy. He and his wife did not at all mind travelling economically, but poor Baronin Wurmb amused Mademoiselle Cochelet much by her upcast eyes and hands and cries of horror, as she saw a princess of Bavaria handed into her own carriage by her own husband. There was some gaiety at Constance to greet the New Year of 1817. A ball given by the city attracted lustrous guests from as far afield as St. Galle and Winterthur. The Prince and Princess of Hohenzollern Sigmaringen came with their son and daughter. Princess Amélie, born Princess of Salm Kyrburg, was a very old friend. She was the kind lady who had offered to take the children of Josephine to safety in England and had asked them to her palace on the quayside opposite the guillotine every Sunday . . . Hortense's guests were shown the historic council chamber of Constance and taken for sledge-rides and skating on the frozen lake. This was a pleasure to which they were accustomed when they stayed for winter sports with the Queen of Bavaria at her favourite castle at Biederstein.

They returned home to a political upheaval, not unexpected. The King had done what the Crown Prince and Wrede had long been pressing upon him. Montgelas had been dismissed. He had been born French. It was a blow for Eugène, but his father in law remained staunch, and he had always been on good terms with Count Rechberg the successor to Montgelas. His brother in law objected that even in the royal shooting-brake, going out for a day after pheasants, everyone spoke French. But it was the language of courts and diplomacy, and King Max stuck to it for his family. He was going to give his kingdom a Constitution; but he had always been an enlightened monarch, and he did not intend any breach with the European policy of his old minister. Bavaria was going to be the defender of the smaller states against Austria and Prussia. There were to be two Houses of Parliament, and articles about the equality of religions and protection of the rights of the Protestant minority. These soon brought thunders from Rome.

In the spring of 1817 Eugène at last began to see daylight about his own future. He expected income from four sources, but the story was immensely complicated. It had taken the newly-restored King of Naples six months to reply on the subject of carving a principality of fifty thousand inhabitants out of his territories. In the end the great decision had been reached that the prince should receive from Naples not land and subjects, but an indemnity. The sum of twelve hundred thousand francs was at first suggested. Lavalette always said that he understood that the Czar had promised Prince Eugène a territory of fifty-five thousand souls and that in the end he had got one with seven thousand. His eventual principality was perhaps no larger, but he did also get the indemnity, though Auguste's diary received violent stabs from her indignant pen as she recorded that the sum had been reduced to five hundred thousand, to be paid over a period of several years. Soulange Bodin wrestled with Paris over Malmaison and Navarre effects. Comte Ré dealt with the question of Eugène's personal possessions in the Papal States, and Baron Bataille had a long stay in Milan. Méneval and Darnay both reported the saga with interest. Méneval believed that the prince retained the estates which he derived from the Kingdom of Italy and the endowments which the Emperor had bestowed upon him in Lombardy and Rome. "Two million seven hundred francs left behind by him in the Italian treasury were restored to him." Darnay knew better, and wrote bitterly:

"The court of Vienna unhappy at seeing Prince Eugène enjoying property in Lombardy, and jealous of the lustre attached to his name there, imagined that by buying up all his belongings they could efface all memory of his beneficent rule. Prince Eugène consented nobly to demands of the Emperor Francis, and sold him his domains in Lombardy. Vain hope on the part of Austria! There remain in Milan and in Venice too many monuments initiated by the prince; too many hearts retain memories which ensure that the name of Eugène will be for ever popular in their country."

Eugène, wishing to fall in with the declared intentions of the Emperor Francis, sold to his government, by means of a direct agreement, all his goods and furniture left in Milan and the neighbouring provinces. Simultaneously, by a clause in the agreement, he had been credited with the sum which he had deposited in the Italian treasury, proceeds of a loan made by him, out of his own money and savings, to the War Department for the requirements of the Army of Italy. (Fifteen years later Darnay was still indignant on behalf of a beloved employer.) "In spite of the clauses in the agreement which acknowledged the sum of two million seven hundred thousand francs in the Lombard treasury it has not yet proved possible to obtain repayment. Austria continually gives us promises that the debt will be repaid in the immediate future, but she wants all the rest of the Italian states which have been restored to her sovereignty to contribute to the repayment, and goes on convoking meetings of commissioners from every state, which for one reason or another are aborted. Meanwhile the debt remains unpaid. It would be quite simple if Austria, employing her superior powers, took the responsibility of assessing the several contributions, and herself guaranteed repayment."

In 1860 the editor of Eugène's diary said the last word on the subject. "This debt has never been repaid."[7]

Within a year of his arrival in Munich as a homeless wanderer he had mentioned one day at table in the Residenz how he would like to build a house here. The result had been rather comic. His father in law had been enchanted, and deeply moved. Crown Prince Ludwig was an enthusiast on the subject of building in the classic style. In his mind's eye he saw Munich a second Rome or Athens. But to have a Beauharnais in one of these lordly pleasure houses seemed to him a heavy price to pay for an architectural amenity. Auguste sadly confided to her diary that when the beloved parent was taken from them, as in course of time he must be, she wondered whether Eugène would want to stay in Munich. But she had under-estimated her husband's devotion. As soon as he could, he gave her a home where she would be surrounded by her family. His first purchase in the village of Ismaning, a few miles to the south-east of Munich, was romantic. Before the secularisation of Bavarian church property in 1803, this little estate had belonged to a Bishop of Freising and long before that, to the monastery of Tegernsee. A small castle dating from the sixteenth century had been rebuilt in the baroque style. Eugène bought it in 1816 hardly knowing if he would ever inhabit it. He had realized that since the death of the infant Caroline, the house lent to them by Auguste's father had been disliked by her. It was also inconvenient to have to be a guest at Berg for every summer holiday. As soon as he knew he was not to be a poor relation for life, humiliatingly dependent on his wife's family, he ordered alterations at Ismaning. The expert whom he employed first on this small affair was Leo von Klenze, court architect to the kings of Westphalia.[8]

While work was going on her brother turned to the problem of Hortense. Her situation was rather more depressing than usual. She too had bought a country estate, but in Switzerland, on the shores of her favourite lake Constance. "The château of Arenenberg was very small, very dilapidated, but its situation pleased me." The authorities of the canton of Thurgau allowed her to make the purchase, but after an awkward silence, which she interpreted as an intrigue against her by Talleyrand, it was suggested to her that she should not take up residence until times were more peaceful. Then it appeared that she could not go on staying in Constance. An engagement made by Grand Duke Karl and Stéphanie to visit her was cancelled, also owing to French machinations, and at the same time she was informed that she must leave Baden. "I wrote to my brother to tell him my position. He spoke to the King of Bavaria who offered to let me live in his country. My brother bought me a house in Augsburg ... I chose this place because I had been told there was no social life there. I had retired from the world and all I needed was tranquillity and kindness." Before settling in Augsburg she went for a week to Munich. King Max showed her every attention. He invited her to his beautiful palace of Nymphenburg, and drove with her in its park. He entertained her at the Residenz in Munich and displayed to her the famous Schatzkammer of the house of Wittelsbach. In the evening she made music for the family. Eugène and his whole staff were included at a dinner in the Pavillon Royal, and a box at the theatre was put at her disposal. On her last day they all went out to Ismaning. The children had been there some days, living in an annexe, a little summer-house.

Hortense left for Augsburg and a two months' visit from her elder son from Italy. Auguste took stock of her new home. She saw at once that it was going to become very dear to them. She was delighted with her rooms—"furnished, not luxuriously but with distinguished simplicity." She was happy to see Eugène so happy, though she found it a little pathetic that "he who had ruled the Kingdom of Italy and commanded armies with so much success and renown was now taking the closest interest in every detail of the economy of so small a concern. As always, he was at work to do his best for all employed by him." The village seemed to have realized already that he was their guardian. Their first party was a dinner for the birthday of King Max, May 27. It was disappointing that a tremendous hailstorm burst upon the scene, breaking many windows and causing havoc in the kitchen garden and newly sown fields. Prince Ludwig and his wife on their road from Vienna to Würzburg were the next guests. Then calm settled until Auguste's birthday.

Birthdays at Ismaning became a great feature of family entertainment and the preparations for June 21 entailed much loving forethought. Auguste was woken on the happy morn by a salute of thirty shots under her newly mended windows. She had entered her thirtieth year. The kindly-meant greeting had been the idea of her son Augustus Charles, who took a keen interest in the wonders of science and natural history. Her present from Eugène was very French—a hat from the celebrated Herbaut of Paris, enormous and decorated with exotic birds.[9] This was the latest fashion: Hortense had one which she admired so much that she had executed a miniature of herself wearing it. Hers had a life-size sea-gull apparently just alighted on her brow. Prince Karl came for breakfast bringing a bracelet with a miniature of himself. An idyllic touch was added by an appearance of the pastor of the village with two assistants, bringing a lamb for the children. It was terribly hot, but an elegant meal was enjoyed by King Max, his queen, two of their daughters, Montgelas and many other worthies. Eugène had arranged the theatrical performance which followed, a comedy by Marivaux, "The Game of Love and Chance." He took part himself, assisted by Bataille, both the Taschers, Méjean's wife and Auguste's new young lady in waiting, Fräulein von Caumont, whom the Baronin was soon going to banish. The play, quite in the style of old Malmaison days, went with surprising dash. After supper came the fireworks and after them the thunderstorm. It was tragic that the summer was being so unpredictable. 1817 was to be remembered as a hunger-year.

Auguste had an aunt, a sister of the King of Saxony, the widow of King Max's elder brother. This venerable lady lived in some state in a massive baroque schloss on the Danube in the Franconian Jura. Eugène and Auguste seized the opportunity this summer of combining a call upon "Tante von Neuburg" with an incognito tour of inspection of two places suggested as possible sites for their future principality. Bayreuth had long been dismissed from consideration. The scenery of Upper Franconia was fine but even the Neues Schloss was uninhabitable. Both castles had been built by Margraves of Brandenburg Kulmbach before Bayreuth had become Bavarian in 1810, and neither had received any attention since. Eugène had sad experience of the enormous expenditure made by his mother on Navarre, which was now his, and fast

The Residenz, Eichstätt

Photographs by permission of Fritz Lauterback, Fürth

dropping back into disrepair. Auguste had a cogent reason for begging to be excused from taking her family to live at Bayreuth. The place was a Protestant stronghold.

Dillingen, also on the Danube, but far to the west, almost on the Württemberg frontier, seemed to them small and sad. The schloss which had been converted into a palace for the Bishops of Augsburg in the sixteenth century, dated in its lower parts from the thirteenth. Eichstätt, their third candidate, had obvious good points. It was much the least remote, less than sixty-five miles north-west of Munich. They could move into the palace without undue delay. It had been built two hundred years ago but had never been uninhabited and had modern conveniences. "It seems," wrote Auguste "that the old Bishop, Freiherr von Stubendorf, who has laid down his office as overlord, now rules his former subjects only as an ecclesiastic, and that the inhabitants would like us to have their town. Thus we are sure of a welcome."[10]

Darnay, accompanying them, shrewdly noted that with the prince the deciding factor was that the place stood some one thousand two hundred and seventy feet up in good hunting country, with the princess that it had a holy history. It was not perhaps ideal that the ecclesiastical palace which would be their home was absolutely attached to the fine cathedral. The chime of bells would seldom be absent. But the Gothic cloisters of two storeys were of surprising beauty, and the Residenz was, even more surprisingly, already rather worldly in style. There was a palatial grand staircase with ornamental iron-work balustrading, and the life-size marble figures of cheerful nude male infants placed at strategic intervals. On the second floor there was a Mirror Hall—if not quite worthy of Versailles, at any rate reminiscent. There were two large adjoining reception rooms. It would be possible to entertain there in suitable style. The little Residenz Platz on which the windows of the palace looked out on the opposite side from the cloisters, was miniature, but fit for a fairytale. There were two imposing sentry boxes, solid stone even to the plumes on their tops. They seemed only waiting for handsome guardsmen.

The façade was a pale brick-red, and the houses all round the square were pea-green, and lilac and yellow, and had glancing gleaming windows in neat rows—far more glass than wall. On a grass plot there was a tall pillar surmounted by a Madonna, erected as a thank-offering after a visitation of plague. The smiling holy figure was silhouetted against a background of hills and woods and an old castle, far away. Eichstätt sat almost in a saucer on the gently flowing river Altmühl. There was a fringe of trees round the edge of the saucer, and mediaeval town walls, with occasional square towers, climbing up the hill. There were four principal squares, all full of coloured houses and each with a character of its own. That in the market place was presided over by St. Willibald, nephew of St. Boniface who had founded the bishopric in 741. The see boasted two more saints, and from many corners of narrow cobbled steep streets there were madonnas inclining perilously from niches, in royal blue robes with hoops of golden stars behind their big top-heavy crowns. A little outside the town there was a famous convent and a summer residence on the river belonging to the bishopric. The whole place seemed only waiting for the arrival of a prince to wake it from sleep. They returned to Ismaning having gratefully decided for Eichstätt.

Hortense had been down to Italy to see her husband. His suit for divorce was still dragging on. She had come back without either of her sons. But he promised to return the younger. She was in a miserably nervous condition. On September 1, Hortense came for her brother's birthday at Ismaning, and again they had theatricals, but this time the living pictures which he had admired at Vienna.

In September crates arrived from France. They contained another consignment of Josephine's treasures from Malmaison. Munich heard with edification that Canova's "Pan" and "Three Graces" now decorated the Bavarian capital.

On October 3 Prince Karl waited in an antechamber of the house in the *Schwabingergasse* until he was given the glad news with which to hurry to the Residenz. Auguste had completed her family. The news was indeed glad, for at last she had another son. He had tactfully chosen his grandfather's name-day for his appearance, but in any case he would have been Prince Max.

Eight days later a solemn but happy little ceremony took place on a piece of land not yet developed though not far from the town centre, which was to become the Odeons Platz almost opposite the Hof Garten. Prince Eugène was laying the foundation of his town house in his wife's country. He had said that he had wanted something like the Villa Napoleon in Milan, an hôtel, a family home, not a palace; but Von Klenze who had already worked for him at Ismaning had large ideas, and knew that he now had a wealthy patron.

It was fortunate that the Crown Prince had gone on to Greece from Italy, for ex-Queen Hortense had been to stay in Munich three times this year, and was now settled in Augsburg, and Comte Lavalette, although still disguised as M. Cossar, had moved into the town and went to the theatre and afterwards supper with the royal family. Moreover, at the christening of one more male Beauharnais, the child received as his final name "Napoleon". The beaming grandfather brought to the function a long-expected, welcome gift for the whole family. "The affair of Eugène is now at an end," he wrote to the absent Crown Prince. The document presented to the exile told him that he was now His Royal Highness the Duke of Leuchtenberg, Prince of Eichstätt. The last Landgraf of Leuchtenberg had died in 1700 and his territory had fallen in to the then Elector of Bavaria. Actually all that remained of Leuchtenberg in October 1817, was a ruined fortress in the Oberpfalz. It was further announced that the duke would rank as the premier peer of the kingdom taking precedence after the princes of the blood, and that all his children would be Serene Highnesses. Finally, the father in law who had always signed himself "Your best friend", bestowed upon the duke the command of a regiment of Bavarian *chasseurs*.[11]

III

In February, 1818, the Duke of Leuchtenberg wrote to the Czar, "Sire, Thanks to your constant protection my uncertainties are at last at an end." This year was to have happy hours but two causes for grave disturbance. In May, Crown Prince Ludwig returned from his Italian tour. Prince Wrede and Count Alois Rechberg were relieved to get him back in time for the ceremonies attending the grant of a Constitution to the kingdom. Unfortunately things began to go very badly from the start. A great deal of publicity was being given to the occasion. Heralds made announcements from street corners, bells rang noisy joy-peals. "The Duke of Leuchtenberg is not yet here," said Prince Karl nervously as he followed his father and elder brother in procession to the Council hall in the Residenz. "Why should he be here?" asked Prince Ludwig. "He is not a Prince of the Blood, or a Minister or a Councillor or the President of a Tribunal?" The King took his stand under a canopy on a dais and made a short speech. His two sons were the first to swear allegiance. The next public engagement was a service of thanksgiving in the Michaelskirche. It had been arranged to coincide with the King's birthday; but he did not appear. He had learned that his son in law had not been invited. Both the Duke and Duchess of Leuchtenberg sat down at the first banquet at the Nymphenburg palace, but the party was very large. When Auguste advanced to congratulate her father, she was so upset that her voice failed. Eugène whose temper was more even, went to a ball in the Museum, but she retired in dudgeon to Ismaning. The French Resident reported to Paris that at an encounter next morning such high words had passed between Ludwig and Eugène that a challenge was likely. It was most unlikely. Eugène wrote a courtly letter to Rechberg asking for clarification as to protocol. The assembly duly ended. Ludwig went back to his wife in Würzburg. But in Munich Eugène had given Von Klenze orders to cease work on the Palais Leuchtenberg. The scandal was great. He had been becoming popular in the city and his wife was well known and much loved. She wrote one of her best and most lengthy letters to Ludwig. Amongst her winning points was a reminder that although he might be the next king of Bavaria, this country would not have been a kingdom but for her marriage to Eugène de Beauharnais. She and her husband went off with the whole family for the usual holiday on the Tegernsee and the foundations of the house in Munich remained untouched. On her birthday party in the Pavillon Royal, the king told his daughter briefly that he had spoken to her elder brother. Later Prince Karl divulged that the Director of Police had been given an audience to explain that the cessation of work on the palace had meant that three hundred men had been unemployed. Auguste told her diary that she was thankful that this unmerited trouble was over, but was afraid that her brother would hate her for the rest of her life.[12]

It was a relief to be off for Eichstätt, and her feelings were soothed by their reception there. From the moment that they entered the principality, villages were decorated with flags and greenery. They were greeted under triumphal arches by chanting schoolchildren. The climax was reached in Eichstätt itself. Here the old Bishop stood waiting to receive them on the steps of the palace. They were escorted up the Grand Staircase to give audience to a deputation including more singing infants who had bouquets to present. Auguste recorded that her apartments were very comfortable, and her new home was beautiful. She gave audience to the wives of the principal local noblemen and citizens. Her father's proclamation allowing religious processions and pilgrimages had caused great joy in a devout town. "Eichstätt is small, very small, but big enough for us to do good in it, and the duke has no other wish than to make this little tiny corner of the world as happy as possible!"

They gave their first dinner party. The decoration of the Mirror Hall was charming. There were designs of Chinamen, birds, beasts and flowers, all as white and fresh as sugar icing. One of the adjoining rooms had a classical wall-paper of a procession and temples, another a *trompe l'oeil* imitation of ginger-coloured hanging curtains. On June 25, the Duchess went for a tour of the Cathedral and the town, which seemed to possess many fine houses as well as four lesser churches. The garden of her palace was unusually pretty and well arranged. The theatre at which they attended a performance was fairly large but unprovided with boxes. They were received with hand-clapping and a local artiste, Fräulein Nanette Heinrichmaier, spoke a Prologue.

The sunny days passed without a cloud. While Eugène went out of the town inspecting the possibilities for *la chasse*, Auguste was escorted by the Bishop and the Head of the Capuchin college to the famous Benedictine nunnery of St. Walburga—a long tug uphill. This establishment was imposing. She was met at the gates by the local clergy and shown the convent, crypt-chapel, and relics, and then the church which was brilliant after the chapel. It was a master-piece of baroque, with shell pink and sky blue as predominating colours, and many large all-gold saints. From a most beautiful little loggia she was called upon to admire a view. She saw all over the convent buildings, and after dinner in the Refectory walked to the foot of a hill where there was the beginning of a walk over the hills which could be made wonderful.

The summer Residenz promised to be a most suitable home for a large young family. It had a dark and cavernous hall (cool in hot weather) and a very large staircase, but the rooms which looked out over gardens and orchard to the river, which was wide and smooth here, were of moderate size. The ceiling in the Festsaal was well chosen. The frescoes represented Flora—a rosy goddess sitting on azure clouds surrounded by nymphs and cupids. At the bottom of the garden there was a Gloriette with three pavilions and a semi-circular grille, with pineapple finials and a fountain. Eugène chose sites for little Swiss châlets for the children. The duke and duchess visited local industries and received gifts. On their last night they gave a ball for a hundred and the town provided dancers in native costume, and singers.

The two residences did not complete the amenities of Eichstätt. There were two hunting boxes—Prünn and Hirschberg. Prünn was not likely to be much visited by the princess. It literally towered above the Altmühl in ideal country for wild-boar. Hirschberg, which had belonged to Counts bearing that title, had a rococo castle built by an Italian architect for a Prince Bishop in 1760, with attractive stucco work and panelling. It was near the confluence of the Altmühl and Sulz which it overhung from a rocky height. Both lay north-east of Eichstätt. Hirschberg was opposite Beilngries.[13]

After their entirely successful first visit to their principality they went on to Baden to fulfil an engagement which must be painful and might be very unpleasant. The Duke of Leuchtenberg had an appointment with a gentleman from St. Helena. He had told King Max, as he must. He much hoped nobody else might know, at least until he had made up his own mind about the authenticity of the Marquis de Las Cases. The Emperor had originally been allowed three officers and twelve servants. He had taken Bertrand as Grand Marshal, as chamberlains the Marquis de Montholon the Marquis de Las Cases, and as aide de camp, Colonel Planat de la Faye. Las Cases had been admitted as a civilian. At the last moment Baron General Gourgaud had been substituted for Planat as he had made such jealous scenes. Naturally, with so small a staff, all cooped up together, people had got on one another's nerves. The first "Voice from St. Helena" to be heard in Europe had been that of a valet dismissed by the Governor. A member of the Opposition in England had got hold of Santini who was illiterate. His *Appeal to the English Nation* had caused a sensation in London. Ingenuous readers learned that St. Helena was a lump of volcanic granite rising out of distant seas. It was only twenty-eight miles in circumference and most unhealthy. The Emperor was terribly ill and ill-treated. He had at first occupied a pavilion belonging to a villa called The Briars, but had in December, 1816, moved to Longwood which was creaky, rotten and rat-ridden. A new Governor had been sent out in April 1816, as Lord Bathurst, the Colonial Secretary, had heard that the first appointed had been too lenient.

Santini, who hated Sir Hudson Lowe with true Corsican fervour, painted him in the blackest colours and some of the paint was destined to stick. More knowledgeable English who regarded the Emperor as a menace, pointed out that General Sir Hudson Lowe had good service and family connections but small private means. He was certainly not a brilliant officer. No officer of promise would have accepted such a post. But he no doubt had sufficient intelligence to realize that if he let Boney escape his career was over. He had arrived with instructions to address the Emperor as General Bonaparte and they had soon ceased to meet. This certainly did not sound reassuring. Santini had been arrested at Como on his way to Rome and Madame Mère, and removed into Austria. Judging by Darnay's accounts he was the only visitor from St. Helena who did not get money out of Prince Eugène.

Las Cases had a curious record. On the Revolution he had fled from France after training in the military schools of Vendôme and Paris, and serving in the navy. He had spent several years as an exile in England and Germany and joined Napoleon during the Consulate. His languages were good. He had once applied for the post of tutor to the children of Queen Hortense. He had retired to England again when the Emperor had gone to Elba and rejoined him for the Hundred Days. He had strongly urged him to throw himself on the mercy of the British nation. He had stayed in St. Helena one year, acting as Secretary and taking notes of his conversations with the great man. He had not been able to get on with Montholon or Gourgaud but his expulsion had come, not from the Emperor, but from Sir Hudson Lowe. He had been forbidden to re-enter France. He was fifty-two, of considerable address and apparently a worshipper of the Emperor. Gourgaud's pet name for him had been "The Jesuit". He was going to win, after the death of his hero, fame and a fortune with his extremely dubious *Memorial of St. Helena*. Eugène met him twice, incognito at Baden. Méneval, who believed him to be "virtuous", believed also that he had brought a message from the Emperor to his stepson. He got letters of exchange for twenty-one thousand eight hundred and twenty francs in June 1818, and next year Frs. three hundred and seventy thousand.

Despite all Eugène's care, Baron Hruby reported to Metternich within a few days of the first secret interview, that the Duke of Leuchtenberg had sent Napoleon, by way of London, ten thousand louis d'or. Newspapers took up the rumour. Catherine of Württemberg, the ex-queen of Westphalia, had stuck to Jerome Bonaparte, who had commanded a wing with courage at Waterloo. They were living in Italy in a very small way when she chanced to meet Hortense, who enlisted her to sign a petition to be presented from the Bonaparte family to the Congress of Powers sitting at Aix la Chapelle. They had heard that the Emperor was having to sell his plate. Catherine said that she supposed Eugène could not join, and Hortense said on the contrary he was heart and soul with them, but could not declare it.

The Austrian authorities were enquiring after Lavalette again and another refugee, Comte d'Erlon, who was living in a country house outside Munich. But King Max was not to be intimidated. He replied that no persons bearing those names were in his domains. He had only one newcomer, M. Cossar, whose papers were in order. At one moment there seemed a possibility that they might have to go down to one of the king's Silesian castles, and they doubted if they would be safe, in the heart of a Prussian province. Luckily the diplomatic correspondence relaxed by degrees.

From Baden the Duke and Duchess of Leuchtenberg returned to Ismaning and were astonished to see how much very young children can grow in six weeks. But they had only a few days there before they set off for the longest holiday journey of their lives. They were going up to Dresden to pay a visit to the restored uncle and aunt there. They left the children happily settled in at Eichstätt for the first time, all delighted with their rooms. At Pillnitz, King Max's sister was so pleased to see Auguste that she took her into her arms wrecking her attempt at kissing the hand. It was the same route that Eugène had followed on his way to Russia in 1812. Now he was happy, with his wife by his side, and September was a lovely month for Saxony. They came home by Chemnitz and Kulmbach. Nürnberg received them with great ceremony. The guard was turned out and Eugène was invited to dine with the General and regiment in garrison. They had to pass Ellingen on their way to Eichstätt, so had to pay a courtesy call on Prince Wrede, though he had behaved so badly in backing up Ludwig. They found the Marschallin and all her sons at home and were asked to dine and shown the schloss. Auguste had never seen

The Leuchtenberg Palace, Munich,
built by Eugène 1817-1821, by F. Hablitschek after
H. Adam

By permission of the Stadtmuseum, Munich

such luxury in a country house. The Residenz in Munich was nothing to it. All was silk, gold, mahogany and bronze. Even the washing utensils in the guests' rooms were of such fine porcelain that they deserved to be in show-cabinets. An army of servitors hovered around. But to do the Marschallin justice, Auguste believed that she preferred her eight children to her husband's luxury.

The duke and duchess had moved back into Munich for the winter when Darnay came in one day in the beginning of November with one of those letters which reached him by unusual channels and always made his master miserable. It was in fact a packet of four letters, though all were written in the same hand. The first was signed General Baron Gourgaud and was addressed to The Empress Marie Louise.

"Madame,

"If your Majesty is graciously pleased to recall the conversation I had with her at Grosbois in 1814 when seeing her, unluckily for the last time, I recounted to her all that had befallen the Emperor at Fontainebleau, I venture to hope that she will excuse the sad duty which I fulfil at this moment when I tell her that the Emperor Napoleon is dying in torment of the most frightful and most prolonged agony. Yes, Madame, he whom divine and human law unite to you by the most sacred ties, he whom you have seen receive homage from almost every crowned head in Europe, he for whose sake I have seen so many tears shed when he separated from you, is dying the cruellest death, a prisoner on a rock in the middle of the ocean, separated by two thousand leagues from his loved ones, alone, without friend or relative, without news of his wife or his son, and bereft of every consolation . . ."

Marie Louise had given birth to a daughter on May 1, 1817, in Parma, and the event had been announced in the court circular. The name of the father had not been given but everyone knew that it had been Neipperg. The remaining letters from Gourgaud were to her father, the Czar, and Prince Eugène, upon whom he wished to call.

His wish was granted, and when he did present himself, his story was disconcerting. He had left St. Helena expedited by Sir Hudson Lowe, who had made him a loan and had given him an introduction from the French commissioner in St. Helena to the French Ambassador in London. This he had used. He had made statements that he had left the Emperor very well and able to send letters out of the island with ease. He could easily escape. But after a few weeks he had thrown off the mask. He was on a secret mission from the Emperor Napoleon! He had been promptly banished from England and came now from Hamburg. His story might not hold water but there could be no doubt at all of the handwriting of a little pencil note which he produced. "My son, you will oblige me by granting every year to Madame Gourgaud (the mother) in Paris, the sum of Frs. 12,000 beginning on January 1, 1817. (To Prince Eugène at Munich.)"

It was dated July 12, 1817. The invaluable Darnay preserved it and in the course of time the excellent Hennin attached it to the Leuchtenberg archives, together with the whole *dossier* about payments by Prince Eugène on the instructions of the Emperor Napoleon from the secret hoard left with Comte Lavalette at the château of La Verrière. Gourgaud got six thousand francs for himself also in 1819, and twelve thousand francs in 1820. The moneys paid out to a dozen pensioners were remitted from Messrs. Matheus of Frankfort and Paris, and Eichthal of Munich, and even by Messrs. Holm of London and Baring *frères*.

There was another immediate result of the talkative Baron Gourgaud's secret call. The Czar was on his road to the Congress at Aix. A letter from Munich might just catch him.

"Sire,

"Newspapers in various countries report that the Emperor Napoleon is being kept without the primary necessities of life and that his health is being impaired by the rigours which are imposed on him.

"If these reports are correct, it cannot have been the intention of the Heads of State (and I am sure it is not yours) to make him suffer these privations.

"In this position of anxiety and doubt, it is my duty to make an appeal in respect of the fate of the man who married my mother, who was my first tutor in my profession of arms and my guide in administration; who loaded me with kindnesses. I must appeal for the interest and attention of Your Majesty.

"Far be it from me to have the temerity to ask for anything which might disturb the peace of Europe, but doubtless it is possible to find a means of reconciling the interests of Europe with those of humanity, and Your Majesty will have no difficulty in using Your Majesty's qualities of heart and head to find them.

"I ask no favour for myself, Sire, when I take the liberty of writing to you today. Your Majesty has been good enough to bring me within the circle of your acquaintance. I am sure, therefore, that far from taking exception to my plea Your Majesty will realize the justice of the feelings which have impelled me to write."

Upon reflection, the stepson of Napoleon decided to follow up his letter by a personal call. He caught the Czar at the best inn in Mergentheim on the Tauber, a pleasant little watering-place in Württemberg. The roads were still open, but the sudden journey at a season when days were short had to be largely performed in darkness. Auguste recorded the result in her diary for December 5, with disappointing discretion.

"Eugène got back last night at ten . . . He had arrived in Mergentheim just before the Czar, who received him privately and treated him as a friend. In their conversation which lasted until two a.m. the Emperor said pleasant things about me . . . Eugène also spoke about our troubles in Bavaria. The Czar said that he had bargained as his conscience dictated. At eight a.m. next morning he was off again. My husband saw him off and had to give a faithful promise to visit him in St. Petersburg. Eugène was startled by the style in which the Czar travelled nowadays, much more pompous and showy than before. It reminded him of the *cortège* accompanying the Emperor Napoleon." Darnay, surprisingly, wrote that the Duke had mentioned the visits of Las Cases.[14]

Early in the New Year the Duke of Leuchtenberg began to sell pictures from his mother's collection to grace the Imperial galleries at the Hermitage.

1818 had ended sadly. Karl of Baden had died suddenly. He had left three daughters: tragedy had overtaken his infant sons. King Max made a long-meditated attempt to claim the Grand Duchy but there was a Duke of Hochberg, a cousin of the late Duke by a morganatic marriage, who was preferred by Austria. The dispute was referred to Aix.

IV

On February 3, 1819, the King opened the new Parliament. "Eight coaches each with six horses," wrote Auguste with satisfaction. Max Joseph went alone in his splendid coronation coach. His son in law as well as his sons, accompanied him to the Michaelskirche and to the steps of his throne. Balls, concerts and a performance of Rossini's "La Cenerentola" in a new theatre occupied the evenings till the 7th, when there was a State Banquet in the *Grüne Galerie* at which a hundred and eighty-six sat down. "This was the gallery in which the civil contract of my marriage took place and in which on my wedding day we supped," wrote Auguste.

After some alarming scenes during which advanced radicals demanded that the army should swear allegiance to the Constitution, Bavaria gradually settled down to the new order and King Max prepared to become a model constitutional monarch. His son in law and daugher dined with him every Thursday while they were in the capital. The figure of the Crown Prince riding out to pay a morning call at Ismaning became a familiar sight. On Auguste's birthday he presented her with a Nymphenburg breakfast service. In the same month Eugène braved up to speak in the Upper Chamber. Auguste wrote proudly, "He explained briefly why he agreed to the nomination of District Councillors. All would have gone well if Prince Wrede, without authority from several members of the Council, had not said that the King did not want this ... He had completely forgotten that the motion must be unanimous. Now the Second Chamber is so enraged that they say they will not sanction the Budget." That trouble blew over and at their next meeting Ludwig told his sister that he regretted he had not had an opportunity to congratulate Eugène. "He spoke like a man who knows only one path, that of honour. A pity he is not more master of the German tongue. He could render us great service in the House."

They stayed with Hortense at Augsburg twice that year and on the second occasion took their two eldest daughters, who were of the age to appreciate a masked ball, however provincial. Hortense had been quite mistaken in thinking that she could live the life of a hermit in her German small-town home. She was her mother's daughter and would have attracted guests on a desert island. Princess Fugger Babenhausen soon found her out. Auguste and Eugène attended a ball for a hundred guests on the night after their first arrival, and danced till one a.m. "Very passable people," commented Auguste, "and no etiquette observed. Everyone spoke to everyone."

In July, Parliament was dissolved and an announcement came from the Aix Congress about the Baden succession. The Hochberg candidate had won. By the Treaty of Frankfort, Bavaria received a small strip of land to connect the kingdom with the Palatinate. Bavarian troops were allowed to garrison the federal fortress of Mainz. The house of Leuchtenberg was settling down harmoniously. Auguste remembered with gratitude the picture of her old father sitting on his birthday in their theatre at Ismaning, laughing till he cried at his French son in law performing a character part in a French farce.

Their years were beginning to follow a regular pattern— Munich for the winter, early summer out at Ismaning and on the Tegernsee, spring, high summer and autumn at Eichstätt. They still had not got a lakeside holiday home of their own. At the end of this summer Eugène approached the Swiss authorities of the canton of Thurgau with an offer to buy land on which to build a house near Lake Constance, and his sister. It would indeed be so near her Swiss château that he could ride over from her home to his own without leaving their joint property, and without disturbing anything except perhaps a roe deer. He had been very much taken with Arenenberg. It was already a sort of Napoleonic family museum, packed tight with association objects, rousing happy memories for him. It was really an exaggeration to call it Schloss Arenenberg. (The odd name was a corruption of "*Narrenberg*"—Fool's Hill.) It was a two-storey, square, butter-coloured house with a red roof and verandahs, set high on a promontory above the inner lake a few miles west of Constance and the Baden frontier. It was so small that the staircase from the hall to the first floor had to be one of the spiral variety common in libraries. But there had been one like that in Josephine's *nid* in the Rue Chantereine. There was much here reminiscent of her. Hortense had made some additions, and there was a succession of four good-sized rooms opening out of one another in which she was able to hang life-size family portraits including her beloved never-forgotten first-born. Her house at once reminded anyone who had ever been there of Malmaison, for she had tent-like rooms with striped material covering walls and ceiling, and crystal chandeliers and circular tables and mahogany and ormolu Empire chairs and cabinets, and bronzes and busts and bookcases. There was evidence of her artistic tastes—a pianoforte and collections of songs, and portfolios of sketches. Her bedroom was so small it might have been a room in an inn, and the dressing-room adjoining was even tinier. Its walls were covered with pleated cashmere. She had an indifferent copy of an English child-picture, "The Infant Samuel" by Reynolds, over her bed.[15]

She had become rather devout since her troubles had descended upon her, and was calmer. She knew now that she was living for her sons. The younger was pursuing his studies with a tutor at the University of Augsburg. The elder came for visits from Italy. Her love-affair with Flahaut had begun to die a lingering death after Waterloo. He had ceased to call while the Czar was with her daily. He had said he did not care for the company of the conquerors of France. He had betaken himself to Mademoiselle Mars for comfort, and then to England. His old stepfather, Ambassador de Souza, had said in a mutter, almost as if ashamed of the idea, that Charles might now make an advantageous alliance. And that was exactly what he had done. Hortense had behaved with typical dignity. "Tell me her names that I may mention them in my prayers." She was Miss Margaret Mercer Elphinstone, and when her old father the Admiral died she would become the Viscountess Keith and immensely rich. She was the bosom friend of the heiress to the throne of Britain, the Princess Charlotte, and her marriage to a French refugee, the reputed son of Talleyrand, aide de camp of Boney, who had been the lover of the Queen of Holland and the Queen of Naples had almost caused a political upheaval. Hortense spoke of her as an English *jeune fille* but in fact she had been Scottish and twenty-nine. She kept a beautiful water-colour of the Duchess of St. Leu, by Isabey, in her bed-chamber and Flahaut proved, as Hortense had always expected he would, an excellent husband. Her letter of congratulation on their fifth daughter was only faintly patronizing. "It must be embarrassing to have such a lot of girls."[16]

The views from Hortense's Swiss home were dazzling, opalescent and rather more clear-cut than her sketches of them. In September, mist generally covered all but the nearest pale blue satin waters. But when the sun broke through there suddenly appeared men in boats, and swans, and bright green orchards with apple-trees, so loaded with bright red fruit that their branches had to be supported by crutches, and a little church on a little hill, and grazing cows with bells which tinkled gently every time they moved. The garden was gay with flowers, and a fountain played, and here in the warm evenings she would sit with her guests while they declaimed poetry under the stars and moon or played on the harp. It was a very small kingdom, but the Duchesse de St. Leu had a *salon* again.

Eugensberg,
built by Eugène on Lake Constance, 1821
Photograph by permission of P. Zaugg, Solothurn

Lavalette had been spending the last few years between Augsburg and Eichstätt. In the spring of 1820 he decided to go back to France. He wanted to look after his invalid wife. He had been advised that it would be quite safe so long as he behaved quietly. King Max said goodbye to him with emotion. "I embrace M. Cossar but I require of M. de Lavalette to return to thank me within two years. I am growing old. Do not wait too long."

They got their most distressing claimant for the Emperor's secret money, before Lavalette set off for France. Doctor Barry O'Meara was of Irish extraction and had served as an assistant surgeon in both the British army and navy. The Emperor, attracted by his proficiency in Italian, had engaged him when his own surgeon Maingaud had refused to folllow him to St. Helena owing to extreme *mal de mer* on their passage from Rochefort. O'Meara was a plausible fellow, but had been unable to pull with Las Cases or Montholon or Lowe, who had expected him to report his private conversations with his patient and had detected him in irregularities. He had been dismissed in July 1818, and provided by the Emperor with a letter recommending him to Marie Louise. He had told the Admiralty that Lowe had orders to murder the captive, and the Admiralty had court-martialled and dismissed him, but his championship of Bonaparte had gained him a certain popularity in Opposition circles in England. It was impossible to tell how far he was truthful, and most unsatisfactory to learn that the Emperor was now left to the mercies of a Corsican whose qualifications were doubtful. But the man had been sent out by Madame Mère. According to Darnay's accounts, he collected for Dr. Stokoe, naval surgeon, 24,565 francs 65 centimes and for himself 2,370 francs 36 centimes. He was soon persuaded by Lowe that the Emperor was feigning illness as part of his policy of non-co-operation. Afterwards Princess Pauline explained that her mother had been convinced that her son was no longer on St. Helena. He had escaped to Malta. Joseph had a plot for rescuing him, conceived by French refugees in Texas. A house had been built for him in New Orleans ... Lucien thought he could combine with his brothers in an effort to conquer Mexico ... But Gourgaud knew that his master was still on the accursed rock, looking out through his telescope from a bleak plateau on the windward side of the windswept little island, pinning his hopes on the collapse of the Bourbons and a change of heart in the English Parliament.

Auguste's diary continued to record everything that happened at home or abroad. She was horrified by the murder of the Duc de Berri at the Opera in Paris, apparently a political assassination. Eugène, who had first met the Bourbon heir-presumptive at the time of the death of Josephine, sent a courtly letter of condolence to Louis XVIII. On Easter Sunday morning after mass Eugène set off on horseback for the delightful Englischer Garten, one of the joys of Munich. He had arranged to meet Auguste for a walk there. In front of the Hof Garten her carriage had to pull up to let a riderless horse charge past. "At once I recognized Eugène's horse. I almost stopped breathing. I urged the postilion on to look for Eugène. At last I found him with his four daughters. He was already on his feet. To assure me that he was all right he mounted the groom's horse. As soon as he is restored he travels to Thurgau to lay the foundation stone of Eugensberg."

She was not entirely happy about his project of his building what he called a little house so near his sister. She could not help feeling that Hortense was possessive. And she mistrusted her household—her penniless, arch, young lady companions all naturally hoping for good husbands and not likely to find them amongst the company she kept. Hortense had always been so kind to young people—artists, musicians, poets, dramatists.

There was another disadvantage in their having Swiss property. Enemies said that a nest of Bonapartes was now forming in Thurgau. But it was impossible to forestall the ingenuity of illwishers. When Eugène had delighted Eichstätt by spending his last birthday in the little town and giving a splendid ball, one of Metternich's spies had written to Vienna that in Eichstätt the Viceroy, as all his staff still called him, was ruling like a king, and when his sister came she was always given the title she had borne in Holland. It was possible that devoted and not young servants did still so address the children of the Empress Josephine. Auguste herself was meticulous always, even in her diary, to speak of her husband as "the duke" and no more. He was very tactful in his miniature principality. An English guest accompanied him on his hunting expeditions, the Right Honourable Sir Brook Taylor, P.C., newly appointed Minister to Bavaria. Of her husband's kinswomen Auguste much preferred Stéphanie, now a still beautiful and pathetic widow, living in retirement with her three daughters at Mannheim. A visit to Baden this summer was not considered advisable but Eugène took his devout wife to witness

the Passion play at Oberammergau.[17] Eichstätt had its best
festivities yet this autumn, as the King and Queen of Bavaria
visited the city on their road to Neuburg. Eugène took King Max
out shooting. Auguste showed her stepmother everything in the
Residenz. The children all behaved like models. The occasion
was a complete success. Everyone was happy.

The Munich court was plunged in mourning in February 1821.
By his second marriage King Max had seven daughters, twice
twins. It might have been thought that with so ample a supply,
the death of one, aged eleven, might not have caused undue
lamentation. But the Wittelsbachs were a devoted family. Thorwaldsen was commissioned to execute a beautiful conversation
group, showing her sisters visiting the little invalid, for her tomb
in the Michaelskirche. She had been her mother's favourite child.
The Czar sent Tschernitscheff on a mission of condolence and
Eugène had long conferences with him. There was going to be
another Congress to settle the peace of Europe. France, Spain,
Naples were all seething with discontent. In Piedmont King
Victor Emmanuel of Sardinia, the ruler appointed after the
Congress of Vienna, had abdicated. The Leuchtenberg family
were all on holiday at Baden on July 11 when Auguste noted in
her diary the death of the Emperor Napoleon. He had died on
May 5 after an illness of forty days, according to her information.
"We all shed sincere tears. One great man the less. My father is
much affected." She did not say what were her husband's feelings.
Her own considered judgment was that as well as many wrong
things, the Emperor had done many which were admirable. She
said they had wept also in memory of the good Empress Josephine.

They broke off their holiday to return to Ismaning and assume
mourning. A memorial service there was attended by the French
minister. When they got to Tegernsee in August they found the
Empress of Austria there. Eugène was concerned for the King of
Rome. Unfortunately Auguste's sister was now even more anti-
French than her brother. Auguste wrote that everyone said the
little Napoleon was now a charming child. There had been a
horrible rumour that his uncles were going to force him to become
a priest. Méneval had believed it. But the Emperor Francis had
refused to consider such a solution. There were plots in France.
The name of the Duc d'Orléans, who was known to have been a
personal friend of the late Vicomte de Beauharnais, was whispered.
The King of Rome, now Duc de Reichstadt, was another candi-

date. But choosing him might mean civil war. Auguste wrote discreetly, "He will always find in Eugène a zealous defender ... No one will succeed in making my husband follow the devious paths of intrigue and 'Fronde' even to attain what he most desires."[18]

In September 1821, at last they were told that their Munich house was ready for inspection. Eugène took Stéphanie on a tour of the premises on the night of September 24. Next day he wrote to Auguste, who was still at Eichstätt, that he had spent five hours there making last corrections before she arrived. She liked to be surprised by her French husband's taste, and set great store by it. The Palais Leuchtenberg was to become one of the sights of Munich, and aquarelles were performed of both the façade and interior. These showed that without, it was a massive square building of three storeys, with well nigh a hundred tall windows, and that within, the duke's bedchamber was that of a soldier— very plain. It was almost sparsely furnished with an Empire semi-circular writing table, a long-shaped dressing table, two big chairs and two small. There was a bust of the Empress Josephine behind the head of his uncanopied bed, and on the wall beside it a painting of five of his children as a cherub choir. On the opposite wall, so that he saw it when he opened his eyes, hung the large full-length portrait of his wife taken in her one visit to Paris, by Gérard. There was a very fine cut-glass chandelier and a ceiling of Pompeian design.

The palace contained a large library, a picture gallery, a map room, a small and a large dining room, a ball room, a theatre and a chapel. The large dining hall had a frieze by Thorwaldsen. The picture gallery exhibited several of the finest Italian pictures from Josephine's collection. Ill-disposed people said the duke had looted these from churches when he was Viceroy. There was an exact replica of his mother's bedroom at Malmaison with the original furniture.[19] He had simply the initial E inside cartouches on furniture and walls.

He wrote to his wife that Max, who was now four years old, had the most beautiful wall-paper in his bedroom. When Auguste saw her *suite* she said that the bedroom was too small; luckily it was only begun and could be enlarged. She thought all the furnishings rich and elegant. Most of them came from Werner of Paris. She had now finished working seats and backs for four chairs. Two of them were installed in her husband's bedroom and two in her own.

They went back to Eichstätt for a fortnight until the house was ready for occupation, and while they were there were puzzled by a call from a character whom they hardly knew whether to write down as dotty or an impostor. Baron von Bönen who had not resided in his own country, Sweden, for thirty-four years, wanted a daughter of Prince Eugène to marry his Crown Prince. They gave him an evasive answer and nearly forgot him. Josephine would not enter her sixteenth year until next March. But for a princess, as Auguste well knew, that was not at all too young to expect suitors. Augustus Charles had got a commission from his grandfather as a second lieutenant in his father's cavalry regiment and had put on his first uniform in highest spirits.

They took up residence at the Palais Leuchtenberg in the end on October 26, 1821, at ten a.m., attended by Prince Karl. The king and queen and their younger daughters came at one o'clock. Guests began to be invited daily—first the family, then the diplomatic corps, next leading townsfolk. General Gourgaud came again on December 7 and got six thousand francs at the desire of General Bertrand. Auguste found him a tremendous talker and thought he seemed to regard Eugène as no longer a good Frenchman because he would not listen to tirades about freeing France. The last present to arrive for Christmas 1821 was sad—a silver candlestick from St. Helena left to his stepson in the Emperor's will. Following it came a letter from Bertrand and Montholon, executors, telling Prince Eugène that in a codicil the Emperor had appointed him to collect and distribute amongst his devoted followers all his belongings in Italy. This meant sending Darnay to Paris, where he was in any case due to see the completed monument to Josephine in Rueil church. As Eugène had never himself been able to get any of his Italian belongings, the outlook was not hopeful. The whole of Lavalette's hoard was now distributed and for some months Eugène had been drawing on his own income.

Barry O'Meara had published his first volume of *Napoleon in Exile*. Hortense had read what she called the horrible book and said that people should know that the Emperor's family had never ceased to torment the English Minister responsible to get Sir Hudson Lowe recalled. The vulgarity of O'Meara's supposed conversations with the Emperor were incredible, but nobody could put the book down. Another and larger edition was soon called for. "Fouché is a bad man, an ex-priest, a terrorist. He will worm your secrets out of you with an air of unconcern. He is very rich but his fortune is ill-gotten . . . Talleyrand is the vilest of agitators and basest of flatterers, wary and circumspect, but always a traitor. Nothing can be got from him except by bribes. Both the kings of Bavaria and Württemberg complained to me of his rapacity and extortions . . . The King of Württemberg was wicked, but clever; the King of Bavaria a good plain man. The Emperor of Austria is a good man led by the nose by Metternich, who is not a great man but an intriguer and a liar. The Czar is an extremely false character, very ambitious. At Tilsit he and the King of Prussia discussed at length the number of uniform buttons on a dragoon's jacket. The King of Prussia, who is a blockhead, had fifty or sixty jackets hanging up on pegs . . . Bernadotte has been ungrateful, but I cannot say he betrayed me, as he in a manner became a Swede, and never promised what he did not intend to perform. He was not treacherous. Neither he nor Murat would have declared against me if they had thought it would cost me my throne . . . I would have made my second son king of all Italy including Naples, and put Murat elsewhere . . . My great fault was not having made peace in Dresden. That armistice was an error . . . But I should have succeeded but for the treachery of Marmont.

"Everything Josephine put on appeared elegant . . . She was grace personified. Eugène was the only one of my family who never made trouble . . . He was promised a principality in Italy but never got it . . ."[20]

CHAPTER EIGHTEEN

The Grandfather of Europe
1822 : 1824

I

AMONGST the many callers at the Palais Leuchtenberg early in
the New Year 1822 was the Baron von Bönen again. He had been
perfectly genuine. He came with a friendly letter from the King
of Sweden for his old comrade-in-arms the Duke of Leuchtenberg, the Order of the Seraphim, and authority to discuss an
alliance for Crown Prince Oscar with Her Serene Highness, the
Princess Josephine. (The prince's romantic name was the result
of the late Emperor Napoleon's admiration for the works of
Ossian.) There seemed to the parents of Josephine everything in
favour of such a match and very little against it. The Bernadottes
did not compare with the Wittelsbachs or even the Beauharnais,
but they were secure on their throne. Desirée *née* Clary, mother of
Prince Oscar, had always been a favourite with the family,
indeed with all who knew her, for she was an amiable and
virtuous woman. The Emperor Napoleon was said in his earlier
years to have desired to marry Desirée who had a fortune as well
as beauty. His brother Joseph had married her sister Julie.

To turn to Prince Oscar himself, he was entirely French by
origin but he had been educated in Sweden and spoke and wrote
the language of his future kingdom like a native. He was twenty-
two, reported to be the most accomplished prince in Europe and
of blameless character. A miniature which accompanied the offer
showed that he was dashingly handsome. He was preparing to
tour Germany, Switzerland and Italy this summer. There would
be no difficulties about religion, for although Sweden adhered to
the Lutheran belief, the present Queen was Catholic and had
always had freedom to exercise her own faith. Von Bönen
returned to Stockholm with a portrait of Josephine. In the same

457

week the French and Austrian Residents in Munich reported another Bonapartist officer installed at the Palais Leuchtenberg. Eugène had a new Secretary. Colonel Nicolas Louis Planat de la Faye had been imposed upon him, by Lavalette, and particularly Hortense. This was the poor nobleman who had volunteered for St. Helena and exile with the Emperor and been pushed out by the egregious Gourgaud on their passage. He had suffered detention at Malta and Smyrna. When he had got back to Paris he had found that he had been dismissed from the army for quitting the country. He must be given employment by the Bonapartes and where better than in Munich? He was of a very old family of Auvergne and had a long sad face of distinguished features. He was a bachelor, aged thirty-seven. He appeared startled and half-starved, and no wonder. He was a martyr to migraine. He wrote long letters home to an elder married sister. If Prince Eugène's family could have seen them, they would have known their worst fears realized. This poor fellow who looked like a death's head was indeed as bitter as a lemon. He told his sister that he had never seen such a set of old by-gones. He enumerated them carefully. First there was the widow of the Duke of Zweibrücken, King Max's elder brother's wife, "Tante Neuburg", on a visit. She was as old as they make them, but an excellent good woman, which was more than could be said for her two ladies in waiting. Next in seniority came the Baronin Wurmb, with watery pale eyes which, however, missed nothing. She was ignorant of all except etiquette of past courts, suffered from indigestion and was terribly wheezy, but her motto was "Better dead than not on duty." The Comtesse Tascher de la Pagerie was a truly good wife and mother, a little inflated by her noble birth. (She had been born a princess Van der Leyen, a niece of the Prince-Primate, Grand Duke of Frankfort, and her husband was going to succeed an uncle as Duc Dalberg.) Unfortunately her countenance was the colours of the old Republican flag for she had a white face, blue eyes and a red nose. Poor Comtesse Sandizell had been crossed in love in youth and never recovered. She was now as deaf as a post with a nutcracker profile. But it was in describing the gentlemen of the household that Planat's acidity overflowed. Baron Triaire, Court Marshal, was an old cavalry type, a booby uttering absurdities by the dozen. Comte Louis Tascher de la Pagerie, cousin and long aide de camp to the Prince, was a clever soldier, honourable, loyal but an inveterate grumbler. He had begun to have gout at thirty-four. Comte Maurice Méjean, junior, had a vulgar set of features which he strove to improve with a pair of fine moustachios and a Henri IV beard; his talk could be coarse. His father, Comptroller of the Household, was a sort of stage caricature of a diplomatist, with a moon face, round belly and beautiful little white hands which he waved about as he interfered in everybody's business. The new secretary had to admit that he had been very much impressed by his welcome from the Prince and Princess. But he had soon got the measure of the education with which the royal lady had been provided by the Baronin Wurmb—detestable, typical of that thought enough for princesses—all for show. Princess Auguste, that famous beauty, looked older than he had expected. It was difficult to see why, for he went on to say that she still had the figure and grace of a girl. Gay King Max astonished the sour gentleman from Paris. Apparently his idea of bliss was to sit down to an ample meal surrounded by as many as possible of his family at the uncouth hour of three thirty p.m.

For the first eight days after Planat's arrival, Prince Eugène preserved a calm aloofness which the secretary understood was habitual. Then he said quietly, "Well, now you will have had the time to see how we get along here. You will find the Baron (Bataille) the most discreet person—devoted . . . You will gradually undertake his duties . . ."

Planat did not live on the premises. He had been found a most desirable lodging opposite the Englischer Garten. He was enchanted with Ismaning when they moved out there, and almost startled out of his wits in his bedroom at Eichstätt on a fine August morning, to find Prince Eugène presenting him in his nightshirt with a turquoise tie-pin. The family, who were keen on anniversaries, had discovered that it was the feast of St. Louis, his name-day. He tried to pass the scene off as ridiculous in his letter home but he was deeply touched. He was accepted. He was a member of a family.

When Prince Oscar arrived on August 23, he had not a word to say against him; on the contrary, he drew the picture of a Prince Charming. The suitor had expressive large black eyes, the best teeth in the world, curly black hair and an elegant figure. From the moment he had got out of his carriage at seven p.m. fresh, modest, respectful yet ardent, he had enchanted all in the little court at Eichstätt. There had been a delay of a month in his coming and Planat had noticed that both the Princess Auguste and her eldest daughter had red eyes. Princess Josephine, it was understood had wept a little when told that she was to go to Sweden, because it was so far off, but she had wept more when it had seemed that perhaps she was to be slighted. She had been brought up to understand that her parents would dispose of her for her own good and that of her family. There were three pens recording every detail of Prince Oscar's arrival at the Residenz, for as well as Planat with his weekly letter, Darnay had arrived and Auguste poured out her feelings to her diary.[1] All were agreed that the future son in law seemed perfection.

Planat thought that the first evening was rather sticky. Auguste said that while the prince talked easily with her eldest son she noticed his eyes straying to Josephine. Baron Böden had reported that when his young master had seen the likeness of the young lady sent to Stockholm he had exclaimed, "That face will bring me joy." Eugène had been on the steps to greet the prince.

"I received him in the first drawing room," recorded Auguste, "with my children and ladies. I was so overwhelmed I had to pull myself together. Nothing is so wearing as anxiety, especially when it concerns the happiness of a daughter." Two days later her uncertainties were at an end. "Prince Oscar has spoken with touching openness to Eugène. He said he had been against this marriage prospect, because he considered it would have been more favourable politically to ally himself with a daughter of a ruling monarch. But his father had been convinced that he could not do better than with a daughter of Prince Eugène, whose spotless reputation was of greater worth than the crown of which he had been deprived." Eventually father and son had agreed that Oscar should go and judge for himself. In spite of this he had nearly not come. Newspaper reports had worried him with their premature conclusions and made him feel that he was being coerced. He had to admit that he had come resolved not to submit to anything of that sort. But when he had seen the princess, and her family behaving with such reserve and tact, he had been ashamed of his hesitation. 'Now,' he said, with a smile, 'he would allow no third person to meddle with his future any more.' His mind was made up and if the princess, who appeared to resemble her mother in everything, would have him, he would be the happiest of men." Eugène tried to calm him, telling him that he should not decide in a hurry, and should consider whether our daughter would make him happy. He said, "I have decided. She is still very young; but in a year she will be able to marry, will she not?"

He was sent off, according to plan, to pay his respects to Tante Neuburg. On his return Auguste told him that he must give himself time. She said she had not yet spoken to her daughter. Planat noticed that already the young man seemed to have fitted into the family. The sons and daughters of the house all accompanied him on strolls on foot in the little town, where his appearance had roused excitement to fever-pitch. They performed theatricals together. Josephine, as Raphael's Madonna in *tableaux vivants* looked her most lovely. Auguste, who had been a little shaken by the size of the *suite* attending the prince, decided that it showed a proper regard of occasion. He had brought seven noblemen, some of whom bore names of the most renowned families in Sweden, and they had all brought attendants. She thought Oscar had a fine Italian cast of features and colouring. While her two elder daughters played the piano, and later Josephine and Oscar sang a duet, Eugène had a quiet talk with Count von Wetterstädt. Planat thought that when the Swedish prince sang alone, a Swedish song, he expressed exactly the grave and plaintive landscape of his far northern country. The prince was known to have composed considerable serious music. Auguste had a private conversation with Count Oxenstierna and learned that the prince would like to address Josephine. He confirmed to the mother that there would be no religious difficulties. An occasion was made after the Italian Opera and Josephine replied, "I am at the disposal of my parents, but for my own part it would make me very happy." Auguste told the prince in her daughter's presence that she believed she was getting a son of whom she would become very fond.

He rode away for Italy, having trysted to return for the announcement in November, and they had a very gay and grand stay at Tegernsee. Both the Czar and the Emperor Francis were there *en route* for the next Congress which would be at Verona.

Planat was getting to know his employer. He became the recipient of some confidences which surprised him. "If I had not married a princess," said the duke one day, "I should have liked to go to America." On another occasion he mentioned that of all professions he would have preferred that of a sailor.[2] The sea and all to do with it had always had a great fascination for him.

Planat thought that he had certainly possessed the necessary sang-froid, quick eye and quick decision. The tutor wondered what might have become of him if he had not been doomed to be the eternal apprentice to the Emperor. As Viceroy even as young as twenty-five he had shown considerable talent as an administrator. "I know," said the duke slowly, "that my position now is false and dependent, in spite of the generosity of the King of Bavaria, but I must sacrifice my independence for my wife and children." He spoke of the Czar. "I am much indebted to the Czar and I have promised him not to enter into any political intrigues. I have given him my word, so henceforward I must occupy myself with the education and establishment of my children."

Of all the shocks he had suffered on arrival, Planat had found the change in Prince Eugène the most remarkable and painful. He had not seen him since the ghastly Russian campaign, the Battle of Malo Jaroslavetz.

"There was a great alteration in him. When I had left him he had been spare, pale and slim; now he was fleshy and corpulent and his face had filled out and was ruddy, giving all the appearance of excellent health. But the change in his *morale* was even more noticeable. This prince who had previously been so expansive and animated, had now become so apathetic and careful over the words he used, that except in private conversation he uttered only *clichés*, and made statements of no consequence. The downfall of the Imperial régime and the humiliations to which he had been forced to submit for the sake of his children, had broken his spirit and seemed to have taken all the life out of him."[3]

It never entered the new secretary's head that his employer was mortally ill and had only a few months of life left.

II

Darnay had been commissioned to buy the trousseau in Paris. It was to be fit for a queen. Auguste thought she had never had a busier, happier Eastertide. One of her causes for joy was that her husband did not slip away to his sister at Augsburg this year. On Easter Sunday, March 23 he went to service with the King and both his brothers in law. The ladies of the royal family sat apart. Suddenly, Auguste heard a disturbance. Looking round she saw her brother Karl helping Eugène out. "I rushed after them. My

husband had lost the power of speech. I took him to the window
and the working of his mouth at once ceased, but it was half an
hour before he could say a word. The King's surgeon said he
must be bled and taken home. Father, brothers, all abounded in
sympathy. It is impossible for me to express my apprehension.
Yet I realized that he had never for a moment lost consciousness,
that he had been able to go up and down stairs unassisted . . .
it was not a case of a real stroke." She had learned a little about
strokes recently, for her father had suffered a slight one last
October. To her great relief Eugène was so much better so soon
that the king and queen were able to leave for a trip to the Dresden
court. Her hopes were vain. During the night of April 13 another
attack ensued, much worse. She listened frantic with alarm while
four specialists asked her to try to remember about accidents,
falls from horse-back . . . But he must have had so many. Long
years before she had set eyes upon him he had been buried alive
in Egypt . . . The doctors sympathetically told her she must
prepare for recurrences. Still, she could not believe that she was
to lose him. Karl said, "Eugène cannot die, God will have pity
on us." She sent the six children to a service at the Herzogs-
spitalkirche where prayers were to be offered at her request, and
heard with gratitude that the attendance had been so great that
people had not been able to kneel. Crowds had followed the
children to the coach expressing simple hopes that they would
soon hear better news of the good duke. When, at last after six
weeks, she was able to drive out to take the air for the first time,
the square outside the palace was full of people. They were too
restrained to cheer, but she could read sympathy on every face.
At last came the great day when the invalid was allowed out. He
tackled the stairs almost unassisted. This time people did cheer.
"It was a triumphal progress."

He had made a wonderful recovery, but they had to make very
careful arrangements for the wedding. The guests began to arrive
on May 20, the bridegroom and *suite*, followed by Hortense, and
her younger son. In the procession to the chapel two days later
the bride was led in by her mother as well as her father. "Our
ladies carried our trains," mentioned Auguste grandly. Hortense
came next in the procession walking with Eugénie, her god-
daughter. The Archbishop, Freiherr von Gebsattel, had agreed
owing to the ill-health of the bride's father, to omit the usual
address. Eugène did not attend the banquet but appeared later

and spoke to many people. They were very unhappy about his parting from the Crown Princess. Father and daughter must both guess that it was for life. But it was managed briefly without witnesses and afterwards it was the bride's mother who had to be almost carried back into the palace.

The wonderful recovery was maintained. He went on doctor's orders, attended by his secretary and personal physician, to Marienbad for a cure, and stayed there three weeks. He wrote to tell his anxious wife that it rained and rained, and they said he need only stay for three weeks this time, but next year ought to take the full treatment of six weeks. He found a most extraordinary link with the past amongst the other old invalids—"My brother in law the Count of St. Leu"—Hortense's husband, very old and very lame. There was a famous author living at Marienbad—Herr von Goethe was seventy-four but still very spry. He had interesting conversations with the ex-Viceroy of Italy on rather an unlikely subject, the junction of the Rhine and the Altmühl by a canal. The author said modestly, a few months later, that Prince Eugène had appeared to him to be one of those great characters who are becoming rarer and whom we are allowed to keep for a very short time. "He was a fine man, about forty-two years old, but looking much more—and no wonder if one considers what he had endured—one campaign after another, and one great deed after another. His life had been crowded."[4]

It was very nearly ended, but he refused to give up the fight. He escorted his wife to his "new little Swiss house" in September. They had an alarmingly rough passage across the lake from Meersburg and arrived after dark. Next morning Auguste drew the curtains of her room before six a.m. and beheld the most beautiful view that she had seen from any home yet. Eugensberg was much larger than her expectations—a country gentleman's home; it would have fitted in well to an English landscape. He was planting splendid woods and avenues around it. It had balconies and verandahs and flanking wings, a *temple d'amour* on a mound and a sundial . . .[5] He was riding again, and spoke of going after the wild boar again with the English Minister. The snows came, and they had to use sledges from romantic Prünn. In the end they had quite a large party and a very merry time of it—Count Anton Rechberg, Chief of Staff, Count Ludwig Arco from Neuburg, Louis Tascher, Prince Woronzov, Count Pappenheim. They got a record bag—sixty-four. But on his return the duke had to confess

The Last Portrait
Eugène de Beauharnais, Duke of Leuchtenberg, Prince of Eichstätt. Many versions exist, and on one was based the full-length statue by Dumont, cast in bronze by Thiebaut, erected in Paris in 1863 by command of his nephew the Emperor Napoleon III. Since 1873 this stands outside the Hotel des Invalides.
By François, Baron Gérard.

By permission of the Napoleon Museum, Arenenberg

he had suffered from giddiness. He had to break off dictating his memoirs. He made his will. His sight and hearing were impaired. He was ordered to bed and the quiet life, which he scorned. Hortense had been so much impressed by his apparent recovery and high spirits that she had gone off for the winter to Italy.

Auguste's diary became more and more desperate. She dreaded Christmas and the New Year, but he got through them well, even attending services in the chapel where he had suffered his first seizure. Nearly every night, now that the snows had come, there was the sound of bells and trotting hooves outside the new palace, and her good father came in to play games with the invalid. Sometimes Eugène could hardly limp round the billiard table; his left leg and arm were affected. Devoted staff with expressionless faces quickly rearranged the superb Paris furniture on carpets so thick that footsteps were as noiseless as on the snow clad streets outside. Two old soldiers (though of different generations) sat together in the kind candlelight, and played *ombre*.

Eugène saw to it that his wife took Eugénie Hortense to balls. He would not be dull. He had letters from the Crown Princess of Sweden. The Baronin who had accompanied the newly married couple as far as Lübeck had brought back the most reassuring accounts. Her mother in law, Queen Desirée, had met Josephine there, and like the bridegroom had found the daughter of Prince Eugène even more beautiful than report. The Crown Princess had sailed up between the lovely clustering islets set in sparkling waters around her new home, to a harbour where she had been met by a gold and purple state coach pulled by eight white horses. When she had arrived at the pretty little château of Haga outside Stockholm, she had made a little speech in Swedish; but she had been obliged to ask one of her Swedish ladies what was the meaning of a certain Swedish word. Everyone said it the moment they caught sight of her. The lady had to tell her it meant "Sweet!"[6]

Eugène had a ball in his house in the end of January, and insisted on doing the honours. He stayed up till midnight and paid for it. But he would not cancel another, planned for February 2. Most unfortunately, a burst of celebrations had to take place in February. It was Max Joseph's Jubilee—twenty-five years as father of his people. His son in law had to be helped to the window to see the illuminations, the bonfires, the fireworks. They had an ingenious revolving star over the Palais Leuchtenberg. On February 19, Auguste's heart almost broke when her husband indicated to her that he wanted the priest. Her father and step-mother came and he took their hands and held them against his heart. Next evening his speech had so much improved he was able to beg her not to wait up. He knew that she had scarcely slept for the past ten days. He said to her quite clearly, "I hope that we are going to have a good night." Next morning, King Max with trembling hand and face of woe began a letter to Prince Ludwig in Italy. "I have lost my poor Eugène."[7]

III

The Princess Auguste, Duchess of Leuchtenberg, outlived Prince Eugène by more than quarter of a century. Her erect, slight figure accompanied by affectionate sons and daughters was to be seen during that period in many unexpected places. She visited the tomb of the Emperor Napoleon at the Invalides, and that of the Empress Josephine at Rueil, staying incognito at 10 Rue de Courcelles and at the Hotel Bristol, Place Vendôme. She thought that the genial Citizen-King Louis Philippe seemed very rocky on his throne.

After two years of mourning (for the late duke had always been strict about that, and his lightest word was now law in the house of the widow), she began to entertain for her children. Their father had been anxious about their education. Tutors and governesses abounded. Prince Karl was guardian. The girls had Mlle. Maucomble, "Fanny", and Fräulein Miego. Augustus Charles had Méjean and Planat, and outside professors. Even Prince Max, aged seven, had an army tutor, Lieut. Schau. All the Old Guard remained on duty. The Méjeans, father and son were known by the children as Grandpapa Méjean and Papa Méjean. Papa's wife, a Viennese, was an accomplished pianist. Triaire, Hennin, Ré, all performed their duties, and there was a new Swiss financial expert, the Chevalier Roux de Damien. The Baronin died before they were out of mourning but the Comtesse Sandizell and Freiin Rosa von Aretin remained, as did all three of the Taschers. Colonel Planat de la Faye had, as Hortense pointed out, like herself lost his best protector and guardian in this world. "Short though his experience had been, he had become absolutely devoted to Prince Eugène who had been like a brother to him, the best and easiest employer in the world. Everyone said so who had ever served him—a character without stain." But the widowed

Princess had further work for him. General Comte d'Anthouard, who had always been in her black books, began to show the cloven hoof before 1827, when he came out with an anonymous article in the *Spectateur Militaire* denigrating the late Viceroy. He had left Eugène's service in a hurry, at his own request, on urgent personal affairs in the darkest Mantua days. He had gone to Paris and flourished exceedingly under the new régime. When he had obtained posts carrying very high emoluments he had continued to draw a pension as aide de camp. He had been indignant when Darnay had written to say that this was going to cease. He had lost heavily speculating on the Bourse. The Duchess of Leuchtenberg emerged from her house of mourning to defend the rights of her orphan cubs with all the ferocity of the lioness bereaved. D'Anthouard's accusations included her, for he had said that Prince Eugène had been seduced by his wife's family from loyalty to the Emperor, and that she had always been anti-French. Planat, briefed by her, replied energetically. The *Spectateur Militaire* refused his article, but in August 1827, the *Journal des sciences militaires* printed it.

Any reasonable reader must conclude that he had completely demolished the slander, but mischief had been done. Authors who wrote with a political slant had picked up tales. M. Thiers, statesman and most verbose historian, repeated inaccuracies in his *Histoire du Consulat et de l'Empire*.

This paper-war was one of Auguste's chief interests in life. Her features had always been good and she stayed wonderfully well preserved. A portrait of her at the age of fifty-two, in a Marie Stuart costume of black velvet slashed with white satin, white quilled ruff, cap with a sweeping ostrich feather, and a large jewelled cross, showed that her blue eyes and chestnut hair were still brilliant. The Prince de Croy who had offered for her before her marriage had offered again, despite the six children, but had been refused. She occupied her time in foreign travel, looking after her family and in defending the memory of Prince Eugène. But for the religious question it seemed that she might have married her elder son to the heiress of England. Augustus Charles appeared at Windsor on his way to his wedding in Lisbon with Maria da Gloria, Queen of Portugal, and according to Méjean père, the Duke of Wellington himself had audibly regretted to the Spanish Minister that they could not have had this very fine young man for our little heiress here. In virtues and appearance, the stepson of Napoleon had, in fact, curiously resembled the future Albert the good, Prince Consort. Even allowing for the fact that both their parents had been renowned for their looks, the children of Prince Eugène were remarkably handsome. Augustus Charles died of diphtheria two months after his wedding, and it was an abiding grief to his mother that her younger son, Max, became Russian, even to his faith, on marrying the Grand Duchess Marie, daughter of the Czar Nicholas I. She lived in terror that he might have to fight against France. The match was otherwise lustrous, though gentle Theodolinde was startled when her sister in law, who insisted on being addressed as Mary as if she was an English girl, and had a countenance of extraordinary pallor, offered to teach her to smoke cigars. She also seemed to Theodolinde to be more in love with her young husband than he was with her—passionately.[9]

Auguste was faintly disappointed in the marriage made by her second daughter, but Eugénie Hortense whilst they were still in mourning had insisted on accepting Prince Friedrich Wilhelm of Hohenzollern Hechingen. She was just eighteen and had hardly seen the world. The wedding was their first occasion for entertainment at Eichstätt since her father's death. It took place quietly. He was a sovereign prince but his territories were small, and as her years advanced Princess Auguste's ideas on the subject of the Beauharnais became grander and grander. She was doubtful of accepting a Hohenzollern. She seemed to have infected Queen Victoria, for in the next generation when three of Max's children visited England, the young princes of Leuchtenberg were pronounced "nice intelligent boys," and "Maroussy" their sister was found by Queen Victoria "ravishing". The Princess Royal of England, wife of Prince Frederick William of Prussia, got a severe set down by her mother for suggesting that a match between a Hesse nephew and this beauty would be a *mésalliance*. Her Majesty held the Taschers and Beauharnais in high esteem, and when she met the Emperor Napoleon III, youngest son of Hortense, was to fall a complete victim to his charm.

Auguste had a delightful last year of Theodolinde's maidenhood. In Venice they stayed at Danieli's hotel. In Rome she visited the studio of Thorwaldsen and she noticed again that his statuary seemed to her to have a cold quality. He had performed a splendid tomb for Eugène in the Michaelskirche, but it had disappointed her. It had his motto "Honour and Fidelity" very large, and Fame inscribing his deeds, and attendant angels. The prince himself was represented as a noble Roman warrior, and his face and form were as they had been in his last years, somewhat heavy. He had always been so gay. It was not quite him.

At the court of Naples the visiting German princesses were invited to dine by the Sicilian Bourbon queen who had been an Austrian archduchess. There were blue skies and waters, and a terraced garden and many people. Suddenly, as they sat at table, a Guards regiment struck up. Auguste was almost overcome. "It reminded me of our home at Milan."

They paid a duty call on Madame Mère in Rome. The old lady had broken her hip and was confined to her sofa on her balcony. She was almost blind, but not at all deaf. There was quite a collection of Bonapartes in Florence and they met Caroline Murat on the Lungarno. She was now the Countess of Lipona. The two daughters had married Italian noblemen and the two sons were farming in America, from where they still wrote very polite letters in English to their invaluable governess Miss Davies, now an unwilling resident of her native Beaumaris, and a martyr to rheumatoid-arthritis contracted during the siege of Gaeta. The Countess of Lipona had, like Marie Louise, a retired military man in constant attendance. Some people said she was secretly married to General Francesco Macdonald, a kinsman of the Marshal. Jerome was now Comte de Montfort, and had a daughter Mathilde and a fat little Napoleon born in Trieste. His long-suffering Württemberg wife still adored him. Pauline and Elisa had died, the younger sister of the same dire malady which had carried off the Emperor's father and reputedly the Emperor, and was soon to claim Caroline.

Auguste met Marie Louise at Berchtesgaden and was horrified by her appearance. She was only forty-nine, but she looked like nothing but a decrepit, stout old peasant. She had given Neipperg a successor, and safely borne three children since the King of Rome. The doctors had been mistaken. Her married life with the Emperor had been remarkably short and unsatisfactory from her point of view but Auguste had never forgiven her as the supplanter of Josephine.

The Duchess of Leuchtenberg lived to hear of the births of fourteen of her sixteen grand-children. A century later their descendants were to be the monarchs of Denmark, Sweden, Norway, and Belgium, and the heirs-apparent of Britain and

Greece. She missed by six years the publication of the last volume of the Memoirs of Marshal Marmont, Duke of Ragusa. This brought Planat and d'Anthouard back into the arena again. Planat was now happily married to a Bavarian lady of French connections, young enough to be his daughter and delighted to combine the duties of wife with those of amanuensis. In 1858 he published his master-work *Le Prince Eugène en 1814*. This was a counterblast to Marmont, who had related all d'Anthouard's old denigrations and more. The Marshal had been the oldest army friend of the Emperor Napoleon, but no one in France had trusted him since, with twenty thousand men, he had drawn back in that last battle before Paris, and entered into a secret convention with the invading Allies. The Bourbons had employed him, but never shown confidence in him. He was understandably embittered, but it seemed particularly inappropriate that he should accuse Prince Eugène of treachery. For there was a new word in the French language now, *raguser*. It meant to betray. As he had died four months before the publication of the volume which contained the offending paragraphs, his editor was the sufferer when the Queen of Sweden, the widowed Empress of Brazil, and the Duke of Württemberg, widower of the Princess Theodolinde, brought and won a legal action. The case created an enormous sensation. There were some curious repercussions. Numbers of shops in principal cities of France, and licensed premises in lesser places, were named *"Au Prince Eugène"*. A nephew of Prince Eugène now ruled the French Empire. The name of Eugène de Beauharnais became popular as never before. On December 2, 1863, a statue of the hero by the popular sculptor Augustin Dumont, was unveiled in front of the Mairie of the 11th arrondissement on a new carriage-way called the *Boulevard du Prince Eugène*. It was cast in bronze and was said to weigh 3,110 kilos and to have cost the Emperor Napoleon III 18,000 francs. It was mounted on a block of Corsican granite, and represented the prince with his martial cloak around him holding in his hand a scrap of paper. On this were inscribed historic words. It was a transcript of his letter to his father in law the King of Bavaria, refusing the crown of Italy.[10]

Notes on the Chapters

1. *Le ménage Beauharnais, Joséphine avant Napoléon, d'après des Correspondences inédites,* Jean Hanoteau, Paris 1935, hereafter cited as Joséphine Beauharnais, Hanoteau 1-82. *Joséphine de Beauharnais 1763–1796,* Frédéric Masson, Paris 1913, hereafter cited as Masson, *Joséphine de Beauharnais,* 15–18. Hanoteau quotes largely from manuscripts of the Tascher de la Pagerie family, owned by the Duc de Tascher de la Pagerie, and the Leuchtenberg manuscripts owned by descendants of Eugène de Beauharnais's son, Maximilian. His work is therefore more valuable for reference than Masson's more exhaustive and devoted volume, the first official biography using the Tascher manuscript, and eclipses two earlier efforts, *Histoire de l'Impératrice Joséphine,* Joseph Aubenas, 1857 and *L'Impératrice Joséphine,* R. Pichevin, Paris, 1909.

2. The Rue Thévenot is gone. The portion of it in which the Beauharnais hôtel stood was opposite the Rue Dussoubs and was demolished in 1895 to make room for the modern Rue Réaumur.

3. The description of Josephine as a child-bride carrying round her jewellery comes from the memoirs of Constant, valet first to Eugène and then to Napoleon, (2 vols., Paris 1830, hereafter cited as *Constant*) ii 157. The description of the jewellery given her on her marriage comes from an inventory presented to her by Lambert, the jeweller who had supplied it, at the instance of her husband who had asked for the return of it on the separation. Some was not yet paid for. Hanoteau, *Joséphine de Beauharnais,* 205–6 from letter in the Bibliothèque Nationale Feb. 17 and March 8, 1786.

4. Hanoteau, *Joséphine de Beauharnais,* 101–107; Masson, *Joséphine de Beauharnais,* 97–101.

5. Eugène de Beauharnais believed his mother had been sixteen, not eighteen, when he was born. She had said she was barely fourteen at the date of her wedding. "These precocious marriages are not infrequent amongst Créoles who are nubile well before Europeans."

1. The site of the Beauharnais hôtel in the Rue Neuve St. Charles is now occupied by the Rue de la Boëtie. At the time the family moved there the street continued beyond the Place St. Augustin to the Rue du Faubourg St. Honoré.

2. Hanoteau (166–201) quotes Alexandre Beauharnais' letters from the

Leuchtenberg mss. which descended to Eugène's sons. Masson (*Joséphine de Beauharnais*) devotes a whole chapter, '*La Séparation*' to the unhappy story.

3. *Mémoires et correspondance politique et militaire du Prince Eugène* ed. A. Du Casse, 10 vols.: Paris 1858, hereafter cited as Du Casse; *Mémoires de la Reine Hortense, publiés par le Prince Napoléon* with notes by J. Hanoteau 3 vols., Paris 1927, hereafter cited as Hortense.

4. Du Casse, I, 29.

5. No record shows that Josephine was ever presented at court and Madame Junot in her memoirs states that she never was. Some curious fancy prompted Alexandre de Beauharnais as late as May 1786 when he had already parted from his wife, to apply for the right to ride in the king's carriages on hunting expeditions. The Duc de Coigny had to reply that the Beauharnais, a good bourgeois family of the Orléannais, could not aspire to this honour reserved for the ancient noblesse. Masson, *Joséphine de Beauharnais*, 95; Hanoteau, *Joséphine Beauharnais*, 84.

6. On the site of the present 226 Boulevard St. Germain.

7. Hanoteau, *Joséphine Beauharnais*, 235: Masson, *Joséphine de Beauharnais*, 167–8; *Lettres de Napoléon à Joséphine, pendant la première campagne d'Italie, le Consulate et l'Empire, et lettres de Joséphine à Napoléon et à sa fille.* 2 vols. ed. Didot, London and Leipzig 1833, hereafter cited as *Lettres, Napoléon, Joséphine, Hortense, ed. Didot*, ii 199–201.

Josephine, who was always good at remembering people who had been kind in her days of misfortune never forgot the courage and generosity of the Princess Hohenzollern. When this lady visited the Tuileries orders were given that the doors should be flung open *à deux battants*. Bonaparte saw that the young Prince of Salm was restored in fortune, and gave to the son of the Princess Hohenzollern the hand of his niece, Marie Antoinette Murat, whom he raised to the rank of Imperial Highness and equipped with the dowry of a Daughter of France.

8. Du Casse, I, 29.

9. Masson, *Joséphine de Beauharnais*, 201.

10. Hortense, I, 19.

11. Ibid., 24–27.

12. Ibid., 30. Valiant attempts have been made to prove that a reconciliation took place between Alexandre and Josephine in prison. But in his farewell letter he states that he feels for her only "fraternal" love. He had never set up house with Madame de Longpré. She had married the Governor of St. Kitts, "*le beau Dillon*" (and had a daughter, Fanny, who became the wife of Marshal Bertrand, attendant on Bonaparte in St. Helena). The Empress Josephine was once brought a list of applicants for pensions which included the name of the woman who had so deeply wronged her. She wrote "This lady is now very infirm" and the supplication was granted.

Six years after Alexandre's death Josephine began to provide for the result of another of his *affaires*, a child born in 1786 to an unmarried girl of good family living at Cherbourg. She found "Adelaide de La Ferté" a husband and a farm. According to fragments of burning love-letters preserved by the beautiful Marquise de Custine, daughter in law of the general whom Alexandre had succeeded, she was undoubtedly his last love. She recorded that Josephine had made a poor impression in prison, bewailing her lot and playing cards in an attempt to read her fate. But she was so harmless, everyone had liked her.

13. Hortense, I, 32–33.
14. Du Casse, I, 31. Hortense, I, 19.

CHAPTER THREE   THE STEPFATHER

1. Du Casse, I, 31; Hortense, I, 36; Constant, I, 15.
2. Masson, *Joséphine de Beauharnais*, 230.
3. *Mémoires de Madame Junot, Duchesse d'Abrantès.* 3 vols, 1883; hereafter cited as Junot, I, 245–7.
4. Masson, *Joséphine de Beauharnais*, 249–254. The site of number 6 Rue de Chantereine, demolished in 1859, is now occupied by number 66 Rue de la Victoire.
5. Napoleon told the story of Eugène and the sword twice, with slight variations, in exile, after many years. *Napoleon in Exile or a Voice from St. Helena*, Barry O'Meara. 2 vols., 1822, hereafter cited as O'Meara, I, 180. Hortense's account (I, 142) differs little from that of Eugène (I, 32) except that he alone says that the general himself brought the permission. He appears to think that Napoleon found his mother at home, but the stepfather is sure that Josephine called to thank him. Lavalette's version is confirmatory. *Mémoires de Comte de Lavalette*, 2 vols., 1831, hereafter cited as Lavalette, I, 194–196. Barras ridicules the sword story (*Mémoires* ed. G. Duruy, 4 vols. Paris 1895), but his memoirs, collected by a literary executor, are so defaced by jealousy on the subject of Josephine and Bonaparte as to be almost valueless.
6. *Mémoires de Mlle. d'Avrillon*, Paris, 1833, 2 vols., hereafter cited as Avrillon, I, 64n. Constant, I, 16.
   Hortense, I, 42; *Journal inédite de St. Helene 1815–1818*, Baron Gourgaud, hereafter cited as Gourgaud, II, 329.
7. Hortense, I, 44. *Mémoires du Maréchal Marmont, Duc de Raguse*, Paris 1857, hereafter cited as Marmont, I, 282.
8. *Mémoires du Comte Miot de Melito*, 2 vols., Paris 1858, i. 159, 184. Lavalette, I, 210–216, 288; *Souvenirs d'Un Sexagénaire*, A. V. Arnault, 4 vols., Paris 1833. *Mémoires de Louis Antoine Fauvelet de Bourrienne*, Paris 1831, hereafter cited as Bourrienne.
9. The Villa Cerutti is now a mental home. There are illustrations of it and of Bonaparte's bedroom at the Palazzo Serbelloni on p. 46 in *Napoleon I*, an anonymous illustrated volume, Munich and Leipzig 1914.
10. Junot, II, 31–36; Lévy 41.
11. Du Casse, I, 35–38; Prince Adalbert, *Eugen*, 23–24.
12. Junot, I, 166.

CHAPTER FOUR   EGYPT

1. Du Casse, I, 40.
2. The bibliography of contemporary accounts of Bonaparte's Egyptian campaign is impressive, but not all the eyewitnesses (some of whom wrote

down their experiences many years later) are to be relied upon. Eugène himself is completely reliable, but, as he often repeats, he was inexperienced at the time and he recorded only what he himself saw. One of the most colourful accounts is that of Bonaparte's private secretary, Bourrienne. He took office under Louis XVIII in 1814, and his memoirs, written after he had deserted Bonaparte, show strong signs of his change of allegiance. In 1830 two French Generals published a volume *Bourrienne, his errors, voluntary and involuntary*. It is necessary before accepting any statement deleterious to the reputation of Bonaparte in his volumes, to check the evidence. Berthier is sound, but his account is brief: *Relation des Campagnes du Général Bonaparte en Égypte et en Syrie*, Pierre A. Berthier, Prince de Neuchatel. Paris 1801, hereafter cited as Berthier. *See also* Marmont and Lavalette, Jonquière, C. de la, *L'Expédition d'Égypte*, Paris 1899, 5 vols., Desvernois, Nicolas, Baron, *Mémoires*, Paris 1898. *Mémoir of Baron Larrey*, L. A. Leroy-Dupré 1861.

3. Lavalette, I, 311 says Mourad Bey's wife sent a shawl and arms to Bonaparte; Bourrienne, I, 144 says she gave Eugène a ring worth a thousand louis.

4. *Copies of Original letters from the army of General Bonaparte in Egypt intercepted by the Fleet under the command of Admiral Lord Nelson*, 2 vols., London 1798-1799. Du Casse, I, 43. Bourrienne, I, 175 says that Bonaparte confided in him in great distress of mind that he had just discovered he must divorce Josephine, but the date and place which he gives is unacceptable—the wells of Messodiah on the way to El Arish, February 1794. Bonaparte's letter to Joseph, and Eugène's letter, are dated in the previous July. As usual with Bourrienne's stories, however, this one is probably founded on fact, only misdated and exaggerated.

5. Lavalette, I, 316 says "Everyone soon appeared reconciled to the event, and nobody talked any more of it."

6. Du Casse, I, 45.

7. Berthier, 39 says that the Arabs cut the throats of all French whom they met, but only mentions Bonaparte's pardon. Lavalette, I, 319, was absent on an expedition to Lake Mensale but heard that Sulkowski had volunteered for duty out of turn. Bourrienne, I, 167, says that the aides de camp Beauharnais and Croisier were ordered to wipe out the village from which the murderers of Sulkowski came and bring the heads of the culprits to Cairo, and that he saw the sacks containing them arrive.

8. Du Casse, I, 53.

9. Ibid., I, 55. Bourrienne, I, 180, says that aides de camp Croisier and Beauharnais on their own authority, although the decree of death had been pronounced against the whole Jaffa garrison, brought in two divisions of prisoners amounting to four thousand men and were severely reprimanded. Bonaparte himself (O'Meara, *A Voice from St. Helena*) said that he had ordered about twelve hundred men to be shot. They had broken their parole, and when he sent in a flag of truce, had cut off the head of the bearer and stuck it on a pole above the walls.

10. Du Casse, I, 56-62, Lavalette, I, 332-359.

11. The story that Bonaparte gave orders for his hopeless-case plague victims to be poisoned, sooner than let them fall into the hands of the Turks, has continued to vex historians. Desegnettes, First Physician, entered into a paper war on the subject with Larrey, Surgeon in Chief. According to Desegnettes, Bonaparte enquired as to the possibility; Desegnettes recoiled in horror. He

also thought some of the patients might recover. At the last there were fifty patients left, and Bonaparte got laudanum from Hadj Mustafa, a Turkish doctor from Constantinople, to be administered by Royer, chief pharmacist. The dose was either by design or mischance not lethal. Some of the patients recovered. Royer died, in Turkish employment, in Egypt in 1802. Desegnettes applied to go home but was refused. He did not leave Egypt until the wholesale evacuation in 1801. Bonaparte resolutely refused to give him publicity by taking any notice of his accusation but created him a Baron, together with Larrey. Larrey, Chief Surgeon, accused Desegnettes of slander, so did Lavalette and Savary. Eugène's testimony does not seem to have been noticed by historians. He was by his own account sent by Bonaparte to Larrey to ask for the final report on the victims, and when he left the hospital, last man out, there were fifteen. When Sir Sidney Smith unexpectedly trod in, having dissuaded the Turks from murdering them, he found, according to his report to Nelson "seven poor wretches left alive in the hospital; they are protected and shall be taken care of." Bonaparte, in St. Helena, at a date when he often talked for effect and contradicted himself, said he had not poisoned his plague victims but he would not have thought it a crime. Personally he would have welcomed it. He said Larrey at first thought it would be an act of charity, but later that perhaps Desegnettes was right.

Of the witnesses who declare that he was guilty, not one had such an opportunity as Eugène for judging. Hortense, I, 76. Du Casse, I, 54, Lavalette I, 359–363, Bourrienne, I, 193–197; La Jonquière, iv. 284–285, 555–577; *Mémoires du Duc de Rovigo*, viii vols., Paris 1820, hereafter cited as Rovigo. Rovigo, I, 106; Marmont, II, 12; O'Meara, I, 329–332 and II, 128.

12. As soldiers' wives were forbidden on the expedition Madame Pauline Fourès arrived in Egypt in the uniform of a chasseur à cheval of the 22nd (her husband's) regiment, and frequently wore this costume in Cairo. She had been a milliner in Carcassonne. On her return to France in 1800 Bonaparte refused to see her but made provision for her until 1812. She remarried a retired Major of the Turkish army in the Consular service, obtained a separation from him and took up the profession of novelist and artist and survived until 1869.

13. See also *Memoir of Baron Larrey, Surgeon in Chief of the Grande Armée*, L. A. H. Deroy-Duprèe, 1861, hereafter quoted as Larrey. This interesting little memoir does not mention the plague victim story.

CHAPTER FIVE   FROM THE ORANGERY TO MARENGO

1. *Lettres au Prince Eugène*, ed. J. Hanoteau; *Revue des Deux Mondes*, 1933, 305–306; *Mémoires de Madame de Rémusat*, 2 vols., 1880, I, 41–42, hereafter cited as Rémusat.

2. Du Casse, I, 75–76; Junot, I, 260–263; Bourrienne, I, 359. Hortense does not mention the painful scene on Bonaparte's return from Egypt.

3. Constant thought Eugène was twenty-one when he was really just eighteen and he must surely have been mistaken when he gave his master's height at that age as five foot three-to-four inches. All other contemporaries describe him as tall or very tall and in pictures he towers above his stepfather whom Constant says was five feet two. Constant, I, 13-24.

4. Bourrienne (I, 232) states that Bonaparte said "Bernadotte has Moorish blood in his veins. He is bold and enterprising. He has been to see my brothers. He does not like me and I am almost sure will oppose me. If he should become ambitious he will venture anything. And yet remember in what a lukewarm way he behaved on 18 Fructidor when I sent him to Augereau. He is the devil of a fellow; not to be seduced — disinterested — clever."

5. Du Casse, I, 78; Lavalette, I, 385–400; Constant, I, 25–26; Bourrienne, I, 245–258; Marmont, II, 92–99. *Mémoires de Lucien Bonaparte, Prince de Canino*, Paris 1835; 78 *et seq*: *Mémoires et Correspondance du Roi Joseph* ed. A. Du Casse, Paris, 1855, 3 vols., *Oeuvres du Comte P. L. Roederer*, viii, Paris, 1854; *Mémoires du Prince de Talleyrand*, ed. Duc de Broglie, Paris 1891, hereafter cited as Talleyrand. See also — *Le dix-huit Brumaire*, Albert Ollivier. Paris 1959; Junot, I, 278 *et seq.*; Rovigo, I, 152–156.

6. Rémusat, I, 44.

7. Du Casse, I, 79–80; Hortense, I, 68–69; Constant, I, 47.

8. Du Casse, I, 80–85; Marmont, II, 124–144; Rovigo, I, 171–181; Bourrienne, I, 359–370. These eyewitnesses do not at all agree over the timing of Desaix's arrival. Bonaparte's despatch makes him arrive about three p.m. He altered the despatch three times in the next eight years. Eugène's timing has here been quoted.

CHAPTER SIX   CONSULATE

1. Du Casse, I, 86.

2. Constant, I, 27–33; Bourrienne, II, 88; Hortense, I, 85–91.

3. Du Casse, I, 87–88; Hortense, I, 78–79; Bourrienne, II, 20.

4. Junot, I, 409–412.

5. Hortense, I, 79–81; Bourrienne, II. 21–22.
   Galignani's New Paris Guide or Stranger's Companion through the French Metropolis, 12th Edition, September 1824.

6. Du Casse, I, 86–88, *Eugen Beauharnais, der Stiefsohn Napoleons, Ein lebensbild*, Adalbert, Prinz von Bayern, hereafter cited as Prinz Adalbert, *Eugen*, 51.

7. Hortense, I, 91.

8. Ibid., 92.

9. Bourrienne, I, 64–65; Hortense, 112–115.

10. Ibid., 107–113.

11. *Memoirs of Baron Claud François de Méneval*, 2 vols., 1894, hereafter cited as Méneval, I, 97 *et seq.*; 113, 129, 176.
    The accounts of Méneval and Bourrienne about the retirement of Bourrienne differ. Bourrienne declared that he was persuaded to stay on for another year, after resigning in 1801.

12. Louis suffered according to his wife from "one hand (the right) which wasted and grew weaker and caused him anxiety".   Bonaparte refused to allow him to depart within a few months of his wedding on one of his cures. "People will say I have given my stepdaughter to a cripple and an invalid." Docteur Cabanès who made exhaustive researches into Louis's medical history, came to the conclusion that his affliction was a form of rheumatism, following several falls from his horse, and dismissed the suggestion that it was due to a

syphilitic infection contracted in Egypt. Nevertheless, the story continued to be repeated.

Cabanès, Auguste, *Légendes et curiosités de l'Histoire*. 2nd series Paris 1914, and 5th series, n.d.

See also Baron Du Casse *Les Rois frères de Napoléon I*, Paris 1883–91 and *Louis Bonaparte en Hollande*, André Dubosc, Paris 1911. Dubosc dismissed tuberculosis and syphilis, and inclined to a diagnosis of scrofula.

13. The Hotel de Villeroy, 78 Rue de Lille presented to Eugène by Bonaparte in 1802 is now the German Embassy. It is next door but one to the Palais de la Légion d'Honneur.

14. Du Casse, 50; Lévy, Arthur, *Napoléon et Eugène de Beauharnais*, Paris 1926, hereafter cited as Lévy, 59.

15. *An Englishman in Paris, the Journal of Bertie Greatheed*, ed. J. Bury and J. Barry, 1953.

CHAPTER SEVEN   PARIS DAYS

1. Du Casse, I, 89–91; Méneval, I, 244–278; Hortense, I, 156–161; Rovigo, I, 11–14, 32–64; Rémusat, I, 168–208; Bourrienne, II, 157–67, 172–205, 222–245; O'Meara, I, 335–6, 453; Lavalette, II, 17 *et seq.*

2. Du Casse, I, 91–92; Hortense, I, 141–181; Rémusat, I, 221–5, 253–56, 297; Méneval, I, 318. Bourrienne.

3. Rovigo, I, 317, 5–6; Méneval, I, 306–313; Junot, I, 327–9; Masson, F., *Madame Bonaparte*, 317; Bourrienne, II, 252–256.

4. Hortense, I, 183–4; Constant, II, 4–5, 19–29, 34–35.

5. *Journal du Comte P. L. Roederer*, Paris 1909, 214.

6. Rémusat, I, 304–310, 214.

7. Du Casse, I, 93.

8. Hortense, I, 198–200; Junot, II, 334–348; Rovigo, I, 75; Rémusat, I, 312–330; Constant, II, 140.

9. Marie Antoinette Adèle Papin was born at Aire in the Landes, 1782 and died in Paris 1860. She was married in 1802 to Charles Jacques Nicolas Duchâtel who held various civil appointments before the Revolution and after, and was still in office in 1815. She was named Dame du Palais, June 1804. The story is difficult to disentangle as Rémusat alludes to her generally as "Madame X" and Hortense never mentions in her memoirs that Eugène had been her victim. Masson, *Napoléon et les Femmes*, devotes a whole chapter to her as "Madame X". But in a long letter to Eugène (*Revue des Deux Mondes*, July 1933, 309) Hortense expands on the subject of their mother's sufferings, "*C'est une femme méchante et dangereuse*," and the malevolence of the Murats towards Josephine. It appears that Madame Duchâtel may have cherished a *grande passion* for the Emperor, though their *liaison* was short. She was one of the few who came to offer their sympathy after his abdication. Baron Gourgaud, speaking to the Emperor in exile about this *affaire* ventured to suggest that Madame Duchâtel seemed to have shown sensitivity. She had never even asked for a diamond necklace. To this the Emperor replied. "Yes, and she would have got some diamonds, which in fact she did not get. But she wanted to put herself on the same level as myself. I had written her some love letters which I claimed back from her, through Duroc. I did not want her to print

them some day, as I had seen happen in the case of other sovereigns. However, they did belong to her, all the more so since she had given me what I wanted." Gourgaud, II, 169; Hortense, I, 202–206; Rémusat, I, 322–342, 365–390; *The First Napoleon* (Bowood Papers), ed. Earl of Kerry, 1925, hereafter cited as Bowood, 2–5.

CHAPTER EIGHT

VICEROY OF ITALY

1. *Revue des Deux Mondes*, vol. 35, 1916, 738.
2. Du Casse, I, 94–97.
3. *Revue des Deux Mondes*, 35, 1916, 739.
4. *Correspondance de Napoléon Ier*, 32 vols., Paris 1862, hereafter cited as Napoleon, Correspondence, vol. 10, 8691, 8720, 8727, 9732; Méneval, I, 318–346; Rémusat, I, 319; Avrillon, I, 183; Constant, II, 196.
5. Hortense, I, 218. Hortense wrote to her brother two months before his wedding. "No doubt you will have heard that I have seen someone who is often in your thoughts. She asked how you were, and I was only too glad to see someone who is fond of you, and you of her. She is a pretty little creature and I felt sorry for her; soon the poor thing will be very sad. But I will take her under my wing for there is no guile in her. She never sees anyone here and if she had not made her little trip, she would have died of disappointment at not seeing you." *Revue des Deux Mondes*, vol. 16, July 1933, pp. 322–333.
6. Avrillon, I, 196.
7. *Napoleon, Correspondence*, 10, 8852.
8. Darnay's volume *Notices historiques sur S.A.R. Le Prince Eugène Vice-Roi d'Italie*, Paris 1830, is dedicated to the widow and august infants by their very humble, very devoted and very faithful servant, and privately printed in an edition of twenty-five copies. (Hereafter cited as Darnay.) The British Museum has the copy presented with the author's homage to the Duchess of Ragusa, and also one of a less profound contemporary rarity which, however, is valuable as it provides a Who's Who catalogue of characters Italian and French, at the Viceregal court and a calendar of events: *Mémoires sur la cour du Prince Eugène et sur le Royaume d'Italie pendant la domination de Napoléon Bonaparte, par un Français attaché à la cour du Vice-Roi*, Charles Jean Lafolie, Paris 1826, hereafter cited as Lafolie.
9. *Lettres inédites de Napoléon I*, 2 vols., Paris 1897 ed. Léon; Lecestre, I, 53.
10. Du Casse, I, 115, 123, 125–6, 165, 178, 195–6, 237.
11. Constant II, 200–205.
12. Du Casse, I, 238.
13. Ibid., 237–247; Prince Adalbert *Eugen*, 82–88.
14. Geheimes Hausarchiv, Munich, hereafter cited as H.A., I.A. 6, 76, v. 12 April 1805.
15. *Revue des Deux Mondes*, ed. F. Masson, vol. 35, Sept.–Oct. 1916, 742–3.
16. Ibid., ed. J. Hanoteau, vol. 16, June 1933, 310–318.
17. Du Casse, I, 360, 373, 385, 395, 416.
18. *Lettres de Joséphine à Napoléon et sa Fille*, vol. ii, 246–248; *Revue des Deux Mondes*, 35, Oct. 1916, 748–750, and 16 July, 1933, 320–324.
19. *Austerlitz*, Claude Mancereau, Paris 1963.

CHAPTER NINE   THE PRINCESS AUGUSTE

1. *Napoleon, Corresp.*, XI. 9636.
2. Du Casse, II, 18–19.
3. Ibid., 15–17.
4. *Max. I Joseph von Bayern*, Adalbert, Prinz von Bayern, Munich 1957, here-after cited as *Max Joseph*, 503.
5. Darnay, 40; Avrillon, I, 304–306; Prinz Adalbert, *Eugen*, 109; Rémusat, II, 40; Lèvy, 116.
6. Darnay who had not yet arrived, believed that the Emperor sent for the barber the moment he set eyes on Eugène and this has been repeated by many authors. But Avrillon, who was on the spot, knew that it was not until he had been to see Josephine that the barber was ordered. Avrillon, I, 301.
7. *Napoleon, Corresp.*, XI, 247.
8. Prinz Adalbert, *Eugen*, Chap. VI; *Max Joseph*, 506–509.

CHAPTER TEN   PRINCE OF VENICE

1. *Napoleon Corresp.* XI, 545.
2. The picture of the arrival of the bridal couple in Venice is reproduced opposite p. 113 in the 1940 edition of the life of Eugen Beauharnais by Adalbert, Prinz von Bayern. The artist is stated to be unknown and acknowledgment for permission to reproduce is made to Countess Eugénie von Blanckenstein, *née* Countess Enzenberg, Schloss Battelau (Mähren). Prinz Adalbert, *Eugen* 116.
3. Lévy, A., 124.
4. The Villa Bonaparte suffered from war damage in Feb. 1943 but has now been restored and houses the important Gallery of Modern Art with paintings and statuary of the Lombard school of the nineteenth and twentieth centuries. These include an oil-portrait by Serangeli of the eldest daughter of Eugène, Josephine, who was born in the house, and one of Auguste by Spalla, and busts of Eugène, Auguste and Napoleon.
5. Prinz Adalbert, *Eugen*, 118, 124.
6. Ibid., 122.
7. Rémusat, II, 116–120; Constant, II.
8. *Revue des Deux Mondes*, 16. July 1933, 326–333.
9. *Napoleon Corresp.* XII, 541.
10. Ibid., 285; Prinz Adalbert, *Eugen*, 128.
11. Ibid., 427. Auguste's letter to which this is the reply is not to be found in the collection lent by her daughter-in-law to Du Casse and to the editor of the official Correspondence of Napoleon I published by order of Hortense's son, Napoleon III.
12. Hortense, I, 236, 239. Prinz Adalbert, *Eugen*, 129–132.
13. *Napoleon Corresp.*, XIII.
14. *Lettres de Napoléon a Josephine*, etc., Leipzig 1833, II, 268.
15. Prinz Adalbert, *Eugen*, 137.
16. Ibid., 138.

17. *Les Beauharnais et l'Empereur*, Jean Hanoteau, Paris 1936, hereafter cited as Hanoteau, *Beauharnais*, pp. 48–49.
18. The beds of Napoleon and Eugène are still to be seen in the Ducal Palaces at Mantua and at Strà.
19. Méneval, II, 122.

1. Hortense II, 6; Rovigo, II, 228.
2. Rémusat, 2, 286–500; Méneval II, 144–151; Oman, C. W. C., *A History of the Peninsular War*, IX vols., hereafter cited as Oman, *Peninsular War*, I, Chapters I–II and IV and V.
3. Avrillon, II, 15–23; Rémusat, II, 467–468.
4. Rémusat, II, 464–465; Hortense, I, 217; Méneval, II, 125–126; Rapp, 17; Hortense, I, 235–6. Both Rapp and Stéphanie Tascher remarried with better success. Stéphanie, born at Fort-Royal 1788, was a daughter of Robert Tascher de la Pagerie, uncle of Josephine. She married as second husband a year after her first marriage was annulled, Gui, Marquis de Chaumont Quitry who had occupied a post in Josephine's household. Lucien Bonaparte's eldest daughter, Charlotte who was fourteen at the time that she wrote the fatal letters home about the Imperial Court married in Italy Prince Gabrielli.
5. Hanoteau, *Beauharnais*, 244.
6. Du Casse, IV, 425, 431–2, 442–443. This collection of 1809 letters from Eugène to his wife passed by inheritance to his daughter Josephine who became Queen of Sweden. Prince Adalbert of Bavaria when working on his life of Eugène 1940 saw the originals in the Bernadotte archives, Stockholm, and ascertained that Du Casse when editing them for his *Mémoires et Correspondance du Prince Eugène* 1859 took some liberties. Copies of some of Auguste's letters to her husband were inherited by her second son and are in the Leuchtenberg Archives.
7. *Napoleon Corresp.*, XVIII, 509, 524–5.
8. Hortense, II, 35; *Revue des Deux Mondes*, XVI, 1933, 565.
9. Méneval, II, 209.
10. Du Casse, V, 181.
11. Méneval, II, 219.
12. Du Casse, V, 275–289 demolishes the claims of Thiers, *L'histoire du Consulat et de l'Empire* with regard to the part played by Macdonald at the battle of Raab. These errors have been followed by other authors, including Ségur in his *éloge* at the funeral of the Duke of Taranto 1841. Macdonald commanded only the right wing of the Army of Italy and was sent orders by Eugène emanating directly from the Emperor to advance and leave Broussier's division at Gratz. He did not come spontaneously to Raab owing to prescience. Aide de camp Méjean searched in vain for him at Papa; he was in a château five miles to the right. His troops arrived on the battlefield of Raab in time to assist at the triumph, with the exception of Lamarque's division who came up after dark. On June 16 the Emperor wrote to Eugène that he had no doubt sent Macdonald's troops to pursue the enemy "because they are fresh".

13. Du Casse, 5, 377–387; 271–279; Du Casse gives the final casualty figures as Austrian nearly 4,000 dead and wounded, more than 2,500 prisoners; Army of Italy 600 dead, 2,300 wounded. Méneval, II, 220 gives the enemy loss as 6,000 killed and wounded. Rovigo, II, 105 states that the Viceroy's personal firmness in leading his troops to the charge not only held the plateau but also broke the Austrian army.

14. The Emperor's letters to Auguste, *Napoleon Corresp.*, 19, 262 and Du Casse, V, 310–311. Eugène's to Auguste: Du Casse, V, 221, 244, 315, 359, 384, 391, 424, 448, 471.

CHAPTER TWELVE   CAMPAIGN AGAINST AUSTRIA AND THE DIVORCE

1. Du Casse, VI, 3–14; 37–38; Rovigo, II, 112–124; Méneval II, 221–222.
2. Du Casse, V, 409; VI, 39, 43; 46–47; 49; 57.
3. Altered in 1867, the palace now houses the Albertina Collection.
4. Du Casse, VI, 58, 60, 74, 77, 79.
5. Prinz Adalbert, *Eugen*, 168.
6. Hortense, II, 39; Rovigo, II, 175.
7. Prinz Adalbert, *Eugen*, 175.
8. Du Casse, VI, 104–107; 170–175; 183–186.
9. This attractive conversation piece is reproduced opposite p. 161 of the 1940 first edition of his biography of Eugène Beauharnais, by Adalbert, Prince of Bavaria, and the owner is there stated to be Graf von Enzenberg, Schwaz, Tyrol. A daughter of Eugène, Theodolinde, had a daughter Auguste who became Gräfin von Enzenberg. Exhaustive enquiries at Schwaz, Innsbruck and Munich have failed to discover the present ownership and whereabouts of this picture. After the death in 1916 of Auguste Eugénie, Gräfin Thun-Hohenstein, born Fürstin von Urach, it was inherited by her son Constantin, Graf Thun-Hohenstein, and was until 1945 in his villa in Innsbruck. During successive military occupations it disappeared.
10. Du Casse, VI, 177–179; 182; 247; 259; 269; 277.
11. Ibid., 282.
12. Hortense II, 47.
13. Du Casse, VI, 289; Hortense II, 64. Constant, II, 165. Méneval, II, 255 states: "Prince Eugène told me at Vienna (1814) that in the first interview that he had with his mother in Napoleon's presence after the divorce had been decided upon, Empress Josephine had asked for the Crown of Italy for her son. Eugène fearing that the favour might be considered as the price of his mother's divorce, had begged her not to insist. The Emperor, touched by his reserve had assured him that he did well to trust himself to his tenderness."
14. Hortense, II, 47–56; Avrillon, II, 130–136; 144–150; Méneval, II, 246–263; Du Casse, VI, 283–294; 296; 311–315. Constant, III, 198–199.
15. Du Casse, VI, 277. Prinz Adalbert, *Eugen*, 183. Hofer's body was removed from Mantua to Innsbruck in 1823 and a marble statue was erected above his tomb in the Franciscan church. In 1893 a bronze memorial was set up on the Iselberg, and at Meran he became the hero of an annual outdoor festival play.

1. Lévy, 175.
2. Hortense, II, 61–71.
3. Méneval, II, 295; Rovigo, II, 196.
4. Hortense, II, 70; Méneval, II, 296–298. The Emperor exiled to their various departments the thirteen Cardinals who had refused to attend his second marriage pleading that the Pope had refused to grant a dissolution of his first. They were forbidden to wear their customary scarlet robes and were hereafter known as "The Black Cardinals". Rovigo, II, 199–203.
5. The Château of Navarre had belonged to the Duc de Bouillon until the Revolution. On the death of Josephine it passed to the sons of Eugène, but they were never able to take up residence in France, and in 1835 the elder died. The house had been severely damaged by fire in the previous year and in the next year the ruins were pulled down. The park and dukedom could not, by a decision of the Minister of Finance in France, be inherited by the male issue of Eugène's second son as he had married the Grand Duchess Marie of Russia and they were in direct descent to the Russian throne.
6. Avrillon, II, 191–204; Hortense, II, 74; Méneval, II, 303.
7. Prinz Adalbert, *Eugen*, 203.
8. *Eleven years residence in the family of Murat, King of Naples*, Catherine Davies, 1841, 2–6, 16.
9. Du Casse, VI, 308 states that except in the biography by Darnay he could find no trace in correspondence or documents of the story that the crown of Sweden was offered to Eugène in 1810. But the story is fully told by Méneval, II, 331.
10. *Max Joseph*, 603.
11. Junot III, 270–272; Méneval II, 317; Lavalette, II, 56.
12. Méneval, II, 383–385; Hortense, II, 125–127.
13. Du Casse VII, 102, Hortense II, 132, Prinz Adalbert, *Eugen*, 223. Until Adalbert, Prince of Bavaria, quoted this letter dated September 17, 1811, from the Geheimes Hausarchiv, Munich (E.A.6), the birthplace of Hortense's son by Flahaut remained a matter of conjecture. Lord Kerry (*The First Napoleon, Bowood Papers*, 241 *et seq.*:) quotes letters which show that Flahaut's mother Madame de Souza took charge of the child early in 1813. According to the *Journal de Paris* Hortense returned to Paris, October 10, 1811. The child was registered on October 21 as the son of a St. Dominique landowner (actually a pensioner of Josephine) named De Morny, and his wife *née* Fleury, now returned to Philadelphia. He was baptized Charles Auguste Louis Joseph. The supposed father applied to Flahaut for funds in June 1813 and died April 1814. Charles Auguste (1811–1865) was a constant guest of the Flahaut family and was created Duke de Morny by his half brother Napoleon III. He represented the Emperor at the coronation of the Czar Alexander II and married Princess Sophie Troubetzkoy. The secret of his birth was well kept. The principal go-between to whom Flahaut addressed letters to Hortense was her son's tutor, the Abbé Bertrand. Hortense in her memoirs says evasively that illuminations and festivities awaited her on Lake Maggiore and her brother anxious on hearing

that she had fallen ill came over the Simplon, but she had to abandon her hope of going to stay with him. Hanoteau quotes a paragraph from the *Archives Nationales* (F7 2685) in which Baron Finot, Prefect of Mont Blanc states that the queen left Aix August 31 for a fifteen days' stay at Prégny, and that the Viceroy came up to the Borommean isles to conduct her to Monza.

14. Du Casse VII, 260–264.

CHAPTER FOURTEEN

1. Hortense, II, 148; Darnay, 162.

2. The letters of Eugène to Napoleon in 1812 were apparently destroyed at Orscha when the Emperor burnt his papers; but all to the Vicereine survive, and Du Casse was given permision to publish them by Eugène's daughter, the Queen of Sweden. Du Casse, VII, 260.

3. Ibid., VII, 327–337.

4. Ibid., 338–343; 357–358; 370–375; 388.

5. Hanoteau, *Beauharnais*, 105. *Lettres, Napoléon, Joséphine, Hortense*, ed. Didot, 356–363.

6. Du Casse, VII, 452, 463.

7. De Ségur, General Comte Philippe Paul, *Histoire de Napoléon et de la Grande Armée pendant l'année 1812*, hereafter cited as Ségur, 102. Baron Agathon Fain, *Manuscript de Mil Huit Cent Douze etc. pour servir a l'Histoire de l'Empereur Napoléon*, 2 vols., Paris 1827, hereafter cited as Fain, I, 440; Constant, III, 292–298.

8. De Ségur (114) says that the Emperor was suffering from dysuria, retention of urine. Constant says he was not as bad as De Ségur made out, but acknowledges that he had a shivering fit and had to lie down on the morning of Borodino at four a.m.

9. Accounts of the battle of Borodino by eyewitnesses differ considerably. The casualty figures given here are those from Prussian reports. De Ségur says (138) that the trophies of victory were only seven or eight hundred prisoners and a score of guns. Twenty thousand wounded were left on the field and those who could be moved were taken to the Abbey of Kolotskoi. Fain, II, 47 has a good map.

10. The seven eyewitness accounts principally drawn upon here are Ségur, 139–178; Fain, II, 1–40; Méneval, III, 56–63; Du Casse, VIII, 46–48; Rapp, 169–258; Constant, III, 319–327 and Caulaincourt, *Mémoires du Générale de Caulaincourt, Duc de Vicen*, ed. J. Hanoteau, 2 vols., hereafter cited as Caulaincourt, I, 208–225.

11. Hanoteau, *Beauharnais*, 107–108.

12. Du Casse, VIII, 56–57.

13. Ibid., 56; Méneval, III, 63–69; de Ségur, 179–206.

14. *Lettres de Napoléon à Marie Louise*, ed. C. de la Roncière, 120; *Lettres de Napoléon de Joséphine et de Joséphine à sa fille*, ed. Didot, 372; Bowood, 25; Fain, II, 242–252.

15. The Emperor's accusation that Wintzingerode was a spy was not entirely without foundation. He had been discovered wearing a civilian topcoat over his uniform, making enquiries from Mortier's troops and from inhabitants of Moscow after the Grande Armée had marched. Caulaincourt, III, 307; Fain, II, 169–171.

16. Du Casse, VIII, 56; Méneval, III, 63–69; de Ségur, 179–206; Caulaincourt, III, 227–289; Constant, III, 151–159.

17. Du Casse, VIII, 82–159; Méneval, III, 71–89; Caulaincourt, III, 335–411; de Ségur, 263–416; Constant, IV, 11–36; *Lettres interceptées par les Russes durant la Campagne de 1812.*

CHAPTER FIFTEEN   HONOUR AND FIDELITY

1. Caulaincourt, III, 403–4; de Ségur, 383, 422; Hortense, II, 152–153; Bowood Papers, 28; Junot, III, 336.

2. A lithograph of a sketch by Albrecht Adam of this incident is reproduced opposite page 265 of the 1940 edition of Prinz Adalbert's *Eugen Beauharnais.*

3. Du Casse, IX, 71, 376–408.

4. Du Casse, VIII, 108, 159, 212, 216, 389, 411; IX, 7, 20, 58, 65, 70, 72, 75, 79, 82, 93–96; Darnay, 187, 190. Bowood Papers, 36–47.

5. Junot's wife (Junot III, 347) said that she had received a letter from him only four days before his death which showed no signs of mental disturbance, but other contemporary evidence is against her. He had been noticed to be behaving strangely for months.

6. *Précis Historique des opérations militaires de l'Armée d'Italie en 1813 et 1814, par le chef de l'Etat Major Général de cette Armée,* (*Le Général Comte de Vignolles*), *Journal Historique sur la Campagne du Prince Eugène en Italie pendant les anneés 1813 et 1814 par L. D. . . Capitaine attaché à l'état major du Prince et Chevalier de la Légion d'Honneur,* both Paris 1817; *Prince Eugène en 1814,* Planat de la Faye, 4 vols., 1858, hereafter cited as Planat de la Faye; Vaudoncourt, Général de *L'Histoire politique et militaire du Prince Eugène* 2 vols., Paris 1828; Weil M. H. *Le Prince Eugène et Murat 1813–1814,* 5 vols., Paris 1902, hereafter cited as Weil. Vignolle and Weil give day to day bulletins. Weil's five volumes are invaluable. For an adverse view see *Dernière campagne de l'Armée Franco-Italienne sous les ordres d'Eugène Beauharnais en 1813 et 1814 par le Chevalier S. J. . . témoin oculaire.* Darnay demolishes this brochure which really does not accuse the Viceroy of more than a tendency to parsimony in his household expenses, of obliging owners to sell him acres to aggrandize the park at Monza and churchwardens to part with a superb picture to add to his collection (one of the most magnificent in Italy) and of gradually becoming less accessible to petitioners. The absurd story of his escaping from Italy in an Austrian uniform also comes from this source. pp. 127–128.

7. Prinz Adalbert, *Eugen,* 288, Du Casse, IX, 283–295.

8. Prince Taxis supplied Princess Auguste with a detailed description of his mission in 1836. Du Casse, IX, 300–306. See also Darnay, 216; Weil, III, 100–7.

9. Darnay, 221; Du Casse, IX, 435.

10. Du Casse, IX, 317.

11. Hortense, II, 174.

12. Du Casse, X, 123.

13. Vignolle, 120–132; *Journal Historique sur la campagne du Prince Eugène,* 38–39, 65–66; Weil, IV, 1–194.

14. *Journal Historique sur la campagne du Prince Eugène en Italie Par L. D. Capitaine.*

15. Du Casse, X, 85–100; Weil, IV, 213–218.
16. Du Casse, X, 125–129; Weil, IV, 234–235. Du Casse and Weil have got the name of this messenger wrong and call him Poni. Prinz Adalbert gives him correctly as Pocci.
17. Du Casse, X, 129–133, 102.
18. Ibid., 134, 230.
19. Ibid., 208.
20. Ibid., 136, 215.
21. *Journal Historique sur la campagne du Prince Eugène*, 73–74, 76.
22. Ibid., 236; Weil, IV, 527 and Annexe LXVIII; Hanoteau, *Beauharnais*, 118.
23. Du Casse, X, 170–174; Darnay, 252–5; Weil, IV, 500, 561; *Sulla Rivoluzione di Milano sequita nel Giorno Venti Aprile 1814 sul Primo suo Governo Provvisorio etc.*, Paris 1814.

CHAPTER SIXTEEN   "CUTTING UP THE CAKE"

1. Du Casse, X, 255, 288–291; Hortense, II, 227.
2. Caulaincourt, II, 329–337, 340.
Caulaincourt's account of the attempted suicide of Napoleon was not published until 1934. Up to that date the only eyewitness description was that of Constant (whose memoirs are a compilation from the pens of various ghostwriters). Bourrienne, Madame Junot, Ségur, Belliard and Méneval spoke from hearsay. Hortense wrote, "I have been told, but I have never had any proof of the statement that he made an attempt to end his days," II, 220.
Since 1808 the Emperor had carried poison in a small heart-shaped packet worn round his neck. After being nearly captured by Cossacks on the night after Eugène's victory at Malo Jaroslawetz he had obtained from Dr. Yvan a mixture of opium, belladonna and hellebore, which he had carried first round his neck, later in his pocket or in the case with his pistols.
3. Caulaincourt II, 383; Hortense, II, 209, 215.
4. Hortense, II, 231–4; 238; Avrillon, 362–373.
5. Hortense, II, 240, 242–244, 247–250; Du Casse, X, 292–295; Avrillon, 376–380, 390; *Mémoires sur la Reine Hortense*, Mlle. Cochelet, Paris 1907, hereafter cited as Cochelet, 87–95.
6. Josephine's monument in white marble, by Gilet and Dubuc, is surmounted by her kneeling figure, by Cartellier. It was not erected until two years after the death of Eugène. Hortense's tomb, opposite bears the inscription "*A la Reine Hortense, son fils Napoléon III.*" Except that it faces in the opposite direction Josephine's figure resembles that in David's coronation picture.
7. *Inventaire après décès de l'Impératrice Joséphine à Malmaison, Préface de Pierre Schommer*, ed. Serge Grandjean. Paris 1965; Lavalette, II, 140–150; Darnay, 296.
8. Prinz Adalbert, *Eugen*, 375; Prinz Adalbert, *Max Joseph*, 543–546; 581–614; Méneval, II, 264–5.
9. Cochelet, 123–140; Hortense, II, 269–273.
10. *Souvenirs du Congrès de Vienne*, Comte S. L. de la Garde Chambonas, Paris 1901, 10 *et seq.*
11. Prinz Adalbert, *Eugen*, 351; *Les dessous du Congrès de Vienne*, M. H. Weil,

2 vols., 1917, hereafter cited as Weil *Congrès*, I, 206, 362.

12. Du Casse, X, 303–326.

13. *Revue des Deux Mondes*, Vol. 16, 1933, 582.

14. Du Casse, X, 256–262; 327–338; Darnay, 274; Hortense, II, 343; Hanoteau, *Beauharnais*, 279; Méneval, II, 373–374. Hortense also gave Boutiaguine, the Russian chargé d'affaires in Paris, a letter for his master expressing her desires for peace, and according to Mademoiselle Cochelet delivered to an officer of Wellington's staff a brush for Eugène in the handle of which was concealed a list of Bonapartist supporters.

15. Du Casse, X, 263.

16. Méneval, II, 380–388. Hager's spies supplied the following letter intercepted by them, dated Vienna night of the 6th–7 April, 1815, attributed to Prince Eugène.

"Allow me, dear and good Séraphine, to say farewell in a note. It would be too sad to have to tell you myself that I leave tonight with the king. I wish you good health and a prompt return to your family. Keep for me a few kind thoughts. I deserve them, for I love you well and shall never forget you. Perhaps we may meet again in happier times." Weil, *Congrès*, II, 435. Séraphine or Sophie is variously described as beautiful and talented and as small, yellow and plain. Hager's spies believed she had been the mistress of the Grand Duke Constantine, Karl of Baden, Prince Narischkine, the Prince of Hesse Darmstadt, and perhaps Metternich. She wanted to go to Russia. The Baronne de Montete declared that her extravagance had ruined Comte Maurice de Fries and broken the heart of his wife, a princess of Hohenlohe. A rumour spread by Séraphine that he had married her after he became a widower (although he was by then a pauper in a garret) was declared by the Baronne to be a falsehood as Séraphine was herself already married to a Monsieur de G . . . Weil, *Congrès*, I, 372, 484, 709, 753, 816.

17. Prinz Adalbert, *Eugen*, 338. The *Hypotheeken und Wechselbank* now stands on this site.

18. Méneval, II, 380–381, 449.

CHAPTER SEVENTEEN   DUKE OF LEUCHTENBERG, PRINCE OF EICHSTÄTT

1. Du Casse, X, 340.

2. Lavalette, II, 240–246.

3. Ibid., II, 347–403.

4. Hortense, III, 133.

5. Ibid., 114.

6. Auguste's diary was left to her daughter Josephine, afterwards Queen of Sweden and is now in the Bernadotte Archives in Stockholm. Prinz Adalbert, *Eugen*, 377.

7. Méneval II, 390; Darnay, 288–91; Du Casse, X, 273–274.

8. Prinz Adalbert, *Eugen*, 387. Eugène's country home at Ismaning was given by Freiherr von Poschinger to the city of Munich in 1899 and is now absorbed into the suburbs, but there were two rooms decorated by Klenze still visible in 1941.

9. Prinz Adalbert, *Eugen*, 388.

10. Ibid., 387.
11. Ibid., 392.
12. Ibid., 403–411.
13. Ibid., 398–401, 412–413.
14. Ibid., 413–418; Du Casse, X, 278–280, 408–411; Méneval, III, 390; Gourgaud, 230, 340–346, 348–353, Darnay, 294; *Narrative of the Surrender of Bonaparte and of his residence on board H.M.S. Bellerophon*, Captain F. L. Maitland, 1826, 52–54, 108, 193, 198, 228, 230.
15. *Die Familie Bonaparte auf Arenenberg*, Jakob Hugentobler, 1961; *Musée Napoléon, Arenenberg*, Jakob Hugentobler, Frauenfeld, 1961.
16. Bowood Papers, 253–256, 267.
Flahaut's son by Hortense became a familiar figure, staying with his father and family in Scotland. His half-brother Napoleon III created him Duc de Morny.
17. Prinz Adalbert, *Eugen*, 429–430.
18. Ibid., 439.
19. Upon second thoughts he sent some of this back to Malmaison in the following year. When his son sold Malmaison, it made its second journey to Munich. Ibid.
20. O'Meara, Vol., I, 421, 243, 356, 500; II, 9, 100, 157, 364.

CHAPTER EIGHTEEN   THE GRANDFATHER OF EUROPE

1. *Vie de Planat de la Faye, Souvenir par sa veuve. Lettres et Dictées recueillis et annotés*, Paris 1895, hereafter cited as Planat, IX, 411–413, 430–437; Prinz Adalbert, *Eugen*, 447–451.
2. Planat, 418.
3. Ibid., 416.
4. Prinz Adalbert, *Eugen*, 460, 471.
5. *Schloss Eugensberg und seiner Erbauer*, Jakob Hugentobler, Thurgauer Jahrbuch, 1937, 13–22.
6. *Ätten Bernadotte*, J. Almén, Stockholm, 1893.
7. Prinz Adalbert, *Eugen*, 267.
8. *Die Herzen der Leuchtenberg*, Adalbert, Prinz von Bayern, Munich 1963, 106.
9. Ibid., 241.
10. In 1873, the Emperor Napoleon III died in exile and the Prefect of the Seine offered the statue of Prince Eugène to the War Minister for the Invalides. The Boulevard du Prince Eugène had become the Boulevard Voltaire and the monumental barracks which had also been named after the hero, had become the Caserne du Château d'Eau. The statue was moved and re-established in much more appropriate surroundings, outside the Musée de l'Armée, where it still stands backed by greenery and an oblique glimpse of the Eiffel Tower.

TASCHER DE LA PAGERIE

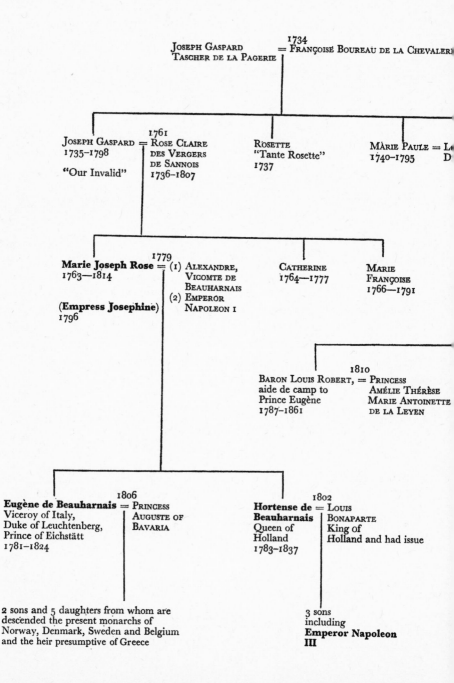

JOSEPH GASPARD
TASCHER DE LA PAGERIE
= 1734 FRANÇOISE BOUREAU DE LA CHEVALERI

JOSEPH GASPARD
1735–1798

"Our Invalid"

= 1761 ROSE CLAIRE
DES VERGERS
DE SANNOIS
1736–1807

ROSETTE
"Tante Rosette"
1737

MÀRIE PAULE = L
1740–1795   D

Marie Joseph Rose
1763—1814

(Empress Josephine)
1796

= 1779 (1) ALEXANDRE,
VICOMTE DE
BEAUHARNAIS
(2) EMPEROR
NAPOLEON I

CATHERINE
1764—1777

MARIE
FRANÇOISE
1766—1791

BARON LOUIS ROBERT,
aide de camp to
Prince Eugène
1787–1861

= 1810 PRINCESS
AMÉLIE THÉRÈSE
MARIE ANTOINETTE
DE LA LEYEN

Eugène de Beauharnais
Viceroy of Italy,
Duke of Leuchtenberg,
Prince of Eichstätt
1781–1824

= 1806 PRINCESS
AUGUSTE OF
BAVARIA

**Hortense de
Beauharnais**
Queen of
Holland
1783–1837

= 1802 LOUIS
BONAPARTE
King of
Holland and had issue

2 sons and 5 daughters from whom are
descended the present monarchs of
Norway, Denmark, Sweden and Belgium
and the heir presumptive of Greece

3 sons
including
**Emperor Napoleon
III**

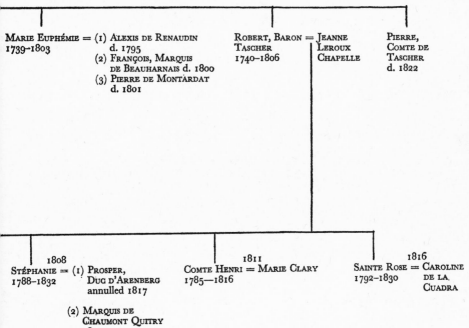

MARIE EUPHÉMIE = (1) ALEXIS DE RENAUDIN
1739–1803   d. 1795
               (2) FRANÇOIS, MARQUIS
                    DE BEAUHARNAIS d. 1800
               (3) PIERRE DE MONTARDAT
                    d. 1801

ROBERT, BARON = JEANNE
TASCHER   LEROUX
1740–1806   CHAPELLE

PIERRE,
COMTE DE
TASCHER
d. 1822

1808
STÉPHANIE = (1) PROSPER,
1788–1832   DUC D'ARENBERG
               annulled 1817

        (2) MARQUIS DE
             CHAUMONT QUITRY
             1817

1811
COMTE HENRI = MARIE CLARY
1785—1816

1816
SAINTE ROSE = CAROLINE
1792–1830   DE LA
               CUADRA

BEAUHARNAIS

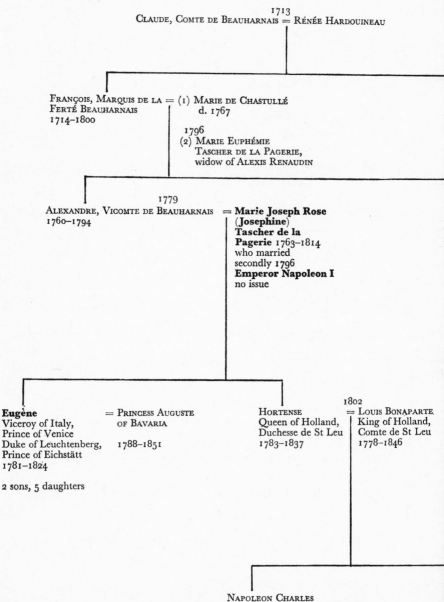

1713
CLAUDE, COMTE DE BEAUHARNAIS = RÉNÉE HARDOUINEAU

FRANÇOIS, MARQUIS DE LA = (1) MARIE DE CHASTULLÉ
FERTÉ BEAUHARNAIS   d. 1767
1714–1800

1796
(2) MARIE EUPHÉMIE
TASCHER DE LA PAGERIE,
widow of ALEXIS RENAUDIN

1779
ALEXANDRE, VICOMTE DE BEAUHARNAIS = **Marie Joseph Rose**
1760–1794   **(Josephine)**
                                          Tascher de la
                                          Pagerie 1763–1814
                                          who married
                                          secondly 1796
                                          Emperor Napoleon I
                                          no issue

Eugène   = PRINCESS AUGUSTE   HORTENSE   = LOUIS BONAPARTE
Viceroy of Italy,   OF BAVARIA   Queen of Holland,   King of Holland,
Prince of Venice   Duchesse de St Leu   Comte de St Leu
Duke of Leuchtenberg,   1788–1851   1783–1837   1778–1846
Prince of Eichstätt
1781–1824

2 sons, 5 daughters

1802

NAPOLEON CHARLES
1802–1807

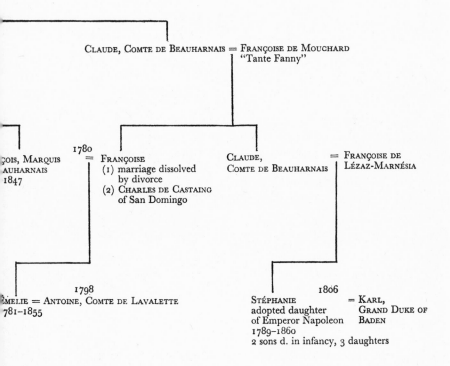

CLAUDE, COMTE DE BEAUHARNAIS = FRANÇOISE DE MOUCHARD
"Tante Fanny"

                              1780
ȮOIS, MARQUIS   = FRANÇOISE   CLAUDE,   = FRANÇOISE DE
ꞮAUHARNAIS   (1) marriage dissolved   COMTE DE BEAUHARNAIS   LÉZAZ-MARNÉSIA
1847   by divorce
                       (2) CHARLES DE CASTAING
                            of San Domingo

                 1798   1806
ꞮMELIE = ANTOINE, COMTE DE LAVALETTE   STÉPHANIE   = KARL,
781–1855   adopted daughter   GRAND DUKE OF
                                              of Emperor Napoleon   BADEN
                                              1789–1860
                                              2 sons d. in infancy, 3 daughters

          NAPOLEON LOUIS   CHARLES LOUIS NAPOLEON
          1804–1831   (EMPEROR NAPOLEON III)
                                          1808–1873

BONAPARTE

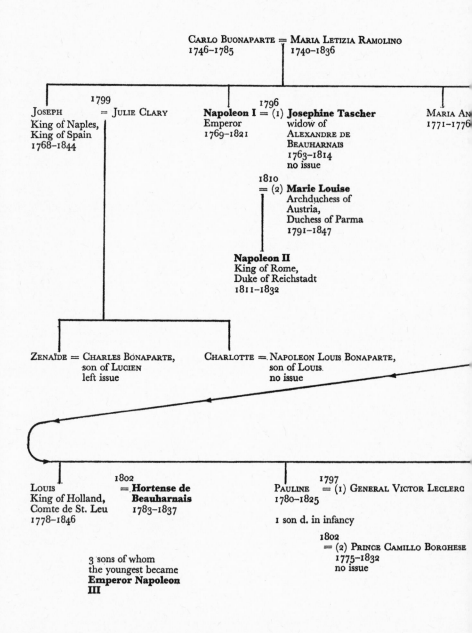

CARLO BUONAPARTE = MARIA LETIZIA RAMOLINO
1746–1785   1740–1836

1799
JOSEPH = JULIE CLARY
King of Naples,
King of Spain
1768–1844

1796
Napoleon I = (1) **Josephine Tascher**
Emperor   widow of
1769–1821   ALEXANDRE DE
                    BEAUHARNAIS
                    1763–1814
                    no issue

MARIA AN
1771–1776

1810
= (2) **Marie Louise**
Archduchess of
Austria,
Duchess of Parma
1791–1847

Napoleon II
King of Rome,
Duke of Reichstadt
1811–1832

ZENAÏDE = CHARLES BONAPARTE,
         son of LUCIEN
         left issue

CHARLOTTE = NAPOLEON LOUIS BONAPARTE,
            son of LOUIS.
            no issue

1802
LOUIS = **Hortense de**
King of Holland,   **Beauharnais**
Comte de St. Leu   1783–1837
1778–1846

3 sons of whom
the youngest became
**Emperor Napoleon
III**

1797
PAULINE = (1) GENERAL VICTOR LECLERC
1780–1825

1 son d. in infancy

1802
= (2) PRINCE CAMILLO BORGHESE
      1775–1832
      no issue

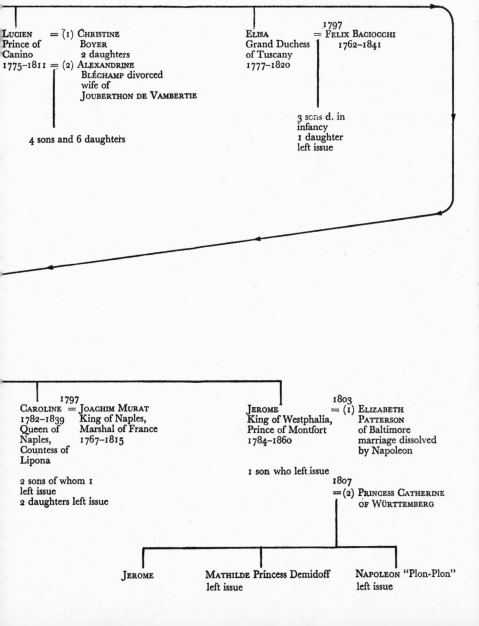

LUCIEN = (1) CHRISTINE
Prince of   BOYER
Canino   2 daughters
1775–1811 = (2) ALEXANDRINE
                 BLÉCHAMP divorced
                 wife of
                 JOUBERTHON DE VAMBERTIE

4 sons and 6 daughters

ELISA   1797
Grand Duchess = FELIX BACIOCCHI
of Tuscany   1762–1841
1777–1820

3 sons d. in
infancy
1 daughter
left issue

                    1797
CAROLINE = JOACHIM MURAT
1782–1839   King of Naples,
Queen of   Marshal of France
Naples,   1767–1815
Countess of
Lipona

2 sons of whom 1
left issue
2 daughters left issue

                    1803
JEROME   = (1) ELIZABETH
King of Westphalia,   PATTERSON
Prince of Montfort   of Baltimore
1784–1860   marriage dissolved
                       by Napoleon

1 son who left issue
                    1807
               = (2) PRINCESS CATHERINE
                     OF WÜRTTEMBERG

JEROME   MATHILDE Princess Demidoff   NAPOLEON "Plon-Plon"
                left issue   left issue

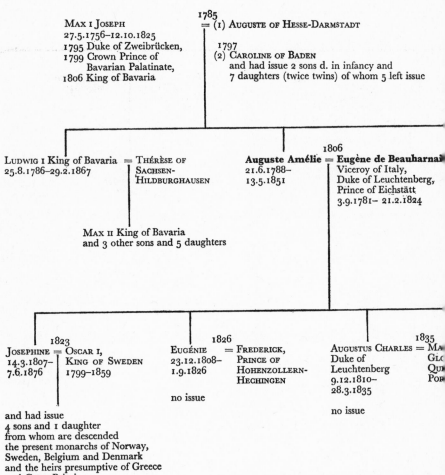

MAX I JOSEPH
27.5.1756–12.10.1825
1795 Duke of Zweibrücken,
1799 Crown Prince of
Bavarian Palatinate,
1806 King of Bavaria

1785
= (1) AUGUSTE OF HESSE-DARMSTADT

1797
(2) CAROLINE OF BADEN
and had issue 2 sons d. in infancy and
7 daughters (twice twins) of whom 5 left issue

LUDWIG I King of Bavaria = THÉRÈSE OF
25.8.1786–29.2.1867   SACHSEN-
                            HILDBURGHAUSEN

1806
Auguste Amélie = Eugène de Beauharnai
21.6.1788–   Viceroy of Italy,
13.5.1851   Duke of Leuchtenberg,
                  Prince of Eichstätt
                  3.9.1781– 21.2.1824

MAX II King of Bavaria
and 3 other sons and 5 daughters

1823
JOSEPHINE = OSCAR I,
14.3.1807–   KING OF SWEDEN
7.6.1876   1799–1859

1826
EUGÉNIE   = FREDERICK,
23.12.1808–   PRINCE OF
1.9.1826   HOHENZOLLERN-
              HECHINGEN

no issue

1835
AUGUSTUS CHARLES = MA
Duke of   GLC
Leuchtenberg   QUI
9.12.1810–   POR
28.3.1835

no issue

and had issue
4 sons and 1 daughter
from whom are descended
the present monarchs of Norway,
Sweden, Belgium and Denmark
and the heirs presumptive of Greece
and Great Britain.

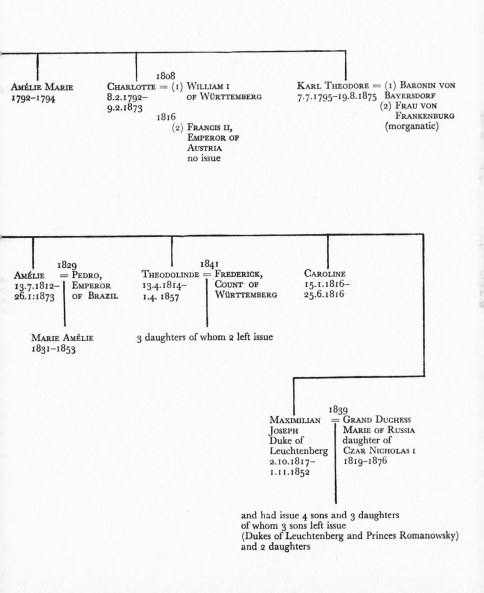

AMÉLIE MARIE
1792–1794

CHARLOTTE = (1) WILLIAM I
8.2.1792–   OF WÜRTTEMBERG
9.2.1873
              1816
              (2) FRANCIS II,
              EMPEROR OF
              AUSTRIA
              no issue

1808

KARL THEODORE = (1) BARONIN VON
7.7.1795–19.8.1875 BAYERSDORF
                    (2) FRAU VON
                    FRANKENBURG
                    (morganatic)

AMÉLIE   = PEDRO,
13.7.1812–   EMPEROR
26.1:1873   OF BRAZIL

1829

THEODOLINDE = FREDERICK,
13.4.1814–   COUNT OF
1.4. 1857   WÜRTTEMBERG

1841

CAROLINE
15.1.1816–
25.6.1816

MARIE AMÉLIE
1831–1853

3 daughters of whom 2 left issue

MAXIMILIAN = GRAND DUCHESS
JOSEPH   MARIE OF RUSSIA
Duke of   daughter of
Leuchtenberg CZAR NICHOLAS I
2.10.1817–   1819–1876
1.11.1852

1839

and had issue 4 sons and 3 daughters
of whom 3 sons left issue
(Dukes of Leuchtenberg and Princes Romanowsky)
and 2 daughters

Index

Abano near Padua, famous mud baths at, visited by Vicereine, 314; successfully, 319; again, 359, 364–5

Acre, siege of, 90–2; Eugène wounded at, 91

Adam, Albrecht, official war-artist to Viceroy, 275; performs a sketch for Queen of Holland, 277; on Russian campaign, 326, 339, 358

Aldini, Antonio, Secretary of State for kingdom of Italy, 176, 180

Alexandria, Eugène describes capture of, 75–6; plague in, 87; departure from, 96

Alexander I, Czar of Russia, orders court mourning for Duc d'Enghien, 152; too late at Austerlitz, 192–3; has secret alliance with King of Prussia, 224; Emperor Napoleon, 231; is deaf, 246; refuses his sisters in marriage to Emperor Napoleon, 292, 316; his diplomacy, 329; scorns peace-offers from Emperor Napoleon, 325 et seq.; thinks crown of Italy tempting to Eugène, 370; Eugène calls upon in Paris, 391; his manners and appearance, 393–4; becomes constant guest at Malmaison, 393–8; outstanding supporter of Eugène at Congress of Vienna, 410; furious with Queen Hortense, 418, 423; Madame Krüdener advises him, 424; Eugène appeals to on behalf of exiled Emperor, 446–7; sees for last time, 461

Amalia, Princess of Hesse Darmstadt, widow of Prince Karl of Baden, mother of Caroline, Queen of Bavaria and Karl, Grand Duke of Baden; opposes Princess Auguste's marriage to Eugène, 199, 204, 206; at Baden-Baden, 404

Amiens, Peace of, 132, 140, 143–8, 199, 305

Angoulême, Louis, Duc d', elder son of Charles X, King of France, 391

Aosta, Eugène first visits, 116–7

Appiani, Andrea, Painter in Chief to Viceroy, 176; presented to Emperor at Milan, 235

Arckinger, Friar, secretary to Hofer, 277–82

Arena, Joseph, Corsican conspirator, 130

Arnault, Antoine, poet, reports on Bonaparte's Mombello headquarters, 59, 62

Artois, Charles, Duc d', afterwards Charles X, King of France, 150; recalls his friendship with Eugène's father, 390; see Angoulême, Berri

Asturias, Prince of, see Ferdinand VII, King of Spain

Auguste Amélie, Princess of Bavaria, Vicereine of Italy, daughter of Maximilian Joseph, King of Bavaria, wife of Prince Eugène, engaged to Karl of Baden, 175; scorns "le Boharnet", 184; Josephine sees her portrait, "could not be more beautiful", 185; meets her, "a charming character", 192; her suitors, 198–9; resolves to sacrifice herself for her country and marry "le Boharnet", 202; the Emperor struck dumb by her beauty, 203; bargains with him, 204; her letters of renunciation to

Beauharnais, Vice-Admiral Claude Louis, Comte de Roches Baritaud, great uncle of Eugène, 13, 21

Beauharnais, Claude, Comte de, son of Claude Louis, uncle of Eugène, 13, 50; father of Stéphanie, 216, 398

Beauharnais, Émilie de, Comtesse de Lavalette, daughter of Comte François, first cousin of Eugène; an unlucky child, 16, 50, 56, 59, 113; her arranged marriage, 70–1, 133–4; takes waters with Josephine and Hortense, 137; at Josephine's funeral, 398; her heroic rescue of her husband from prison, 425–6

Beauharnais, Eugène de, birth of, 24–5; child of a broken home, 26–8; a brave boy, 31; attends Assembly with his father, 31–2; "*Violà le Dauphin*", 32; his mother schemes to evacuate him to England, 33–5; his father orders him to Strasbourg, 35; protector of his mother and sister during Revolution, 39–45; reveres his father's memory, 44; apprenticed to a carpenter, 45, 47; at Collège Irlandais, St. Germain, 49; begins his military career under Hoche, 46–8; first meets General Bonaparte, 52–5; entreats his mother not to marry him, 55; joins him in Italy as aide de camp, 59; sent to Corfu, Naples, Rome, Venice, 65–7; goes on Egyptian campaign, 69–97; describes Battle of the Pyramids, 78; writes to beg his mother to be discreet, 82; objects to his stepfather's mistress, 84; forms friendship for life with Duroc, 88; wounded at siege of Acre, 90–1; witnesses massacre of prisoners after sack of Jaffa, 8<; and plague at, 93; distinguishes himself at Battle of Aboukir, 95; leaves Egypt, 96–7; persuades his stepfather to forgive his mother, 101; his account of 18 Brumaire, 104–8; appointed to Consular Guard, Captain of *chasseurs à cheval*, 112; describes Battle of

Marengo, 124; praised by his stepfather and promoted, 122; helps to frustrate plot to murder First Consul, 129–30; hears of Hortense's marriage, 137–40; present at birth of her first son, 141; his stepfather gives him a palace in Paris, 142; first efforts to find him a wife, 142–3; the *danseuse* Bigottini, 142; his views on conspiracy of Cadoudal, execution of Duc d' Enghien and Coronation of Emperor Napoleon, 149–63; has no status, 161–2; reconciles his stepfather and mother, 63; appears in David's picture of coronation, 167; Madame Duchâtel, 168; sent to Italy, 167–8; appointed Serene Highness, Arch Chancellor of State, 169; Viceroy 174; his instructions, and staff, 175–81; scolded by Emperor, 172, 179; reports on Crown Prince of Bavaria, National Guard, new roads, 182–90; Commander in Chief, Army of Italy, 194; summoned to Munich, 195; raised to rank of Imperial Highness, adopted by Emperor, heir-presumptive to throne of Italy, 201; his romantic mid-winter ride and arrival, 204; love at first sight, 205; his marriage to Princess Auguste of Bavaria, 208–9; Prince of Venice, 221; his happiness, 215; activity as Viceroy, 221 et seq., birth of Princess Josephine, 229; comforts his mother who fears divorce, 232; his sister on death of her son, 233; said by Emperor to be not clever enough to bargain at Erfurt, 243; ardently desires to take part in next campaign, 247; defeated by Archduke John at Sacile, 252–5; the Emperor's wrath, 255–7; makes a brilliant recovery, 259; outstrips his baggage on his advance, 260; arrives in Vienna "on the crest of the wave", 261; wins Battle of Raab, 261–5; at Battle of

Beauharnais, Eugène de, *continued*
Wagram, 206-9; dreadful service in Tyrol, 277-82; his happy homecoming wrecked by summons to Paris, 282; his support of his mother and dignified refusal of any promotion or emolument on her divorce, 285 et seq.; at marriage of Emperor to Marie Louise, 294; Château of Navarre, 301; refuses offers of thrones of Sweden, 317; Poland and Greece, 320; a son at last, 313; makes arrangements for birth of Hortense's son by Flahaut, 319; on Russian campaign, 326; anxious for troops short of food and decimated by dysentry, 326; in action near Vitebsk; hears at Smolensk of birth of Princess Amélie, 328; Battle of Borodino, 331-2; begs Emperor to quit burning Kremlin, 335; admires Moscow, 336; but writes to his children that there are no toys in Russia, only bears, 337; distinguishes himself in command at Battle of Malo Jaroslawetz, 342-3; horrors of retreat, 347-51; his junction with Ney, 349; Commander in Chief of what is left of Grande Armée, 358; at Battle of Lützen, 301; fights to save Italy for Emperor, 364 et seq.; refuses Allies' secret offer of Crown of Italy, 368-9; defends himself against Emperor's accusations of lethargy, 378-9; his proclamation to Army of Italy, 375; hears of Emperor's abdication and addresses troops in farewell, 387; escorts his family to Munich and sets out for Paris on news of his mother's illness, 388; calls upon Louis XVIII and family, 390; not a Marshal of France or Marquis de Beauharnais, 390; promised a principality outside France, 391-3; attends his mother's death-bed, 397-8; inherits Malmaison and Navarre, 399; his prospects at Congress of

Vienna wrecked by Emperor Napoleon landing in France, 411; and indiscretion of Hortense, 418; writes in defence to Metternich, 419; retires to Munich where his father in law welcomes him, 420 et seq.; provides for innumerable Bonapartists on the run after Waterloo, 426; created Duke of Leuchtenberg, Prince of Eichstätt, 439; receives messages from St. Helena, 442, 445, 451; appeals to Czar by letter and personally on behalf of his stepfather, 447; speaks in Bavarian Parliament, 448; builds Eugensberg, 449; 452; Palais Leuchtenberg, 439, 455; has cerebral haemorrhages, 462-5; death and funeral of, 466; his good appearance and excellent manners, 102, 111, 131, 160; high spirits and sense of humour, 289, 315, 357; resonant voice on parade ground, 127; care for troops, wounded and refugees, 222, 265; "best and easiest employer in the world", 102, 111, 406; his modesty and courage, 213, 238, 309, 345, 347-8; loves his children and calls them *"mes petits choux"* and *"marmosets"*, 249; loves music and theatricals, 127, 128, 365, 410, 436; horses, 154, 326; good maps, 328, 337; Paris, 115; promotes arts and sciences, 243; plants trees, 101, 184, 223; his letters to his wife, from Italy, 249-59; Vienna, 1809, Hungary and Tyrol, 261-81; Paris 286-9; Poland and Russia, 324-50; Prussia, 356-62; Vienna 1814, 408-9; his portraits: by Gros, 61; Ménageot, 208; Locatelli, Calliano, Bosio, 243; Gérard, 243; Isabey, 410; monument by Dumont, 470; monument by Thorwaldsen, 468; "Honour and Fidelity" marching song in his honour, 377

Beauharnais, François, Comte de, uncle of Eugène, 13, 22, 31, 36, 39, 137, 398

Bleyberg, Eugène goes down a lead-mine at, 280

Blücher, Marshal Gebhard Leberecht Prince of, Prussian commander, 361, 377, 423

Bonaparte, Caroline, wife of Joachim, King of Naples, sister of Napoleon, *see* Caroline Murat

Bonaparte, Charles Louis Napoleon, *see* Napoleon III

Bonaparte, Napoleon I, Emperor of the French, *see* Napoleon I

Bonaparte, Pauline, *see* Pauline

Bonaparte, Charlotte, daughter of Lucien, Princess Gabrielli, sent to live with her grandmother, 238; writes wittily home about the Bonapartes, 245; marries, 480

Bonaparte, Elisa, wife of Felix Baciocchi, Princess of Lucca and Piombino, sister of Napoleon, *see* Baciocchi, Elisa, 133, 154, 393

Bonaparte, Jerome, King of Westphalia, at school with Eugène, 55, 63; performs in theatricals at Malmaison, 128; in the Navy, 136; marries Betsy Patterson, 155; the marriage annulled, 191; a royal bride is sought for, 198; King of Westphalia, 231; marries Catherine of Württemberg, 234; present in Paris for divorce of Josephine, 285 et seq.; marriage of Marie Louise, 29, 310; will not be chosen King of Poland, 322; retires from Russian campaign, 328, 393; at Waterloo, 444; Comte de Montfort, leaves issue, 469

Bonaparte, Joseph, King of Naples, King of Spain, brother of Napoleon, 61, 64-6, 83, 101, 104, 125, 133-4, 146, 153-4, 155, 172, 193, 207, 237, 241, 247, 393, 451, 457

Bonaparte, Julie, *née* Clary, wife of Joseph, King of Naples, King of Spain, 66, 133-4, 153-4, 288, 300, 307, 457

Bonaparte, Letizia, mother of Napoleon, "Madame Mère", dislikes Josephine, 61-3; but "always amiable", 99, 136; does not attend coronation, 165; supports Jerome, 172; entertains her grand-daughter Charlotte, 238, 245, 480; present at divorce of Josephine, 288; wedding of Marie Louise, 299; her lady in waiting burnt to death, 310; provided for by treaty of Fontainebleau, 393; exiled, 428; sends a surgeon to St. Helena, 451; Auguste calls on in Rome, 408

Bonaparte, Louis, King of Holland, youngest brother of Napoleon, best looking of the sons, 62; goes on Egyptian campaign, 69, 70; invalided home, 97, 98; unfriendly to Josephine, 100; a hypochondriac, 135-6, 476; married to Hortense, 137-40; birth of their first son, 141, becomes Imperial Prince, 153-4; refuses to let his son be adopted by the Emperor, 155; his insane jealousy, 156, 172, 186; Governor of Paris, 187, 191; Eugène takes precedence of, 207; forbids Hortense to go to her brother's wedding, 207, 217; King of Holland, 218; death of his eldest son and birth of future Emperor Napoleon III, 232-33; refuses crown of Spain, 241; present at divorce of Josephine, 288; wants a separation, 295; deserts his kingdom and family, 311; lives in Styria, 318; provided for, 393; rallies to Emperor, 411; wants a divorce, 430; very aged, 464

Bonaparte, Lucien, Prince of Canino, brother of Napoleon, makes an unsuitable marriage, 61; supports Napoleon on Brumaire, 18, 106-9; sent to Madrid, 134; described by Madame Junot, 134; refuses to divorce his second wife, Alexandrine Jouberthou, 155, 165, 173, 181

Bonaparte, Napoleon Charles, Prince, eldest son of Louis Bonaparte and Hortense, "le Dauphin", 141; Emperor wishes to adopt, 155;

528